C(... CAL
... E LATE
... 533

Warfare and dislocation are obvious features of the break-up of the late Roman West, but this crucial period of change was characterised also by communication and diplomacy. The great events of the late antique West were determined by the quieter labours of countless envoys, who travelled between emperors, kings, generals, high officials, bishops, provincial councils, and cities. This book examines the role of envoys in the period from the establishment of the first 'barbarian kingdoms' in the West, to the eve of Justinian's wars of reconquest. It shows how ongoing practices of Roman imperial administration shaped new patterns of political interaction in the novel context of the earliest medieval states. Close analysis of sources with special interest in embassies offers insight into a variety of genres: chronicles, panegyrics, hagiographies, letters, and epitaphs. This study makes a significant contribution to the developing field of ancient and medieval communications.

ANDREW GILLETT is Research Fellow in the Department of Ancient History, Macquarie University, Sydney.

Cambridge Studies in Medieval Life and Thought
Fourth Series

The series Cambridge Studies in Medieval Life and Thought was inaugurated by G. G. Coulton in 1921; Professor D. E. Luscombe now acts as General Editor of the Fourth Series, with Dr Christine Carpenter and Professor Rosamond McKitterick as Advisory Editors. The series brings together outstanding work by medieval scholars over a wide range of human endeavour extending from political economy to the history of ideas.

For a list of titles in the series, see end of book.

ENVOYS AND POLITICAL COMMUNICATION IN THE LATE ANTIQUE WEST, 411–533

ANDREW GILLETT

CAMBRIDGE
UNIVERSITY PRESS

CAMBRIDGE UNIVERSITY PRESS
Cambridge, New York, Melbourne, Madrid, Cape Town, Singapore, São Paulo, Delhi

Cambridge University Press
The Edinburgh Building, Cambridge CB2 8RU, UK

Published in the United States of America by Cambridge University Press, New York

www.cambridge.org
Information on this title: www.cambridge.org/9780521813495

First published 2003
Reprinted 2004
This digitally printed version 2008

A catalogue record for this publication is available from the British Library

ISBN 978-0-521-81349-5 hardback
ISBN 978-0-521-09638-6 paperback

CONTENTS

Contents

TABLES

PREFACE

This study sprang from several coincidences. I chanced to read Hydatius, Priscus, and Senarius' *Epitaph* (tucked away in the indexes of Mommsen's edition of Cassiodorus) at much the same time, and was struck not only by the importance of 'diplomacy' to all three texts, but also by the fact that while diplomatic communication was a prominent feature in modern literature on the Byzantine East, it was not much evident in studies of the early medieval West. At much the same time, we were all wakened each morning by radio news of the 'shuttle diplomacy' preceding the Gulf War of January–February 1991. These tense events suggested parallels with the repeated embassies in Hydatius, and with Senarius' boast of visiting eastern and western capitals twice within one year; more significantly, they focused the mind on the interconnectedness of communication and warfare. Some time later I began to research 'diplomacy in the West', but soon became convinced that the fragmentary nature of the sources precluded any meaningful 'diplomatic history' of the period, if the purpose of such a history was to gain insight into what our sources call the *arcana* and *secreta* of the imperial and royal courts. The most expansive sources tend to describe the policy intentions of the centres of power at best superficially and very rarely with any real claim to insider knowledge; what they are interested in is the importance of embassies to the careers of envoys themselves, or to their local communities. Fergus Millar's elucidating articles on the 'internal diplomacy' of Roman imperial administration, however, struck me as providing the proper context for understanding 'diplomatic' activity in the period of the empire's break-up: not as a primitive forebear of European international statecraft, but as the continued practice of communications between different levels of authority in the classical world. This study, then, focusses on the activity, not the issues, of 'diplomacy'. The nature of the sources also dictated the methodology used in the main chapters, which foregrounds the interaction of sources, their genre, and their historical setting.

I owe many thanks to instructors and friends. Not unusually, this book descends from a doctoral dissertation, presented in 1994 at the Centre for Medieval Studies, University of Toronto. There I was privileged to be guided by erudite and generous instructors: my supervisor Walter Goffart, Timothy Barnes, Jocelyn Hillgarth, and Alexander C. Murray. I could not imagine a more luminous constellation of scholars from whom to learn, and I am greatly indebted for their invaluable and continued counsel. At Toronto, too, I was fortunate to enjoy the instruction of M. Edouard Jeauneau; the help of staff of the Pontifical Institute of Mediaeval Studies Library; the guidance of the directors of the Centre for Medieval Studies, in particular Roberta Frank; and discussions and companionship with many fellow students, of whom I wish to mention in particular Ann Kuzdale, Catherine Conybeare, and Michael Kulikowski. The work of revising and extending this study took place in the Ancient History Documentary Research Centre of Macquarie University, a warm haven for the study of late antiquity. I am most grateful for the guidance there of Alanna Nobbs, Ted Nixon, Edwin Judge, Sam Lieu, and Robert Tannenbaum; the bonhomie of Rosalinde Kearsley, Lea Benness, Tom Hillard, and Geraldine Herbert-Brown; the cheerful assistance of Beth Lewis and Pat Geidans; and the unflagging service of the Macquarie University Library staff. To Paul Barnwell, Peter Brennan, Brian Croke, Carman Cardelle de Hartmann, Walter Kaegi, Fergus Millar, Andreas Schwarcz, Roger Scott, and Phil Wynn, I am indebted for valuable discussions and advance copies of publications, and I am particularly grateful for the encouragement of Peter Brown. The book has gained much from the comments of the series editor Rosamond McKitterick, from Doug Lee, and from the anonymous readers from Cambridge University Press. None of the above, of course, bears any liability for the content or approach of this book. At various stages, this study has been generously supported by the Canadian Commonwealth Fellowship and Scholarship scheme, the Canadian Association for Graduate Studies/Association canadienne pour les études avancées, the Australian Academy for the Humanities, the Australian Research Council, and Macquarie University. My warmest thanks to Don Gillett and Dora Gillett for their constant interest. Finally, I am deeply grateful for the advice and support of Antonina Harbus.

ABBREVIATIONS

SOURCES AND MODERN STUDIES

AASS	Acta sanctorum (Antwerp, 1643–)
AB	*Analecta Bollandiana*
Altaner, *Patrologie*[7]	B. Altaner and A. Stuiber, *Patrologie: Leben, Schriften und Lehre der Kirchenväter*[7] (Freiburg im Breisgau, 1966)
Amm. Marc.	Ammianus Marcellinus, *Rerum gestarum libri qui supersunt*, ed. Wolfgang Seyfarth, 2 vols. (Teubner; Leipzig, 1978)
Anderson	Sidonius, *Poems and Letters*, trans. W. B. Anderson, 2 vols. (LCL; London, 1936, 1965)
Anon. Val.	*Excerpta Valesiana*, ed. J. Moreau, rev. V. Velkov (Teubner; Leipzig, 1968)
Bagnall *et al.*, *Consuls LRE*	Roger S. Bagnall, Alan Cameron, Seth R. Schwartz, and Klaas A. Worp, *Consuls of the Later Roman Empire* (Atlanta, 1987)
Bede, *HE*	Bede, *Historia ecclesiastica*, ed. and trans. B. Colgrave and R. A. B. Mynors (Oxford, 1969)
BHL	*Bibliotheca hagiographica latina* (Brussels, 1898–9); *Novum supplementum*, ed. H. Fros (Brussels, 1986)
Budé	*Collection des universités de France* (Paris, 1920–)
Burgess, *Chronicle*	R. W. Burgess (ed.), *The* Chronicle *of Hydatius and the* Consularia Constantinopolitana: *Two Contemporary Accounts of the Final Years of the Roman Empire* (Oxford, 1993)
Burgess, 'Hydatius'	R. W. Burgess, 'Hydatius: A Late Roman Chronicler in Post-Roman Spain: A Historical Study and New Critical Edition of the Chronicle' (diss., University of Oxford, 1988)

Bury	J. B. Bury, *History of the Later Roman Empire: From the Death of Theodosius I to the Death of Justinian*, 2 vols. (London, 1923; repr. New York, 1958)
Cameron, *Claudian*	Alan Cameron, *Claudian: Poetry and Propaganda at the Court of Honorius* (Oxford, 1970)
Cardelle de Hartmann *Philologische Studien*	Carmen Cardelle de Hartmann, *Philologische Studien zur* Chronik *des Hydatius von Chaves* (Palingenesia 47; Stuttgart, 1994)
Cass., *Variae*	Cassiodorus, *Variae epistolae*, ed. T. Mommsen (MGH AA 12)
CCSL	Corpus christianorum. Series latina, 176 vols. (Turnhout, 1953–)
CIL	Corpus inscriptionum latinarum, ed. T. Mommsen *et al.*, 17 vols. (Berlin, 1863–1986)
Claudian	Claudian, *Carmina*, ed. J. B. Hall (Leipzig, 1985)
Clover, *Merobaudes*	Frank M. Clover, *Flavius Merobaudes: A Translation and Historical Commentary* (Philadelphia, 1971)
Cod. Just.	*Codex Justinianus*, in *Corpus iuris*
Collectio Avellana	*Epistulae imperatorum pontificum aliorum (Collectio Avellana)*, ed. Otto Guenther (CSEL 35; Vienna, 1895)
Constantius, *Vita Germani*	Constantius, *Vita Germani episcopi Autissiodorensis*, ed. W. Levison (MGH SRM 7); ed. and trans. R. Borius (Sources chrétiennes 112)
Corpus iuris	Justinian, *Corpus iuris civilis*, ed. T. Mommsen, P. Krüger, R. Schöll, and W. Kroll, 3 vols. (Berlin, 1872–1895; repr. Dublin and Zurich, 1968–70)
CSEL	Corpus scriptorum ecclesiasticorum latinorum, 90 vols. (Vienna, 1860–)
CTh	*Theodosiani libri XVI*[3], ed. T. Mommsen and P. Kruger (Berlin, 1962)
De cer.	Constantine VII Porphyrogenitus, *De cerimoniis aulae Byzantinae libri duo*, ed. J. J. Reiske, 2 vols. (Corpus scriptorum historiae Byzantinae 7; Bonn, 1829–30)

Demougeot	E. Demougeot, *La Formation de l'Europe et les invasions barbares*, 2 vols. (Paris, 1979)
Dessau, *ILS*	*Inscriptiones latinae selectae*, ed. Hermann Dessau, 3 vols. (Berlin, 1892–1916)
Digest	Justinian, *Digesta*, in *Corpus iuris*
Du Cange, *Gloss.*	Charles du Fresne Du Cange, *Glossarium mediae et infirmae latinitatis*, ed. C. P. Carpenter and G. A. L. Henschel, 10 vols. (Niort, 1883–7; repr. Graz, 1954)
Ennodius, *Vita Epiphani*	Ennodius, *Vita beatissimi Epiphani episcopi Ticinensis ecclesiae*, ed. F. Vogel in Ennodius, *Opera* (MGH AA 7)
Ep. Austr.	*Epistolae Austrasicae*, ed. W. Gundlach (MGH Epp. 3)
Eusebius/Jerome	*Die Chronik des Hieronymus*, ed. Rudolf Helm (GCS 47 = Eusebius' Werke 7; Berlin, 1956)
Fr. Class. Hist.	*The Fragmentary Classicising Historians of the Later Roman Empire: Eunapius, Olympiodorus, Priscus, and Malchus*, ed. and trans. R. C. Blockley, 2 vols. (ARCA Classical and Medieval Texts, Papers and Monographs 6 and 10; Liverpool, 1981, 1983). Where necessary, reference is given to the page number as well as fragment number.
Fredegar, *Chron.*	Fredegarius Scholasticus, *Chronicarum libri IV*, ed. B. Krusch (MGH SRM 2)
GCS	Die Griechischen Christlichen Schriftsteller der erstern Jahrhunderte
Gregory the Great, *Registrum*	Gregory the Great, *Registrum epistolarum*, ed. P. Ewald and L. M. Hartmann (MGH Epp. 1, 2)
Gregory of Tours, *Hist.*	Gregory of Tours, *Historiarum libri X*, ed. B. Krusch and W. Levison (MGH SRM 1.1²)
Haenel, *Corpus legum*	*Corpus legum ab imperatoribus Romanis ante Iustinianum latorum*, ed. Gustav Haenel (Leipzig, 1857)

Harries, *Sidonius*	Jill Harries, *Sidonius Apollinaris and the Fall of Rome* (Oxford, 1994)
Harrison, 'Verse Panegyrics of Sidonius Apollinaris'	Geoffrey Harrison, 'The Verse Panegyrics of Sidonius Apollinaris: Poetry and Society in Late Antique Gaul' (diss., Stanford University, 1983)
Hyd.	Hydatius, *Continuatio chronicorum Hieronymianorum*, ed. T. Mommsen (MGH AA 11, 1–36); Burgess, *Chronicle*, 70–123. References give Mommsen's section numbering, followed by Burgess' in square brackets, except where these coincide.
Isidore, *Hist. Goth.*	Isidore of Seville, *Historia Gothorum Wandalorum Sueborum*, ed. T. Mommsen (MGH AA 11, 267–303)
Jedin and Dolan	*History of the Church*, ed. Hubert Jedin and John Dolan, vol. II: *The Imperial Church from Constantine to the Early Middle Ages*, trans. Anselm Biggs (New York, 1980)
John Lydus, *De magistratibus*	John the Lydian, *On Powers, or The Magistracies of the Roman State*, ed. and trans. A. C. Bandy (Philadelphia, 1983)
Jones, *LRE*	A. H. M. Jones, *The Later Roman Empire, 284–602: A Social, Economic and Administrative Survey*, 3 vols. (Oxford, 1964)
Jordanes, *Get.*	Jordanes, *Getica*, ed. T. Mommsen (MGH AA 6.1)
Justinian, *Nov.*	Justinian, *Novellae*, in *Corpus iuris*
Kal. Autiss.	*Kalendarium Autissiodorensis*, in *Martyrologium Hieronymianum*, ed. J. B. de Rossi and L. Duchesne, AASS Nov. II pars 1 (Brussels, 1894)
LCL	Loeb Classical Library (London, 1912–)
Lewis and Short	*A Latin Dictionary*, ed. Charlton T. Lewis and Charles Short (Oxford, 1879)
Liber pont.	*Liber pontificalis*, ed. L. Duchesne, 2 vols. (Paris, 1886), I

Loyen, *Recherches*	A. Loyen, *Recherches historiques sur les panégyriques de Sidoine Apollinaire* (Paris, 1942; repr. Rome, 1967)
Loyen, *Sidoine*	Sidoine Apollinaire, *Poèmes et lettres*, ed. and trans. André Loyen, 3 vols. (Budé; Paris, 1970)
Malalas, *Chron.*	*The* Chronicle *of John Malalas: A Translation*, trans. E. Jeffreys, M. Jeffreys, R. Scott *et al.* (Byzantina Australiensia 4; Melbourne 1986)
Matthews, *Western Aristocracies*	John Matthews, *Western Aristocracies and Imperial Court, AD 364–425* (Oxford, 1975)
Menander Protector	*The History of Menander the Guardsman*, ed. and trans. R. C. Blockley (ARCA Classical and Medieval Texts, Papers and Monographs 17; Liverpool, 1985). Where necessary, reference is given to the page number as well as the fragment number.
MGH AA	*Monumenta Germaniae Historica. Auctores antiquissimi*, 15 vols. (Berlin, 1826–)
MGH Epp. 3	*Monumenta Germaniae Historica. Epistolae*, vol. 3: *Epistolae Merowingici et Karolini aevi I*, ed. E. Dümmler, W. Gundlach *ct al.* (Berlin, 1892) [the texts used here are all edited by Gundlach]
MGH SRM	*Monumenta Germaniae Historica. Scriptores rerum Merovingarum*, 7 vols. (Hanover, 1885–)
Muhlberger, *Fifth-Century Chroniclers*	Steven Muhlberger, *The Fifth-Century Chroniclers: Prosper, Hydatius, and the Gallic Chronicler of 452* (ARCA Classical and Medieval Texts, Papers and Monographs 27; Leeds, 1990)
Niermeyer, *Lexicon*	*Mediae latinitatis lexicon minus*, ed. J. F. Niermeyer (Leiden, 1976)
Not. dig.	*Notitia dignitatum*, ed. Otto Seeck (Berlin, 1867; repr. Frankfurt-am-Main, 1962)

NPNF	A Select Library of Nicene and Post-Nicene Fathers of the Christian Church, 28 vols. (Buffalo and New York, 1886–90)
PCBE I, II	*Prosopographie chrétienne du Bas-Empire*, I: *Prosopographie de l'Africa chrétienne (303–533)*, ed. Andre Mandouze (Paris, 1982); II, part 1: *Prosopographie de l'Italie chrétienne (313–604)*, ed. Charles Pietri, Luce Pietri *et al.* (Paris, 1999)
PIR	*Prosopographia imperii Romani saec. I. II. III.*, ed. E. Klebs *et al.*, 3 vols. (Berlin, 1897–8); 2nd edn, E. Groag *et al.*, 5 vols. to date (Berlin and Leipzig, 1933–87)
PL	*Patrologiae cursus completus. Series latina*, ed. J.-P. Migne, 221 vols. (Paris, 1841–64)
PLRE I, II, III	*The Prosopography of the Later Roman Empire*, ed. A. H. M. Jones, J. R. Martindale *et al.*, 3 vols. (Cambridge, 1971–92)
Portmann, *Geschichte in der spätantiken Panegyrik*	Werner Portmann, *Geschichte in der spätantiken Panegyrik* (Europäische Hochschulschriften, series 3: Geschichte und ihre Hilfswissenschaften, vol. 363; Frankfurt-am-Main, 1988)
Priscus, *Fr.*	Priscus, *Fragmenta*, in *Fr. Class. Hist.*
Procopius	Procopius, *Opera omnia*, ed. Jakob Haury, rev. G. Wirth, 4 vols. (Teubner; Leipzig, 1963–4)
RE	*Realencylopädie der classischen Altertumswissenshaften*², ed. A. F. von Pauly, G. Wissona *et al.* (Stuttgart and Munich, 1893–1978)
RIC	*Roman Imperial Coinage*, ed. Harold Mattingly *et al.*, 10 vols. (London, 1923–94)
Schanz-Hosius	*Geschichte der römischer Litteratur bis zum Gesetzgebungswerk des Kaiser Justinians*, ed. Martin Schanz, Carl Hosius, and Gustav Krüger, 4 vols. (Munich, 1914–35)
Seeck, *Regesten*	Otto Seeck, *Regesten der Kaiser und Päpste für die Jahre 311 bis 476 n. Chr.: Vorarbeit zu einer Prosopographie der christlichen Kaiserzeit* (Stuttgart, 1919)

Seeck, *Untergang*	Otto Seeck, *Geschichte des Untergangs der antiken Welt*, 6 vols. (Berlin and Stuttgart, 1910–21)
Senarius, *Epitaph*	see pp. 195, 293 below
Sid. Ap., *Carm.* and *Ep.*	see Loyen, *Sidoine*
Sirmond	Sidonius, *Opera*, ed. Jacques Sirmond (Paris, 1602) = *PL* 58, 435–752
Stein	Ernst Stein, *Histoire du Bas-Empire*, trans. J.-R. Palanque, 2 vols. (Paris, 1959)
Stevens, *Sidonius*	C. E. Stevens, *Sidonius Apollinaris and His Age* (Oxford, 1933)
Teubner	Bibliotheca scriptorum graecorum et romanorum Teubneriana (Leipzig, 1849–)
Thiel, *Epistola*	*Epistolae Romanorum pontificum genuinae*, ed. Andreas Thiel (Brunsberg, 1867; repr. Hildersheim, 1974)
ThLL	*Thesaurus linguae latinae*, 10 vols. to date (Stuttgart and Leipzig, 1900–)
Thompson, *Romans and Barbarians*	E. A. Thompson, *Romans and Barbarians: The Decline of the Western Empire* (Wisconsin, 1982)
Tranoy I, II	Hydace, *Chronique*, ed. and trans. Alain Tranoy, vol. I [French trans.], vol. II [notes] (Sources chrétiennes 218, 219; Paris, 1974)
TTH	Translated Texts for Historians (Liverpool, 1985–)
TU	Texte und Untersuchungen zur Geschichte der altchristlichen Literatur (Leipzig and Berlin, 1882–)
Vita Orientii	*Vita (I) sancti Orientii episcopo Ausciorum in Novempopulania*, ed. G. Henskens, AASS Mai I
Vita Viviani	*Vita Bibiani vel Viviani episcopi Santonensis*, ed. B. Krusch (MGH SRM 3, 92–100)
Wolfram, *History of the Goths*	Herwig Wolfram, *History of the Goths*, trans. T. J. Dunlap (Berkeley, 1989)

CHRONOLOGICAL TABLE

Canones *of emperors, Western kings, and Popes, 390s–550s*

	Western emperors	Eastern emperors	Visigoths (in Italy, Gaul, Spain)	Sueves (in Spain)	Vandals (in Gaul, Spain, Africa)	Burgundians (in Gaul)	Ostrogoths (in Italy)	Franks (in Gaul)	Popes
390	Theodosius I 378–95		[Alaric I 395–410]		(to Gaul and Spain)				Siricius 384–99
	Honorius 395–423	Arcadius 395–408							Anastasius I 399–401
400	Constantine III 407–11	Theodosius II 408–50		Hermeric? 409–41	Gunderic 406–28				Innocent 401–17
410			Athaulf 410–15						Zosimus 417–18
			Segericus 415						Boniface I 418–22
			Vallia 415–18 (in Gaul)						
			Theoderic I 418–51						

420	Constantius III 421				(to Africa)			Celestine 422–32
	John 423–4				Geiseric 428–77			
	Valentinian III 425–55							
430				Rechila 438–48				Sixtus III 432–40
440								Leo I 440–61
				Rechiarius 448–56				
450	Petromius Maximus 455	Marcian 450–7	Thorismod 451–3	Maldras 456–60		Gundioc and Chilperic I 455–? 474	Childeric I? 456–*c*.481	
	Avitus 455–6	Leo I 457–74	Theoderic II 453–67	Framtane 457				
	Majorian 457–61			Rechimund? 459–61				
460	Libius Severus 461–5		Euric 467–84	Frumarius ?460–5				Hilarus 461–8
	Anthemius 467–72			Remismund 465–? 469				Simplicius 468–83

(cont.)

(*cont.*)

	Western emperors	Eastern emperors	Visigoths (in Italy, Gaul, Spain)	Sueves (in Spain)	Vandals (in Gaul, Spain, Africa)	Burgundians (in Gaul)	Ostrogoths (in Italy)	Franks (in Gaul)	Popes
470	Olybrius 472	Leo II 474		unknown *c*.470–*c*.550	Huneric 477–84	Gundobad ?474–516	[Odoacer 476–93]		
	Glycerius 473–4	Zeno 474–91				Godigisel ?474–500			
	Julius Nepos 474–80	Basiliscus 475–6				Chilperic II ? 474–?			
	Romulus 475–6					Godomar I ? 474–?			
480			Alaric II 484–507		Gunthamund 484–96			Clovis I ?481–511	Felix III 483–92
490		Anastasius 491–518			Thrasamund 496–523		Theoderic *c*.474–526		Gelasius 492–6
							(in Italy 489/93–526)		Anastasius II 496–8
									Symmachus 498–514
500			(in Spain) Gesalic 507–11						

510	Justinus I 518–27	Amalric 511–31 (under regency of Theoderic)		Sigismund 516–23		Theuderic I 511–33 Chlodomer 511–24 Childebert I 511–58 Lothar I 511–61	Hormisdas 514–23
520	Justinian 527–65		Hilderic 523–30	Godomar II 524–32 (conquest by Frankish kings)	Athalaric 526–34 (regency of Amalasuntha)		John I 523–6 Felix IV 526–30
530		Theudis 531–48 (regent for Theoderic)	Gelimer 530–4 (conquest by Belisarius)		Amalasuntha 534–5 Theodahad 534–6 Vitigis 536–40	Theudebert I 533–47	Boniface II 530–2 John II 532–5 Agapitus 535–6 Silverius 536–7 Vigilius 537–55

(cont.)

(*cont.*)

	Western emperors	Eastern emperors	Visigoths (in Italy, Gaul, Spain)	Sueves (in Spain)	Vandals (in Gaul, Spain, Africa)	Burgundians (in Gaul)	Ostrogoths (in Italy)	Franks (in Gaul)	Popes
540			Theodisclus 548–9 Agila I 549–54				Ildibad 540–1 Eraric 541 Totila 541–52	Theudebald 547–55	
550			Athanagild 551–68	Charric ?550s Ariamir *c*.558–after 561			Theia 552 (conquest by Belisarius)		Pelagius I 555–61

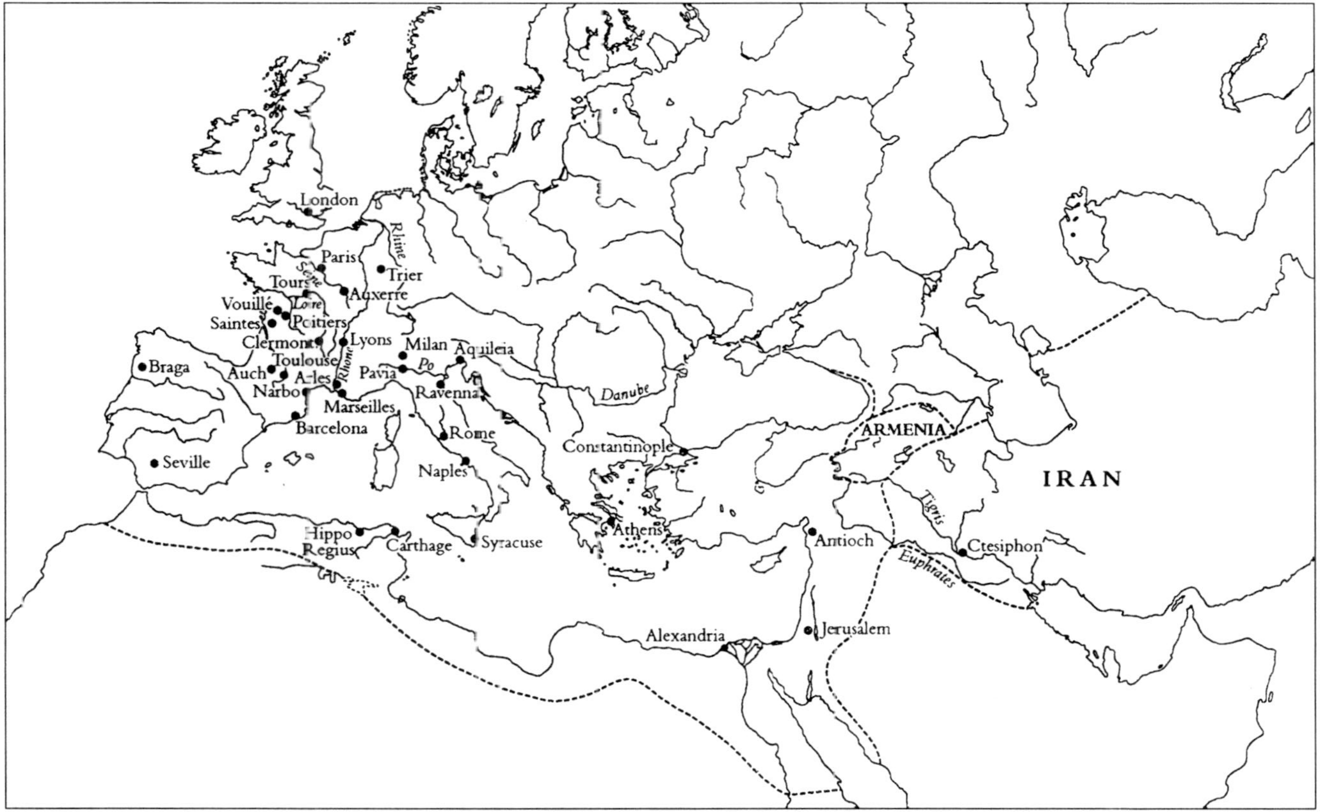

Map 1. Major centres named in the text

Map 2. Fifth-century Spain (based on E. A. Thompson, *Romans and Barbarians: The Decline of the Western Empire,* 138)

Chapter 1

EMBASSIES AND POLITICAL COMMUNICATION IN THE POST-IMPERIAL WEST

INTRODUCTION

Embassies were ubiquitous, constant, and crucial during the break-up of the late Roman West and the establishment of the first medieval kingdoms in the fifth and early sixth centuries. The conduct of political communication through formal conventions was a shaping force in this period of change, more frequent if less obvious than warfare. This study examines the literary monuments for the envoys who carried out the task of communication. Their story brings to the fore new aspects of political processes in the late and post-imperial world. Late antique embassies present uninterrupted continuations of Greco-Roman public oratory and administration, functioning in new and complex circumstances. The patterns of communication traced by envoys reveal a wide range of participants in political affairs. Envoys had long been the voice of cities and provinces to imperial authorities; in late antiquity, municipal envoys spoke not only of taxation and civic honours, but also of war and peace. Envoys now became also, as one himself put it, the 'voice of kings': with the rise of a multiplicity of states, rulers required forms of representation not needed by emperors in earlier centuries.[1] Many constituents of the western polities employed envoys as their instruments, participating in classical conventions of communication which remained common to all regions and all parts of society in the West, long past the fragmentation of political boundaries. Rewards accrued to those who successfully undertook embassies, either on palatine service or for local communities. Their missions moulded both the grand and the local politics of the late antique West.

Embassies were important cumulatively. Regularity and ubiquity of political communication, constantly sustaining relations among the gamut of participants in public life, characterise the role of embassies in the politics of the West. Sources, however, often present narratives of embassies

[1] Senarius, *Epitaph*, line 4.

as dramatic and pivotal moments; so too do many modern studies, which incorporate embassies into their accounts and analyses of political events. It is not usually acknowledged that the relatively few embassies attested by our sources represent only a small fraction of the constant flow of legations in the period, and that embassies were so common an event as to be generally ignored by contemporary authors. As a result, specific embassies which appear in the sources are often misinterpreted by modern commentators by being presented as outstanding; modest events are turned into decisive moments of history. Such reconstructions wrongly interpret the specific case; but they also misconstrue the general functioning of political processes and communication in the period. A 'diplomatic history' of the fragmentation of the Roman West would be profoundly revealing, but the materials available are very inadequate for the task. The same envoy cited above, a court servant of Theoderic king of Italy, states that he himself undertook twenty-five legations for the king; narrative sources do not record this many embassies for the whole of Theoderic's reign, though more embassies are attested to and from the Ostrogothic court than any other western centre of power.[2] Not only is there a lack of anything like a representative record of the number of embassies exchanged, but the nature of the available sources does not lend itself to a reconstruction of political events. Most western texts which mention legations were not intended as records of the issues negotiated, but as eulogistic monuments to the individuals who carried out the onerous task of the embassy.

This study seeks to turn this emphasis to an advantage, by focusing not on 'diplomacy' but on its agent, the envoy. The sources foreground the political and social patterns which determined the conduct of legations, rather than the issues of negotiation. Examining these patterns offers valuable insight into the role of communication in the unravelling of imperial authority in the West, a role traditionally overshadowed by communication's counterpart, military force.[3] Because many of the sources are formally eulogistic, they are examined in the chapters below as much through literary as historical analysis, in order to reveal the ways in which the undertaking of embassies fulfilled social functions.

[2] Senarius, *Epitaph*, line 9.

[3] For the identification of communication as a new field of research in late antique and medieval history, see Marco Mostert (ed.), *New Approaches to Medieval Communication* (Utrecht Studies in Medieval Literacy 1; Turnhout, 1999), esp. 15–37, 193–297; Michael McCormick, *Origins of the European Economy: Communications and Commerce, AD 300–900* (Cambridge, 2001), esp. 15–19. The study of political communication is a complement, not an alternative, to the study of warfare; cf. the salutary comments of Bernard S. Bachrach, *Early Carolingian Warfare: Prelude to Empire* (Philadelphia, 2001), ix.

Envoys and political communication

Embassies and envoys were important during the fragmentation of the West because disunity gives rise not only to conflict but also to communication. Throughout antiquity, relations among the Mediterranean states and neighbouring powers had been managed by peaceful communications and alliances as well as by warfare. For several centuries, when the entire Mediterranean basin was subject to the Roman empire, formerly independent regions interacted politically with each other only little, looking primarily towards their common master, the emperor or his provincial representatives. In the fifth century AD, however, the western half of the empire was divided into several autonomous regions under the control of monarchs, the barbarian kingdoms.[4] The political unity of the empire was replaced by a multiplicity of powers, and constant political interaction again became necessary throughout these former parts of the empire. Political communication and negotiation were the inevitable products of the break-up of the empire, and were fundamental to the nature of the barbarian kingdoms and of the Roman empire in the fifth and early sixth centuries.

Relations between the fifth-century states were undertaken in a variety of ways, some continuing classical practices unchanged, others products of their time. The empire and the kingdoms established formal alliances which, to the extent that they can be understood from the limited sources, resemble the truces, defensive and offensive alliances, and 'friendships' of the Greek states and the Roman republic.[5] Hostages, as in classical antiquity, were held in order to facilitate cultural and political ties as much as to provide sureties.[6] Pseudo-familial ties, including both marriage alliances among royalty and military and civilian elites, and 'adoption-in-arms' of one ruler by another, were a new development in imperial foreign affairs, influenced or imported by the influx of barbarian aristocracies. The function of these alliances, however, was appreciated by Romans, not least because of traditional Mediterranean practices of aristocratic marriage ties

[4] Despite its pejorative overtones and Romanocentric perspective, I find 'barbarian' the most convenient label for these states; it has the virtue of being a contemporary term. The designations 'successor' and 'post-Roman states' are only superficially more neutral; they imply a break and new start which down-plays the cultural and other continuities from imperial to early medieval times. 'Post-imperial', restricting discontinuity to the form of overarching political structure, is more appropriate. 'Germanic' is quite misleading; see Michael Kulikowski, 'Nation versus Army: A Necessary Contrast?' in Andrew Gillett (ed.), *On Barbarian Identity: Critical Approaches to Ethnicity in the Early Middle Ages* (Studies in the Early Middle Ages 4; Turnhout, 2002), 69–70 n. 2.

[5] For overviews of recent work on *foedera*, see Walter Pohl (ed.), *Kingdoms of the Empire: The Integration of Barbarians in Late Antiquity* (The Transformation of the Roman World 1; Leiden, 1997), with papers by Pohl, Wirth, Heather, and especially Chrysos.

[6] David Braund, *Rome and the Friendly King: The Character of the Client Kingship* (London 1984), 12–16; A. D. Lee, 'The Role of Hostages in Roman Diplomacy with Sasanian Persia', *Historia* 40 (1991), 366–74.

and adoption, and the ancient concept of 'kinship diplomacy', in which ties were established between cities or states through the manufacture of common descent from prominent historical peoples.[7] Baptismal sponsorship constituted a new, Christian form of kinship diplomacy which was to have a vigorous continuity throughout the Middle Ages.[8]

The most basic instrument in all forms of contact, however, was the envoy, the individual who acted as an authority's representative, and so as the vehicle for communication. Even formal, diplomatic letters were of secondary importance to the envoys who bore them as their credentials and as overtures to their speeches. The political shifts of the fifth century rode upon the pronouncements and persuasions of countless, largely unrecorded representatives dispatched by emperors, kings, generals, bishops, cities, and provincial councils. Examining these individuals reveals how embassies shaped the framework of events during the fifth century, and how the demands of communication and negotiation among the western powers were impressed upon their careers as court officials, clergy, or provincial magnates.

Embassies were *legationes* in Latin, πρεσβεῖαι in classical Greek; envoys *legati* (also, by the mid-sixth century, *legatarii*) or πρέσβεις. Each term had also a wider range of meanings.[9] There was, however, no classical term equivalent to the familiar modern word 'diplomacy', although the word has classical origins.[10] Formalised management of relations among authorities was so ubiquitous a feature of classical and late antique civilisation

[7] Ekkehard Weber, 'Die trojanische Abstammung der Römer als politisches Argument', in Eckart Olshausen and Hildegard Biller (eds.), *Antike Diplomatie* (Wege der Forschung 462; Darmstadt, 1979), 239–55; C. P. Jones, *Kinship Diplomacy in the Ancient World* (Cambridge, MA, 1999); Andrew Erskine, *Troy between Greece and Rome: Local Tradition and Imperial Power* (New York, 2001), esp. 256 (on the Trojan origins of the Franks).

[8] Joseph H. Lynch, *Christianizing Kinship: Ritual Sponsorship in Anglo-Saxon England* (Ithaca, 1998), 205–28 on sponsorship by emperors and kings of other rulers. A somewhat different example: Nikephorus, *Short History*, ed. and trans. Cyril Mango (Corpus fontium historiae Byzantinae 13; Washington, DC, 1990), IX: under the direction of the emperor Heraclius, Constantinopolitan nobles sponsor their visiting 'Hunnic' counterparts.

[9] I.e. *legati* (literally, 'the ones sent or appointed') was a standard term for military commanders during the Roman republic and early empire; *legationes* and *legatarii* were also used for legacies and heirs. On the adoption of *legatus* as the term for envoys (replacing the early republican, and partly religious, term *orator*): Jerzy Linderski, 'Ambassadors Go to Rome', in E. Frézouls and A. Jacquemin (eds.), *Les Relations internationales* (Paris, 1995), 457–66. The original sense of πρέσβεις as 'seniors' or 'elders of a council' was retained in late antiquity, and applied also to Christian presbyters.

A Gothic term for 'embassy' is shown by the glosses for πρεσβεία and the verb πρεσβεύειν in the New Testament: *airus* and *airinon*, cognate with modern English 'errand'; the sense is closer to the Latin than the Greek (*airus* also glosses ἄγγελος in its root sense of 'messenger'); Luke XIV. 32, XIX.14; Corinthians V.20; Ephesians VI.20 in *Die Gotische Bibel*, ed. Wilhelm Streitberg, I 2nd edn, II 3rd edn (Heidelberg, 1919; repr. Heidelberg, 1960).

[10] On 'diplomacy', see e.g. Jones, *Kinship Diplomacy*, 17–18.

that no one context for the deployment of these skills was distinguished with a separate title. The individual envoy's talents in communication were a part of his *paideia*, his exertions in undertaking an embassy one aspect of *negotium*; relations between states or other authorities constituted one facet of *res publica*.

The modern word 'diplomacy' has several connotations which are anachronistic or misleading in the context of this study. It can mean the instruments of the modern system of international relations which originated in the high-medieval contact between Venice and Byzantium, developed in France during the seventeenth and eighteenth centuries, and further evolved under the aegis of the League of Nations and United Nations in the twentieth century. These instruments and conventions include foreign policy formulated by centralised national governments, bureaucratic control of foreign affairs, permanent overseas consulates, career diplomats, international conventions, and diplomatic recognition as an exclusive acknowledgement of sovereignty. Many of these aspects of modern diplomacy have counterparts in the ancient and medieval world, but none was institutionalised as they are in the modern world. 'Diplomacy' can also mean, more generally, 'warfare by other means' (reversing Clausewitz's dictum): not a cynical statement but an accurate summary of the deployment by states of non-combatant means to achieve security or hegemony, a constant and intrinsic complement to actual military engagement. Diplomacy, in this sense, is strategic; it embraces for example payment of subsidies to client polities, or involvement in the domestic politics of another state in order to support an allied regime. It also includes the exploitation by states of the potential of their military force as leverage for negotiating their aims.[11]

Many of the embassies examined below set out to achieve 'diplomatic' purposes in this latter sense; the negotiations of the Gothic king of Italy, Theoderic, with the eastern emperors to achieve recognition of his rule, and with other western kings to prevent armed conflict, are examples. But for other legations, the implications of our term 'diplomacy' as the conduct of state-to-state relationships are inappropriate. Some of the most interesting embassies of which we have record, particularly in saints' *Vitae*, were dispatched not from heads of state but from local communities such as provincial cities. Their aims were to negotiate with authorities on

[11] For the interrelationship between warfare and these types of diplomacy, see e.g. Hugh Elton, *Warfare in Roman Europe AD 350–425* (Oxford, 1996), 175–98; John Haldon, *Warfare, State and Society in the Byzantine World, 565–1204* (London, 1999), 36–9, 277–9. The observations of Edward N. Luttwak, *The Grand Strategy of the Roman Empire from the First Century AD to the Third* (Baltimore and London, 1976), e.g. 1–5, remain instructive, even if his thesis of a 'grand strategy' is not accepted.

behalf of their citizens; by and large, such provincial bodies had no military counterpart to their supplications. Other levels of public authority such as bishops, generals, and senior officials, barred from participation in modern diplomacy by the concept of national sovereignty, also dispatched and received embassies on important political issues. There is no differentiation in vocabulary between 'internal' embassies, such as provincial legations to government magistrates, and communications between heads of state; indeed, some of the most dramatic and detailed accounts of embassies describe 'internal' rather than 'foreign' embassies. The conventions which governed these 'internal' embassies also determined legations between rulers; as discussed below, these conventions directly continued Roman administrative practices. In order to avoid the distracting modern associations of the word 'diplomacy', that term is avoided here, as much as possible, in favour of the phrase 'political communication'.[12] This term should be taken to encompass formal contact between parties of various levels of authority concerning public matters. It too imposes on ancient sources a terminology reflecting modern interests, but it has this virtue at least, that it avoids referring implicitly to an established set of concepts which are anachronistic to the period being studied.

The temporal limits of this study are the years 411 and 533, beginning with the establishment of the first barbarian kingdoms in the West, those of the Vandals, Alans, and Sueves in Spain; and ending with the commencement of Justinian's wars in North Africa, Italy, and Spain. These dates delineate a distinct phase of the history of the western Mediterranean which, for the purposes of this study, had two salient characteristics. On the one hand, continuity of Roman cultural and administrative patterns provided the modes of political communication: embassies, audiences, declamations, and letters. On the other hand, this was a period of incremental political change as first parts, then all of the West passed under the government of new monarchies, reaching a brief period of equipoise before Justinian's brusque intrusion. The frequent lurches in political boundaries generated new causes for contact and new combinations of parties in communication. Envoys were special actors in the politics of this time. Embassies and political communication were important in the post-Justinianic West also, as the many references to legations

[12] By the same token, the term 'envoy' is to be preferred to 'ambassador'; both are representatives dispatched by a principal, but conventionally 'ambassador' refers to a permanent resident in the recipient's realm, rather than an agent travelling between parties; *Oxford English Dictionary*, 2nd edn (Oxford, 1989), I, 382 s.v. 'ambassador' § 2; V, 316 s.v. 'envoy 2'. The institution of ambassadorial residence arguably originates in late antiquity with papal *apocrisiarii* at Constantinople (see below, chapter 6 at nn. 208–12), but this was the exception rather than the rule. 'Envoy' more closely approximates the terms *legatus* and πρέσβυς.

in the *Histories* of Gregory of Tours and the *Chronicle* of Fredegar demonstrate; evidence from the later sixth century is drawn upon below for comparative purposes.[13] But the envoys of the Merovingian period travelled between relatively stable political blocs.[14] Their predecessors in the long fifth century grappled with traditional tools in situations of recurrent novelty.

The geographic scope of this study is the former western provinces and Constantinople. It is not a study of 'Constantinople *and* the West'; it is a central characteristic of the period that political communication was multilateral, not radiating from one imperial centre. The former western provinces, though divided among a multiplicity of states, shared with each other and with the east Roman empire a common history and culture which included, among other things, uniform practices of political communication. In an important sense, negotiations among the various states, including the eastern imperial court, were not foreign relations but the internal negotiations of a cultural and diplomatic bloc.[15]

Political communication throughout this bloc was conducted within a variety of contexts, both geopolitical and social. To modern eyes, these contexts include both foreign relations and internal governmental administration, but those distinctions do not necessarily hold fast for the period of transition between empire and kingdoms. It is useful to sketch the major routes of communication discussed in the following chapters. At the highest level of administration and formality, the courts of the two halves of the late Roman empire communicated through formal channels including embassies, in order to maintain the complex relationship between two centres representing one authority. As the western provinces, and finally Italy, came under the rule of multiple kings, the role of the western emperor in this relationship was assumed by the barbarian courts, especially that of the kingdom of Italy; the propaganda of the Ostrogothic king Theoderic refers to *utraeque res publicae*, East and West.[16]

A second venerable and formal channel of communication was that between the Roman empire and the empire of Iran, which the Romans referred to as Persia, ruled and reinvigorated by the Sassanian dynasty since the early third century. Throughout the fifth and sixth centuries, the forms by which relations between the two 'superpowers' were conducted evolved, developing more elaborate diplomatic concepts and

[13] On Gregory and Fredegar: below, chapter 6.

[14] Notwithstanding the internal divisions of the Merovingian kingdom into *Teilreiche*: Ian Wood, *The Merovingian Kingdoms, 450–751* (London, 1994), 54–5, 60–3, 88–101.

[15] Cf. Garth Fowden, *Empire to Commonwealth: Consequences of Monotheism in Late Antiquity* (Princeton, 1993), 6 on the Byzantine and Islamic 'commonwealths'.

[16] Cass., *Variae* 1, 1.4; cf. Maximianus (below, n. 82): *geminum . . . regnum*.

procedures.[17] Rome's dealings with Persia affected political relationships and diplomatic practice in the West; the appeal of the Ostrogoths, besieged in Italy by Belisarius in the late 530s, to the shah Chosroes I for help is only the most dramatic example.[18]

With the fragmentation of the western provinces and establishment of smaller, autonomous kingdoms, established routes of internal communication, from imperial centre to provinces, were superseded by multilateral relations between imperial and royal courts – multilateral, because not only did the imperial courts and their senior civil and military magistrates in the provinces conduct relations with each of the new states, but each new kingdom negotiated with its peers also. To call these states 'foreign' to the empire is misleading: all parties recognised the cultural, political, and demographic continuities shared by the imperial East and the post-imperial West, and though the ruling elites of each kingdom were distinguished – by Romans – with barbarian labels, this did not preclude administrative and social ties operating across the nominal borders.[19]

The imperial government had always needed to attend to relations with barbarian groups outside its borders. During the course of the fifth century, the rise to power of the Hunnic khanate made dealings with European barbarians high priority. Contacts with the Huns were characterised by extreme sensitivity to the niceties of diplomatic procedure.[20] Again, patterns of communication were not restricted to contact between the two imperial courts and the Hun leadership; apart from the semi-independent relations with the Huns conducted by the *magister militum* Aetius, the Huns were also involved in a complex network of alliances and conflicts with the rulers of the new western kingdoms. In 451, Attila turned his attention from the imperial provinces in the Balkans towards the West; later writers record his pretexts of war as an alliance with the Vandals in North Africa, a quarrel with the Goths of Toulouse, involvement in factional disputes within the Frankish nobility in northern Gaul, and a claim to marriage with the Theodosian dynasty.[21] The western kingdoms were constantly in contact not only with each other and with the imperial court, but also with groups outside former imperial territories. In the collection of the official correspondence which he had

[17] R. C. Blockley, *East Roman Foreign Policy: Formation and Conduct from Diocletian to Anastasius* (ARCA Classical and Medieval Texts, Papers and Monographs 30; Leeds, 1992).

[18] Procopius, *Wars* II, 2.1–11, 14.11; VI, 22.17–20. Cf. the hyperbole of Sid. Ap., *Ep.* VII, 9.5, *Carm.* 45–54.

[19] The interrelationship between 'Roman' and 'barbarian' identities (and populations) in this period is a topic of valuable if controversial debate; see Patrick Amory, *People and Identity in Ostrogothic Italy, 489–554* (Cambridge, 1997); and the papers in Gillett (ed.), *On Barbarian Identity*.

[20] E.g. B. Croke, 'Anatolius and Nomus, Envoys to Attila', *Byzantinoslavica* 42 (1981), 159–70.

[21] Jordanes, *Get.*, 184–6; Priscus, *Fr.*, 20–1.

written for the Ostrogothic rulers of Italy, Cassiodorus prominently displays diplomatic letters to rulers, giving pride of place equally to eastern emperors, kings governing former imperial provinces, and rulers beyond imperial boundaries.[22]

Warfare constituted a specific venue for foreign diplomacy. In late antiquity as before, generals in the field possessed a certain latitude in dealing with enemy powers. Few battles were fought to extinction; after a demonstration of resources and an initial trial of strength, commanders were in a position to negotiate a settlement, to establish a truce and perhaps the framework for a permanent agreement. This authority was an important element in the foreign relations of the fifth century, when military engagements were sometimes resolved by permanent settlement of barbarian groups on Roman soil. The activities of generals represent an extension of imperial authority in foreign affairs.

Within the empire, the Christian church employed means to communicate between its major and peripheral centres, and with secular authorities, derived from the conventions of civic embassies. Bishops regularly dispatched envoys to communicate with other ecclesiastical and secular authorities; the only extant set of instructions to envoys written under the later Roman empire are those of Pope Hormisdas to clerics sent to the emperor Anastasius in 515 and 519.[23] The role of embassies within the Church itself and between the Church and secular rulers is a complex issue which is not treated in full here; it calls for a separate study. Here may it suffice to note that these points of contact, too, comprise what contemporaries called *legationes* and *negotium*. Very likely, some of the twenty-five embassies declared by Theoderic's envoy, mentioned above, consisted of journeys to the bishops of Rome and perhaps to Constantinople in order to resolve Church schisms, alongside the representations to hostile western kings which the same envoy certainly undertook.[24]

Of all the contexts within which political communication operated, it is most important for this study to stress the domestic: the many aspects of late Roman society and government which were regulated by negotiations conducted through envoys according to recognised conventions. Imperial provinces were administered not only through centralised bureaucratic machinery, but also by constant interchange between provincial cities and their imperial or royal rulers. Provincial approaches to the imperial court always retained the forms of foreign embassies. The Senate of

[22] See chapter 5, below.

[23] *Collectio Avellana*, 116 (with *Collectio Avellana*, 115, 116a, 116b); 158 (= Hormisdas, *Indiculi* of 515, 519). John Matthews, 'Gesandtschaft', trans. R. Werner-Reis, *Reallexicon für Antike und Christentum* x (Stuttgart, 1977), 675–84. See below, chapter 6, pp. 227–30.

[24] Below, chapter 5.

Rome, too, dispatched formal legations to the emperors. 'Such embassies, undertaken by leading citizens on behalf of their communities, are among the best-attested civic functions of Roman society.'[25] The civil administration of the empire has been viewed as 'a diplomatic system', and the constant traffic of petitions and rescripts between the provinces and the court as 'internal embassies', equivalent to the empire's communications with other nations.[26]

In the fifth century, the internal diplomacy of provincial administration became the interstate communication of the western kingdoms. Provincial bodies now played a role in negotiating the major political and military changes of the period, alongside imperial and royal courts, generals in the field, and ecclesiastical networks. In antiquity and the Middle Ages, communication with foreign powers was not the exclusive right of governments. The following description of the later Middle Ages well outlines the situation in late antiquity:

> The right of embassy was not spoken of in theory or regarded in practice as diplomatic representation, a symbolic attribute of sovereignty. It was a method of formal, privileged communication among the members of a hierarchically ordered society, and its exercise could be admitted or denied according to the relations of the parties concerned and the nature of the business at hand.[27]

When the barbarian monarchs assumed control of the West, most administrative structures and patterns of authority remained intact. New centres of authority were superimposed over late Roman society without displacing the existing network of communication. Provincial communities negotiated not only with their barbarian rulers but also, as before, with imperial authorities; provincial bishops under non-Catholic kings appealed to the bishop of Rome to settle schisms within the orthodox church. Following the paths and practices of traditional provincial embassies, the negotiations of these bodies were as important to the political development of the fifth century as the actions of monarchs.

Emperors and kings wielded immense authority, and foreign policies, like internal ones, may often have reflected the personal outlook of individual monarchs. The *rapprochement* of Theodosius I with the Goths in the Balkans, Marcian's avoidance of war with the Vandals, and Justinian's aggression towards the same barbarians, were all policies divergent from those of their immediate predecessors, described by contemporary

[25] John Matthews, 'Roman Life and Society', in John Boardman *et al.* (eds.), *The Oxford History of the Classical World* (Oxford, 1986), 754.

[26] Fergus Millar, 'Government and Diplomacy in the Roman Empire during the First Three Centuries', *International History Review* 10 (1988), 352–7.

[27] Garrett Mattingly, *Renaissance Diplomacy* (Boston, 1955; repr. New York, 1988), 23.

writers as the initiatives of each emperor. Nevertheless, though emperors and kings may have been the source of foreign policy, many officials and private persons were involved in its implementation. The ruling elites of the provinces in which the new kingdoms were situated also shaped the course of events, by accepting or rejecting annexation, and by their relations with the new rulers. A constant stream of emissaries between the imperial palace, officials in the provinces, military commanders, royal courts, ecclesiastical sees, cities, and provincial assemblies formed the context in which political events occurred. The intentions of monarchs can only be seen at a distance through official propaganda and the record of their deeds. But the experience of several individuals of a more modest position, who served as envoys or drafted diplomatic correspondence, can be fleshed out by close examination of literary sources, providing an insight into the nature of communication throughout the West, rather than a reconstruction of central policy.

THE FRAMEWORK AND CONVENTIONS OF EMBASSIES IN THE CLASSICAL WORLD

Though the circumstances giving rise to political communication in the fifth- and early sixth-century West were new, a millennium of exchanges between political powers throughout the Mediterranean world lay behind the forms and conventions of late antique embassies. The practices of the fifth and sixth centuries are best appreciated in the light of two earlier periods of Mediterranean civilisation, classical Greece and the early Roman empire. The forms and patterns of communication developed in these periods were the basis for the practices in the different political conditions of the fifth and early sixth centuries.

Classical Greece

Despite the intellectual adoption of a biblical past by Christian writers, the late Roman empire remained culturally and politically the product of classical civilisation.[28] Late antique conventions of communication had a cultural pedigree leading back to the Greek city states of the fourth and fifth centuries BC.[29] Embassies were among the most common political

[28] Biblical past: e.g. most bluntly, Gregory of Tours, *Hist.* I. Averil Cameron, 'Remaking the Past', in G. W. Bowersock, P. Brown and O. Grabar (eds.), *Late Antiquity: A Guide to the Postclassical World* (Cambridge, MA, 1999), 1–20.

[29] For the following: Dietmar Kienast, 'Presbeia', *RE* Suppl. XIII, 499–628; D. J. Mosley, *Envoys and Diplomacy in Ancient Greece* (Historia Einzelschriften 22; Wiesbaden, 1973); Frank Adcock and D. J. Mosley, *Diplomacy in Ancient Greece* (London, 1975); and Matthews, 'Gesandtschaft', 653–85.

phenomena in the classical Greek states. The multiplicity of Greek powers, their alliances and leagues, the extension of the Athenian empire, and contacts with Persia, Macedonia, and Rome necessitated a constant interchange of emissaries. Greek historical writing after Thucydides evolved into 'diplomatic history' in order to embrace the development of the whole Hellenistic world.[30]

The practices for dispatching and receiving embassies, πρεσβεία, in Athens are naturally the best recorded. Like most public business, foreign affairs were first considered by the Athenian council, before being put to the general assembly. Foreign envoys arriving in Athens were received by the city council; after consideration of the issues raised, they were permitted to address the general assembly. The council provided recommendations for a response, which, though not binding on the general assembly, usually were followed. For reasons of expediency, formation of foreign policy and the selection of envoys to represent the city were often delegated by the assembly to the council. The envoy, 'authorised by the council and the people', executed the formal decrees of these bodies. Consequently, envoys were subject to public audit, and to punishment for failure to adhere faithfully to their briefs or for corruption.[31]

The legal position of the envoy was customary but extraordinary. Few statutory requirements other than a minimum age (usually thirty)

See also: Coleman Phillipson, *The International Law and Custom of Ancient Greece and Rome*, 2 vols. (London, 1911); V. Serguiev, 'La diplomatie de l'antiquité', in M. Potiemkine (ed.), *Histoire de la diplomatie*, trans. X. Pamphilova and M. Eristov, I (Paris, 1953), 7–76; a series of articles by D. J. Mosley, including 'The Size of Embassies in Ancient Greek Diplomacy', *Transactions of the American Philological Association* 96 (1965), 255–66; 'Greeks, Barbarians, Language, and Contact', *Ancient Society* 2 (1971), 1–6; 'Diplomacy and Disunion in Ancient Greece', *Phoenix* 25 (1971), 319–30 (a number of Mosley's articles are collected and translated into German in *Antike Diplomatie*); E. Frézouls and A. Jacquemin (eds.), *Les Relations internationales* (Paris, 1995); Anthony Bash, *Ambassadors for Christ: An Exploration of Ambassadorial Language in the New Testament* (Tübingen, 1997); and Jones, *Kinship Diplomacy*, 17–80.

30 Charles William Fornara, *The Nature of History in Ancient Greece and Rome* (Berkeley, 1983), 33–4.

31 Pierre Briant, 'La Boulè et l'élection des ambassadeurs à Athènes au IVe siècle', *Revue des Etudes Anciennes* 70 (1968), 7–31; Adcock and Mosley, *Diplomacy in Ancient Greece*, 165–70; Matthews, 'Gesandtschaft', 656. On the passage of topics for debate from the Athenian *boulé* to the *ekklesia*: P. J. Rhodes, *The Athenian Boule* (Oxford, 1972), 52–81; Mogens Herman Hansen, *The Athenian Assembly in the Age of Demosthenes* (Oxford, 1987), 35–7. Delegation of responsibility for foreign affairs to the *boulé*: Hansen, *The Athenian Democracy in the Age of Demosthenes* (Oxford, 1991), 264–5. On public audit (*euthynai*) and charges of corruption during an embassy (*parapresbeia*): Mosley, *Envoys and Diplomacy*, 39–42; Kienast, 'Presbeia', 577–8; Mogens Herman Hansen, '*Rhetores* and *Strategoi* in Fourth-Century Athens', *Greek, Roman, and Byzantine Studies* 24 (1983), repr. in his *The Athenian Ecclesia* II (Copenhagen, 1989), cited here, 28–9; Hansen, *Athenian Assembly*, 69. The prosecution and (successful) defence speeches in a charge of *parapresbeia* are preserved in Demosthenes, *Oration 19: De falsa legatione*, in *Demosthenes* II, trans. C. A. Vince and J. H. Vince (LCL; London, 1926) and Aeschines, *Oration 2: De falsa legatione*, in *The Speeches of Aeschines*, trans. Charles Darwin Adams (LCL; London, 1919); see also Hyperides, *Oration 4: In Defence of Euxippus*, in *Minor Attic Orators* II, trans. J. O. Burtt (LCL; London, 1954), cc. 29–30, summarising a charge of *parapresbeia*, related to that brought against Aeschines, against Philocrates.

restricted the choice of an emissary. Unlike other public functionaries, Greek envoys did not hold a formal office, an ἀρχή. No restrictions prevented the reappointment of a former envoy, or limited the duration of his appointment, which terminated when he returned from his mission. Whereas holders of most Athenian offices ideally were selected by lot, envoys were chosen by election in the assembly. Only generals were similarly free from the standard restrictions surrounding public offices.[32]

Though envoys did not enjoy the status of generals, neither were they mere functionaries. On return from their mission, envoys reported to the council and assembly, and made recommendations. Their addresses were considered of equal standing to those of *rhetores*, movers of proposals in the council or assembly, and were therefore an important part of the Athenian political process. Envoys were held responsible for the policies they advocated, and were liable to the penalties applicable against *rhetores*. They were also subject to the same public audit which all holders of public office were obliged to undergo at the expiry of their term. Envoys were thus treated simultaneously as special agents, as politically influential public speakers, and as civic office holders.[33]

Considerations of domestic and foreign politics determined the selection of an envoy. Election was first an acknowledgement of popular respect for the individual concerned. The envoy's knowledge of the recipient state, and his existing contacts with influential persons there, was the main practical consideration in selection; where possible, envoys were chosen for their influence in the state to which they were to be sent. An individual who had introduced a motion concerning another power was eligible to be chosen as the envoy to implement the resultant decree.[34]

Practices for the reception of foreign envoys were customary and formal but, in contrast with later states and Rome in particular, characterised by little ceremonial and minimal public expense. Neither the dispatch nor the reception of envoys seems to have been marked by public formalities. Envoys could expect to receive the customary courtesies of hospitality,

32 Mosley, *Envoys and Diplomacy*, 39–49; David Stockton, *The Classical Athenian Democracy* (Oxford, 1990), 105–7.

33 Phillipson, *International Law and Custom* I, 343–6; Mosley, *Envoys and Diplomacy*, 78–9; Hansen, '*Rhetores* and *Strategoi*', 29–31, 32 §9. Processes against *rhetores*: Mogens Herman Hansen, 'The Athenian "Politicians", 403–422 BC', *Greek, Roman, and Byzantine Studies* 25 (1983), repr. in his *Athenian Ecclesia* II, 9–10. An example of an envoy's address to the assembly on return from a mission: Andocides, *Oration 3: On the Peace with Sparta*, in *Minor Attic Orators* I, trans. K. J. Maidment (LCL; London, 1941); cf. Demosthenes' statement of the responsibilities of an envoy, *Oration 19: De falsa legatione*, cc. 4–5. Note that the (lost) collection of public speeches made in the late fifth century BC by Demetrius of Phalerum included both the speeches of *rhetores* in the assembly and the addresses of envoys: *RE* IV.2, 2829–30.

34 Mosley, *Envoys and Diplomacy*, 43–9; Adcock and Mosley, *Diplomacy in Ancient Greece*, 157; Hansen, '*Rhetores* and *Strategoi*', 30.

divinely sanctified by Zeus Xenios, extended to other guests, but these were generally proffered by private individuals, not the state. No accommodation, transport, or provisions were provided at the public expense of the receiving state. Except in Sparta, foreign envoys appear to have enjoyed the complete freedom of movement available to all other visitors. Many customary acts of hospitality, in particular the giving of gifts, were not observed by the public authorities because of the potential implication of bribery. Only at the conclusion of his business could an envoy expect to attend a formal meal as guest of the state to which he had been sent. Otherwise, the envoy had either to provide for himself, supplementing with his own resources the minimal amounts paid to him by his own state for expenses, or to look to the hospitality of a local citizen.

Hospitality could be extended by an individual with whom the envoy had prior personal contact, through either business or familial connections, and with whom he shared the obligations of guest-friendship. A more formal institution which could provide for the wants of envoys was *proxenia*. A *proxenos* was a citizen of one state, recognised by a second as a representative of its interests; for example, a Theban citizen who was granted *proxenia* by Athens would extend hospitality to Athenians visiting Thebes on private or official business, and would be expected to advocate policies friendly to Athens in the Theban assembly. *Proxenia* remained an essentially private institution, for although, in this example, the grant of *proxenia* was an official action on the part of Athens, it did not formally involve the council or assembly of Thebes. In regard to diplomatic communication, *proxenoi* provided assistance to envoys from the state to which they were connected, and might be chosen to act as envoys to that state because of the prestige they already enjoyed there. They might also wield a special authority influencing policies towards the other state.[35]

A second institution which affected the conduct of diplomacy was the tradition of heralds. Originating before historic times, the herald's office was essentially religious; though heralds performed functions on behalf of their communities, they were not officers of state. Their functions were hereditary, in Athens passing through the family of the *Kerykes*, in Sparta through the *Talthybioi*. In the fifth and fourth centuries BC, heralds were most associated with the formalites of warfare, delivering declarations of war and petitioning for the recovery of the dead and wounded. Religious sanctions protecting heralds in times of war did not extend to regular envoys; nevertheless, envoys were often conveyed

[35] F. Gschnitzer, 'Proxenoi', *RE* Suppl. XIII, 629–730; Kienast, 'Presbeia', 581–7; Adcock and Mosley, *Diplomacy in Ancient Greece*, 160–3.

between belligerents under the safe conduct of heralds.[36] Even without the protection of heralds, however, envoys were usually considered to be protected from mistreatment by the common consent of all states, though the origin of this moral force is unknown.[37]

The framework within which embassies were carried out in ancient Greece was ultimately religious and private, not official or governmental. Though dispatched and received by the general assembly, their tasks were not undertaken as part of an office. The reception and treatment of foreign envoys was determined by obligations of hospitality or private connections, and in times of war the religious sanctions of heralds protected envoys. There was little involvement of government in facilitating communications between states.

Elements of this framework continued into later Hellenistic and Roman times. The moral protection of envoys' inviolability, considered to be part of *ius gentium* in Roman jurisprudence, is evidenced by both Roman and barbarian rulers.[38] Even under the bureaucratic late Roman state, embassies were performed as special commissions, not as the duties of an office. But there are few parallels to the private and religious context of Greek embassies in late antiquity.[39]

The conventions governing the selection of envoys and the execution of their commissions, however, show much greater continuity from classical to late antiquity. Though any citizen of the democratic Greek states was theoretically eligible for selection as an envoy, the choice was for the most part restricted to the wealthiest members of society. Practical considerations played a part in this restriction. Envoys were chosen for their familiarity and contacts with a foreign state; this implied foreign commercial interests, or other connections generally limited to the wealthy elite (an occasional exception was made for actors, whose trade carried them to all parts of Greece). Social patterns were important in other ways. Leading citizens sought election to an embassy for the prestige associated with the appointment. Participation in embassies was an important expression of citizenship by the leading members of the community. A large proportion of the politically active citizens of Athens served on diplomatic missions. A list of some 368 known politically active individuals

[36] Mosley, *Envoys and Diplomacy*, 84–7; Adcock and Mosley, *Diplomacy in Ancient Greece*, 152–4; J. Oehler, 'Keryx 2', *RE* XI.1, 349–57; von Geisau, 'Talthybios 2', *RE* IV A.2, 2090.

[37] Mosley, *Envoys and Diplomacy*, 81–92; Adcock and Mosley, *Diplomacy in Ancient Greece*, 184; Matthews, 'Gesandtschaft', 657.

[38] Phillipson, *International Law and Custom* I, 70–9, 328, 331–4; A. M. von Premerstein, 'Legatus', *RE* XII.1, 1134–5; Matthews, 'Gesandtschaft', 659. In late antiquity: below, chapter 6, at nn. 181–94.

[39] The language of guest-friendship, *xenia*, is used by Procopius, *Wars* III, 9.5: guest-friendship of the Vandal prince Hilderic and Justinian, then still *magister utriusque militiae*.

from fourth-century BC Athens shows that the sixty-seven recorded *strategoi* rarely served as envoys; but almost a third of the remaining 300-odd rhetors did, fifteen of them undertaking three or more embassies. These proportions are an indication as much of the honour associated with embassies as of the frequent need for diplomatic interchange.[40]

The need for oratorical skills also tended to restrict candidacy to the better-educated aristocracy. The task of envoys was 'political advocacy', the persuasive promotion of the proposals of their state, rarely participation in actual negotiation. Diplomacy 'by conference', the meeting of representatives authorised to negotiate a settlement, was little practised, and even so-called plenipotentiaries, *autocratores*, were empowered only to reach agreements within previously defined limits.[41] The task of advocacy should not be underestimated, however, for it involved more than the mere communication of the decisions of one state to another. The letters borne by envoys, which served as their proof of credence, probably only related the assembly's decree in sparse style.[42] It was the envoy's task to persuade his recipient to agree with his own state's proposals.

The importance of formal rhetorical training in this task of persuasion can be seen in the change of personnel selected as envoys from the fifth to the fourth centuries BC. In the early fifth century BC, most Athenian envoys were current or former generals; a century later, as a result of increased professionalism, embassies were dominated by *rhetores*, including 'professional' politicians, philosophers, and other figures trained in eloquence. Many fourth-century generals never served on an embassy, and almost no lesser military figures did.[43] Oratorical skill was established as the essential element of the envoy's duty: 'Odysseus . . . [was] . . . the mirror of a diplomatist, eloquent and resourceful.'[44] The association of eloquence and diplomatic representation was maintained throughout antiquity.

[40] Mosley, *Envoys and Diplomacy*, 43; Adcock and Mosley, *Diplomacy in Ancient Greece*, 158; Matthews, 'Gesandtschaft', 658. Athenian political figures: Hansen, '*Rhetores* and *Strategoi*', 32–64.

[41] D. J. Mosley, 'Diplomacy by Conference: Almost a Spartan Contribution to Diplomacy?', *Emerita* 39 (1971), 187–93; Mosley, *Envoys and Diplomacy*, 14, 30–8 (on plenipotentiaries); Adcock and Mosley, *Diplomacy in Ancient Greece*, 155 (quote); Matthews, 'Gesandtschaft', 656. For a statement of the relative responsibilities of the envoy and the assembly: Andocides, *Oration 3: On the Peace with the Spartans*, c. 41.

[42] Mosley, *Envoys and Diplomacy*, 21.

[43] Mosley, 'Diplomacy and Disunion', 321; *Envoys and Diplomacy*, 21–9, 43; Adcock and Mosley, *Diplomacy in Ancient Greece*, 10, 126–7; Kienast, 'Presbeia', 590–6; Matthews, 'Gesandtschaft', 657. *Rhetores* and *strategoi* as envoys: Hansen, 'Athenian "Politicians"', 20–1. Only seven of the sixty-seven fourth-century BC *strategoi* in the prosopographical list of Hansen, '*Rhetores* and *Strategoi*', 32–64, are attested as serving as envoys. Known Attic and Spartan envoys are listed in Kienast, 'Presbeia', 595–628.

[44] Adcock and Mosley, *Diplomacy in Ancient Greece*, 9.

Republican and imperial Rome

Diplomatic relations under the Roman empire, up to the battle of Adrianople, were conducted within substantially different political and administrative frameworks from that of the classical Greek cities. But the mode of comunication, the Greek model of the envoy as an eloquent advocate, persisted throughout the Roman imperial period into late antiquity. These conventions affected not only embassies to foreign powers, but also internal embassies among communities and authorities within the empire.[45]

Even before its imperial expansion, republican Rome played an important part in the diplomatic traffic of the Mediterranean world. According to Varro and other antiquarians, the earliest Roman relations with other polities were conducted within a religious framework; both the conduct of embassies and the conclusion of treaties were carried out by priests of the college of *fetiales*. By the late republican period, this framework was long superseded, the *fetiales* retaining only a ceremonial religious role in the conclusion of treaties. Roman political dominance shifted the conduct of interstate relations from a quasi-religious sphere to a more explicitly military and state context. The Roman state exercised greater control over embassies than did the Greek cities. Envoys of allied states were supported at state expense; those of enemy powers had to seek permission to enter Roman territory, were excluded from the central precincts of the city itself (within the *pomerium*), and sometimes were required to travel under Roman escort. Unlike the Greek cities, only the Senate received foreign envoys, not the assemblies of the *populus Romanus*. Though in the early republic the *populus* voted on prosecuting war or concluding peace treaties, foreign policy was primarily the domain of the Senate.[46]

[45] For the following: in addition to Matthews, 'Gesandtschaft', 660–72 and Kienast, 'Presbia', 587–90: von Premerstein, 'Legatus', *RE* XII.1, 1133–41; Fergus Millar, *The Emperor in the Roman World (31 BC – AD 337)* (London, 1977), 341–55; Millar, 'Emperors, Frontiers, and Foreign Relations, 31 BC to AD 378', *Britannia* 13 (1982), 1–23; 'Government and Diplomacy'; Richard J. A. Talbert, *The Senate of Imperial Rome* (Princeton, 1984), 408–30; John F. Matthews, 'Hostages, Philosophers, Pilgrims, and the Diffusion of Ideas in the Late Roman Mediterranean and Near East', in F. M. Clover and R. S. Humphreys (eds.), *Tradition and Innovation in Late Antiquity* (Madison, WI, 1989), 29–49; Linderski, 'Ambassadors Go to Rome' and Jean-Louis Ferrary, '*Ius fetiale* et diplomatie', in Frézouls and Jacquemin (eds.), *Les Relations internationales*, 411–32; Elton, *Warfare in Roman Europe*, 175–98; Jones, *Kinship Diplomacy*, 81–121; Richard Duncan-Jones, *Structure and Scale in the Roman Economy* (Cambridge, 1990), 100–6.

[46] Polybius, *Histories* III, trans. W. R. Paton (LCL; London, 1923), VI, 13, 6–8; Theodore Mommsen, *Römisches Staatsrecht*, 3rd edn, III.1 (Leipzig, 1887; repr. Graz, 1952), 590–606, 1147–73; Erich S. Gruen, *The Hellenistic World and the Coming of Rome* (Berkeley, 1984), I, 203–49, esp. 231–44; Arthur M. Eckstein, *Senate and General: Individual Decision Making and Roman Foreign Relations, 264–194 BC* (Berkeley, 1987), xviii–xx.

The founding of the principate altered the political framework of Roman foreign policy making and diplomatic practice. The power of the triumvirs was recognised by neighbouring rulers, whose representatives sought out the *imperator* best able to offer Rome's favour, rather than the Senate. Octavian's monarchy stabilised the situation, establishing a single individual and sequence of successors whom 'client' kings and dynasts could approach. Until the mid-second century, the Senate continued occasionally to receive foreign envoys, and was advised, and sometimes consulted, on the emperors' dealings with other powers. This involvement appears to have been little more than a formal acknowledgement of the Senate's republican responsibilities. Augustus' *Res gestae* displays the shift in real authority. The Senate formally voted the emperor authority to conclude treaties in the mid-first century, a right possibly confirmed at each succeeding imperial accession. By the early third century, the Senate's former role in the creation and execution of foreign policy was a matter of nostalgia.[47]

The emperors' control of foreign relations was only one consequence of the true basis of their authority, the exclusive control of the army. Military force, actively employed or used indirectly as coercion, was the determining factor in international relations; the military authority concentrated in the person of Augustus and his successors inevitably bestowed the central role in foreign relations upon the emperors.[48] Just as they acted as commander-in-chief of the army, so the emperors alone received foreign representatives or rulers, and dispatched responses. From the late second century, the 'irreducibly personal character' of the emperors' command of military and diplomatic functions increased, as the delegation of special commands to lesser generals became uncommon. The imperial court was relocated from the Italian heartlands to the northern and eastern borders, the scene of the emperors' major campaigns, and from the time of Marcus Aurelius and Lucius Verus, sharing of imperial authority between co-emperors, each situated on a different frontier, became

[47] *Res gestae divi Augusti*, in *Documents Illustrating the Reigns of Augustus and Tiberius*, ed. Victor Ehenberg and A. H. M. Jones, 2nd edn (Oxford, 1955), cc. 31–3; cf. *ibid.*, chap. 7, 'Foreign Kings', 101–4; G. W. Bowersock, *Augustus and the Greek World* (Oxford, 1965), chap. 4, 'Kings and Dynasts', 42–61; Millar, 'Emperors, Frontiers, and Foreign Relations', 4–5 and n. 25, citing Cassius Dio LII, 31.1 on the former role of the Senate, 11–12; Millar, 'Government and Dipomacy', 348–51, 366–8; Talbert, *Senate of Imperial Rome*, 425–30. On Roman relations with foreign nations under the early empire: Luttwak, *Grand Strategy*; Braund, *Rome and the Friendly King*; Lynn F. Pitts, 'Relations between Rome and the German "Kings" on the Middle Danube in the First to the Fourth Centuries AD', *Journal of Roman Studies* 79 (1989), 45–58.

[48] Luttwak, *Grand Strategy*, 2–3; J. B. Campbell, *The Emperor and the Roman Army, 31 BC–AD 235* (Oxford, 1984), 348.

common. At the same time, the rare reception of foreign representatives by the Senate ceased.[49]

Not only did the emperor receive foreign envoys: he also often acted as the representative of the empire to hostile or allied peoples. The meeting on the Danube between the emperor Valens and the Gothic leader Athanaric in 369, and that of Valentinian I and the Alamanni king Macrianus on the Rhine five years later, are indicative of the military–diplomatic practices of the second to fourth centuries: personal confrontations between emperors and foreign leaders at one of the three riverine frontiers (Rhine, Danube, and Euphrates) of the empire.[50] Such meetings obviated diplomacy. The emperor's presence dispensed with the need for representation, and the location of the confrontation on or within the empire's borders avoided the projection of a Roman presence into foreign territory. Initial contacts between the adversaries preceded these meetings, but only as the battlefield diplomacy of antagonists in close proximity, not on-going negotiation at a distance. Of course, emperors were not necessarily present on the frontiers of the empire for every settlement; but even alliances and treaties negotiated by leading generals seem to have required subsequent personal ratification between the emperor and highly ranked representatives of the other party in person.[51]

It seems likely that frequent political communications other than military conflicts between the empire and the many powers adjacent to its frontiers must have existed. Certainly, imperial frontiers hosted constant communication in the form of trade.[52] There is, however, remarkably little evidence from the late second to the fourth centuries of diplomatic communication, or of responses to foreign states from the political centre of the empire. Rather, initial and perhaps most contact was presumably carried out by provincial governors and especially frontier military

[49] Millar, 'Emperors, Frontiers, and Foreign Relations', 14–15, 23 (quote); Millar, 'Government and Diplomacy', 375–7; Campbell, *The Emperor and the Roman Army*, 317–62.

[50] Valens: Amm. Marc. XXVII, 5.9; Themistius, *Orationes*, ed. H. Schenkl, G. Downey, and A. F. Norman, 2 vols. (Leipzig, 1951), I, *Or.* 10.201–6. Valentinian I: Amm. Marc. XXX, 3.5. Cf. the negotiations concluding the caesar Julian's campaign against the Chamavi in 358, held on the banks of the river Meuse; Eunapius, *Fr.*, 18.6. A later example of negotiations conducted from mid-stream of an (albeit temporary) water border: Nikephorus, *Short History* VI: the emperor Heraclius and the Persian general Shahin parlay from their ships on the Bosporus in 615; cf. *Chronicon Paschale, 284–628 AD*, trans. Michael Whitby and Mary Whitby (TTH 7; Liverpool, 1989), s.a. 615. Millar, 'Emperors, Frontiers, and Foreign Relations', 14; Millar, 'Government and Diplomacy', 369.

[51] Elton, *Warfare in Roman Europe*, 183.

[52] C. R. Whittaker, *Frontiers of the Roman Empire: A Social and Economic Study* (Baltimore, 1994), 113–31; Peter S. Wells, *The Barbarians Speak: How the Conquered Peoples Shaped Roman Europe* (Princeton, 1999), 224–58.

outposts. It is perhaps not solely the result of the sources' silence that foreign relations under the empire appear to be 'Romanocentric'. Even in its relations with newly powerful Sassanian Iran, the imperial government seems not to have maintained regular communications. Before the relatively well documented fourth century, there are few examples of imperial emissaries dispatched to foreign peoples, and it has been argued that much of the contact which did occur between Roman and Persian territories was essentially the outcome of private initiatives such as religious pilgrimage rather than of formal government initiatives.[53] Nevertheless, the fourth-century evidence suggests that the use of civilian and military officials, and also private individuals, as envoys to Persia and to the northern barbarians was a standard if not frequent practice in times of military confrontation.[54]

Four factors involved in the selection of the emperors' envoys to foreign rulers are illustrated in the accounts of Ammianus Marcellinus and Eunapius of Sardis of two embassies sent in 358 by Constantius II to the shah Shapur II, concerning Persian claims to Mesopotamia and Armenia.[55] The first embassy, consisting of the *comes rei militaris* Prosper, the *tribunus et notarius* Spectatus, and the philosopher Eustathius, failed to deter Shapur's preparations for war; a second mission, comprising the former *comes domesticorum* Lucillianus and the *tribunus et notarius* Procopius, was no more successful.

Just as generals were often sent as envoys to former antagonists in fifth-century BC Greece, so the choice of the two military officers, the *comites* Prosper and Lucillianus, probably exploited their military experience with the Persians. Lucillianus at least had previously commanded troops against

[53] Evidence of contacts from early to late empire: Monica Affortunati, 'Ambasciaṭori germanici in Italia dal II sec. a.C. al II sec. d.C', in Barbara and Piergiuseppe Scardigli (eds.), *Germani in Italia* (Rome, 1994), 105–15 (for northern European tribes). Primarily 'private' nature of Roman contacts with foreign regions: Matthews, 'Hostages, Philosophers, Pilgrims', esp. 45 (though several of the 'informal' factors of contact discussed operated under a governmental umbrella, i.e. hostages, and the Christian missionaries supported by the emperor Constantius II). Roman–Sassanian relations to fourth century: Benjamin Isaac, *The Limits of Empire: The Roman Army in the East* (Oxford, 1992); M. H. Dodgeon and S. N. C. Lieu (eds.), *The Roman Eastern Frontier and the Persian Wars, AD 226–363: A Documentary History* (London, 1991); for attested embassies: 17, 19–20 (Alexander Severus), 131–4 (Galerius).

[54] Millar, 'Emperors, Frontiers, and Foreign Relations', 5–6 (to the list at n. 36 of fourth-century evidence of Roman envoys, add Claudian, *Cons. Stil.* I, 51–68: Stilicho's mission to Persia *c.* 383), 18; Millar, 'Government and Diplomacy', 370–2.

[55] Amm. Marc. XVII, 5.1–15, 14.1–3 (first embassy); XVII, 14.3; XVIII, 6.17 (second embassy); Eunapius, *Vitae sophistarum*, ed. G. Giangrande (Rome, 1956), VI, 5–10, trans. in Philostratus and Eunapius, *Lives of the Sophists*, trans. Wilmer Cave Wright (LCL; London, 1921), 395–9. See also *Consularia Constantinopolitana* (MGH AA 11), s.a. 358: Persian envoys visit Constantinople in April 358.

the Persians, and Prosper had been stationed on the empire's eastern front.[56] Senior military commanders, *comites* or *magistri*, are prominent in other embassies recorded by Ammianus, and Eunapius states that it was usual for emperors to select as envoys 'men who had won distinction in the army, or *magistri militum*'.[57]

Eunapius' observation presents a second factor determining the selection of envoys, for he continues: 'or men who were next in rank to these and had been selected for [civilian] office'. Status was important; not, as in the Greek cities, the individual's position in regard to his aristocratic peers or the urban community, but his rank in the service of the emperor and the perception of his seniority in the eyes of foreign rulers. Shapur dismissed the first embassy on the pretext that its members were insufficiently distinguished (though the composition of the second mission was almost identical).[58]

Thirdly, the Roman administration, as is well known, had no equivalent to a specialised department of foreign affairs for policy creation or implementation.[59] No office in the imperial bureaucracy embraced the duties of a 'professional' diplomat. Rather, officials were chosen to undertake missions *ad hoc* at the emperor's pleasure or on the advice of his *consistorium*; Eustathius, who held no public office at all, was included on the first mission on the advice of Constantius' praetorian prefect Musonianus.[60] Mere proximity to the emperor was an important factor in selection. Two members of Constantius' embassies to Shapur were *tribuni et notarii*, and other *tribuni* feature as legates elsewhere in Ammianus.[61] The position of *tribunus et notarius*, though primarily a stenographic post, seems often to have served as a factotum for the imperial consistory, and it is not surprising that holders of this office should be chosen as the emperor's emissaries. From the fourth century, *magistri officiorum* often feature in accounts of embassies. Their role, however, was only to provide support facilities for embassies and to arrange the emperors' audiences with foreign envoys. The office was not vested with responsibility for foreign

[56] *PLRE* I, 'Lucillianus 3', 517–19; 'Prosper', 751. [57] Eunapius, *Vitae* VI, 5.3.

[58] Cf. R. Mathisen, 'Patricians as Diplomats in Late Antiquity', *Byzantinische Zeitschrift* 79 (1986), 34–49.

[59] Millar, 'Emperors, Frontiers and Foreign Relations', 4–7; Matthews, 'Gesandtschaft', 665; Gruen, *The Hellenistic World*, 203–49; Eckstein, *Senate and General*, xviii–xx; A. D. Lee, 'Diplomacy', in Bowersock *et al.* (eds.), *Late Antiquity: A Guide*, 411–12.

[60] Amm. Marc. XVII, 5.15. For Eustathius' career: *PLRE* I, 'Eustathius 1', 310; he is not even known to have held a teaching position, unlike his wife Sosipatra; *PLRE* I, 849.

[61] Amm. Marc. XIX, 11.5: Constantius II sends two *tribuni* to the Sarmatian Limigantes in 359. A fifth-century example is Consentius, *tribunus et notarius* in the consistory of Valentinian III, used as an envoy to Constantinople; Sid. Ap., *Carm.* XXIII, 214–32.

policy creation or implementation, although individual *magistri*, such as Peter *patricius*, evidently took a particular interest in foreign affairs.[62]

Eustathius' presence in the first mission raises the final factor determining selection of envoys: rhetorical skill. The philosopher was nominated as a member of the embassy for his talents in persuasion, *ut opifex suadendi*, remarkable testimony to assumptions of cultural assimilation between the Sassanian court and the Greek East.[63] The classical practice of selecting envoys for their skill in oratory continued to operate under the Roman empire. At the time of the embassies to Shapur, the praetorian prefect Musonianus had already been engaged for some time in negotiations with Persia. His suggestion to send the philosopher reflects the judgement of an experienced officer on how best to constitute an embassy. Though philosophers and sophists are not frequently attested as envoys to foreign powers, the criterion by which Eustathius was selected was not unusual. Rhetorical training was the key to success for a civil public career; when selecting a representative, the emperor had at his disposal a pool of individuals with conventional rhetorical training within the imperial service. Eustathius' companion on the journey to Ctesiphon, the *tribunus et notarius* Spectatus, is elsewhere described as an able orator, as may be expected from a cousin of the sophist Libanius of Antioch.[64] Spectatus' fellow *tribunus* Procopius was sufficiently regarded by his close relative the emperor Julian to be considered as a potential successor to the throne.[65] Eloquence, indeed, was the most characteristic trait of envoys.

Though the emperors engaged in frequent diplomatic communications with foreign powers, they were far more often the recipients of formal embassies from within the empire: approaches from cities, provincal and diocesan councils, the Senate, and other bodies. There are no terminological distinctions between formal *legationes* within the empire and those without; the same conventions and conceptions regulated

[62] Rudolf Helm, 'Untersuchungen über den auswärtigen diplomatischen Verkehr des römischen Reiches im Zeitalter der Spätantike', *Archiv für Urkundenforschung* 12 (1932), repr. in Olshausen and Biller (eds.), *Antike Diplomatie*, 343–5 and n. 323; Jones, *LRE* I, 369, III, 75 n. 8; Manfred Clauss, *Der Magister officiorum in der Spätantike (4.–6. Jahrhundert): das Amt und sein Einfluss auf die kaiserliche Politik* (Vestigia 32; Munich, 1980), 63–72. See below, chapter 5 at n. 41, and chapter 6 at nn. 10–17, 30, 52.

[63] Amm. Marc. XVII, 5.15 (quote); the theme is much developed in Eunapius, *Vitae* VI, 5–10. Cf. R. C. Blockley, 'Doctors as Diplomats in the Sixth Century', *Florilegium* 2 (1980), 89–100; S. N. C. Lieu, 'Captives, Refugees and Exiles: A Study of Cross-Frontier Civilian Movements and Contacts between Rome and Persia from Valerian to Jovian', in P. Freeman and D. Kennedy (eds.), *The Defence of the Roman and Byzantine East* (BAR International Series 297; Oxford, 1986), 492–3.

[64] Libanius, *Epp.*, 331 (trans. Dodgeon and Lieu, *Roman Eastern Frontier*, 223–4); *PLRE* I, 'Spectatus 1', 850.

[65] *PLRE* I, 'Procopius 4', 742–3.

both.[66] This tradition of 'internal diplomacy' was essential to developments in the West in the fifth century.

Formal approaches to the emperor from his subjects were an intrinsic element of the administrative structure of the empire. The imperial court, whether residing in Rome or on campaign, was always thronged by crowds of provincial emissaries and litigants. Absence on a mission to the emperor was accepted as a normal duty for provincial aristocrats; under imperial legislation, members of urban or provincial councils who had undertaken an embassy were exempt from serving on another mission for two years, an indication of the frequency with which journeys to the court could be required.[67]

Embassies from the cities and provinces constituted the dynamic impetus of most imperial governmental activity, for the bulk of the emperors' non-military actions were responses to initiatives from local communities, concerning issues such as disputes between cities, complaints about provincial governors, or requests for privileges. The political cohesion of the empire, also, was maintained by this traffic, as urban and provincial councils dispatched delegations to the emperors on all ceremonial occasions – imperial accessions, victories, decennaliae, dynastic events such as marriages and births – as expressions of loyalty. Under the empire, individual *honorati* and land-owners as well as municipal magistrates and imperial officials were accustomed to expressing their views to the central government, either directly or through provincial assemblies, via delegated *legati* if necessary.[68]

Cities and provincial communities appear generally to have been able to approach the emperor directly, bypassing, with some restrictions, their provincial governors. Direct appeal to the emperor was a form of administration parallel to the hierarchical system of provincial government, one 'ascending' from the provinces rather than 'descending' from the central authority. By these approaches, the needs of cities and provincial

66 For the following: von Premerstein, 'Legatus'; Jones, *LRE* II, 763–6; Kienast, 'Presbia'; Matthews, 'Gesandtschaft', 661–72; Talbert, *Senate of Imperial Rome*, 408–25; Joyce Reynolds, 'Cities', in David Braund (ed.), *The Administration of the Roman Empire, 241 BC–AD 193* (Exeter, 1988), 28–31, 39–46; Tor Hauken, *Petition and Response: An Epigraphic Study of Petitions to Roman Emperors 181–249* (Monographs from the Norwegian Institute at Athens 2; Bergen, 1998), esp. 296–317; Clifford Ando, *Imperial Ideology and Provincial Loyalty in the Roman Empire* (Berkeley, 2000), 93–4, 168–9, 175–205; most importantly, Millar, *Emperor in the Roman World*, 342–50, 363–463, esp. 363–8, 375–94, and Millar, 'Government and Diplomacy'.

67 Millar, *Emperor in the Roman World*, 363, 375, 379; Paulus, *Responsa* I *apud* Justinian, *Digest* L, 7.8.1. For imperial law on provincial embassies: *CTh* XII, 12.1–16; Justinian, *Codex* X, 63.1–6; *Digest* L, 7.1–17.

68 E.g. *Constitutio* of Honorius, 17 April 418, establishing the *Concilium septem provincarum: vel honoratos confluere, vel mitti legatos . . . si earum iudices occupatio certa tenuerit, sciant, legatos iuxta consuetudinem esse mittendos*; MGH Epp. 3, 13–15. On provincial assemblies: Jones, *LRE* I, 763–6.

assemblies came to the attention of the emperor without active investigation on the part of his bureaucracy; the imperial court's role was essentially passive and reactive, typical of Roman imperial government.[69] Imperial bureaucracy and provincial embassies were recognised as being complementary elements of administration. A *subscriptio* of the emperor Caracalla in 213 states that 'those who are performing the duties of an embassy enjoy the same privilege as those who are absent on behalf of the state'. Success in pleading the case of an embassy could lead to reimbursement of costs by the emperor. In the fourth century, imperial sponsoring and control of embassies was regularised. The costs of embassies were no longer the burden of either the envoy or his community, but were reimbursed from imperial funds. Envoys were issued with warrants (*evectiones*) permitting them to travel by the *cursus publicus*.[70] Imperial legislation controlled the expenses of embassies and provided legal protection for envoys. In this way, the appeals of provincial communities were coopted into the structure of imperial administration.[71]

Embassies from provincial cities originated as appeals to Rome from free cities and communities. The extension of Roman power and the process of provincialisation transferred the business of most important political affairs from the cities, the traditional units of social organisation of much of the Mediterranean world, to the imperial authorities. In the late first century AD, Plutarch observed:

> Nowadays, then, when the affairs of the cities no longer include leadership in wars, nor the overthrowing of tyrannies, nor acts of alliances, what opening for a conspicuous and brilliant public career could a young man find? There remain the public lawsuits and embassies to the emperor, which demand a man of ardent temperament and one who possesses both courage and intellect.[72]

The incorporation of regions into the Roman empire turned cities' embassies to Rome from 'foreign' to 'internal' communications, but contemporary sources do not make this distinction. The diplomatic forms of foreign embassies were always maintained in approaches to the emperors from provincial bodies and, indeed, from the Senate. Before Caesar and Augustus, missions to Rome had approached the Senate; by the mid-second century, provincial embassies, like missions from foreign powers,

69 Peter Garnsey and Richard Saller, *The Roman Empire: Economy, Society and Culture* (Berkeley, 1987), chap. 2: 'Government Without Bureaucracy', 20–40; Hauken, *Petition and Response*, 298.

70 Caracalla: *Cod. Just.* II, 53.1, cited in Millar, *Emperor in the Roman World*, 383. Fourth century: *CTh* VIII, 5.32, XII, 12.6.9, cited in Matthews, 'Gesandtschaft', 664.

71 Millar, *Emperor in the Roman World*, 363; Matthews, 'Gesandtschaft', 663–4.

72 Plutarch, *Precepts of Statecraft*, in *Moralia* X, trans. Harold North Fowler (LCL; London, 1936), 805a–b, cited in Reynolds, 'Cities', 28; cf. Strabo, *Geography*, trans. H. L. Jones, VI (LCL; London, 1929), XIV, 3.3, cited in Jones, *Kinship Diplomacy*, 106.

seem no longer to have sought out the Senate even as a gesture of courtesy, an indication of the conceptual equality of embassies from within or without the borders of the empire.[73]

As in earlier antiquity, so under the Roman empire, representation of a community was the prerogative of the aristocracy. An embassy represented both a burden, for the expense involved and the strain of travelling, and an honour, to represent the community and possibly to gain personal rewards from the emperor. For both reasons, provincial councillors chose emissaries from their own ranks. But the essential quality determining the selection of an envoy was still rhetorical skill. The movement known as the Second Sophistic, which developed and flourished in the first two centuries after Augustus, provided its students with technical skills to produce a range of oratorical occasional pieces. The genres and forms defined by the Sophists shaped the conduct of public speech within the empire; both orators and their audiences were conscious of the conventions to be observed. The late third-century handbook attributed to Menander Rhetor outlines the forms of panegyrics to be delivered to public magistrates, including the emperor.[74] These rhetorical practices were intrinsically tied to public administration under the empire:

> all might depend on the favour with which the emperor greeted the oration; hence arose that well-attested role of the orators of the Second Sophistic on embassies before the emperor. It is impossible to over-emphasise both the fact that these endlessly-repeated journeys to the emperor were the essential means by which the cities and other groups communicated with him, and that they required on the part of the ambassador a comportment, diction and choice of words in accordance with the exacting canons of Graeco-Roman culture.[75]

The oration, not the mere journey to the court or any letters delivered to the emperor, was the essential component of an embassy. When the emperor was in residence in Rome, provincial communities sometimes sent a letter by a carrier to a fellow-citizen already residing in the imperial city, asking him to present an oration to the emperor; it was the orator, not the carrier of the letter, who was paid the *viaticum*, the expenses

[73] Talbert, *Senate of Rome*, 411–25; Millar, *Emperor in the Roman World*, 343–50.

[74] *Menander Rhetor*, ed. and trans. D. A. Russell and N. G. Wilson (Oxford, 1981), Treatise II, 1–2 (imperial panegyric), 12 (speech for delivery of *aurea coronarum*), 13 ('envoy's speech' on behalf of a city 'in trouble'). G. W. Bowersock, *Greek Sophists in the Roman Empire* (Oxford, 1969), esp. 43–58; G. Anderson, *The Second Sophistic: A Cultural Phenomenon in the Roman Empire* (London, 1993).

[75] Millar, *Emperor in the Roman World*, 382–5 (quote at 385); for examples of the sophists as envoys to the emperors. *ibid.* 385 n. 69, references from Philostratus, *Lives of the Sophists*; also Peter Brown, *Power and Persuasion in Late Antiquity: Towards a Christian Empire* (Madison, 1992).

owing to an envoy.[76] The oratorical nature of diplomatic missions was in accord with the primacy given to oral pronouncements in all imperial decisions and other public business.[77] The fortunes of Sophistry declined with those of the empire during the mid-third century, but flourished again in the fourth century with the talents not only of pagan rhetoricians such as Libanius of Antioch and Themistius of Constantinople, but also of their Christian pupils, including John Chrysostom. In the shadow of these great figures, however, many nameless holders of civic or imperial office regularly put into practice the techniques of rhetoric in the constant communication between government and its constituents.

CONTEMPORARY PERSPECTIVES

The conventions covering embassies in classical Greece and imperial Rome, and the administrative arrangements of the latter, formed the background to the patterns of political communication in the kingdoms of the post-imperial West.[78] Many traditional practices and attitudes are evident in the fifth and early sixth centuries. In the 460s, a Gallic aristocrat described in a letter the honour accruing to a member of a provincial council when he represented his city to the imperial authorities; his addressee was obviously more conscious of the burden an embassy entailed.[79]

Perhaps the most obvious continuity was skill in traditional rhetoric as the essential criterion for selection as an envoy, for representatives of provincial communities as much as those of kings and emperors. Despite the contraction of publicly supported schools, grammar and rhetoric remained the core of the educational curriculum, providing not only one of the most important distinguishing features of the governing classes, the

76 *Digest* L, 1.36; Millar, *Emperor in the Roman World*, 363 (oration), 379 (letters).

77 Millar, 'Government and Diplomacy', 358.

78 The best accounts of diplomatic procedures in late antiquity are Helm, 'Untersuchungen über den auswärtigen diplomatischen Verkehr'; F. L. Ganshof, 'Merowingisches Gesandschaftswesen', in *Aus Geschichte und Landeskunde: Forschungen und Darstellungen* [*Festschrift* for Franz Steinbach] (Bonn, 1960), 166–83; Ganshof, *The Middle Ages: A History of International Relations*, trans. R. I. Hall (New York, 1970), esp. chaps. 1 and 3; Matthews, 'Gesandtschaft'; Blockley, *East Roman Foreign Policy*, chap. 4: 'Policy and Its Instruments', 129–63; P. S. Barnwell, 'War and Peace: Historiography and Seventh-Century Embassies', *Early Medieval Europe* 6 (1997), 127–39. The discussion of strategic information collection in A. D. Lee, *Information and Frontiers: Roman Foreign Relations in Late Antiquity* (Cambridge, 1993), addresses many aspects of foreign policy and diplomacy. Several of the articles in Jonathan Shepard and Simon Franklin (eds.), *Byzantine Diplomacy* (Society for the Promotion of Byzantine Studies Publication 1; Aldershot, 1992) offer useful if later comparanda; see especially E. Chrysos, 'Byzantine Diplomacy, AD 300–800: Means and Ends', 25–39. No study has focused on the fifth- and sixth-century West and the Latin sources. For earlier and later periods, see n. 107 below.

79 Sid. Ap., *Ep.* V, 20.

honestiores, but also the conventions for communication in all spoken or written public media.[80] Italy retained the highest level of education in the West, but Gaul, Spain, and North Africa all also continued to produce young men trained in a classical curriculum, at least during the pre-Justinianic period.[81] The rise of episcopal and monastic schools, prompted by the shrinkage of public schools, shifted emphasis of the purpose of education, but not necessarily of its content. Rhetorical education and literary proficiency on the one hand, and engagement in public life on the other, remained mutually linked. It is not surprising to find the poet Maximianus, apparently a contemporary of Boethius in Ostrogothic Italy, opening an elegy on a particularly infelicitous love affair with the lines:

> Sent to the lands of the dawn on the duty of an envoy,
> To weave for the sake of all a tranquil work of peace,
> While I strove to bring together covenants of the two-fold realm
> I met with impious wars of my own heart.[82]

Conventions of education and rhetoric shaped not only the conduct of communication, but also thereby the works which we use as sources for the period.[83]

The context of political embassies, however, grew more complex after the establishment of the barbarian kingdoms. During the early empire, the administration of conquered territories as provinces transformed

[80] On late antique education: Pierre Riché, *Education and Culture in the Barbarian West: Sixth through Eighth Centuries*, trans. J. J. Contreni (Columbia, 1976); Robert A. Kaster, *Guardians of Language: The Grammarian and Society in Late Antiquity* (Berkeley, 1997); Robert Browning, 'Education in the Roman Empire', in *The Cambridge Ancient History* XIV: *Late Antiquity: Empire and Succesors*, ed. Averil Cameron, Bryan Ward-Perkins and Michael Whitby (Cambridge, 2000), 855–83; J. H. W. G. Liebeschuetz, *The Decline and Fall of the Roman City* (Oxford, 2001), 318–41. For late public schools and episcopal schools in the West: Riché, *Education and Culture*, 15–135; Riché, 'La survivance des écoles publiques en Gaule au Ve siècle', *Le Moyen Age* 63 = 4th ser. 12 (1957), 421–36; Martin Heinzelmann, '*Studia sanctorum*: éducation, milieux d'instruction et valeurs éducatives dans l'hagiographie en Gaule jusqu'à la fin de l'époque mérovingienne', *Haut Moyen-Age: culture, éducation et société* (Nanterre, 1990), 105–38. Rhetoric: G. A. Kennedy, *Classical Rhetoric and Its Christian and Secular Tradition from Ancient to Modern Times* (Chapel Hill, 1980).

[81] For the sixth to ninth centuries: see the articles by Ian Wood, Thomas F. X. Noble, and Roger Collins in Rosamond McKitterick (ed.), *The Uses of Literacy in Early Mediaeval Europe* (Cambridge, 1990).

[82] Maximianus, *Elegia* V, in *Poetae latini minores* V, ed. E. Baehrens (Leipzig, 1879), lines 1–4: *Missus ad Eoas legati munere partes/Tranquillum cunctis nectere pacis opus/Dum studeo gemini componere foedera regni/Inveni cordis bella nefanda mei.* Date: *PLRE* II, 'Maximianus 7', 739–40. Cf. the careers of the Gallic aristocrats Arator and Parthenius, who acted as representatives to the court of Theoderic in Ravenna on behalf of Provence and Dalmatia respectively; *PLRE* II, 126–7, 833–4; below, chapter 6 at n. 102.

[83] Two examples of the impact of late antique educational conventions on genres of source materials are Alan Cameron, 'Wandering Poets: A Literary Movement in Byzantine Egypt', *Historia* 14 (1965), 470–509 (for panegyric); and Geoffrey Greatrex, 'Lawyers and Historians in Late Antiquity', in Ralph W. Mathisen (ed.), *Law, Society, and Authority in Late Antiquity* (Oxford, 2001), 148–60 (for *historia*).

'foreign' embassies into 'internal' communications; an integral part of the process of 'Romanisation' was the use of conventions of communication by the elites of former independent regions as a means to display their participation in the political system of the empire.[84] In an obvious, political sense, the establishment of the kingdoms was a process of 'de-provincialisation'. Regions that were once imperial dioceses or provinces now constituted autonomous polities representing regional interests. The interaction among the kingdoms and the empire, now no longer part of a single, hierarchical system, can be called 'foreign relations'.[85] But the 'shifting frontiers' of the post-imperial West are not to be understood simply as a redrawing of the traditional *limes* along new military border-zones between the empire and the kingdoms.[86] The western kingdoms had a marked propensity to replicate the former administrative borders of the Roman provincial administration.[87] The antithetical terms *Romania* and *barbaricum* which appear in fourth-century sources have no equivalents in the fifth and sixth centuries; indeed, sources from the western kingdoms refer to their polities and the eastern empire jointly as *res publicae* and *regna*.[88]

More important to the present context are the continuities in cultural and political practices which overlaid military and administrative borders. Inhabitants of former provinces, now the subjects of new rulers, could approach imperial authorities, expecting and sometimes receiving the emperor's aid. Perhaps the best-known embassy of late antiquity is that of the 'groans of the British' to the *magister militum* Aetius in or after 446,

[84] For recent work on 'Romanisation': Greg Woolf, *Becoming Roman: The Origins of Provincial Civilization in Gaul* (Cambridge, 1998); Ando, *Imperial Ideology and Provincial Loyalty*; Ramsay MacMullen, *Romanization in the Time of Augustus* (New Haven, 2000).

[85] Braund, *Rome and the Friendly King*, 6, usefully suggests that the foreign relations of the late empire can be understood in the light of the 'client' kingdoms of the late republican period.

[86] For the quoted phrase: Hagith S. Sivan and Ralph W. Mathisen, 'Introduction', in Ralph W. Mathisen and Hagith S. Sivan (eds.), *Shifting Frontiers in Late Antiquity* (Aldershot, 1996), 1–7; see the chapters by Drinkwater, Harries, and Olster, and esp. David Harry Miller: 'Frontier Societies and the Transition between Late Antiquity and the Early Middle Ages', 158–71.

[87] As one example, note the letter of Remigius of Rheims to Clovis, congratulating his assumption of the administration of Belgica secunda; *Ep. Austr.* 2. Clovis' later conquests are conventionally recognised as roughly prefiguring the borders of modern France, but it is more pertinent to note that they reintegrated most of the two imperial dioceses of Gaul and the Seven Provinces.

[88] For the dichotomy of *Romania* and *barbaricum*: *Scolies Ariennes sur le concile d'Aquilée*, ed. and trans. Roger Gryson (Sources chrétiennes 267; Paris, 1980), [*Epistula Auxenti de fide, vita, et obitu Ulfilae*] 37–8, 165. For other attestations (some sixth century, but not with regard to the western kingdoms), see the entries s.vv. in *ThLL* II, 1733; Lewis and Short, 222; G. W. H. Lampe, *A Patristic Greek Lexicon* (Oxford, 1961), 289, 1219; Henri Chirat, *Dictionnaire Latin–Français des auteurs chrétiens* (Turnhout, 1954), 110, 725. *Barbaricum* was a variant of the classical *barbaria*. *Res publicae*: as at n. 16 above; cf. the letters of the Burgundian king Sigismund to either Anastasius or Justin I, which strive to portray the Burgundian realm as within the *termini* of the empire (Avitus of Vienne, *Epp.*, 78, 93, 94).

recorded by Gildas as an indication of British degeneracy and pointedly repeated by Bede. This vain attempt to gain Roman imperial military support against barbarian raids was the last of three legations sent to imperial authorities, after the withdrawal of direct Roman administration and the establishment of independent rule.[89] There are less melodramatic examples of embassies sent to imperial officials by individuals, cities, and local bodies in Spain, several generations after the establishment of autonomous kingdoms there.[90] At the same time, provincials still under direct imperial rule could present petitions at the courts of neighbouring barbarian monarchs.[91] The approaches of kings themselves to the emperor often resemble the appeals of any other subject, albeit a highly placed one, to his legitimate ruler; yet an experienced envoy could speak of addressing the emperor and barbarian rulers in the same terms.[92] The establishment of the new kingdoms did not terminate the constant motion of embassies throughout the western provinces, but expanded its range of participants. Legatine traffic in the fifth and early sixth centuries was both a sign of administrative and social continuity from imperial to royal rule, and itself an instrument of the political changes of the period.

Formal interstate diplomacy, the most obvious example of political communication, is more studied in relation to the late Roman East than the West. This is not only because of the evident importance of Roman foreign relations with its neighbouring empire, Sassanian Persia, but also because the extant eastern sources foreground embassies and treaties. The East proffers 'diplomatic histories' and administrative monuments, including archives and formulae for ceremonial, which the West lacks.[93] The extant sections of the classicising Greek historians Olympiodorus of

89 Gildas, *De excidio Britonum*, ed. T. Mommsen, trans. M. Winterbottom (Arthurian Period Sources 7; London, 1978), XIV–XX, quotation at XX, 1. Bede, *Chronica maiora*, ed. T. Mommsen (MGH AA 13, 303), 484; Bede, *HE* I, 13.

90 For Spain: see below, chapter 2 and Table 1 nos. 1, 3, 16, 24–5, 40. For Gaul, cf. below, chapter 4, on Orientius of Auch.

91 Sid. Ap., *Ep.* I, 2.8; IV, 8.5.

92 Kings' addresses to emperors: e.g. Cass., *Variae* I, 1; II, 1; VIII, 1 (Theoderic to Anastasius; Athalaric to Justin); Avitus of Vienne, *Epp.*, 46A, 78, 93, 94 (Sigismund to Anastasius or Justin I). Experienced envoy: Senarius, *Epitaph*, lines 4–13.

93 Archives: Peter *patricius, magister officiorum* under Justinian and an experienced envoy to the Persians and Goths (*PLRE* III, 'Petrus 6', 994–8), published an account of his mission to Persia in 561, and may also have lodged minutes of meetings and other papers concerning the same mission in imperial archives; Blockley, Introduction to Menander Protector, 19–20 and *Fr.* VI, 2. The lengthy account in Malalas, *Chron.* XVIII, 56 of the embassy of an unnamed envoy sent by Justinian to the king of the Axumites, dated *c.* 530, was also based on a report written by the envoy himself; the style and emphasis on exoticism suggest a literary publication rather than an archival report. Peter *patricius*' history of the office of the *magister officiorum* preserved descriptions of ceremonial for various court events, including the dispatch and reception of envoys: *De cer.* I, 84–95 (envoys: I, 87–90); see below, chapter 6, at nn. 8–20.

Thebes, Priscus, Malchus, Nonnosus, and Menander Protector all have valuable, detailed accounts of diplomatic interchange between the eastern Roman empire and its neighbours.[94] It has been suggested that these authors illustrate a shift in fifth- and sixth-century eastern historiography from warfare to diplomacy as the main emphasis of *historia*, a shift which in turn reflects the increasingly formalised relations between the Roman and Persian states.[95] While the development of regularised relations between the great powers is sufficiently well attested, it is less certain that eastern historiography underwent a corresponding shift of emphasis.

Most of the extant fragments of the classicising historians owe their survival to later Byzantine excerpters and readers who had particular interests in diplomatic exchange. This is explicit in the cases of Priscus, Malchus, and Menander Protector; the significant fragments of their works are mediated by deliberate selection in the *Excerpta de legationibus Romanorum* and *Excerpta de legationibus barbarorum* (*Excerpts concerning the Embassies of the Romans and the Barbarians*), part of the series of *Excerpta* from classical and late Greek authors ordered by the tenth-century Byzantine emperor Constantine VII Porphyrogenitus.[96] The selection criteria for extracts from earlier works were defined by the well-educated emperor, and reflect the strategic preoccupations of tenth-century Byzantium. Constantine VII himself, no soldier emperor, was the author of a diplomatic manual.[97] Olympiodorus and Nonnosus owe their partial survival to Photius, the ninth-century Constantinopolitan scholar (and, later, imperial bureaucrat and Patriarch), and to his massive 'good book guide', the *Bibliotheca*, which summarises nearly 400 books, many now otherwise lost.[98] Photius too had a personal and professional interest in embassies

[94] Olympiodorus of Thebes, Priscus and Malchus: ed. and trans. in Blockley, *Fr. Class. Hist.* II. Nonnosus: ed. and trans. in Photius, *Bibliothèque*, ed. René Henry, 8 vols. (Paris, 1959–77), I, *codex* 3; English trans. in Photius, *The Bibliotheca*, trans. N. G. Wilson (London, 1994), 27–9. Menander Protector: *The* History *of Menander the Guardsman*, ed. and trans. R. C. Blockley (ARCA Classical and Medieval Texts, Papers and Monographs 17; Liverpool, 1985).

[95] Historiography: Blockley, *Fr. Class. Hist.* I, 61; Blockley, *The* History *of Menander*, esp. 17–18; cf. the reviews by Brian Croke, *Phoenix* 37 (1983), 175–8 and Averil Cameron, *Phoenix* 42 (1988), 282. Cf. the title of a German translation of Priscus: *Byzantinische Diplomaten und östliche Barbaren*, trans. Ernst Doblhofer (Byzantinische Geschichtsschreiber 4; Graz, 1955). Roman–Persian relations: Blockley, *East Roman Foreign Policy*; Dodgeon and Lieu, *Roman Eastern Frontier and the Persian Wars*; Lee, *Information and Frontiers*; Geoffrey Greatrex, *Rome and Persia at War, 502–532* (ARCA Classical and Medieval Texts, Papers and Monographs 37; Leeds, 1998).

[96] *Excerpta historica iussu imperatoris Constantini Porphyrogeniti confecta*, ed. U. Boissevain, C. de Boor, and T. Buttner-Wobst, 4 vols. (Berlin, 1903–10), I: *Excerpta de legationibus*, ed. C. de Boor (1903).

[97] Constantine VII Porphyrogenitus, *De administrando imperio* I, ed. G. Moravcsik, trans. R. J. H. Jenkins, 2nd edn (Corpus fontium historiae Byzantinae 1; Washington, DC, 1967); II: *Commentary*, ed. R. J. H. Jenkins (London, 1962).

[98] Photius, *Bibliothèque, codices* 3 (Nonnosus) and 80 (Olympiodorus). Other fragments of Olympiodorus are listed and translated by Blockley in *Fr. Class. Hist.* I, 107–12; II, 153–220.

which affected his presentation of earlier historical works, though less drastically than in Constantine's *Excerpta*. The *Bibliotheca* was compiled at the request of Photius' brother Tarasius shortly after Photius had been chosen to participate in an imperial embassy to the 'Assyrians', probably the Abbasid caliphate.[99] That his impending voyage was prominent in Photius' mind is indicated in his prefatory and concluding addresses to his brother, mentioning not only the circumstance of composition and the alacrity with which he had fulfilled his brother's request prior to departure, but also the possibilty of his dying during the journey.[100] Photius had a particular interest in histories, the only genre of work he specifies in his preface, and in accounts of voyages; his historical summaries dwell on accounts of embassies and preserve the most picturesque details.[101]

The selections of Photius and Constantine VII illustrate how contemporary geopolitical concerns informed readers' use of the classical and late Roman cultural heritage of Constantinople; they also valuably preserve a huge proportion of our sources for late antique history. But their predilections for diplomacy distort our image of their sources. The works of those classicising historians which are fully extant, Procopius, Agathias, and Theophylact Simocatta, also feature detailed accounts of embassies, but their embassy narratives are set in a broader context of military history and imperial politics.[102] Sections of the fragmentary authors which survive outside the *Excerpta* of Constantine VII indicate the range of their concerns other than embassies and diplomacy; again, they concern imperial dynastic affairs and military campaigns in particular.[103] The selections of Procopius' *Wars* in the *Excerpta* convey only a very partial representation of Procopius' interests, and Photius' summary of the first two books

[99] Warren T. Treadgold, *The Nature of the* Bibliotheca *of Photius* (Washington, DC, 1980), 16–36, 51; for date (843/58 and likely 845): 25–36.

[100] Photius, *Bibliothèque* I, *Praef.*, p. 1; VIII, *fin.* 214.

[101] Treadgold, *Nature of the* Bibliotheca, 100–2; Henry's note to Photius, *Bibliothèque* I, 4 n. 2; Tomas Hägg and Warren Treadgold, 'The Preface of the *Bibliotheca* of Photius Once More', *Symbolae Osloenses* 61 (1986), 137, for the reading of the part of the preface mentioning histories. Details: e.g. in Olympiodorus: fossils in the Egyptian oases, difficulties in sea travel, St Elmo's fire, a talking parrot, and emerald mines (*Fr.*, 32, 35.1, 35.2 [33, 36, 37]); in Nonnosus: again dangers in travelling, herds of elephants, climatic changes between north and central Africa, and pygmies (Photius, *Bibliothèque* I, *codex* 3).

[102] Procopius, *Wars*; Agathias, *Historiarum libri quinque*, ed. Rudolf Keydell (Corpus fontium historiae Byzantinae 2; Berlin, 1967); trans. J. D. Frendo (Corpus fontium historiae Byzantinae 2a; Berlin, 1975); Theophylact Simocatta, *Historiae*, ed. C. de Boor and P. Wirth (Leipzig, 1887; repr. 1972); trans. M. Whitby and M. Whitby (Oxford, 1986).

[103] E.g. Blockley, *Fr. Class. Hist.* I, 118–23, conspectus of fragments of Priscus: accounts of eastern and western imperial dynastic matters, other court affairs, events in Constantinople, and many military issues not involving embassies come from sources other than the *Excerpta* (*Fr.*, 3, 7–8, 18, 19, 28–30, 32, 34–5, 42–3, 50, 54–66). Similarly *ibid.*, 126–7, conspectus of fragments of Malchus.

of Procopius, while generally accurate, is brief on military points but evidently interested in embassies, treaties, and ethnography (Photius retains, for example, the embassy of the Gothic king Vitigis to the Persian shah Chosroes).[104] The stress on diplomacy in the extant versions of the classicising authors is not a direct reflection of their own emphases or of a climate of increasing formality in relations between Constantinople and Ctesiphon; in addition to Persia, the fragments and summaries narrate in detail Roman relations with important and lesser barbarian neighbour groups, most famously Priscus' account of his embassy to Attila.[105] The classicising historians are extremely valuable sources; the conditions of their survival in fact serve modern interests to an extent which is rare for study in this period. But it is important to recognise the bias in their preservation.

The West has no equivalent even to these selective 'diplomatic' histories. This is largely because of different literary traditions in East and West: a classicising Latin historiography may have existed in the Latin West during the fifth century, but it did not flourish and has barely been transmitted to posterity.[106] A word about sources and methodology is therefore in order. Because of the inadequacy of Latin *historiae*, a detailed narrative account of diplomatic politics throughout the West – a diplomatic history – cannot be written without invalidating lacunae or excessive speculation. Similarly, a full, systematic analysis of the functions of embassies cannot be written for the late antique West, though a survey of available data is offered at chapter 6 below.[107] To compile an inventory of desirable areas of enquiry, most of which remain blank through lack of data, or which are filled with specific examples from which generalisations can be drawn only perilously, would not be useful.

Although diplomatic narratives are lacking, certain western writers do display a special interest in diplomatic exchange and the role of the envoy. Their interests are all the more striking for appearing in texts representing

[104] Procopius: Photius, *Bibliothèque* I, *codex* 63; Tomas Hägg, *Photios als Vermittler antiker Literatur: Untersuchungen zur Technik des Referierens und Exzerpierens in der Bibliotheke* (Uppsala, 1975), 184–94. Gothic embassy: see below, chapter 6, at nn. 1–5.

[105] Priscus, *Fr.*, 11–14 [7–11].

[106] Latin classicising historiography: the *historiae* of Renatus Profuturus Frigeridus (written probably before 454) and of Sulpicius Alexander (extending to at least 395), fragments of both preserved only in Gregory of Tours, *Hist.* II, 8–9.

[107] For systematic analysis of other periods: for classical Greece: Mosley, *Envoys and Diplomacy*; Adcock and Mosley, *Diplomacy in Ancient Greece*; for the early Middle Ages and Carolingian period: McCormick, *Origins of the European Economy*, esp. 123–236, 470–4; for the central Middle Ages: Krijnie N. Ciggar, *Western Travellers to Constantinople: The West and Byzantium, 926–1204: Cultural and Political Relations* (Leiden, 1996); for late Middle Ages: Donald E. Queller, *The Office of Ambassador in the Middle Ages* (Princeton, 1967); for Renaissance Europe: Mattingly, *Renaissance Diplomacy*.

genres which, unlike classical *historiae*, were not traditionally concerned with embassies and political communication: chronicles, panegyric, hagiography, letters, and poetic epitaph. Instead, for the most part the works belong to genres concerned with encomium, and the activities of envoys register as part of this purpose. The works are not deposits of historical data, but literature 'in action', engaged with both their literary and sociopolitical contexts in order to fulfil specific purposes. The following chapters explore the role of embassies during the break-up of the West as much through literary as historical analysis. The phenomenon of political communication which the sources describe can only be elucidated by analyses appropriate to each source. The functions each text sought to fulfil, and the ways in which it differs, in its attention to embassies and envoys, from other works in the same genre, provide insight into the political and social contexts of political communication to which narrative histories pay little attention. Close analysis of these works and their unusual features brings to the fore an important aspect: the significance to the participants themselves of undertaking embassies.

In chapter 2, the testimony of Hydatius' *Chronicle* to the frequency and ubiquity of legations throughout the fifth-century West, unique among late antique chronicles, provides a case-study of one small part of the fifth-century West. It also shows some of the patterns of communication in the period, both geopolitical and social, revealing the variety of levels of authority – rulers, officials, provincial bodies, ecclesiastics, local magnates – which dispatched and received embassies from each other. The following three chapters concern the interaction of the envoy and the society for which he acts, whether provincial community or palatine court. Both provincial councils and imperial or royal courts relied on envoys, who stood to reap significant rewards in terms of social status. Chapter 3, on Sidonius Apollinaris' idiosyncratic *Panegyric* on the emperor Avitus, examines a literary exploitation of the high status held by envoys by the mid-fifth century. Sidonius seeks to supplant traditional *topoi* of praise for emperors with a new image, of the emperor as a legate; his portrait is the more striking because false. Very similar literary strategies and exploitations of social status are evident in the four Gallic and Italian saints' *vitae* discussed in chapter 4. The authors appropriate for the bishops they praise the same image of the envoy to which Sidonius appeals – a portrait of an eloquent and commanding statesman who protects his community and repeatedly accepts mission after mission. Their works demonstrate the desire of provincial elites for the social credit gained by undertaking embassies. Both Sidonius and the hagiographers present artificial representations of their subjects as envoys, though for different ends: for Sidonius, as political propaganda; for the hagiographers, to promote saints' cults. A similar respect within a different context is evidenced in the writings of Cassiodorus and Senarius, two palatine officials of the Ostrogothic court of Italy, the subjects of chapter 5. The successful completion of legations is exploited as part of a professional ethos, and brings tangible rewards in terms of career advancement and wealth. The study of Senarius' career sheds light on the extensive role of embassies in one of the most important upheavals of the early sixth century, the Frankish defeat of the Visigoths at Vouillé in 507. In chapter 6, a survey of sources permits a reconstruction of some of the mechanics and protocols of undertaking embassies, highlighting in particular the role of ceremonial in their dispatch and reception.

Close attention to contemporary texts shows that embassies were not occasional events, but were the regular currency of all levels of political life in the fifth- and early sixth-century West. Much modern scholarship silently assumes that unrecorded embassies must have preceded events of which we do know, such as dynastic marriages and warfare. But because the ubiquity of political communication through embassies has not been sufficiently acknowledged, evidence for individual legations is often misconstrued by being viewed in isolation and, ironically, overestimated. The embassies sent by the Gothic king Euric at the time of his accession (recorded by Hydatius), and embassies sent to him from Italy in the 470s (particularly that recorded in Ennodius' *Life of Epiphanius of Pavia*), are examples of such misinterpreted evidence. Seen as isolated and exceptional instances of diplomatic contact, both sets of embassies have been read as crucial moments in relations between the western empire and the Gothic kingdom, revealing decisive steps in Euric's hostile policy towards the empire. In fact, in neither case did the embassies mark a pivotal change: both sets of embassies arose from regular contact and continued existing patterns of relations; both are recorded for specific literary and historiographical reasons as part of the structure of individual texts. Euric's real moments of change from cooperation with the empire to aggression remain unrecorded; the accounts of embassies show him engaged in different activities.[108]

Envoys fulfilled functions of both importance and status; magnates, bishops, and palatine officials all sought the duties and prestige conveyed by the successful completion of legations. A corollory of the importance of envoys to regional communities is the extent of political activity conducted by provincial and city councils; provincial bodies appear in

[108] For Euric's accession embassies, see Andrew Gillett, 'The Accession of Euric', *Francia* 26.1 (1999), 1–40, esp. 19–32, and below, chapter 2, at nn. 142–50. For embassies of 470s, see below, chapter 4, at nn. 224–8.

the sources sometimes fighting and resisting barbarian armies, sometimes establishing treaties, often sending and receiving envoys. The most comprehensive contemporary overview of the function of embassies in the politics of the empire and the western kingdoms comes not from a major political centre such as Rome or Ravenna, but from a very provincial origin, written by a lamenting bishop unhappily conscious of living on the very edge of Mediterranean civilisation.

Chapter 2

THE PROVINCIAL VIEW OF HYDATIUS

In 467, the Gothic army of Toulouse assembled before its new king Euric. The soldiers, fully armed, were watched by several envoys sent to Euric by Remismund, king of the Sueves in western Spain. Circumstances were tense, for the Sueves and the Goths were on the verge of conflict. As the assembly proceeded, the envoys witnessed a strange sight, which they took to be a portent. The metal blades of the Goths' weapons changed colour; the natural metallic hues drained away, replaced for a time by green, rose-red, saffron-yellow, or black.

This story is recorded by Hydatius of Lemica, a bishop of the western Spanish province of Gallaecia, towards the end of his continuation of the *Chronicle* of Eusebius and Jerome. It is fitting that the most picturesque incident in Hydatius' *Chronicle* concerns an embassy, for embassies are an important topic in his record.[1] Late antique chronicles are generically brief, yet Hydatius gives considerable room to accounts of embassies. His presentation of events is unique; no other western narrative source gives such prominence to the actual mechanics of political communication. This apparently minor difference in content deserves to be recognised and underscored, for it is the key to gaining insights into the nature and conduct of fifth-century developments. Extensive patterns of communication, though characteristic of the time, would be barely discernible but

[1] For editions, see 'Note on Editions, Commentaries, and Translations' below. The incident was one of three prodigies witnessed and reported by the Suevic envoys (Hyd., cc. 242–4 [238] at 243). Unlike the other two, it is not a common topos (Carmen Cardelle de Hartmann, *Philologische Studien Zur* Chronik *des Hydatius von Chaves* (Palingenesia 47; Stuttgart, 1994), 146). There is a near-contemporary comparandum: Procopius, *Wars* IV, 2.5–7 (the effect may be explicable by natural chemical change of the metals). Later writers exploited the ambiguity of the portents: Fredegar, *Chron.* II, 56 (portending Gothic defeat at the battle of Vouillé); Isidore, *Hist. Goth.*, 34 (part of a generally encomiastic account of Euric). Jacek Banaszkiewicz, 'Les hastes colorées des Wisigoths d'Euric (Idace c. 243)', *Revue Belge de Philologie et d'Histoire* 72.2 (1994), 225–40, strains the text to present a triumphalist view of Euric (for a more modest view of Euric at the time of his accession: Gillett, 'The Accession of Euric').

Important topic in *Chron.*: Muhlberger, *Fifth-Century Chroniclers*, 211; Suzanne Teillet, *Des Goths à la nation gothique: les origines de l'idée de nation en Occident du Ve au VIIe siècle* (Paris, 1984), 222–3; Burgess, 'Hydatius', 69–70.

for this one source. Indeed, Hydatius' accounts of embassies are preserved in only one manuscript; his description of political events did not accord with the historiographic practices of medieval users and redactors any more than with that of his contemporaries.[2]

Though he records events throughout the Roman empire, Hydatius is best informed on his own, relatively unimportant province in western Spain, the seat of the kingdom of the Sueves since 411. Until recently, modern scholarship has tended to bypass his work in favour of sources concentrating on Italy and Gaul, the centres of the old empire and the new Frankish kingdom, and from general disdain for the genre of the Christian chronicle. But of late Hydatius has been better appreciated as arguably the best source for the history of the West in the fifth century. He provides a relatively lengthy and reliable narrative of events; perhaps more importantly, the details of his account offer the richest basis for analysing the constituent elements of public affairs in his time: the conventions and participants of the business of politics. Notwithstanding his provincial focus, the outline Hydatius gives of the patterns of relationships between authorities within and outside Gallaecia is valuable, for it is an outline lacking for almost all other fifth-century barbarian kingdoms.

Two aspects of Hydatius' *Chronicle* are instructive for the role of diplomatic communication in the fifth century. The author's unique attention to embassies as political phenomena demonstrates the importance which a provincial community leader recognised in communications among barbarian and Roman authorities, and highlights the general but misleading omission of diplomatic embassies from other sources. The patterns of contact revolving around Suevic Gallaecia in Hydatius' account, though falling far short of a full diplomatic history of the West, reveal the complex infrastructure of communication underlying the break-up of the late Roman West. Both aspects deserve detailed investigation.

HYDATIUS AND EMBASSIES

Hydatius records some forty-two embassies. The first, sent by the Persian shah Shapur III to the emperor Theodosius I in 384, is recorded in the *Consularia Constantinopolitana*, an annotated list of Roman consuls. Hydatius drew information for the first few years of his *Chronicle* from a version of this *fasti* list.[3] The forty-one remaining embassies are recorded

[2] Manuscript: Phillipps 1829, Deutsche Staatsbibliothek, Berlin; see Burgess, *Chronicle*, 11–26 (11 n. 4 for date) and cf. 154–72.

[3] Hyd., c. 11; cf. the extant recension of the *Consularia Constantinopolitana* (MGH AA 9 and Burgess, *Chronicle*, 215–45), s.a. 384; Marcellinus *comes* and the *Chronicon Paschale* (both in MGH AA 11), s.a. 384, are also drawn from the same source. On the *Cons. Const.* and its relations with other

under the years from 431 onwards. In his preface, Hydatius states that he was dependent upon written sources and *relationes* for the period 379 (the conclusion of Jerome's continuation of Eusebius) to 427; thereafter, following his elevation as bishop, he wrote 'from the knowledge which the mournful times of my own life now provide'.[4] His accounts of the forty-one embassies come from his own observations or from contemporary reports.[5]

Diplomatic missions constitute a large proportion of Hydatius' *Chronicle*.[6] This attention is unique among late antique chroniclers; it is not a usual topic of the genre. Neither Hydatius' model, Jerome's translation and continuation of the *Chronicle* of Eusebius, nor his only extant written source, a recension of the *Consularia Constantinopolitana*, accords significant space to embassies.[7] The dispatch and reception of embassies are not topics regularly entered by late antique chroniclers. Eusebius' model established more or less standardised topics for inclusion in Christian chronicles (many derived in turn from earlier chronographic traditions), including imperial and episcopal successions, battles, the writings of leading churchmen, earthquakes, and portents.[8] All are

late antique historical sources: Mommsen, Introduction to Hyd., 199–204; Brian Croke, 'City Chronicles of Late Antiquity', in G. Clarke (ed.), *Reading the Past in Late Antiquity* (Rushcutters Bay, 1990), 182–91; Muhlberger, *Fifth-Century Chroniclers*, 23–46; Burgess, *Chronicle*, 175–207, esp. 178–86. Hydatius did not use the extant version of the *Cons. Const.*, traditionally attributed to his editorship, but an earlier recension; Burgess, 'Hydatius', 35–50; Burgess, *Chronicle*, 199–202; Cardelle de Hartmann, *Philologische Studien*, 24–38.

4 Hydatius, *Praefatio*, §§ 5–7 [5–6]: *ex cognitione quam iam lacrimabile propriae vitae tempus offendit.* On Hydatius' sources: Thompson, *Romans and Barbarians*, 142–50; Muhlberger, *Fifth-Century Chroniclers*, 206–9; Burgess, 'Hydatius', 33–72; Cardelle de Hartmann, *Philologische Studien*, 17–38. Hyd., *Praef*., 7 [6] implies that he became bishop in 427 or 428; this is not confirmed in the body of the *Chron.* itself, but the entries for the years 426 and 427 are lacunose, as Burgess' edition demonstrates.

5 See Table 1 for a list of these embassies.

6 Of 165 sections in Mommsen's edition from 427 onwards, twenty-nine directly mention embassies, but the presence of embassies in the text is greater than this statistic suggests because of indirect references in other sections (e.g. cc. 242–4 [238]) and the clustering of accounts of embassies (e.g. Table 1, nos. 1–4, 34–9); cf. Muhlberger, *Fifth-Century Chroniclers*, 211: 'Hydatius' chronicle after [455] is almost a history of these embassies and the news they brought.'

7 The *Consularia Constantinopolitana* records only two embassies: Persian envoys to Constantinople in 358, and again in 384 (= Hyd., c. 11), concerning the partition of Armenia; *Cons. Const.*, s.aa. That part of the *Cons. Const.* thought to have been continued in Spain contains no accounts of embassies. The few embassies recorded in Jerome's translation and continuation of Eusebius' *Chronicle* occurred in distant antiquity; neither author listed embassies in his account of recent history (Eusebius/Jerome, *Chron.*, 128, lines 7–9: envoys of Ptolemy I to Rome, seeking *amicitia*, 293 BC; 132, lines 16–23: envoy of the Jews to Ptolemy III, 246 BC; 137, lines 15–18: Antiochus the Great sends legates to Hannibal, 186 BC; 156, lines 17–19: embassy of the Jews to Rome, seeking *amicitia*, 46 BC). For an instance where a known foreign embassy is not mentioned: Eusebius/Jerome, *Chron.*, 247, lines 23–4 s.a. 375, cf. Amm. Marc. XXX, 5.15: death of Valentinian I, while receiving a Quadi embassy.

8 Eusebius defined the categories of topics in his *Canones*: Eusebius/Jerome, *Chron.*, 18–19.

recorded by other fifth-century continuators of Eusebius and Jerome. Only Hydatius regularly notes the dispatch and return of embassies.

Embassies are not altogether absent from other chronicles and annotated consular lists. Embassies appear occasionally: in works derived from city chronicles as records of ceremonial events; as elements of rhetoric; and, on rare occasions, as specific, politically important events. But none of Hydatius' peers paid the same regularity of attention to the passage of embassies.

City chronicles were local records of public religious and ceremonial occasions and of other recurring or singular special events important to urban life, maintained by municipal authorities and used as sources by a number of both eastern and western chronicles.[9] Only a few legations are recorded in extant city chronicles. The city chronicle tradition of Constantinople noted the arrival at the imperial city of embassies from foreign peoples bearing gifts and seeking the emperors' *amicitia*.[10] The city chronicles of Constantinople and Italy also recorded the unwilling embassy of Pope John I to the emperor Justin I on behalf of Theoderic in 525, an unprecedented visit of the bishop of Rome to the eastern imperial capital and a major ceremonial occasion.[11]

Several authors of chronicles choose to colour particular events or themes with accounts of individual embassies. Prosper, a contemporary of Hydatius who abridged and continued Eusebius/Jerome, does not regularly record embassies, although he gives much attention to relations between the empire and the new barbarian kingdoms in the West in the first half of the fifth century. But he does describe, in some detail, two embassies, both undertaken by Pope Leo I (the first while still a deacon of Rome), one to the leading general Aetius in Gaul in 440, the other, more famously, to Attila in northern Italy in order to prevent his march on Rome. Prosper was an enthusiastic supporter of Leo, who is praised elsewhere in the *Chronicle*; the embassies are mentioned solely in Leo's honour.[12] Similarly, Cassiodorus in his annotated consular list records

[9] Croke, 'City Chronicles'; Croke, *Count Marcellinus and His Chronicle* (Oxford, 2001), 177–8.

[10] Marcellinus *comes*, *Chron.*, s.aa. 384.1 (above, n. 3); 448.1, 496.2: gifts to the eastern emperors from 'India'; cf. *Chronicon Pascale*, s.a. 384. Malalas, *Chron.* XVIII, 73, 106: 'Indian' embassies bearing gifts, presumably Axumites, cf. XVIII, 15, 56. Victor of Tunnuna, *Chronica* (MGH AA 11), s.a. 563.2: first Avar envoys in Constantinople. John of Biclar, *Chronica* (MGH AA 11), s.aa. 569.1, 573.6, 575.3: envoys from the Garamantes, Maccurritae, and Saracens seek *amicitia*. Croke, 'City Chronicles', 175, 179; Croke, *Count Marcellinus*, 113, 119.

[11] Constantinople: Marcellinus *comes*, *Chron.*, s.a. 525. Italy: *Anon. Val.* XV, 88–93; Andreas Agnellus, *Liber pontificalis ecclesiae Ravennatis*, 39, both given in MGH AA 11 (Mommsen's *Consularia Italica*), pp. 328, 333. Novelty and ceremonial: *Liber pont.*, 55 (the embassy was greeted by the emperor Justin I at the fifteenth milestone before Constantinople).

[12] Prosper Tiro, *Epitoma Chronicon* (MGH AA 9), 1341, 1367; cf. 1375: Leo's *supplicatio* to Geiseric before the gates of Rome in 455. See below, chapter 4, at nn. 3–6.

the embassy from Constantinople to Italy in 519 of one Symmachus, possibly the current eastern *magister officiorum*. Cassiodorus mentions the eastern envoy's presence as part of his description of the lavish celebrations attending the consulship in that year of Theoderic's nominated successor, Eutharic, whose colleague in the consulate was the emperor Justin I and to whom Cassiodorus' consular list was dedicated.[13] In the chronicles of both Prosper and Cassiodorus, embassies are mentioned as elements of praise, either of the recipient or of the legate himself.

There is a limited number of embassies recorded in chronicles as individual, politically significant events. Marcellinus *comes* mentions important embassies sent by the emperor Theodosius I, by Attila, and by Justinian. The chronological spread of these embassies – 385, 448, 533 – highlights the irregularity of Marcellinus' attention to diplomatic traffic.[14] The anonymous account of the reign of Theoderic which forms the second part of the *Anonymus Valesianus*, and which draws upon Italian chronicle sources, records three embassies to Constantinople between 490 and 497, headed by leading senators of Rome; they represent Theoderic's protracted attempts to gain recognition of his rule in Italy from the emperor Anastasius.[15] The enforced embassy of Pope John I to Justin is also described, as part of the invective which the latter part of the work constitutes.[16] Other important embassies received or dispatched during Theoderic's rule and attested *inter alia* by Cassiodorus' *Variae* are not mentioned, though the author does describe the outcomes of such communications, including marriage alliances with western kings, changing relations with the emperors, and resolution of ecclesiastical conflicts. Few other individual embassies are recorded in western chronicles.[17]

Altogether, this list of embassies in fifth- and sixth-century chronicles is very short: a score of references, about half the number Hydatius gives. Two features are striking. First, embassies were not regularly recorded by any of these sources, but only sporadically inserted for specific reasons arising from the purposes of the individual source. Reciprocal exchanges of embassies are not described; the embassies appear as isolated, ceremonial occasions. Secondly, for the most part, the value and function of

[13] Cassiodorus, *Chronica* (MGH AA 11), c. 1364, cf. *PLRE* II, 'Symmachus 4', 1043.

[14] Marcellinus *comes*, *Chron.*, s.aa. 385: Theodosius I subdues eastern regions *per legatos suos* (see *The Chronicle of Marcellinus: Translation and Commentary*, trans. Brian Croke (Byzantina Australiensia 7; Sydney, 1995), p. 59, s.a. 385); 448.1: Attila sends envoys to Theodosius II to protest the curtailment of payment of tribute to the Huns; 533: envoys sent to the Persians to conclude the 'Endless Peace'. Cf. *Additamentum* to Marcellinus, s.aa. 535.2: Pope Agapitus sent to Constantinople by Theodahad; 547.1: the besieged Goths in Italy send an envoy to Justinian.

[15] *Anon. Val.* XI, 53; XII, 57, 64 (s.aa. 490, 492, 497). [16] Above, n. 11.

[17] John of Biclar, *Chron.*, s.a. 576.3: the Suevic king Miro sends envoys for peace to the Gothic king Leuvigild.

embassies in each of these texts is as a marker of prestige. Foreign legates paying homage to imperial authority, and the imperial envoy attendant at the consular celebrations of Theoderic's appointed successor, signify the status of their recipients; Pope Leo's role as deliverer of the western empire displays his secular as well as spiritual authority.

Not only Hydatius' models and near contemporaries, but his users, too, omitted embassies from their historical accounts. The *Chronicle* of 511, an exiguous revision and continuation of Eusebius/Jerome composed either in Gaul or in Spain, is the earliest extant work to use Hydatius as a source; it deletes all his references to embassies.[18] So too do most manuscript traditions of Hydatius. His early medieval redactors display little interest in preserving record of embassies: they either wholly omit Hydatius' chapters describing embassies, or retain his general account of relevant events but leave out mention of embassies themselves.[19]

Hydatius differs from his models, other chroniclers of his time, and his users in his regular attention to exchanges of embassies. The contrast is significant. Embassies, part of the mechanics of communication by which major events were brought about, were not of themselves considered to be topics appropriate for inclusion in chronicles. In chronicle writers besides Hydatius, reference to embassies is incidental to other purposes. Given the generic brevity of late antique chronicles and their focus on major events, this omission is understandable; outside Hydatius, embassies appear regularly only in lengthy historical works such as Procopius, Malalas, or Gregory of Tours.[20] In many ways, Hydatius was the faithful continuator

18 *Chronica Gallica ad a. 511* (MGH AA 11, part of Mommsen's *Chronica Gallica*); for the possibility of a Spanish origin. Gillett, 'Accession of Euric', 36–8.

19 The texts of the six main redactions of Hydatius' work are conveniently presented in Burgess, *Chronicle*, Appendix 4, 154–72. Three, the *Chronica Gallica 511*, the lost Alcobaciensis MS, and the *Chronicon Luxoviense* (M), omit all twenty-nine chapters in Hydatius directly relating to embassies. Texts descended from a late sixth-century Spanish epitome (H) omit all but one (the capture of Censorius while on an embassy; Table 1, no. 6). Isidore, *Hist. Goth.* preserves four, mostly relating to the Goths of Toulouse (Table 1, nos. 23 [probably], 28 and 29, 33, and 34). Only the second book of the *Chronicle* of Fredegar preserves a significant number of chapters describing embassies: ten, again mostly about the Goths; about half differ considerably from the best MS of Hydatius (Table 1, nos. 9, 11, 13, 17–20, 21–3, 33, 39, possibly 41). For embassies in Fredegar: below, chapter 6, at nn. 219–22.

20 On the impact of genre on record of embassies, cf. Barnwell, 'War and Peace', esp. 131–2.

Malalas, *Chron.* includes embassy accounts in a range of chronographic, historical, and literary styles: brief notes from city chronicle sources (*Chron.* XVIII, 73, 106; Elizabeth Jeffreys, 'Chronological Structures in the *Chronicle*', in Elizabeth Jeffreys, Brian Croke, and Roger Scott (eds.), *Studies in John Malalas* (Byzantina Australiensia 6; Sydney, 1990)); a summary of an envoy's account of his reception in an exotic court (*Chron.* XVIII, 56); detailed records of exchanges, in one instance perhaps drawing on personal knowledge (*Chron.* XVII, 9–10; XVIII, 57; XVIII, 34, 36, 44, 50, 53–4, 56, 60–1, 65, 68, 70, 72, 76; on the latter, see Roger Scott, 'Diplomacy in the Sixth Century: The Evidence of John Malalas', in Shepard and Franklin (eds.), *Byzantine Diplomacy*, 159–65); and dramatic fictions (*Chron.* XIV, 10, 23). Malalas' detailed accounts occur

of the Eusebian model he portrayed himself to be, particularly regarding chronographic technicalities. Yet he wrote a much lengthier narrative than his model, more clearly shaped by authorial aims and expressing sharper judgements on his *miserabile tempus*. He shows the beginning of the early medieval trend to employ the chronicle format as a structure for a full historical narrative, seen for example in Fredegar.[21] Hydatius is an autonomous voice, using but adapting the dominant Christian genre of historiography to offer an independent view of public and spiritual life.

The difference between Hydatius and other writers in the same genre in treatment of embassies is partially the result of circumstances. Most of the embassies recorded by Hydatius passed to or from Gallaecia. The Suevic kingdom is almost invisible in other fifth-century sources; it is not surprising that few other records of missions between Gallaecia and Roman or Gothic authorities have survived.[22] Nevertheless, the essential difference between Hydatius and other chroniclers is one of selection, not of available information. Contacts between imperial authorities, barbarian rulers, and provincial elites occurred in all the western kingdoms. Hydatius alone regarded these contacts as a topic for inclusion in a chronicle. The attention he gives to diplomatic communication is on par with that given to battles of armies, or conflicts between the Sueves and Spanish provincials. Embassies have an intrinsic part in Hydatius' understanding of western politics.

The bishop's individual perception is largely attributable to his provincial position. This can be seen in the differences between his account of events and that of other writers more closely attached to the imperial authorities. Merobaudes, a panegyrist of the western imperial court, mentions a victory over the Sueves won by a subordinate of the *magister utriusque militiae* Aetius. Unless this event passed unnoticed by Hydatius,

only in the reigns of Justin I and Justinian, and his treatment is irregular: he provides a detailed account of Roman/Persian embassies of 529–33, and one lengthy entry on embassies prior to Justinian's war against the Vandals; but he includes no account of embassies prior to the commencement of Justinian's war in Italy (cf. *Chron.* XVIII, 88, 97, 110, 116) or the recommencement of Roman/Persian hostilities in 540 (cf. *Chron.* XVIII, 87 and 147). Malalas' world chronicle is in many respects, notably length and literary treatment, more similar to Gregory of Tours' *Historiae* and Fredegar's *Chronica* than the brief chronicles of e.g. Prosper, Hydatius, or Marcellinus *comes*.

21 Hydatius and his model: Hyd., *Praef.*, 1–5; Burgess, *Chronicle*, 6–9, and 31–3 on possible apocalyptic themes; cf. on other early chroniclers' treatment of Eusebius/Jerome: Muhlberger, *Fifth-Century Chroniclers*, 19–23, 60–73, 138–40.

22 Conversely, Hydatius was often unaware of embassies outside Gallaecia. He seems not to have known that the Gallic noble Avitus, when proclaimed emperor by the Goths at Toulouse, was there as envoy of the emperor Petronius Maximus; Hyd., c. 163; cf. Sid. Ap., *Carm.* VII, 375–418. Other records of embassies in Gallaecia: Jordanes, *Get.*, 231 (presumably = Table 1 no. 12), 234 (Gallaecian bishops sent to Theoderic II after the death of Aioulf, cf. Hyd., cc. 180, 187 [173, 180]). The latter, if factual, is not recorded by Hydatius.

which is unlikely, Merobaudes can only be referring to one of several occasions, described by Hydatius, on which Aetius sent envoys to negotiate a cessation of hostilities between the Sueves and the Spanish provincials.[23] Merobaudes' transformation of negotiated peace into military victory is characteristic of the 'victory ideology' permeating late antique political rhetoric, and may reflect Aetius' own representation of events.[24] Hydatius was free from the need to present the general's actions in this light, and, in this instance, received information locally rather than through imperial propaganda. As a leading figure in a provincial community, he was conscious that peaceful conditions in Gallaecia depended on the constant maintenance of relations between imperial authorities, Suevic rulers, and provincials, not upon any single military or diplomatic success. This awareness informed Hydatius' attention to the mechanics of communication which sustained these relations.

Hydatius had personal experience of the business of political communication. The first embassy which he records in the section of the *Chronicle* not dependent on written sources was undertaken by himself in 431–2. Hydatius, as bishop, sought aid for the Gallaecian provincials against the Sueves, who had broken a recently negotiated *pax*.[25] He approached the general Aetius, then campaigning against the Franks in Gaul. Hydatius' embassy was the first of several occasions on which the provincials sought such intervention, first from the Roman authorities in Gaul and subsequently from the Gothic kings of Toulouse.

Success was mixed. Once Aetius had subdued the Franks and could spare resources, he sent the *comes* Censorius to the Suevic king Hermeric. Hydatius, apparently having wintered in Gaul, returned to Gallaecia with Censorius. He does not state whether he was also involved in Censorius' discussions with the Suevic king, but his participation appears probable. While Censorius was in Gallaecia, fighting broke out in Italy between Aetius and his rival, the *magister utriusque militiae* Boniface. Censorius abandoned his mission and left Spain, giving civil war priority over

[23] *PLRE* II, 'Aetius 7', 25, citing Merobaudes, *Panegyric* I *Fr.* IIA, 22–3 (ed. F. Vollmer, MGH AA 14), probably delivered in 439 (*PLRE* II, 25–6); cf. Jordanes, *Get.*, 176 (a victory over the Sueves by Aetius before 436). Embassies from Aetius to the Sueves: Table 1 nos. 3, 5, and 6. The only recorded Roman military campaign against the Sueves in Aetius' time was that of 446 (Hyd., c. 134 [125]), a disaster for the Romans.

[24] On 'victory ideology' in late antiquity: Michael McCormick, *Eternal Victory: Triumphal Rulership in Late Antiquity, Byzantium, and the Early Medieval West* (Cambridge and Paris, 1986), esp. 47–64 on the increasing frequency of victory celebrations in the early fifth century, despite declining military success. Of course, such sleight-of-hand had a long tradition, as commemorations of Augustus' 'victory' over the Parthians in 20 BC show.

[25] Table 1 no. 1; cf. Hyd., c. 91 [81]. Hydatius also appears earlier in his narrative: cc. 40 [33], 62b (omitted by Burgess, but cf. *Journal of Roman Studies* 87 (1997), 313), cf. Muhlberger, *Fifth-Century Chroniclers*, 196–9.

relations with the Sueves. After his departure, Hermeric was convinced to restore the *pax* with the Gallaecians by 'episcopal intervention', presumably a delegation of bishops, one of whom was sent by the Suevic king to the imperial authorities to confirm the agreement.[26] One imagines Hydatius among the bishops who reached agreement with Hermeric.

In the preface to his *Chronicle*, Hydatius cites his position as bishop to give authority to his personal knowledge as a historical source: 'called to episcopal office, [I am] not unaware of all the toils of a wretched age'.[27] The truth of this claim is illustrated by his mission of 431–2. On becoming a bishop, Hydatius gained access to ecclesiastical sources of information, not least the network of letters circulated throughout the Mediterranean by his fellow bishops.[28] More importantly for the writing of the *Chronicle*, Hydatius entered the ranks of those whose position brought them into contact with the flux of political power. Like many historians and chroniclers of antiquity, Hydatius wrote with experience in public life, but unlike fourth-century writers such as Ammianus Marcellinus, Eutropius, Festus, Aurelius Victor, or Nicomachus Flavianus, his experience was not in high-level military, legal, or administrative affairs.[29] His authority was as a bishop, at a time when the episcopal office was increasingly assuming the responsibilities of provincial aristocracies and municipal offices. Like his contemporaries Priscus and Sidonius Apollinaris, and his near-contemporary Olympiodorus of Thebes, Hydatius' most important foray into public life was as an envoy and orator.

Hydatius' attention to embassies in the *Chronicle*, however, does not merely reflect his personal experience; he does not relate solely those embassies with which he was personally involved. Instead, he consistently endeavours to relate exchanges of embassies as an important element of all political affairs. The far fuller *historiae* of Procopius and Gregory of Tours pay similar attention to exchanges of embassies as intrinsic, shaping elements of events. It is not so much Hydatius' personal experience as his awareness that such communications are a crucial factor in the politics of his own province and the empire as a whole that determines Hydatius' choice to include a new category in his *Chronicle*.

The description of embassies in the *Chronicle* is not formulaic. Whereas the *Consularia Constantinopolitana* records embassies with specific day

[26] Table 1 nos. 3–4: *sub interventu episcopali*.

[27] Hyd., *Praef.*, §7 [6]: *adlectus ad episcopatus officium, non ignarus omnium miserabilis temporis aerumnarum*.

[28] Denys Gorce, *Les Voyages, l'hospitalité, et le port des lettres dans le monde Chrétien des IVe et Ve siècles* (Paris, 1925), 193–247; Catherine Conybeare, *Paulinus Noster: Self and Symbols in the* Letters *of Paulinus of Nola* (Oxford, 2000).

[29] For the professional backgrounds of late antique historians of a later period: Geoffrey Greatrex, 'Lawyers and Historians in Late Antiquity', in Ralph W. Mathisen (ed.), *Law, Society, and Authority in Late Antiquity* (Oxford, 2001), 148–61.

dates, as it does the *adventus* of emperors and relics, Hydatius records no precise dates for events concerning embassies.[30] Instead he sets down a range of different details about each embassy: the sender and recipient; details of the envoys themselves, such as their name and social rank, whether they had undertaken similar journeys before, and whether they travelled with a party; the return of the embassy, its route, duration, and incidents during the journey; the purpose, the recipient's response, and the success or failure of the mission; whether the embassy repeated an earlier mission or responded to previous contact; whether the embassy was undertaken jointly with representatives of a second power, or if it coincided with representatives dispatched by a third party on the same issue. Hydatius describes some missions at length, but merely notes the occurrence of others. Most other sources refer only to the arrival of an embassy at its destined court, but Hydatius regularly notes the envoys' return journey also.[31]

The embassies in the *Chronicle* primarily concern Gallaecian affairs. Hydatius records twelve missions involving relations between the Gallaecians and the Sueves, twenty-one other embassies to or from the Suevic kings, and one to a Gothic king while in Gallaecia.[32] The number of other embassies he records is small.[33] Hydatius knows the name of the principal envoy of every mission representing the Gallaecians, and of the envoys sent by imperial authorities in reply to the Gallaecians. He also names one of the Gothic envoys sent in reply to the Gallaecians, and several of the imperial and Gothic envoys to the Sueves. But of the envoys sent by the Suevic kings, only two are named; both are Roman provincials, not Sueves.[34]

[30] For *Cons. Const.*: n. 3 above. Hydatius did record precise dates for certain other events, e.g. the entry of the Vandals, Sueves, and Alans into Spain (c. 42 [34], preserving two different dates); eclipses and comets (cc. 64, 136, 151, 191, 214, 225 [56, 128, 143, 184, 209, 221]); the capture of Carthage (c. 115 [107]); an earthquake in Gallaecia (c. 149 [141]); battles during Theoderic II's campaign against the Sueves (cc. 173, 174, 186 [166, 167, 179]); and Hydatius' own captivity (c. 201 [196]).

[31] Return journeys: Table 1 nos. 1–3, 6, 10–11, 14–15, 21–2, 24–7, 31–3, 35–6, 38–40.

[32] Concerning Gallaecians and Sueves: Table 1 nos. 1, 3–5, 16, 24–6, 32, 40; probably 6, 33. Other embassies to or from the Sueves: nos. 2, 7, 8, 10–12, 14–15, 17, 19, 21–2, 28–31, 35, 36–8, 41. To Theoderic II in Gallaecia: no. 13.

[33] Seven in all. Hydatius would have known of several of these non-Spanish embassies from simultaneous embassies to the Sueves, i.e. Table 1 nos. 18, 20 (to the Vandals; cf. nos. 17, 19), 34, 39 (to the western emperor and the Vandals; cf. no. 35). Other embassies: nos. 9 (between the western and eastern emperors), 23 (between Geiseric and the western emperor), 27 (between the *comes* Aegidius and Geiseric).

[34] Gallaecian envoys: Table 1 nos. 1 (bishop Hydatius), 24 (the *vir nobilis* Palogorius, not explicitly named as *legatus*), 40 (Opilio – assuming that he represented the *plebs Aunonensis*). Imperial envoys responding to Gallaecians: nos. 3 (the *comes* Censorius), 5 (Censorius and Fretimund). Gothic envoy responding to Gallaecians: no. 25 (Cyrila); cf. nos. 11, 12, 32 (unnamed Gothic envoys).

Hydatius only intermittently addresses the subject of most interest to modern students, the purpose of individual embassies. Sometimes he is forthcoming: his own embassy to Aetius was undertaken because of Suevic *depraedationes*; several later missions of imperial or Gothic envoys also seem to have sought to intervene in relations between the Sueves and the provincials. There is no clear statement what sort of settlement the provincials desired, but in several cases conflict appears to terminate with the re-establishment of a formal treaty, a *pax*, between the provincials and the Sueves. The imperially backed foray of the Goths into Gallaecia in 456, the fullest narrative in the *Chronicle*, was disastrous; Hydatius' description can hardly be seen as advocating military intervention to control or even remove the Sueves.

The *Chronicle* contains no remarks on the motives of many embassies, but this need not mean that Hydatius was uninformed.[35] In the great brevity of late Roman chronicles, much information is conveyed paratactically. The *comes* Censorius undertook his third, fatal embassy to the Sueves in 440 after the Suevic occupation of Lusitania; the simultaneous embassies of the Vandals and the Goths to the Sueves in 458 came after the Gothic occupation of Baetica, the strategic stepping-stone to North Africa.[36] The motivation of these missions is clearly implied. Embassies outside Spain are curtly characterised: Avitus' envoys to Marcian went *pro unanimitate imperii*; Geiseric's envoys to Majorian sought a *pax*.[37]

Hydatius makes no comment on the purpose of the most intriguing missions, the multiple embassies *ad gentes* sent by Valentinian III after his murder of Aetius, and those sent by the Gothic king Euric to at least the Sueves, the Vandals, and the western emperor, after his accession.[38] Perhaps, to Hydatius, no explanation is needed. Hydatius records these multiple embassies as the most important consequences of the deaths of Aetius and Theoderic II. He accords them a significance given by no other source for the period, not because of the missions' unstated outcomes but as events politically significant in themselves. The embassies were the actions of governments in a time of crisis. Irrespective of the instructions given to each mission, the embassies shared a common purpose: the maintenance of relations between powers.

Imperial envoys to the Sueves: nos. 6 (Censorius, probably concerning the Suevic occupation of Lusitania), 7 (the *comites* Mansuetus and Fronto), 8 (Iustinianus), 10 (Fronto). Gothic envoys to the Sueves: no. 33 (Salla); possibly no. 2 (Vetto; see below, Table 1, 'Note on *Legatus* and *Legatio*'). Suevic envoys: nos. 4 (bishop Symphosius), 41 (Lusidius, a leading citizen of Lisbon, cf. c. 246); cf. the unnamed envoys of nos. 26, 28, 30–1, 36–8.

[35] Cf. Thompson, *Romans and Barbarians*, 190.

[36] Table 1 nos. 6, 14–15 (cf. below at nn. 105, 118, 127).

[37] Table 1 nos. 9, 23.

[38] Table 1 nos. 8 (Valentinian III), 34, 35, 39 (Euric), with the consequential embassies sent by the Suevic king Remismund, nos. 36–8. Gillett, 'Accession of Euric', 29–30.

The frequency of embassies recorded by Hydatius increases as the *Chronicle* progresses. The work falls into two parts, distinguished by many changes, including the regularity of record of embassies. The first part reaches to 456, the year of a devastating Gothic assault on the Suevic kingdom, which Hydatius clearly found traumatic but which passed with little attention in other extant sources; the second consists of the final dozen years.[39] Thirteen embassies are recorded in the first part, within the three decades from Hydatius' advancement to the episcopacy and the beginning of his independent historical account, to 456. Most belong to one of two clusters, the first concerning disputes between the Sueves, Gallaecians, and imperial authorities in the 430s, the other as part of the prelude to the Gothic assault of 456. No embassies at all are recorded for over a decade between these two clusters, from 440 and 453.[40] For the second section of the *Chronicle*, 457 to 468, some twenty-seven embassies are recorded, all but two directly or indirectly concerning Gallaecia.[41] The record of legations is more evenly spread in the second half than in the first: almost every year entry features at least one mission, and the *Chronicle* records more or less consistent reciprocal exchange of embassies, rather than clusters of accounts. Statistically, embassies appear four times more frequently in the second part of the work than in the first.

This abrupt increase in the frequency of embassies recorded by Hydatius is best explained by the structural composition of the *Chronicle*. The events of 456 are a dividing point of the work. Hydatius' narrative of the Gothic attack is much lengthier than previous entries, and his description of events is fuller and more detailed. The length of entries for each year expands again for the final few years of the *Chronicle*, but without a sustained narrative equivalent to that of the Gothic assault on Gallaecia. This expansion and contraction of detail, together with the shift to almost annalistic record of embassies concerning Gallaecia, suggests that the account of 456 marks a juncture in the composition of the *Chronicle*. Other technical and thematic differences, too, distinguish the latter part of the *Chronicle*: a severe restriction in non-Spanish material and ecclesiastical reports, and irregularities with the chronology.[42] Hydatius makes

[39] Goths in Gallaecia: Hyd., cc. 168–86 [161–79]. Other sources: *Auctarium Prosperi Hauviensis* (MGH AA 11, 305), s.a. 457.1–2; Jordanes, *Get.*, 229–34. Cf. Burgess, 'Hydatius', 229–40, esp. 237.

[40] Table 1 nos. 1–13. Cluster in 430s: nos. 1–4 (431–3), 5, 6 (437–8, 440); cluster leading up to 456: nos. 9–13.

[41] Table 1 nos. 14–41; exceptions: nos. 23 (Geiseric to Majorian), 27 (Aegidius to Vandals). Other legations not directly involving the Sueves form part of multiple embassies which do concern Gallaecia (e.g. nos. 17–20, cf. 16; no. 39, cf. 34–8).

[42] Burgess, 'Hydatius', 87, 93 (though thoroughly dismissing the view that Hydatius' chronology is basically accurate to 455 and confused thereafter; Mommsen, Introduction to Hyd., 4–6),

no explicit statement indicating when he began or completed composition of his work. Though he is often assumed to have written the whole work retrospectively in the late 460s, he may have written a first version in the mid-450s, prompted by the traumatic events of the Gothic attack; the remainder of the *Chronicle* may have been added in the late 460s, using notes kept in the intervening period, including records of embassies to and from Gallaecia. At both stages of composition, Hydatius wrote lengthier entries for recent events, by no means an uncommon historiographic tendency.[43]

One formal feature of the *Chronicle* preserves evidence of this two-stage composition. In his account of the Gothic attack on the Sueves in 456, Hydatius describes how Theoderic II won a pitched battle, then pursued and captured the Suevic king Rechiarius and accepted the surrender of his army; consequently, he adds, *regnum destructum et finitum est Suevorum*, 'the kingdom of the Sueves was destroyed and ended'.[44] The finality of this statement is at odds with Hydatius' subsequent record of the activity of the Sueves, unambiguously referring to the Suevic *regnum* and its *reges*.[45] The phrase *regnum destructum et finitum est* is not Hydatius' own, but is derived from a formal feature of Jerome's translation and continuation of the *Chronici canones* of Eusebius. In Eusebius/Jerome, this phrase was regularly used to mark the collapse of ancient *regna* such as Lydia, Egypt, and Achaemenid Persia. In the original format developed by Eusebius for his *Canones* and maintained by Jerome (but abandoned by their continuators), the chronologies of contemporaneous empires were set out in parallel columns; the phrase *regnum destructum et finitum est* closed the column assigned to each empire as it reached its end.[46] The use of

135–6, 224–6, 238–40; thematic differences are discussed *passim*, e.g. 134, 179, 190; Cardelle de Hartmann, *Philologische Studien*, 47–9, 61–5.

[43] Cf. Burgess, *Chronicle*, 5–6. Cardelle de Hartmann, *Philologische Studien*, 64–5 suggests *c.* 450 as the date for a first draft of the *Chronicle*, maintained annually thereafter. The argument is based in part on the greater length of entries in the latter part of the work. Hydatius' account of the Gothic assault on Gallaecia is certainly much longer than earlier entries, but few subsequent entries are in fact longer than pre-456 material. The length of the account of 456 suggests that it was originally the final entry to an early version of the text.

[44] Hyd., c. 175 [168].

[45] References to the *regnum* of the Sueves post-456: Hyd., cc. 187, 203 [180, 198]; to their *reges*: 181, 188, 230, 232, 237, 238, 240, 249 [174, 181, 226, 228, 233, 234, 236, 243]. The possibility of composition in stages and the significance of this phrase was first pointed out by Thompson, *Romans and Barbarians*, 140–1 and 290 n. 10; not followed by Muhlberger, *Fifth-Century Chroniclers*, 194 n. 3, 264, or Burgess, 'Hydatius', 65, 229–40; briefly discussed by Cardelle de Hartmann, *Philologische Studien*, 64–5.

[46] E.g. Eusebius/Jerome, *Chron.*, 103b (Lydia), 121 (Egypt), 124 (Persia). The complex structure of parallel columns used by Eusebius/Jerome was abandoned by most continuators and many copyists, but the formula for the end of states was commonly employed by continuators and users, e.g. *Chronica Caesaraugustana* (MGH AA 11) *ad a.* 507: *regnum Tolosanum destructum est*, the

this phrase in Hydatius' account of the Gothic assault on Gallaecia, which evidently did not end the autonomy of the Suevic kingdom, appears to be fossilised from an earlier version of the *Chronicle* written soon after 456.

The events of 456 clearly appeared catastrophic from a Gallaecian perspective, and can readily be understood as a spur to the composition of a work of Christian historiography, with its teleological emphasis; Hydatius compares the Gothic sack of Braga with divine wrath against Jerusalem.[47] By contrast, the end of the *Chronicle* describes changing circumstances, with the collapse of Gothic tutelage of the Sueves and renewed hostilities between the barbarian armies and Gallaecian provincials; the outcome of these events was uncertain when Hydatius wrote, and indeed remains unknown. As it stands, the work has no distinct ending, either a chronological summary like Eusebius/Jerome and many continuators, or a terminal comment such as Hydatius' description of the events of 456. The final entry, listing natural phenomena as omens of ambiguous significance, is reminiscent of the last chronological entry to Gregory of Tour's *Histories*, with a similar (perhaps accidently) inconclusive tone.[48] The second part of Hydatius' *Chronicle* has every appearance of being a continuation of a work extending originally only to 456; Hydatius was not alone among continuators of Eusebius/Jerome in adding extensions to his own work.[49] The more regular record of embassies in the latter

Frankish defeat of the Goths at Vouillé and end of the old Gothic kingdom of Toulouse (but not of the kingdom of the Goths itself, subsequently restricted to Spain).

47 Hyd., c. 174 [167], identified with 'the abomination of desolation' of Daniel IX.27 and Matthew XXIV.15 by Tranoy II, 105.

48 Renewed hostilities: Hyd., cc. 230, 233, 245–6, 249–50 [226, 229, 239–40, 243–4]. Omens: 253 [247]; Gregory of Tours: *Hist.* X, 30 (the final chapter is a review of the acts of the bishops of Tours, Gregory's own writings, and a chronological summary); Walter Goffart, *The Narrators of Barbarian History (AD 550–800): Jordanes, Gregory of Tours, Bede, and Paul the Deacon* (Princeton, 1988), 186.

49 E.g. Prosper wrote versions of his *Chronicle* in 433, 445, possibly 451, and 455; Marcellinus *comes* in 518 and 534. Hydatius thought it possible that Jerome had also; *Praef.*, 4.

The *Chronicle* of 511, the earliest extant user of Hydatius, seems to preserve extracts from only the first half of his work (Burgess, *Chronicle*, 167–8, though cf. MGH AA 9, 664, c. 634, citing Hyd., c. 198, *recte* 200 [195]; Gillett, 'Accession of Euric', 37). The *Chronicle* of 511 shows interest in the extension of Gothic control in north-eastern Spain and southern Gaul in the 470s (cc. 651, 652, 657), yet does not use material from the second half of Hydatius concerning Gothic influence in Gallaecia, Baetica, Lusitania, and Narbonensis in the 460s (172–86, 192–3, 201, 217, 245–6, 250 [165–79, 185, 188, 196, 212, 239–40, 244]), suggesting that the author of the chronicle may not have had that part of Hydatius' text.

For a different interpretation of the structure of the *Chronicle*: Burgess, 'Hydatius', 229–40, seeing the conflict of 456 as the dramatic climax of a unified work written in the late 460s with a classical literary structure, implying composition retrospectively in the 460s. This reading does not explain Hydatius' use of the phrase *regnum destructum et finitum est Suevorum*; composition in the late 460s is a rather delayed reaction to the events of more than a decade before.

part highlights Hydatius' developed awareness of the importance of embassies as political events, perhaps directly as a result of composing the first version of the *Chronicle*.

How did Hydatius know of each embassy? As a bishop of the province, important enough to be chosen as an envoy on one occasion and exiled on another, Hydatius was probably involved in negotiations other than those of 431. Imperial and Gothic embassies to the Suevic kings concerning their treatment of the Gallaecians came in response to provincial appeals (not all of them noted in the *Chronicle*). Hydatius knew of such missions through his episcopal office and these contacts.

It is less clear how Hydatius knew of other embassies to and from the Suevic court. There is no reason to think that leaders of provincial communities would have been consulted by the Sueves on the permutations of political and military alliance between the barbarian kingdoms and the empire, nor would one assume that Hydatius had frequent access to the Suevic court at Braga. In a few cases, the Suevic rulers employed provincials, including bishops, to act as their legates, but this seems to have been rare.[50] Hydatius' main source of knowledge may have been public: the display of court ceremonial. Several entries explicitly record the public ritual surrounding the reception of embassies. The imperial envoy Hesychius, sent by the emperor Avitus to the Gothic king Theoderic II after his defeat of the Sueves in 456, conveyed 'sacred rewards' to the king while he was still in the field. At the same time, Hesychius proclaimed a recent defeat of the Vandals, a traditional bulletin of an imperial victory delivered to provincials and allied kings.[51] Hydatius' knowledge of imperial, Gothic, and Vandal embassies to the Suevic kings probably came from similar ceremonial occasions. Attestation of such ceremonial in fifth-century sources is clear though rare: the formal announcement of the arrival of an Italian envoy to Toulouse, not to the court but to 'public notice'; public receptions in provincial centres and imperial residences for the *adventus* of bishops undertaking embassies, recorded in hagiographical sources; in Hydatius, the display of a Gothic army parade before the Suevic envoys to Euric in 467, and a similar display seen by envoys visiting the western imperial court at the same time.[52] It is likely that the

[50] Table 1 nos. 4 (Hermeric sends bishop Symphosius to the imperial consistory, 433), 41 (Remismund sends Lusidius, a *praesens civis* of Lisbon, to the emperor Anthemius, 468). Cf. Jordanes, *Get.*, 234: the Sueves send 'bishops of their regions' to Theoderic II after the death of the Gothic puppet Aioulf, 457.

[51] Table 1 no. 13. On victory bulletins: McCormick, *Eternal Victory*, 39–41 and 41 n. 22, 192–3, 234; to foreign powers: 3 n. 9.

[52] Announcement: Ennodius, *Vita Epiphani*, 85: *cum summo gaudio adventum pontificis indicavit notitiae publicae*. On *adventus* ceremonies for embassies: below, chapter 6 at nn. 138–43. Displays to Suevic envoys: Hyd., cc. 243, 247 [238, 241].

dispatch and reception of envoys was attended by ceremonial and display at Braga and other barbarian courts as it was at the imperial capitals.

Embassies were a source of information as well as a topic of Hydatius' *Chronicle*. Information in some entries was taken directly from envoys in Gallaecia.[53] Other travellers to western Spain, too, provided Hydatius with information.[54] Such visitors must have been a welcome source of knowledge to Hydatius, especially after he began composition of the work. Given Hydatius' prefatory remarks on his geographical distance from the rest of the Roman world, it is tempting to attribute much of the unsourced material in the *Chronicle* to contact between Hydatius and envoys. But in fact, Hydatius is quite explicit about what information he derived from envoys; less than half a dozen entries are sourced to envoys, and there is no reason to assume that any other data are based upon news from embassies where they are not mentioned.[55] Only once did envoys bring news of an imperial succession, which could have contributed to the chronological structure of the work: the death of the emperor Libius Severus in 465, reported by Suevic envoys returning from Toulouse.[56] For no other imperial accession or death does Hydatius indicate the source for his information.[57] That Hydatius mentions how Severus' death was discovered suggests that the haphazard transmission of such news through diplomatic missions was exceptional.

Some of the information Hydatius did acquire from travellers came from private interview, but this need not have been the case for news gained from visiting or returning embassies.[58] The purpose of certain

53 For the following: contrast Muhlberger, *Fifth-Century Chroniclers*, 211; Burgess, 'Hydatius', 67–70; Burgess, 'The Third Regnal Year of Eparchius Avitus: A Reply', *Classical Philology* 82 (1987), 337 and n. 10; Margarita Vallejo Girves, 'Relaciones del reino visigodo de Tolosa con el imperio. El papel de las embajadas', in Antonio Mendez *et al.*, *Los Visigodos y su mundo* (Madrid, 1997), 76.

54 E.g. the priest from Arabia, Germanus; Hyd., c. 106 [97].

55 Only Hyd., cc. 177, 197 [170, 192] (in both cases, envoys visiting Gallaecia specifically to make public pronouncements), 230–1, 242–4, 247 [226–7, 238, 241] (Suevic envoys bearing news on their return from Gaul) explicitly cite *legati* as the source for information.

56 The Suevic envoys presumably had been sent about Gothic–Suevic tensions over the Suevic expansion into Lusitania; Table 1 no. 31; Hyd., c. 231 [227]; cf. Muhlberger, *Fifth-Century Chroniclers*, 310. Burgess, 'Hydatius', 81 and n. 19, conjectures that information on the dating of Anthemius' reign came from the Suevic envoys of Table 1 no. 36.

57 Hydatius' list of imperial dynastic events includes not only the elevation and deaths of the emperors, but also the deaths of the *augustae* Galla Placidia in 450 (c. 148 [140]) and Pulcheria in 453 (c. 157 [149]). As Burgess points out ('Hydatius', 68), the hostility towards Valentinian III in the entry concerning the murder of Aetius makes it unlikely that the envoys subsequently dispatched by the emperor were Hydatius' source (cc. 160, 161 [152, 153]). Other examples of major political news being received in Gallaecia before the arrival of envoys dispatched in association with the events include Ricimer's naval victory over the Vandals (cc. 176, 177 [169, 170]) and the fratricidal accession of Euric (cc. 237, 238 [233, 234]).

58 Private interview: e.g. Hyd., 106 [97]: Hydatius received news of certain eastern ecclesiastical affairs from the priest Germanus and 'other Greeks' (*relatione comperimus*). Cf. the prefatory remarks

embassies was precisely to proclaim news publicly. This is the case with the only two incoming embassies recorded by Hydatius from which he drew information: the mission of the tribune Hesychius to Theoderic II in Gallaecia, and of the imperial and Gothic envoys to Gallaecian provincials and the Suevic and Vandal courts, announcing the new *pax* between Majorian and Theoderic II.[59] The information was gathered from a public source, not personal interview; Hydatius reproduces official propaganda, not inside information. Elsewhere, Hydatius relates news 'announced' without reference to envoys, possibly indicating less formal dissemination of information.[60] Several envoys and messengers from the emperor Avitus visited Gallaecia; Hydatius' sparse account of the Gallic usurper's reign in Italy gives no indication that he had interviewed the visitors for information.[61]

on the use of *aliquantorum relatus* and *relationes indicantium*, *Praef.*, 5, 6, though *relationes* could include written material, e.g. episcopal letters.

Other examples of authors citing envoys as sources of information include *The Chronicle of Pseudo-Joshua the Stylite*, trans. Frank R. Trombley and John W. Watt (TTH 32; Liverpool, 2000), 25 (unnamed envoys to the eastern emperor and the Persian shah among sources of Pseudo-Joshua's account of recent affairs); Gregory of Tours, *Hist.* v, 43; vi, 18, 40 (Gregory speaks personally with both visiting and Frankish envoys, mainly however about the state of Trinitarian belief in Gothic Spain); vi, 33, possibly iv, 28 (items of news explicitly reported by returning envoys).

59 Hyd., cc. 177, 197 [170, 192]. Another possible example of embassies used for official proclamations is c. 226 [222]: in 464/5, Theoderic II sends envoys to Remismund, the Gothic nominee as ruler of the Sueves, conveying weapons, gifts, and Remismund's wife, kept in Gaul while Remismund established his power in Gallaecia. The bestowal of *munera*, and Hydatius' very knowledge of this transaction, suggest that the reception of the embassy was staged as a public statement of the Gothic king's support for the Sueves' new ruler (cf. the *munera* sent by Avitus to Theoderic II in c. 177 [170]).

60 Hyd., cc. 176 (*magna multitudo Vandalorum . . . regi Theudorico nuntiatur occisa per Avitum*), 186 (*Theudoricus adversis sibi nuntiis territus . . . de Emerita egreditur*) [169, 179]. In both cases, news is given to Theoderic II while in Gallaecia, without reference to envoys or the original source of the information (cf. preceding note). The message of c. 176 [169] appears to have been separate from the later formal victory legation of the *tribunus [et notarius]* Hesychius, sent to Theoderic by Avitus (c. 177 [170]; Table 1 no. 13), *contra* Ralph W. Mathisen, 'The Third Regnal Year of Eparchius Avitus', *Classical Philology* 80 (1985), 330 = his *Studies in the History, Literature and Society of Late Antiquity* (Amsterdam, 1991) (making the two messages refer to two different naval victories) and Tranoy ii, 105–6 (seeing cc. 176 and 177 [169, 170] as a doublet, reporting the same victory and the same announcement twice); cf. Burgess, 'Reply', 337–8 and n. 11.

The news of Euric's accession also seems to have reached Gallaecia before he dispatched envoys there; Hyd., cc. 237–8 [233, 234], Table 1 nos. 33, 35.

The bearers of episcopal correspondence recorded in the *Chronicle* are similarly anonymous: cc. 109, 133, 135, 145, 151 [100, 125, 127, 137, 143]; cf. Muhlberger, *Fifth-Century Chroniclers*, 207–9.

61 Envoys and messengers from Avitus: Hyd., cc. 170, 176, 177, possibly 186 [163, 169, 170, 179]. Details of Avitus' rule: proclamation in Gaul; 'summons' and acknowledgement in Rome; alleged recognition by the eastern emperor Marcian; commission and reward of Theoderic II for supression of Sueves; naval victory by Ricimer over the Vandals; departure from Italy and (intention to reach) Arles (Burgess, 'Reply', 339). All these details appear to reflect Avitus' own public propaganda rather than inside reports from Rome; Hyd., cc. 163, 166, 169, 173, 176–7 [156, 159, 162, 166, 169–70].

The ceremonial forms of legations ensured that they acted as a public medium for dissemination of information. Towards the end of the *Chronicle*, Hydatius specifies other information acquired from Suevic envoys returning to Gallaecia from missions abroad: the prodigies seen by Suevic envoys at Toulouse, and political and military events witnessed or heard of by Suevic envoys to the emperor Anthemius (some of these reports were inaccurate or already outdated). Exactly how Hydatius learnt of news brought back to Gallaecia by the Suevic envoys to Gaul and Italy remains problematic.[62] His care to specify the source of his information here and elsewhere, however, suggests that it is unlikely that embassies served as the basis of his information for chapters where they are not specified; his other sources remain unknown. The proclamations of visiting and returning envoys in Gallaecia is evidence of the public role of embassies as a medium for political communication, propaganda, and even disinformation.

Hydatius' attention to embassies is itself testimony to the frequency, importance, and public nature of diplomatic communication in the fifth-century West. The predominance of embassies in the *Chronicle* is a substitute for documentary sources, such as diplomatic archives, as evidence that formalised diplomatic exchange was a characteristic feature of public life at the time of the break-up of the Roman West. Hydatius' independent approach to describing public events captures the diplomatic infrastructure of political developments almost unseen in other contemporary chronicles. His provincial position shapes his outlook: he is freed from intentionally propagandistic purposes; he is a member of the provincial episcopacy increasingly shouldering legations along with other imperial and municipal duties. His record is the product of a provincial bishop who knows that security, both for his own provincial community and in the wider arena of the empire and barbarian kingdoms, depends on the outcome of such missions. Like warfare and imperial dynastic events, embassies are major political events. Hydatius brings us closer than any other western author to the actual conduct of relations between powers.

PATTERNS OF CONTACT

The numerous embassies in the *Chronicle* were part of a complex network of contact throughout the West. The modern tendency to envisage political relations in the fifth century as radiating out from the two imperial

[62] Hyd., cc. 242–4, 247 [238, 241]. Inaccuracy: Thompson, *Romans and Barbarians*, 223–6. Hydatius and Suevic envoys: cf. Cardelle de Hartmann, *Philologische Studien*, 137–8, perhaps overestimating factors preventing contact.

courts is deceptive. Hydatius demonstrates vigorous contact throughout many levels of authority in the provinces; provincial imperial authorities, municipal communities, episcopal assemblies, and the barbarian royal courts all communicated with each other. Envoys travelled not only from the barbarian courts to the imperial capitals, but also across the provinces. The *Chronicle* records more missions between Toulouse and Braga than along any other route. To each centre of authority in the provinces, the position of the imperial court, though unique, was not necessarily central. A diagram of relations in the West would look less like the radii of a circle than a cat's cradle.

Yet Hydatius' vision was circumscribed. He mentions only one embassy to an eastern emperor.[63] The intense negotiations preceding Attila's invasion of Gaul in 451 seem to have been unknown to him.[64] Diplomatic exchanges between barbarian peoples in the West other than the Sueves, Goths, and Vandals – those who impinged upon affairs in Gallaecia – were beyond his knowledge. While Hydatius' authority on contact between southern Gaul and Gallaecia is presumably reliable, his awareness of interactions among other western powers is demonstrably sporadic.[65] Hydatius describes only one small part of the mosaic of the West in the mid-fifth century, detailed for north-western Spain but fragmentary beyond. His account is all the more valuable for the richness of information it nevertheless provides for this one, relatively unimportant region.

Some idea of the extent of political interaction between the different regions and social strata of the West can be gained by setting out the various bilateral channels of communication which appear in the *Chronicle*. The empire is by no means a player in all dialogues; even when it is, senior imperial officers in the provinces form a quite distinct entity from the two imperial courts. Hydatius' own class, the Gallaecian provincials and their episcopacy (not necessarily a uniform body), is seen in contact with authorities in Gaul, first with imperial magistrates, then with the Goths; they treat also with their Suevic rulers. The Sueves negotiate with the Goths of Toulouse, sometimes in association with their relations with

[63] Table I no. 9 (Avitus to Marcian, 455).

[64] Cf. Jordanes, *Get.*, 184–9, 191, 194–5, 197–9; Sid. Ap., *Carm.* VII, 328–56; Prosper, *Chron.*, c. 1364. Aetius' manipulations in 451 became a leitmotiv in early medieval histories: Gregory of Tours, *Hist.* II, 7; Fredegar, *Chron.* II, 53; *Addimenta ad Prosperum Hauniensis* (MGH AA 9), 302, s.a. 451; S. Barnish, 'Old Kaspars: Attila's Invasion of Gaul in the Literary Sources', in Drinkwater and Elton (eds.), *Fifth-Century Gaul*, 43–4.

[65] E.g. he recorded Geiseric's overtures for peace to Majorian in 460 (Table I no. 23), seemingly unaware of earlier treaties between the Vandals and the empire in 435 and 442; cf. F. M. Clover, 'Geiseric the Statesman: A Study of Vandal Foreign Policy' (diss., University of Chicago, 1966), 53–60, 88–102.

the provincials or the empire, sometimes not. Contact between all the western courts and the Vandals in Africa are recorded with tantalising brevity. The combinations and permutations of these diplomatic principals indicate the complex networks underlying political and military developments.

Gallaecian provincials and imperial and royal authorities

Relations between the western powers differed in many ways from modern international relations. The Roman aristocracies, especially in the provinces, played a part duplicated by no modern private individuals. This is well illustrated by the embassies to and from the provincials of Gallaecia. The Gallaecians repeatedly appealed to the imperial government, and later to the Goths of Toulouse, for intervention between themselves and the Sueves. Yet it is evident that they could also treat with their barbarian neighbours on their own authority.

Provincial embassies are first seen in the mission to Aetius undertaken by Hydatius and the return legation sent by the general in 431–2.[66] In 430 (soon after the departure of the Vandals from Baetica to North Africa), the Sueves under King Hermeric violated a *pax* with the Gallaecian provincials, attacking inland areas where certain provincials retained strongholds. The provincials defended themselves and defeated the Sueves, and the *pax* was restored.[67] The following year the Sueves again abrogated the *pax*. Presumably lacking confidence that they could again defeat the Sueves, the provincials sought imperial intervention. Bishop Hydatius was sent to northern Gaul to seek the general Aetius.

This repetitious conflict and Hydatius' description of the Sueves as a 'treacherous tribe' have cast the barbarians as untrustworthy raiders, oblivious to the obligations of treaties, 'marauders, nothing else'.[68] But Hydatius' elliptical presentation is tendentious. During the first conflict, it was the Sueves, not the Gallaecians, who suffered the worst from 'slaughter and captivity'. The *pax* restored in 430 is previously unmentioned in the *Chronicle*. Hydatius may indicate that the Sueves, the following year,

[66] Table I nos. I and 3.

[67] Hyd., c. 91 [81]. The *mediae partes Gallaeciae* perhaps refers to the inland region of the *conventus* of Braga, where Aquae Flaviae, Hydatius' putative episcopal see, was located; Tranoy II, 63, Map iii. This would explain why Hydatius was chosen as envoy in 431.

[68] Hyd., c. 208 [203]: *gens perfidia*, cf. c. 219 [215]: *Suevi promissionum suarum ut semper fallaces et perfidi*. Thompson, *Romans and Barbarians*, 164 (quotation), 209; cf. e.g. 'La Galicia sueva vista por los escritores indígenas contemporáneos', in Erwin Koller and Hugo Laitenberger (eds.), *Suevos-Schwaben: Das Königreich der Sueben auf der iberischen Halbinsel (411–585)* (Tübingen, 1998), 27–9. Vituperation of barbarians as untrustworthy was an ancient commonplace with much currency in the fifth century (e.g. Sid. Ap., *Ep.* VI, 6.1).

claimed an unspecified pretext to breach this renewed agreement.[69] Like the Goths of Toulouse, the Sueves demanded hostages from the provincial population as part of the *pax* with the Gallaecians.[70] Stripped of pejorative rhetoric, Hydatius' descriptions of peace settlements, before and after 430–1, suggests that treaties were formally concluded by both the Sueves and the Romans.[71] The *paces* were not mere reprieves from constant raids.

Hydatius travelled not to the western imperial court resident in Italy, but to the field camp of one of the western *generalissimos*. This has been seen as an early sign of Aetius' assumption of quasi-imperial authority in dealing with barbarian peoples in the provinces, and part of his personal dominion of western politics.[72] Aetius' role was not without precedent. As the successors of Theodosius I did not lead military campaigns, the traditional role of the emperor in treating personally with barbarian leaders devolved onto the leading commanders of the mobile forces.[73] Most famously, the settlement of Vallia's Goths in Aquitania Secunda in 418 was arranged by the then *magister utriusque militiae* and *patricius* Constantius.[74]

The approach to Aetius was necessitated by conditions of imperial administration in Spain. The reorganisation of western armies in the 410s and 420s, following the suppression of the usurpers in the time of the emperor Honorius, established new infantry forces and a new commander in

69 Provincials' defeat of Sueves and restoration of *pax*: Hyd., c. 91 [81]: *Suevi . . . pacem quam ruperant . . . restaurant* (429); cf. certain Gallaecians' successful defence against a Gothic band, inflicting large casualties, in 457; c. 186 [179].

Pretext for renewed hostilities: *Rursum Suevi initiam cum Callaecis pacem libata sibi occasione conturbant* 96 [86] (431). For examples of *occasio* with the sense of *causa* in late Latin: *ThLL* 9.2 332 IBa; A. Blaise and H. Chirat, *Dictionnaire latin–français des auteurs chrétiens* (Turnhout, 1954), 571 §§ 3–4.

70 Hostages: Hyd., c. 100 [91]. Hostages held by Goths of Toulouse: Sid. Ap., *Carm.* VII, 215–18, with chapter 3, n. 63 below (Roman provincials given as hostages to Gothic settlers during or after 418 settlement in Aquitaine). Cf. Paulinus of Pella, *Eucharisticos*, ed. W. Brandes, in *Poetae Christiani minores* I (CSEL 16; Vienna, 1888), lines 379–82 (during the siege of Bazas by Goths under Athaulf in 414/15, an unnamed Alanic king, who occupies the city in order to repel the besiegers, gives his wife and one son as hostages to the citizens as sureties of his good intentions). Other possible examples of hostage-taking in Hydatius: Hyd., c. 91 [81] (when the Sueves first broke the *pax* in 430, they seized Gallaecian *familiae*, perhaps to serve as *obsides*); Hyd., c. 131 [123] with n. 129 below (possible forced taking of Gallaecean hostages by Vandals in 445); Hyd., cc. 188, 196 [181, 191] (after the devastating Gothic attack of 456, the divided Sueves again successfully approached the provincials for a *pax*, which soon collapsed when the Sueves killed certain provincial *honesti*; these may have been luckless hostages given over for the renewed *pax*).

71 E.g. Hyd., c. 113 [105]: *Suevi . . . pacis iura confirmant.*

72 E.g. O. Seeck, 'Flavius Aetius', *RE* I, 701; J. M. O'Flynn, *Generalissimos of the Western Roman Empire* (Edmonton, 1983), 89–90.

73 John Lydus, *De magistratibus* II, 11. Michael Whitby, 'From Frontier to Palace: The Personal Role of the Emperor in Diplomacy', in Shepard and Franklin (eds.), *Byzantine Diplomacy*, 295–303.

74 Later proclaimed emperor. Prosper, *Chron.*, s.a. 419; Hyd., c. 69 [61].

Spain, the *comes Hispaniarum*.[75] This army, known only from its attempts to check the Asding Vandals, was not destined for a glorious future. Its intervention in conflicts between the Vandals and the Sueves precipitated the Vandal occupation of Baetica in 419, and its subsequent attempt to dislodge the barbarians resulted in defeat.[76] In 429 the Vandals decimated the imperial forces in Spain, probably attempting to prevent the Vandal passage to North Africa.[77] The Sueves' ambitions in 429–31 to expand beyond Gallaecia and to overthrow existing arrangements with the Roman provincials were encouraged by the simultaneous destruction of the imperial military in Spain and the departure of the Vandals.

In 431, as a former *magister utriusque militiae per Gallias* and now *magister utriusque militiae praesentalis*,[78] Aetius was not only one of the supreme

[75] Possibly upgraded 419/21 to a *magister utriusque militiae* equivalent to the *magister utriusque militiae per Gallias*; Jones, *LRE* I, 192, 196–7; III, 36 n. 44, 353–4; Hyd., cc. 74 [66] (the *comes Hispaniarum* Asterius), 77 [69] (the *magister utriusque militiae* Castinus); *Not. dig.* Oc. VII, 118–34 (*comes Hispaniarum*, not listed in the *distributio* of *ibid.* V). The *comes* Asterius occupied a *praetorium* in Tarragona in ?419; Augustine, *Epistolae ex duobus codicibus nuper in lucem prolatae*, ed. Johannes Divjak (CCSL 88; Vienne, 1981), *Ep.* 11* 8.2, cf. lviii–ix. The exclusive assignment of Castinus and other *magistri utriusque militiae* to Spain is disputed by A. Demandt, 'Magister Militum', *RE Suppl.* XII, 635, 667–9, 671; cf. J. Sundwall, *Weströmische Studien* (Berlin, 1915), 51 no. 44, 'Fl. Asturius'. Cf. Javier Arce, 'La *Notitia dignitatum* et l'armée romaine dans la *diocesis Hispaniarum*', *Chiron* 10 (1980), 605–6.

[76] In 421; Hyd., cc. 74, 77 [66, 69].

[77] *Chron. Gall. 452*, c. 107 (s.a. 431); Seeck, *Untergang* VI, 111–12; Norman H. Baynes, 'A Note on Professor Bury's *History of the Later Roman Empire*', *Journal of Roman Studies* 12 (1922), 220–1; Stein I, 320. The evidence of *Chron. Gall. 452* has been dismissed as a duplicate of Castinus' campaign of 421, Hyd., c. 77 [69] (L. Schmidt, *Histoire des Vandales*, trans. H. E. del Medico (Paris, 1953), 36 n.1; Christian Courtois, *Les Vandales et L'Afrique* (Paris, 1955), 55 n. 4, cf. 56 n. 5, 156; Thompson, *Romans and Barbarians*, 172–3, 299 n. 70). But there is no reason to attribute a chronological error of eight years to the author of *Chron. Gall. 452* (cf. Clover, 'Geiseric the Statesman', 9–10 n. 1). The entry has also been interpreted as a reference to the battle in 429 between the Vandals and the Sueves, Hyd., c. 90 [80] (Clover, *ibid.*, 9–10 n. 1; Muhlberger, *Fifth-Century Chroniclers*, 171 n. 77), but the passage refers to the defeated army as *milites*; it is unlikely that the author would refer to the Sueves so, when elsewhere he consistently refers to barbarians by tribal names.

Cassiodorus, *Chron.*, c. 1215 (s.a. 427) records a campaign against the Vandals by the Goths immediately prior to the crossing into Africa. This is clearly a separate campaign from that of 421; cf. Cass., *Chron.*, 1203; Jordanes, *Get.*, 166 (the date of 427 in both sources is derived from Prosper's dating of the Vandal entry of Africa). The Goths were probably auxiliaries to a Roman force, as they had been in 421. It is possible that the Suevic forces in Lusitania, which Geiseric attacked before departing Baetica, were also Roman allies (Hyd., c. 90 [80]; Courtois, *Vandales*, 56 n. 5), but it is more likely that this was the beginning of the Suevic push to occupy the rest of the peninsula.

Salvian, *De gubernatione Dei*, ed. F. Pauly (CSEL 8; Vienne, 1883), VII, 11.46, 12.53, links the crossing to Africa with a Vandal defeat of the Romans and their Gothic auxiliaries, but does not indicate how close in time these events were.

[78] Epigraphic evidence of Aetius' tenure as *magister utriusque militiae per Gallias*: *L'Année Épigraphique*, 1950 (= *Revue Archéologique* ser. VI, 36 (1950)), no. 30. His tenure was either 425–9, during which he is attested only as *comes* (W. Ensslin, 'Zum Heermeisteramt des spätrömischen Reiches', *Klio* 24 (1931), 476–7; *PLRE* II, 'Aetius 7', 22), or 429–30, between his attested appointment as a *magister*

military commanders in the West, but also the senior officer with competence over the military affairs of Spain, part of the prefecture of Gaul.[79] The provincials sought his assistance in the absence of local military forces. The military commanders in Spain in the 410s and 420s had been allied with the Sueves against the Vandals.[80] Perhaps they also served to mediate relations between the barbarians and the provincials. If so, the provincials in 431 desired Aetius to assume the same role from Gaul. Certainly Hydatius shows no sign of disappointment that Aetius responded to the provincials' appeal with a diplomatic mission rather than a military offensive.[81]

What authority did Hydatius represent as envoy? Usually when Hydatius portrays a body politic of Gallaecian provincials – sending or receiving envoys, negotiating with the Sueves – he refers to it only as the *Gallaeci*.[82] The simplicity of this term is deceptive. During occasions of hostility, the Sueves were in conflict not with all the Roman inhabitants of the province but with specific smaller areas. There were also divisions among the Gallaecians which Hydatius chose not to emphasise.[83] The *Chronicle* records no local imperial or municipal officers involved in negotiations on behalf of the Gallaecians, either in 431 or later.[84] Several times, Hydatius refers to regional divisions of Gallaecia, the *conventus* of Braga, Lugo, and Astorga. These appear to be the old local juridical and administrative units of the early empire, still functioning in the fifth century.[85] None of the embassies to or from the provincials is associated

and the murder of the senior *magister utriusque militiae praesentalis* Felix (T. Mommsen, 'Aetius', *Gesammelte Schriften* IV (Berlin, 1906), 535 n. 9; Sundwall, *Weströmische Studien*, 41; Demandt, 'Magister militum', 654); cf. O'Flynn, *Generalissimos*, 78. For Aetius' position in 431: Ensslin, 'Heermeisteramt', 477–8; Demandt, 'Magister militum', 654–5; Sundwall, *Weströmische Studien*, 41; *PLRE* II, 22–3.

79 Cf. Demandt, 'Magister militum', 667. There is no *magister utriusque militiae per Gallias* attested between 430 and 437 (cf. *PLRE* II, 1289), during which Aetius campaigned several times in Gaul.

80 Hyd., cc. 71, 74 [63, 66]; cf. Bury I, 204, 208–9.

81 Table I no. 3; cf. Thompson, *Romans and Barbarians*, 290 n. 8.

82 E.g. Hyd., cc. 96, 100, 135, 188, 196, 197, 204, 220 [86, 91, 127, 181, 191, 192, 199, 216].

83 Thompson, *Romans and Barbarians*, 178–87, 211; Muhlberger, *Fifth-Century Chroniclers*, 245–60.

84 The only possible imperial official in Gallaecia in the *Chronicle* is the *rector* of Lugo, killed by a Suevic attack in 460; Hyd., c. 199 [194]; cf. Tranoy I, 46; Thompson, *Romans and Barbarians*, 169. A *consularis Callaeciae* is listed in the *Not. dig. Oc.* I, 67: XXI.10, but does not appear in Hydatius' narrative.

85 Hyd., cc. 102, 194, 202 [93, 189, 197] (*conventus* of Lugo, cf. the *Lucensis urbs* of c. 219); 179, 214a [172, 213] (of Braga); 249 [243] (of Astorga, cf. cc. 130, 173 [122, 166]: *Asturicensis urbs*). Tranoy II, Map iii. For the *conventus* and *conventus civium Romanorum* in the early empire: E. Kornemann, 'Conventus', *RE* IV.1 (Berlin, 1900), 1173–1200 (note the lists of juridical *conventus* assemblies and of *conventus civium Romanorum*, 1177, 1184); W. Kunkel, *An Introduction to Roman Legal and Constitutional History*, trans. J. M. Kelly, 2nd edn (Oxford, 1973), 41–2; A. N. Sherwin-White, *The Roman Citizenship*, 2nd edn (Oxford, 1973), 225–7; for the *conventus* of Spain: Eugene Albertini, *Les Divisions administratives de l'Espagne romaine* (Paris, 1923), 83–104;

with an authority representing the *conventus*. Nor is there any reference to municipal magistrates acting as the principals of the embassies.

Hydatius does, however, mention other bodies which he called *plebes*. It was one of these bodies, a *plebs* of inland Gallaecia, that the bishop represented in 431.[86] The classical meaning of the word *plebs* has prevented correct interpretation of Hydatius' evidence. *Plebs* in Hydatius has been read pejoratively, as socially or heretically divisive groups, but this is inconsistent with the description of the *plebs* in the *Chronicle*.[87] The *plebs* of inland Gallaecia was able to dispatch envoys recognised by imperial authorities, which suggests some official standing.[88] It could also treat with the Suevic king. Hermeric concluded *paces* with the *plebs* of inland Gallaecia in 430, 431, and 438, the latter two times after imperial persuasion.[89] In a parallel case in the 460s, a different *plebs*, called the Aunonians, also dispatched and received envoys, and concluded a *pax* with a Suevic king.[90] The negotiations of 431–2 between the *plebs* and the Sueves were carried out by members of the Gallaecian episcopacy; the *plebs* cannot have been opposed to either the church or the aristocracy of the province.[91]

Hydatius' *plebes* represent officially recognised local authorities separate from the *conventus* and cities. In later Latin, *plebs* was often used to

Nicola Mackie, *Local Administration in Roman Spain AD 14–212* (BAR International Series 173; Oxford, 1983), 8–9, 136–9. Isidore, *Etymologiae*, ed. W. M. Lindsay (Oxford, 1911), XIV, 5.21 lists different examples of Spanish *conventus*. The town of Aquae Flaviae (probably Hydatius' see) appears to be described as a *conventus* in Hyd., c. 201 [196], in which an attack on it by the Sueves is reported; cf. Thompson, *Romans and Barbarians*, 170. But in the early empire it was part of the *conventus* of Braga. It seems likely that Hydatius means that Aquae Flaviae was attacked as part of a general Suevic assault on the eastern part of the *conventus* of Braga, differentiating this from the attack on the *conventus* of Lugo mentioned earlier in the same entry.

86 Hyd., cc. 91, 96 [81, 86] (Table 1 no. 1). The wording of c. 96 [86] indicates that the provincials attacked by the Sueves in 431 and represented by Hydatius were the *plebs* of c. 91 [81]: the Sueves breached the *pax* they had made the previous year with the *plebs* of the *mediae partes Gallaeciae*. This *plebs* is described as *quae castella tutiora retinebat*. For *castella* as early imperial municipalities: Mackie, *Local Administration*, 5–8, 14 n. 12, 22–4.

87 Thompson, *Romans and Barbarians*, 271 n. 52, sees the *plebs* as Bagaudae; Tranoy II, 74 as rural Priscillianist heretics; Muhlberger, *Fifth-Century Chroniclers*, 249 as 'lesser folk' acting without official authority.

88 I.e. by Aetius in 431 and probably 438. The Gothic king Theoderic II responded to the *Aunonensis plebs* in 466.

89 The *plebs* of Hyd., c. 113 [105] (Table 1 no. 5) appears to be the *pars plebis Callaeciae* of cc. 91, 96 [81, 86]; cf. Tranoy II, 74.

90 Hyd., cc. 233, 239, 249 [229, 235, 243] (Table 1 nos. 32 and 40): in 466, the *Aunonensis plebs* is attacked by the Sueves (the Aunonian region has not been identified). It sends envoys to the Gothic king Theoderic II, who responds by dispatching envoys to the Sueves. In 469, the Aunonians contract a *pax* with the Sueves.

91 Hyd., cc. 96 (Bishop Hydatius' embassy), 100 (a *pax* made with king Hermeric *sub interventu episcopali*), 101 (Bishop Symphosius is sent by Hermeric after concluding the *pax*) [86, 91, 92]. For Hydatius' aristocratic background: Muhlberger, *Fifth-Century Chroniclers*, 196–8.

refer to a specific Christian congregation, whether of a diocese, parish, or bishopric.[92] In the negotiations of the *pars plebis Callaeciae* in 430–1, however, several bishops were involved, while no clergy are mentioned in relation to the Aunonian *plebs*. Hydatius' *plebes* do not appear to represent ecclesiastical administrative units. A closer comparandum to Hydatius' use of the word occurs in the *Vita S. Severini* by Eugippius, written 509/11, in which *plebs* appears as an alternative to *Romani* and *habitatores oppidi*, to refer to the inhabitants of the town of Comagenis in Noricum. These provincial *Romani* had formed a *foedus* with a group of barbarians.[93] Late in the sixth century, Gregory of Tours, who usually uses *plebs* in the senses either of *vulgus* or congregation, reproduces a legal judgement of 590, in which *plebs* refers to an urban community under the governance of a *comes*.[94] The uses of *plebs* by both Eugippius and the document reproduced by Gregory are similar to Hydatius' term, though both refer to the communities of specific towns, whereas Hydatius' *plebs* seems to refer to a wider region, and there is no reference in the *Chronicle* to a governor or any other single magistrate with authority for the *plebs*. The *plebes* of Gallaecia appear to be a remnant of Roman provincial administrative structures, a local assembly or council. *Plebes* are the only provincial organisation attested in Hydatius' *Chronicle* with the authority to send representatives to treat with imperial authorities and the Suevic court, and may be the body acting in Hydatius' other references to the *Gallaeci*.

Hydatius' embassy and the subsequent negotiations between the imperial envoy, the Sueves, and the provincial bishops had limited success.

[92] Niermeyer, *Lexicon minus*, s.v. §§ 6–16; Du Cange, *Gloss.*, VI, 363–4; attestations for *plebs* designating a specific community begin in the ninth century. Isidore, *Etymologiae* IX, 4.5–6 gives the classical definition of *plebs*.

[93] *Plebs*: Eugippius, *Vita Severini* II, 2 (cf. *Romani* in I, 4, II, 1; *habitatores oppidi* in II, 1); for the *foedus*: I, 4.

Elsewhere in *Vita Severini*, *cives* of the town of Tiburnia are able to fight a band of Goths to a standstill (reminiscent of the success of Gallaecian provincials in defeating Sueves and Goths; Hyd., cc. 91, 186 [81, 179] and cf. at nn. 67–71 above) and to establish a truce: XVII, 4 (*cives Tiburniae vario cum obsidentibus Gothis certamine dimicantes vix initi foederis pactione*); the truce required the townspeople, *inter cetera*, to hand over to the Goths clothing which had been collected for distribution to the poor, an insight into the scale of barbarian raids in post-Roman Noricum.

On these passages from Eugippius: Thompson, *Romans and Barbarians*, 119 and nn. 16, 18; R. A. Markus, 'The End of the Roman Empire: A Note on Eugippius, *Vita Sancti Severini*, 20', *Nottingham Medieval Studies* 26 (1982), 4 and n. 17. (Markus errs in describing the *benivola societas* between Rugi and Norican provincials in *Vita S. Severini* XXXI, 6 as a treaty negotiated by Severin; the saint only provides safe passage for the provincials whom the Rugian king relocated to territories tributary to him.)

[94] Gregory of Tours, *Hist.* X, 16 508, lines 9–10 (referring to Poitiers); for *plebs* as *vulgus*: III, 18 118, line 4; as a congregation: e.g. IV, 5 138, line 12; VII, 31 398, line 7; cf. X, 1 479, lines 3, 4, 8 (the *Oratio* of Pope Gregory I).

Plebs is attested from the early eighth century with the meaning 'legal community' or *pagus*: Niermeyer, *Lexicon minus*, s.v. §§ 3–5; Du Cange, *Gloss.* VI, 354: *conventus publicus*.

Although the agreement reached by the bishops and the Sueves does not seem to have been ratified by the imperial government,[95] Hydatius recorded no further conflict in Gallaecia for five years. Then, in 437, the *comes* Censorius was sent a second time, presumably again in response to a provincial embassy, to broker a settlement between the Sueves and the same *plebs* of inland Gallaecia.[96] This was the last appeal of the Gallaecians to the imperial authorities. When the Gallaecians and the Sueves next came into conflict, almost two decades later in the late 450s and 460s, it was no longer from imperial authorities but from the Gothic court of Toulouse that the provincials sought intervention.

Although Hydatius records provincial embassies from the Gallaecians to the imperial authorities and to the Goths, he never refers to any embassy representing the Gallaecians to the Sueves, or the Sueves to the Gallaecians. The conflicts and treaties between the Sueves and Gallaecians indicate that even after six decades of Suevic settlement in north-western Spain, the Gallaecians preserved a corporate identity separate from the royal court of Braga.[97] Yet during periods of conflict, the *Chronicle* records no representation or intercession for the provincials before the Suevic kings; no Gallaecian was sent as *legatus ad Suevos*.

The Sueves and the provincials clearly interacted, not as ruler and subject, but as two relatively equal parties.[98] Although Hydatius refers to his province as *infelix Gallaecia*, conflict between the two parties was sporadic, its timing dependent upon the external actions of the Sueves. Hydatius describes the initial settlement of the Vandals, Sueves, and Alans

[95] Table I no. 4: Hermeric sent Bishop Symphosius *ad comitatum*, in vain. Hydatius' terminology is careful. The Gallaecians and Sueves had negotiated with a representative of the *magister utriusque militiae* in Gaul, not directly with the western imperial court. But Hermeric was unable to ratify the agreement with Aetius. In 432–3, Aetius' fortunes were fluctuating wildly as he fought with his rivals Boniface and Sebastian; *PLRE* II, 'Aetius 7', 23–4. Hydatius distinguished between the *palatium*, the household of Galla Placidia and Valentinian III which the generals sought to dominate (Hyd., cc. 99 twice, 100 [89, 91]), and the *comitatus*, the emperor's court of high magistrates including Aetius, the ultimate victor of the struggle for power (cf. Jones, *LRE* I, 366–73). Hermeric's approach to the *comitatus* should be seen as an attempt to conclude negotiations with Aetius or, if necessary, his successor in these uncertain conditions, not as an appeal to the emperor himself (contrast the embassies of Euric and Remismund, unambiguously described as *ad imperatorem*; Table I nos. 34, 36, 41). The embassy fell foul of the violent politics of the western imperial court; cf. Tranoy II, 68; Thompson, *Romans and Barbarians*, 179; Muhlberger, *Fifth-Century Chroniclers*, 221.

[96] Table I no. 5.

[97] *Paces* between the Sueves and provincials: Hyd., cc. 91, 100, 113, 188 (a Suevic assault *sub specie pacis*, 'under the appearance of a peace'), 204, 219 (*promissa*), 223, 249 [81, 91, 105, 181, 199, 215, 219, 243]. It was perhaps these reports of Hydatius which convinced Isidore that, after the Suevic occupation of all Gallaecia in 429, *Gallici autem in parte provinciae regno suo utebantur*; *Hist. Goth.*, c. 85.

[98] For a thorough discussion of Suevic–provincial relations: Muhlberger, *Fifth-Century Chroniclers*, 245–60.

in Spain in 409–11 in apocalyptic terms, but relates no specific incidents. In 429, Geiseric led the Vandals from southern Spain into North Africa, and the Sueves unsuccessfully attempted to occupy Lusitania.[99] In the following year, the first conflict between the Sueves and the Gallaecian provincials recorded in the *Chronicle* broke out; it was not finally resolved until 438.[100] Hydatius notes no further conflicts for almost twenty years.

During that time, Suevic power expanded rapidly under kings Rechila and Rechiarius. The Sueves gained control of Lusitania, Baetica, and Carthaginiensis – most of the Iberian peninsula – despite imperial military opposition. In Hydatius' account, the Suevic expansion immediately follows the 438 *pax* between the Sueves and the Gallaecians.[101] Renewed Suevic expansion in 455/6 brought a sharp reaction by the emperor Avitus and the Goths under Theoderic II, who in 456 defeated the Suevic army and executed Rechiarius.[102]

As the Sueves' expansionist ambitions collapsed, conflict and negotiation with the Gallaecians reappeared. In the confusion following the Gothic assault, several shadowy figures sought to gain control of the Sueves. Their first recorded actions were to establish a *pax* with the Gallaecians, before attempting to reimpose their authority on the southern parts of Gallaecia and Lusitania.[103] But in 459, conflict erupted between the Sueves and the provincials in the northern region of Lugo, spreading to other parts of Gallaecia and continuing until the end of Hydatius' record. Throughout the 460s, the security of the Suevic kingdom was again challenged by Gothic opposition, as the Goths occupied the provinces of Baetica in the south of the peninsula, at Theoderic II's orders in 458, and Lusitania, under Euric in 468. The Goths also sought to intervene in the disputes between the Sueves and the Gallaecians.[104]

[99] Hyd., c. 90 [80].

[100] Hyd., cc. 91, 96–101, 111 and 113 [81, 86–92, 103, 105] (Table 1 nos. 1–5).

[101] Under Rechila, the Sueves gained control of Lusitania, Baetica, and Carthaginiensis after occupying the capital cities of each province (Hyd., cc. 114, 119, 121, 123: *Rex Rechila Hispali obtenta Baeticam et Carthaginiensem provincias in suam redigit potestatem* [106, 111, 113, 115]). Rechiarius campaigned in Terraconensis in 448–9, but does not seem to have gained control (cc. 137, 140, 142; cf. 158: the Goths operate freely in Terraconensis against Bagaudae in 454 [129, 132, 134; 150]). The return of Carthaginiensis to imperial control may have been negotiated in 453 (so Tranoy II, 95 at §155.3; cf. Hyd., cc. 155, 168 [147, 161]). After the political upheavals of 454–5, Rechiarius again sought to occupy Carthaginiensis and Terraconensis (cc. 168, 170, 172 [161, 163, 165]).

[102] Hyd., cc. 173–8 [166–71].

[103] *Pax*: Hyd., c. 181, 188: *Suevi in partes divisi pacem ambiunt Gallaecorum*; cf. the Gothic nominee Remismund in 464, c. 223 [174, 181; 219]. Expansion: c. 188; cf. 190, 193, 195 [181; 183, 188, 190].

[104] Conflicts in Lugo and other regions: Hyd., cc. 196–208 (460), 219–20 (463), 233, 237, 239, 249 (465–8) [191–203, 215–16, 229, 233, 235, 243]. Gothic occupation of Baetica as threat to Sueves, particularly in Lusitania: cc. 192, 193 (*Theudoricus . . . ad Baeticam dirigit manum . . . Suevi*

It seems that the Sueves needed peaceful relations with the provincials in Gallaecia before attempting to expand. During the 440s and 450s, when the Sueves occupied most of Spain, no domestic conflict is recorded in Gallaecia. Even in the confused conditions after the Gothic attack of 456, Suevic leaders endeavoured to secure *paces* with the provincials. Yet Hydatius never mentions embassies between the provincials and the Sueves to negotiate these agreements. Hydatius may have viewed contact between Sueves and provincials differently from other relations. Terminology used for formal embassies may have been inappropriate to describe communication and negotiation at a local level between the provincials and their barbarian neighbours, precluded not least because of Hydatius' bitter view of the Sueves.

Sueves and external affairs

The Sueves as well as the provincials communicated with imperial authorities and the Goths on the internal affairs of Gallaecia. But other issues too generated Suevic diplomatic traffic: control of the Iberian peninsula, and military alliances between Braga, Toulouse, and the western imperial court. In response to the Suevic expansion into Lusitania, Baetica, and Carthaginiensis after 438, the *comes* Censorius undertook his third journey to the Sueves, probably again sent by Aetius. Censorius had previously brokered settlements between the Sueves and the Gallaecians, but Rechila, far from treating with the imperial envoy, took Censorius captive.[105] A subsequent attempt in 446 to remove the Sueves from southern and eastern Spain by force also failed, and when Rechila died in August 448 in the Suevic-occupied city of Mérida in Lusitania, his son and successor Rechiarius immediately set out to subdue remaining areas of resistance.[106] Nevertheless, the return of Carthaginiensis to Roman authority was achieved through negotiation, probably in 453.[107] When Rechiarius attempted to reoccupy Carthaginiensis three years later,

nihilominus *Lusitaniae partes . . . depraedantur*) [186, 188]; Thompson, *Romans and Barbarians*, 189; *contra* R. W. Burgess, 'From *Gallia Romana* to *Gallia Gothica*: The View from Spain', in Drinkwater and Elton (eds.), *Fifth-Century Gaul*, 23–4. In 468, the Goths attacked the Sueves on two fronts, through Astorga in the north and from Mérida, newly occupied, in the south; it is unclear whether the Goths in Astorga were part of the force sent to occupy Lusitania or were a separate band from Gaul: cc. 245–6, 249–50 [239–40, 243–4].

105 Table I no. 6; cf. nos. 3 and 5.

106 Imperial campaign: Hyd., c. 134; Rechiarius: c. 137 [126, 129]. In the same year, the *comes* Censorius, held captive for eight years, was put to death, possibly as a show of hostility to the empire; c. 139 [131].

107 Hyd., c. 155 with 168 [147, 161]; cf. Tranoy II, 95.

imperial envoys were sent to protest. They travelled in a joint embassy with envoys of the Gothic king Theoderic II – a pivotal moment in relations between the Sueves, the empire, and the Goths.[108]

The Sueves' dealings with the western imperial authorities cannot be understood separately from the simultaneous development of their relations with the Goths. In the 410s, Vallia's Goths campaigned for the empire in Spain against the Asding and Siling Vandals, Alans, and Sueves, but were recalled by the *magister utriusque militiae* Constantius in 418, after extirpating the Alans and the Siling Vandals. The Sueves and Asding Vandals were left intact, in Gallaecia. The basis for this withdrawal was probably a tripartite alliance between the empire, Goths, and Sueves. The Sueves, like the Goths, were accepted as imperial federates, and were tied to the Goths by a marriage alliance between the two barbarian royal houses; a similar three-way alliance was to operate in the 450s (from the union of the 410s was born Ricimer, later *generalissimo* of the western empire). The Sueves benefited from their federate status with the empire: imperial forces defended the Sueves from Asding Vandal aggression in 419. But the marriage alliance with the Goths was short-lived, ruptured when Vallia died shortly before the settlement of the Goths in Aquitania and the new dynasty of Theoderic I assumed rule of the Goths.[109] Subsequent relations between the Sueves and Goths are obscure. In 421 and 429, Gothic auxiliaries assisted imperial forces campaigning against the Asding Vandals, enemies of the Sueves, in Spain.[110] In the unsettled conditions caused by the Vandal departure for North Africa in 429, the Goths may have sought to interfere in relations between the Sueves and the empire, but the details are unclear.[111]

In the 440s, the Goths were willing to support the empire in its attempt to regain Carthaginiensis and Baetica from the aggressive Suevic king Rechila. A large Gothic force accompanied the *magister utriusque militiae* Vitus into Spain in 446, but was put to flight by the Sueves.[112]

[108] Table 1 nos. 10 and 11.

[109] On the question whether the Sueves were federates after 411: Muhlberger, *Fifth-Century Chroniclers*, 248 n. 120 for bibliography, with Demougeot II, 448–9. Ricimer's parentage as evidence of a tripartite alliance in 417/18: Andrew Gillett, 'The Birth of Ricimer', *Historia* 44 (1995), 380–4. Alliance of 450s: below, n. 116. Imperial assistance to Sueves against Asding Vandals: Hyd., cc. 71 and 74 [63, 66].

[110] 421: Hyd., c. 77 [69]; 429: as at n. 77 above.

[111] Table 1 no. 2: in 431, while the Gallaecians sought imperial assistance against the Sueves, *Vetto, qui de Gothis dolose ad Gallaeciam venerat, sine aliquo effectu redit ad Gothos.* It is unclear whether Vetto acted on behalf of the Gothic king; cf. Table 1, 'Note on *Legatus* and *Legatio*'.

[112] Hyd., c. 134 [126]. Hydatius accused the Goths of following Vitus only for plunder, but they would have been observing their obligations as federates, reconfirmed by the settlement of the

Three years later, when Rechila died, the Gothic king Theoderic I entered into an alliance with the Sueves, marrying one of his daughters to Rechila's son and successor, Rechiarius.[113] Rechiarius was already expanding the territory taken by his father, undertaking expeditions into the Pyrenees and Terraconensis.[114] Theoderic appears to have reneged on his obligations to the empire in favour of this alliance.[115]

The imperial elevation of Avitus in July 455 altered this relationship. The Goths, now ruled by Theoderic I's son, Theoderic II, nominated and supported Avitus as emperor. For a brief time, imperial and Gothic interests were joined as never before. In 456, when Avitus sent envoys to Rechiarius to protest the Suevic reoccupation of Carthaginiensis, Theoderic sent his own envoys in support. The imperial envoy told the Sueves to withdraw from Carthaginiensis, but the real threat came from the Goths, who stated that the Sueves 'should observe the promises of the sworn alliance, both with themselves and with the Roman empire, since they were joined in one alliance of peace'.[116] Theoderic's ties with Avitus altered relations between the Goths and the Sueves. The Goths' marriage alliance with the Sueves was now subordinate to their *foedus* with the empire; and the Goths treated with Spain in a quasi-imperial capacity. When Rechiarius rejected Theoderic's envoys and instead extended his activities into Terraconensis, a second embassy was sent later the same year, not from the imperial authorities but from Theoderic II alone. Rechiarius imprudently rejected this embassy also. Theoderic promptly (*mox*) led an army into Gallaecia, overthrew the Suevic army, and captured and executed his brother-in-law. The attack was not only condoned but publically ordered by Avitus. Its aim was the destruction of the Suevic

436–9 war in southern Gaul; Thompson, *Romans and Barbarians*, 53, 272 n. 66; Wolfram, *History of the Goths*, 176–7. Theoderic I may also have been disturbed by the growing power of the Sueves, who had now ruled all the Iberian peninsula except Terraconensis for five years.

113 Hyd., cc. 140, 142 [132, 134]. The ceremony appears to have taken place in Toulouse, a sign that the Goths were the superior party in the alliance; cf. Valentinian III's offer to relocate the site of his wedding to Theodosius II's daughter, Licinia Eudoxia, in 437 from Thessalonica to Constantinople, out of respect for Theodosius; Socrates, *Ecclesiastica historia*, ed. Robert Hussey (Oxford, 1853), VII, 44.

114 Hyd., cc. 137 (*obtento tamen regno sine mora ulteriores regiones invadit* [sc. Rechiarius] *ad praedam*), 140 (attacks Gascones), 142 (joins with Bagaudae in attacking Zaragossa and Lérida in Terraconensis) [129, 132, 134].

115 Cf. the reluctance of Theoderic I to assist the empire against Attila two years later; Wolfram, *History of the Goths*, 178. The Goths resumed their service to the empire as federates after the accession of Theoderic II in 453. His brother Frederic led an army against Bagaudae in Terraconensis that year, on behalf of the empire, but apparently not under a Roman commander; Hyd., c. 158 [150].

116 Table 1 no. 11 (Hyd., c. 170 [163]): *ut tam secum quam cum Romano imperio, quia uno essent pacis foedere copulati, iurati foederis promissa servarent.*

monarchy and the establishment of a Gothic-nominated governor over the Sueves, an attempt which, in the event, was unsuccessful.[117]

Avitus appears to have delegated diplomatic and military authority in dealing with the Sueves to his Gothic allies. Gothic envoys represented the empire's interests; the Gothic army went to Gallaecia in 456 not as the auxiliaries of an imperial general, but under the command of their own king. Avitus' successor Majorian seems to have concurred in this arrangement, perhaps largely through necessity, after initial conflict with the former supporters of the emperor he had overthrown.[118] The Goths' new authority over Iberian affairs, confirmed by a Gothic embassy announcing the reconciliation of Majorian and Theoderic II, was recognised by the Gallaecian provincials: when conflicts with the Sueves again arose in the 460s, the Gallaecians no longer sought the intervention of imperial authorities but instead appealed to Toulouse.[119] Theoderic II, first approached by the provincials in 463, repeatedly sent envoys to the Suevic kings on the Gallaecians' behalf.[120] In 464 the Sueves accepted as their king Remismund, nominated by Theoderic. His first act was to restore

[117] Table I no. 12 (second embassy); Hyd., c. 173–8 (campaign of Theoderic II *et cum voluntate et ordinatione Aviti imperatoris*; death of Rechiarius; *regnum destructum et finitum est Suevorum*), 180, 187 (failure of Aioluf, the Gothic-nominated governor of the Sueves; cf. Jordanes, *Get.*, 229–34) [166–71, 173, 180].

[118] Initial conflict: in 456, Theoderic II saw Majorian as a threat. The 'adverse news' Theoderic received while besieging Mérida, causing him to withdraw from Spain (Hyd., c. 186 [179]), was probably Avitus' deposition and death at the hands of Ricimer and Majorian; cf. cc. 183, 185 [176, 178] (though Hydatius' wording links the withdrawal to the cult of Eulalia in Merida; cf. the use of *terreo* in c. 182 [175]). Theoderic recognised the loss of his ally Avitus as a threat to his own security.

Concurrence in arrangements: after two years, Theoderic and Majorian agreed to a *pax*; cf. c. 197 [192]; Ralph W. Mathisen, 'Resistance and Reconciliation: Majorian and the Gallic Aristocracy after the Fall of Avitus', *Francia* 7 (1979), 619–20 (repr. in his *Studies*); Wolfram, *History of the Goths*, 179–80. This settlement allowed the Goths to retain possession of Baetica, where they posed a constant threat to the Sueves; above, n. 104. Majorian's campaign in Carthaginiensis in 460, *en route* to attack the Vandals in North Africa, seems to have been coordinated with an attack on the Sueves in northern Gallaecia by Gothic forces; Hyd., c. 200–1 [195–6]; cf. n. 128 below. Theoderic appointed *comites* and *magistri militum* in Spain in the 460s. Whether of Roman or Gothic origin, these commanders appear to have been solely under Theoderic's command; Hyd., cc. 197, 201, 212, 213 [192, 196, 207, 208]; Stein I, 381 ('En sa qualité de commandant des forces impériales en Espagne, Théodoric disposait aussi des troupes de ce pays').

[119] Table I no. 16.

[120] The Gallaecian noble Palogorius approached Theoderic in 463, presumably for assistance against the Sueves, now split among several rulers. Theoderic responded by sending as envoy to Gallaecia Cyrila, a general who had previously campaigned in Spain on Theoderic's behalf; Palogorius accompanied him back to Spain (Hyd., cc. 192, 193 [185, 188]). But Cyrila's mission was unsuccessful; Table I nos. 24–6. He was subsequently sent back to Gallaecia; Hyd., c. 220 [216]. Often seen as a second embassy (*PLRE* II, 'Cyrila', 334 and 'Remismund', 939; Burgess, 'Reply', 337 n. 10; Burgess, 'Hydatius', 69; Muhlberger, *Fifth-Century Chroniclers*, 255 n. 132), this was more likely a military campaign. Hydatius does not specify that Cyrila was sent as a *legatus* (cf. Table I, 'Note on *Legatus* and *Legatio*'). He was accompanied by the future king Remismund, and they were preceded by *aliquanti Gothi*, 'not a few Goths', i.e. a military force (Hyd., c. 220

the *pax* with the provincials, securing his position locally and complying with Theoderic's wishes.[121] Renewed Suevic expansion in the 460s drew protests not from imperial authorities but from Theoderic.[122] From 456 to the death of Theoderic II in 467, the Goths stood in the same relation to the Gallaecians and the Sueves as had the imperial army in Gaul under Aetius in the 430s and 440s.

Vandal diplomacy

The focus of Hydatius' account is the relations between the provincials, the Sueves, the imperial authorities, and the Goths. On the periphery of his vision are contacts with the Vandals. Hydatius records embassies to or from the Vandals on six occasions after their occupation of North Africa. That he preserves any record at all of the Vandals is testimony to the dangerously prominent role played by the long-lived Vandal king Geiseric; the Vandals were, geographically, as far from Gallaecia as the Franks, who are barely mentioned in the *Chronicle*, and the actions of the Vandals rarely affected the Sueves in Gallaecia.[123] But politically and militarily, the Vandals in Carthage posed a constant threat, real or potential, to Rome, Constantinople, and indeed the Sueves. Despite periodic treaties with the empire and even a proposed marriage alliance between the families of Valentinian III and of the Vandal king Geiseric, the Vandal control of Rome's historic nemesis Carthage, the main granary of the West and port to a major fleet, offered the Vandal king too much autonomy and too great an opportunity for extortion and naval warfare for any alliance to be more than conditional.[124] Vandal piracy throughout

[216]). Cyrila's purpose is revealed by the succeeding events: the Suevic factional ruler Frumarius dies, and Remismund, clearly tied to Theoderic, is accepted as their king by the Sueves (Hyd., c. 223, cf. 226 [219, 222]). This parallels the events of 456: once attempts to negotiate failed, Theoderic sent a military force to replace an uncooperative Suevic ruler with a Gothic nominee. (On Courtois' arguments for a lacuna in the manuscripts at this point: Muhlberger, *Fifth-Century Chroniclers*, 285–99.)

Subsequent Gothic embassies concerning the Sueves' treatment of the Gallaecian provincials: Table 1 nos. 32, 33, 40. It is unclear on whose behalf the envoy Opilio acted (Table 1 no. 40); the fact that Hydatius names him may mean that he was a provincial rather than a Goth or a Sueve (above, at n. 34), but in c. 237 [233] Hydatius also names a Gothic envoy; cf. *PLRE* II, 807; Tranoy I, 172; II, 125; Burgess, *Chronicle*, 119.

121 Hyd., c. 223 [219]: *Remismund . . . pacem reformat elapsam*; Muhlberger, *Fifth-Century Chroniclers*, 254–5. But by the following year the Sueves were harassing the Aunonian *plebs*; Table 1 nos. 32, 40.

122 This seems the best explanation for Table 1 nos. 21, 22, 30–1.

123 Embassies: Table 1 nos. 14, 18 and 20, 23, 27, 37, 39. Franks: Hyd., c. 98 [88]. Vandal actions directly affecting Sueves: Table 1 no. 14 (embassy in 458); Hyd., c. 131 [123] (a Vandal raid on the Gallaecian coast in 445).

124 On the Vandals under Geiseric: Schmidt, *Histoire des Vandales*, chap. 2, 54–122; Courtois, *Les Vandales et l'Afrique*, part 2, chap. 1, 155–214; Clover, 'Geiseric the Statesman'; Philip de Souza,

the Mediterranean in the 440s and the destructive sack of Rome in 455, sharp demonstrations of Geiseric's power and potential hostility, made him the single most disruptive element in western politics until his death in 477.[125] News of the Vandals travelled. Nevertheless, Hydatius does not record enough information to reveal clearly patterns in the Vandals' contacts. Only one diplomatic exchange, in 460, between Geiseric and the empire is recorded; earlier treaties, and the betrothal of Valentinian III's daughter Eudocia to Geiseric's son Huneric, are unmentioned.[126]

Direct contacts between the Vandals and the Sueves are twice recorded by Hydatius. On the first occasion, Vandal and Gothic envoys arrived in Gallaecia after the Gothic occupation of Baetica in 458.[127] *Post quod propter quod*: the timing suggests that the Goths' actions not only posed a threat to the south of the Sueves and a potential check on their renewed ambitions on Lusitania, but also caused unease to the Vandals, now facing the sometime imperial allies across the narrow straits of Cadiz. The Vandal mission to the Sueves probably sought their friendship in the face of a mutual foe.[128] The Sueves themselves had controlled Baetica from 441 to the mid-450s, and there is some evidence that this occupation of the province also had caused hostility with the Vandals.[129]

Piracy in the Graeco-Roman World (Cambridge, 1999), 231–8. The historic antagonism of Punic Carthage was recalled by Prosper, *Chron.*, 1339. For the strategic importance of control over the African grain supply: Elton, *Warfare in Roman Europe*, 195.

125 Andrew Gillett, 'Rome, Ravenna, and the Last Western Emperors', *Papers of the British School in Rome* 69 (2001), 164.

126 Hyd., c. 209 [204]; on other treaties: above, n. 65. Similarly Hydatius does not record the imperial campaign against the Vandals in 441, although he does record the campaigns of Majorian and Leo in 460, 467, and 469 (cc. 200, 236, 240, 247 [195, 232, 236, 241]). He records several Vandal naval raids or battles (cc. 86, 131, 176–7, 227 [77, 123, 169–70, 223]), and Geiseric's release of Licinia Eudoxia, Valentinian III's widow, to the eastern court in 462, after arranging the marriages of the empresses' two daughters (c. 216 [211]).

127 Table 1 no. 14. Goths in Baetica: Hyd., c. 192 [185].

128 Goths as strategic threat to Vandals: the rationale of Avitus' alliance with the Goths of Toulouse, as presented by his propagandist Sidonius, was to use Gothic support to defeat the Vandals; cf. chapter 3 below, at nn. 39–43, 51–3; and Clover, 'Geiseric the Statesman', 156–68. Events following the Gothic seizure of Baetica justified any Vandal concerns. The Goths were hostile to the emperor Majorian for two years after the deposition of Avitus (cf. n. 118 above). When Majorian and Theoderic II concluded a *pax* in 459, imperial and Gothic envoys were sent jointly to announce the settlement to the Vandals and the Sueves (Table 1 nos. 17–20). Soon afterwards, Majorian commenced his campaign against the Vandals (Hyd., c. 200 [195]; Priscus, *Fr.*, 36.1, 2). The campaign was staged in the south-eastern Spanish province of Carthaginiensis, unlike the imperial campaigns against the Vandals of 441, 467, and 469, which were staged in Sicily (Hyd., c. 200 [195]; Marius of Avenches, *Chron.*, s.a. 460; *Chr. Gall. 511*, cc. 633–4; Priscus, *Fr.*, 36.1; for 441 and 467–9 campaigns: Clover, 'Geiseric the Statesman', 80–4, 194–9). Majorian's alliance with the Goths, together with their hold of strategic Baetica, may explain the decision to advance on North Africa from south-east Spain.

Goths in Baetica as a threat to the Sueves in Lusitania: above, nn. 104, 118.

129 Suevic occupation of Baetica: Hyd., c. 123 [115]. Suevic/Vandal contact: possibly the explanation of the Vandal raid on coastal Gallaecia and the capture of *familiae* (perhaps as hostages, cf. n. 70

The second embassy between Carthage and Braga attested by Hydatius also suggests more regular contact than the *Chronicle* records. In 467, following Euric's usurpation of the Gothic kingship at Toulouse, the Suevic king Remismund sent envoys to the Goths, the emperor Anthemius, and the Vandals.[130] At the commencement of his reign, Remismund had been supported by Theoderic II, now killed by Euric; he was rightly concerned about Euric's intentions on Spain. His dispatch of envoys to Carthage indicates Braga's need to determine the position of the main players in the western Mediterranean in the face of the sudden change at Toulouse.

Hydatius preserves the only record of a further embassy to the Vandals. In 464, the *comes et magister utriusque militiae per Gallias* Aegidius sent envoys to Geiseric.[131] Aegidius had been incensed at Ricimer's murder of the emperor Majorian in 461. Retaining his military command in Gaul but refusing to recognise Ricimer's puppet emperor Libius Severus, Aegidius threatened to attack Italy and overthrow Ricimer. To gain the support of the Goths against Aegidius and to block his path to Italy, Ricimer condoned the ceding of Narbonne to Theoderic II. Thereafter Aegidius was occupied fighting the Goths, winning a major battle at Orléans in 463.[132] The following year Aegidius sent envoys to Geiseric, doubtless to seek Vandal support against the Goths or Ricimer or both. The envoys sailed *per Oceanum*, along the Atlantic coast, avoiding hostile territories under imperial or Gothic control.[133] Leaving in May, they did not return until the end of summer; Aegidius must not have anticipated coordinated action with the Vandals until the following year. It never occurred, for he was murdered later that year.[134]

How did Hydatius learn of this maritime embassy? It is unlikely that the legation landed at Gallaecia on its way.[135] Remismund had just been installed as king of the Sueves through the influence of Theoderic II and with the help of a Gothic army. Envoys of Aegidius would have been

above) in 445, some four years after the Suevic occupation of Baetica; Hyd., c. 131 [123]. Suevic loss of Baetica: presumably during the assault of Theoderic II on Gallaecia 456/7, though it is possible that the Sueves retained control of the south of Spain until the Gothic expeditions of 458.

[130] Table I nos. 36–8. [131] Table I no. 27.

[132] On Aegidius: Priscus, *Fr.*, 39.1; Hyd., cc. 217, 218, 228 [212, 214, 224]; Marius of Avenches, *Chron.*, s.a. 463; *Chron. Gall.* 511, c. 638; Gregory of Tours, *Hist.* II, 12, 18, 27; Stein I, 378–9, 381–2; Clover, 'Geiseric the Statesman', 182–4; *PLRE* II, 11–13.

[133] This is the only occasion on which Hydatius specified the route or duration of an embassy. The sea-route from northern Europe to the Mediterranean was also used by Heruli pirates; Hyd., c. 194 [189]. Cf. Gregory of Tours, *Hist.* VIII, 35 (ships from Gaul to Gallaecia attacked by orders of Gothic king Leuvigild of Spain).

[134] Hyd., c. 228 [224].

[135] Cf. Thompson, *Romans and Barbarians*, 172; Muhlberger, *Fifth-Century Chroniclers*, 310.

sensible to give wide berth to the kingdom of the Goths' client. It is more probable that news of the embassy came from contact with the Goths. Hydatius records three other entries on Aegidius, each concerning his battles with the Goths in Gaul. Of the general's conflict with Ricimer and Severus, or his earlier triumphs over the Franks, Hydatius appears unaware.[136] The perspective is that of Toulouse, not of the imperial court or of Aegidius himself. So, too, news of the maritime embassy may have come from Toulouse. Secrecy was not a major characteristic of ancient communications. Aegidius may well have advertised the embassy after its return, in order to spread concern among his enemies. During 463 and 464, there were communications between the Gallaecian provincials, the Sueves, and the Goths.[137] News could well have reached Hydatius from the courts of Toulouse or Braga.

Multiple embassies

Two entries unique to Hydatius indicate the range of political relations simultaneously maintained by western powers. Both describe multiple embassies dispatched at times of crisis. In September 454, Valentinian III murdered the general Aetius in the imperial palace at Rome. Aetius had dominated western politics for almost thirty years, largely through his personal relations with the Huns. In 454, while attempting to form a dynastic union with the imperial family, he fell victim to a court faction which spurred Valentinian against him.[138]

Aetius' removal had many consequences; Valentinian's own death six months later was one. Of the several sources recording the aftermath of Aetius' death, only Hydatius notes the following: 'After [murdering Aetius and his followers], Valentinian sent envoys to the *gentes*. Justinian was the envoy who went to the Sueves.'[139] Contact with barbarian groups was necessitated by Aetius' death not because he had been the power behind the imperial throne, but because he had for so long been a general in the field. The role of the empire's representative on the frontier, which had been that of the emperors until the end of the fourth century, had been assumed by the long-serving *magister militum*.[140] The embassies did not prevent strife. Barbarian groups both within and outside imperial

[136] Hyd., cc. 217 (surrender of Narbonne), 218 (battle of Orléans), 228 (Goths take areas previously held by Aegidius after his death) [212, 214, 224]. Cf. Muhlberger, *Fifth-Century Chroniclers*, 233–4.

[137] Table 1 nos. 24–6, 28–9.

[138] *PLRE* II, 28; Stein I, 349; Seeck, *Untergang* VI, 319–20; B. L. Twyman, 'Aetius and the Aristocracy', *Historia* 19 (1970), 480–503; O'Flynn, *Generalissimos*, 95.

[139] Hyd., c. 161 [153]: *His gestis legatos Valentinianus mittit ad gentes, ex quibus ad Suevos venit Iustinianus.*

[140] Cf. Seeck, 'Flavius Aetius', *RE* 1.1, 702–3; O'Flynn, *Generalissimos*, 86–7, 89–90.

territories attacked or prepared to attack imperial territory. They were quelled only by the appointment of a new *magister utriusque militiae per Gallias*, Avitus, who set about re-establishing the disturbed alliances.[141]

Hydatius describes at greater length the series of embassies resulting from the accession of the Gothic king Euric in 467. Euric came to power by murdering his elder brother, Theoderic II. His first recorded act was to dispatch envoys to other western rulers.[142] Hydatius knew of embassies to the new western emperor Anthemius, to the Suevic king Remismund, and to the Vandals. Remismund quickly dismissed Euric's envoys and sent his own legations to Anthemius, to the Vandals, and to Euric.[143] Hydatius records nothing further of the Gothic mission to Rome, but he states that the Gothic envoys to Carthage withdrew upon hearing of the military campaign being prepared against the Vandals by the emperors Leo and Anthemius.[144] The Suevic mission to the Goths was disastrous: on its return, it was closely followed by a Gothic army which contested control of Lusitania with the Sueves, while from the north a second Gothic force attacked Gallaecia.[145] Remismund subsequently sent a second embassy to Anthemius.[146]

[141] External threats: raids by the Alamanni, Ripuarian Franks, and Saxons on northern Gaul and the Atlantic coastline: Sid. Ap., *Carm.* VII, 369–75. Internal: preparations for war by the Goths of Toulouse: *ibid.* VII, 361–2, 398–400; the Sueves reoccupied Carthaginiensis, surrendered to the empire the previous year: Hyd., c. 168 with c. 155 [147, 161] and Tranoy II, 101. Cf. Stein I, 349; Seeck, *Untergang* VI, 319–20 (wrongly citing the assault on Arles by the Gothic king Thurismund, who had been killed the previous year; *PLRE* II, 1116).

It is unclear whether the death of Aetius in September 454 or that of Valentinian III in March 455 prompted these aggressions. Sidonius' description seems to place the actions of the Alamanni, Ripuarian Franks, and Saxons after Valentinian's death (*Carm.* VII, 360), but the winter of 454/5 would in any case have delayed reaction to Aetius' death until the spring, especially in northern Gaul. The Goths seem to have reacted to the news of Valentinian's death, not Aetius'. The *magister utriusque militiae* Avitus did not find it necessary to approach the Goths until May or June 455 (according to Sidonius, he went three months after his appointment as *magister*, which was soon after Petronius Maximus' imperial accession on 17 March; Avitus was still in Toulouse when news of Maximus' death in Rome on 31 May arrived; Sid. Ap., *Carm.* VII, 391–3, 450–1). Cf. Loyen, *Recherches*, 53–5; Wolfram, *History of the Goths*, 179 (on the Goths as 'legitimistic').

[142] On the date (467, not 466), participants (the emperor involved was Anthemius in Rome, not Leo I in Constantinople), and significance of these embassies: Gillett, 'Accession of Euric'. Hyd., cc. 237–8 [233–4] seems to indicate that the news of Euric's usurpation had reached Gallaecia before Euric dispatched his envoys.

[143] Table 1 nos. 34–9.

[144] Hyd., c. 240 [236], cf. 236 [232]. The campaign was abandoned because of bad weather. A subsequent collaboration between Leo, Anthemius, and Marcellinus, *de facto* ruler of Dalmatia, also failed; c. 247 [241]; Priscus, *Fr.*, 53.3.

[145] Hyd., cc. 245–6, 249–50 [239–40, 243–4].

[146] Table 1 no. 41. Hydatius dedicates long entries to news brought back to Gallaecia by the Suevic envoys to Toulouse and Rome; Hyd., cc. 242–4, 247 [238, 241]. This is probably because they were recent events at the time when he wrote the final segment of the *Chronicle*; cf. the similar expansion of the narrative for 456, when the first section of the work was probably composed; nn. 42–6 above.

Modern reconstructions of the events of 467 often mistakenly credit Hydatius with omniscience concerning political relations throughout the West. Hydatius describes a four-way traffic between Toulouse, Braga, Carthage, and Rome; this traffic is explained as various combinations of alliance and aggression between the parties mentioned.[147] But Hydatius falls far short of being a 'universal' chronicler. In his description of the embassies of 467, as elsewhere in the *Chronicle*, his view is restricted to Gallaecia. He knows and describes only the effects of Euric's actions on the Suevic kingdom. There is no reason to believe that the diplomatic flurry after Euric's accession was restricted to the recipients recorded in the *Chronicle*. Hydatius knew that Euric had sent embassies to the western emperor and to the Vandals because it was to these powers that the Suevic king also sent envoys. But it would be odd if Euric, upon taking the Gothic throne, communicated with the Sueves and Vandals to his south but not with the Burgundians to his east, the independent Roman territories of northern Gaul under Syagrius, the Bretons in Armorica, and even the Frankish rulers. Hydatius' account of these events shows the limits of his provincial position.

The Gothic embassies to Rome and to the barbarian kingdoms need not have been related. The change of ruler at Toulouse seems to have been of no immediate concern to the imperial government, which continued with its existing plans for an assault on the Vandals. Gothic and Suevic nervousness at the mustering of the imperial forces indicates that neither kingdom felt secure from Rome.[148] The interchange of embassies between the Goths and the Sueves merely continued attempts begun by Theoderic II to intervene in the Sueves' conflicts with the provincials and to limit their attempts to expand. Euric ultimately chose to send an armed force against the recalcitrant Sueves, as had his brother in 456 and 463.[149] Euric's embassies to Anthemius, Remismund, Geiseric, and

[147] For references: Gillett, 'Accession of Euric', 21–2 and n. 71, to which add Vallejo Girves, 'Relaciones del reino visigodo', 75. The 'chassé-croisé d'ambassades' is schematised by Tranoy II, 124.

[148] Hyd., c. 240 [236]. Cf. Harries, *Sidonius*, 142.

[149] In 466 Theoderic II had sent envoys to Remismund concerning the Suevic attacks on the *plebs* of Aunonensis. Remismund spurned the envoys and sent them back quickly: *legati . . . spretique ab eo [sc. Remismundo] mox redeunt*; Table 1 no. 32. Cf. Remismund's reception of Euric's envoys the following year: *quibus [legatis] sine mora a Remismundo remissis*, Table 1 no. 35 (Demougeot II.2, 631: 'Remismond . . . congédia les ambassadeurs'). The Aunonian provincials sent representatives, presumably to Euric; Table 1 no. 40. Despite the Gothic embassy, the Sueves continued their assaults on the Gallaecians and tried to occupy Lusitania, pausing only in uncertainty over Anthemius' intentions. Euric responded by sending an army against the Sueves; Hyd., cc. 240, 245 [236, 239]. For parallel resorts to force by Theoderic II after the failure of negotiations: above, at nn. 117 (456), 120 (463). There is no reason to think that Euric deviated from his brother's attitude to the Sueves. Both the Sueves and the Goths contacted the Vandals, probably because of their potential for interference with the Gothic stronghold in Baetica.

probably other rulers, indicate not a 'diplomatic assault' on the empire, but the new king's active pursuit of Gothic interests with each of the major powers of the West.

The significant feature of Euric's and Remismund's embassies is that in each case several missions were sent simultaneously. The multiple embassies dispatched by Valentinian III provide a direct parallel to those of Euric. Like Valentinian's, Euric's embassies were *ad gentes*, sent to a wide range of friendly or hostile powers after a sudden change in rule. The missions need not have been motivated by any single policy. Rather, Euric pursued bilateral relations with several rulers concurrently.[150]

To construe the embassies of 467 as part of a single plan by Euric is to miss the significance of Hydatius' evidence. The dispatch of simultaneous embassies by a ruler at his accession cannot have been uncommon. Surrounded by many neighbours, all western rulers constantly needed to sustain many relations at once. Like Valentinian III in 454, Euric showed that, despite recent domestic upheavals, his realm would continue uninterruptedly to pursue its interests. But of the contemporary sources, only Hydatius chose to record this variety of political practice.

A MODEL OF POLITICAL COMMUNICATION IN THE BARBARIAN KINGDOMS

Hydatius' sparse *Chronicle* presents the fullest picture we have of the complex patterns of political communication in a western kingdom. These patterns do not solely reflect the particular circumstances of Suevic

[150] Cf. Gregory of Tours, *Hist.* IX, 1: the Gothic king Reccared, on succeeding his father Leuvigild in 586, sends two separate embassies simultaneously to the Frankish kings Guntram and Childebert II (they are received very differently). This is another example of a new king resuming his predecessor's simultaneous, bilateral ties (cf. *Hist.* IX, 16: Reccared sends one group of envoys successively to Guntram and Childebert, their mission modified according to how they are received by the former). Cf. also Priscus, *Fr.*, 20 (Attila, on learning of the death of Theodosius II, sends to Marcian to continue uninterrupted his demands for Roman tribute; *Fr. Class. Hist.*, 305).

The regular dispatch of embassies notifying neighbouring rulers of a new monarch's accession, perhaps customary between the eastern imperial court and Persia (E. Chrysos, 'Byzantine Diplomacy, AD 300–800: Means and Ends', in Shepard and Franklin (eds.), *Byzantine Diplomacy*, 31–3), may have been practised by the western kings as well (e.g. Cass., *Variae* VIII, 1; Procopius, *Wars* V, 4.11; Barnwell, 'War and Peace', 136–7). Even Roman–Persian accession embassies, however, appear to have been largely pretexts for maintaining on-going negotiations, e.g. Priscus, *Fr.*, 52; Malalas, *Chron.* XVIII, 34 with Roger Scott, 'Diplomacy in the Sixth Century: The Evidence of John Malalas', in Shepard and Franklin (eds.), *Byzantine Diplomacy*, 160 (Justinian's accession embassy sent to Ctesiphon two years after he comes to power, indicating that the protocol need not be taken too seriously); the accessions of the shahs Chosroes and Hormisdas did not interrupt on-going negotiations with the Roman empire about a variety of issues (Procopius, *Wars* I, 21–2; Menander Protector, *Frag.*, 9.1, 23.9 Blockley).

Gallaecia; the political actors present in Hydatius' Spain were represented in all the western states. Hydatius' unique record may be used as a descriptive model for the diplomatic activity which underlay fifth-century history. Several main characteristics of political communication in the late antique West are evident in his account: the frequency and importance of diplomatic traffic, albeit neglected by other historical sources; the complex interaction of authorities, both among the monarchs of the western kingdoms and the empire, and between various social groups within individual kingdoms; the concurrent maintenance of many bilateral relations by each power; and the political functions of embassies other than negotiation of immediate issues.

Political communication dominates Hydatius' account, especially in the latter half. Despite his evident and self-confessed limitations as a historian, Hydatius knew of many embassies throughout the fifth-century West. The same must have been true of other writers whose chronicles survive. Some, like Prosper and Marcellinus *comes*, who had contacts to the papal or imperial courts, clearly had greater potential than Hydatius to be informed on secular affairs. But conventions of genre and individual agenda precluded record of diplomatic traffic. Formal communication between realms was, to Hydatius, as important a political activity as warfare. If he is not forthcoming on the purpose of embassies, neither is he on the aims of war; modern students are obliged to infer the motives behind most battles in this period, as they must for Hydatius' embassies. Certain events which appear in other sources as military victories register as diplomatic settlements in Hydatius, an indication not only of the inseparable ties between war and diplomacy but also, again, of the constraints of late antique literary genres.[151]

Surviving narratives or references to embassies should be recognised as almost randomly preserved evidence of a phenomenon so common as to be, in general, undeserving of record. They should not be treated as exceptional, and consequently given distorted significance when exploited in modern accounts. Almost all major political events must have been preceded by many busy embassies, mostly unrecorded. It is inconceivable, for example, that marriage alliances between barbarian royalty were not negotiated at length through exchanges of embassies, though we hear of almost no such negotiations until the late sixth-century *Histories* of Gregory of Tours. It is clear from other sources that the repeated embassies prior to the Goths' assault on the Sueves in 456 were typical of

[151] Cf. I. N. Wood, 'Continuity or Calamity? The Constraints of Literary Models', in Drinkwater and Elton (eds.), *Fifth-Century Gaul*, 9–18.

attempts to avert open conflict.[152] Only in Hydatius' *Chronicle* do we see the busy network of communication which formed the infrastructure for all developments in the late and post-imperial West. This infrastructure is revealed not only in the legations heralding specific wars or treaties, but also in less conclusive, regular contact: when the Sueves and Vandals consult each other as a matter of course following significant actions by the Goths, or in the multiple embassies dispatched by rulers' courts to announce shifts in domestic power politics. The regularity of such contact contributed to its absence from most records.

The political structures of the fifth-century West were very complex. Neither the old centres of imperial authority nor the new barbarian courts formed exclusive centrepoints for political activity. Participation in political affairs was open to senior civil and military officials, members of municipal or other provincial bodies, and clergy, acting for their local communities or for the Church. The interaction of many levels of authority characterises political communication in the fifth century.

Each barbarian kingdom maintained multiple, bilateral relations with neighbouring and distant powers. Policies regarding other states might be interdependent, as with the tripartite relations between Sueves, Goths, and empire in the 410s and 450s; or relations could instead be separate and simultaneous. Long distances did not preclude diplomatic relations. The division of the western half of the Roman empire into autonomous kingdoms did not result in isolationism. Constant, complex interchange replaced imperial rule as a political force binding the West together into a diplomatic system.

The 'external' and 'internal' affairs of each state had no clear demarcation. The geographical borders of the barbarian kingdoms were overrid den by patterns of communication which survived the Roman empire. Gallaecian envoys to Gothic rulers in Gaul travelled the routes that their forefathers had taken to the courts of the senior imperial magistrates in the provinces. Regional communities had an acknowledged role to play in relations between states. In Hydatius' record, provincial authorities unmentioned in other sources, the *plebs*, not only dispatch representatives to imperial and barbarian courts, but are paid the respect of receiving embassies from these bodies to inform them of recent developments. The assumption of responsibility for the welfare of neighbouring provincials

[152] Pre-marital negotiations: for the fifth century, evidenced only for the marriage of Valentinian III and Licinia Eudoxia; *The Life of Melania the Younger*, trans. Elizabeth A. Clark (New York, 1984), 50–5; sixth century: Gregory of Tours, *Hist.* II, 28; IV, 27–8; VI, 29, 33–4, 45; IX, 16, 20, 28, 25, 28. Embassies prior to conflict: e.g. Theoderic of Italy's letter to Clovis in 506/7; Cass., *Variae* III, 4.3 (discussed below, chapter 5 at nn. 123–39); Procopius, *Wars* III, 9–10; V, 3–7.

by the Goths in the mid-450s was one element of the devolution of imperial authority to Toulouse. Communication consequently crossed the borders of Gothic, Suevic, and imperial territories; what had been an 'internal' responsibility now became an 'external' issue.

Relations between barbarian rulers and Roman elites in the provinces were conducted by an 'internal diplomacy' reminiscent of the early empire. As with provincial embassies of the earlier empire, governmental actions – imperial and Gothic protection of the Gallaecians – were initiated by the petitions of regional communities. Repeated references to *paces* between the Sueves and the Gallaecians indicate a formality comparable to that of the Sueves' *foedera* with the empire and the Goths. We have little knowledge of the constitutions of either the provincial authorities or the Suevic court, partly because of what may be conscious exclusion by Hydatius of reference to negotiations between the two. But it is evident that the maintenance of formal relations between barbarian military rulers and provincial aristocracies was the precondition for the stability and expansion of the Suevic kingdom; this too is true of other western kingdoms.

Notwithstanding Hydatius' bitter references to the Sueves, the provincials' appeals to imperial and Gothic authorities for intervention in domestic politics appear to have sought diplomatic, not military, resolution: the confirmation of their *paces*. It was Suevic expansion outside Gallaecia, not internal relations with the provincials, which prompted imperial and Gothic military campaigns against the Sueves. Hydatius' detailed account of the effects of the Gothic assault of 456–7, lamenting what would now be called collateral damage and the plundering of uncontrolled troops, shows sufficiently why the civilian provincial population would not seek outside military intervention. There is no reason to believe that Gallaecian legates to Gaul anticipated the requests to eastern emperors by sixth-century bishops of Rome, under Gothic and Lombard occupation of Italy, to 'exterminate our cruel enemies'.[153]

The dispatch and reception of embassies served 'less obvious ends' alongside the immediate settlement of conflict or alliances.[154] The reception of envoys could be attended by ceremonial display, performances aimed at impressing foreign and perhaps domestic audiences with authority and power. Military parades impressed visiting envoys, as the reports of Suevic legates to Toulouse and Italy show.[155] The presence of foreign

[153] Gregory the Great, *Registrum epistolarum*, ed. Dag Norberg (CCSL 140, 140A; Turnhout, 1982), Ep. XIII, 38, to Phocas on the Lombards, 603. Cf. Procopius, *Wars* VII, 35.9–10.

[154] Cf. P. Antonopoulos, 'The Less Obvious Ends of Byzantine Diplomacy', in Shepard and Franklin (eds.), *Byzantine Diplomacy*, 315–19.

[155] Hyd., cc. 243 (cited at the beginning of this chapter), 247 [238, 241].

envoys at court was itself an indication of a ruler's potency.[156] The status of an envoy was consequently important, indicating sensitivity to the recipient's domestic needs; known imperial envoys to the Sueves all held the rank of *comes*, while Gallaecian legates to Gaul included a bishop and a *vir nobilis*. Other aspects of diplomatic communication too may have been for domestic consumption. Hydatius' knowledge of particular details of embassies to or from the Suevic royal court suggests that those incidents had been intentionally noised abroad. Did Hydatius' record of Suevic kings' brusque dismissal of certain Gothic embassies originate in well-publicised bluster of the court of Braga in the face of opposition to its expansionist aims? Embassies evidently were a source of information as well as political phenomena themselves. As such, they could be exploited by their principals as channels of propaganda while simultaneously fulfilling their obvert purpose. Public circulation of the news of Avitus' embassy to Marcian for imperial recognition, and of Aegidius' approach to Geiseric, are perhaps cases of disinformation and brinksmanship conducted through embassies, examples of the use of communications for political or strategic aims. So too may be the reports of military musters seen at Toulouse and at Rome by Suevic envoys.

Hydatius' *Chronicle* shows through the eyes of a contemporary how relations between authorities throughout the West were conducted. It is a model for understanding a period of busy communication and negotiation, conducted along lines of traditional administrative embassies, now operating in a new context. The political circumstances Hydatius describes for the Suevic regions can be taken as an example for other parts of the fifth-century West. Hydatius' younger contemporary Sidonius Apollinaris describes, however differently, the same world, with its carefully negotiated relations between local aristocracies, regional imperial officers, barbarian rulers, and imperial authority. In various writings, Sidonius demonstrates an aspect of western political communication only hinted at by Hydatius: the high prestige associated with successfully completing embassies, and the social capital this conveyed. Sidonius and other Gallic and Italian writers seek keenly to exploit this status, for both literary and social gains.

156 E.g. Sid. Ap., *Ep.* VIII, 9, *versus* lines 19–54.

Table 1 *A list of embassies in Hydatius' Chronicle*

The embassies recorded by Hydatius are tabulated below with commentary. As above, Mommsen's chapter numbers are followed by Burgess' in square brackets. For dates after 455, cf. Muhlberger, *The Fifth-Century Chroniclers*, 308–11; Burgess, 'Hydatius', 274–7, and *Chronicle*, 70–122 (noting that the marginal AD dates in the translation refer to Hydatius' chronology, not necessarily actual dates of events, e.g. Hyd., c. 148 [140]). Entries from Fredegar, *Chron.* II, 50–6 (based primarily on Hydatius) which appear to contain information not preserved in the fullest MS of Hydatius are included; see nos. **11, 17–20, 22, 41** and notes.[1]

Cross references to other embassies are shown thus: (**5**). Groups of related embassies are indicated thus: ***1–4***. The sign † indicates doubt whether the entry refers to a formal embassy.

384 c. 11	*Persian legates sent to Theodosius I at Constantinople (from* Consularia Constantinopolitana, *s.a. 384)*
1–4 431–3	
1 431 cc. 96, 98 [86, 88]	Bishop Hydatius undertakes an embassy to the *magister utriusque militiae* Aetius in Gaul, concerning the Suevic breach of a *pax* made with the Gallaecian provincials the previous year; he returns to Gallaecia with the *comes* Censorius (**3**).
†2 431 c. 97 [87]	Vetto comes to Gallaecia from the Goths *dolose*, and returns to Gaul 'without effect'. (Cf. 'Note on *Legatus* and *Legatio*' below.)
3 432–3 cc. 98, 100 [88, 91]	The *comes* Censorius is sent by Aetius to the Sueves in response to (**1**); he returns *ad palatium*, apparently without resolving the conflict between the Sueves and the Gallaecians, because of Aetius' conflicts with Boniface and Sebastian in Italy.
4 433 c. 101 [92]	King Hermeric re-establishes the *pax* with the Gallaecians, under episcopal mediation, having received hostages. Bishop Symphosius is sent by Hermeric *ad comitatum* (n. 95 above); the purpose of his mission, unstated, is not achieved.
5 437–438 cc. 111, cf. 113 [103, 105]	The *comes* Censorius is sent on a second mission to the Sueves, presumably by Aetius, in the company of Fretimund (despite his name, an imperial rather than a Gothic envoy, since at this time the Goths and Aetius were engaged in the prolonged war of 436–9; cf. Hyd., cc. 107, 108, 110, 112, 116, 117 [98, 99, 101, 104, 108, 109]). The *pax* between the Sueves and *pars plebis Callaeciae* (c. 113 [105]) appears to result from this mission.

Beginning of Suevic expansion under Rechila: conquests of Lusitania, Baetica, and Carthaginiensis (438–441; cc. 114, 119, 123 [106, 111, 115])

Table 1 (*cont.*)

6 440 c. 121 [113]	The *comes* Censorius, returning from an embassy to the Sueves, is besieged at Mertola in southern Lusitania by the Suevic king Rechila and surrenders himself. Cf. c. 139 [131]: Censorius is killed at Seville in 449 (date: Burgess, *Chronicle*, 44).
Imperial campaigns against Bagaudae in Terraconensis 441–3 (cc. 125, 128 [117, 120])	
The magister utriusque militiae *Vitus campaigns against the Sueves in Carthaginiensis and Baetica, but is defeated 446 (c. 134 [126])*	
The new Suevic king Rechiarius expands into the ulteriores regiones, *forms a marriage alliance with the Gothic king Theodoric I, and attacks Terraconensis*[2] *448–9 (cc. 137, 140, 142 [129, 132, 134])*	
7 453 c. 155 [147]	The *comes Hispaniarum* Mansuetus and the *comes* Fronto are sent to the Sueves and successfully obtain prescribed terms. Possibly this refers to the return of Carthaginiensis from Suevic to imperial authority; cf. c. 168 [161], Tranoy II, 95.
8 454	(Multiple embassies)
c. 161 [153]	After the murder of Aetius, Valentinian III sends envoys *ad gentes*; Hydatius names only the envoy Justinian, sent to the Sueves.
9 455 c. 166 [159]	The western emperor Avitus sends envoys to the eastern emperor Marcian 'on behalf of the unity of the empire'. Cf. 169 [162]; Tranoy II, 101.
Sueves attack Carthaginiensis, previously returned to imperial authority, 455 (c. 168 [161])	
10–12 456	
10 and **11**	(Joint embassies)
456 c. 170 [163]	The emperor Avitus sends the *comes* Fronto (cf. (**7**)) to the Sueves (**10**). At the same time the Gothic king Theodoric II also sends envoys to the Sueves (**11**), asking the Sueves to observe their alliances with both the Romans and the Goths (cf. cc. 140, 142; 155 [132, 134; 147]). The embassies presumably concern renewed Suevic expansion into the province of Carthaginiensis (cf. c. 168 [161]). The Suevic king Rechiarius rejects both the imperial and Gothic envoys and attacks Terraconensis.
12 456 c. 172 [165]	Theodoric II again sends envoys to Rechiarius. They are ignored as the Sueves further their assault on Terraconensis. (cf. Jordanes, *Get.*, 231).
The Goths, at the order of the emperor Avitus, enter Gallaecia, and attack and defeat Rechiarius (cc. 173–5 [166–8])	

(*cont.*)

Table 1 (*cont.*)

13 456 c. 177 [170]	The emperor Avitus sends a legation under the *tribunus* Hesychius to Theodoric II, bringing imperial rewards to Theodoric and formally announcing the *magiter utriusque militiae* Ricimer's victory over the Vandals in Corsica. (The latter news had already been reported to Theodoric; cf. c. 176 [169] and Burgess, 'Reply', 338 n. 11.)

End of the first edition of the Chronicle*?*

The Sueves, fragmented after the death of Rechiarius, form a pax *with the Gallaecian provincials, 457 (c. 188 [181])*

A Gothic army occupies Baetica, 458 (c. 192 [185])

14 and **15**	(Simultaneous embassies)
458 c. 192 [185]	Embassies are sent by both the Vandals (**14**) and the Goths (**15**) to the Sueves; they return. These legations appear to concern the Gothic occupation of Baetica.

Renewed conflict between Sueves and Gallaecian provincials; Goths intervene in Gallaecia and also enter Lusitania, 459–60 (cc. 196, 199, 201–7 [191, 194, 196–202])

16–20 459[3]	
16 459 c. 197 [192]	Envoys are sent to the Gallaecian provincials by the *Magister militum* Nepotian and the *comes* Suneric to announce the new alliance between the emperor Majorian and Theodoric II, after the defeat of the Goths in battle.
17–18 and **19–20** = Fredegar, *Chron.* II, 55, p. 76, lines 22–3	*(Joint embassies?)* Envoys are sent by Majorian (**17, 18**) and Theodoric II (**19, 20**) to the Sueves and the Vandals to announce the new *pax*.
21–22 460 **21** 460 c. 205 [200]	Theodoric II sends envoys to the Sueves; they return.
22 460 c. 208 [203]	Suevic envoys sent to Theodoric II; they return. (Cf. Fredegar, *Chron.* II, 55, p. 76, lines 28–9, suggesting that these envoys sought and obtained a *pax* from the Goths; the passage, however, is unclear.)
23 460 c. 209 [204]	Geiseric seeks a *pax* from Majorian through envoys.
24, 25, 26 463 c. 219 [215]	The Gallaecian *vir nobilis* Palogorius travels to Theoderic II (**24**). Theodoric II sends the general Cyrila to Gallaecia; Palogorius returns with him (**25**). Rechimund, one of the leaders of the fragmented Sueves, sends envoys to Theodoric II (**26**). Meeting Cyrila and Palogorius *en route*, they return to Lugo in northern Gallaecia where they

Table 1 (*cont.*)

	receive Cyrila. Cyrila departs from Gallaecia. His mission does not prevent the continuation of conflict between the Sueves and the provincials. (Cf. c. 220 [216]: Cyrila and Remismund are sent to Gallaecia by Theodoric II. This is a military assault, not a further embassy; see at n. 120 above and 'Note on *legatus* and *legatio*' below.)
27 464 c. 224 [220]	The *comes* Aegidius sends envoys from Gaul to the Vandals via the Atlantic. They set out in May and return in September.
28 and **29** 464 c. 226 [222]	Remismund (the Gothic nominee as ruler of the Sueves) sends envoys to Theodoric II (**28**). Theodoric II sends back his own envoys, conveying arms, gifts, and Remismund's wife (**29**).
30 and **31** 465–6 cc. 230–231 [226–7]	Remismund twice sends envoys to Theodoric II. On its return, one of these embassies reports the death of the emperor Libius Severus.

Conflicts between Sueves and plebs *of Aunonensis begin, 466 (c. 233 [229])*

32 466 c. 233 [229]	Theodoric II sends envoys to Remismund concerning the conflicts of the Sueves and the *plebs* of Aunonensis; the Sueves reject the Gothic envoys, who soon depart.
33 467 c. 237 [233]	Theodoric II sends one Sulla to Remismund, presumably on the same issue. During Sulla's absence from Gaul, Theodoric II is murdered.

34–9 Euric's accession
(see Gillett, 'Accession of Euric')

34, 35 467 c. 238 [234]	Euric, after becoming king of the Goths, sends envoys to the western emperor Anthemius (**34**) and to the Sueves (**35**). The latter envoys are immediately sent back by Remismund.
36, 37, 38 as above	Remismund, after receiving Euric's envoys, sends his own to the emperor Anthemius (**36**), to the Vandals (**37**), and to the Goths (**38**). (Cf. cc. 242–4: prodigies seen at Toulouse by the Suevic envoys; c. 245: the Suevic envoys return from Toulouse, 468; c. 247: return of the Suevic envoys to Anthemius, 468 [238, 239, 241]).
39 467 c. 240 [236]	Gothic envoys to the Vandals, presumably sent at the same time as Euric's legations to Anthemius and to the Sueves, return to Gaul after hearing of the imperial campaign to Africa planned for 467.
40 467 c. 239 [235]	Opilio returns either to or from the *plebs* of Aunonensis, accompanied by other envoys sent with him and by men sent by the king (probably a legation from the provincials to either Theodoric II or Euric); cf. c. 249 [243]: the Sueves and the Aunonenses agree to a *pax*.

(*cont.*)

Table 1 (*cont.*)

Gothic army enters Spain and pressures the Sueves from Lusitania to the south and from north-eastern Gallaecia, 468 (cc. 245–6, 250 [239–40, 244])

41 469	
c. 251 [245]	Remismund sends Lusidius, a *praesens cives* of the Lusitanian city of Lisbon, together with Suevic envoys, to the emperor Anthemius. (Cf. Fredegar, *Chron.* II, 56, p. 77, line 21: Richymund 'crosses to' [*transeuntem*] the emperor.[4])

Note on legatus *and* legatio

Hydatius consistently uses these terms to identify formal embassies. They are used in every embassy listed above except nos. **†2, 24**, and **39**, usually with a part of *mitto*. Where an envoy is named, the title *legatus* is given in apposition, e.g. *Censorius comes legatus mittitur* (no. **3**). It is clear from the wording of no. **39** (*Gothi . . . missi*) that the subjects had been sent as envoys. The *vir nobilis Galleciae* Palogorius (no. **24**) was almost certainly an envoy from some element of the Gallaecian provincials, though the passage is difficult to construe. Like Hydatius in 431 (no. **1**), he travelled to southern Gaul, and returned in the company of an envoy; only by then, the Gallic envoy's principal was the Gothic king Theoderic II, not the emperor's leading general.

The wording of no. **†2** is ambivalent, and it is possible that Vetto in fact travelled to Gallaecia not as an envoy of the Gothic king (cf. the Arian missionary Aiax, never stated to have been sent by Theoderic II; Hyd., c. 232 [228]). Hydatius' careful use of the terms *legatus* and *legatio* makes it improbable that Cyrila's second mission to Gallaecia was diplomatic (Hyd., c. 220 [216]; cf. above no. **26**).

Notes:

1. Table 1 differs somewhat from the enumeration of embassies in Burgess, 'Hydatius', 69–70. Table 1 omits:
   (a) Hyd., cc. 176, 186 [169, 179], refering to 'announcements' made to Theodoric II while in Spain. Hydatius' terminology does not indicate that this news was conveyed by formal embassies; cf. at n. 60 above.
   (b) Hyd., c. 220 [216], the dispatch of Remismund and Cyrila to Gallaecia. The passage refers to a military expedition, not an embassy; cf. Table 1 no. **26** and n. 120 above. (Cf. 'Note on *legatus* and *legatio*' above.)
   Table 1 includes:
   (c) Fredegar, *Chron.* II, 55, p. 76, lines 22–3, printed by Mommsen parallel to Hyd., c. 197 [192] (Table 1 no. **17–20**). Fredegar's entry is too different from Hydatius' to be a variant of the same text, and it appears to preserve a fragment lost from the other MSS of Hydatius; cf. n. 160 below.
2. Terraconensis is not occupied by the Sueves at this time; cf. Hyd., c. 158 [150]: the Goths operate on the empire's behalf in Terraconensis. The *ulteriores regiones* perhaps refers to the Pyrenees region; cf. c. 140 [132].

Notes to Table 1 (*cont.*)

3. It is possible that the embassy sent by Nepotian and Suneric recorded by Hydatius (**16**) is the same as the joint imperial/Gothic embassy to the Sueves mentioned by Fredegar (**17, 19**). Both Nepotian and Suneric, however, appear to have operated under Theodoric II, not Majorian. In Hyd., c. 193 (459), Theodoric sends Suneric with an army to Baetica; in c. 201 (460), Nepotian and Suneric jointly command a Gothic army operating against the Sueves in Gallaecia; and in c. 213 (462) Theodoric II appoints a successor to Nepotian as *magister utriusque militiae* [188, 196, 208]. It seems unlikely that Nepotian and Suneric would be described as the representatives of the emperor and the Gothic king (cf. Tranoy II, 112). At the time of embassy (**16**), the Sueves and the provincials of Gallaecia were again in conflict; Hyd., c. 196 [191]. It is quite possible that the provincials had communicated with Theodoric II or his generals for assistance, as they did later; cf. (**24**) and (**40**). The generals may have notified the provincials of Majorian and Theodoric's reconciliation independently of the rulers' formal notification to the royal courts of Braga and Carthage. Cf. *PLRE* II, 778; Burgess, 'From *Gallia Romana* to *Gallia Gothica*', in Drinkwater and Elton (eds.), *Fifth-Century Gaul*, 23–25.

Fredegar's account (**17–20**) appears to refer to a separate set of missions. It describes two joint embassies: an imperial/Gothic embassy to the Sueves, and another imperial/Gothic embassy to the Vandals. Possibly the same envoys who travelled to Gallaecia continued on to North Africa.

4. Richymund may be the same person as Rechimund, one of the contestants for leadership of the Sueves after the Gothic incursion of 456; Hyd., cc. 193, 202, 203, 219 [188, 197, 198, 215]; (**26**) (not in *PLRE* II). Possibly Lusidius and Richymund were sent together to the emperor; if so, Fredegar preserves the name of a different envoy from the one (uniquely) recorded in the Berlin MS of Hydatius. It is also possible, however, that Fredegar's verb *transeo* here means that Richymund entered the service of Anthemius. In this case, Fredegar reports a completely unrelated incident.

Chapter 3

THE HERO AS ENVOY: SIDONIUS APOLLINARIS' *PANEGYRIC* ON AVITUS

> Will future races and peoples ever believe this?
> – a Roman's letter annulled a barbarian's conquests.
> Sidonius, *Carm.* VII, lines 310–11[1]

The response of modern critics to Sidonius' rhetorical question has been remarkably positive. In 439, three years of hostilities between the Goths of Toulouse and the empire ended through the intercession of Eparchius Avitus, then praetorian prefect of Gaul, later, briefly, emperor of the western half of the empire. Where the army had failed, Avitus succeeded by exercising his personal influence over the court of Toulouse. This, at least, is the version given by Sidonius in his *Panegyric*, delivered sixteen years later to celebrate the imperial consulate of his father-in law, Avitus.

With some reservations, Sidonius' version of the events of 439 generally has been accepted – a small victory for a poem described as possessing 'a very moderate portion either of genius or of truth'.[2] This acceptance reflects less Sidonius' credibility than the rarity of well-informed testimony of the relations between the empire and the barbarian settlers in the West in the mid-fifth century. The *Panegyric* on Avitus is an almost unique portrait of contacts between the Gallic aristocracy and the Gothic monarchy of Toulouse. Most of the political elements active in Hydatius' Gallaecia are present: regional aristocracy, civil and military imperial officers in the provinces, barbarian rulers and army, and the western imperial court in Italy (but not the Church, which has no role to play in the genre

[1] For editions, see 'Note on Editions, Commentaries, and Translations' below. For Sidonius' life: A. Klotz, 'Sidonius 1', *RE* II A.2, 2230–8; Stevens, *Sidonius*; Harries, *Sidonius*; *C. Sollius Apollinaris Sidonius: Brief, Buch I*, ed. and trans. Helga Köhler (Bibliothek der klassischen Altertumswissenschaften n.s. 2, 96; Heidelberg, 1995), 3–6; see too F. Prévol, 'Deux fragments de l'épitaphe de Sidoine Apollinaire découverts à Clermont-Ferrand', *Antiquité Tardive* 1 (1993), 223–9.

[2] Edward Gibbon, *The History of the Decline and Fall of the Roman Empire*, ed. David Womersley, 3 vols. (London, 1994), II, 368 (c. 36); cf. 363 n. 12. Acceptance: e.g. by Bury I, 250; Stein I, 324. Rejection of Sidonius' account: Michel Rouche, *L'Aquitaine des Wisigoths aux Arabes, 418–781: naissance d'une région* (Paris, 1979), 28 (concerning related events of 437); Harries, *Sidonius*, 68–9.

of poetic panegyric). The narrative of the poem is structured on incidents of political communication.

Sidonius offers far more generous details than does Hydatius in his accounts of embassies, but the importance of his *Panegyric* to understanding the place of embassies in fifth-century politics does not lie in individual items of data. Rather, it is the assumptions underlying the literary construction of the poem which are telling. Indeed, despite the frequent exploitation of Sidonius' work in modern accounts of Roman–Gothic relations, analysis of the *Panegyric* shows it to be least reliable as a historical source precisely when it addresses the workings of embassies and communication between the imperial government, Gallic provincials, and the Gothic monarchy. Sidonius' hero, Avitus, is a literary creation who must be always separate in our minds from the real Gallic noble. His journeys and influence on the Goths of Toulouse are crucial to a work of propaganda engineered with a delicacy belied by Sidonius' derivative and overwrought style. Many of the main elements of Sidonius' narrative depend, if not on untruths, at least upon consistently false impressions. These impressions are built upon common notions which are informative of the vitality of traditional patterns of political communication in the new circumstances of the fifth-century West.

For the investigation of certain historical topics, 'fiction occupies a privileged position'.[3] The value of the *Panegyric* for this study lies in its disingenuous presentation of Avitus. Sidonius' portrait of the emperor retains many traditional features of imperial panegyric. But the poet substitutes the most basic 'virtue' of an emperor, the quality of victory, with an unusual image. Avitus is presented primarily as an envoy, a *legatus*, whose oratorical skills and personal authority protect Rome more effectively than military strength. Sidonius appeals, sincerely or otherwise, to an ideal of a diplomatic alternative to military means of dealing with the barbarian presence in the West. Praising the rhetorical and persuasive talents of a subject as an element of eulogy was by no means new with Sidonius. But his panegyric on Avitus is perhaps the most sustained employment of this topos, and certainly its only application to an imperial subject, in ancient literature. The fact that it is odd has made the topos harder to recognise, and so more deceptive. Sidonius' portrait displaces a less generous interpretation of Avitus' rise: a provincial magnate stepping into the place of the *generalissimo* Aetius and supporting his usurpation of the throne by the threat of the sometime hostile Goths. Though the *Panegyric* often seems laborious, Sidonius skilfully manipulates the

[3] Keith Hopkins, 'Novel Evidence for Roman Slavery', *Past and Present* 138 (1993), 6, cited in G. W. Bowersock, *Fiction as History: Nero to Julian* (Berkeley, 1994), ix.

narrative to manufacture this image of Avitus as envoy. It is the assumptions behind Sidonius' literary presentation of his hero as an envoy, not the elusive details of Avitus' dealings with the Goths, which are most informative of the role of political communication in the politics of the West in the mid-fifth century.

The literary nature of the *Panegyric*, and the circumstances of its delivery, are often and unwisely ignored when assessing the information it provides. The *Panegyric* is not a record like a formal history or a chronicle. It is an ornately literary and political work that happens to treat real events rather than, for example, mythology. Modern critics, failing to take proper account of the work's literary and ceremonial nature, have sometimes misconstrued the poem as a poor attempt at a historical sketch of the early fifth century, or as a personal political manifesto expressing the aspirations of the south Gallic aristocracy.[4] Ignoring the circumstances of the delivery of the *Panegyric* has led to dismissal of its political message as mere flattery.[5]

The poem can be understood only in the immediate political context of its delivery. In Rome on 1 January 456, Sidonius celebrated a provincial usurper who had claimed power at a time of great upheaval, supported by barbarian auxiliaries. The audience of the poem was the senatorial aristocracy of Rome, whose influence on imperial politics increased in the mid-fifth century. Sidonius was conscious of criticisms of Avitus' legitimacy, and in particular of his relations with the Goths. In his later *Panegyric* on the emperor Majorian, also the product of a period of

[4] Historical sketch: Samuel Dill, *Roman Society in the Last Century of the Western Empire*, 2nd edn (London, 1906), 334; A. Arnold, 'Sidonius Apollinaris', *Realencyklopädie für protestantische Theologie und Kirche* XVIII (Leipzig, 1906), 303: '[the *Panegyric*] spiegelt die Zeitgeschichte seit *c.* 420 aus seiner Art wieder'.

Political manifesto: Marc Reydellet, *La Royauté dans la littérature latine de Sidoine Apollinaire à Isidore de Séville* (Rome, 1981), 50–5: 'une grande unité . . . de pensée' behind all Sidonius' panegyrics expresses a 'senatorial and republican' idea of imperial power; Rouche, *L'Aquitaine*, 29–30: the *Panegyric* expresses the 'optimisme' of the south Gallic nobility (cf. Dill, *Roman Society*, 335: 'The poem reflects the general gloom'); Teillet, *Des Goths à la nation gothique*, 195: '[Avitus] apparaît, aux yeux de Sidoine, comme un intermédiaire tout désigné entre Rome et la capitale wisigothique, entre l'Empire et les nations'; Rigobert Günther, 'Apollinaris Sidonius – Eine Untersuchung seiner drei Kaiserpanegyriken', in G. Wirth *et al.*, *Romanitas–Christianitas: Untersuchungen zur Geschichte und Literature der römischen Kaiserzeit* (Berlin, 1982), 660: 'Romm kann von Gallien gerettet werden'; H. S. Sivan, 'Sidonius Apollinaris, Theoderic II, and Gothic–Roman Politics from Avitus to Anthemius', *Hermes* 117 (1989), 87–90: the poem expresses 'Sidonius' advocacy of Gallo-Gothic cooperation'; Harries, *Sidonius*: the main purpose of the poem at the time of delivery was to justify Avitus' 'policy' of cooperation with the Goths, in contrast with Aetius' efforts to contain the barbarians (67–8). These analyses generally focus on the poet's presentation of the Gothic kings, not his image of Avitus, the subject of the *Panegyric*.

[5] E.g. Thomas Hodgkin, *Italy and Her Invaders* II (Oxford, 1880), 375–6. Two valuable analyses of the literary nature of the *Panegyric* are the brief account of Sabine MacCormack, *Art and Ceremony in Late Antiquity* (Berkeley, 1981), 223–4 and, in greater detail, Harrison, 'Verse Panegyrics of Sidonius'.

tension, Sidonius avoided direct mention of contentious issues. The *Panegyric* on Avitus, however, directly addressed delicate issues by focusing on Avitus and the Goths. Rather than a profession of provincial patriotism, the *Panegyric* was propaganda, serving as a channel of communication between the emperor and the Roman aristocracy. It sought, and at least temporarily gained, confirmation of political support. Sidonius' literary creation of an envoy who became emperor was part of the work's success.

THE CIRCUMSTANCES OF THE *PANEGYRIC*

In March 455, the Roman noble and *patricius* Petronius Maximus contrived the murder of Valentinian III and assumed the throne. By May, news reached Rome of an impending Vandal assault on the city. The Vandal king Geiseric, whether urged by Valentinian's widow Licinia Eudoxia as some sources claim, or exploiting the recent deaths of Aetius and Valentinian, ignored the treaty he had made with the western court in 442. Maximus did not try to resist Geiseric's threat. Fleeing Rome as the Vandals reached Italy, he was mobbed by servants of the palace and killed, leaving a 'city devoid of all defence'. Geiseric's forces seized the city and, for fourteen days, systematically sacked it, removing major treasures, seizing captives, and kidnapping the *augusta* Licinia Eudoxia and her two daughters.[6]

One month later, Eparchius Avitus was elevated as emperor.[7] In the 430s, Avitus had held three military posts, including *magister utriusque militiae*, under Aetius; in *c.* 439/40 he was praetorian prefect of Gaul. Avitus had the rare honour of holding both the senior military and civilian posts of the Gallic provinces. Between 440 and 455 he held no public office, though he was involved in negotiations with the Goths of Toulouse at the time of Attila's assault on Gaul in 451. Petronius Maximus, after assuming the throne, appointed Avitus *magister utriusque militiae*.[8]

Sidonius, the sole source for Avitus' pre-imperial career, makes no comment on Avitus' return to public life after fifteen years' *otium*.[9] Long

[6] Prosper, *Chron.*, c. 1375 (quote); *Fasti Vind. prior.*, s.a. 455; *Fasti Vind. post.*, s.a. 455; *Addit. ad Prosp. Havn.*, s.a. 455; Hyd., cc. 162, 167 [154, 160]; Marcellinus *comes*, *Chron.*, s.a. 455; Cass., *Chron.*, cc. 1262–3; Victor of Tunnuna, *Chron.*, s.a. 455; Priscus, *Fr.*, 30 (= John of Antioch, *Fr.*, 201), states that the treaty of 442 ended with the death of Valentinian III; Procopius, *Wars* III, 5.2; Bury I, 292–300; Stein I, 365–7; Clover, 'Geiseric the Statesman', 136–62.

[7] On Avitus: A. Jülicher, 'Eparchius Avitus 5', *RE* II.2, 2395–7; *PLRE* II, 'Eparchius Avitus 5', 196–8; Stein I, 367–9.

[8] *PLRE* II, 'Eparchius Avitus 5', 197–8; Sundwall, *Weströmische Studien*, 55 (incorrectly stating that Avitus actually fought under Aetius in 451).

[9] In fact, Sidonius silently passes over Avitus' period out of office, except for the events of 451; Sid. Ap., *Carm.* VII, 316–21.

periods between public offices were not unusual for the Roman aristocracy, but it is striking that Maximus, in a time of political and military disturbance, selected as *magister utriusque militiae* a provincial so long out of office. Avitus was living on his country estates when appointed by the new emperor.[10] Maximus had *clientes* in Gaul, but there is no evidence of patronage or personal connections between Maximus and Avitus.[11]

Avitus' withdrawal to private life may not have been entirely voluntary. Possibly, like Majorian, he was forced from public life by Aetius, jealous of rivals for dominance in the western provinces.[12] Unlike Majorian, however, Avitus came from an aristocratic background. His departure from office is perhaps best seen as a voluntary and customary retirement after a successful career, and his selection as *magister utriusque militiae* by Maximus as the result of the same close ties between Avitus and the Gothic court of Toulouse emphasised by Sidonius in the *Panegyric*. The deaths of Aetius and Valentinian III disturbed relations with barbarian groups inside and outside the empire's borders.[13] Maximus, in choosing Avitus, was probably mindful of his success in gaining Gothic assistance against Attila four years previously. Relations with the Goths were important for the security of the western half of the empire; Avitus' appointment was a consequence of this.

The first few months of Avitus' commission were spent securing peace with barbarian groups on the empire's northern borders; possibly Avitus used the former imperial capital of Trier as a base.[14] Probably in late June,

[10] Sid. Ap., *Carm.* VII, 378–87, casting Avitus as a new Cincinnatus.

[11] *Clientes*: Sid. Ap., *Ep.* II, 13.1 (the otherwise unattested Serranus); cf. 4 (before his elevation, Maximus' *patrocinia florebant*).

Petronius Maximus and Avitus have recently been described as brothers-in-law: T. S. Mommaerts and D. H. Kelley, 'The Anicii of Gaul and Rome', in Drinkwater and Elton (eds.), *Fifth-Century Gaul*, 111–21, at 118. This lacks foundation. The silence of all sources, especially of Sidonius (who would thus have been related to the Anicii), is more than usually compelling. The postulated kinship of Petronius Maximus and Avitus assumes that Maximus was the father of Magnus, praetorian prefect of Gaul under Majorian and consul in 460 (*ibid.*, 118; *PLRE* II, 'Magnus 2', 700–1). Sidonius states that, of Magnus' family, only his grandfather had been consul before him (Agricola, 421), and that Magnus' son, Magnus Felix, was the first *patricius* in the family since his ancestor Philagrius (dated to the fourth century by *PLRE* I, 'Philagrius 4', 693; to the third by T. D. Barnes, '*Patricii* under Valentinian III', *Phoenix* 29 (1975), 153–4); Sid. Ap., *Carm.* XV, 150–3; *Ep.* II, 3.1. Petronius Maximus was twice consul, in 433 and 443, and *patricius* by 445; therefore he cannot have been an ancestor of this Gallic family; *PLRE* II, 'Petronius Maximus 22', 750. Other claims for ties between Avitus and the Anicii are tendentious, e.g. the appearance of the name Eparchius among the children of Ruricius, bishop of Limoges, could indicate a relationship of the family of Avitus with that of Ruricius' wife Hiberia rather than with the Ruricii (Mommaerts and Kelley, 'Anicii', 111; cf. Sid. Ap., *Carm.* XVII to Hiberia's father Ommatius).

[12] *PLRE* II, 'Fl. Iulius Valerius Maiorianus', 702. Cf. Gibbon, *Decline and Fall* II, 363.

[13] Cf. above, chapter 2, at nn. 138–41.

[14] Sid. Ap., *Carm.* VII, 369–75, 388–91; Stevens, *Sidonius*, 27 n. 1; Stein I, 367.

Avitus travelled to Toulouse to convince the Goths – so Sidonius says – to maintain the alliance they had observed under Valentinian III.[15] Just then, Sidonius adds, news of Maximus' death and the Vandal attack on Rome arrived in Toulouse. The Gothic king Theoderic II urged Avitus to assume the purple; Avitus displayed the reluctance for advancement becoming to imperial candidates.[16] Soon after, an assembly of Gallic nobles at Beaucaire, near the provincial capital Arles, nominated Avitus as emperor, and two days later, on 9 or 10 July, Avitus was proclaimed by the 'Gallic army'.[17]

Avitus travelled to Rome later in the summer, entering Italy on 21 September.[18] In Rome, he was received and recognised by the Senate. Proclaiming himself consul for the following year, in accordance with the usual practice of new emperors, Avitus was accordingly voted consular honours by the Senate.[19] During the celebrations for the beginning of Avitus' consular year, 1 January 456, his son-in-law Sidonius delivered before the Senate the extant *Panegyric* on the emperor's consulate.[20]

Sidonius' *Panegyric* was delivered six months after Geiseric had systematically looted the imperial city and seized the family of Valentinian III,

[15] *PLRE* II, 198 incorrectly states that Maximus '*immediately* sent [Avitus] as his envoy to the Goths at Toulouse' (my emphasis).

[16] News of Maximus' death: Sid. Ap., *Carm.* VII, 450–1: *captivum imperium ad Geticas rumor tulit aures* (cf. 378: the announcement to Avitus of his appointment as *magister utriusque militiae* is described as *collati rumor honoris*; Anderson misleadingly translates *rumor* at 451 as 'rumour', at 378 as 'tidings'; Loyen better translates both as 'la nouvelle'). Theoderic II and Avitus: *Carm.* VII, 506–19. On the topos of reluctance: MacCormack, *Art and Ceremony*, 180 with 348 n. 105, 199, 209, 223, 249.

Cf. Gregory of Tours, *Hist.* II, 11: *[Avitus] Romanum ambisset imperium.*

[17] Sid. Ap., *Carm.* VII, 519–80. Date: *Addit. ad Prosp. Havn.*, s.a. 455 (9 July); *Fasti Vind. Priores*, s.a. 455 (10 July); cf. *Continuatio Prosperi Reichenaviensis ad a. 457* (MGH AA 9, 490), cc. 29–30: Avitus elevated *post aliquos dies* after Geiseric occupied Rome (2–14 July).

Victor of Tunnuna, *Chron.*, s.a. 455 states that Avitus came to power on the 75th day after Geiseric entered Rome, i.e. 14 August, which contradicts all other sources. This appears to be an error, accepted only by Bury I, 326. Seeck, *RE* II.2, 2396 and *Untergang* VI, 476 n. 18, explains the figure LXXV as a scribal error for XXV, i.e. Avitus came to power on the 25th day after Geiseric *left* Rome. The figure could also be an erroneously transferred duplicate of the length of Maximus' reign, given by Victor as *diebus* LXXVII (cf. other records of the length of Maximus' reign: *Continuatio Prosperi ad a. 462* (MGH AA 9, 491), line 4: 75 days; *Cont. Prosp. Reich.*, s. 28: 72 days; *Chron. Gall. a. 511*, c. 623: 70 days). Hodgkin, *Italy* II, 376, takes 14 August as the date on which the news of Avitus' elevation reached Rome, but a delay of five weeks from southern Gaul to Italy is unlikely, and Victor's sources were probably eastern, not Roman.

Presumably 9 or 10 July is the date of Avitus' acclamation by the army. On Avitus' acclamation: MacCormack, *Art and Ceremony*, 223–4 and below, at nn. 90–9.

On Avitus' accession: Bury I, 326; Seeck, *Untergang* VI, 328; Stein I, 368; Jones, *LRE* I, 240; Demougeot II.2, 576–7; Stevens, *Sidonius*, 28–9; Loyen, *Recherches*, 55; Karl Friedrich Stroheker, *Der senatorische Adel im spätantiken Gallien* (Tübingen, 1948), 53, 153; Harries, *Sidonius*, 54.

[18] *Addit. ad Prosp. Havn.*, s.a. 455.

[19] Hyd., c. 163 [156]: *Avitus . . . Romam pergit et suscipitur*; Sid. Ap., *Carm.* VII, 7–10. Avitus' consulate was not recognised in the East, nor by Majorian; Bagnall *et al.*, *Consuls LRE*, s.a. 456.

[20] Date: Sid. Ap., *Carm.* VII, 10–13.

and three months after Avitus had arrived from Gaul as emperor. Like all imperial panegyrics, it was the product of a specific ceremonial occasion. As part of the consular celebrations, the *Panegyric* addressed the civilian aristocracy of Rome with an account of Avitus' accession, emphasising the legitimacy and efficacy of his authority. Panegyrics were deployed in imperial public events for functions ranging from ceremonial flourish and affirmation of dominant sociopolitical values, to propaganda advancing specific policies or claims to legitimacy. Authors of panegyrics may often have had little official or personal connection with the emperors they praised; few late antique panegyricists were, like Sidonius, personally related to their imperial subjects.[21] There is no doubt that the panegyric to Avitus was propaganda, addressed to a specific, Roman audience.

Rome's status as a political centre, eclipsed during the later third and early fourth centuries, had improved since the late fourth century. This steady revival reached its zenith in the mid-fifth century, as Rome again became the regular residence of the western emperors. Although Ravenna was the administrative capital of the West under Honorius and the early part of Valentinian III's reign, from about 440 Valentinian frequently resided in Rome, and relocated there definitively in 450.[22] This shift is reflected also in the role of the senatorial aristocracy. Roman aristocrats of the mid-fifth century were more frequently honoured than their predecessors with the western consulate.[23] The ambitions of Petronius Maximus, and the machinations in Rome following the death of Valentinian, are only the most melodramatic evidence of increased senatorial participation in imperial administration and politics.[24] Avitus' establishment in Rome, and the celebration of his consulate there, attests his recognition of the need to placate interests in the ancient capital.[25] The *Panegyric* is testimony of the emperor's relations with the aristocracy of Rome.

[21] Sabine MacCormack, 'Latin Prose Panegyrics', in T. A. Dorey (ed.), *Empire and Aftermath: Silver Latin II* (London and Boston, 1975), 163; MacCormack, *Art and Ceremony*, 223–4; modified by C. E. V. Nixon and Barbara Saylor Rodgers (trans.), *In Praise of Later Roman Emperors: The* Panegyrici Latini (Berkeley, 1994), 7, 26–33. Imperial panegyric delivered by a relative: Julian, *Panegyric on the Emperor Constantius II* and *On Royalty*, in *Œuvres complètes*, ed. and trans. J. Bidez, I (Budé; Paris, 1932).

[22] Seeck, *Regesten*, 368–400; Stewart Irving Oost, *Galla Placidia Augusta: A Biographical Essay* (Chicago, 1968), 254 n. 11; Gillett, 'Rome, Ravenna', 142–8.

[23] Bagnall *et al.*, *Consuls LRE*, 4–6, 354–445; Gillett, 'Rome, Ravenna', 163 n. 145.

[24] Priscus, *Fr.*, 30.1 = John of Antioch, *Fr.*, 201. For the background to the Senate's rising influence in the early fifth century: Matthews, *Western Aristocracies*, esp. 253–7, 352–61, 381–8.

[25] Cf. Portmann, *Geschichte in der spätantiken Panegyrik*, 105. Avitus remained in Rome until forced to leave Italy: Priscus, *Fr.*, 32 = John of Antioch, *Fr.*, 202; Gillett, 'Rome, Ravenna', 149.

PANEGYRIC AND PROPAGANDA

How did the *Panegyric* function as propaganda? It was surely not an attempt to 'convert' its hearers to support the emperor. The political persuasiveness of poetry should not be overestimated, and in any case, the Roman Senate had already demonstrated its consent to Avitus' rule.[26] Rather, the poem functioned as a medium for its audience to express support of the new emperor. Sidonius, providing a baroque decoration to the celebrations of the imperial consulate, exploited the occasion to restate Avitus' claim to rule. The poet's detailed and tendentious narrative of the emperor's accession probably elaborated claims which Avitus had already put forth in Gaul and Italy the previous summer; the consular celebrations were surely not their first airing.[27] Sidonius' delivery of the panegyric offered the Senate the opportunity, or perhaps obligation, to reaffirm its support of Avitus through its reaction. The Senate displayed this reaffirmation by following a precedent established in the time of Stilicho and revived under Valentinian III: the erection of a bronze statue of the ruler's panegyricist in the Forum of Trajan.[28] The statue, honouring the emperor's advocate, was a public gesture of support. The *Panegyric* was a focus of the symbolic communications between the emperor and the Roman aristocracy.

Late antique panegyrics generally followed well-established but flexible conventions.[29] The *Panegyric* on Avitus preserves the basic structure recommended by rhetorical handbooks, though it is set in an epic, narrative framework. The *laudatio* of the emperor, delivered by Jupiter himself, follows the traditional order of topics: an introduction (discussing the roles of fate, fortune, and divine aid in Rome's history) and short accounts

26 On the function of panegyric as propaganda: C. E. V. Nixon, 'Latin Panegyrics in the Tetrarchic and Constantinian Periods', in Brian Croke and Alanna M. Emmett (eds.), *History and Historians in Late Antiquity* (Sydney, 1983), 88–99. Senatorial consent: above, at n. 19.

27 *Contra* Michael Mause, *Die Darstellung des Kaisers in der lateinischen Panegyrik* (Palingenesia 50; Stuttgart, 1994), 100.

28 Statue of Sidonius: Sid. Ap., *Carm.* VIII, 7–10 (written before Avitus' downfall); *Ep.* IX, 16.21–8. Precedents: in Stilicho's time, the statue of his spokesman Claudian: Claudian, *Bellum Geticum*, in *Carmina*, ed. John Barrie Hall (Teubner; Leipzig, 1985), Praef. 7–9; CIL VI, 1710 = Dessau, *ILS*, 2949; Cameron, *Claudian*, 248–9. In Valentinian's time, the statue of the court eulogist Merobaudes: Merobaudes, *Pan.* I, *Fr.* IIA, 2–3; Hyd., c. 128 [120]; Sid. Ap., *Carm.* IX, 300–1; CIL VI, 1724 = Dessau, *ILS*, 2950; Clover, *Merobaudes*, 39–40.

29 Lester B. Struthers, 'The Encomia of Claudius Claudian', *Harvard Studies in Classical Philology* 30 (1919), 49–87; MacCormack, 'Latin Prose Panegyrics', 145; Cameron, 'Wandering Poets', 478–81; Cameron, *Claudian*, 22–3, 253–5; Mause, *Darstellung des Kaisers*, 63–204. On literary techniques of the Latin panegyrists: W. S. Maguinness, 'Some Methods of the Latin Panegyrists', *Hermathena* 47 (1932), 42–61; Maguinness, 'Locutions and Formulae of the Latin Panegyrists', *Hermathena* 48 (1933), 117–38. The best-known rhetorical handbook is that attributed to Menander Rhetor, ed. and trans. Russell and Wilson, Treatise II.

of Avitus' homeland, ancestry, birth, and education, are followed by his public deeds, the main part of the poem; a brief epilogue concludes the work.[30]

Sidonius' structure is copied directly from his undoubted model, Claudian, rather than from a rhetorical handbook.[31] The poetic panegyrics of Claudian, panegyricist at the western imperial court and propagandist for the *magister utriusque militiae* Stilicho from 396 to 404, differed structurally from the prose panegyrics of the third and fourth centuries. His epic style transformed the lengthiest part of the encomium, the account of the subject's deeds, from a list categorised under different thematic subheadings into a narrative, comprising sequential speeches and tableaux. Sidonius closely follows Claudian, borrowing his dramatic setting for the *Panegyric* on Avitus, the council of Olympians and Roma's supplication before Jupiter, from Claudian's epic *De bello Gildonico* and his mythological poem *De raptu Proserpinae*.[32] But Sidonius' debt to Claudian goes deeper than structure and imagery. Claudian was a master propagandist; like him, Sidonius employs rhetorical bombast, narrative structure, allusion, and omission for the purposes of propaganda.

Claudian's success not only revived the genre of Latin poetic panegyric, but created a new role for political poetry in the West. The prose panegyrics of the fourth century, ubiquitous in public ceremonies, gave many aspiring orators entry into public life; offices were granted to panegyricists both as reward for praise and in recognition of rhetorical virtuosity. Stilicho's relationship with Claudian, however, was more sustained than was customary between patron and panegyricist. After discovering Claudian, Stilicho used the poet as a mouthpiece not just once or twice, but continuously throughout most of a decade; the stream of propaganda was cut off probably by Claudian's death.[33] Stilicho's successors as *generalissimo* followed his lead in securing the exclusive services of a single poet to produce panegyrics and other works on their behalf. The *magistri utriusque militiae* Boniface and Sebastian had a Gallic panegyrist to sing their praises, while their rival, Aetius, was lauded by an Italian soldier-poet, Quintianus. Valentinian III, too, enjoyed the praises of a panegyrist,

[30] Introduction: Sid. Ap., *Carm.* VII, 123–38; *patria*: 139–52; *gens*: 153–62; birth and youth: 162–206; deeds: 207–584; epilogue: 585–98. Cf. Harrison, 'Verse Panegyrics of Sidonius', chapter 4, 100–56.

[31] André Loyen, *Sidoine Apollinaire et l'esprit précieux en Gaule aux derniers jours de l'Empire* (Paris, 1943), 32–3; Cameron, *Claudian*, 255.

[32] Cameron, *Claudian*, 253–66; MacCormack, 'Latin Prose Panegyrics', 186; MacCormack, *Art and Ceremony*, 6–7. Sidonius on Claudian: *Carm.* IX, 274–6.

Council of Olympians in Claudian: Claudian, *De raptu Proserpinae* III, 1–17; Roma before Jupiter: *In Gildonem*, 17–127; cf. Portmann, *Geschichte in der spätantiken Panegyrik*, 99–100.

[33] Panegyrics as entry to public office: Cameron, 'Wandering Poets', 484–91, 497–507. Stilicho and Claudian: Cameron, *Claudian*, 37–62, 415–18.

though the surviving works of his poet, the Spaniard Merobaudes, praise Aetius as much as the emperor. Sidonius himself records the patronage of poets by *generalissimi* throughout the early fifth century.[34] Avitus' use of his son-in-law's talents should be seen in the context of this tradition, the use of a specific poet as spokesman, rather than in the more general convention of panegyric as an occasional literary work.

Panegyricists sought to impress on the Roman elite the legitimacy and success of their rulers. Their approach varied with the basis of emperors' claims to legitimacy. When referring to an imperial accession, the propagandist could emphasise such qualities as the new emperor's dynastic ties to his predecessors; his military successes – the essential quality of victory; his support among different sections of society; portents associated with his rise; and his 'virtues'.[35]

How circumstances forced panegyricists to vary the aspects of rule they emphasised can be seen by comparing Sidonius' *Panegyric* on Avitus with Claudian's on the third consulship of Honorius. The latter was delivered in January 396, the first year of Arcadius' and Honorius' independent rule after the death of Theodosius I eleven months before. Throughout the poem, Claudian emphasises the obvious basis of Honorius' legitimacy: his descent from Theodosius, his birth to a ruling emperor (an honour not shared by his brother Arcadius), and Theodosius' arrangements for rule of the empire to descend upon his two sons. No less emphasised is Theodosius' charge to Stilicho to guard his successors.[36] In his later poems, Claudian praises the victories of the *generalissimo* Stilicho, even when his nominal subject was Honorius.[37]

Sidonius can claim for Avitus no ties to the Theodosian dynasty, and though he praises Avitus' military prowess, it is not his main theme. In the political conditions of the 450s, greatly different from those of Claudian's time, the audience of the panegyricist had new concerns. Sidonius' portrait of Avitus combines traditional and new elements. Attention to Avitus' military prowess reflects Roman military culture and

[34] Sid. Ap., *Carm.* IX, 277–301 (following his description of Claudian's *De raptu Proserpinae*).

[35] MacCormack, *Art and Ceremony*, part III, 'Accessio', 161–266, esp. 164, 179, 209.

[36] Claudian, *Panegyricus dictus Honorio Augusto tertium consuli.*

[37] E.g. *Panegyricus dictus Honorio Augusto quartum consuli*, 439–83; *De consulatu Stilichonis* I, 94–137, 170–385; III; *Panegyricus dictus Honorio Augusto sextum consuli*, 210–330, 440–90.

Claudian includes the successful completion of an embassy to Persia among the achievements of Stilicho (Claudian, *De consulatu Stilichonis* I, 51–68); this passage is very closely imitated by Sidonius in regard to the general Procopius, father of the future emperor Anthemius (Sid. Ap., *Carm.* II, 75–88). Both passages, describing non-imperial honorands, concentrate on the impression made by the envoys on their hosts and, especially, the Persian oaths sealing the treaties won by the envoys. There is no parallel to Sidonius' innovative depiction of the envoy wielding a personal influence over another power or his central theme, the elevation of contact with neighbouring powers to a claim for authority. Cf. Mause, *Darstellung des Kaisers*, 107–8.

conventions of panegyric. The portrait of Avitus as an envoy, however, is unprecedented in imperial encomium. Its uniqueness suggests that the portrait served a specific purpose, and is the key to understanding the issues which Sidonius addressed in his public declamation.

THEMES AND PLOT OF THE *PANEGYRIC*

As a work of fiction, the *Panegyric* communicates its message through the repetition of central themes and the development of its plot. The central theme of the poem is the need for military action against the Vandals, presented as the overriding political issue of the day. The plot traces the development of relations between Avitus and the Goths of Toulouse. Theme and plot meet in the climax: Avitus' elevation and his personal ties with the Goths promise new strength for the western empire against the threat from Carthage.[38]

The central theme of the work is established in the opening lines of the poem. Rome's destiny is to grow greater out of adversity: this ancient image, employed by Sidonius in the opening address, tactfully broaches the subject of the recent disaster while simultaneously introducing Avitus' potential as Rome's restorer.[39] The Vandals are not named until later in the poem; mere allusion to recent adversities is sufficient. Avitus is identified as the cause of the city's destined restoration: 'Now she begins to rise once more with an emperor for consul.'[40] The Senate will see Avitus not only in his consular celebrations, but also in his triumph over the barbarians.[41]

The first speech of the poem, delivered by Roma to Jupiter, develops this theme. Again the Vandals are not mentioned, Roma's appearence – stumbling, bowed, dishevelled – sufficing to indicate the historical context.[42] Jupiter promises renewal, in the person of Avitus.

This opening is a statement of policy. It defines political priorities: the Vandal attack is the most important issue in the West. The purpose of

[38] Cf. Harrison, 'Verse Panegyrics of Sidonius', 126–45; Lynette Watson, 'Representing the Past, Redefining the Future: Sidonius Apollinaris' *Panegyrics* of Avitus and Anthemius', in Mary Whitby (ed.), *The Propaganda of Power: The Role of Panegyric in Late Antiquity* (Leiden, 1998), 177–98, esp. 188–90: Watson rightly notes that treaties, rather than military conquest, are important in the *Pan.* But as a literary theme, treaties are very secondary to the presentation of the person of Avitus as an envoy.

[39] Sid. Ap., *Carm.* VII, 5–7. The image goes back to Livy; for references: MGH AA 8, 390 (*Loci similes* to *Carm.* V, 63), 395 (to *Carm.* VII, 5ff). The use of this image most recent in time to Sidonius is Rutilius Claudius Namatianus, *De reditu suo sive iter gallicum*, ed. Ernst Doblhofer, 2 vols. (Heidelberg, 1972), I, 129–30.

[40] Sid. Ap., *Carm.* VII, 7–8: *modo principe surgit consule.*

[41] Sid. Ap., *Carm.* VII, 8–10.

[42] Sid. Ap., *Carm.* VII, 45–9; at 116 Roma calls herself *capta.*

Avitus' rule is to bring renewal to Rome by defeating the Vandals.[43] The opening of the poem excludes from consideration the other major issue arising from the events of mid-455: with the death of Valentinian III, ninety years of dynastic succession from Valentinian I and Theodosius I ended.[44] No mention of the break is made in the opening lines, and Valentinian's death is never mentioned, although those of Aetius and Petronius Maximus are.

The Theodosians, however, are not ignored. Roma's speech blames not foreign attack for her distress, but the ineptitude of her rulers. Her state has come about *de Caesare*, 'through the emperors'.[45] Throughout the *Panegyric*, the Theodosian dynasty is repeatedly criticised. In Roma's speech, the Theodosians are implicitly compared to the standard 'bad emperors'. Just as Trajan followed Nero and Vitellius, so now a new Trajan is needed.[46] The first explicit reference to the extinct dynasty is Sidonius' famous description of Valentinian III as *semivir amens*, as he murders Aetius.[47] The speech of the leader of the Gallic assembly before Avitus blames the Theodosians, and the 'boy emperor' Valentinian III in particular, for the 'cruel fortune' suffered by Gaul.[48]

These harsh remarks may reflect genuine Gallic resentment against the rule of Valentinian III.[49] Their primary role in the *Panegyric*, however, is to compensate for Avitus' lack of a dynastic claim to the throne.[50] Sidonius exploits one of the potentials of the panegyric genre, the substitution of invective for praise. But the invective comes only in passing references.

43 Pierre Courcelle, *Histoire littéraire des grandes invasions germaniques*, 3rd edn (Paris, 1964), 167. Stein I, 369 contrasts the 'bellicose' spirit of the *Panegyric* with Avitus' dispatch of envoys to seek redress from the Vandals (Priscus, *Fr.*, 31.1), but there is no real contradiction. No war could be opened without at least a formal attempt at reconciliation; cf. at chapter 2 above, nn. 117, 120, 149.

44 For indications of contemporary consciousness of the dynastic break: Hyd., c. 164 [157] (probably written in 456): *Usque ad Valentinianum Theodosi generatio tenuit principatum.*

45 Sid. Ap., *Carm.* VII, 103; cf. Reydellet, *La Royauté*, 54 n. 25.

46 *Carm.* VII, 104–18.

47 *Carm.* VII, 358–9. Cf. *Carm.* V, 305–11. Reydellet, *La Royauté*, 52–3, 55–8, sees criticisms of the Theodosians as expressions of Sidonius' personal disapproval of the dynasty, which failed to live up to his ideal of 'hommes d'action'. This ignores the function of such comments as propaganda exploited in specific situations. Elsewhere Sidonius described Valentinian III positively: *Carm.* IX, 300 (*carus popularitate princeps*); *Carm.* XXIII, 214 (*pius princeps*).

48 *Carm.* VII, 532–43. The rhetoric of this passage is reminiscent of descriptions of the travails of Gaul under the barbarian attacks and usurpations of the early fifth century by Gallic poets such as Orientius and the author of the *Carmen de providentia Dei*; cf. Courcelle, *Histoire littéraire*, 85–8, 96–101; M. Roberts, 'Barbarians in Gaul: The Response of the Poets', in Drinkwater and Elton (eds.), *Fifth-Century Gaul*, 97–106.

49 Cf. Strohecker, *Der senatorische Adel*, 51–2; Stevens, *Sidonius*, 21, 35.

50 Avitus had no known western competitor who could claim to be a legitimate heir to Valentinian III. Before Petronius Maximus' elevation, however, the candidature of Majorian had been supported by the *augusta* Licinia Eudoxia; Priscus, *Fr.*, 30 [= John of Antioch, *Fr.*, 201]. Cf. the situation in the East in 450, after the death of Theodosius II, when the support of the *augusta* Pulcheria gave dynastic legitimacy to Marcian; Kenneth G. Holum, *Theodosian Empresses: Woman and Imperial Dominion in Late Antiquity* (Berkeley, 1982), 208–9.

Avitus' position is insufficiently consolidated to give too much attention to the break from the past. Here and elsewhere, Sidonius is nervous about perceptions of Avitus' legitimacy.

Established in the opening lines as the central issue, the Vandal theme is latent until the penultimate scene of the poem. The account of Avitus' duties as *magister utriusque militiae* under Petronius Maximus and his trip to the Goths in Toulouse is interrupted by the only explicit reference to the Vandal attack on Rome.[51] It is placed here in the narrative to show the alleged significance of this event in relations between Avitus and Theoderic II. News of the attack and Petronius Maximus' death dictates the Goths' response to Avitus' overtures for peace. Knowing that the imperial throne is vacant, Theoderic agrees to peace on condition that Avitus becomes emperor. Only Avitus' elevation will ensure that the empire has the support of the Goths, specifically against the Vandals. This is emphasised by the somewhat clumsy contrast between the Gothic sack of Rome in 410 and recent events.[52] Jupiter's final speech reiterates this theme: the imperial acclamations of Gaul bring fear to the Vandals.[53]

These themes reflect Avitus' approach to the Senate. As emperor, Avitus can offer the alliance and support of the Goths, with whose aid the West has the opportunity to defeat the Vandals. No other consideration of legitimacy should count, and no other candidate for the throne can offer this military strength.

The plot of the *Panegyric* is a carefully crafted vehicle for these themes of renewal and deliverance. Like the speeches and the mythological framework, the plot is a literary contrivance; it ought not be confused with historical developments, however much the contrivance draws upon reality. The dramatic sequence does not reflect true historical development. Sidonius' style permits him to manipulate historical events freely. The mythological frame removes the narrative from reality, and this abstraction also affects the account of Avitus' *gesta*. Events happen sequentially but timelessly. Temporal indicators introducing each episode obscure the passage of time between actual events.[54] The years between 439 and 451 pass without notice, and Avitus, addressing the Goths in 455, refers to his office as praetorian prefect in 439 as if it recently preceded his current military appointment.[55] The epic tone of the poem enables Sidonius to shape characters and events into a historical fiction. Details are provided

[51] Sid. Ap., *Carm.* VII, 441–51.

[52] Condition: Sid. Ap., *Carm.* VII, 499–509; sack of 410: 504–6.

[53] Sid. Ap., *Carm.* VII, 585–91.

[54] Sid. Ap., *Carm.* VII, 230: *interea*; 243: *vix*; 316 and 319: *iam . . . subito*; 357: *iam*; cf. 295: *haec post gesta*.

[55] Sid. Ap., *Carm.* VII, 464–7.

to give the impression of accuracy – Avitus' offices; the presence of the Gothic king's brother in discussions in 455; the auguries taken after Avitus' elevation. But the events of the story, while presumably 'true', are presented without regard for real historical significance.[56] Conflict and alliance between Aetius and the Goths are shown only to demonstrate Avitus' superior abilities to reach concord with the barbarians; the causes of conflict, or the conditions of alliance, are irrelevant to the narrative development.

The plot follows the progress of Avitus' relations with the Gothic court of Toulouse. Behind this plot lie fundamental tensions. Avitus' claim to authority rested on his military strength, which in turn depended in large part on the support given to him by the Goths, potentially the most significant military force in the West. But Sidonius had to make clear that the emperor controlled the Goths, not vice versa. Before the settlement of the Goths in Aquitaine in 418, Gothic and Burgundian leaders in Italy and Gaul had supported a series of imperial usurpers.[57] Memory of the political turmoil this caused had not disappeared by Sidonius' time.[58] Moreover, it was necessary that Avitus' alliance with the Goths in 455 did not appear to have been cultivated for the purpose of seizing power. Sidonius tried to resolve these tensions by showing Avitus' contacts with the Goths only in a context which was civilian and predominantly private, not in military circumstances which would emphasise the realities of power. Several generals in the fourth and fifth centuries had attempted to usurp the throne with the aid of barbarian backing; Avitus' similarity to them was all too obvious. As an alternative model, Sidonius chose to portray Avitus as an envoy, whose oratorical skill and personal qualities command the unselfish following of the Goths.

A chronological account of Avitus' *cursus honorum* provides the structure of the plot. After the brief outline of Avitus' *patria* and youth, Sidonius relates Avitus' public life, his *gesta*, in seven episodes. Four of the episodes concern Avitus and the Goths, while two concentrate on

56 Truth: there are, however, many assertions in the poem which, merely for want of other evidence, are assumed to be factual, e.g. the statement that no one tried to claim the imperial power after the death of Maximus; Sid. Ap., *Carm.* VII, 512–14. Yet after the death of Valentinian III, several candidates had struggled for power; Priscus, *Fr.*, 30.1 = John of Antioch, *Fr.*, 201; above, n. 50.

57 Attalus elevated (and deposed) by the Gothic leaders Alaric I, 409–10, and Athaulf, 414–15; Jovinus supported by the Burgundian and Alan leaders Guntiarius and Goar, 411; supported (and deposed) by Athaulf, 412/13. Matthews, *Western Aristocracies*, 295–9, 313–18; Michael Kulikowski, 'The Visigothic Settlement in Aquitania: The Imperial Perspective', in Ralph W. Mathisen and Danuta Shanzer (eds.), *Society and Culture in Late Antique Gaul: Revisiting the Sources* (Aldershot, 2002), 31–2.

58 Sid. Ap., *Ep.* III, 12.5; V, 9.1 (with Harries, *Sidonius*, 28–30); cf. *Narratio de imperatoribus domus Valentinianae et Theodosianae* (MGH AA 9, 630), 6, line 13 (written post-424).

his military career; the first episode acts as a prelude. The episodes can be grouped as three pairs, followed by a longer climax:

1 (Prelude) Early embassy to Constantius (lines 207–14)
2 (Goths i) First journey to Toulouse (lines 214–29)
3 (Military i) Military career under Aetius (lines 230–40)
4 (Military ii) Incident of 437 (lines 241–94)
5 (Goths ii) Peace settlement with Goths in 439 (lines 295–315)
6 (Goths iii) Embassy to Goths in 451: Attila (lines 316–56)
7 (Goths iv) Embassy to Goths in 455: elevation (lines 357–584)

The two military episodes provide an intermission to the main plot, Avitus' growing influence over the court of Toulouse.[59]

The distinction of military and Gothic episodes reflects Sidonius' careful approach to his subject. When in contact with the Goths, Avitus is never portrayed as a military figure, though this involves an element of prevarication. Instead, relations between Avitus and the Goths are always portrayed in the context of official embassies. Sidonius makes a subtle change to one of the conventions of panegyric to facilitate this portrayal. Rhetorical handbooks and influential models of panegyric commonly divided the account of the public life of the subject into deeds 'of war and of peace'. Sidonius instead introduces the narrative of Avitus' mature life as a record of *pugnae et foedera regum*, 'of wars and compacts with kings'. Sidonius quietly adapts the traditional dichotomy in order to assimilate Avitus' Gothic dealings with actions 'of peace', and so catalogue them as civilian, not military, achievements.[60]

The first episode serves as a prelude. Avitus, on behalf of the Auvernians, undertakes a mission to the *magister utriusque militiae* and *patricius* Constantius, at some time before the latter's elevation as emperor in February 421. Though a youth, Avitus successfully seeks the remission of an onerous tax levied on his homeland.[61] The passage dwells on

[59] For a somewhat different structural analysis: Harrison, 'Verse Panegyrics of Sidonius', 126–45, 225–6. Though valuable, Harrison's analysis is misleading in seeing lines 214–315 (but not lines 207–14) as Avitus' *gesta* in war and peace, with the remainder of the poem 'outside the limits of a Menandrian panegyric'; 137–8. Sidonius is more free with panegyrical structure than Harrison maintains. Sidonius does not structure his account of Avitus' deeds into 'war' and 'peace' (lines 214–29, the first mission to Toulouse, cannot be described as military), but presents a chronological narrative; the 'civil' episodes (nos. 1–2, 5–7 above) are interrupted by the two military ones (nos. 3–4 above). The *gesta* begin with line 207, the embassy to Constantius (seen by Harrison as part of the account of Avitus' education), introducing the unifying theme of Avitus as envoy.

[60] Sid. Ap., *Carm.* VII, 214–15. On 'deeds of war and of peace': MacCormack, 'Latin Prose Panegyrics', 145; Menander Rhetor, *Treatise* II, 1–2, 12, 13 (Russell and Wilson, 85–93, 179–80, 181). Avitus' Gothic dealings are accepted as 'civil virtues and deeds' by Mause, *Darstellung des Kaisers*, 107.

[61] For the circumstances: Loyen, *Recherches*, 36–9, associating the mission with the establishment of the council of Seven Provinces in 418. Agricola, a relative of Avitus, was then praetorian prefect of Gaul.

Avitus' skills of persuasion, an inborn talent (*indole*). These oratorical skills are the defining quality of the character of Avitus. With this first mission, Sidonius establishes the context in which Avitus will most often be portrayed.[62]

The following episode describes Avitus' first trip to the Gothic court of Toulouse. It is here that the phrase 'wars and compacts with kings' appears. By implication, it appears that the first journey to Toulouse constitutes part of Avitus' public life and duties, and is therefore an 'official' mission, like the preceding journey to Constantius and the later approaches to the Goths. But this is deceptive. Avitus visits Toulouse to see his relative Theodorus, one of several Gallic hostages given to Theoderic I as part of a settlement between the Goths and the empire.[63] There is nothing in Sidonius' language to indicate that Avitus represented either imperial or provincial authorities, or that his aim was to demand the return of Theodorus, as is often assumed.[64] If Avitus' purpose had been to seek the surrender of the Gallic hostages, Sidonius would have commented on the outcome, as he does for all the official missions. His task was private, carried out *pro pietate propinqui*.[65]

This episode establishes in the plot of the poem the beginnings of the ties between Avitus and the Gothic monarchy.[66] The Gothic king Theoderic I is charmed by Avitus, as may be expected from the praise, in the preceding episode, of the young Gaul's eloquence. But this nascent liaison is immediately qualified. Theoderic is so impressed by the young

[62] Sid. Ap., *Carm.* VII, 207: *[Avitus] eligitur primus, iuvenis, solus*. Loyen has been misled by the structure of Sidonius' poem into translating the passage as 'Il est alors choisi, *pour la première mission*, malgré sa jeunesse, comme unique délégué'; cf. Anderson: 'young though he was, he was chosen first and alone'.

[63] Sid. Ap., *Carm.* VII, 215–29. For the circumstances: Loyen, *Recherches*, 39–43; *PLRE* II, 1087. On hostages given between rulers and provincial communities, see above, chapter 2, n. 70. Loyen's objections to 425 as the date when hostages were given to the Goths are inadequate. Prosper's report (*Chron.*, c. 1290) that Aetius defeated the Goths after their siege of Arles is not incompatible with a mutually agreed settlement in which the Goths received hostages as guarantees against whatever concern prompted their attack on the provincial capital (on the causes for Gothic assaults on Arles: Wolfram, *History of the Goths*, 175; Peter Heather, 'The Emergence of the Visigothic Kingdom', in Drinkwater and Elton (eds.), *Fifth-Century Gaul*, 84–5).

[64] Anderson I, 136–7 n. 1 rightly insists that *expetis* in Sid. Ap., *Carm.* VII, 219 should be understood as 'to seek out', not 'to demand back', as translated by e.g. Mommsen, MGH AA 8 Index personarum 436 s.v. 'Theodorus' (*repetitur*); Loyen, *Sidoine* I, 63 ('le réclamer'). Elsewhere, Sidonius uses *expetere* in the sense of 'to seek out', e.g. *Epp.* I, 2.4; II, 4.3; V, 20.3; VII, 2.2; cf. *ThLL* V.2, s.v. *expetere* I.B.2.a.

[65] Sid. Ap., *Carm.* VII, 218. Rouche, *L'Aquitaine*, is forced to assume that 'Théodoric accorda probablement la libération demandée'; cf. Jülicher, 'Eparchius Avitus', 2396; Harries, *Sidonius*, 68.

[66] So Loyen, *Recherches*, 39–40, though discussing the scene as a source rather than a literary contrivance: 'L'importance de cette visite est capitale, puisqu'elle est à l'origine d'une amitié qu'Avitus mit parfois au service de Rome, parfois de son ambition personnelle.'

man that he wishes to make Avitus *suus*. What this offer involves is unclear – his friend, his follower? In any case, Sidonius implies that it would compromise Avitus' loyalty to the empire.[67] Avitus rejects the proposition.

Sidonius emphasises this rejection. The poet concludes many of his episodes with a short exemplum, often drawing upon a classical literary image. The exemplum is not a mere rhetorical flourish, but encapsulates the essential point of the preceding episode, summing up what Sidonius wishes to communicate.[68] In the exemplum at the end of the second episode, the poet compares the first meeting between Avitus and Theoderic I to that of the Roman envoy C. Fabricius Luscinus and the Epirot king Pyrrhus in 280 BC. Fabricius, who refused gifts offered by the king, is the classical model of incorruptibility.[69] The comparison is an assertion of Avitus' independence from the power which supported his rise to the throne. The first episode presents Avitus as a persuasive orator and successful emissary. The second establishes Avitus' personal connections with the Gothic monarchy, while emphasising Avitus' autonomy.

The following two episodes interrupt Avitus' relations with the Goths in order to relate his military career of the 430s. The first briefly mentions wars in which he engaged under the generalship of Aetius. Sidonius avoids details, devoting half this passage to a catalogue of Avitus' martial qualities. His virtues are contrasted with those of different barbarian races, some contemporary, others drawn from literary sources.[70] The following, longer episode expands upon Avitus' prowess. In this lengthy

67 Sid. Ap., *Carm.* VII, 224. It is tempting to interpret Theoderic's proposition as an indication of Gothic recruitment of Roman administrative and military talent not otherwise attested before the 450s; cf. Heather, 'Emergence', 89–91.

68 Cf. Portmann, *Geschichte in der spätantiken Panegyrik*, 99, for a less positive view, which considers only historical exempla from the republican period, not mythic or other literary exempla (e.g. the image of the Phoenix; below at n. 82). The proponderance of republican models among the historical exempla (cf. *ibid.*, 105) reflects the long-standing literary role of early Roman history as a reservoir of moral instruction, catalogued by handbooks such as that of Valerius Maximus and its epitomes; for historical exempla from the imperial period in the *Pan.*: Mause, *Darstellung des Kaisers*, 51–2.

69 On Sidonius' use of exempla: Harrison, 'Verse Panegyrics of Sidonius', 162–7; Michael Roberts, *The Jeweled Style: Poetry and Poetics in Late Antiquity* (Ithaca, NY, 1989), 37. Fabricius: the *locus classicus* is Plutarch, *Pyrrhos* XX, 1–3, in Plutarque, *Vies*, ed. and trans. Robert Flacelière and Emile Chambry, VI (Budé; Paris, 1971). Fabricius was often cited by Latin writers, including Cicero; cf. Eutropius, *Breviarium* II, 12.2–4. On the danger posed to envoys in classical antiquity by the acceptance of gifts: Adcock and Mosley, *Diplomacy in Ancient Greece*, 164–5; Mosley, *Envoys and Diplomacy*, 39–40.

70 Sid. Ap., *Carm.* VII, 230–40. Cf. Loyen, *Recherches*, 43–4. Anderson I, 138 n. 3 is wrong to imply that Avitus did not take part in the campaigns against the Iuthungi, Nori, and Vindelicians. Lines 231–2 imply that he did, and *iunctus tibi* in 235 is probably best seen qualifying the whole of 232–5, not just *Belgam . . . absolvit*. For barbarians as points of comparison for martial virtues: Statius, *Achilleis*, ed. A. Marastoni (Leipzig, 1974), II, 132–3; MGH AA 8, 397 (*loci similes* to *Carm.* VII, 237ff).

set-piece, describing an incident which occurred in 437, Avitus avenges the death of a servant by defeating a marauding Hunnic auxiliary in single combat. These two episodes present Avitus as an experienced military commander, a claim which could not be made for either Valentinian III or Petronius Maximus, and a counterpoint to Avitus' oratorical skills.

The military episodes are more carefully crafted than first appears. The anecdote of the single combat lends itself to heroic treatment, suitable to the epic tenor of the poem. Sidonius digresses to compare his hero to Achilles avenging Patroclus. Yet in itself, the fight is a minor incident in a career which had seen several major wars and three military appointments in less than a decade. Sidonius does not expand upon any of the campaigns which Avitus undertook with Aetius, nor mention any of the three military offices held by Avitus in the 430s, stating only that he is now *vir inlustris*.[71] The poet's purpose becomes evident only with the realisation that at this point Sidonius is guilty of an inconsistency. Though the narrative appears to follow 'un ordre rigoureusement chronologique', in fact Sidonius did not relate all events in correct sequence.[72] The Hun whom Avitus defeated was one of the auxiliaries attached to the *comes* Litorius as he advanced on Narbo, then besieged by the Goths, in 437.[73] Together with Aetius, Litorius relieved the seige. Avitus also was involved in the relief of Narbo, convincing Theoderic I to withdraw from the city.[74] The *Panegyric* mentions Avitus' participation, not in chronological sequence, following his fight with the Hunnic soldier in the fourth episode, but later, in the speech which he later delivers at Toulouse in 455, in the seventh episode of the poem. There Avitus' involvement is assimilated with other peaceful ties between himself and the Goths. Yet his actions at Narbo were undertaken in a military capacity, for at the time Avitus held the last of his three military appointments under Aetius.[75] The re-ordering of events, and the epic treatment of the single combat with the Hun, conceal Avitus' actions in a military capacity against the Goths.

The third and fourth episodes praise Avitus' military abilities, but without associating the Goths with his military career. Avitus, in the *Panegyric*,

[71] Sid. Ap., *Carm.* VII, 241; the three military posts of the 430s are mentioned at line 462, during events of 455. Though little is known of the campaigns against the Nori and Iuthungi (lines 233–5), they were significant enough to be recorded by Hydatius (cc. 93, 95 [83, 85]); in the *Chron. 452* (c. 106); and probably in the extant inscription of the statue of the *comes* Merobaudes (Dessau, *ILS* I, 2950: *inter arma litteris militabat et in Alpibus acuebat eloquium*). For the Burgundian campaign: Loyen, *Recherches*, 44.

[72] Loyen, *Recherches*, 40. [73] Sid. Ap., *Carm.* VII, 246–8; Hyd., c. 110 [101]; Stein I, 323.

[74] Sid. Ap., *Carm.* VII, 475–80. Siege: Prosper, *Chron.*, s.a. 436; Hyd., cc. 107, 110 [98, 101].

[75] Sid. Ap., *Carm.* VII, 255, cf. 462. *PLRE* II, 197 suggests that Avitus was *magister utriusque militiae per Gallias* in 437, explaining his *inlustris* rank (Sid. Ap., *Carm.* VII, 241); he was not only 'a local leader'; Harries, *Sidonius*, 75.

treats with the Goths only in a private or civilian capacity, and only in a context of alliance, never of aggression.[76]

The narrative returns to the Goths with the fifth episode. In 439, after three years of conflict between the Goths and the imperial forces in Gaul, peace is concluded through the agency of Avitus. The former general is now praetorian prefect of Gaul, an exceptional transition from military to civil authority. This is the first of three occasions on which Avitus bends the Goths to cooperation with the empire. Though Sidonius may exaggerate the seriousness of the Gothic threat, there is no reason to doubt the historicity of Avitus' central role in the settlement.[77]

The significance of this episode, however, is the nature of Avitus' relations with the Goths as depicted by Sidonius. The respect which Avitus previously had earned from Theoderic I has blossomed into a commanding authority. It is a sleight of hand; the two intervening military accounts enable Sidonius to redefine the nature of the relationship he had earlier established. Avitus did not travel to Toulouse himself in 439. The peace was achieved by his *pagina*. But the constant imagery of Avitus' eloquence and authority assimilates this episode with earlier and later embassies to the Goths.

Avitus' success is contrasted with the failure of the military to resolve the conflict. Litorius is captured; Aetius' military and diplomatic approaches have failed.[78] But Avitus can resolve the conflict peacefully. In this instance, Sidonius explicitly distances Avitus, whose martial prowess he has recently praised, from 'savage battles'.[79]

The sixth episode develops this presentation of Avitus. Again Aetius is at a loss, now unable to secure the support of the Goths against Attila

[76] Jülicher, 'Eparchius Avitus', 2396 makes Avitus' involvement in the relief of Narbo an embassy to Toulouse, which is certainly the impression Sidonius wishes to give.

[77] While most sources focus on the defeat and capture of the pagan Litorius at Toulouse (e.g. Cassiodorus, *Chron.*, c. 1232; Salvian, *De gubernatione Dei* VII, 9.39–10.44; *Vita Orientii* 62), the subsequent settlement between the empire and the Goths is recorded by Prosper, *Chron.*, 1335; Hyd., c. 116–17 [108–9]; Jordanes, *Get.* XXXIV, 177; possibly Merobaudes, *Pan.* II, 144–97, esp. 186–7 (cf. Clover, *Merobaudes*, 58–9 and Harries, *Sidonius*, 69, though *PLRE* II, 'Avitus 7', 25 identifies the passage with Avitus' victory the previous year). Jordanes states that the conflict had reached a stand-off (*utrique fortes et neuter infirmior esset*) and this is implied also by Prosper's account (*anceps pugna*). Prosper makes the Goths the initiators of the settlement, but this does not necessarily mean that they were overwhelmed by the imperial forces. Both Salvian and the *Vita Orientii* state that the Goths also had sought peace *before* Litorius' ill-fated attack on Toulouse. The death of Litorius, who had refused these overtures, may have enabled a settlement desirable to both sides to be reached (cf. Loyen, *Recherches*, 49–50 and 50 n. 2). Jordanes clearly refers to a negotiated, mutually agreed settlement. On Jordanes' account: Olivier Devillers, 'Le conflit entre Romains et Wisigoths en 436–439 d'après les *Getica* de Jordanès: fortune et infortune de l'abréviateur', *Revue de Philologie de Littérature et d'Histoire Anciennes* 69 (1995), 111–26.

[78] Sid. Ap., *Carm.* VII, 299–300: *nil prece, nil pretio, nil milite fractus agabat/Aetius.*

[79] Sid. Ap., *Carm.* VII, 312–15: *fera proelia.*

in Gaul in 451. Before an assembly of Gallic nobles, Aetius seeks Avitus' aid.[80]

The speech placed in Aetius' mouth reiterates Avitus' authority over the Goths. Avitus acts as an envoy, having no official post.[81] It is his first journey to Toulouse as an imperial envoy, but Sidonius' earlier descriptions of the second and fifth episodes obscures this fact. The exemplum at the end of the episode encapsulates the message: as ordinary birds flock after the fabled Phoenix, so the Goths willingly follow Avitus.[82]

The fifth and sixth episodes draw two contrasts: Avitus, with his personal authority over the Goths, is distinguished from the ineffective generals; and the self-defeating attempt to force the Goths into submission through warfare is contrasted with the pursuit of peace through alliance. Though a capable military commander, Avitus does not resort to battle with the Goths, able instead to command their alliance.

The seventh and final episode occupies over a third of the total length of the poem. It has the most complex narrative, shifting between Italy, Arles, and Toulouse. Four speeches constitute the greater part of the episode, which opens with the political turmoil of 454–5 in Rome and closes with Avitus' elevation at Arles. Avitus, appointed *magister utriusque militiae* by the new emperor Petronius Maximus following the deaths of Aetius and Valentinian III, makes peace with barbarian groups on the Rhine border, then travels to Toulouse to prevent hostilities with the Goths. Theoderic II surprises Avitus by urging him to take the throne which has again, suddenly, become vacant with the death of Petronius during the Vandal sack of Rome. Returning to Arles, Avitus is proclaimed emperor by the Gallic magnates and army.

The established elements of Avitus' character – his role as an envoy for the empire and his relations with the Gothic royalty – become the vehicle for his imperial elevation. Sidonius emphasises that, though Avitus is *magister utriusque militiae*, he approaches the Goths not in a military capacity but as an envoy of the empire, as he had in the earlier scenes: 'Avitus, armed with an imperial writ, was already entering the home of

[80] Sid. Ap., *Carm.* VII, 336–8. This Gallic assembly has attracted little attention. Possibly Aetius convened a council of nobles of southern Gaul to select an envoy to be sent to Toulouse (Harries, *Sidonius*, 70, suggests a meeting of the *concilium septem provinciarum*). Ennodius, *Vita Epiphani*, 53–8 and 81–2, presents two Italian provincial councils, summoned by the *magister utriusque militiae* Ricimer and the emperor Nepos, to select envoys; below, chapter 4, n. 201. Sid. Ap., *Ep.* V, 20, refers to an assembly gathered to choose an envoy; *Epp.* VII, 6.10, 7.4 mention a southern Gallic assembly, including bishops, with authority to oversee the exchange of embassies and agreements between the empire and Toulouse; below, chapter 4, n. 224.

[81] Sid. Ap., *Carm.* VII, 352–3.

[82] Sid. Ap., *Carm.* VII, 353–6. For negotiations with the Goths in 451: cf. Jordanes, *Get.* XXXVI, 186–90, and, in a lighter vein, Fredegar, *Chron.* II, 53.

the Goths and, having laid aside for a little the pomp of the Master's office, had taken upon himself the authority of an envoy.'[83] Addressing the *coetus* of Theoderic II, Avitus states '[when appointed *magister utriusque militiae* by Petronius Maximus], then did I most readily embrace the duty, that I might go as envoy to you'.[84] As in the fifth episode, Sidonius portrays Avitus' contacts with the Goths as civil, not military. The speech of a Gothic warrior restates this message: though a brave general, Avitus resolves conflict with the Goths through ties of alliance, not war.[85]

In the brief scene of Avitus' arrival at Toulouse, imagery functions to convey the episode's message. Avitus' mere arrival is enough to quell Gothic aggression. Sidonius compares the effect of his arrival on the Goths with the thunderbolt which struck down Phaethon from the wild chariot of Phoebus.[86] It is perhaps not the happiest simile (the thunderbolt was hardly *clemens* to Phaethon), but it conveys the idea of a superior being resolving a temporary breach of the natural order. The description of the reception of Avitus by Theoderic II and of their joint entry into the city suggest an *adventus* ceremony, an urban ritual of welcome and submission.[87] When entering the city, 'Avitus kept on one side of him the king, on the other side the king's brother, and with joined hands they entered Toulouse.'[88] These lines are suggestive of another image familiar from imperial art: an imperial college, with senior and junior rulers side-by-side in *concordia*.[89] Another image of concord, the unification of the Sabines with the Romans, concludes the scene. The presentation of

[83] Sid. Ap., *Carm.* VII, 400–2: *succinctum . . . diplomate Avitum/iam Geticas intrare domos positaque parumper/mole magisterii legati iura subisse.*

[84] Sid. Ap., *Carm.* VII, 467–8: *promptissimus istud/arripui officium, vos quo legatus adirem.*

[85] Sid. Ap., *Carm.* VII, 423–5: *pacem fortis amas.*

[86] Sid. Ap., *Carm.* VII, 405–10. Traditionally the thunderbolt was thrown by Zeus, not (as in Sidonius) by Phoebus.

[87] Sivan, 'Sidonius Apollinaris, Theoderic II, and Gotho-Roman Politics', 87–8 and n. 13. Cf. MacCormack, *Art and Ceremony*, 17–22.

[88] Sid. Ap., *Carm.* VII, 435–6: *hinc germano regis, hinc rege retento/palladiam implicitis manibus subiere Tolosam* (the brother mentioned was probably Frederic; cf. Marius of Avenches, *Chron.*, s.a. 455; Sirmond, *PL* 58, 689–90 n. e; *PLRE* II, 'Fredericus 1', 484).

[89] The association of *concordia* with adjacent figures also appears in other contexts, e.g. portraits of married couples.

Imperial coin types depicting two or more emperors were common from the Diocletianic period through the fourth and fifth centuries. Variants of the reverse legend CONCORDIA AUGG were frequent during the Tetrachy and Constantine's periods of shared rule. CONCORDIA legends were not used by Constantine's sons nor by Valentinian I and Valens, but reappeared after the death of Valentinian I and continued to the death of Honorius; *RIC* VI–X; R. A. G. Carson, *Coins of the Roman Empire* (London and New York, 1990), 194–9.

Neither this coin type nor this legend, however, was common during the time of Theodosius II and Valentinian III. Theodosius II's coins issued during the reign of Honorius featured both, but after Valentinian III's accession, these features appeared only on the issues celebrating the joint imperial consulship of 426. Valentinian III's coins used neither this type nor this legend; Philip Grierson and Melinda May (eds.), *Catalogue of Late Roman Coins in the Dumbarton Oaks*

Avitus' arrival exploits images of submission and concord, the essential nature of the Goths' relationship with Avitus in the *Panegyric*.

There is little doubt that Sidonius' presentation of the Goths' unpremeditated nomination of Avitus is intentionally misleading. Petronius Maximus died in Rome on 31 May, and Geiseric entered Rome on 2 June.[90] Avitus was proclaimed five weeks later. Sidonius implies (without stating) that Avitus was unaware of the recent events in Rome before setting out to Toulouse, for he places the announcement of the news among the Goths during his account of the general's visit, and makes Theoderic II mention Maximus' death to Avitus, as if informing him.[91] The length of time between Maximus' death and Avitus' elevation make it unlikely that Avitus did in fact travel to Toulouse 'for a dead man'.[92] So too does Sidonius' own chronology. Sidonius states that Avitus went to Toulouse just over three months after his appointment as *magister utriusque militiae*.[93] This means that Avitus set out in mid to late June at the earliest, already several weeks after the death of Maximus.[94] Sidonius' narrative is carefully constructed, misleading without stating actual falsehoods.

Chronicle sources offer different, if brief, versions of Avitus' accession. Hydatius states that Avitus was twice acclaimed emperor by the army of Gaul and the Gallic *honorati*, first at Toulouse and subsequently at Arles.[95] If Hydatius' report is accurate, either he counted the Goths as part of the *exercitus Gallicanus et honorati*, or Avitus travelled to Toulouse with a contingent of the imperial army, which acclaimed him there. In either event, Hydatius' account contradicts Sidonius', for Sidonius mentions

Collection and in the Whittemore Collection: From Arcadius and Honorius to the Accession of Anastasius (Washington, DC, 1992), 136–51, 233–41, plates 12–17, 33–4; *RIC* X, 59, 64, 72–3, 145.

The image of the emperors side-by-side, associated with the 'virtue' *Concordia*, may, however, have continued to appear in other imperial art during the time of Theodosius II and Valentinian III: cf. Merobaudes, *Carm.* I, 1–2, an ekphrasis of a mosaic or fresco in an imperial palace, presumably in Rome or Ravenna, in the early 440s.

90 Seeck, *Regesten*, 402.

91 Sid. Ap., *Carm.* VII, 450–1, 512–14; but cf. 464 and Loyen, *Sidoine* I, 185 n. 83: Sidonius makes Avitus describe Maximus ambiguously as *princeps modo* – emperor 'now' or 'formerly'? The narrative is often accepted at face value, e.g. Stevens, *Sidonius*, 28.

92 Wolfram, *History of the Goths*, 179.

93 Sid. Ap., *Carm.* VII, 391–2: *vixque hoc* [sc. the pacification of barbarian groups] *ter menstrua totum luna videt.*

94 The date of his appointment is not known. Maximus came to power on 17 March; Avitus was in Gaul at the time, so he could not have received news of his appointment earlier than late March; *PLRE* II, 751. Sidonius was aware that Maximus' reign had finished before Avitus travelled to Toulouse; cf. Sid. Ap., *Ep.* II, 13.4: Maximus' reign was *paulo amplius quam bimenstris* (cf. Cass., *Chron.*, c. 1262: *Maximus intra duos menses . . . extinctus*, and the enumerations of days at n. 17 above).

95 Hyd., c. 163 [156]: *Ipso anno in Galliis Avitus Gallus civis ab exercitu Gallicano et ab honoratis primum Tolosa, dehinc apud Arelatum Augustus appellatus*; c. 183 [176]: *Avitus . . . Gallis et Gothis factus fuerat imperator.*

no acclamation in Toulouse, only those of Arles. According to Marius of Avenches, when Avitus was proclaimed emperor, Theoderic II entered Arles 'in peace'.[96] The presence of the Goths at Arles when the Gallic nobles agreed to Avitus' elevation does not feature in Sidonius' version of events.[97]

The ability to mobilise the military strength of the Goths was the basis of Avitus' claim to authority. Sidonius, however, carefully distances the Goths from the legitimate acclamations of Avitus, just as he is particular to employ the familiar topos of the new emperor unwillingly sought out. The description of the acclamations in Arles is unusual amongst late antique panegyrics for its 'legalistic emphasis on the constitutional process of election'.[98] The scene presents a claim: despite Avitus' unusual basis for authority, his election was a purely Roman affair, observing all traditional norms.[99] By recognising Avitus, the Senate accepted this misrepresentation as true.

This claim is the climax of the poem. The narrative ends in Arles, rather than continuing to recount Avitus' journey to Italy and arrival in

96 Marius of Avenches, *Chron.*, s.a. 455.

97 Avitus was accompanied by a Gothic bodyguard, in addition to part of the Gallic army, when he went to Italy; Priscus, *Fr.*, 32 = John of Antioch, *Fr.*, 202.

98 MacCormack, *Art and Ceremony*, 232, cf. 223–34.

99 Avitus, arriving at the assembly of Gallic nobles greeting his return from Toulouse, is addressed by *procerum . . . maximus unus, / dignus qui patriae personam sumeret* (*Carm.* VII, 530–1). Whereas the Gothic warrior who speaks at *Carm.* VII, 411–30 is a fictitious, composite character (cf. Claudian, *De bello Gothico*, 485–517), the Gallic spokesman is probably real. Loyen identifies this person as Tonantius Ferreolus, praetorian prefect of Gaul in 451; Loyen, *Sidoine* I, 186 n. 91, followed by Reydellet, *La Royauté*, 56; Rouche, *L'Aquitaine*, 30. There is no evidence to support this identification, which seems based solely on the assumption that the description of the speaker is flattery, consistent with Sidonius' praise of Tonantius elsewhere (*Carm.* XXIV, 35; *Ep.* VII, 12). But Sidonius' terminology is more exact. *Proceres* refers to imperial office holders, not just 'magnates'; cf. *Carm.* VII, 210: Constantius, then senior *magister utriusque militiae* and *patricius*, is *procerum . . . potentior*. The 'greatest of [civil] leaders' in Gaul must be the current praetorian prefect of Gaul. Only the praetorian prefect would be fit to 'assume the character of his homeland'. The description invokes the familiar figures of the personifications of provinces, as seen e.g. in the illustrations to *Not. dig.* Oc. II and Or. III, and probably appearing on the codicils of office. Unfortunately, the identity of the praetorian prefect of Gaul for 455 is unknown; he may have been Priscus Valerianus, a relative of Avitus (*PLRE* II, 'Priscus Valerianus 8', 1142–3; Sid. Ap., *Carm.* VIII, title, 1–2).

Avitus was formally nominated as emperor by the highest civil officer in the Gallic prefecture. This is another aspect of the 'legalism' of the Arles scene.

The assembly at which Avitus is elevated has been identified as a regular meeting of the *Concilium septem provinciarum* (Gibbon, *Decline and Fall* II, 364; Demougeot II.2, 576; cf. Bury's note to his edition of Gibbon (7 vols., London, 1926), IV, 10 n. 21), but this is unlikely. When established in 418, the *Concilium* met from mid-August to mid-September, not in July, when Avitus was proclaimed; MGH Epp. 3, 13–15. The 455 assembly included nobles from the Rhine provinces, which do not appear to have been included in the *Concilium*; Sid. Ap., *Carm.* VII, 527. Moreover, Sidonius states that the meeting was assembled solely to welcome Avitus (and, no doubt, proclaim him emperor); *Carm.* VII, 521–30.

Rome.[100] Sidonius foregoes the opportunity of a scene of Avitus' *adventus* into Rome, a standard element of late Latin panegyric, showing Avitus' reception by the Senate and populace of Rome.[101] Possibly the circumstances of Avitus' arrival were too delicate to recall so soon after the event. But Sidonius had no need to portray local events to his Roman audience. He described earlier events in which the Senate did not participate. His purpose was not to convince the Senate of the truthfulness of his narrative, but to gain the senators' acquiescence in the events in Gaul through a public gesture of approval of this 'official' version.

Sidonius' epic tone and his portrait of Avitus enable him to assimilate Avitus' private and military contacts with the Goths to his formal embassies. Avitus represented his provincial community in his appeal to the general Constantius in *c.* 418; he went to Toulouse in 451 on behalf of the imperial government. His other journeys to the Goths were either in a private capacity (on his first journey to Toulouse), or in military office (during his involvement in the relief of Narbo in 437). In 439 Avitus acted as praetorian prefect, but did not travel to Gothic territory himself. Sidonius blurs the distinction between these contacts, casting them all as official, civilian embassies.[102]

This deceptive account provides a context for his presentation of Avitus' journey to Toulouse in 455: once again, Avitus acts in a civilian capacity to use his personal influence over the Goths in the interests of the empire. In fact, Avitus' bid for power, supported by the Goths, was the first involvement of a barbarian leader and his troops in the politics of the western imperial succession since the settlement of the Goths in Toulouse in 418 (which had ended, among other political disturbances, a decade of Gothic-supported imperial usurpations in the West). To Italian eyes, Avitus probably appeared as a usurper who had gathered the support of the Gothic king by exploiting his position as a major land-owner

[100] Sid. Ap., *Carm.* VII, 589–91, is the only allusion to Avitus' actions after the Gallic acclamation; cf. Loyen, *Recherches*, 57–8.

[101] Cf. MacCormack, *Art and Ceremony*, 224: 'The only constitutional element which could not be mentioned [in the scene of the Arles acclamation] was the Roman Senate.'

[102] Avitus' formal embassies were clearly distinguished by Sirmond, *PL* 58, 683 n. c, 687 n. a, 689 n. b. Subsequent users of the *Panegyric* were not so careful, e.g. Gibbon, *Decline and Fall* II, 363: Avitus concluded 'the most important embassies' before his appointment as praetorian prefect in 439 (he had in fact only undertaken one, to Constantius); Stevens, *Sidonius*, 22: Avitus had been sent to the Goths 'on several occasions' before 455 (in fact only once, in 451). Harries, *Sidonius*, 97, sums up Sidonius' literary creation well: a 'pro-Gothic civilian diplomat'; cf. (more cautiously) Ralph W. Mathisen, *Roman Aristocrats in Barbarian Gaul: Strategies for Survival in an Age of Transition* (Austin, 1993), 54. Sidonius' evocation of a negotiated approach to relations with the Goths addressed the specific circumstances of Avitus' barbarian-supported usurpation in 455, not a general 'policy' of cooperation with the Goths, as envisaged by Harries, *Sidonius*, 67–75, cf. 14, 101.

in southern Gaul, his local influence as a former and current imperial magistrate, and even his earlier military activities against the Goths. The misleading epic of Avitus and the Goths was a tactful way of denying this charge.[103]

THE PORTRAYAL OF THE ENVOY

The social and political forces shaping Sidonius' world are the same as those in Hydatius' Gallaecia. Relations between local aristocracies and barbarian rulers have become the focus of political action in the provinces. The empire has a stronger presence in southern Gaul than in western Spain, and the authority of imperial office supports the influence of local magnates such as Avitus, just as it had in previous centuries. But relations between Avitus and the Goths are primarily unofficial, determined by Avitus' standing as a local magnate. Where Hydatius portrays only conflict between Gallaecian leaders and the Sueves, Sidonius' writings reveal a range of relations between Gauls and Goths, from hostility to cooperation. The presentation of these relationships to a non-provincial audience had to be very carefully crafted.

Understandably, Sidonius' panegyric on Avitus is a mixture of old and new: the traditional imagery of Roman military prowess, and the innovative presentation of barbarian alliance as a basis of authority. The new circumstances are carefully qualified. Avitus is shown as independent of the Goths, swaying them with his personal authority. His fitness to command the imperial army is fully established, yet his relations with the Goths are consistently dissociated from his military career. The value of his personal contacts with Toulouse is contrasted with the failure of exhausting warfare as a way to control the Goths. The plot of the *Panegyric* determines the character of its protagonist. At some expense to the truth, Avitus is portrayed repetitively fulfilling the functions of an envoy; doing so is the defining feature of the literary character of Avitus.[104]

[103] The emphasis on Avitus' private contact with the Goths explains the quaint portrait of Avitus teaching Roman law and Virgil to the young Theoderic II; Sid. Ap., *Carm.* VII, 495–9, taken literally by almost all modern accounts. Theoderic II's liberal education, however, need not be fictitious. Sidonius suggests that Toulouse maintained a tradition of secular education; *Carm.* VII, 436, *Palladia . . . Tolosa*; cf. Ausonius, *Parentalia* III, 11, *Commemoratio professorum Burdigalensium* XVII, 7; XIX, in *The Works of Ausonius*, ed. R. P. H. Green (Oxford, 1991), 28, 54. See in general Pierre Riché, 'La survivance des écoles publiques en Gaule au Ve siècle', *Le Moyen Âge* 63 = 4th ser. 12 (1957), 421–36.

[104] Mause, *Darstellung des Kaisers*, 100–1, correctly observes that '[Sidonius] lobt . . . nicht den *Kaiser* Avitus, sondern seinen *Weg* zum höchsten Amt . . . [According to Sidonius, Avitus comes to power] durch eine permanente Rastlosigkeit', though it is misleading to see Avitus' defining activities as 'vor allem . . . die kriegerische Betätigung' (101, cf. 104).

The *Panegyric* is an experiment. Of all the activities of the real Avitus – land-owner, general, administrator – Sidonius selected the role of envoy as the most flexible and appropriate means to portray Avitus' relations with the Goths. The *Panegyric* casts the familiar figure of the *legatus* as a hero with the trappings of political authority. The envoy is portrayed as a powerful figure: persuasive, authoritative, able to build and maintain alliances crucial to the strength of the empire. The personality of ties between Rome and barbarian allies is vested in the envoy, not in the emperor he represents. Sidonius' envoy is a statesman, elevated above a mere messenger or skilled spokesman.[105] This figure is constantly contrasted, explicitly or not, with the image of a victorious general. Sidonius draws on well-established portraits of epic heroes, whose outstanding qualities are *fortitudo* and *sapientia*. Aetius and Litorius are not criticised by Sidonius; their wars demonstrate their *fortitudo*. But Avitus prevails because he, like Aeneas, combines wisdom with strength.[106] The envoy acquires strength through alliance with barbarians, not crushing them in battle. Alliance is not disguised as *philanthropia*; rather, it is a very traditional means of acquiring barbarian service to Roman power.[107]

No ideological shift from military to diplomatic solutions underlies Sidonius' portrait of Avitus. The approach to the West's most immediate problem, the Vandals, remains military. Sidonius merely attempts to exploit the role of the envoy to find an acceptable formula describing Avitus' rise to power, by elevating the envoy to the status of a victorious general. At the time of delivery, Sidonius' experiment in propaganda succeeded in manipulating traditional and current political concepts. Sidonius' choice of literary strategy in presenting Avitus as a *legatus*, and the formal acclaim of his poem in Rome, give evidence that the frequency of embassies throughout the West was so commonly understood that Sidonius could exploit it in his deceptive account of Avitus' journeys to Toulouse. More, Sidonius' propaganda relied upon a perception, shared by the provincial magnate and his Roman senatorial audience, of a role for envoys in the politics of the mid-fifth century West which was central and prestigious. The *legatus* was an image which could be associated with imperial power.

[105] Contrast the description of the role of rhetors as emissaries of their communities in Brown, *Power and Persuasion in Late Antiquity*, esp. chap. 2, 35–70: however skilful rhetors might be, the effectiveness of their appeals ultimately depends on the goodwill of governors who know how to '[play] the game correctly' (45).

[106] Cf. Ernst Robert Curtius, *European Literature and the Latin Middle Ages*, trans. Willard R. Trask (Bollingen series 36; New York, 1953), 167–78.

[107] On *philanthropia* in relations with barbarians: Blockley, *East Roman Foreign Policy*, 108; P. J. Heather, *Goths and Romans, 332–489* (Oxford, 1991), 167–8, 177–8; cf. Lawrence J. Daly, 'The Mandarin and the Barbarian: The Response of Themistius to the Gothic Challenge', *Historia* 21 (1972), 351–79. Barbarian service: Sid. Ap., *Carm.* VII, 429–30 (speech of a Gothic elder): [*Avito*] *auxiliaris ero: vel sic pugnare licebit.*

The juxtaposition of Avitus with Aetius entails not criticism of the *generalissimo*, but rather the acceptance of communication and negotiation as complements to military engagement. Avitus' dealings with the Goths had to be cast in an acceptable formula to dismiss open charges of usurpation by sheer force or subordination to barbarian interests, but Sidonius did not seek or need to justify provincial relations with barbarian rulers in general. Rather he exploited these contacts, showing Avitus as an emperor able to muster the force needed to resist the Vandals, by ensuring the active support of the Goths and the quiescence of other barbarians. In its fictitious as much as its historical elements, the *Panegyric* is evidence of the rising status of envoys in the politically fragmented West.

As a basis for panegyric, Sidonius' portrait of Avitus finds no echo in subsequent extant imperial panegyric, despite his influence on later Latin writers. His letters and poems, however, all written later than the *Panegyric* to Avitus, contain intermittent references to envoys and political communication, which are analogous to the positive image of envoys from which Sidonius constructed his portrait of Avitus.

Sidonius refers several times to the functions and high status both of envoys dispatched by city or provincial councils, and of palatine legates. In a letter encouraging a fellow townsman, Pastor, to accept his nomination by the city council of Clermont for a legation to the praetorian prefect of Gaul in Arles, Sidonius describes the competition and intrigue carried out in order to secure such nominations by those seeking the *popularitas* which attends the completion of an embassy.[108] Nevertheless, provincial embassies could be viewed as a burden, notwithstanding the availability of official transport and travel costs.[109] Sidonius himself performed at least one embassy to the imperial court, using official transport, on behalf of the Auvergne. His well-known description of the Gothic king Theoderic II is written from the point of view of a petitioner, though whether on his own or others' behalf is unclear.[110] He describes one provincial council in the 470s as having not only a supervisory role in embassies between

[108] Sid. Ap., *Ep.* v, 20 to Pastor (not in *PLRE* II). Loyen's identification of Pastor's proposed embassy with that of Sidonius to the emperor Anthemius in Rome in 467 is erroneous; Loyen, *Sidoine* II, 208, 257. Sidonius does not intend to accompany Pastor (who is *missus a nobis*), and the mission is to Arles, not Rome. Loyen underestimates the frequency of traffic between provincial communities and governmental authorities.

[109] *Evectio* and *sumptus*: Sid. Ap., *Ep.* v, 20.2–3; *onus*: v, 20.1.

[110] Embassy to court: in 467, to the emperor Anthemius: Sid. Ap., *Epp.* I, 5.2 (*cursus publicus*), 9.5 (provincial embassy); *PLRE* II, 117. It is not clear in what capacity Sidonius acted when pleading to Majorian in 458 for relief from punishments imposed for rebellion; Sid. Ap., *Carm.* v, 574–603. To Theoderic II: Sid. Ap., *Ep.* I, 2.8.

the empire and the Goths of Toulouse, but even authority to treat, delegated from the imperial government.[111] When writing a lengthy eulogy of Consentius, a friend and host, and describing his tenure as *tribunus et notarius praetorianus* in the consistory of Valentinian III, Sidonius chooses to dwell on the embassies which Consentius undertook to the court of Theodosius II, which he praises in hyperbolic terms.[112] Simplicius, a former minor official, later a candidate for metropolitan bishop, is similarly praised in a public address for the embassies he had undertaken on behalf of his city to both imperial and royal courts.[113]

Just as Sidonius portrays Avitus, misleadingly, as repeatedly undertaking embassies, so in his letters and poems he emphasises the numerous legations undertaken by those he praises for serving as envoys.[114] He praises envoys' eloquence, and portrays them not as messengers but as peace-makers.[115] Closely reminiscent of the *Panegyric* on Avitus is Sidonius' praise of Tonantius Ferreolus, former praetorian prefect of Gaul in the early 450s.[116] During Ferreolus' prefecture, Thorismod, king of the Goths after the death of his father Theoderic I in 451, besieged Arles.[117] The siege of 452/3 was lifted, according to Sidonius, by Ferreolus' eloquence in negotiating with Thorismod. The situation was parallel to that of Avitus, as praetorian prefect, treating with Theoderic I in 439. Like Avitus in the *Panegyric*, Ferreolus is contrasted with Aetius, whose military strength was useless: 'by means of a banquet you removed from the gates of Arles one whom Aetius had been unable to remove by war'.[118]

Describing the *quaestor* Licinianus, sent by the emperor Nepos to negotiate with the Gothic king Euric, Sidonius outlines the characteristics of an effective legate: he is already known by his good reputation, his speech is forthright and impressive (though Licinianus is praised for

[111] Sid. Ap., *Ep.* VII, 6.10, 7.4.

[112] Sid. Ap., *Carm.* XXIII, 214–62. *PLRE* II, 'Consentius 2', 308–9. Consentius was also *cura palatii* under Avitus, but Sidonius does not elaborate on this post; *Carm.* XXIII, 428–33. Loyen, *Sidoine* I, 152 n. 19 mistakenly reads *militia ampla* (222) as a promotion to higher office; Sidonius in fact refers to the completion of Consentius' service.

[113] Sid. Ap., *Ep.* VII, 9.19 (Simplicius): *non ille semel pro hac civitate stetit vel ante pellitos reges vel ante principes purpuratos.*

[114] Sid. Ap., *Carm.* XXIII, 233; *Ep.* VII, 9.19.

[115] Eloquence: Sid. Ap., *Carm.* XXIII, 233–40. Peace-maker: *ibid.*, 241–62 (a list of barbarians whom Consentius could have bound to the empire if necessary; they are mostly standard literary figures taken from Statius, with the exception of the Vandals and their disruption of Mediterranean trade, an uncharacteristic reference to a pressing current issue); *Ep.* III, 7.4 (the *quaestor* Licinianus, sent by Nepos to Euric).

[116] *Ep.* VII, 12 (written in the 470s); *PLRE* II, 'Tonantius Ferreolus', 465–6.

[117] *Chron. Gall. 511*, c. 621; cf. Hyd., c. 156 [148]: *Thurismo rex Gothorum spirans hostilia* (Burgess' translation misconstrues the text; Gillett, *Journal of Roman Studies* 87 (1997), 313); Prosper, *Chron.*, c. 1371.

[118] *Ep.* VII, 12.3: *ab Arelatensium portis quem Aetius non potuisset proelio te prandio removisse.*

severitas rather than *linguae rotunditate*), and he is faithful. At the same time, Sidonius criticises the faults of *plurimi* undesirable envoys: unimpressive in their delivery, more concerned for their reputation than the success of their mission, and worst, treacherous and profiteering: 'those who, bartering the secrets of the princes who have sent them, hope to do well from the barbarians for the legate rather than for the legation'.[119] In his well-known letter to the bishops involved in the negotiations with Euric which resulted in the ceding of the Auvergne to the Goths, Sidonius similarly accuses the bishops of using their role in the communications 'not to relieve public dangers so much as to pursue their private fortunes'.[120]

The heroic image of the envoy which Sidonius drew upon in the *Panegyric* on Avitus is echoed in these minor eulogies and invectives of the 460s and 470s. Though there are no lengthy analogues to Sidonius' literary exploitation of the status of envoys in extant panegyric, there are close comparanda in contemporary works of another eulogistic genre: hagiography. Sidonius' letters, like Hydatius' *Chronicle*, indicate the importance of negotiation in the duties of bishops. Adjudicating a disputed episcopal election in the 470s, Sidonius claims that a monk would not be acceptable to the laity (notwithstanding the Gallic tradition of monk-bishops trained at Lérins) for fear that a monk 'would be better able to intercede with a heavenly judge on behalf of souls than with an earthly judge for bodies'.[121] Contemporary Gallic hagiography not only demonstrates the importance of bishops' secular intercessions, but exploits the same image of the envoy used by Sidonius – of the legate as eloquent, repeatedly undertaking missions, and delivering his communities from the greatest calamities – in order to praise their subjects.

[119] *Linguae rotunditate*: *Carm.* XXIII, 237. Treachery and profiteering: Sid. Ap., *Ep.* III, 7.2–3: *qui secreta dirigentium principum venditantes ambiunt a barbaris bene agi cum legato potius quam legatione.*

[120] Sid. Ap., *Ep.* VII, 7.4: *non tam curae est publicis mederi periculis quam privatis studere fortunis.*

[121] Sid. Ap., *Ep.* VII, 9.9: *intercede magis pro animabus apud caelestem quam pro corporibus apud terrenum idicem potest.*

Chapter 4

THE SAINT AS ENVOY: FIFTH- AND SIXTH-CENTURY LATIN BISHOPS' *LIVES*

Through the intercession and merit of the priest, a king was restrained, an army recalled, provinces spared from devastation.

Constantius, *Vita Germani Autissiodorensis*, 28

Besides Sidonius' *Panegyric* on Avitus, the most extensive dramatisations of embassies in late antique Latin literature occur in several hagiographic *Lives* of bishops. Scenes of bishops undertaking legations to rulers on behalf of their communities are well-known attestations of the increasing involvement of the episcopacy in public functions, in turn a reflection of the annexation of the office of bishop by members of the provincial aristocracy.[1] Such tableaux also appear to give evidence of a concomitant ebb of municipal and imperial authority, a vacuum filled perforce by the church. This latter impression is misleading.[2] Embassies appear in late fifth- and early sixth-century hagiography precisely because the undertaking of legations was a common but prestigious political occurrence in secular centres of power, carried out by non-ecclesiastics

[1] On bishops and aristocracy: M. Heinzelmann, *Bischofsherrschaft in Gallien: zur Kontinuität römischer Führungsschichten vom 4. bis zum 7. Jahrhundert* (Beiheft der Francia 5; Munich, 1976); S. J. B. Barnish, 'Transformation and Survival in the Western Senatorial Aristocracy, c. AD 400–700', *Papers of the British School in Rome* 56 (1988), 138–40.

There is no single overview of late antique/early medieval hagiography pending the completion of the multi-volume *Hagiographies*, ed. Guy Philipart, 2 vols. to date (Corpus Christianorum; Turnhout, 1994, 1996), but valuable surveys of recent work include: P. Fouracre, 'Merovingian History and Merovingian Hagiography', *Past and Present* 127 (1990), 3–38; Julia M. H. Smith, 'Early Medieval Hagiography in the Late Twentieth Century', *Early Medieval Europe* 1 (1992), 69–76; Patrick J. Geary, *Living with the Dead in the Middle Ages* (Ithaca, NY, 1994), 9–29; I. N. Wood, 'The Use and Abuse of Latin Hagiography in the Early Medieval West', in E. Chrysos and I. Wood (eds.), *East and West: Modes of Communication* (The Transformation of the Roman World 5; Leiden, 1999), 93–109. For literary analysis of the genre: F. Lotter, *Severinus von Noricum: Legende und historische Wirklichkeit* (Stuttgart, 1976), 37–59; C. Stancliffe, *St Martin and his Hagiographer: History and Miracle in Sulpicius Severus* (Oxford, 1983), 86–102; W. Berschin, *Biographie und Epochenstil im lateinischen Mittelalter*, 3 vols. (Stuttgart, 1986–91), esp. I, section IV, 'Bischofsleben der Spätantike', 193–266.

[2] Cf. the cautions against exaggerating the degree of municipal secular authority held by bishops prior to the mid-sixth century (for the West) in Liebeschuetz, *Decline and Fall of the Roman City*, esp. 143, 144, 154, 156–7.

including provincial magnates and palatine officials. Authors of episcopal biographies sought to appropriate for their subjects the social credit attached to this function. The impression that bishops shouldered the burden of municipal duties in undertaking embassies stems from the general invisibility of non-ecclesiastic envoys in the sources. A series of *Vitae* show the growth of a new saintly image, a distinct extension of earlier hagiographic types, which flourished between the late fifth and mid-sixth centuries. These *Vitae* were a reaction to the increasing social value of the role of envoy in public life.

THE EMBASSY OF POPE LEO I TO ATTILA

A convenient illustration of the appropriation by hagiographers of the social credit due to those who carried out embassies is the story of the meeting of Pope Leo I with Attila. Most hagiographic accounts of embassies are the sole testimonies of the legations concerned, but for a few, instructive comparanda are available. The *Chronicle* of Prosper records an embassy of 452 to Attila in northern Italy. The journey was undertaken, on behalf of the *senatus populusque Romanus* and the emperor Valentinian III, by three envoys: Trygetius, perhaps formerly prefect of Rome or praetorian prefect of Italy, who had previously negotiated with Geiseric in North Africa; Gennadius Avienus, a member of the highest Roman nobility who had shared the consulate with Valentinian two years previously, later described by Sidonius Apollinaris as one of the two most powerful senators in Rome; and Pope Leo I.[3] Prosper, an enthusiastic supporter of Leo, credits the success of the mission to Leo's divine support and Attila's joy at the presence of the bishop. In an earlier edition of the *Chronicle*, published before these events occurred, Prosper had already portrayed Leo as a peace-maker of the great when, as a deacon of Rome in 440, he was sent to Gaul on a *legatio publica* to settle a quarrel between the *magister utriusque militiae* Aetius and the praetorian prefect of Gaul, Fl. Albinus.[4] Prosper's partisanship may have led him to exaggerate Leo's pre-eminence over his notable companions on the legation of 452; Leo's role was perhaps to negotiate the ransoming of captives, a duty

[3] Prosper, *Chron.*, 1367. *PLRE* II, 'Gennadius Avienus 4', 193–4; 'Trygetius 1', 1129.

Other attestations to the embassy: Otto J. Maenchen-Helfen, *The World of the Huns: Studies in Their History and Culture*, ed. Max Knight (Berkeley, 1973), 129–30, 134–5, 140–2 (probably Leo, *Sermo*, 84.1, *PL* 54, 433–4; Leo, *Ep.*, 113, *PL* 54, 1024; *Epistola orientalium episcoporum ad Symmachum*, *PL* 62, 59–60).

On the hagiographic elements of Prosper's account of Leo throughout the *Chron.*: Muhlberger, *Fifth-Century Chroniclers*, 131–5.

[4] Prosper, *Chron.*, 1341. Muhlberger, *Fifth-Century Chroniclers*, 111 (erroneously identifying Albinus as a general).

often undertaken by bishops in time of war.[5] Later redactions of the story went further than Prosper, not only in introducing miraculous aid to the Roman embassy, but in erasing altogether the presence of Trygetius and Avienus, along with Leo's imperial commission.[6]

This is an instructive literary evolution. Even stripped of legendary qualities, later versions of Leo's embassy portray him as the sole and self-motivated protector of Rome. Prosper's original version, though written in Leo's favour, better displays the real historical context: embassies undertaken on behalf of a secular authority by *optimates* whose social standing was derived from a range of backgrounds – in this case, a senior palatine official, a member of the highest Roman aristocracy, and a patriarch – at least two of whom had experience with embassies of similar importance previously. The later hagiographical portrait of Leo as sole protector of his community, acting without reference to secular authority, is a literary construct, which retains functions to which social prestige adheres, while washing away the historical residue. A similar selectivity in other hagiographic sources also has the effect of making the actions of bishops appear egregious, by isolating the deeds of saints from the context of common provincial political communications.

'THE HERO WORN OUT BY HIS LABOURS': CONSTANTIUS, *LIFE OF GERMANUS OF AUXERRE*

A cluster of four texts from late fifth- and very early sixth-century Gaul and Italy share images and narrative structures in which the undertaking of embassies is central to the presentation of a bishop. They include Constantius' account of Germanus of Auxerre; the anonymous *Vitae* of Orientius of Auch and of Vivianus of Saintes; and the *Vita* of Epiphanius of Pavia by Ennodius. The *Vita* of Germanus of Auxerre seems to be the earliest of these texts; in view of the literary ingenuity displayed by the author, Constantius, it is very likely that this image was his creation. This new aspect of hagiographic portraiture was added comfortably to existing saintly types, of the saint as ascetic and as thaumaturge, though it was not easily compatible with one established mode of sanctity, the prophet in Old Testament mould. The aspect of the saint as a busy and frequent

[5] Leo's role: *Ep. orien. episc. ad Symm.*, *PL* 62, 59–60. Bishops ransoming captives: William Klingshirn, 'Charity and Power: Caesarius of Arles and the Ransoming of Captives in Sub-Roman Gaul', *Journal of Roman Studies* 75 (1985), 183–203, esp. 184–7.

[6] E.g. Victor of Tunnuna, *Chron.*, s.a. 449; *Liber pont.*, 47; Jordanes, *Get.*, 223 (with details of location not in Prosper); Paul the Deacon, *Hist. Rom.* XIV, 11–12. Later legend: Maenchen-Helfen, *Huns*, 141; Joaquín Martínez Pizarro, *Writing Ravenna: The* Liber pontificalis *of Andreas Agnellus* (Ann Arbor, 1998), 117.

envoy was a reflection of the authors' milieu; they stressed those deeds of their bishop which currently earned great social capital. This facet of the saints, more directly comparable with Sidonius' Avitus than with the well-established hagiographic types of Anthony or Martin of Tours, is a careful literary construct. It need not be unfactual, but it is none the less a product of conscious selection, which exploits the secular prestige of participation in embassies between provincial communities and centres of government.

The dates of neither Germanus' episcopate nor the composition of his *Vita* are certain.[7] Traditionally, Germanus' tenure as bishop has been assigned to 418–48, but (as the round figure of a thirty-year episcopate intimates) the evidence is tenuous, and alternative dates as early as 437 have been proposed for his death, though on no firmer grounds.[8] The period of composition is equally uncertain. The only relevent evidence is provided by two letters, which precede the *Vita* in the manuscript tradition, addressed by Constantius to the current bishops of Lyons and Auxerre; but the dates of the bishops' episcopates are unknown. Both were correspondents of Sidonius Apollinaris in the 470s.[9]

[7] For editions, see 'Note on editions, commentaries, and translations' below. On Germanus, Constantius, and the *Vita*: Wilhelm Levison, 'Bischof Germanus von Auxerre und die Quellen zu seiner Geschichte', *Neues Archiv* 29 (1903), 97–175; Levison Introduction to *Vita Germani*, 225–46; L. Duchesne, *Fastes épiscopaux de l'ancienne Gaule* II: *L'Aquitaine et les Lyonnaises* (Paris, 1910), 430–52, esp. 445; *Saint Germain d'Auxerre et son temps* (Auxerre, 1950), esp. Gustave Bardy, 'Constance de Lyon, biographe de saint Germain d'Auxerre', 89–108; Nora K. Chadwick, *Poetry and Letters in Early Christian Gaul* (London, 1955), 240–74; Paul Grosjean, 'Notes d'hagiographie celtique 27–29', *AB* 75 (1957), 158–85; Borius, Introduction to *Vie de Germain*; E. Griffe, 'L'hagiographie gauloise au Ve siècle: la *Vie de saint Germain d'Auxerre*', *Bulletin de Littérature Ecclésiastique* 66 (1965), 289–94; Griffe, *La Gaule chrétienne a l'époque romaine* II: *L'Eglise des Gaules au Ve siècle*, 2nd edn (Paris, 1966), 289–301; Wilhelm Gessel, 'Germanus von Auxerre (um 378 bis 448): die *Vita* des Konstantius von Lyon als homiletische Paränese in hagiographischer Form', *Römische Quartelschrift für Christliche Altertumskunde und Kirchengeschichte* 65 (1970), 1–13; *PLRE* II, 'Germanus 1', 504–5; R. Mathisen, 'The Last Year of Saint Germanus of Auxerre', *AB* 99 (1981), 151–9; Martin Heinzelmann, 'Neue Aspekte der hagiographischen Literatur', *Francia* 1 (1973), 27–44; Heinnzelmann, 'Gallische Prosopographie, 260–527', *Francia* 10 (1982), 615–16; E. A. Thompson, *Saint Germanus of Auxerre and the End of Roman Britain* (Studies in Celtic History 6; Woodbridge, Suffolk, 1984); Ian Wood, 'The End of Roman Britain: Continental Evidence and Parallels', in M. Lapidge and D. Dumville (eds.), *Gildas: New Approaches* (Studies in Celtic History 5; Woodbridge, Suffolk, 1984), 8–17; Arne Søby Christensen, 'The *Vita* of Saint Germanus of Auxerre and Fifth-Century History', *Studies in Ancient History and Numismatics Presented to Rudi Thomsen* (Aarhus, 1988), 224–31.

On the chronology of the *Vita*: see Appendix 1.

[8] The dates 418–48 appear in most reference works, e.g. *PLRE* II, 'Acolius 2', 6; Martin Heinzelmann, 'Gallische Prosopographie, 260–527', *Francia* 10 (1982), 615–16. On the dates of Germanus' episcopate: see Appendix 1.

[9] Constantius, *Epp.* to Patiens and Censurius. Dates: see Appendix 1.

Little certain is known about the author. He is usually identified with a correspondent of Sidonius Apollinaris and dedicatee of eight out of his nine books of letters, possibly Sidonius' former teacher in rhetoric, and said to be a priest from Lyons. Each element of this description is speculative.[10] Sidonius never explicitly refers to *Vita Germani*, though possibly he alludes once to the work.[11] None the less, it is safe to picture Constantius in the same circle as Sidonius; the dedicatees of *Vita Germani* were correspondents of Sidonius; Constantius' style, though far more limpid than Sidonius', reflects the same preciosity; and *Vita Germani* shares motifs with certain of Sidonius' letters and especially his *Panegyric* on Avitus.

[10] Description: e.g. T. Mommsen, 'Index personarum' to Sid. Ap., *Epistulae et carmina*, MGH AA 8, 423; Bardy, 'Constance', 89; Borius, Introduction to *Vie de Germain*, 13–16; *PLRE* II, 'Constantius 10', 320. Cf. Levison, Introduction to *Vita Germani*, 230 n. 8; Thompson, *Saint Germanus*, 78–9.

Sidonius' Constantius: Sid. Ap., *Epp.* I, 1; III, 18; VII, 18; VIII, 16; IX, 16.1 (dedications and invitation to correction). Priest of Lyons: based on the sole poetic composition of Constantius mentioned by Sidonius, a set of verses written to be inscribed on the walls of a basilica newly built in Lyons (Sidonius mentions this in the context of passing on to a friend his own verses for the same church); Sid. Ap., *Ep.* II, 10.3; and Sidonius' reference to Constantius' 'continual reading of sacred literature' and description as 'venerable in your faith'; Sid. Ap., *Epp.* VII, 18.4; III, 2.3. This is insufficient proof of Constantius' position, for the following reasons:

Sidonius never alludes to any clerical office occupied by Constantius; the lack of such detail is striking in the panegyrical letter Sidonius wrote to Constantius after the latter travelled to Clermont to help resolve civic discord in the town; Sid. Ap., *Ep.* III, 2 (the closest is the description of Constantius as *nobilitate sublimis religione venerabilis*, III, 2.3). Constantius' reading and composition of Christian literature need not mark him as ordained; laity as well as clergy read sacred literature (e.g. Sid. Ap., *Epp.* II, 9.4; IV, 9.3; Sulpicius Severus, author of the *Vita* of St Martin of Tours, was a layman). The basilica in Lyons featured verses written by three poets, Constantius, Sidonius, and one Secundinus, of whom the latter two at least were at the time laymen; Constantius may well have been also (Harries, *Sidonius Apollinaris*, 112, 115–17; *PLRE* II, 'Secundinus 3', 985; Heinzelmann, 'Gallische Prosopographie', Secundinus 2, 690). The verses for the basilica do not localise Constantius in Lyons; cf. poetic works written for the cult of St Martin by poets who were not resident in Tours (Sidonius, who also wrote verses for inscription in the Tours basilica of St Martin as a layman; Paulinus Petricordus, possibly from Aquitania, who set Sulpicius' *Vita Martini* to verse). Fifth-century lay poets wrote to support the flourishing cults of certain Gallic saints without necessarily living in the town hosting the cult.

Identification of the two Constantii: the name was common (eighteen Constantii in *PLRE* II, plus two cases of 'Constantius' standing other than in the final position of a name; four Gallic Constantii in Heinzelmann, 'Gallische Prosopographie' (all in *PLRE* II); five Constantii in André Mandouze, *Prosopographie chrétienne du bas-empire*, I: *Prosopographie de l'Afrique chrétienne (303–533)* (Paris, 1982) (none in *PLRE* II); cf. Bardy, 'Constance', 89–90, dismissing other known Gallic Constantii as possible authors of *Vita Germani*). To be sure, the Latinity of the hagiographer is such as would warrant the deference of Sidonius to his friend (Sid. Ap., *Epp.* I, 1.1; IX, 16.1; for appreciations of Constantius' Latinity: Levison, Introduction to Constantius, *Vita Germani*, 231; Bardy, 'Constance', 98–9; Borius, Introduction to *Vie de Germain*, 23–4, 60–1). The identification is at best a comfortable hypothesis; even if correct, we know less than is often assumed about Sidonius' friend.

[11] See Appendix 1.

Vita Germani has a very clear structure. Two dedicatory letters precede the work in the manuscript tradition; the *Vita* itself comprises three unequal parts. It begins with a short preface, followed by a brief account of Germanus' youth, ordination, and episcopacy. The following account of five miracles forms a distinct second section.[12] The main part of the *Vita* is the narrative of five journeys undertaken by Germanus, including many miracles and incidents which occur *en route*, culminating in the bishop's death in Italy and the return of his body to Auxerre. The structure of the *Vita* is tabulated below:[13]

I	Two letters of Constantius, to Patiens bishop of Lyons and Censurius bishop of Auxerre, which describe Patiens' commission to Constantius to write the work and Censurius' publication of it.	
II	Conventional modesty topos.	Preface
III	The youth, civil career, and episcopal ordination of Germanus; his personal asceticism; foundation of a monastery across the river Yonne from the main town of Auxerre.	1–6
IV	Miracles performed by Germanus, not set in chronological context.	7–11
V	(Voyage 1). Germanus' first voyage to Britain, with Bishop Lupus [of Troyes], to repress Pelagianism; they are chosen by a synod of Gallic bishops. After defeating the Pelagian bishops in public debate, Germanus visits the shrine of St Alban and helps the Britons defeat raiding Picts and Saxons in the 'Alleluia victory'.	12–18
VI	(Voyage 2). Germanus' journey to the praetorian prefect of Gaul Auxiliaris in Arles, to seek relief for Auxerre from new taxation.	19–24
VII	(Voyage 3). Germanus' second trip to Britain, with Bishop Severus [identified by Bede, *HE* I, 21 as bishop of Trier; but cf. Levison, 'Bischof Germanus von Auxerre', 129], again to repress Pelagians.	25–7
VIII	(Voyage 4). Germanus travels to confront the Alan leader Goar, commissioned by the *magister utriusque militiae* Aetius to inflict reprisals for rebellion in Armorica.	28

[12] Wood, 'End of Roman Britain', 9 insightfully interprets these five miracles as moving schematically between different spheres: the official, the communal, the monastic, the supernatural, and the animal. The miracle stories contain some elements which will become prominent features of the longer embassy-narratives: Germanus' association with senior imperial officials (Constantius, *Vita Germani*, 7: Ianuarius, *princeps praesidalis . . . officii*; not in *PLRE* II) and travels (*ibid.*, 10–11).

[13] Cf. Borius, Introduction to *Vie de Germain*, 40–2. Numbering on right is Levison's; section chapter headings in Roman numerals on left are my own, for convenience of reference.

IX (Voyage 5). In order to confirm the settlement reached with Goar, Germanus journeys to the imperial court of Valentinian III at Ravenna. 29–40

X Death of Germanus in Ravenna; preparations for the funeral cortège; return of the body to Auxerre. 41–6

XI Epilogue.

Constantius' narrative has several prominent features to which attention should be drawn. First, the greater part of the *Vita*, recounting the bishop's five journeys, is striking for its flowing narrative sequence, very different from the thematically structured forms of earlier hagiography, in which narrative is largely episodic. A range of techniques achieves this flow. The journeys are not timeless; the sequence of one after the other is made plain. There are causal relationships between individual voyages: Germanus' success during the first trip to Britain prompts his selection to undertake the second; the embassy to the Alan leader Goar necessitates the journey to the imperial court.[14] Situations and characters recur from one journey to another, and contrasts between the different journeys are drawn.[15] Journeys are described, however briefly, from inception to return; the bishop's routes from Auxerre to Arles and from Auxerre to Ravenna can be mapped, because of the many localised incidents which occur *en route*.[16] Most of these incidents – which, indeed, constitute the bulk of the embassy narratives – consist of miracles and other deeds of piety performed by Germanus *en route*. Many of the miracles are modelled directly on Sulpicius Severus' *Vita* of Martin of Tours; but, unlike the incidents there or in earlier fourth- or early fifth-century hagiography, the miracle accounts are not presented timelessly or linked to each other thematically.[17] They are firmly made part of the embassy narratives, occurring at particular stages during Germanus' travel. Some are incidents specific to travelling, such as the miraculous return of the bishop's stolen horse, or his humble assistance to an old man at a river crossing in the Italian Alps.[18] Others are directly related to the outcome of the missions. A recurring motif, derived from the Gospels, is Germanus' healing of

[14] Constantius, *Vita Germani*, 25, 28.

[15] Recurrences: the two debates with the British Pelagians; Germanus' friend Senator; Constantius, *Vita Germani*, 14, 27; 22, 29. Contrasts: Constantius, *Vita Germani*, 30: *Erat iter illius comitatu proprio solitarium*, a reference back to his companions on the trips to Britain, Lupus and Severus.

[16] Borius, Appendices to *Vie de Germain*, 212.

[17] Earlier hagiography: alongside Latin compositions such as Sulpicius' *Vita Martini* and Paulinus' *Vita Ambrosii*, a large number of Latin translations of earlier eastern saintly biographies and *sententia* circulated in the West, which should be understood as forming the generic context for new western works; many of these translations were assembled together and augmented in the sixth-century collection known as *Vitae patrum*; *PL* 73; *Lexikon des Mittelalters* VIII (Munich, 1997), 1765–6.

[18] Constantius, *Vita Germani*, 20, 31.

members of senior officials' households; some of these cures precipitate the successful conclusion of Germanus' missions.[19] Like other late antique saints' lives, each of these incidents vividly demonstrates the working of divine power in the world.[20] But each miracle account could have been related in isolation, without a narrative framework, and its didactic value perhaps enhanced by being presented in an isolated tableau, as Sulpicius Severus and many other hagiographers chose. Constantius provides *Vita Germani* with an unusually strong context for the individual tableaux it presents, through his strongly articulated narrative sequence.

A second aspect of Constantius' narrative is the sense of urgency which arises from this sequence. Constantius specifies not only that each voyage occurs after the preceding account, but that it occurs *immediately* afterwards. Each new journey is introduced with a time-indicator phrase which, while providing no details to establish an absolute chronology for the events of Germanus' episcopate, creates an internal progression.[21] When Germanus returns from his first voyage to Britain, he meets the 'anticipation' of the populace of Auxerre, already waiting to ask him to travel to Arles; the resurgence of the Pelagian bishops in Britain 'at the same time' as Germanus is in Arles prompts his second mission to Britain; 'barely had he returned' from this trip when 'already' the Armorican legation seeks his aid against Goar; and, after halting the assault on Armorica, he 'straightaway' sets out for the imperial court in Italy.[22] By thus compressing the events of Germanus' life – artificially[23] – Constantius creates a sense of urgency and haste, which provides an underlying timbre to the individual embassy narratives and their events. This tension is central to the image of Germanus developed by Constantius.

[19] Constantius, *Vita Germani*, 15 (first trip to Britain: daughter of a *vir tribuniciae potestatis*); 24 (Arles: wife of the praetorian prefect of Gaul Auxiliaris); 26–7 (second trip to Britain: son of Elafus, *quidam regionis illius primus*). Germanus cures household members of other men of rank during his ultimately unsuccessful embassy to Ravenna; 33–4 (*en route* from Milan to Ravenna: entire *familia* of the *vir spectabilis* Leporius); 38 (Ravenna: son of Volusianus, *patricii Segisvulti cancellis praeerat*); 39 (son of Acolus, *praepositus regalis cubiculi*). New Testament models for miraculous healings of members of eminent households: John IV.46–54 (nobleman's son); Matt. VIII.5–13, Luke VII.1–10 (centurion's servant); Matt. IX.18–26, Mark V.22–42, Luke VIII.41–56 (priest's daughter).

[20] Gessel, 'Die *Vita* des Konstantius als homiletische Paränese', 9–11.

[21] Lack of absolute chronology: Bardy, 'Constance', 107: 'une imprécision désespérante'. But Bardy uses the Bollandists' text, which obscures Constantius' structure; he also presupposes a New Testament model of 'relative chronology' (cf. Marc van Uytfanghe, 'Heiligenverehrung II', *Reallexikon für Antike und Christentum* 14 (1988), 164). The 'formules de transition' he cites do not include any of the connective phrases between journeys (see next note).

[22] Constantius, *Vita Germani*, 19 (return from Britain: *expectatio propriae civitatis*); 25 (resurgence of Pelagianism in Britain *interea* Germanus is in Arles); 28 (Armoricans seek Germanus' aid *vixdum domum de transmarina expeditione remeauerat, et iam . . . legatio . . . fatigationem . . . antistis ambiebat*); 29 (*exin Italiam petiturus egreditur*). This technique is more emphatic than Sidonius' similarly misleading practice in the *Pan.* on Avitus; above, chapter 3, at nn. 54–5.

[23] See Appendix 1.

A third aspect of Constantius' narrative is its drama: the drama not only of the public performance of miracles, but also of worldly events, skilfully elaborated by Constantius' prose.[24] The repulse of the Picts and Saxons in the 'Alleluia victory' well displays Constantius' talent for narrative, but perhaps the best piece of dramatic narrative from the fifth-century West is Germanus' bold confrontation with the Alan war-leader Goar:

> Barely had he returned from his overseas expedition, and already an embassy from the Armorican tract sought out the weariness of the blessed bishop. For the magnificent Aetius, who then ruled public affairs, was offended by the insolence of that proud region, and had committed it to be overthrown, in punishment for its rebellious presumption, by Goar, the most fierce king of the Alans, who lusted after it with barbarian greed. And so, against a bellicose tribe and an idol-worshipping king, was opposed an old man, alone; yet by Christ's aid, greater and stronger than all.
>
> Without delay he hastily set out, since the weapons of war were at hand. Already the tribe had advanced, and iron-clad horsemen filled the whole route, yet our priest was borne along his way until he reached the king himself whom he pursued. He met him already advancing on his journey, and stood before the armed general amongst the throngs of his followers. Through an interpreter, he first poured forth a prayer of supplication; next, he rebuked the one who rejected him; finally, thrusting forth his hand, he seized the reins of the bridle, and thus brought to a halt the entire army.[25]

Here and elsewhere, Constantius skilfully injects a sense of escalating drama absent from earlier saintly biography.[26]

A final aspect of Constantius' narrative is the image of Germanus. The bishop, while in many respects presented within the stiff imagery of hagiographic convention, personifies consensus. Germanus' requests are won – or lost – by unanimity: the praetorian prefect of Gaul Auxiliaris 'sought from the most blessed man that he should deign to accept what he was about to ask for'; even with Goar, once his attention has been caught, 'the weapons of war and the clamour of arms gave place to the

[24] Drama of public miracles: Peter Brown, *The Cult of the Saints: Its Rise and Function in Latin Christianity* (Chicago, 1981).

[25] Constantius, *Vita Germani*, 28: *vixdum domum de transmarina expeditione remeauerat, et iam legatio Armoricani tractus fatigationem beati antistitis ambiebat. Offensus enim superbae insolentia regionis vir magnificus Aetius qui tum rem publicam gubernabat Goari ferocissimo Alanorum regi loca illa inclinanda pro rebellionis praesumptioe permiserat, quae ille aviditate barbaricae cupiditatis inhiauerat. Itaque genti bellicossimae regique idolorum ministro obicitur senex unus sed tamen omnibus Christi praesidio maior et fortior. Nec mora festinus egreditur, quia imminebat bellicus apparatus. Iam progressa gens fuerat totumque iter eques ferratus impleuerat, et tamen sacerdos noster obvius ferebatur donec ad regem ipsum qui sequebatur accederet. Occurrit in itinere, iam progresso, et armato duci inter suorum catervas opponitur, medioque interprete primum precem supplicem fundit, deinde increpat differentem, ad extremum manu iniecta, freni habenas invadit atque in eo universum sistit exercitum.*

[26] Borius, Introduction to *Vie de Germain*, 22–3, 38–42, 63.

civilised behaviour of counsel'; while, in Ravenna, Germanus acquiesces in the imperial decision ultimately to punish the rebellious Armoricans without apparent protest.[27] Yet Constantius drew heavily from models which presented a very different archetype of the bishop as prophet, railing against worldly rulers.

For all his borrowings from earlier works, Constantius' narrative structure and its related portrait of Germanus is without real precedent in late antique hagiography. To be sure, both the undertaking of intercessions and a saint's association with powerful worldly figures were early features of hagiography; St Anthony himself corresponded with the emperor Constantine and his sons, the *caesares* Constantius and Constans, albeit reluctantly.[28] *Vita Germani* is often viewed in the context of the western tradition of bishops' *Vitae*, and regarded as closely adhering to the influential antecedents of the *Vitae* of Martin of Tours by Sulpicius Severus, and of Ambrose of Milan by Paulinus.[29] Constantius' debt to the miracle-narratives of *Vita Martini* is clear, and it is probable that he used elements of *Vita Ambrosi*. In their *Vitae*, Martin and Ambrose confront secular authorities, but, while these scenes are striking, they serve a different narrative function from embassy scenes in *Vita Germani*.

Appeals by Martin to secular authority are mentioned in only one scene of *Vita Martini*, describing relations between the bishop of Tours and the imperial usurper Magnus Maximus. The purpose and persons concerned in the appeals are not specified; most of the section concerns a meal which Martin reluctantly attends at Maximus' request.[30] Structurally, *Vita Martini* and *Vita Germani* are dissimilar. *Vita Germani* is constructed with prolonged narrative sequences, whereas *Vita Martini* comprises clusters of episodes with strong thematic links, underscoring Martin's spiritual and thaumaturgical prowess. The 'action' of any one

27 Auxiliaris: Constantius, *Vita Germani*, 24 (*ambiuitque a beatissimo viro ut dignaretur accipere quod querebat*; cf. *ibid., fin.*: *acceptis itaque ex voluntate beneficiis*); 28 (*apparatus bellicus armorumque commotio ad consilii civilitatem, deposito tumore, descendit*); Armoricans: 40 (*intercessio sacerdotis evanuit*).

28 Athanasius, *Vie d'Antoine*, ed. and trans. G. J. M. Bartelink (Sources chrétiennes 400; Paris, 1994), 81; see also 48, 57, 61, 86 for senior civil and military magistrates (on the authorship of the *Life* of Anthony: T. D. Barnes, 'Angel of Light or Mystic Initiate? The Problem of the *Life of Anthony*', *Journal of Theological Studies* n.s. 37 (1986), 353–69). Powerful worldly figures and intercessions: among many analogues (including scenes in the *vitae* of Martin, Ambrose, and Severinus, discussed below), cf. the very prominent role of the emperor Leo I and other court figures throughout the *Life of St. Daniel the Stylite*, in *Three Byzantine Saints*, trans. Elizabeth Dawes and Norman H. Baynes (New York, 1948); and note the passing reference in *Vies des Pères du Jura* [*Vita Lupicini*], ed. F. Martine (Sources chrétiennes 142; Paris, 1988), 63, to intercessions undertaken by the abbots of Condat to the court of the Burgundian kings (dramatised at 92–5; cf. 96–110).

29 E.g. Borius, Introduction to *Vie de Germain*, 31–8, 42–3, 65; Heinzelmann, 'Neue Aspekte', 35–44; Stancliffe, *St. Martin and his Hagiographer*, 90–1; Berschin, *Biographie und Epochenstil* I.

30 Sulpicius Severus, *Vie de saint Martin*, ed. Jacques Fontaine, 3 vols. (Sources chrétienne 133–5; Paris, 1967), I, XX, 1–9.

scene is isolated; its links with preceding or following scenes are anagogical, not causal or chronological.[31] There are no verbal echoes or uses of motifs from the scene of Martin and Magnus Maximus in *Vita Germani*, though Constantius had read Sulpicius' work and drew heavily from other sections of it, and later Latin hagiographers would combine motifs from this scene with elements of Germanus' *Vita* when composing their own narratives.[32] More significantly, the imagery and purpose of Sulpicius' account differ radically from embassy scenes in *Vita Germani*. Sulpicius presents Martin as an Old Testament prophet. His meetings with the emperor are 'affrontements publics', during which the bishop berates the emperor for his sins in taking the throne by violence, and denounces the 'adulation' of other bishops attending the emperor's court: 'if it was necessary for [Martin] to appeal to the emperor on others' behalf, he commanded rather than requested, and, though frequently asked, he abstained from [Maximus'] feasts, saying that he could not be a fellow of the table of one who had expelled one emperor from his realm, the other from his life'.[33] The following narrative, in which Martin ultimately agrees to attend Maximus' *convivium*, focuses on Martin's charged gesture in passing a goblet, given to him at the command of the emperor, not to Maximus but to his own priest, 'judging that no-one was more worthy to drink after himself, and that it would compromise his integrity were he to prefer over his priest either the emperor himself or those near him'.[34] This 'témérité spectaculaire . . . gratuit et . . . pittoresque' is far from Constantius' portrait of the winning eloquence of Germanus' gracious supplications and his consensual successes.[35] So too are the scenes of Martin's meetings with emperors in Sulpicius' *Dialogi*, a later companion to *Vita Martini*: Martin

[31] Fontaine, Introduction to Sulpicius Severus, *Vie de saint Martin* I, 59–96, 244–5; Stancliffe, *St Martin and his Hagiographer*, 86–7.

[32] Constantius' use of Sulpicius: Levison, 'Bischof Germanus von Auxerre', 114–17; Levison, Introduction to Constantius, *Vita Germani*, 231 and nn. at 248 n. 1; 249 n. 4; 253 n. 2; 254 n. 2; 255 nn. 3, 5; 256 n. 2; 257 n. 2; 258 n. 1; 264 n. 1; 267 n. 2; 268 n. 2; 273 n. 1 (bis); 279 n. 1; 282 n. 2; Borius, Introduction to *Vie de Germain*, 31–8, 42, 65 n. 4. The majority of uses of Sulpicius concern imagery or details of Martin as thaumaturge.

Later uses: see below, on *Vita Viviani* and *Vita Orientii*.

[33] Sulpicius, *Vita Martini* xx, 2: *Nam et si pro aliquibus regi supplicandum fuit, imperauit potius quam rogauit, et a conuiuio eius freqenter rogatus abstinuit, dicens se mensae eius participem esse non posse, qui imperatores unum regno, alterum vita expulisset.*

On this scene: J. Fontaine, 'Une clé littéraire de la *Vita Martini* de Sulpice Sévère: la typologie prophétique', *Mélanges offerts à Mademoiselle Christine Mohrmann* (Utrecht, 1963), 84–95, esp. 89–90; Fontaine, 'Hagiographie et politique, de Sulpice Sévère à Venance Fortunat', *Revue d'Histoire de l'Eglise de France* 62 (1976), 118–19 ('affrontements publics'); Fontaine, Introduction to Sulpicius, *Vita Martini* I, 92–5; III, 907–46; Berschin, *Biographie und Epochenstil* I, 204–6.

[34] Sulpicius, *Vita Martini* xx, 6: *Sed Martinum, ubi ebibit, pateram presbytero suo tradidit, nullum scilicet existimans digniorem qui post se prior biberet, nec integrum sibi fore si aut regem ipsum aut eos, qui a rege erant proximi, presbytero praetulisset.*

[35] Quotation from Fontaine, 'Une clé littéraire', 90.

imposes his will on a hostile Valentinian I through divine violence; and, again attending Maximus' court, Martin knows that his *virtus* has diminished after exactly the sort of compromise of his integrity he fears in the *Vita*.[36] Germanus, by contrast, can part amicably even from the barbarian idolater Goar. The benefits of Germanus' voyages for the various communities on whose behalf he acts is made patent; by contrast, *Vita Martini* does not even name those on whose behalf Martin acts (it is in the later *Dialogi* that the followers of Priscillian are named). Sulpicius' *Vita* of Martin did not provide a precedent for either the narrative structure or the imagery of Constantius' work.

Constantius may have used Paulinus of Milan's *Vita Ambrosii*, a work lacking the stylistic skills of Sulpicius' or Constantius' writings, as a model for his brief outline of Germanus' *cursus publicus* prior to his assumption into the clergy.[37] In *Vita Ambrosii*, the bishop confronts the emperors Magnus Maximus, Theodosius I (three times), Valentinian II, and Eugenius.[38] Some of these confrontations arise from embassies during which Ambrose acts on behalf of a second imperial court, or of sections of the Italian populace; others, occurring within Milan, stemmed from Ambrose's assertive interpretation of the duties and authority of his office as bishop of the city. The work has a sense of chronology alien to *Vita Martini*; many episodes are datable, and these are usually placed in chronological order. But this chronology is a function of Ambrose's historical engagement with the imperial court of Milan, not the product of a literary design. Paulinus emphasises Ambrose's involvement in the major imperial events of the 380s and 390s and the influence he claimed to wield over the imperial court on ecclesiastical and secular affairs. In doing so, Paulinus follows Ambrose's lead in his own writings, which Paulinus frequently uses and often cites.[39] The chronology of *Vita Ambrosii* is not an 'internal' sequence, constructed by the hagiographer to give form to his narrative. How much time elapses between, for example, Ambrose's embassy to Magnus Maximus and his confrontation with Theodosius I over the destruction of the synagogue of Callinicum would be unknowable were these events not dated from other sources. *Vita Ambrosii* is not unlike

[36] Sulpicius Severus, *Dialogi* II, 5 (Valentinian I); III, 11–13 (Maximus).

[37] Levison, nn. to Constantius, *Vita Germani*, 251–2 n. 5; Borius, Introduction to *Vie de Germain*, 33–5. Doubts: Chadwick, *Poetry and Letters*, 265. On *Vita Ambrosii*: Emilien Lamirande, *Paulin de Milan et la* Vita Ambrosii: *aspects de la religion sous le Bas-Empire* (Montreal, 1983).

[38] Paulinus, *Vita Ambrosii*, *PL* 14, cc. 19, 22–4, 26, 31.

[39] Neil McLynn, *Ambrose of Milan: Church and Court in a Christian Capital* (The Transformation of the Classical Heritage 22; Berkeley, 1994), esp. xvii, 371–2. On Ambrose's embassies (to Magnus Maximus on behalf of Valentinian II, and to Theodosius I on behalf of the supporters of Eugenius after the latter's death): *ibid.*, 160–3, 354.

a selective *breviarium* of western imperial history during two busy decades, a summary of those major events in which the bishop of the main western imperial residence participated. The sequential narrative of *Vita Germani*, by contrast, is focused exclusively on Germanus himself; the failure of all attempts to establish a chronology for Germanus' episcopate proceeds precisely from the want of reference to datable historical events. Paulinus' presentation of the aristocratic Ambrose, while not the same as Sulpicius' portrait of the eremitical Martin, is very different from Constantius' Germanus. Martin's meetings with Magnus Maximus present him as an Old Testament prophet confronting satanic forces; Ambrose, who sought to cast himself as the prophet Nathan to the emperor Theodosius' David, claimed *victoriae* over the four emperors whom he confronted.[40] Not surprisingly, there are no verbal echoes of the confrontation scenes of *Vita Ambrosii* in *Vita Germani*.

The narrative structure chosen by Constantius, new to western hagiography, was not merely a means to organise his material. Its importance has been only obliquely recognised in modern scholarship. *Vita Germani*, though providing rather little in the way of useful historical data, has been regarded as an important text for understanding the fifth-century West, partly because it features two ill-attested regions, post-Roman Britain and Armorica, as dramatic settings, and important personages, including the *augusta* Galla Placidia, as characters. In particular, the *Vita* holds an important place in British historical writing since Bede.[41] But the work's agreeable narrative sequence is also an important part of the modern appeal of *Vita Germani*: Constantius' style creates the illusion of historicity.[42] Constantius, however, does not strive for mimesis. His firm structure is

[40] Paulinus, *Vita Ambrosii*, 24: *cuius* [*sc.* Theodosius I] *correctionis profectus secundam paravit victoriam*. Berschin, *Biographie und Epochenstil* I, 218; McLynn, *Ambrose*, 291–360.

[41] Bede, *HE* I, 17–21; on his use of *Vita Germani*: Robert W. Hanning, *The Vision of History in Early Britain: From Gildas to Geoffrey of Monmouth* (New York, 1966), 77–8, 83; Goffart, *Narrators of Barbarian History*, 302–3; Jacques Elfassi, 'Germain d'Auxerre, figure d'Augustin de Cantorbéry: la réécriture par Bède de la *Vie de saint Germain d'Auxerre*', *Hagiographica* 5 (1998), 37–47. Modern exploitation: e.g. Peter Salway, *Roman Britain* (Oxford, 1981), 462–9, 479–80.

Limited historical data: Levison, 'Bischof Germanus', 118. Most twentieth-century articles on *Vita Germani* have been concerned with dating the text, rather than with extracting information from the work. Cf. Christensen, 'Germanus and Fifth-Century History', 224–7.

[42] Chadwick, *Poetry and Letters*, 254: 'The admirable narrative style of Constantius still today succeeds in imposing this fantastic story [the 'Alleluia victory'] on our sober historians.' Cf. Borius, Introduction to *Vie de Germain*, 42–3: 'il y a un Constance historien qui se manifeste dans la *Vita Germani*, et qui ne doit rien aux œuvres de ses prédécesseurs . . . son originalité apparaît déjà dans son souci de composition selon un plan cohérent, et dans son goût pour la belle *narratio*' (cf. *ibid.*, 63–4, defending the credibility of Constantius' narrative: 'le prêtre lyonnais était un homme estimé et respecté, sa culture certaine, son autorité reconnue, et il n'y a pas de raison majeure de suspecter a priori sa bonne foi').

one vehicle among several for the construction of central literary elements of his work, notably the *persona* of Germanus.

Late antique hagiography, though generally offering little in the way of characterisation of subjects, does present firmly delineated *personae*, largely idealised and static, expressed through the actions and 'patterned lives' of its subjects.[43] Severe ascesis, prophetic candour, miraculous powers, authority, and respect are dominant characteristics of such portraits. Though lacking the abrasive outspokenness of biblical prophets, the *persona* of Germanus exhibits these other conventional elements. If any of these qualities has a claim to historical verisimilitude, it is ascesis. It is likely that Germanus was associated with the monastic movement of southern Gaul which radiated out from Lérins and Marseilles. This is suggested by his establishment of a monastery adjacent to Auxerre, and perhaps by his connection with Hilary of Arles. The only contemporary attestation of Germanus, a brief entry in *Chronica Gallica* of 452, praises his miracles and 'the strictness of his life'.[44] But ascesis is not a major theme of *Vita Germani*. A short section of the early part of the work describes how Germanus 'preserved the desert while engaged with the world'; there are a few later references to his modesty.[45] Germanus the thaumaturge is a far more dominant image, very closely adhering to the pattern provided by Sulpicius Severus; many of Germanus' miracles are directly modelled on those of Martin in *Vita Martini* and *Dialogi*.

One major aspect of the *persona* of Germanus in the *Vita* is less conventional than ascesis or miracle-working. Constantius presents Germanus as a hero in a classical sense, a leader who performs strenuous deeds on behalf of his community. This image is cultivated through a range of techniques, including the exploitation of the narrative structure of the *Vita*. At the simplest level is vocabulary. Germanus is twice described as a *heros*, a term

43 Two partial exceptions to the undifferentiated presentation of saints are Possidius' occasionally intimate portrait of Augustine (*Vita Augustini*, *PL* 32, 33–66), and the *Vita Fulgentii* of Ruspe (*PL* 65, 117–50), which exhibits an unusual degree of individual psychological development. Quotation: Elissa R. Henken, *The Welsh Saints: A Study in Patterned Lives* (Cambridge, 1991).

44 Germanus and Lérins: Gessel, 'Die *Vita* des Konstantius als homiletische Paränese', 8; R. Mathisen, 'Hilarius, Germanus, and Lupus: The Aristocratic Background of the Cheldonius Affair', *Phoenix* 33 (1979), 160–9, with Wood, 'End of Roman Britain', 15 (on the limited value of *Vita Hilarii*). Hilary of Arles: Constantius, *Vita Germani*, 23. *Chron. Gall. 452*, s.a. 433: *Germanus episcopus Altisiodori virtutibus et vitae districtione clarescit*. Some eighth-century authors believed Germanus was a monk of Lérins: Levison, 'Bischof Germanus von Auxerre', 150.

45 Ascesis: Constantius, *Vita Germani*, 3–4, 6 (*heremum in saeculi conversatione servavit*). Modesty: 5 (washes feet of guests); 19 (content with a small company for journey to Arles); 21, 31, 32, 35 (attempts to keep his actions anonymous); 33 (charity); 38 (embarrassed at being asked to perform miracle). *Vita Germani*, 3–4, 6 loosely parallels Sulpicius, *Vita Martini*, 10, as an account of the ascetic practices of the bishop and his monks, following the subject's episcopal election. Gessel, 'Die *Vita* des Konstantius als homiletische Paränese', 7–9.

in itself not unusual as a Christian epithet in late antiquity.[46] He is also referred to several times as *dux*, a term with resonances of the commonplace imagery of *miles Christi*.[47] More specific to Constantius' description of Germanus are the terms used to describe the bishop's deeds. Germanus performs many *labores*: 'it sufficed for him that he should never be free from labour to enjoy peace'.[48] Other than *virtus*, 'miracle', the characteristic terms associated with Germanus' actions are *labor* and its synonyms, *discrimina* and *necessitas*.[49] These terms, mostly clustered at the outsets of Germanus' travels, are specifically identified with his voyages, and repeatedly set in opposition to the *quies et requies*, 'peace and rest', from which Germanus is kept by the constant flow of petitions for his aid.[50] Constantius' narrative structure, with its succession of scenes of Germanus undertaking one journey after another, contributes to the building-up of this aspect of Germanus' *persona*, and is reflected in the author's descriptive language. Just as the bishop's five voyages follow immediately one after the other, so too Germanus undertakes each journey as soon as it is enjoined upon him: his labours are shouldered *festinus*, *promptius*, with

46 *Heros*: Constantius, *Vita Germani*, 12 (Germanus and Lupus are *eroes devotissimi*), 42 (*eroas*). For this orthography: *ThLL* VI, 2661; for other Christian usages: *ibid.*, 2663. Wolfgang Speyer, 'Heros', *Reallexikon für Antike und Christentum* 14 (1988), 875.

47 *Dux*: 9, 13, 17 *ter*. *Dux* is also used of Christ: *ibid.*, 13; cf. 17: *Christus militabat in castris*; and of Goar: 28. Cf. 2 (*deseritur mundi militia, caelestis adsumitur*), 18 (the British army is *miles religiosus*). *Miles Christi*: A. Harnack, Militia Christi: *The Christian Religion and the Military in the First Three Centuries*, trans. I. M. Gracie (Philadelphia, 1981), chap. 1, 27–64; in fourth-century hagiography. e.g. Sulpicius, *Vita Martini* IV, 3. In *Vita Germani*: Chadwick, *Poetry and Letters*, 263–5.

Constantius, *Vita Germani*, 1, states that the apex of Germanus' secular career was *ducatus culmen et regimen per provincias*. This has been variously accepted as evidence of a military post, the *dux tractus Armoricani et Nervicani*, attesting an unusual civilian, military, and ecclesiastical career (e.g. Chadwick, *Poetry and Letters*, 257; *PLRE* II, 'Germanus 1', 504–5); as an error (Levison, 'Bischof Germanus von Auxerre', 117; Levison, Introduction to Constantius, *Vita Germani*, 231, 251–2 n. 5; cf. Griffe, 'La *Vie de saint Germain d'Auxerre*', 289–94); or as a carry-over from a parallel section of *Vita Ambrosii* (J. Gaudemet, 'La carrière civile de saint Germain', in *Saint Germain d'Auxerre et son temps*, 114–16; Borius, Introduction to *Vie de Germain*, 34–5). The problem remains intractable, but it should be noted that the passage serves a literary purpose. In the lines immediately following the reference to his *ducatus*, each element of Germanus' prior secular life is assigned a divinely planned purpose preparing him for episcopal office: 'He was instructed, by the secret design of God, so that he should want nothing to perfect him in his imminent, apostolic priesthood. His eloquence was in preparation for preaching, his knowledge of law for justice, and the company of his wife as proof of his chastity' (Constantius, *Vita Germani*, 1). The only exception is the most important, the *ducatus*, implying that the *ducatus* is preparation for the episcopate itself.

48 Constantius, *Vita Germani*: *cui* [*sc. Germano*] *id solum sufficeret, ne umquam labore vacuus quiete frueretur*.

49 *Virtus*: Borius, 'Index de quelques mots latins', in *Vie de Germain*, 220. *Labor* (not in Borius' index, nor Levison, 'Lexica et grammatica', MGH SRM 7): 12 (*labroriosior necessitas*), 16, 19, 25, 29, 42. *Discrimina, necessitas*: 12, 19, 40.

50 Constantius, *Vita Germani*, 16 (*itineris labor*). *Quies et requies*: 19, 29. At 32, a possessed member of the congregation in Milan urges Germanus to cease exorcising demons: '*Quiesce, ut nos quieti esse possimus*'; *quiescere* is the opposite of Germanus' working of *virtutes*. Cf. 10, 41 (*quies* as eternal life).

celeritas, nec mora; 'instead of peace and rest . . . after his overseas exertions he entered into the labours of a journey on land'.[51] Both the repetitiveness of the demands for Germanus' advocacy, and his appearance as a traveller, are lightly underscored by one of Constantius' few explicit biblical citations, describing Germanus' journey to Ravenna: 'this alone sufficed for him, that he should never be free from labour to enjoy peace, but, as the prophet says, "he travelled from strength to strength" (Psalms 83 [84] 8)'.[52]

Though Germanus 'delighted in his labours and gladly expended himself for Christ', such exertions prove exhausting: returning from Britian for the second time, he is fatigued, and on the journey to Ravenna he needs to pause for rests.[53] Ultimately Germanus' *labores* kill him, for he dies exhausted after a short illness, 'worn out by his labours'.[54] Constantius employs the image of Germanus constantly undertaking tiring journeys not only to shape his *persona*, but also to prepare the 'climax' of the *Vita*, the saint's death and passage to eternal life:

When, on a certain day, following the solemnity of Matins, a discussion on faith was being held with the other bishops [also in Ravenna], Germanus raised a sad subject, saying, 'Dearest brothers, I commend to you my passing. In my sleep at night, I saw myself, about to sojourn abroad, receiving from our Lord supplies for the journey; and when I asked for the business [*causa*] of my departure, he said, "Fear not. I send you to your homeland, not on a foreign sojourn. There you will have eternal peace and rest." ' The bishops sought another interpretation of the dream, but he more firmly commended to them his end, saying, 'I know well what homeland God promises in reward to his servants.'

Some days later an illness followed; as it grew worse, the whole city was troubled. He who was calling him to glory hastened his passing, and the Lord invited the hero worn out by his labours to his rewards . . . On the seventh day of his illness, his faithful and blessed soul was borne to the heavens.[55]

[51] Constantius, *Vita Germani*: 19 (*pro quiete vel requie . . . post marina discrimina labores terranae expeditionis ingreditur*), 25, 28 (*festinus*), 12 (*promptius, celeritas*), 28 (*nec mora*). On *celeritas* as a panegyrical topos: G. M. Cook (trans.), *Ennodius: Life of St Epiphanius* (Washington, DC, 1942), 174–5.

[52] Constantius, *Vita Germani*, 29: *cui id solum sufficeret, ne umquam labore vacuus quiete frueretur; sed ut propheta ait, ambulabat de virtute in virtutem*. Borius, n. *ad loc.*, cites the Vulgate: *ibunt de virtute in virtutem* (*Biblia sacra iuxta vulgatam versionem*, ed. R. Weber and R. Gryson, 4th edn (Stuttgart, 1994), Psalm 83.8, 876), but several *vetus Latina* versions of the Psalms give *ambulabunt* (*Bibliorum sacrorum Latinae versiones antiquae*, ed. P. Sabatier (Rheims 1743–9; repr. Turnhout, 1983), II, 170, Psalm 84.8).

[53] Constantius, *Vita Germani*, 25: *et laboribus delectatur et Christo se gratanter inpendit*; 28: *fatigatio*; 33: *iter sensim moris felicibus carpit* (cf. 34: *interea gradum accelerant*).

[54] Constantius, *Vita Germani*, 42: *fessus . . . laboribus*.

[55] Constantius, *Vita Germani*, 41–2: (41) *Quadam die, matutinale sollemnitate perfecta, dum cum episcopis sermo de religione confertur, tristissimam protulit mentionem, inquiens: 'Commendo vobis, fratres karissimi, transitum meum. Videbar mihi per nocturnum soporem a Domino nostro viaticum peregrinaturus accipere, et cum causam profectionis inquirerem: "Ne metuas", inquit, "ad patriam, non ad peregrinationem te dirigo, ubi*

At the level of imagery, this passage elevates to a spiritual plane Germanus' constant travels on behalf of various *causae*;[56] and at the level of plot, it brings a conclusion to his travels. The language of dispatch (*viaticum, causa, dirigo, praemia*), of travel (*peregrinor, peregrinatio, transitum*), and of return (*patria, quies et requies*) serves as metaphor for worldly and eternal life, playing on Christian imagery employed in particular by Augustine.[57] Germanus' heroic aspect and his exhausting labours are emphasised in the epithet *fessum eroam laboribus*. Throughout the *Vita*, Germanus' miracles are prominent, but the imagery used in his death-scene indicates that Constantius' central literary conception of Germanus is as a traveller on behalf of the causes of others – an envoy.

Constantius explicitly eulogises Germanus' efficacy in dealing with secular affairs: from his meeting with the praetorian prefect of Gaul, Germanus 'bore back to his own city what had been hoped for'; on his embassy to Goar, 'through the intercession and merits of the priest, the king was constrained, the army recalled, provinces released from devastation'.[58] But the author also works his material in less obvious ways to heighten the image of Germanus as an agent of constant and exhausting travels, including the false impression that Germanus' journeys occurred rapidly one after the other. All of Germanus' missions are presented as commissions – by the synod of Gallic bishops; by the populace of Auxerre; by the Armorican embassy; even by Goar, whose request for imperial confirmation of the understanding reached between the bishop and the king propels Germanus to Ravenna. Germanus is never seen initiating any of his actions. By contrast, neither Martin nor Ambrose is ever depicted in the *Vitae* responding to a request, even when explicitly

habebis quietem et requiem sempiternam." ' Dirivabant intellectu alio somnium sacerdotes; sed ille studiosius commendabat extrema, dicens: 'Bene novi, quam patriam Deus suis famulis repromittet.'

(42) *Factum est, ut post dies aliquot sequeretur incommodum; quo ingravescente, civitas tota turbatur. Accelerabat transitum, qui vocabat ad gloriam, et fessum eroam laboribus Dominus invitat ad praemia . . . Septimo incommodi die ad caelos anima fidelis et beata transfertur.*

Other fifth-century metaphoric uses of *viaticum* are listed in Blaise and Chirat, *Dictionnaire latin–françois des auteurs chrétiens* (Turnhout, 1954), s.v. § 1.

The topos of the saint warned of his impending death by a divine vision or dream appears in other late antique Latin hagiography, e.g. Honoratus Massiliensis, *Vita Hilarii episcopi Arelatensis*, ed. S. Cavallin, *Vitae sanctorum Honorati et Hilarii episcoporum Arelatensium* (Publications of the New Society of Letters at Lund 40; Lund, 1952), 19–20.

56 *Causa* appears in the passage immediately prior to Germanus' vision: Constantius, *Vita Germani*, 40: *Causam sane Armoricanae regionis quae necessitatem peregrinationis* [*sc. ad Ravennam*] *indixerat*. The proximity and collocation with *peregrinatio* indicates that its meaning in c. 41 is semi-technical, 'business' or 'case', not more generally 'cause'.

57 Peter Brown, *Augustine of Hippo: A Biography* (London, 1967), 323–4. Cf. (with caution) R. Van Dam, *Leadership and Community in Late Antique Gaul* (Berkeley, 1985), 145–6 and n. 16.

58 Constantius, *Vita Germani*, 24 (*optatum levamen propriae detulit civitati*), 28 (*per intercessionem et meritum sacerdotis rex compressus est, exercitus revocatus, provinciae vastationibus absolutae*).

undertaking an embassy; they are always portrayed as actively prosecuting causes under their own initiative.[59] Similarly, Pope Leo's function in the embassy to Attila as representative of the emperor Valentinian III and the *senatus populusque Romanus* is omitted by sources later than Prosper. Germanus, however, responds to others' petitions.

Constantius casts his subject as a legate through a further literary ploy. The five journeys served different purposes, yet they are assimilated by Constantius through his selection of vocabulary and narrative technique, creating an artificial homogeneity. During the two voyages to Britain, which formed part of the early fifth-century dispute within the church on Pelagianism, Germanus travelled in order to participate in public *disputationes* (by chance, Germanus' voyage to Britain is the only incident of the *Vita* of which record exists in another source, the *Chronicle* of Prosper[60]). The context is firmly ecclesiastical; though the 'Alleluia victory' introduces an important secular element, this is not part of Germanus' actual mission. Germanus' other three missions continued different traditional patterns of communication. When travelling to Arles to seek tax relief for his *patria* from the senior imperial magistrate of Gaul, Germanus fulfilled a characteristic function of provincial aristocrats in the Roman empire, part of the administrative structure of imperial government.[61] Precedents exist, too, for the more dramatic events of Germanus' involvement in Armorican affairs, in which a leading figure sought to avert imperial punishment of a whole community. The rush of various parties in Antioch to claim responsibility for successfully allaying the wrath of the emperor Theodosius I after the Riot of the Statues in 387 is an indication of the social capital to be gained from such an undertaking.[62] Though the term *legatio* is not used to describe the journeys to either Arles or Ravenna – or indeed to Britain, though ecclesiastic representations were also commonly referred to as *legationes* – the formal context of the trips to imperial centres is indicated by other terminology and by allusions

[59] E.g. Paulinus, *Vita Ambrosii*, cc. 19, 31 (embassies to Magnus Maximus and Theodosius I) contain no reference to Ambrose being approached by the beneficiaries of the embassies, Valentinian II and Roman senators associated with Eugenius respectively.

[60] Prosper, *Chron.*, 1301, usually assumed to refer to Germanus' first journey to Britain, though it could as easily refer to the second. On the differences of the two sources: Levison, Introduction to *Vita Germani*, 227 n. 5; Borius, Introduction to *Vie de Germain*, 79–85; Wood, 'End of Roman Britain', 10; Muhlberger, *Fifth-Century Chroniclers*, 84–5; Christensen, 'Germanus and Fifth-Century History', 228. The only known comparandum for a Gallic bishop travelling to Britain for ecclesiastical controversy is Victricius of Rouen, *De laude sanctorum*, 1 (*PL* 20, 443).

[61] On provincial and imperial administration and embassies seeking tax relief: above, chapter 1, at nn. 67–77.

[62] Libanius, *Selected Works*, trans. A. F. Norman, II (LCL; London, 1977), 237–43; Brown, *Power and Persuasion*, 105–9. The late third-century treatise of Menander Rhetor includes an address to the emperor on behalf of a city 'in trouble' as a standard genre; Menander Rhetor, *Treatise* II, 13.

to receptions for the bishop's *adventus* into towns along his route.[63] The three journeys, to Arles, to Goar, and to Ravenna, have little in common with the two trips to Britain other than travel and oratory. Germanus' experiences awaiting entry to the imperial presence, only for his request to be refused, must have been most unlike his participation in public debate in a provincial synod of bishops in Britain. The journeys differ both in content, involving affairs of municipal and imperial government or of the church, and in form: some were embassies carrying out formal supplications to authorities, others public debates.

None the less, Constantius' presentation of the scenes diminishes the differences between these various activities. The generalising terminology of *labores* and haste common to the accounts of each of Germanus' journeys, and the fast-paced narrative structure of the work, emphasise the similarities, not differences, of the trips. This assimilation is reminiscent of Sidonius' *Panegyric* on Avitus, in which the differences between communications of an equally disparate nature are elided to convey the impression of a series of embassies, following in rapid succession.[64]

A final literary ploy used by Constantius to cast Germanus in a heroic mould is his choice of stories. Germanus leading the British army to victory, albeit bloodless, against the overwhelming forces of the Picts and Saxons; seizing the reins of a barbarian leader's horse to bring a whole army to halt; carrying a man on his back through a swollen mountain river: these are not motifs from earlier Christian literature, and strongly suggest quite different literary genres, of romance or epic. The 'Alleluia victory' and the confrontation with Goar, the most dramatic scenes in the *Vita*, notably lack miracles. Even if regarded as *fabulae*, these stories are clearly of a piece with Constantius' image of Germanus.[65] They may not be Constantius' creation, for some analogues exist. The motif of a spurned suppliant grabbing the reins of a general's horse to stop him and his army appears also in the early sixth-century *Ecclesiastical History* of Theodore Lector. There, the scene involves the emperor Valens, riding out to his fatal battle with the Goths at Adrianople, and the Constantinopolitan monk Isaac. Theodore's source is unknown; it is none of the fifth-century ecclesiastical historians whose parallel accounts he sought

[63] *Legatio* is, however, used for the appeals to which Germanus responds, i.e. from the British and the Armoricans (Constantius, *Vita Germani*, 12, 28). Formal terminology: i.e. *evectio*, official travel warrants, also the actual horses used for transport (cf. Niermeyer, *Lexicon*, 383 s.v. *evectio* § 2); Constantius, *Vita Germani*, 19, 20, 44. *Adventus* and receptions: Constantius, *Vita Germani*, 24: '[the praetorian prefect of Gaul Auxilianus] *ingrediente* [*sc. Germano*] *longissimo praeter consuetudinem famulatur occursu*'; also 21, 23, 30: '[populaces of towns *en route*] *advenienti* [*sc. Germano*] *occur*[*unt*]'; 31–2: Germanus attempts to avoid recognition in Milan; 35: *adventus* into Ravenna; see also chapter 6 below, at nn. 137–43.

[64] Above, chapter 3, at n. 102. [65] *Fabulae*: Chadwick, *Poetry and Letters*, 251.

to unify.[66] The reverberating cry which frightens off the Picts and Saxons in the 'Alleluia victory' is reminiscent of the Indian expeditions of Dionysus, the war-cries of whose followers puts an ambush to panic. The story is related in the *Dionysiaca*, the fifth-century Greek mythological epic of Nonnos of Panopolis, and Dionysus' Indian campaign formed part of the legendary cycles exploited by contemporary Gallic poets.[67] From what, if any, sources Constantius derived these stories is unclear, but it is evident that he wrote with attention to literary genres besides earlier Latin hagiography.

Constantius' preface to *Vita Germani* does not hint that the work would differ from previous western saints' *Vitae*. To write the *vita gestaque* of Germanus, Constantius says, was a fearful task, because of the *miraculorum numerositate*, 'the great number of his miracles'.[68] Miracles are the main emphasis of Constantius' prefatory remarks, and indeed miracle-narratives constitute the greater part of the *Vita*. Yet Constantius chose to write his work using a structure and devices of literary characterisation which clearly emphasise Germanus' travels, the legatine nature of those journeys, and an aspect of Germanus' deeds which was heroic in a secular sense, not in the Christian sense of martyrdom or ascesis. As the imagery of Germanus' dream vision indicates, the journeys are not merely a framing device for the miracle accounts, but are central to a carefully constructed representation of the saint.[69] This image is not suggested in the preface. It is the emphasis on Germanus' travels which most firmly

[66] Theodoros Anagnostes, *Kirchengeschichte*, ed. G. C. Hanson, 2nd edn (GCS n.s. 3; Berlin, 1995), 216; followed by Theophanes, *Chron.* AM 5870. The confrontation between Isaac and Valens appears in several of Theodore's main sources (Sozomen, *HE* VI, 40; Theodoret, *HE* IV, 34; but not Socrates, *HE*) and in Cassiodorus/Epiphanius, *Historia tripartita*, *PL* 69, 1119; but without the detail of Isaac seizing Valens' reins. (Unlike Germanus, Isaac does not win respect for his boldness, but is cast into prison, where he has the satisfaction of miraculously smelling burning when the defeated Valens is consumed in a blazing hut.)

[67] War-cry: Nonnos, *Dionysiaca*, ed. and trans. N. Hopkinson and F. Vian, VIII (Paris, 1994), XXI, 315–XXII, 70, XXIV, 147–61 (the cry 'alleluia' of the Naiads is eye-catching though probably coincidental; XXII, 8, XXIV, 156); cf. Diodorus Siculus, II, 38.6. Dionysus' Indian campaigns featured in imperial iconography of the second century AD: *Lexicon iconographicum mythologiae classicae* III, 1 (Zurich, 1986), 565. Dionysus' Indian expedition in late epic: Rudolf Keydell, 'Nonnos von Panopolis', *RE* XVII.1, 905; in fifth-century Gallic literature: Sid. Ap., *Carm.* XXII, ep. 2, *carm.*, 22–63 (not mentioning the scene of the war-cry).

[68] Constantius, *Vita Germani*, Praef.; cf. further in the same passage: *religionis contemplatio et innumerabilium miraculorum*, and the letter to Patiens: *sanctum virum inlustrare virtutibus suis desideras et profectui omnium mirabilium exempla largiris*. Heinzelmann, 'Neue Aspekte', 38–9; Christensen, 'Germanus and Fifth-Century History', 224.

In his letters and preface, Constantius does not invoke any precedents to the writing of a *vita*, as earlier Latin hagiographers had, e.g. Sulpicius, *Vita Martini*, Praef. (pagan *de viris illustribus*); Sulpicius, *Dialogi passim* (accounts of the Egyptian monks); Paulinus, *Vita Ambrosi*, Praef. (the *Vita* of Anthony; Jerome's *Vita* of Paul; Sulpicius, *Vita Martini*); Possidius, *Vita Augustini* (earlier Christian biographies in general).

[69] Journeys as framing device: Christensen, 'Germanus and Fifth-Century History', 224.

differentiates *Vita Germani* from its influential Gallic predecessor, *Vita Martini*. Even in recounting Germanus' journeys, Constantius could have chosen to stress his role as a theologian or exegete, in his debates with the British Pelagian bishops; instead, the *disputationes* in Britain are assimilated with the secular journeys for tax-remission and amelioration of punishment. The image of Germanus as a 'homme d'action au service de la communauté' is no less a literary artifice than that of the saint as thaumaturge.[70]

Why did Constantius choose to craft his portrait of Germanus in this way? Although classical legatine functions feature in parts of the New Testament, Constantius does not follow a biblical model in his portrait of Germanus as an envoy.[71] It is natural for the historian to look to the wider political context of late fifth-century Gaul, rapidly passing out of imperial control. The author of a sensitive reading of the *Vita*, after considering what is known of Sidonius' friend Constantius (in particular his assistance to Sidonius during a Gothic seige of Clermont), states: 'the author might be expected to have an eye to the role which a cleric might play in times of crisis... [and to produce] a work whose central concern was episcopal behaviour in a period of crisis, almost a handbook for bishops in the 470s or 480s. And this is what the *Vita Germani* is.'[72] Does *Vita Germani* indeed invoke a sense of 'crisis'? Modern scholars seem to expect that it should, but not all find that it does: '[a characteristic of Constantius' writing is] his serenity, or at least his apparent tranquility. To read him, one would not imagine that his hero had lived, and he himself still lived, in the terrible fifth century which saw the Roman empire of the West collapse... [It is impossible to see in Constantius' letters to Patiens and Censurius or in his preface] the least allusion, the least reference to contemporary events.'[73]

Indeed, Constantius' general portrait of the West – and one has no reason to believe that the author himself in fact intended to produce any sort of general political or social account – seems rather sunny. The churches of various provinces communicate with each other, and though a heresy exists, it is rapidly dispelled. No paganism lurks in the towns or countryside of Constantius' Gaul. Germanus' sanctity and authority

70 Quotation from Borius, Introduction to *Vie de Germain*, 69; cf. Chadwick, *Poetry and Letters*, 266.

71 Bash, *Ambassadors for Christ*, chapters 6–8, 81–151. On biblical models for hagiography: M. van Uytfanghe, 'Modèles bibliques dans l'hagiographie', in *Bible de tous les temps* IV: *Le Moyen Age et la Bible* (Paris, 1984), 449–88.

72 Wood, 'End of Roman Britain', 9, 12.

73 Borius, Introduction to *Vie de Germain*, 24: 'Un dernier trait de caractère de ce lettre que fut Constance de Lyon demande que l'on s'y attarde quelques instants: c'est sa sérénité ou du moins son apparente tranquillité. A le lire, on n'imaginerait pas que son héros a vécu, et que lui-même vit encore, dans ce terrible ve siècle qui voit disparaître l'Empire Romain d'Occident.' Ibid., 26: 'pas la moindre allusions, pas la moindre référence aux événements contemporains'. Borius attributes this apparent ommision to 'l'illusion, qui n'est pas sans grandeur', of the eternity of Rome.

are respected wherever he goes. Senior imperial magistrates are only too pleased to assist Germanus, and the imperial court itself is a place of great piety. It is true that barbarians, a subject presumably of keen interest to Gauls of the late fifth century, appear twice. Barbarians appear twice in both *Vita Martini* and *Vita Ambrosii* also.[74] The first barbarians in *Vita Germani* are the Picts and Saxons in far-off Britain, traditional raiders who are repelled bloodlessly by a ruse; if Britain was bothered any further by these looters, Constantius seems unaware of it.[75]

More complex is the scene concerning the second group of barbarians, the Alans of Goar. What is significant here is that the barbarians themselves are not the problem. Greedy and warlike though the Alans are, their king is easily won over, not by a miracle, but through Germanus' audacity and eloquence. The Alans are only an instrument in an internal Roman dispute: a provincial rebellion (Constantius does not use the word 'Bagaudae') and its repression by the imperial government. Germanus' missions to Goar and to the imperial court are a bid not to repel invading barbarians or insurgent peasants but to ameliorate the brutality of imperial justice. In this attempt he is unsuccessful, because of the fickleness of the provincials. Neither the imperial government nor the Alans is at fault, nor of course is Germanus' supplication any less efficacious than before.[76] The fault is laid with the Armoricans and specifically the rebel leader Tibatto, whose just punishment removes the sole cause of trouble, as had the expulsion of the Pelagian bishops from Britain. Germanus' acquiescence in the imperial decision to inflict punishments on the Armoricans is made plain: 'the intercession of the priest vanished'.[77] The verb used to represent the bishop's failure to prevent what may very well have been a bloodbath, *evanuit*, is studiously ambiguous, but Constantius makes very clear that events caused no rupture in relations between Germanus and the imperial court.[78] When Germanus had first arrived in Ravenna, he

[74] Sulpicius, *Vita Martini*, 4, 18. Paulinus, *Vita Ambrosii*, 30, 36.

[75] Constantius, *Vita Germani*, 18 *fin.*, 27 *fin.* On the artificial closure of these sections: Christensen, 'Germanus and Fifth-Century History', 226.

[76] Constantius, *Vita Germani*, 40: *obtenta venia et securitate perpetua ad proprium obtinuisset arbitrium.* For a review of interpretations of the fifth-century Bagaudae: John Drinkwater, 'Patronage in Roman Gaul and the Problem of the Bagaudae', in Andrew Wallace-Hadrill (ed.), *Patronage in Ancient Society* (London, 1989), 189–203.

[77] Constantius, *Vita Germani*, 40: *intercessio sacerdotis evanuit. Contra* Wood, 'End of Roman Britain', 10 ('a section of text which is so carefully crafted as to lead the reader . . . into overlooking the fact that the legation was useless'), Constantius' recapitulation of the causes of Germanus' journey to Ravenna in fact emphasises the failure of the embassy to Ravenna; contrast the brief statement of the success of the legation to Arles (Constantius, *Vita Germani*, 24 *fin*).

[78] Bloodbath: cf. e.g. *Chron. Gall. 452*, 99 (Ravenna in 425, punished for supporting the usurper John); Hydatius, *Chron.*, 173–8 [166–71] (Gallaecia punished for Suevic expansionism); Procopius, *Wars* V, 9.23–8 (Belisarius' picture of what citizens of Naples can expect if the city is taken by force).

had been respectfully greeted by the imperial court and particularly by the *augusta* Galla Placidia; when he later fell fatally ill, in the passage immediately following the cessation of his intercession, there was a pious contest between members of the imperial family and court and the Ravennan church to pay homage to his memory.[79] The failure of Germanus' mission caused no breach between the Gallic bishop and the imperial court, nor did Constantius modify his positive portrait of the court (the contrast with Martin, leaving the court of Magnus Maximus with grief and sighs, is sharp[80]). It is difficult to construe a message pertinent to times of crisis from this harmonious tone. The imperial court is pious, merciful, and just; the Alans are no more and no less than standard literary barbarians, of a group which was to play no very significant part in the affairs of late fifth-century Gaul; the Armorican provincials, though 'flighty and undisciplined', were delivered from the 'treachery' of Tibatto by the wise 'circumspection' of the imperial court; even Tibatto is only a device introduced to deflect both the blame and the punishment of the rebellion.

Crisis is far from the literary world of Constantius. The author's portrait of the times is more positive. There is no compelling reason to believe that Constantius' heroic portrait of Germanus was intended as a model for contemporary bishops, any more than the bishop's more fantastic aspect as a thaumaturge was seriously meant for imitation (indeed, it is noteworthy that Constantius' representation of Germanus' ascesis, one aspect which could serve as a practical model for contemporary bishops, is both brief and mild, and largely restricted to his hospitality).[81] The heroic image of Germanus was surely intended to complement, not to challange, his role as a miracle-worker; journeys may determine the structure and the climax of the work, but comfortably familiar miracles fill more pages.[82] Accounts of miracles served an important role in the cult of saints, to be sure, but at a literary level they also served as a form of entertainment, with strong ties to the genre of romance.[83] The heroic aspect of *Vita Germani* may be best construed as a complement to the romance element of hagiographic miracles. Epic imagery was popular with the Gallic literate elite of the late fifth century, as Sidonius' panegyrics

[79] Constantius, *Vita Germani*, 42–4.

[80] Sulpicius Severus, *Dialogi* III, 13.

[81] Cf. Geary, *Living with the Dead*, 22.

[82] The assessment of Chadwick, *Poetry and Letters*, 265–6, 273, too brusquely dismisses the importance of miracles in *Vita Germani*. Christensen, 'Germanus and Fifth-Century History', 227–8.

[83] H. Delehaye, *Legends of the Saints*, trans. V. M. Crawford (1907; repr. Norwood, PA, 1974), 3–4; Borius, Introduction to *Vie de Germain*, 32; Alison Goddard Elliott, *Roads to Paradise: Reading the Lives of the Early Saints* (Hanover and London, 1987); van Uytfanghe, 'Heiligenverehrung II', 168–72.

and some other hagiographical works indicate.[84] From time to time, the duties of bishops required travel, though the nature of their journeys was often far from political. Constantius turns these episcopal duties into a virtue by annexing the status enjoyed by legates in contemporary secular values. Sidonius had earlier employed a similar device in a different context in his panegyric on Avitus.

Sidonius' portrait of Avitus has no known imitators in the genre of panegyric. Constantius fared rather better, for Germanus was to become a popular figure in Gallic hagiography. Besides literary borrowings from the *Vita*, Germanus appears as a character in several *Vitae* of fifth- and sixth-century bishops and ascetics, most famously Genovefa of Paris and Patrick, but also Lupus of Troyes, Hilary of Arles, Amator of Auxerre, and Severus of Vienne; St Martin, by contrast, though much imitated in the narratives of later saints, rarely figured as a character in later *Vitae*.[85] Details of Germanus' episcopate were reworked in later liturgical and other documents produced in Auxerre.[86] Germanus' journeys are not only recalled in the later texts, but exploited as the opportunity for the great bishop to meet other saints: Germanus meets the young Genovefa on both of his journeys to Britain, and encounters Severus, a devout priest and active church-builder in Vienne, *en route* to Italy. A late sixth/early seventh-century mass for Germanus recalled his preaching and miracles in 'all Gaul, Rome, Italy, and Britain'.[87] But the nature of Germanus' voyages changes in these later texts. Germanus' journeys to Britain to repress Pelagianism are recalled in the *Vitae* of Genovefa of Paris and of Lupus of Troyes, Germanus' companion on the first

[84] Other hagiography: e.g. Eucherius of Lyons, *Passio Acaunensium martyrum*, ed. B. Krusch, MGH SRM 3, 20–39 (trans. in *The Lives of the Jura Fathers*, trans. Tim Vivian, Kim Vivian, and Jeffrey Burton Russell (Cistercian Studies 178; Kalamazoo, 1999), 187–96); note Eucherius' comment on his composition *pro honore gestorum stilo*, 'in a style commensurate with their honourable deeds', *Passio*, 1. Eucherius was bishop of Lyons immediately prior to Patiens, who had commissioned Constantius to write *Vita Germani*; Duchesne, *Fastes épiscopaux* II, 163; *Patrology* IV, 504–7.

[85] Levison, 'Bischof Germanus', 143–57. St Germanus in later hagiography: Stephanus Africanus, *Vita Amatoris episcopi Autissiodorensi*, AASS Mai I, 51–61, at cc. 4–5; *Vita Lupi episcopi Trecensis*, ed. B. Krusch, MGH SRM 7, p. 297, c. 4; Honoratus Massiliensis, *Vita Hilarii episcopi Arelatensis*, ed. S. Cavallin, *Vitae sanctorum Honorati et Hilarii episcoporum Arelatensium*; *Vita Genovefae virginis Parisiensis*, ed. B. Krusch, MGH SRM 3, cc. 2–6, 11; *Vita sancti Severi Viennensis*, in *AB* 5 (1886), 416–24, cc. 4–7; Muirchu's *Vita* of Patrick, in *St. Patrick: His Writings and Life*, ed. and trans. A. B. E. Hood (Arthurian Period Sources 9; London, 1978), 6–8. Germanus is also mentioned in Venantius Fortunatus, *Vita Radegundae*, 16, as an example of ascesis.

St Martin: *Vies des Pères du Jura* [*Vita Eugendi*], 159–60; *Vita S. Victurii Cenomanensi Galia episcopi*, AASS Sept. I, 220–3; *Vita Amator*, AASS Mai I, 56. As model: J. Leclercq, 'S. Martin dans l'hagiographie monastique du moyen âge', in *Saint Martin et son temps* (Rome, 1961), 175–87, on medieval monastic hagiography.

[86] See Appendix 1.

[87] *Missale gallicanum vetus (Cod. Vat. Palat. lat. 493)*, ed. L. C. Mohlberg (Rome, 1958), 342.

voyage; but the account of the *Vita Lupi* is far briefer than Constantius', and the *Vita Genovefae*, while only concerned with Germanus' passage through Paris *en route* to Britain, none the less provides a theological account of Pelagianism totally absent from *Vita Germani*.[88] In other sources, the purposes of Germanus' missions are omitted altogether or radically altered; in several texts, Germanus' Italian journey was to Rome, not Ravenna, as a pilgrimage to the martyrs' shrines.[89] Even the *Gesta* of the bishops of Auxerre, compiled in the ninth century on the model of the Roman *Liber pontificalis* and closely following Constantius in its account of Germanus, omits Germanus' journey to Arles, and provides no details on the purpose of the journey to Ravenna.[90] Some later recensions of *Vita Germani*, increasingly interpolated with text from later hagiographies, retained the miracle accounts but removed them from the context of Germanus' journeys, thus overthrowing Constantius' structure.[91]

Constantius' portrait of Germanus is striking for its exaggerated presentation of the bishop as constantly engaged in strenuous journeys and intercession. This image, grafted onto existing models of sanctity, has no known precedent in hagiographical literature; Sidonius' presentation of Avitus, however, is a suggestive comparandum in literary technique. It was an image which appealed for a limited period; by the late sixth century at the latest, the image was superseded within the literary traditions of the cult of Germanus. Within that period, however, other authors of pious biography made use of the typology established by Constantius.[92]

[88] *Vita Genovefae*, c. 2.

[89] *Vita Severi*, c. 4 (pilgrimage to Rome); Gregory of Tours: *Gloria confessorum*, ed. B. Krusch, MGH SRM 1.2, 40 (Germanus died in Rome; yet Gregory's record of the length of time taken for the funeral cortège to reach Auxerre accords with the *Kal. Autiss.*, 98, 124; Grosjean, 'Notes d'hagiographie celtique 29: Le dernier voyage de S. Germain', 180). Cf. *Missale gall. vetus*, 342 (Germanus preached and performed miracles in 'all Gaul, Rome, Italy, and Britain').

[90] *Gesta episcoporum Autissiodorensis* (see Appendix 1), VII.

[91] Levison, Introduction to Constantius, *Vita Germani*, 237 (on MS Paris BN lat. 12598).

[92] The *Vitae* of Lupus of Troyes and of Genovefa of Paris have obvious textual connections with *Vita Germani*: both refer to Germanus' journeys to Britain (Lupus accompanied Germanus on his first voyage; Genovefa, as a child, met the bishop as he passed through Paris on both his journeys to Britain); both are involved with barbarian rulers (Lupus with Attila and the Alamanni king Gebavult, Genovefa with Attila and Clovis); *Vita Lupi episcopi Trecensis*, ed. B. Krusch, MGH SRM 3 (1896) and 7 (1920), 4, 5, 10; *Vita Genovefae virginis Parisiensis*, ed. B. Krusch, MGH SRM 3, 2–4, 9, 10–12, 55. But, though both *Vitae* exploit Germanus' fame, neither displays the influence of Constantius' portrait of the bishop as an effective envoy either in structure or in imagery. (On the dates of these works, now considered to be early sixth century: Eugen Ewig, 'Bemerkungen zur Vita des Bischofs Lupus von Troyes', in K. Hauck and H. Mordek (eds.), *Geschichtesschreibung und geistiges Leben im Mittelalter* (Cologne, 1978), 14–26; M. Heinzelmann and J.-C. Poulin, *Les Vies anciennes de Sainte Geneviève de Paris* (Paris, 1986).)

THE *LIVES* OF ORIENTIUS OF AUCH AND VIVIANUS OF SAINTES

Two Gallic hagiographies display elements derived from Constantius' portrait of Germanus as an envoy: the *Vitae* of Orientius, bishop of Auch, and of Vivianus, bishop of Saintes. Like Germanus, both bishops lived in the first half of the fifth century, but their anonymous *Vitae* were composed later. Estimates of the dates of composition range from the early sixth century to Carolingian times; opinion on the veracity of the events they describe similarly ranges from credence to dismissal. The greatest part of each *Vita* concerns one or more journeys undertaken by the bishop. At a literary level, it is clear that both *Vitae* were constructed from elements drawn from *Vita Germani* and Sulpicius' *Vita Martini* and *Dialogi*.[93]

Orientius of Auch

As with Germanus, the little that is known about the historical Orientius differs sharply from his appearance in *Vita Orientii*.[94] Orientius is usually identified as one of the early fifth-century Gallic Christian poets, the author of an elegiac poem conventionally referred to as the *Commonitorium*.[95] The poem calls for recent disasters to be seen only as particular intimations of the universal approach of death (*per varias mors ruit una vias*), and as spurs for spiritual withdrawal from the world. Praising monasticism as the only true response to signs of temporal destruction, the poet

[93] Courcelle, *Histoire littéraire*, 145–6 and Appendix VII: 'Histoire ou cliché hagiographique? Trois dîners chez le roi wisigoth d'Aquitaine', 339–47, sees *Vita Viviani*, cc. 4–6, and *Vita Orientii*, c. 5, as imitations of Ennodius, *Vita Epiphani*, cc. 85–92. But the common elements cited by Courcelle (primarily the *convivium* scenes) are present also in the earlier *Vita Martini* and *Vita Germani*, and there are other direct echoes of *Vita Martini* and *Vita Germani* in *Vita Viviani* and *Vita Orientii*, which do not appear in *Vita Epiphani* (see below). Ennodius was familiar with *Vita Germani*, and there is no evidence of *Vita Epiphani* circulating in Gaul (cf. MGH AA 7, 333: 'Index scriptores qui Ennodium compilaverunt'). It is very likely that *Vita Martini* and *Vita Germani*, rather than *Vita Epiphani*, served as models for *Vita Viviani* and *Vita Orientii*. Griffe, *La Gaule chrétienne* II, 69–71 nn. 13 and 16, rejects Courcelle's suggestion, seeing the *Vitae* of Vivianus and Orientius as preserving 'la tradition orale', though he admits the similarity of the cup motif in *Vita Martini*, 20 and *Vita Viviani*, 6.

[94] For edition, see 'Note on editions, commentaries, and translations' below. On Orientius: Duchesne, *Fastes épiscopaux* II, 96; Heinzelmann, 'Gallische Prosopographie', 659–60. On *Vita Orientii*: C. Lécrivain, 'Note sur la Vie de Saint Orientius, évêque d'Auch', *Annales du Midi* 3 (1891), 257–8 (dismissing the *Vita* as derived from Salvian and other sources); Griffe, *La Gaule chrétienne* II, 31–4; 69 and n. 13; 276–7 (cautious acceptance of the account of the *Vita*, which he dates to early sixth century); III, 257; Courcelle, *Histoire littéraire*, 146 (dismisses *convivium* scene as a literary imitation, but accepts embassy to Aetius and Litorius).

[95] Orientius, *Commonitorium*, ed. R. Ellis (CSEL 16; Vienna, 1888); trans. M. D. Tobin, (Washington, DC, 1945). On the *Comm.*: Schanz-Hosius IV, 2, 367; Courcelle, *Histoire littéraire*, 98–101; *Patrology* IV: *The Golden Age of Latin Patristic Literature from the Council of Nicea to the Council of Chalcedon* [Quasten], ed. A. di Berardino (Westminster, MD, 1994), 326–8; Wood, 'Continuity or Calamity?', 9–10.

was perhaps influenced by Pelagian moral teaching (*mollia securis ducentes otia rebus/pro merito vivunt nunc bene, post melius*). His gloomy description of the devastation of Gaul after barbarian raids (presumably the Vandals, Alans, and Sueves, 406–9) is much cited.[96]

Vita Orientii, however, does not reflect the literary, moral, or historical milieux of the *Commonitorium*. The bishop of hagiography is active in the world, prosecuting his pastoral duties with zeal, and confronting generals and kings with secular issues. Following is a summary of the brief text:

1 Introduction; Orientius' learning and pastoral care, especially his conversion of pagans among the people of Auch.
2 Exorcism of a pagan temple on a mountain.
3 Embassy on behalf of the Gothic king of Toulouse to the *magistri utriusque militiae* Aetius and Litorius [439].
4 Praise of Orientius.
5 Embassy to the royal court of Toulouse.
6 Posthumous healing miracle.
7 Concluding invocation.

Orientius undertakes two embassies (§§ 3 and 5). The first, during the penultimate stages of the conflict between the Gothic kingdom of Toulouse and the western empire from 436 to 439, is prior to Litorius' fatal attempt to capture Toulouse with the aid of Hunnic auxiliaries.[97] The homilist Salvian, a Gallic contemporary of these events, laments that prior to Litorius' assault on Toulouse, the Goths sent Catholic bishops to negotiate for peace, but these overtures were rejected by the imperial commanders.[98] These events are dramatised in *Vita Orientii*. The unnamed Gothic king (Theoderic I), terrified by the army of Aetius and Litorius, asks Orientius to undertake an embassy to the generals. Aetius, approached by the bishop, dismounts and asks Orientius to pray for him; Litorius disdains to reply to Orientius and continues his assault on Toulouse. Captured by 'the Toulousians', Litorius is executed; Aetius and his army, who seem also to have been captured (a detail not in any other source), are freed unharmed because of Orientius' prayers and *interventus*.[99] As with Pope Leo's embassy to Attila, there is a misleading exclusiveness in the narrative of Orientius' embassy, making him the sole

[96] Quotations: Orientius, *Comm.* II, 192, 339–40. Monastic response: *ibid.*, II, 321–40. Destruction of Gaul: *ibid.*, II, 165–84. Pelagianism: *Patrology* IV, 327–8.

[97] See above, chapter 3, at n. 77. Sources for Litorius' capture and death: Prosper, *Chron.*, 1335; Hydatius, *Chron.*, 116 [108]; Cassiodorus, *Chron.*, 1232; Jordanes, *Get.*, 177; Sid. Ap., *Carm.* VII, 300–1; Salvian, *De gubernatione Dei* VII, 9–10.

[98] Salvian, *De gubernatione Dei* VII, 9. Lécrivain, 'La Vie de Saint Orientius', 257–8, sees *Vita Orientii*, 3, as a fiction constructed from Salvian and chronicle sources; Courcelle, *Histoire littéraire*, 347 n. 1, sees Salvian as an analogue, not a source.

[99] *Vita Orientii*, 3.

actor in the drama. Other sources indicate a variety of participants involved in the ending of conflict: a number of bishops in Salvian; Avitus, then praetorian prefect of Gaul, according to Sidonius; Merobaudes probably attributes it to Aetius.[100]

The second embassy, in which Orientius attends the court of (presumably the same) Gothic king to petition for the life of a Spanish *vir nobilissimus genere* condemned to death on a false accusation, can be roughly paralleled in letters of Sidonius Apollinaris describing petitions to the Gothic kings by provincial magnates.[101] Orientius wins his suit after attending the king's dinner.

That the author was familiar with *Vita Germani* is most explicit in the healing miracle of *Vita Orientii*, c. 6, in which a man who suffers crippling contractions of his legs and hands is cured by praying at Orientius' tomb. This is the only healing miracle, and one of only two miracle narratives, in the *Vita*. Motifs and vocabulary of this scene are derived from *Vita Germani*, c. 30, in which Germanus (*en route* to Ravenna) cures a young girl whose hands are crippled; the most direct borrowing is the grotesque detail that the fingernails of both sufferers had grown into the palms of their hands.[102] The opening words of *Vita Orientii* also borrow a conceit from Constantius, the inability of the author to provide a complete account of the saint's deeds because of their great number.[103]

[100] Salvian, *De gubernatione Dei* VII, 9; Sid. Ap., *Carm.* VII, 295–315; Merobaudes, *Pan.* I with Clover, *Merobaudes*, 32–41 and *PLRE* II, 'Aetius 7', 25–6; cf. *L'Année épigraphique 1950* (Paris, 1951), 30.

[101] Sid. Ap., *Epp.* I, 2.8; IV, 8.5.

[102] (Common words in *BOLD*): *Vita Germani*, 30: *Illic in conventu [sc. Autun] omnium prostrati in terram parentes filiam in annis nubilibus obtulerunt, cui DEBILITATIS POENAM saevissimam* temporis accessione *generaverat. Ab ortu enim nativitatis suae ita CONTRACTIS NERVIS, in PALMAM DIGITI curvabantur, ut, crescentibus introsum nimie unguibus, cedente carnis teneritudine, tot inciperent esse vulnera quot DIGITI, et nisi insistenti acumini ossa obiecta aliquatenus restitissent, PALMAM totam ulcera inmersa transfoderent. Huius dextram conprehensam dum adtrectat sacerdos, tactus salubritate benedixit adprehensosque singillatim digitos, cedentibus nervis, in USUM flexibilem REVOCAVIT, REDDITURQUE ministerio MANUS, quae inferebat sibi ipsa perniciem.*

Vita Orientii, 6: *Quidam peregrinus, arcescentibus NERVIS vim DEBILITATIS incurrens, et CONTRACTIS genibus manibusque constrictis longa POENA languescens, ad solemnitatem beati Orientii episcopi, virtutem caelestis medici dum requireret, invenit: ibique fideli oratione supplicare non cessat. Procedit virtus de tumulo, et in tantum sanitas REDDITUR arefacto, ut redivivo infuso sanguine, vitali calore membra sanitas gratia replerentur. Sic ergo praemortuae MANUS IN USUM pristinum REVOCANTUR: quarum DIGITI ita fuerant ante constricti, ut etiam eorum vestigia, PALMIS infixa debilibus, putrida apparerent.*

Cf. Gregory of Tours, *Gloria confessorum*, 57, attributing a similar miracle to the tomb of Vivianus of Saintes.

[103] *Vita Germani*, *Praef.*: *Plerique ad scribendum, sollicitante materia uberiore, producti sunt . . . mihi inlustrissimi viri Germani antistitis vitam gestaque VEL ex aliqua PARTE dicturo incutitur pro miraculorum numerositate trepidatio.*

Vita Orientii, 1: *Beatissimi Orientii sacerdotis sacratissimos actus VEL PRO PARTE disserere, non peritiae profluitate, sed tantae materiae admiratione, compellor . . .*

Cf. Levison, 'Bischof Germanus', 144–5.

The two embassy accounts in *Vita Orientii* do not form part of an articulated structure as the equivalent narratives in *Vita Germani* do. The *Vita* of Orientius is more episodic; there are no temporal connectives between the episodes, and the only internal indicator of time is the statement, opening the embassy to Aetius and Litorius, that Orientius 'had led a long life in the world before the Lord'.[104] The two embassy accounts, however, comprise most of the length of the short *Vita*, and are the most developed episodes. Moreover, the author's general praises of Orientius (§ 4) stress his role as a securer of peace and effective intercessor, alongside his pastoral duties and success as an exorcist. *Labor*, Constantius' favoured term in describing Germanus, is used repetitively in this eulogy: 'Orientius, this blessed pontifex worthy of God, was greatly needed not only for his preaching, and besides for the liberation of his homeland, but he also liberated the bodies of many besieged by demons... In his time, and by his labour, peace and security, for which he laboured greatly, entered the world.'[105] Orientius was 'salvation to both his citizens and to foreigners'.[106]

Orientius' embassy to Aetius and Litorius contains echoes of Germanus' confrontation with Goar:[107] the advanced age of the bishop is stressed at the outset of the journey; he meets an army on its march to the conflict he seeks to prevent; his appeal is rejected (by Litorius); when it is heeded (by Aetius), the army leader dismounts. The second embassy, to the court of the Gothic king, contains motifs more distinctly drawn from two scenes in Sulpicius' *Vita Martini* and *Dialogi* concerning the emperor Magnus Maximus.[108] In *Vita Martini*, discussed above, Maximus invites Martin to join his *convivium*; in the *Dialogi*, Maximus presses Martin to join in communion with the bishops involved in the condemnation of Priscillian. Though the two episodes are described differently by Sulpicius, in both cases, Martin is forced to compromise his integrity to obtain the success of his petitions. Orientius, similarly, is invited to the king's *convivium* and given the opportunity to gain his request, provided he will partake of the meat dishes, which his frugal regular diet excludes; the bishop compromises by blessing the food. Orientius is threatened during the dinner by leading figures of the court; this seems to be an awkward parallel to the tension of Martin's refusal to pass the cup of wine to the emperor Maximus.[109] The earlier scene of Orientius' embassy

104 *Vita Orientii*, 3: *Et cum praestante Domino vitam longam in seculo produceret.*

105 *Vita Orientii*, 4: *Beatus iste et Deo dignus pontifex Orientius, non solum in praedicatione, nec non et patriae liberatione necessarius multum fuit, sed etiam multorum hominum obsessa a daemonibus corpora liberavit... Eius temporibus, eo laborante pax et securitas, pro qua multum laboravit, in orbem terrae introivit.*

106 *Vita Orientii*, 6. *civibus salus et externis.*

107 Constantius, *Vita Germani*, 28.

108 Sulpicius, *Vita Martini*, 20; *Dialogi* III, 11–14.

109 *Vita Martini*, 20.

to Aetius and Litorius may also contain echoes of Sulpicius' *Dialogi* in the emphasis on the bishop's protection even of heretics: Martin protects the Priscillianists, Orientius the Arian Goths.[110] As is often the case with hagiography, the model is used not by direct reproduction, but through new combinations of existing motifs.

The two embassy scenes in *Vita Orientii* offer limited historical data. The author's intent is not to be descriptive, but to establish tableaux which present charged gestures: Aetius' dismounting and request for the prayers of Orientius; the bishop surrounded by menacing barbarians at the court of the Gothic king.[111] That Orientius in fact fails to prevent the imperial assault on Toulouse seems not to be a difficulty to his hagiographer; Litorius' punishment for disrespect, and Aetius' salvation on account of his faith, are the point of the story.

Orientius' embassy to Aetius and Litorius has often appeared problematic: the approach of a Roman provincial bishop to imperial generals, seeking peace on behalf of a recently aggressive barbarian leader, has raised questions of loyalty.[112] It has been suggested that the work (or a hypothetical source) must have been written before the battle of Vouillé in 507 and the Frankish take-over of southern Gaul in the following years, as the author's sentiment is seen as too dangerously pro-Gothic to have been composed after 507.[113] These considerations overlook the tenor of the *Vita*. The hagiographer takes pains to display Orientius' distance from the Arian Goths.[114] More importantly, the milieu of the *Vita* is civilian and local: Orientius' mission provides freedom for his *patria*; he is the salvation of his fellow *cives*.[115] In describing Litorius' antagonists, the author uses interchangeably the contemporary term *Gothi*, the classicising *Getae*, and the civic label *Tolosani*.[116] The author writes from a standpoint of regional, not ethnic or political, identification. Orientius' embassy is not to support the Gothic regime, but to prevent the outbreak of warfare in his own region; irrespective of which combatant won, the

[110] Sulpicius, *Dialogi* III, 11; *Vita Orientii*, 3 *fin.*

[111] Joaquín Martínez Pizarro, *A Rhetoric of the Scene: Dramatic Narrative in the Early Middle Ages* (Toronto, 1989).

[112] E.g. Thompson, *Romans and Barbarians*, 179, 272 n. 62 ('St. Orientius' sympathies lay with the Visigoths'); Wolfram, *History of the Goths*, 176 ('It is surprising to read in the biography of Bishop Orientius of Auch . . . that its hero had led the delegation to Litorius and had even prayed for the victory of the Goths'); Mathisen, *Roman Aristocrats in Barbarian Gaul*, 125.

[113] Courcelle, *Histoire littéraire*, 347 n. 1; more cautiously, Griffe, *La Gaule chrétienne* II, 32 n. 3.

[114] *Vita Orientii*, 3: *apud Dominum omnes eius* [*sc. Gothorum regis*] *ante confidentia propter fiduciam Arianorum viluerat . . . Quam supplicationem beatus Orientius libenti animo amplectens, non pro haereseon erroris squallore contempsit . . .* [*Orientium*] *antea contempserat haereticorum turba Getarum.*

[115] *Vita Orientii*, 4, 6.

[116] *Vita Orientii*, 3: *Tolosani qui beati Orientii patrocinia postulaverant* (making explicit the identification with the Goths).

civilian residents of Toulouse and its environs would be harmed by the *terribilis impetus* of the imperial army.[117] Even if the author did not have personal knowledge of the destruction wrought on provinces by imperial armies and their barbarian auxiliaries, one of his sources, Sulpicius' *Dialogi*, offers eloquent testimony of the wholesale destruction which could be expected from imperial punitive action.[118] *Vita Orientii* offers a realistic insight into civilian trepidation at the prospect of warfare, to which political allegiances are quite secondary.

The details of the embassy to Aetius and Litorius in the *Vita* beg consideration whether its report is true, notwithstanding the materials reworked from earlier hagiographies, and whether the author was near-contemporary to the subject.[119] Recent commentators have tended to put trust in the *Vita*, in part because Salvian offers approximate corroboration, in part because of the possibility (surely dubious) that 'oral tradition' accurately preserved details from the 430s until the putative early sixth-century composition of the work.[120] Tentative support for a relatively early date may come from the hagiographer's borrowing of the image of the saint as an effective envoy from *Vita Germani*. Writings associated with the cult of St Germanus of Auxerre suggest that the appeal of this image had been lost by the late sixth century. Imitation of that aspect of Constantius' work is more probably early than late.

Vivianus of Saintes

The *Vitae* of Orientius of Auch and of Vivianus (or Bibianus) of Saintes are often paired in modern studies. The two works have in common not only dramatic scenes involving Visigothic kings of Toulouse, but also particular literary motifs which concern embassy narratives.[121] There is no

[117] *Vita Orientii*, 3.

[118] Sulpicius, *Dialogi* III, 11 (Martin anticipates that anti-Priscillianist tribunes to be sent into Spain by Magnus Maximus would not distinguish between heretics and others). For fifth-century examples of wide-scale destruction by imperial forces and auxiliaries: above, n. 78; cf. Ennodius, *Vita Epiphani*, 53, discussed below, at n. 201. Violence to provincials by Litorius' Hunnic auxiliaries is the background for Sid. Ap., *Carm.* VII, 241–94; see chapter 3 above, at nn. 73–74.

[119] Lécrivain, 'La Vie de Saint Orientius', 258 considers the *Vita* erroneous as it is the only source which locates Aetius as well as Litorius at Toulouse at the time of the defeat of the imperial forces in 439. But Sid. Ap., *Carm.* VII, 299–300, strongly implies Aetius' involvement in the final stages of the conflict; cf. also Hydatius, *Chron.*, 112 [104]: Aetius wins a major battle in 438. Aetius must have been involved in the settlement reached by the Goths and the empire later in 439 (Prosper, *Chron.*, 1335; Hyd., c. 117 [109]; Jordanes, *Get.*, 177). The sources concentrate on Litorius because of the shock, and moral exemplum, of his defeat.

[120] Courcelle, *Histoire littéraire*, 347 n. 1 (Salvian is confirmation but not a source); Griffe, *La Gaule chrétienne* II, 69–71 nn. 13 and 16 (oral tradition); Thompson, *Romans and Barbarians*, 265 n. 3; Wolfram, *History of the Goths*, 176.

[121] For edition, see 'Note on editions, commentaries, and translations' below. On Vivianus and the *Vita*: C. Lécrivain, 'Un épisode inconnu de l'histoire des Wisigoths', *Annales du Midi* 1

contemporary attestation of Vivianus' episcopate; he is known only from later liturgical and hagiographic sources.[122] The dates of his episcopate are unknown. In his *Vita*, he meets a Gothic king of Toulouse, Theoderic; there is no clear indication whether this is Theoderic I (418–51) or II (453–67), nor is evidence available of other fifth-century bishops of Saintes.[123] Nor is there any firm internal evidence of the time of composition of the text, which has been dated variously, from close to the saint's life to the Carolingian period.[124]

Vita Viviani is longer than *Vita Orientii*. Vivianus' single embassy, the longest part of the *Vita*, is one of several scenes developed at length. Following is a summary of the *Vita*:

1 Introduction.
2 Vivianus' family and entry into the church.
3 His election.
(The embassy to Toulouse, 4-6)
4 Gothic oppression of citizens of Saintes; Vivianus sets out to Toulouse.
5 His residence in Toulouse near the tomb of the martyr Saturninus; episode of the theft of the oxen which had drawn his cart.
6 The king's *convivium*; success of Vivianus' petition.
7 His prayers free Saintes from attacks by Saxons.

(1889), 47–51; Krusch, Introduction to *Vita Viviani*, 92–3; Duchesne, *Fastes épiscopaux* II, 72–3; F. Lot, 'La *Vita Viviani* et la domination Wisigothique en Aquitaine', in *Mélanges Paul Fournier* (Paris, 1929), 467–77; Courcelle, *Histoire littéraire*, 145–6, 339–47; Griffe, *La Gaule chrétienne* II, 70–1, 274–5; III, 257; Heinzelmann, 'Gallische Prosopographie', 716–17; Goffart, *Barbarians and Romans*, 95–7.

Shared literary motifs: Lécrivain, 'La vie de Saint Orientius', 258; Courcelle, *Histoire littéraire*, 344.

122 *Martyrologium Hieronymianum*, ed. J. B. de Rossi and L. Duchesne, AASS Nov II pars I (Brussels, 1894) (28 August); Venantius Fortunatus, *Carm.* I, 12; Gregory of Tours, *Gloria confessorum*, 57.

123 He is called 'Theodorus' in the text; *Vita Viviani*, 4, 6. In manuscripts of the chronicles, this form is common for Theoderic I, but not for Theoderic II or the Ostrogothic Theoderic; MGH AA 13 Indexes 494, 627.

Theoderic I: Lécrivain, 'Un épisode inconnu', 50 (the tax impositions of *Vita Viviani*, 4, are part of the settlement of the Goths in Aquitaine in 419); Krusch glosses 'Theodorus' with the dates of both Visigothic Theoderics in his note to *Vita Viviani*, 96, n. 1, but identifies the king as Theoderic I in a note to Gregory of Tours, *Gloria confessorum*, MGH SRM 1.2, 330–1 n. 5; Griffe, *La Gaule chrétienne* II, 70–1. Theoderic II: Lot, 'La *Vita Viviani*', 470; Goffart, *Barbarians and Romans*, 96; Mathisen, *Roman Aristocrats*, 99, 100, 122.

The first known successor of Vivianus, Petrus, is attested at the council of Orléans in 511 (Duchesne, *Fastes épiscopaux* II, 73), but given the poor records of the bishops in fifth- and sixth-century Gaul, there could well have been other bishops between Vivianus and Petrus.

124 An early date was proposed by Lécrivain, 'Un épisode inconnu', 48–9 ('un peu après la mort du saint', before the battle of Vouillé in 507; the *Vita* is probably the same text which Gregory of Tours possessed, *Gloria confessorum* 57), but dismissed by Krusch, Introduction to *Vita Viviani*, 92 (Carolingian; certainly after Jonas' *Vita Columbani* so post-640). Lot, 'La *Vita Viviani*', 468, 474–6, argued again for an early date (*c.* 520/30); followed by Levison, *Deutschlands Geschichtsquellen* I, 93 n. 202 (tentatively); Courcelle, *Histoire littéraire*, 344 (who sees *Vita Viviani* as influenced also by *Vita Epiphanii*); Griffe, *La Gaule chrétienne* II, 70–1 n. 15.

8 A trader uses Vivianus' blood as a relic, in the East (during Vivianus' lifetime); construction of a basilica dedicated to Vivianus in the East by the emperor Severus.

9 In his old age, Vivianus builds a basilica in Saintes, with relics from Rome; his death.

As with *Vita Orientii*, close imitation of a miracle account reveals familiarity with Constantius' *Vita Germani* on the part of the author of *Vita Viviani*. *En route* to Arles, Germanus suffers the theft of his horse during the night; but the next day, the thief returns the beast, casting himself at Germanus' feet to confess his sin and stating that he had been miraculously transfixed all night, unable to move in any direction other than to return the horse to its owner. Germanus, recognising that need prompted the theft, gives the horse to the man with his blessing.[125] This quietly humorous scene is emulated in *Vita Vivianus*: at night, after Vivianus has arrived in Toulouse, a thief steals the oxen which had drawn the carriage in which the bishop travelled, but then walks in circles for the rest of the night, realising at dawn that he is again at the same point where he had taken the animals. He confesses his crime at the feet of Vivianus, who mercifully grants the oxen to the man for him to live by his labour, not theft.[126] As in *Vita Germani*, the scene is part of the journey of an embassy. The descent of this scene in *Vita Viviani* from *Vita Germani* seems clear. A less close parallel is discernible also between the accounts of Germanus' and Vivianus' early years.[127]

The embassy narrative of *Vita Viviani* concerns a representation on behalf of the provincials of Saintes to the Gothic king of Toulouse. An *intolerabilis iniunctio* is imposed on the citizens of Saintes, causing the impoverishment and even slavery of both *mediocres* and *nobiles*. Some Goths, seeking to acquire for themselves the forfeited lands of the *nobiles*, eagerly carry imprisoned citizens of Saintes to Toulouse.[128] Vivianus, unwilling for members of his flock to be imprisoned without their bishop, travels also to Toulouse where, finding humble accommodation near the tomb of the martyr Saturninus, he meets and forgives the thief in the

[125] Constantius, *Vita Germani*, 20.

[126] *Vita Viviani*, 5. Though the events are very close to *Vita Germani*, there are no marked verbal echoes; the tone of *Vita Viviani* is harsher than its model. Whereas the thief in *Vita Germani* is unable to move, his counterpart in *Vita Viviani* wanders in circles all night; the change is perhaps derived from Paulinus, *Vita Ambrosii*, 8 (Ambrose's attempt to escape episcopal election; cf. *Vita Viviani*, 3: another echo from *Vita Ambrosii*). The theft scene in *Vita Germani* is anecdotal, loosely linked to the surrounding embassy narrative, but that of *Vita Viviani* has a somewhat greater structural significance, as popular report of the saint's mercy prompts his entré to the king's court.

[127] Constantius, *Vita Germani*, 1, cf. *Vita Viviani*, 2. Levison, 'Bischof Germanus', 144.

[128] On this *iniunctio*: Goffart, *Barbarians and Romans*, 96.

story above. Rumour of this benevolence catches the attention of the king, who invites Vivianus to his *convivium*. There, the king orders the bishops present to drink to him, but Vivianus, seeing the ceremony as communion, refuses, because Theoderic is a heretic and a layman. The king is enraged, but the following night, which Vivianus spends in prayer, the king receives a terrifying vision which prompts him to seek the bishop's forgiveness. He consequently agrees to Vivianus' petition for the release of the captive citizens of Saintes.[129]

Like *Vita Orientii*, *Vita Viviani* borrows from both Sulpicius' *Vita Martini* and Constantius' *Vita Germani* to construct this narrative. Vivianus, like Martin and Orientius, is invited to a ruler's *convivium* where he finds himself in a threatening situation. *Vita Viviani* reuses two further elements from Sulpicius' *Vita Martini*, not used in *Vita Orientii*: the ceremonial cup, the use of which insults the ruler; and comparison between the saint and other bishops in attendance at court, pliant to the king's wishes. The author's borrowings from Constantius' *Vita Germani* are more structural. Like *Vita Orientii*, the embassy narrative is isolated from other incidents in the work; but the author has followed Constantius in developing his account of the stages of the embassy. After a lengthy account of the circumstances necessitating the voyage, the author imitates Constantius' description of incidents *en route* in Germanus' travels: the saint's journey is the opportunity for both a miracle account (the theft of the oxen, imitating the theft of Germanus' horse as he travelled to Arles), and for the saint to visit the tomb of a martyr (Germanus at the tomb of St Alban in Britain; Vivianus at the tomb of St Saturninus in Toulouse).[130] The narrative then moves to the dramatic confrontation, using motifs from Sulpicius' *Vita Martini*. In the concluding sentence of the scene, Vivianus returns with his freed fellow citizens to his *patria* and church, bearing gifts given to him by the king. This jubilant return echoes the triumphal conclusions of several of Germanus' journeys.[131] *Vita Viviani* also uses lesser motifs from *Vita Germani* to embellish the embassy narrative: like Germanus (and Orientius), Vivianus is old when he undertakes his journey, and uses 'humble' transport.[132]

[129] *Vita Viviani*, 4–6. For brief discussion on the status of the bishops at the *convivium*: Ralph W. Mathisen, 'Barbarian Bishops and the Churches *in barbaricis gentibus* during Late Antiquity', *Speculum* 72 (1997), 681 n. 111.

[130] Journey as opportunity for miracles: cf. Constantius, *Vita Germani*, 20: *etiam eius iter clarum fuisse virtutibus* (theft of horse). Martyrs: *ibid.*, 16; *Vita Viviani*, 5.

[131] *Vita Viviani*, 6: *Et cum magnis opibus, ab eodem qui auferre cupiebat rebus plurimus muneratus, reduxit patriae incolomes cives, et sic virtutibus clarum recepit ecclesia sacerdotem.* Cf. Constantius, *Vita Germani*, 19, 24 *fin*.

[132] *Vita Viviani*, 4: *confractus senio; carri vehiculum quamvis altus mente, humilis habitu perquisivit.* Cf. Constantius, *Vita Germani*, 28: *senex*; 19: *contentus parvissimo comitatu et exigua evectione.*

The author has reworked elements from Constantius' embassy narratives and Sulpicius' scenes of secular confrontation in order to describe the appeal of a bishop for release of fellow citizens imprisoned because of onerous taxation. The description of the embassy, however, is ambiguous. The purpose of Vivianus' journey to Toulouse is not explicitly to plead for release of the prisoners, but to share their captivity voluntarily; arriving in the royal city, the bishop does not seek an audience with the king, but is summoned by Theoderic only because of his benevolence towards the thief; at the *convivium*, Vivianus makes no representation to the king. It is only after Theoderic's vision that the author refers to '[Vivianus'] petition for the release of the citizens'.[133] This ambiguity is underscored by the statement that Vivianus achieved the release of the prisoners 'trusting in divine authority rather than in supplication'.[134] The author of *Vita Viviani* seeks to exploit the drama and image of authority which could be drawn from embassy scenes, without portraying his subject in the humbling position of a suppliant. This ambiguity reflects closer adherence to Constantius' Germanus than to Sulpicius' Martin. Though Martin 'commanded rather than requested' when making supplications to the emperor Maximus, his *Vita* and Sulpicius' *Dialogi* show him compromising his views in order to win appeals.[135] Constantius' portrayal of Germanus' embassies to Arles and to Ravenna, however, avoids actually presenting the bishop in supplication.[136]

Though neither *Vita Orientii* nor *Vita Viviani* displays the sustained narrative structure of *Vita Germani*, both imitate Germanus' presentation of a bishop engaged in undertaking embassies to secular rulers on behalf of his local community, to prevent war and oppressive taxation. Both

[133] *Vita Viviani*, 6: *petitio eius* [sc. *Viviani*] *pro absolutione civium*.

[134] *Vita Viviani*, 6: *auctoritate divina potius quam supplicatione fretus*.

[135] Above, at nn. 33, 36.

[136] Cf. later versions of Pope Leo's embassy to Attila, in which, like Theoderic in *Vita Viviani*, Attila is convinced by visions rather than persuasion: Pizarro, *Writing Ravenna*, 117–18.

Vita Viviani clearly influenced the *Life* of Marcellus, bishop of Die in Viennensis (463–510). The extant prose and metric texts of his life are Carolingian but may be based on an earlier *Vita*: François Dolbeau, 'La *Vie* en prose de saint Marcel, évêque de Die', *Francia* 11 (1983), 97–130, esp. 107–9, prose text at 113–30. As in the *Vita* of Vivianus, the citizens of Marcellus' town are deported *en masse* by a Gothic king, though here the king is Euric, and the exiles are taken to Arles not Toulouse; Marcellus secures their release after a healing miracle which restores the king's (unnamed) son to health (*Vita Marcelli* IV–V). More clearly than in *Vita Viviani*, no supplication on the part of the bishop is intimated. In a later episode, however, the bishop does act explicitly on behalf of the city of Die: while in Lyons to attend the dedication of a church (in 506: Dolbeau, n. 44 to *Vita Marcelli* IX, 1), he petitions the Burgundian king Gundobad, seeking *immunitas* for Die from a tax. Gundobad refuses, but reverses his decision after a healing miracle cures a servant of his queen Caratena (*Vita Marcelli* IX; for Caratena: CIL XIII, 2372; *PLRE* II, 'Caratena', 260–1; Heinzelmann, 'Gallische Prosopographie', 574). Healing miracles involving the children or servants of powerful figures are a common hagiographical motif following New Testament archetypes; see n. 19 above. On *Vita Marcelli*, see also chapter 6 below, n. 81.

works were composed probably in the early sixth century. In seeking credit for their heroes by appealing to two images, the thaumaturge and the envoy, the authors attest the appropriation by the provincial church of the social credit associated with the completion of legations.

'AUTHOR OF CONCORD': ENNODIUS, *LIFE OF EPIPHANIUS OF PAVIA*

The lengthiest and most developed accounts of embassies in fifth- and early sixth-century Latin literature appear in a saint's *Life* written in Italy: the *Vita Epiphani* of Ennodius.[137] Epiphanius was bishop of Pavia in northern Italy, 466–96.[138] Nearly the whole narrative of Epiphanius' episcopate in the *Vita* is dedicated to his journeys and involvment in political negotiations in the time of the last western emperors and their successors, Odoacer and Theoderic;[139] the work presents something like a historical novella of the period. Major differences in content and presentation exist between Constantius' *Vita Germani* and *Vita Epiphani*: miracle accounts are negligible in the latter, and none of Epiphanius' many journeys involves ecclesiastical affairs, at least in Ennodius' presentation. Nevertheless, Ennodius can be seen to have made a conscious choice to structure his work on the basis of the Gallic model in presenting his subject as an envoy.

Unlike the other authors discussed in this chapter, Ennodius is well documented, not least from his autobiographical *Confessio* and almost 300 letters.[140] Born in Gaul 473/4, perhaps at Arles, he was of a prominent family whose ancestors included a consul. After his parents died in his youth, he moved to northern Italy, perhaps Milan, where he was brought up by an aunt. The move was probably connected not with Euric's conquest of Arles in 476, but rather with promoting Ennodius'

[137] For editions, see 'Note on editions, commentaries, and translations' below. On *Vita Epiphani*: Reydellet, *La royauté*, 141–82; Teillet, *Des Goths*, 274–80; S. J. B. Barnish, 'Ennodius' *Lives* of Epiphanius and Antony: Two Models for the Christian Gentleman', *Studia Patristica* 24 (1993), 13–19; Cesa, Introduction to *Vita del Epifanio*, 27–36.

[138] On Epiphanius: *PCBE* II, 'Epiphanius 1', 637–41. On early medieval Pavia: Donald Bullough, 'Urban Change in Early Medieval Italy: The Example of Pavia', *Papers of the British School at Rome* 34 (1966), 82–131.

[139] Cf. Cesa, Preface to *Vita del Epifanio*, 5 ('un singolare prelato-diplomatico'), 23–5.

[140] On Ennodius: Hartel, Index nominum et rerum to Ennodius, *Opera*, 620; Vogel, Introduction to Ennodius, *Opera*, summary at xxviii; B. Hasenstab, *Studien zur Ennodius: ein Beitrag zur Geschichte der Völkerwanderung* (Munich, 1890); C. Benjamin, 'Magnus Felix Ennodius 4', *RE* v (1905), 2629–33; J. Sundwall, *Adhandlungen zur Geschichte des ausgehenden Römertums* (Helsinki, 1919), 1–83; Schanz-Hosius IV, 2, 131–48; J. Fontaine, 'Ennodius', in *Reallexikon für Antike und Christentum* V (Stuttgart, 1962), 398–421; *PLRE* II, 'Magnus Felix Ennodius 3', 393–4; Cesa, Introduction to *Vita del Epifanio*, esp. 8–17; *PCBE* II, 'Magnus Felix Ennodius', 621–32. *Confessio*: ed. Vogel, MGH AA 7, 300–4; ed. Hartel, CSEL 6, 393–401.

educational and social prospects.[141] In 489, the year Theoderic entered Italy and Ennodius turned sixteen, Ennodius' aunt died. Ennodius contracted a marriage with an unnamed daughter of a noble family, but the marriage did not eventuate because Ennodius' fortunes collapsed; the disarray caused by the prolonged conflict between Odoacer and Theoderic in northern Italy during 489–93 may have been the cause. Instead of the planned marriage, Ennodius entered the church, *c.* 493. His ordination was urged by Fl. Anicius Probus Faustus 'Niger', a relative and frequent correspondent. Faustus was a powerful patron, particularly at the time of Ennodius' entry to the church: a senior member of the Anicii clan, the last appointment as western consul by Odoacer in 490 and the first attested *magister officiorum* under Theoderic (though whether appointed by Odoacer or Theoderic is unclear), he undertook an embassy on Theoderic's behalf to the emperor Anastasius, *c.* 492–4, to gain imperial recognition of Theoderic's viceroyalty of Italy.[142] Ennodius, Faustus' client, was ordained by Epiphanius, bishop of Pavia. In 494, presumably after his ordination, he accompanied Epiphanius on an embassy to the Burgundian king Gundobad in Lyons to redeem Italian captives.[143] In 495/6, Ennodius declaimed a eulogistic poem in honour of the thirtieth anniversary of Epiphanius' episcopal election; Epiphanius did not live to his next anniversary. Ennodius is next attested, before 499, as a deacon of the church of Milan, under Bishop Laurence (490–512).[144] With the sole exception of his eulogy for Epiphanius' thirtieth anniversary, Ennodius' extant writings begin in 501. The earliest non-epistolary work appears to be the prose speech he delivered in honour of the anniversary of Laurence's ordination, in March 503. Ennodius was active in support of

[141] Gothic conquest of Arles linked to Ennodius' migration: Mathisen, *Roman Aristocrats in Visigothic Gaul*, 63. The valuable education in grammar and rhetoric which Ennodius received in Italy was sought also by a steady stream of nephews who followed him from Visigothic Gaul during the 500s, to be directed by their uncle to the school of Milan. Their mothers, Ennodius' sisters and other female relations, lived in Visigothic Gaul, one sister in Arles, whence the family had perhaps originated (*PLRE* II, 'Euprepia', 426–7 [Arles]; 'Archotamia', 135 [Marseilles]; 'Camilla', 255 [Gaul]; 'Fl. Licerius Firminus Lupicinus 3', 694; 'Parthenius 2', 832–3; Riché, *Education and Culture in the Barbarian West*, 24–6). Ennodius' family demonstrates not aristocratic flight before conquering barbarians, but the gender division in educational ambitions of the late Roman aristocracy.

[142] Urged by Faustus: Ennodius, *Ep.* I, 7 (= *opus* XI Vogel); Barnish, 'Ennodius' *Lives* of Epiphanius and Antony', 17–18. On Faustus: Sundwall, *Abhandlungen*, 117–20, 191; *PLRE* II, 'Fl. Anicius Probus Faustus iunior Niger', 454–6. Faustus and Ennodius: Moorhead, *Theoderic in Italy*, 157; *PCBE* II, 'Magnus Felix Ennodius', 621, 623–5. See further chapter 5 below, at nn. 83–5.

[143] Ordination: Ennodius, *Vita Epiphani*, 199. Gaul: 171.

[144] Vogel, Introduction to Ennodius, *Opera*, makes Ennodius transfer from Pavia to Milan after Epiphanius' death; Cook, *Life of Saint Epiphanius*, 209–10, arguing that such a transfer would have contravened western ecclesiastical practice, suggests that Ennodius was originally attached to Milan but ordained by the bishop of Pavia while Laurence was imprisoned by Odoacer on account of his support for Theoderic.

Pope Symmachus in the Laurentian schism in Rome during the early 500s, as were his patron Faustus Niger and Bishop Laurence of Milan. Ennodius wrote a refutation of criticisms of Symmachus and, together with his bishop, Laurence, he visited Ravenna in late 503 to advance Symmachus' cause; Ennodius provided significant amounts of money for Laurence to disburse there on Symmachus' behalf.[145] Internal evidence indicates that Ennodius' *Vita Epiphani* was written during this period, *c.* 502–4.[146]

Ennodius' later career, not strictly relevent to assessment of the *Vita*, none the less indicates his high status and shows continuities with Epiphanius' own life. Perhaps in late 506, Ennodius was sent on a journey to the Cottian Alps, apparently by his bishop.[147] He enjoyed close contact not only with Faustus Niger but also with other senior palatine officials in Ravenna, from whom he received assistance for clients and valuable information on the itinerary of the royal court and the best means to approach the king to pursue suits.[148] During 507, Ennodius made an extended stay in Ravenna for purposes which are obscure; while there, in April 507, he delivered a panegyric before Theoderic in Ravenna, on behalf of the church of Milan.[149] Not surprisingly, Ennodius was well tutored in the political views of Theoderic's court. Ennodius' Bishop Laurence was also in Ravenna later the same year, and Ennodius contemplated a further trip there early the next year, to present a case before the king.[150] In 511, he was chosen as envoy to represent his province, Liguria, on a mission to Theoderic – it was in this capacity that Epiphanius had twice travelled to Ravenna – but ill health made Ennodius disinclined to undertake the journey, and he hoped, from information passed on by contacts in Ravenna, that Theoderic would soon be travelling to the province of Liguria and so make the trip unnecessary.[151] Throughout

[145] Ennodius, *Opera*, 77, 139, 283, 300 (Ennodius sponsored Laurence's expenses on Symmachus' behalf), 362 = *Epp.* III, 10; IV, 11; VI, 16, 33; VII, 29. In late 508, Ennodius was still seeking reimbursement from Symmachus. *Fragmentum Laurentianum* (Duchesne, *Liber pont.*), 52, accuses Symmachus of bribing Theoderic's court.

[146] Date of *Vita Epiphani*: Vogel, Introduction to Ennodius, *Opera*, xviii–xix; Sundwall, *Adhandlungen*, 21, 74.

[147] Ennodius, *opus* 245 = *Carm.* I, 1, line 6: *Iussus in excursum Gallica lustra sequi*; line 16: *edocuit vates fervidus imperio*. Hartel, Index nominum et rerum to Ennodius, *Opera*, 620; Sundwall, *Abhandlungen*, 39; Barnish, 'Ennodius' *Lives* of Epiphanius and Antony', 18.

[148] *PCBE* II, 'Magnus Felix Ennodius', 623–5.

[149] Ennodius, *Panegyricus Theoderico regi dictus*, ed. Vogel, MGH AA 7, 203–14; ed. Hartel, CSEL 6. On behalf of church of Milan: *Pan.*, 77. Date and place: Sundwall, *Abhandlungen*, 42–4. Suggested political and ecclesiastic contexts for the *Panegyric* are reviewed by Cesa, Introduction to *Vita del Epifanio*, 20–1 n. 33.

[150] Ennodius, *opus* 294 = *Ep.* VI, 27; Sundwall, *Abhandlungen*, 47.

[151] Ennodius, *opus* 433 = *Ep.* IX, 11.6: *legati provincialis nomen*; cf. *opera*, 435, 437 = *Ep.* IX, 13, 14. Barnish, 'Ennodius' *Lives* of Epiphanius and Antony', 18.

the early 500s, Ennodius corresponded with Laconius, a senior palatine official (perhaps *consilarius*) of the Burgundian king Gundobad; Epiphanius and Ennodius had met Laconius during the embassy to Lyons in 494. The correspondence ceases in 506/7, about the time of the outbreak of hostilities leading up to the battle of Vouillé.[152] Ennodius' extant writings terminate in early 513. Probably the next year, he became bishop of Pavia, the second in succession to Epiphanius. Twice in the next three years, in 515 and 517, he and several other bishops were sent by Pope Hormisdas on embassies to the emperor Anastasius, concerning the Acacian schism between Rome and Constantinople; Anastasius treated the second embassy with contempt and Ennodius' return to Italy was uncomfortable. Hormisdas' instructions for the first mission are extant.[153] Ennodius' epitaph records his death in 521.

This outline of Ennodius' career provides some context for the composition of his *Vita Epiphani*. The author was a member of Epiphanius' lower clergy in the last years of the bishop's life. His selection to present a eulogy of the bishop's anniversary after only some two years in orders suggests that Faustus' patronage of Ennodius elevated his standing above his junior level. Ennodius lived in northern Italy during the disturbed years of conflict between Odoacer and Theoderic, vividly described in *Vita Epiphani*, and he accompanied Epiphanius on at least one embassy, to Gaul in 494. It is possible that Ennodius accompanied his bishop on one subsequent journey also, to Theoderic in Ravenna in 496, though Ennodius' account could have been derived from other members of the bishop's entourage. Ennodius had already written a shorter, poetic eulogy of Epiphanius before composing the *Vita*. The *Vita* itself was written within six to eight years of the death of its subject; Ennodius draws attention to how recent some of the events described were.[154] Presumably he maintained contacts with the church of Pavia after Epiphanius' death and his own transfer to Milan, prior to his election as bishop of the city.[155] Such contacts might have prompted the composition of the *Vita*. The

[152] Ennodius, *opera* 38, 86, 252 = *Epp*. II, 5; III, 16; V, 24.

[153] For Hormisdas' instructions, see chapter 6, below, at nn. 21–30. On the embassies: *Liber pont*. 54; W. T. Townsend and W. F. Wyatt, 'Ennodius and Pope Symmachus', in *Studies in Honor of E. K. Rand* (New York, 1938), 277–91.

[154] Ennodius, *Vita Epiphani*, 6.

[155] Evidence of Ennodius' contact with Pavia in the period covered by his extant writings, 501–13, is sparse: only two letters to a recipient in Pavia, the nun Speciosa (possibly the intended spouse of the young Ennodius); Ennodius, *opus* 35, 36 = *Ep*. II, 2, 3; and two *Dictiones* written on behalf of Bishop Maximus, Epiphanius' successor as bishop of Pavia; *Dict*., 3, 4 = *opera* 214, 277; Sundwall, *Abhandlungen*, 72–83. Though Ennodius travelled to Ravenna and Rome, he seems to have visited Pavia only once in the period covered by his extant writings; *opus* 36 = *Ep*. II, 3.

His election as bishop of Pavia perhaps owed much to his earlier support for Laurence of Milan, metropolitan of Liguria, in the Laurentian schism.

work was the first lengthy hagiography Ennodius had written, though he had composed at least the two shorter eulogies for Epiphanius and for Laurence of Milan. He was to write a second *Vita*, of Antony, a monk of Lérins, several years later; this work has resonances with the other well-known hagiographic product of Ostrogothic Italy, Eugippius' *Vita* of Severinus of Noricum.[156] Proximity in time alone makes Ennodius closer to his subject than Constantius was to Germanus; it also significantly affects the presentation of the subject of the biography.

The *Vita* includes lengthy accounts of six embassies undertaken by Epiphanius, brief descriptions of another three, and references to 'many' others; the bishop is also once shown dealing with a ruler on behalf of his province by letter, and four times negotiating other situations of conflict. The following outline indicates the structure of the work:[157]

I	Introduction.	1–6
II	Family; miracle in childhood; entry to church; appearance; subdeaconate.	7–20
	1st embassy: on behalf of church of Pavia, to the land-owner Burco (property dispute; 456/8).	21–5
	Deaconate; ascesis and reading.	26–35
	Episcopal election; ascesis as bishop.	36–50
III	*2nd embassy*: on behalf of province of Liguria and the *magister utriusque militiae* Ricimer, to the emperor Anthemius in Rome (prevention of civil war; 471).	51–75
IV	His sister Honorata; his alms-giving.	76–8
V	*Brief account*: supplication to emperor Glycerius (473/4).	79
	3rd embassy: as representative of *consilium* of Liguria and the emperor Nepos, to the Gothic king Euric in Toulouse (prevention of Gothic raids; 474).	80–94
VI	Siege of Pavia during Odoacer's revolt against Orestes (476).	95–100
	Restoration of damage; two miracles.	101–5
VII	*Two brief accounts of embassies*: on behalf of Pavia to Odoacer for tax relief (probably not undertaken by Epiphanius personally); on behalf of Liguria to Odoacer for relief from	

[156] *Vita Antoni*: Ennodius, *opus* CCXL = *opusculum* IV, written 506 according to Sundwall, *Adhandlungen*, 77; *PCBE* II, 'Antonius 5', 161. Eugippius, *Vita Severini*, ed. P. Regerat (Sources chrétiennes 374; Paris, 1991), begun 509 and completed 511 (Eugippius, *Epistola ad Paschasio*, 1, in *Vita Severini*). For literary comparison and contrast: Steven Muhlberger, 'Eugippius and the *Life of St. Severus*', *Medieval Prosopography* 17 (1996), 107–24.

[157] Numbering on right from Vogel's edition; section chapter headings in Roman numerals on left are my own, for convenience of reference.

The following is the most likely chronology for Epiphanius' career, based on references in *Vita Epiphani* to Epiphanius' age as he progresses through his clerical career:[158]

438: birth
446: entry to the church of Pavia, as Lector, under Bishop Crispinus (aged eight)
456: becomes subdeacon (aged eighteen)
458: becomes deacon (aged twenty)
466: becomes bishop (aged twenty-eight)
496: death (aged fifty-eight).

Constantius' *Vita Germani* provided the template on which Ennodius modelled his portrait of Epiphanius. *Vita Germani* was published in Ennodius' youth, and certainly circulated, at least in southern Gaul, throughout his lifetime. Ennodius could have encountered the work before moving to Italy, or, perhaps more likely, learnt of it in Milan through Gallic contacts; he had access to other recent literature from southern Gaul.[159]

[158] For the construction of this chronology, see appendix II.

[159] Other recent Gallic literature: poems and letters of Sidonius Apollinaris; Vogel, *Index auctorum profanorum quos citavit aut imitatus est Ennodius*, 332; Cook, *Life of St Epiphanius*, 129–30. Sidonius was introduced in Ravenna by Gallic émigrés: Arator, *Epistula ad Parthenium*, lines 48 (*PL* 68, 251); Riché, *Education and Culture in the Barbarian West*, 26.

Unlike *Vita Orientii* and *Vita Viviani*, there are no direct borrowings of whole scenes from *Vita Germani* in Ennodius' work, though several verbal echoes have been detected.[160] Ennodius' familiarity with *Vita Germani* is shown both in his fundamental narrative strategies – the sequential structure of the work and the characterisation of his hero – and in the borrowing of motifs. Neither Constantius nor Ennodius presents his hero exclusively as an envoy: Germanus is also an ascetic and, especially, a thaumaturge; Epiphanius, again an ascetic, is an ecclesiastical administrator, active in building churches.[161] But in each *Vita*, the aspect of the hero as an envoy and rhetor is intrinsic to the overall composition of the work and determines its narrative structure. The presentation of the bishops as legates enables the narratives of the *Vitae* to be sequentially articulated.[162]

Like Paulinus' *Vita Ambrosii*, the only extant earlier *Life* of an Italian bishop and inevitably an influence on any hagiographer writing in Milan, *Vita Epiphani* possesses a chronology discernible to modern scholars from external dating of the succession of rulers and major events in Italian politics in which Epiphanius participates.[163] These great events are mentioned only as they relate to Epiphanius, not to indicate the chronology of Epiphanius' episcopate.[164] Though the succession of rulers provides a general framework for events, the sequential narrative of the *Vita* arises from the links between the accounts of embassies. This is particularly true of the latter half of the work: Epiphanius' embassy to Theoderic in Milan, after his entry to Italy, foreshadows the Gothic and Rugian occupations

[160] Levison, 'Bischof Germanus von Auxerre', 144–5 (description of Epiphanius' *origo*, cf. *Vita Germani*, 1 and *Vita Epiphani*, 7; Aetius and Ricimer *rem publicam gubernabat*, cf. *Vita Germani*, 28 and *Vita Epiphani*, 51; admiration of Auxiliaris and Gundobad that the saint's merits were so much greater than rumour suggested, cf. *Vita Germani*, 24 and *Vita Epiphani*, 152). Levison sees this as unconscious imitation of a work Ennodius knew in his youth.

[161] Building: Ennodius, *Vita Epiphani*, 101–4, 106. Barnish, 'Ennodius' *Lives* of Epiphanius and Antony', 14.

[162] Cesa, Introduction to *Vita del Epifanio*, 32–3, sees *Vita Germani* as 'un probabile modello' of *Vita Epiphani*, but considers that the portrait of Epiphanius 'di diplomatico ed oratore . . . è del tutto nuova'; cf. Reydellet, *La Royauté*, 147–8: 'D'un point de vue littéraire, on ne sent pas des modèles.' Cesa discusses the *tipi* of Germanus and Epiphanius, a dominant approach in modern hagiographic studies, and rightly notes similarities and differences in their portraits. But more telling than the *tipi* considered in isolation is the underlying narrative structure of each *Vita*, which facilitates the presentation of the bishops as intercessors and which is fundamentally different from the thematically articulated structures in *vitae* of 'prophetic' bishops such as Martin or Severinus. It is Constantius' narrative structure which Ennodius appropriates.

[163] Like Ambrose, Epiphanius' protagonists are almost exclusively rulers. Note the inclusion of the emperors Olybrius and Glycerius; Epiphanius has no dealings with the former, and his contact with the latter is mentioned but not dramatised. These emperors seem to be included for a sense of completeness. First Italian episcopal *vita* since *Vita Ambrosii*: Cesa, Introduction to *Vita del Epifanio*, 7; influence of *Vita Ambrosii*: Cesa, Commentary to *ibid.*, 191.

[164] The only chronological details of Epiphanius' episcopate are Ennodius, *Vita Epiphani*, 81: Epiphanius undertakes the mission to Euric in the eighth year of his episcopate; 182: final journey to Theoderic takes place two years after the embassy to Gundobad.

of Pavia; Epiphanius' appeal to Theoderic for restoration of legal rights is the springboard for the mission to Gundobad, which then prompts first the letter, then the final legation to Theoderic; this mission, in turn, is the occasion for Epiphanius' death-scene. References forward and back tie the scenes closely together.[165] Like Constantius, Ennodius presents his hero in an almost constant state of travel and mediation. The presentation of the bishop as a legate is not an element of historical record so much as a plot device, a structural integration of character and narrative borrowed from *Vita Germani*.

Ennodius incorporated more specific borrowings and motifs from *Vita Germani* also. Epiphanius' death-scene is modelled on Germanus': both bishops' deaths result from illness contracted while on an embassy, in both cases to Ravenna (though Epiphanius manages to return to his own see before dying); both suffer for seven days before passing away; the Holy Spirit reveals their imminent deaths to both beforehand (developed at greater length in *Vita Germani*); the multitudes of the towns where both lie ill are disturbed; high officials visit the dying bishops; both chant psalms during their final days.[166] Like Constantius, Ennodius details the separate stages of each embassy undertaken by Epiphanius: the initial request to the bishop; the journey, with reference to events and the fame of the bishop *en route*;[167] the bishop's *adventus* at his destination, and reception either by fellow bishops or palatine officials; the saint's return and greeting at his own see. Each stage is exploited to indicate the high respect in which the bishop is held. As in *Vita Germani*, the account of Epiphanius' episcopal election is followed by a general description of the ascesis he practised as bishop, before beginning the account of his embassies.[168] Elements of imagery and vocabulary recur: Ennodius frequently uses *labor*, a word favoured by Constantius, to describe the embassies, and stresses the *mira celeritate* with which Epiphanius completes his journeys.[169] The familiar

[165] E.g. Ennodius, *Vita Epiphani*, 110 (Theoderic in Milan, anticipating the use of Pavia as a refuge in § IX); 127, 131 (Epiphanius and Theoderic in Ravenna recall the siege of Theoderic's forces in Pavia).

[166] Constantius, *Vita Germani*, 41–2; Ennodius, *Vita Epiphani*, 190–5. (For *Vita Epiphani*, 191: *tamquam ad sepulchri receptaculum properans*, cf. 39: *quasi ad sepulchrum festinans* [sc. Crispinus] *regressus est*.)

[167] Ennodius does not develop any scenes of the journeys, except briefly (*Vita Epiphani*, 177, one of the few miracle accounts). The lengthy accounts of incidents during Germanus' travels are mostly healing miracles; Ennodius does not present Epiphanius as a thaumaturge.

[168] Constantius, *Vita Germani*, 3–5; Ennodius, *Vita Epiphani*, 47–50.

[169] *Labor*: e.g. Ennodius, *Vita Epiphani*, 5, 57, 82, 95, 124, 140, 175, 179, 181; Ennodius uses *studium* and *molestiae* as synonyms (e.g. *Vita Epiphani*, 58, 83). Cf. above, at nn. 48–54 and Cesa, Commentary to *Vita del Epifanio*, 154. *Celeritas*: 151; cf. 51, 57, 58, 59, 72 (*mox, statim, festinans*), 86, 107 (*alacer ambulavit poposcit obtinuit*), 147 (*ex tempore*), 183 (*protinus*); Cesa, Commentary to *Vita del Epifanio*, 161, 200.

motif of the envoy's advanced age is used, as is the conceit that respect for the envoy ensures that his request is granted before being asked.[170] Like Germanus, Epiphanius twice travels with companion bishops, including in each case a figure of great influence at the time of composition.[171] Finally, like Germanus but unlike Martin or Ambrose (or Severinus, in the slightly later *Vita* of Eugippius), Epiphanius is presented as achieving his aims through gaining consensus, not by prophetic castigation; he is, as King Gundobad addresses him, a 'proponent of peace', the 'author of concord', an 'outstanding peace-maker'.[172] Old Testament imagery of divine castigation of unjust kings appears only once in Epiphanius' speeches; Theoderic, his interlocutor, is able to counter with biblical allusions of his own, but none the less grants the bishop's request, out of respect for Epiphanius himself.[173] Germanus and Epiphanius offer consensus, not authority over secular rulers.

Notwithstanding the shaping influence of *Vita Germani* on Ennodius' *Vita Epiphani*, there are significant differences between the composition of the two works. The most striking is the near-absence of miracles from *Vita Epiphani*. While embassy narratives provide the structure for *Vita Germani*, miracle accounts form the bulk of the narrative. *Vita Epiphani*, however, is almost devoid of miraculous elements. Those supernatural events included are mentioned only very briefly. By contrast, Ennodius had already recounted one prodigy, a heavenly light which shone over Epiphanius' cradle when he was a baby, at greater length in his much briefer eulogy of Epiphanius in 496.[174] In one instance, Ennodius states that he will pass over miracles which he knows Epiphanius performed while *en route* to the court of Anthemius in Rome, in favour of recounting the bishop's 'greater deeds' there. This is perhaps a reminiscence of Constantius' explicit omission of miracles worked by Germanus during his travels, but in the context of the paucity of accounts of Epiphanius' miracles, as opposed to the plethora of Germanus', Ennodius seems to

170 Age: Ennodius, *Vita Epiphani*, 183. Conceit: Constantius, *Vita Germani*, 23; Ennodius, *Vita Epiphani*, 54, 61, 71, 141.

171 Constantius, *Vita Germani*, 12 (Lupus of Troyes, on whom see e.g. Sid. Ap., *Epp.* VI, 1; IX, 11), 25 (Severus of Trier). Ennodius, *Vita Epiphani*, 123–4 (Laurence of Milan; cf. *Acta synhodorum habitarum Romae* II, *Praeceptio* I of Theoderic (MGH AA 12), and the signature lists of the *acta* of the councils of 501 and 502); 146, 153 (Victor of Turin).

172 Ennodius, *Vita Epiphani*, 165: *pacis suasor; concordiae auctor; egregie moderator* (also: *Christianae lucis iubar*). Cf. Reydellet, *La Royauté*, 148; Muhlberger, 'Eugippius and the *Life of St. Severus*', 118–20.

173 Ennodius, *Vita Epiphani*, 129, 132.

174 Miracles: Ennodius, *Vita Epiphani*, 8 (glowing light over his cradle; cf. Ennodius, *Carm.* I, 9 = *opus* 43, lines 88–106); 58 (*virtutes* performed *en route* to Rome, mentioned but passed over); 103 (collapsing church vault does not strike workmen); 105 (expulsion of a 'crowd of demons'); 177 (exorcism).

be underscoring his exclusion of miracle accounts.[175] Despite the importance of miracle narratives in highly influential hagiographies including the *Vitae* of Anthony, Martin, and Ambrose, accounts of bishops devoid of supernatural elements were not unprecedented; neither Possidius' *Life* of Augustine nor the *Life* of Fulgentius of Ruspe includes miracle accounts.[176]

The absence of miracles in Ennodius' narrative might in part be a function of his proximity to the saint's own lifetime, to which Ennodius draws attention in his preface – though Sulpicius' *Vita Martini*, the western model of the thaumaturge, was composed during its subject's lifetime.[177] Proximity in time clearly tempers Ennodius' rhetoric. Whereas the embassies of Germanus and Vivianus for taxation relief are completely successful, Ennodius is careful to specify that, in response to Epiphanius' missions, Theoderic does not pardon quite all who had supported Odoacer, or grant to Liguria a complete relief from taxation; nor does Gundobad allow all the Italian prisoners to be redeemed without payment.[178] Nevertheless, more germane to the scarcity of miracles from *Vita Epiphani* may be the purposes of the biography. Ennodius perhaps did not want the romance element of miracle accounts to distract from his narrative. The absence of the miraculous in *Vita Epiphani* affects Ennodius' embassy narratives: Germanus achieves success in his missions after performing healing miracles; Epiphanius wins his cases through oratorical skills and force of personality.[179]

The second major narrative difference between *Vita Germani* and *Vita Epiphani* is Ennodius' use of dramatic speeches. The six major embassy narratives are distinguished not just by their length, but by the inclusion

[175] Ennodius, *Vita Epiphani*, 58: *In quo itinere quid molestiarum sustinuerit quidve virtutum gesserit, festinans ad maiora praetereo*; cf. Constantius, *Vita Germani*, 20: *Operae pretium puto mandare memoriae, etiam eius iter clarum fuisse virtutibus*. Lotter, *Severinus von Noricum*, 57.

[176] Possidius, *Vita Augustini*; *Vita Fulgentii* (the traditional attribution to Ferrandus is disputed), *PL* 65, 117–50, now trans. in *Fulgentius: Selected Works*, trans. R. B. Eno (Washington, DC, 1997), 1–56. *Vita Fulgentii*, 22–3, in fact belittles the importance of miracles in the profile of a bishop, perhaps in line with Augustine's early thought (cf. Brown, *Augustine*, 413–18), though nevertheless attributing by implication healing miracles to Fulgentius; cf. also 6–7 (miraculous recovery of lost *solidi*). On miracles in hagiography: Lotter, *Severinus von Noricum*, 51–9, esp. 57; Stancliffe, *St. Martin and his Hagiographer*, 98.

Augustine's works were much cultivated in Ostrogothic Italy, but the absence of miracles in *Vita Epiphani* is unlikely to have been a result of Augustinian influence; note that Eugippius, a focus for Augustinian scholarship in Italy, included miracles prominently in his *Vita Severini*.

[177] Ennodius, *Vita Epiphani*, 6; Fouracre, 'Merovingian History and Merovingian Hagiography', 11.

[178] Ennodius, *Vita Epiphani*, 134, 170, 187.

[179] These characteristics, like the absence of miracles, are also shared with the portrait of Fulgentius in *Vita Fulgentii*.

of direct dialogue, especially substantial speeches.[180] These formulaic set-pieces, used to heighten the drama of the narrative, assimilate the *Vita* to the genres of epic or *historia*, of no small importance to the high regard for *Vita Epiphani* in modern times.[181] Perhaps significantly, the speeches compensate in length for the omission of miracle accounts.

The speeches reflect a third general difference between *Vita Epiphani* and not only *Vita Germani* but also *Vita Orientii* and *Vita Viviani*. The Gallic works exploit the narrative possibilities of presenting their heroes as envoys, but baulk at actually portraying the bishops in the humbling act of supplication. Ennodius, by contrast, not only dramatises the act of supplication through his speeches, but freely uses the term *legatus*, *legatio*, and *supplicatio* in regard to Epiphanius. Indeed, he explicitly compares Epiphanius with other servants of *principes*, though emphasising the bishop's unselfish superiority in declining rewards for his services; and Ennodius portrays Epiphanius in the act of bowing to a ruler.[182] Ennodius' proximity to the milieux of both an important metropolitan see and the royal court, where the dispatch and reception of legations were common and their undertaking brought prestige and reward, shaped his attitude towards the activity in which he portrayed the saint engaged.

Ennodius, like Constantius, crafts a *persona* for Epiphanius which reinforces his role as an envoy. His characteristic function is forecast in his years before assuming the episcopate. The lengthy account of the young Epiphanius' physiognomy, including praise of his physical comeliness, his *sermo*, and his *vox sonora*, mention that he was, among other things, 'then already adept at intercessions' (the importance of his attractive features to his success as an intercessor is underscored by the testimonial paid him by the Ligurian nobles who later recommend Epiphanius to Ricimer as an envoy to Anthemius).[183] His tenure as deacon was a period of preparatory training in 'the struggles of intercession'.[184] The sole event related from his twenty years in the junior clergy is his first embassy, as representative of his bishop Crispinus, to dispute ownership of property along the Po. He was chosen because 'he would both bravely sustain assertions

[180] Ennodius, *Vita Epiphani* §§ III (dialogue: Ricimer and the *collectio Ligurum nobilitatis*; speeches: Epiphanius and Anthemius), V (Epiphanius and Euric), VIII (Theoderic), X (Epiphanius and Theoderic), XI (Theoderic and Epiphanius; Epiphanius and Gundobad), XIII (Epiphanius and Theoderic). Reydellet, *La Royauté*, 148.

[181] Drama: almost every speech of Epiphanius' interlocutors is bipartite: the first half listing reasons why the bishop's requests should be rejected; the second half suddenly capitulating (e.g. Ennodius, *Vita Epiphani*, 60–1, 67–9/70–1; 131–3/4; 165–6/7; 188 *init.*), thus emphasising, rather stiffly, Epiphanius' overwhelming persuasiveness.

[182] Other servants: Ennodius, *Vita Epiphani*, 179; bowing: 164.

[183] Speech: Ennodius, *Vita Epiphani*, 17: *ad intercessiones iam tunc artifex*. Comeliness: 13–16: *in quo lucem membrorum animae fulgor exuperat*. Testimony of Ligurian nobles: 54: *cui est vultus vitae similis*.

[184] Ennodius, *Vita Epiphani*, 32: *intercessionum etiam tunc certamina proludebat*.

brought against him and temper his replies with mature counsel'.[185] Similarly, the first reported event of his episcopate is his embassy to Rome on behalf of Ricimer. Ennodius emphasises the primacy of this event in Epiphanius' episcopal career by exaggeration; after the careful record of Epiphanius' age during his early years, Ennodius compresses the five years between Epiphanius' election and the embassy to Anthemius with the term *mox*, although he had exact information on the timing of the journey.[186] Epiphanius' episcopate is thus made to begin as it would continue and end, engaged in secular embassies protecting the interests of the province of Liguria. Each of the bishop's interlocutors asserts Epiphanius' irresistible oratory and personality. Gundobad is made to address Epiphanius with the three epithets cited above, describing Epiphanius as a peace-maker; Epiphanius' metropolitan, Laurence of Milan, defers to his junior colleague's experience, for 'the laborious path of frequent legations had wearied his footsteps, and more than once, through the constantly coursing path of such journeys, the dust of the camp had made him grimy'.[187] In his final oration before Theoderic, Epiphanius characterises their relationship as suppliant and ruler: 'Practice fashions me to request necessities, you to grant them.'[188] Like Sidonius' portrait of Avitus, Epiphanius is an envoy who eclipses his principal; Euric, replying to the bishop's speech on behalf of Nepos, accedes to his request, stating: 'Venerable father, I will do as you demand, for the person of the legate is greater to me than the power of the sender.'[189] By both presentation and definition, Epiphanius appears primarily as a legate.

The proximity of Ennodius' image of Epiphanius to a secular ethos is underscored by a chance coincidence. When in the *Vita* Epiphanius approaches Gundobad for the release of Italian captives, the king, persuaded by the bishop's eloquence and saintly bearing, agrees to free without ransom all the captives he possesses, and to encourage those of his men who hold captives to release theirs also, but on payment of ransom, as the

185 Ennodius, *Vita Epiphani*, 21–5, quotation at 22: *qui et fortiter inlatas intentiones exciperet et maturitate consilii inferendas temperaret.*

186 *Mox*: Ennodius, *Vita Epiphani*, 51. Timing: 72 (Epiphanius left Rome to return to Pavia on 9 March. The year must be 471, not 472, as Rome was besieged by Ricimer from February 472; Paul the Deacon, *Historia Romana* xv, 4 with *Fasti Vind. prior*, s.a. 472; Seeck, *Regesten*, s.a. 471).

187 Gundobad: above, n. 172; Gundobad also calls the bishop *Christianae lucis iubar*, one 'Christian' epithet alongside three testimonials of Epiphanius as a peace-maker. Laurence: Ennodius, *Vita Epiphani*, 124: *cuius vestigia frequentium legationum laboriosus callis adtriverat et per tramitem huiuscemodi itineris cursitantem non semel hispidum castrensis pulvis effecerat.* B. Näf, 'Die Zeitbewusstsein des Ennodius und der Untergang Roms', *Historia* 39 (1990), 120.

188 Before Theoderic: Ennodius, *Vita Epiphani*, 185: *et me ad postulanda necessaria et vos ad tribuenda usus informat.*

189 Ennodius, *Vita Epiphani*, 91: *Facio ergo, venerande papa, quae poscis, quia grandior est apud me legati persona quam potentia destinantis.*

captives were part of their war booty.[190] One of the extant fragments of the *Byzantine History* of Malchus of Philadelphia, who was probably an exact contemporary of Ennodius, reports an almost identical story about the Constantinopolitan senator and *patricius* Severus, sent by the emperor Zeno to the Vandal king Geiseric in 474. Geiseric, impressed by Severus' moderation and integrity, particularly his refusal of the conventional gifts offered to him, agrees to release all the Roman captives held by himself and his sons, and to permit Severus to purchase those captives held by his followers, if they are willing to sell.[191] The situation, qualifications, and means of persuasion are almost identical between the two narratives; it is the envoy, not the principal, who earns the king's respect. Malchus, a sophist who wrote from a purely secular, classicising perspective, may have enjoyed contacts with senior court officials at Constantinople, including another of Zeno's envoys. His portrait of the prudent envoy appeals to both the sophistic tradition and the professional ethos of palatine officials.[192] There is no qualitative difference between his presentation of Severus and Ennodius' portrait of Epiphanius in these scenes.[193]

Ennodius could have chosen to portray Epiphanius differently.[194] His poetic declamation in honour of the thirtieth anniversary of Epiphanius' episcopal election was delivered in 495/6, some six to nine years before the composition of the *Vita*.[195] The *dictio* uses, at greater length, themes and images which reappear in the sections of the *Vita* concerning Epiphanius' youth and election: the introductory conceit, the miracle of the glowing light above the cradle, Epiphanius' physical beauty and modesty, his popular election.[196] There may be manuscript evidence that Ennodius consulted the earlier work while composing the *Vita*.[197] But the emphasis of the *dictio* is almost entirely on Epiphanius' election. Only

[190] Ennodius, *Vita Epiphani*, 170. For the historical context: Cesa, Commentary to *Vita del Epifanio*, 195–6.

[191] Malchus, *Fr.* 5; for date of composition: Blockley, *Fr. Class. Hist.* I, 72–3. Cf. Victor of Vita, *Historia persecutionis Africanae provinciae*, ed. K. Halm, MGH AA 3.1 (Berlin, 1879), I, 51.

[192] Contact: Blockley, *Fr. Class. Hist.* I, 78. Professional ethos: below, chapter 5, e.g. following n. 60.

[193] Cf. Faustus of Riez, *De gratia Dei et libero arbitrio* I, 16 (*PL* 58, 809): in a comparison with Christ's redemption of humanity, Faustus envisages an 'envoy or bishop' (*legatus aliquis vel sacerdos*), who seeks the redemption of a city captured in war, receiving the whole population without payment of ransom by a gratuitous act of the victor. (Faustus was one of the four Gallic bishops involved in the ceding of the Auvergne to Euric in 475, Sid. Ap., *Ep.* VII, 6.10; he was himself exiled after Euric took control of Provence; Heinzelmann, 'Gallische Prosopographie', 607.)

[194] Ennodius' choice on mode of presentation of Epiphanius: Reydellet, *La Royauté*, 148.

[195] Ennodius, *Carm.* I, 9 = *opus* 43. Editions: ed. Sirmond, *PL* 63, 322–6; ed. Vogel, MGH AA 7, 40–5; ed. Hartel, CSEL 6, 531–9. On the date: Hasenstab, *Studien zur Ennodius*, 15–18; Benjamin, 'Ennodius', 2631; Sundwall, *Adhandlungen*, 13–14, 73; Schanz-Hosius IV, 2, 145.

[196] Hasenstab, *Studien zur Ennodius*, 15.

[197] Benjamin, 'Ennodius', 2631.

one incident from his episcopate intrudes: Epiphanius' mission to Gaul to ransom the captive Italians, undertaken the year before Ennodius presented the *dictio*. The *dictio* presents in outline the story later developed in full in the *Vita*: Epiphanius secured the return of his captured people from Gaul through the effects of his prayers on a king. There are strong verbal echoes between the accounts of the *dictio* and the *Vita*.[198] But the account in the *dictio* is only eight lines long (in a work of 170 lines), and there is no context to suggest that the bishop had repeatedly undertaken similar journeys. The incident seems to be included because of its topicality. Although the *dictio* gives no temporal indication that this event happened almost three decades after the bishop's election, the subject both was recent and had current ramifications, for the disruption to the economy of Liguria was not resolved by the return of the captives, and would prompt Epiphanius' final embassy to Theoderic for taxation relief. The *dictio* and the *Vita* do not present contradictory portraits of Epiphanius; the difference in emphasis between the two is in part because the *dictio* was an occasional piece. But the divergence suggests a decision by Ennodius, when composing the *Vita* some years after the *dictio*, to take up an incident mentioned in the *dictio* only briefly and on account of its current relevance, and to expand it into a fundamental theme. The process is reminiscent of the contrast between Hydatius and other chroniclers in regard to the record or disregard of embassies: an occurrence so common as to be generally passed over is chosen by an author at a specific time as a useful theme or framework.

This literary decision by Ennodius begs the question, what is his purpose in framing *Vita Epiphani* as he did? Most obviously, portraying Epiphanius as an envoy provides opportunity for many demonstrations of the high respect in which he was held by other bishops, rulers, and the general populace, through the testimonials of Epiphanius' interlocutors and brief dramatisations of ceremonial. Ennodius emphasises this respect by his selectiveness in representing Epiphanius as acting in isolation, just

[198] Ennodius, *Carm.* 1, 9 = *opus* 43, lines 126–33:

> Tu bene transmissum tibi censum possides, heres.
> Res non parva docet triplicatis iuncta talentis:
> Monstrat ab occidui revocatum partibus orbis
> Quod supplex captum transmittit Gallia vulgus.
> Effera te viso didicerunt pectora flecti,
> Armatum precibus superasti, maxime, regem.
> Sic pugnax gladios obtundit verbere lingua,
> Sic ferrum expugnat verborum lammina fortis.

To the last two lines, cf. Ennodius, *Vita Epiphani*, 176: *quantum acutior fuit verborum quam ferri lammina, hinc lector agnosce: expugnavit sermo cui se gladii subduxerunt.*

as the legends of Pope Leo elevate his role in dealing with Attila by erasing all other participants. In fact, Epiphanius' missions took place in a context in which provincial and palatine embassies were very common. Ennodius' narrative misleads. Other embassies between Nepos and Euric, employing palatine officials, are known. Ennodius makes Theoderic select Epiphanius from amongst other bishops for the mission to Gundobad, giving the impression that the king considered only bishops when choosing an envoy, whereas in fact Theoderic freely chose representatives from a wide range of positions: senior and junior palatine officials, aristocrats from the leading families of Rome, as well as clergy including, famously, a pope.[199] Epiphanius, rather than Laurence of Milan, is portrayed as being the principal envoy of the legation to Theoderic to appeal for restoration of legal rights, but the reverse may have been true. An appeal from Laurence would have been weighty: not only was he a metropolitan bishop, but he himself had been exiled from Milan by Odoacer for supporting Theoderic; a petition for clemency from Odoacer's victim would have been hard to dismiss.[200] Ennodius' selective presentation artificially boosts Epiphanius' credit. Taken out of their literary context, Epiphanius' embassies appear rather less exceptional. The prime importance of his missions was at a local level, to their beneficiaries.

This relevance at the local level suggests the milieu in which Ennodius wrote the work. Though Epiphanius acts against a broad landscape stretching from central Italy to western Gaul, it is the province of Liguria which is the focal concern of each mission. An assembly of Ligurian nobles, eager to prevent the destructiveness of civil war, initiates the peace overtures from Ricimer to Anthemius and selects Epiphanius as envoy; another *consilium* of Ligurian magnates, summoned by Nepos, chooses Epiphanius to travel to Euric.[201] Epiphanius is motivated not, as Germanus, by the desire to labour for God, but by 'the love I owe to my homeland'.[202] The embassies for taxation relief are undertaken on behalf of either the bishop's see, Pavia, or the province of Liguria;

[199] Envoys from Nepos to Euric: Sid. Ap., *Epp.* III, 7.2–4 (the *quaestor* Licinianus); VII, 6, 7 (the bishops Basilius of Aix, Leontius of Arles, Faustus of Riez, and Graecus of Marseilles). Theoderic: Ennodius, *Vita Epiphani*, 136; his envoys: below, chapter 5, at nn. 24, 26.

[200] Ennodius, *Dictio* I, 15; Courcelle, *Histoire littéraire*, 203.

[201] Anthemius: Ennodius, *Vita Epiphani*, 53 (*collectio Ligurum nobilitatis*), 54–5 (selection); cf. 64 (Epiphanius casts himself as representative of Italy as well as Ricimer before the emperor). Euric: 81–2. Cf. the Gallic council assembled by Aetius which chooses Avitus to approach the Goths for support against Attila; above, chapter 3, n. 80. On Liguria: Andreas Schwarcz, 'Die Liguria zwischen Goten, Byzantinern, Langobarden und Franken im 6. Jahrhundert', in Laura Balletto (ed.), *Oriente e occidente tra medioevo ed età moderna*, ed. (Genoa, 1997), 1109–31. On the Ligurian provincial council: Cesa, Commentary to *Vita del Epifanio*, 151–2, 169.

[202] Ennodius, *Vita Epiphani*, 57. Cf. Näf, 'Die Zeitbewusstsein des Ennodius', 121.

when dealing with the Roman, Gothic, and Rugian armies occupying Pavia, Epiphanius acts for his city.[203] Somewhat more equivocal are the embassies to Theoderic for restoration of legal rights, and the mission to Gundobad. The former is introduced as a representation on behalf of a class, those who had not supported Theoderic during the war with Odoacer; support for Odoacer and Theoderic was divided throughout the whole of Italy.[204] Yet the speech Ennodius makes Epiphanius deliver before Theoderic presents the province of Liguria as the suppliant.[205] Similarly, though the mission to Gaul to ransom captives is commissioned by Theoderic, who refers to 'the whole of Italy' as ravaged by the Burgundians' plunder, the sequence as a whole strongly emphasises the restoration of Liguria through the legation.[206] Ennodius gives attention to Epiphanius' relations with the province of Liguria also through repeated reference to Milan, the capital and metropolitan see of the province; as Ennodius was attached to the church of Milan at the time of composition, this attention is not surprising.[207] Like the Gallic and Spanish sources discussed in earlier chapters, imperial and royal issues in *Vita Epiphani* are seen through a provincial focus. Regional concerns animate the provinces' main political voice, embassies.

In the *dictio* for Epiphanius' episcopal anniversary, the embassy to redeem the Italian captives is the only deed mentioned from Epiphanius' thirty-year episcopate. The equivalent account in the *Vita*, by far the longest single section, is also the most developed narrative, comprising four long speeches; several other passages of direct dialogue; substantial rhetorical descriptions utilising biblical and classical imagery; the most references to persons of influence in any section; one of the few miracles

203 §§ VI, VII, IX, XII, XIII. Cf. Liebeschuetz, *Decline and Fall of the Roman City*, 156.

204 Divided support: Cassiodorus, *Variae* I, 3.3–4 (support for both Theoderic and Odoacer in Sicily); Gelasius, *Ep.* 95 (*PL* 59, 63) (resistance to Odoacer in Rome; cf. Courcelle, *Histoire littéraire*, 203). Ennodius, *Vita Epiphani*, 109–10; Ennodius, *Dictio* I, 15 (both Epiphanius and his metropolitan, Laurence of Milan, supported Theoderic). Theoderic threatened reprisals in regions other than northern Italy: Sicily (Cassiodorus, as above); possibly Rome (if H. Useners' interpretation of the circumstances of the delivery of the speech *pro allecticiis* by Q. Aurelianus Memmius Symmachius is correct; cited Schanz-Hosius IV, 2, 84; Courcelle, *Histoire littéraire*, 204; Moorhead, *Theoderic*, 31). See Cesa, Commentary to *Vita del Epifanio*, 189.

205 Ennodius, *Vita Epiphani*, 130: *Liguria vestra nobiscum profusa supplicat.*

206 Ennodius, *Vita Epiphani*, 138 (*universa Italiae loca*), cf. 141, 157; 138–9, 141, 162 (Liguria).

207 Ennodius, *Vita Epiphani*, 36–8 (Epiphanius' predecessor Crispinus seeks the approval of Rusticius, bishop of Milan, for Epiphanius to be his successor); 53, 75 (Ricimer at Milan); 123–4 (bishop Laurence of Milan accompanies Epiphanius to Theoderic to plead for restoration of legal rights). Vogel, Introduction to Ennodius, *Opera*, xviii, doubts that Ennodius wrote the *Vita* in Milan as his bishop Laurence is described with *ieiunis verbis*, but cf. the similarly jejune references to Lupus of Troyes in Constantius, *Vita Germani*, 12–19: to Constantius' contemporary Sidonius, Lupus was a leading light of the Gallic church; e.g. Sid. Ap., *Epp.* VI, 1; IX, 11.

in the *Vita*; and the only intrusion of Ennodius himself into his narrative, as a witness of events.[208] Moreover, the redemption of the captives is the only incident recalled at the end of the *Vita*: at Epiphanius' funeral, 'every mother went there and cried that her son had been freed by him; every wife, her husband; every sister, her brother; he who was a single man, himself'.[209] The local focus of the *Vita* is underscored by this concluding pathos.

Because Epiphanius is portrayed as acting against a grand canvas, because the speeches he is made to deliver address political issues, and because Ennodius was clearly well informed about certain issues important to the court of Ravenna, *Vita Epiphani* has been interpreted as having an essentially political purpose, a sort of narrative 'mirror for princes' rising from a rough abutment between Christianity, Roman culture, and barbarian rule in Ostrogothic Italy.[210] To be sure, Ennodius shows himself aware of major political issues of the day, and the speeches contain sentiments of good rule, some specifically Christian in origin or imagery, others more general statements of governance.[211] But this is not the same as a sustained political message. The sentiments of the speeches are conventional.[212] There is no clear division between Roman and barbarian rulers; oratory, seen by some as the badge of distinction between Romans and barbarians, is a characteristic of both Theoderic and Gundobad.[213] Ennodius' presentation of rulers is not simple or consistent; though all the

[208] Length: forty-one sections out of 199 in Vogel's edition; the missions to Anthemius and Euric occupy twenty-four and fourteen, the three missions to Theoderic occupy two, thirteen, and seven sections. Names: bishops Victor of Turin, Rusticianus of Lyons, and Avitus of Vienne; the religious woman Syagria; Gundobad's brother Godigisclus; Laconius, probably Gundobad's *consiliarius*. Witness: Ennodius, *Vita Epiphani*, 171.

[209] Ennodius, *Vita Epiphani*, 197: *quaecumque ibi mater venit, liberatum clamavit ab illo filium; quaecumquae uxor, maritum; quaecumque soror, fratrem; qui caelebs, se ipsum*. That the Burgundian captivity is meant, not the taking of captives during Odoacer's siege of Orestes in Pavia, is indicated by the exclusively male prisoners whose freedom is celebrated; during Odoacer's siege, female citizens were captured for ransom; *Vita Epiphani*, 97, 99 (Honorata and Luminosa; *matres familias*).

[210] E.g. Reydellet, *La Royauté*, 141–82; Cesa, Introduction to *Vita del Epifanio*, 23; cf. Teillet, *Des Goths*, 276–80.

[211] Current issues: e.g. Theoderic's concerns regarding succession: Ennodius, *Vita Epiphani*, 186; his marriage alliance with Gundobad: 163. The mission to Gundobad is seen as negotiating this alliance by e.g. Courcelle, *Histoire littéraire*, 181; Schwarcz, 'Die Liguria', 1112; Danuta Shanzer, 'Two Clocks and a Wedding: Theodoric's Diplomatic Relations with the Burgundians', *Romanobarbarica* 14 (1998), 227–32, 255 (only Shanzer seeks to adduce evidence from the text, though describing the putative negotiations as 'virtually dissimulated' by Ennodius). As a negotiation tactic, the combination of ransom offering and alliance proposal seems unlikely, and the text gives no support. Certainly the marriage alliance is a precondition for the success of Epiphanius' mission: *Vita Epiphani*, 163, 167. Other, unattested embassies will have negotiated the marriage of Theoderic's and Gundobad's children.

[212] Teillet, *Des Goths*, 278.

[213] Gundobad: Ennodius, *Vita Epiphani*, 164 (*erat fando locuples et ex eloquentia dives opibus et facundus adsertor*); Theoderic: dramatised in his speeches: 110, 131–4, 136–41, 188–9.

late emperors and Odoacer are shown as having respect for Epiphanius and being guided by his precepts, nevertheless they are at one point dismissed, for the convenience of a biblical image, as wicked rulers deposed for their faults.[214] Neither is Theoderic presented as an ideal ruler; his obedience to Epiphanius is in the same order as that of all his predecessors, and the praise which Ennodius pays him can be taken as no more than a sign of the conventional prudence concerning a current ruler. The necessity to undertake two embassies to Theoderic of itself precludes any suggestion that he is a model ruler. Theoderic bulks large in the narrative because he is associated with that mission of Epiphanius which receives the most attention both in the *dictio* on the bishop's anniversary and in the *Vita*, namely the redemption of the Italian captives in Gaul. It would be difficult to imagine Ennodius, in 502/4, feeling compelled to offer himself as an educator in governance to Theoderic, in view, on the one hand, of Ennodius' constant recourse to the patronage of court officials and even of the king; and on the other, of the prudent statesmanship displayed by Theoderic in matters including his involvement in both the Laurentian and Acacian schisms, and his triumphal ceremonial visit to Rome in 500.

Indeed, a central element of the literary *persona* of Epiphanius, which Ennodius modelled on Constantius' Germanus, strongly limits any potential there may be for the *Vita* to espouse elaborate political sentiments. Epiphanius, like Germanus, resolves disputes through consensus; he is the *concordiae auctor*.[215] Achieving consensus implies that both parties at dispute have been at fault; Ennodius consistently portrays all rulers as partly culpable for the *causae discordiae*.[216] Ennodius can portray each

[214] Ennodius, *Vita Epiphani*, 129.

[215] Cf. Ennodius, *Vita Epiphani*, 114: *inter dissidentes principes solus esset qui pace frueretur amborum.*

[216] Ricimer and Anthemius: Ennodius, *Vita Epiphani*, 51–2: *invidia et* pars *dignitas causa discordia* . . . mutuo *bella praepararent*. Both Ricimer and Anthemius portray the other as intemperate; 53, 61 (both also exchange conventional ethnic insults: 53, 67; *contra* e.g. Näf, 'Die Zeitbewusstsein des Ennodius', 117, who sees the use of the term *Greculus* for Anthemius as anti-Byzantine feeling). Nepos and Euric: though the initiative rests with Gothic raids to which Nepos responds, *hinc* utrimque *litium coeperunt fomenta consurgere, et dum* neutrae partes *conceptum tumorem vincendi studio deponunt, sic exuperabat causa discordiae*; 80. Theoderic and Gundobad: Theoderic's speech to Epiphanius commissioning the embassy is very circumspect; when the Burgundians are mentioned, Theoderic immediately implicates himself too, by inaction: *haec* [*sc.* the depopulation of Liguria] *quamvis Burgundio inmitis exercuit, nos tamen, si non emendamus, admisimus*; 139. Gundobad is made to claim that the Burgundian raid was a response to *contumeliam* of Theoderic and his betrayal of their former alliance; 166. Ligurian embassies to Theoderic: the repression of legal rights of Odoacer's supporters is described as *universa Italia lamentabili iustitio subiacebat*; 122. Relief is needed from *vix ferenda tributorum sarcina*; 182. Discussions of these passages have generally sought to use them as evidence for the constitutional positions of the emperors and kings (e.g. Cesa, Commentary to *Vita del Epifanio*, 169, 185), but constitutional terminology is not Ennodius' concern; dramatically, the passages present conflicts arising from the clash of two antagonists.

ruler, depending on the dramatic needs of each scene, as pious or enraged, excellent or treacherous.[217] There is very little scope, within this fictive construct of consensus and the rhetorical description of Epiphanius' protagonists, for the author to prefer any model of rule or political figure over another.

It is striking, in a work which takes pains to praise its hero above all for his success as an envoy, that several of Epiphanius' missions appear spectacularly unsuccessful to modern expectations. Epiphanius' embassy to Anthemius did not prevent the ultimate outbreak of civil war and the murder of the reigning emperor; his journey to Toulouse did not avert Gothic annexation of parts of Gaul.[218] The key to understanding how these legations were claimed as successes lies in Ennodius' regional perspective. Civil war erupted in Italy between Anthemius and Ricimer some eight to eleven months after Epiphanius' embassy to Rome.[219] The consequential siege of Rome by Ricimer was recalled in Ennodius' lifetime as one of three catastrophes with which divine judgement had struck Christian Rome, alongside Alaric's infamous sack of the city.[220] Ennodius does not ignore this enormity. Anthemius, after agreeing to observe peace, is made to declare to Epiphanius: 'Henceforth, if Ricimer has deceived even you with the cunning of his wonted guile, let him take up the battle, wounded as he is.'[221] Ricimer did, indeed, take up the battle, bringing war to Rome instead of fighting defensively in northern Italy. The words which Ennodius gives to Anthemius are not neutral, nor do they bring closure to the episode; rather, they anticipate future events. The purpose of Epiphanius' mission on behalf of his *patria* was to restrain the emperor from attacking his rebellious subject in Milan, and so forestall civil war being brought to northern Italy and Liguria becoming a theatre of war, as Rome would be.[222] The aim of Epiphanius' embassy in 471 was to protect Liguria, and in this he succeeded.[223]

[217] E.g. Gundobad: Epiphanius is warned by bishop Rusticius of Lyons of the *astutiae regis* (Ennodius, *Vita Epiphani*, 151), yet when the bishop meets the king *sua utrique visione laetati sunt* (153); Gundobad is later called *rex probatissimus* (164).

[218] Cf. Cesa, Introduction to *Vita del Epifanio*, 31: as 'Ennodio . . . mira a presentare come un successo tutte le azioni del suo eroe', his accounts of Epiphanius' dealings with Anthemius and Euric are 'difficilimente interpretabili'.

[219] Epiphanius left Rome on 9 March 471; Ricimer began his siege of the city in either November 471 or February 472, depending on two variant chronologies in Priscus, *Fr.*, 64.

[220] Gelasius, *Lettre contre les lupercales*, ed. G. Pomarès (Sources chrétiennes 65; Paris, 1959), 13. The third catastrophe is the pestilence of 467. Oddly, Gelasius does not include Geiseric's sack of Rome in 455.

[221] Ennodius, *Vita Epiphani*, 70: *postremo si solitae calliditatis astutia etiam te fefellerit, certamen iam vulneratus adsumat*.

[222] *Patria*: Ennodius, *Vita Epiphani*, 57.

[223] The account of Epiphanius' mission to Rome is followed by the only break in the narrative of his public deeds during episcopate: a description of the sanctity of his sister Honorata, her spiritual

The problematic praise of Epiphanius' embassy to Euric is clarified by attention to the regional focus of *Vita Epiphani* and to the wording of the text. Among the most famous of the letters of Sidonius Apollinaris are those describing first his hopes, then his disappointment in negotiations overseen by four Provençal and Gallic bishops, which resulted in the ceding of the Auvergne to Euric.[224] The accounts by Ennodius and Sidonius of negotiations with Euric have traditionally been read together, but they can be squared only awkwardly, usually by assuming that Epiphanius' mission in fact surrendered the Auvergne, an arrangement subsequently confirmed by the Gallic bishops.[225] Ennodius' youth was probably spent in that part of Gaul taken over by the kingdom of Toulouse shortly after the appeasement of Euric failed to satisfy the king; it is difficult to see how he could genuinely have regarded such a mission on the part of Epiphanius as a success from the point of view of the empire. In fact, the activity of Euric which precipitates conflict with Nepos in *Vita Epiphani* is not the king's attempts to annex parts of Gaul, naturally of concern to

instructor Luminosa, and Epiphanius' own alms-giving. The narrative then resumes, with the tumultuous deaths of Anthemius and Ricimer mentioned solely as time indicators; Ennodius, *Vita Epiphani*, 76–9. The unique digression perhaps serves to underscore the omission of civil warfare. Honorata and Luminosa feature again in Odoacer's siege of Pavia: 97, 99.

224 Sid. Ap., *Ep.* VII, 6, 7. Hodgkin, *Italy and her Invaders* II, 501–7, esp. 504 n. 1; Seeck VI, 376–7; Bury, *LRE* I, 343; Stevens, *Sidonius*, 158, 198–9, 207–11; Ludwig Schmidt, *Geschichte der deutschen Stämme bis zum Ausgang der Völkerwanderung* I: *Die Ostgermanen* (Munich, 1934–41), 491–2, Sundwall, *Eurich*, 77–81, Cook, *Life of St Epiphanius*, 187–9, Anderson, *Sidonius* II, 322–3 n. 2; Courcelle, *Histoire littéraire*, 180; Stein I, 396, 604 n. 182; Loyen, *Sidoine: Lettres* II, 20–1; Demougeot II, 604–5; Harries, *Sidonius*, 237.

Sidonius does not, as is often assumed, state that the four bishops went as envoys to Euric, or, more importantly, that they acted at the behest of the emperor Nepos. The bishops are described as having a supervisory role in the exchange of embassies and the making of treaties, perhaps by virtue of their senior position in a provincial *concilium* (*Ep.* VII, 6.10, 7.4: *cum in concilium conventis . . . primi comprovincialium*. Sirmond, *PL* 58, 573 n. b and Loyen, *Sidoine: Lettres* III, 191 n. 36, see this as a council of the bishops of the diocese of Arles, but Sidonius characterises the proper concern of the *concilium* as *publicis . . . periculis*, which seems more pertinent to a provincial than an ecclesiastical council; cf. Anderson, *Sidonius* II, 329 n. 4). The bishops have authority with regard to negotiations *quamquam principe absente* (*Ep.* 7.4). Sidonius never otherwise mentions the emperor; he blames the surrender of the Auvergne region on the bishops' pursuit of personal interests. Elsewhere, Sidonius expresses concern that intermediaries between the empire and the Goths sought personal profit rather than the empire's interests; *Ep.* III, 7.3.

The only other source for the Gothic annexation of the Auvergne is the very different scenario of Jordanes, *Get.*, 238–41: Euric conquered the Auvergne, in face of opposition from the *patricius* and *magister utriusque militiae* Ecdicius (Sidonius' brother-in-law), who was compelled to withdraw from the region. Nepos had appointed Ecdicius *magister utriusque militiae* in Gaul in recognition of his earlier private efforts, under Anthemius, to resist Euric's expansionism (Sid. Ap., *Epp.* III, 3; V, 16; *PLRE* II, 'Ecdicius 3', 384). According to Jordanes, after Euric's annexation of the Auvergne and Ecdicius' retreat, Nepos transferred military command from Ecdicius to Orestes (*Get.*, 241); *PLRE* II, 'Orestes 2', 811, sees this as command in Gaul. If this scenario is accurate, it indicates that Nepos intended to continue the defence of Gaul, through Orestes, and was not party to the surrender of the Auvergne.

225 Cf. Cesa, Commentary to *Vita del Epifanio*, 166–8.

Sidonius; rather, it is constant intrusions across the Alps into Italy: '[the Goths], taking no heed of the new emperor, did not cease to assail the confines of the Italian empire, which he had stretched across the Gallic Alps; Nepos, for his part, wished to defend strenuously the border given to him by God to rule, lest ill-advised presumption become customary'.[226] Ennodius' apparently limiting description of Nepos' rule over an '*Italian* empire' has attracted more comment than the actual cause of conflict. In 473, before Nepos' reign, Euric had sent a leading general into Italy, where he was defeated and killed by imperial commanders. Ennodius refers to subsequent harassment, after Nepos' accession in early 474, perhaps repeated raids rather than large-scale attempts to annex territory.[227] Since Nepos chose to summon Ligurian nobles to a council of ways and means to discuss the Gothic intrusions, the area concerned must have been the Cottian or Maritime Alps regions, parts of the Italian prefecture which straddled the Alps, and uncomfortably close to the province of Liguria.[228] Epiphanius' mission was to secure an agreement from Euric against further intrusions into Italy. It would therefore have been quite unrelated to the discussions, so scathingly criticised by Sidonius, which ceded the Auvergne region of Gaul to Toulouse.

Epiphanius' missions protect the security of Liguria, not of all Italy or the western empire.[229] There are parallels with the *vitae* of Germanus and of Orientius: Germanus pleads for the Armorican rebels, nothwithstanding their insurgency against the empire; Orientius seeks to prevent the imperial attack on the Goths, though they had recently sought to annex imperial territory, in order to prevent warfare in Aquitania; earlier in *Vita Epiphani*, Ennodius' hero sought to prevent the emperor

[226] Ennodius, *Vita Epiphani*, 80: *illi [sc. Gothi] Italici fines imperii, quos trans Gallicanas Alpes porrexerat, novitatem spernentes non disineret incessere, e diverso Nepos, ne in usum praesumptio malesuada duceretur, districtius cuperet commissum sibi a deo regandi terminum vindicare.* Cf. 88 (Epiphanius' speech to Euric): *Nepos . . . ad haec nos impetranda destinavit, ut . . . terrae sibi convenae dilectionis iure socientur.* For the interpretation which follows, cf. Paul the Deacon, *Hist. Rom.* XV, 5.

For interpretation of *quos . . . porrexerat*, see Stevens, *Sidonius*, 210 and Cesa, Commentary to *Vita del Epifanio*, 165, against Cook, *Life of St Epiphanius*. The passage implies either an otherwise unattested extension of the Italian prefecture west of the Alps by Nepos (perhaps in the sense of restoration of the Alpine provinces after Euric's assault of 473), or a more general assertion of imperial power in Gaul (possibly Nepos' appointment of Ecdicius as *magister utriusque militiae*). Sundwall, *Eurich*, 75.

[227] 473: *Chron. Gall. 511*, 653 (Wolfram, *History of the Goths*, 189, 452 n. 144, redating Vincentius' death to *c.* 476 is unfounded; cf. *PLRE* II, 'Vincentius 3', 1168). Nepos' accession: as *caesar* at Ravenna, early 474 (at which point he presumably controlled north Italy); as *augustus* at Rome, 19 or 24 June 474 (Jordanes, *Get.*, 338; *PLRE* II, 'Julius Nepos 3', 777). It is unclear from Ennodius' account whether Nepos was present at the Ligurian council.

Raids rather than annexation: perhaps indicated by the failure of *Chron. Gall. 511* to mention Gothic incursions into Italy after 473.

[228] Council: Ennodius, *Vita Epiphani*, 81. Alps: Jones, *LRE*, Map 1.

[229] Cf. Näf, 'Die Zeitbewusstsein des Ennodius', 121.

bringing war against a rebel subject in northern Italy. All strive to protect provincial communities from suffering violence in the course of imperial military action. These rare attested embassies, and the meetings of provincial councils which often precede them, are small fragments among the many unattested communications which shaped the course of events.[230] They are recorded in works written for provincial audiences, because they concern the security of those communities.

Ennodius' *Vita Epiphani* has long been highly regarded as a historical document of the fifth century, on account of the political situations dramatised in the narratives of Epiphanius' embassies. But the work must be used with caveats. Despite the bishop's meetings with emperors, kings, and senior officials in Italy and Gaul, the focus of the work, and presumably Ennodius' intended audience, was local: the province of Liguria, and specifically the two leading cities of Milan and Pavia. Notwithstanding Ennodius' contacts with the papal court in Rome and the royal court in Ravenna, *Vita Epiphani* reflects the views of the provinces, like Hydatius and Sidonius, not of the central government. The narrative structure of the work was consciously chosen, using the distinctive and highly literary model of Constantius' *Vita Germani* to portray the bishop's career as a ceaseless series of journeys undertaken for others' sakes. Two suggestions, neither exclusive, may be made as to why Ennodius chose this model to represent his late bishop. Epiphanius' mission to Gaul to redeem captives taken by Burgundian raids was clearly felt to be an outstanding achievement, both during the bishop's lifetime, and some years later when Ennodius composed the *Vita*; the young Ennodius had been personally involved. The model of Constantius' Germanus may have suggested itself to the Gallic-born Ennodius as a way to provide a suitable context and background for Epiphanius' deed. Secondly, to provincials of the empire, the task of undertaking a legation, always prestigious, had grown even more important within local communities during the new circumstances of the fifth century. At the same time, as the next chapter explores, the completion of embassies for imperial and royal courts also rose in social capital. Ennodius, a member of the local aristocracy and church of Liguria enjoying strong connections to senior officials and career servants of the court of Theoderic, sought to exploit the prestige from both these milieux for his hero.

The *Vitae* of Germanus, Orientius, Vivianus, and Epiphanius share the same literary vehicle to praise their subjects. The presentation of the bishops as effective envoys requires omission and exaggeration: ignoring

[230] Cf. Procopius, *Wars* v, 8–10 (negotiations between citizens of Naples and Belisarius).

important aspects of the bishops' careers, assimilating different sorts of activities as legations. In 456, Sidonius' *Panegyric* on Avitus had presented a similar image of the hero as an eloquent and authoritative mediator, engaged in a constant series of embassies. Sidonius used this portrait not only to praise his subject but also to create a highly selective and acceptable background to Avitus' current relations with the Goths. In a similar way, both *Vita Germani* and *Vita Epiphani* may have been constructed to give context to their subjects' final missions. It is possible that this literary device descended through fifth-century Gallic narrative literature from Sidonius via Constantius to his imitators.

Each of these works is a useful source of data for patterns of political communication throughout the fifth-century West, but their main value comes through recognition of their literary artifice. These quasi-fictitious biographies are manifestations of the social credit earned by legates and the desire of provincial *optimates* to enjoy it. They are intended not to be instructive, but to reflect and exploit social values.

The presentation of the bishops need not passively reflect episcopal assumption of secular duties throughout the western provinces in the fifth century. The image of the bishop as envoy is a conscious arrogation of values from secular politics: of the local credit earned by provincial magnates in undertaking legations to imperial authorities, and of the social and pecuniary rewards gained by servants to imperial and royal courts. Just as an earlier generation of clergy appropriated architectural and sartorial trappings of power from municipal and imperial authority, so the image of the bishop as envoy was used to graft the approbation of legatine functions to existing models of sanctity.

The hagiographers, however, also strove to distance their subjects somewhat from the worldliness of their secular model. Constantius never portrays Germanus in the act of supplication; the author of *Vita Viviani* credits the success of the bishop's embassy to the saint's reliance on 'divine authority rather than supplication'.[231] Ennodius, far more comfortable than his Gallic predecessors with the ethos and protocols involved in palatine embassies, none the less praises Epiphanius' selfless superiority to his secular counterparts. In doing so, he creates a silhouette of conventional behaviour and expectations of court servants. After two of his journeys, Epiphanius declines to report the outcome of his missions in person to his principals, 'lest, being present, he should appear to exact public thanks as if it were owed to him'.[232] Returning from the mission to Gundobad which Theoderic had enjoined on him,

[231] *Vita Viviani*, 6 *fin.*

[232] Ennodius, *Vita Epiphani*, 75: *ne velut debitas gratiarum actiones praesens videretur exigere*. Epiphanius does not report to Ricimer or Theoderic. He does, however, report to Nepos and receive high

[Epiphanius] did not wish to go himself in the near future to the unconquered king Theoderic, lest, being before him in person, he should appear to exact a return for his labour, either in public thanks or in a display of rewards. For, after the completion of princes' orders, one who himself announces that he has executed the task demands repayment as if it were owed to him. This the astute and forsightful man keenly desired to shun. Yet he wrote and committed to letters a report of what had occurred, so that he would not be judged either contemptuous by being silent or intemperate by arrogantly presenting himself.[233]

In lieu of a reward for his services, Theoderic granted the modest bishop his request for financial aid to the returned captives. Ennodius uses Epiphanius' abstemiousness to his credit. By contrast, more conventional agents of courts were clearly expected not only to report in person, but to claim public honour and monetary rewards as their due.[234] The writings of officials at the court of Theoderic, including those of a friend and patron of Ennodius, show how contemporary palatine agents cultivated and profited from just such praise and reward.

praise; whether the report is in person is unclear (94: *Nepoti effectum peractae legationis insinuat, et crescente laudum cumulo humilitas in eo pariter sentibat augmentum*).

[233] Ennodius, *Vita Epiphani*, 179–80: *Ad regem invictissimum Theodericum per se mox ire noluit, ne forte laboris sui vicissitudinem in relatione gratiarum aut in exhibitione munerum coram positus videretur exigere. Flagitat enim quasi debitam retributionem, qui profligatis principum iussionibus ipse quid actum sit actor adnuntiat. Hoc ergo ille totius acuminis vir prospiciens declinare gestiebat. Scripsit tamen et quae gesta sint loqui commisit epistulis, ne aut tacendo contemptor aut occurrendo per adrogantiam pronuntiaretur intemperans.*

[234] Report in person to a ruler would often be required to maintain secrecy, just as the initial commission of an embassy was carried out *secretius*; cf. Ennodius, *Vita Epiphani*, 136 and below, chapter 5 n. 44.

Chapter 5

CASSIODORUS AND SENARIUS

Hydatius, Sidonius, Constantius, and Ennodius are concerned with the activities and status of legates acting on behalf of provincial councils, cities, and other regional communities. The two authors discussed here speak from the point of view of the royal court of post-imperial Italy. The status and rewards of palatine emissaries differ from those of provincial legates: they look to achieve status not only within their local community, but also within the ranks of their professional peers, and to gain more tangible returns in terms of career path and financial reward. Cassiodorus and Senarius, demonstrating their part in political communication in the late antique West before the time of Justinian, display a court official's professional ethos. They provide a thumbnail sketch of the career of a court servant who was well seasoned in foreign embassies, and of certain aspects of his public life: the qualities for which he was chosen for such tasks; the nature and scale of the journeys he undertook; the rewards he gained within the civil bureaucracy; and the social capital accrued by success. Some of the intellectual and spiritual concerns which occupied such a Roman official while at the royal court of Ostrogothic Italy can also be glimpsed. Senarius and others like him were not professional ambassadors in the modern sense. They undertook important embassies, at the direction of emperors or kings, as an adjacent duty to their proper palatine office, whether in financial or other administrative posts. Their careers and honours illustrate the fluid structures of late Roman government adapting to the sharply increased necessity for political communication during the fifth and sixth centuries.

Like Hydatius and Sidonius, these two Italian authors attest the importance and frequency of diplomatic communication throughout the Mediterranean world. They present, however, different perspectives, and must be studied in different contexts, from that of their older contemporaries. Whereas Hydatius is almost the sole witness for many of the events he describes, and Sidonius' Gaul is only sporadically illuminated for us, Italy under the Ostrogoths is the best-documented western kingdom of the fifth and sixth centuries, and its foreign relations are the most clearly understood. The negotiations of the Ostrogothic king Theoderic with the emperors Zeno, Anastasius, and Justin are well if not fully attested, and the extensive network of marriage alliances which bound Theoderic to the other major powers of the West draws comment from several near-contemporary writers. Modern narratives of Theoderic's successors concentrate on deteriorating relations with Constantinople up to Justinian's commencement of war, rather than on domestic developments.[1] This historical context for the involvement of Cassiodorus and Senarius in political communication is reasonably well known.

It is not these participants, however, who are the sources for our knowledge of foreign politics or policies. Cassiodorus and Senarius were closely tied to the quasi-imperial court of Ostrogothic Ravenna. Though they were members of the Italian aristocracy, both owed their social positions not to descent from great landholding families, but primarily to service performed for the court by themselves and their immediate forebears. Early sixth-century Italy was home to a vigorous literary culture, which has left behind a wider range of Latin writings than any other part of the West. Works survive from both Cassiodorus and Senarius, in greatly differing quantities; they are considered here in inverse proportion to the length of their extant writings. Cassiodorus not only was the editor of a polished selection of 468 of his own official letters, which are of interest here, but also was the author of an extant chronicle; of panegyrics, two of which are preserved in fragments; of a history, now lost; and, after his retirement into monastic *otium*, of theological, exegetical, grammatical, and didactic works which enjoyed a healthy history of transmission throughout the Middle Ages. From Senarius, there is extant only one eighteen-line poem, and one fragment and a loose paraphrase of a letter; there exist also replies to several lost letters of Senarius

[1] On the Ostrogothic kingdom, in addition to the standard accounts of Bury I, 422–69, Stein II, 107–56, 328–68, Jones, *LRE* I, 245–57, and Demougeot II, 796–833: Theodore Mommsen, 'Ostgothische Studien', *Neues Archiv der Gesellschaft für ältere deutsche Geschichtskunde* 14 (1889), 225–49, 453–544; 15 (1890), 181–6, reprinted in his *Gesammelte Schriften* VI (Berlin, 1910), 362–484, cited here; Sundwall, *Abhandlungen*; Wilhelm Ensslin, *Theoderich der Grosse*, 2nd edn (Munich, 1956); Ensslin, 'Beweise der Romverbundheit in Theoderichs des Grossen Aussen- und Innenpolitik', *I Goti in Occidente* (Settimane di studio del Centro italiano di studi sull'alto medioevo 3; Spoleto, 1956), 509–36; Peter Llewellyn, *Rome in the Middle Ages* (London, 1971), 21–77; Wolfram, *History of the Goths*, 247–362; John Moorhead, *Theoderic in Italy* (Oxford, 1992); Jan Prostko-Prostynski, Utraeque res publicae: *The Emperor Anastasius I's Gothic Policy (491–518)* (Poznan, 1994); Amory, *People and Identity in Ostrogothic Italy*; and the conference proceedings *Teoderico il Grande e i Goti d'Italia*, Atti de XIII Congresso internazionale di studi sull'alto medioevo, 2 vols. (Spoleto, 1993); and *Teoderico e i Goti tra Oriente e Occidente*, ed. Antonio Carile (Ravenna, 1995).

from a number of his correspondents. These various writings convey few data on current international affairs, yet none the less emphasise, in different ways, the importance of their authors' participation in the political communication which enveloped the wars and truces of the time. Cassiodorus and Senarius were concerned to exhibit their own social status and literary skills; references to foreign relations in their writings display the significance of diplomatic duties only for their own careers. By this self-presentation, they reveal the extent to which, a century after the Roman West had begun to be divided among the new kingdoms, the traditional role of embassies in public life had continued and developed vigorously in changed political circumstances, and how the duty of political communication could be exploited in new ways as an indicator of status with the court milieu.

DIPLOMATIC CORRESPONDENCE IN THE *VARIAE* OF CASSIODORUS

Fl. Magnus Aurelius Cassiodorus Senator was a member of the fourth recorded generation of an aristocratic family which had branches in both the eastern and western halves of the empire in the mid-fifth century. His ancestors had perhaps emigrated from the East to Italy during the reign of Valentinian III. His great-grandfather, grandfather, and father had all held public office at first the imperial, then the royal, courts of Ravenna and Rome; his father, as prefect of Italy, induced the young Cassiodorus into public life. Cassiodorus himself held posts at the court of the Ostrogothic monarchs three times over the course of three decades. At a young age, in recognition of the literary eloquence he displayed when delivering a panegyric to Theoderic, Cassiodorus was appointed to the office of *quaestor palatii* (*c.* 506/7–511), a post which, as the ruler's official spokesman, occupied a very senior position in the royal *consistorium*. Over a decade later, he was appointed by the king as *magister officiorum* (523–7), the controller of the civil service, infamously succeeding the incarcerated Boethius, and was retained in this post after Theoderic's death by his successor and grandson Athalaric. The same king reappointed Cassiodorus to office five years later, now as praetorian prefect of Italy (533–7), the chief executive civil minister of the Italian government, and again Cassiodorus was retained in the same office throughout the succeeding and troubled rules of Amalasuntha, Theodahad, and Vitigis. By the end of his public career, Cassiodorus had thus held all three of the most senior civil offices at the court of Ravenna. Between his first and second periods in office, he was appointed sole consul for the year 514, and at some date before leaving his final post he was made *patricius*. At an unknown time during the protracted Byzantine war against the Goths in Italy, Cassiodorus took up religious life, and journeyed to Constantinople. Later he founded a double monastery, including the well-appointed cenobite house of Vivarium, on his family lands in the south Italian province of Bruttium. He was still there, writing grammatical works, at the age of ninety-three.[2]

Prior to completing his tenure as praetorian prefect of Italy in 537, Cassiodorus published a selection of the official letters he had written over the last thirty years, both in the names of the Ostrogothic monarchs and in his own right, gathered into twelve books, together with a thirteenth which was a short philosophical work on the nature of the soul. He chose to emphasise the stylistic diversity of the collection by naming the work *Variae*, and offered it to satisfy the demands of admiring literary friends for publication of his writings, and also to provide model formulae of official letters for later civil servants to imitate.[3] All the letters which he had written in the names of the Ostrogothic monarchs, from Theoderic to Vitigis, were drafted in the capacity of *quaestor*, the publicist of the court. Though he had formally held this post only at the beginning of his career, Cassiodorus had acted in the capacity of *quaestor* when in

[2] On Cassiodorus: L. Hartmann, 'Cassiodorus 1–4', *RE* III.2, 1671–6; Sundwall, *Abhandlungen*, 154–6; Schanz-Hosius IV, 2, 92–109 (*Variae*, 97–9); A. van de Vyver, 'Cassiodor et son œuvre', *Speculum* 6 (1931), 244–92; Arnaldo Momigliano, 'Cassiodorus and the Italian Culture of His Time', in his *Studies in Historiography* (London, 1966), 181–210; *PLRE* II, 'Cassiodorus 1–3', 263–5 (ancestors), 'Fl Magnus Aurelius Cassiodorus Senator 4', 265–9; Averil Cameron, 'Cassiodorus Deflated', *Journal of Roman Studies* 71 (1981), 183–6. See also John Matthews, 'Anicius Manlius Severinus Boethius', in Margaret Gibson (ed.), *Boethius: His Life, Thought and Influence* (Oxford, 1981), 25–31. For a possible context of the emigration of Cassiodorus' ancestors to the West: Andrew Gillett, 'The Date and Circumstances of Olympiodorus of Thebes', *Traditio* 48 (1993), 18–24 and n. 99.

[3] For editions, see 'Note on editions, commentaries, and translations' below. On the *Variae*: B. Hasenstab, *Studien zur Variensammlung des Cassiodor Senator: ein Beitrag zur Geschichte der Ostgothenherrschaft in Italien* (Munich, 1883); Mommsen, *Prooemium* to Cass., *Variae*, v–xxxix; Å. J. Fridh, *Terminologie et formules dans les* Variae *de Cassiodore: études sur le développement du style administratif aux derniers siècles de l'antiquité* (Studia graeca et latina Gothoburgensia 2; Stockholm, 1956); Odo John Zimmermann, *The Late Latin Vocabulary of the* Variae *of Cassiodorus, with Special Advertance to the Technical Terminology of Administration* (Washington, 1944; repr. Hildersheim, 1967); James J. O'Donnell, *Cassiodorus* (Berkeley, 1979), 55–102; Stefan Krautschick, *Cassiodor und die Politik seiner Zeit* (Bonn, 1983), 41–117; Robin Macpherson, *Rome in Involution: Cassiodorus'* Variae *in Their Literary and Historical Setting* (Poznan, 1989); P. S. Barnwell, *Emperor, Prefects, and Kings: The Roman West, 395–565* (London, 1992), 166–9; Beat Meyer-Flügel, *Das Bild der ostgotisch-römischen Gesellschaft bei Cassiodor: Leben und Ethik von Römern und Germanen in Italien nach dem Ende des Weströmischen Reiches* (Berne, 1992); Andrew Gillett, 'The Purposes of Cassiodorus' *Variae*', in Alexander C. Murray (ed.), *After Rome's Fall: Narrators and Sources of Early Medieval History: Essays Presented to Walter Goffart* (Toronto, 1998), 37–50.

Date of publication: Mommsen, Prooemium to Cass., *Variae*, xxx–xxxi.

his later offices also, giving assistance to the current incumbents of the post.[4]

The *Variae* is of crucial importance to modern knowledge of court bureaucracy, administration, prosopography, and innumerable social issues of Ostrogothic Italy and indeed of the later Roman empire in general, but of course this was not the purpose of the work. Cassiodorus' publication is sometimes seen as an apology on behalf of the Ostrogothic regime or of Cassiodorus himself, written with an eye to the conflict between Gothic and eastern Roman forces then raging in Italy. It is more likely, however, that the true motives for publication are those stated by Cassiodorus in several places, with regard to both the official letters and the philosophical tract which constitute the *Variae*: that the work, like other published epistolary collections of the fifth and sixth centuries, was a vehicle for the cultivation of *amicitia*, here within a circle of aristocratic senior bureaucrats, many of whom are named and praised in the letters; moreover, that the collection was a display of literary virtuosity, which would not only provide models for later civil servants to imitate, but also, most importantly, stand as a monument to the talents of the author.[5]

It is with this immodest aim in mind that the diplomatic correspondence in the *Variae* may be considered. The individual letters of the collection fall into three distinct categories: the dispositive letters, including edicts and rescripts; letters of appointment for office holders; and diplomatic correspondence.[6] Envoys and embassies feature occasionally in both the edicts and letters of appointment, but it is the third group which displays, indeed vaunts, the significance of political communication to Cassiodorus. Certain of the diplomatic letters address issues of crucial importance to the survival of the Ostrogothic regime: for example, the first letter of the collection, from Theoderic to the emperor Anastasius, seeking peace between *utraeque res publicae*; and the last letters of Book X, written in the name of Vitigis, concerning the war with the eastern empire which had erupted some two years before Cassiodorus

4 On the quaestorship: Gillett, 'Purposes', 41–3 with references there. For a comparable example of a palatine officer carrying out the duties of *quaestor* while filling another post: *PLRE* II, 'Ambrosius 3', 69. Cassiodorus' letters name four of the five *quaestores* whose tenures overlapped with his four years as *magister officiorum* (Decoratus, Honoratus, Ambrosius, Fidelis; *PLRE* II, *Fasti*, 1259), and one for his time as praetorian prefect of Italy, also held for four years (Patricius, in office 534–5; Cass., *Variae* X, 6–7; *PLRE* II, 'Patricius 12', 839–40; not listed in the *Fasti* of either *PLRE* II or III; cf. Ludwig Traube, 'Index rerum et verborum', to Cass., *Variae*, 576, s.v. *quaestor palatii*). The latter is the last recorded western *quaestor*.

5 Motives: Cass., *Variae, Praef*.; XI *Praef*.; *De anima*, c. 1. Fridh, *Terminologie et formules*, 1–4; Gillett, 'Purposes'; to references there, add Jean-Louis Jouanaud, 'Pour qui Cassiodore a-t-il publié les *Variae*?', in *Teoderico il Grande e i Goti d'Italia* II, 721–41; Amory, *People and Identity in Ostrogothic Italy*, 49.

6 Fridh, *Terminologie et formules*, 8–9.

published his collection. The significance of these and other diplomatic letters to Cassiodorus' aims, however, is not their political content – the probable context of the opening letter to Anastasius can only be deduced on the basis of the chronology of Cassiodorus' career, which is not at all explicit – but their literary finesse. The diplomatic correspondence is not presented in such a way as to offer any sort of comment on the political affairs of Theoderic's time, or on the early stages of the Byzantine war in Italy. Instead, the diplomatic letters exemplify Cassiodorus' prefatory remarks on the need for 'conscious eloquence' in the service of the state.[7] There is no doubt that the letters to rulers are among those which, for Cassiodorus, demonstrated the highest of the three styles of composition he strove to employ, 'elevated to the greatest height of oratory by exquisite sensibilities'.[8] The diplomatic letters are a demonstration of his skills as *quaestor*, for the composition of letters to rulers, like the other types of letters in the first ten books of the *Variae*, was the responsibility of the quaestorship.[9] Modern scholars tend to study the diplomatic letters as documentary evidence from the chancery of the Ostrogothic kings, examined for slim indications of foreign policy; but in the published *Variae*, they appear as Cassiodorus' own epistles to emperors and kings, to be perused as the graceful products of his pen.

Diplomatic correspondence in the *Variae* is distinguished from edicts and letters of appointment not only by its function but also by Cassiodorus' editorial policy. Letters to rulers constitute less than a tenth of the *Variae*'s 468 letters, but Cassiodorus' arrangement of his letters gives them emphasis commensurate with their importance, not their number. It has long been noted that the thirty-two diplomatic letters, nineteen to emperors or empresses in Constantinople and thirteen to western kings, have pride of place in the collection.[10] Book I opens with a letter to the emperor Anastasius, and each following book, with the exception of the *formulae* and the two books written in Cassiodorus' own name as praetorian prefect, also begins with a letter to an emperor or western king. Books I, II, and V also close with letters to kings; Book X presents a variation on this, a series of letters to the emperor and his senior officials.

The placing of the diplomatic letters at the beginning of each book, and at the end of some, is the most obvious organising principle in the

[7] Date of Cass., *Variae* I, 1: Krautschick, *Cassiodor*, 50–1. Eloquence: Cass., *Variae, Praef.*, 8: *conscia facundia*.

[8] Cass., *Variae, Praef.*, 16: *ad summum apicem disputationis exquisitis sensibus elevatur*; Fridh, *Terminologie et formules*, 9. The three styles, however, are distinguished not by the social status of the recipients, but by the addressees' degree of literacy.

[9] Cass., *Variae* X, 6.6; Mommsen, 'Ostgothische Studien', 390.

[10] Mommsen, *Prooemium* to Cass., *Variae*, xxvii; Hermann Peter, *Der Brief in der romischen Literatur* (Leipzig, 1901; repr. Hildersheim, 1965), 209; O'Donnell, *Cassiodorus*, 77–81.

Variae, and overrides the broadly chronological sequence of the letter collection.[11] This framework, however, is closely allied to a second pattern. Following the first two letters of the first book with their imperial themes,[12] Cassiodorus placed two letters of appointment, announcing the elevation of his father to the rank of *patricius*, *c.* 507; at the end of Book IX, in the position occupied in other books by letters to kings, he placed the two letters of appointment for his own elevation as praetorian prefect, in 533. These four letters, our main sources for the biography of four generations of Cassiodori, serve to set out the *cursus honorum* of the author and to eulogise his *stirps*. Few other letters in the collection directly concern Cassiodorus or his family; the final two books, written in his own name as praetorian prefect, are not similarly self-descriptive or formally eulogistic, and serve Cassiodorus' aims in a different way.[13] The two pairs of letters of appointment enjoy the same prominent placement as the diplomatic correspondence, and for the same reasons: as monuments to the career of their author.

Table 2 lists the letters to rulers (indicating first and last letters in each book with bold print) and letters concerning Cassiodorus personally (in italics).

The diplomatic letters are distributed unevenly throughout the collection. Books I to V and VIII to IX, containing letters written in the names of Theoderic and Athalaric, contain only three letters to emperors but all thirteen letters to western kings. Fifteen letters in Book X, almost half the book, are addressed to Justinian or Theodora; there are no letters to kings in this book. Presumably, as Justinian sought opportunity for conflict in Italy, the Ostrogothic monarchs repeatedly used their praetorian prefect Cassiodorus to act as *quaestor* by drafting correspondence appropriate to their delicate and crucial negotiations with the East. None the less, the

[11] Organising principle: no satisfactory suggestion has been made to explain the selection of concluding letters for Books III, IV, and VIII. O'Donnell, *Cassiodorus*, 79–81, is not convincing. He assumes a very subtle pattern which would 'please a Byzantine audience', not a credible motive for the publication of the *Variae* (cf. Gillett, 'Purposes'): the final letter of Book IV is addressed to Symmachus, later executed by Theoderic, and that of VIII concerns riots; neither 'put[s] the very best possible face on the Ostrogothic kingdom'.

Disruption of chronological sequence: e.g. Cass., *Variae* II, 1, written late 510, cf. III, 1–4, written late 506/7, which must in fact have been among the earliest letters written by Cassiodorus; V, 43–4, written *c.* 510/11, but all other letters in Book V (with the possible exception of V, 1–2) appear to have been written *c.* 523–7; Mommsen, *Prooemium* to Cass., *Variae*, xxxvi; Krautschick, *Cassiodor*, 59, Table 3, 77. It is not clear why Cassiodorus placed these letters at the end of Book V, not at the end of Book III or IV, both of which contain letters written in the same period (during his tenure as *quaestor*) but which do not close with diplomatic letters. In general: Krautschick, *Cassiodor*, 73–7, Tables 3 and 4, 102–6.

[12] *Variae* I, 2 concerns the production of purple dye for the *sacra vestis*.

[13] Another letter on Cassiodori: *Variae* III, 28 (summons to court the author's father from Theoderic).

Table 2 *Diplomatic and personal letters in Cassiodorus,* Variae

I 1	**Theoderic to Anastasius**
[I 2	On the manufacture of imperial purple dye]
I 3–4	*Theoderic to Cassiodorus (father of the author) and to the Senate: appointment of Cassiodorus senior as* patricius
I 46	**Theoderic to the Burgundian king Gundobad**
II 1	**Theoderic to Anastasius**
II 41	**Theoderic to the Frankish king Clovis**
III 1	**Theoderic to the Visigothic king Alaric II**
III 2	Theoderic to Gundobad
III 3	Theoderic to the kings of the Heruli, Warni, and Thuringians
III 4	Theoderic to Clovis
(*III 28*	*Theoderic to Cassiodorus [father of the author]*)
IV 1	**Theoderic to the Thuringian king Herminafred**
IV 2	Theoderic to the king of the Heruli
V 1	**Theoderic to the king of the Warni**
V 2	Theoderic to the king of the Haesti
V 43	Theoderic to the Vandal king Transamund
V 44	**Theoderic to the Vandal king Transamund**
[VI and VII	Formulae, containing no diplomatic letters (though note VI 3.6; 6.4; 9.7–8; VII 5.1; 33 – on provisioning of visiting envoys)]
VIII 1	**Athalaric to Justin**
IX 1	**Athalaric to the Vandal king Hilderic**
IX 24–5	*Athalaric to Cassiodorus and the Senate: appointment of Cassiodorus as praetorian prefect*
X 1	**Amalasuntha to Justinian**
X 2	Theodahad to Justinian
X 8	Amalasuntha to Justinian
X 9	Theodahad to Justinian
X 10	Amalasuntha to Theodora
X 15	Theodahad to Justinian
X 19	Theodahad to Justinian
X 20	Theodahad to Theodora
X 21	Gudeliva to Theodora
X 22	Theodahad to Justinian
X 23	Theodahad to Theodora
X 24	Gudeliva to Theodora
X 25	Theodahad to Justinian

(*cont.*)

Table 2 (*cont.*)

X 26	Theodahad to Justinian
X 32	Vitigis to Justinian
X 33	Vitigis to (eastern) *magister officiorum*[a]
X 34	Vitigis to *episcopis suis*[a]
X 35	**Vitigis to (eastern) *praetorian prefect*[a]**
XI and XII	*Letters in Cassiodorus' own name as praetorian prefect*, containing no diplomatic letters (though note XI 13[b])

[a] Letters of credence for the envoys carrying X 32.

[b] *Variae* XI, 13 (in the name of the Senate of Rome to Justinian, seeking to prevent the outbreak of hostilities between Constantinople and Italy) is not treated as diplomatic correspondence by Cassiodorus' editorial principles, for it is not given any significant placing in Book XI. As the letter was included in Book XI, not Book X, it was written by Cassiodorus in the capacity of praetorian prefect, not *quaestor* to Theodahad, and was therefore not regarded by Cassiodorus as a communication from a ruler either in form or origin.

Earlier correspondence between eastern emperors and the Senate of Rome during Ostrogothic rule: *Collectio Avellana*, 113, 114, a. 516.

balance of imperial and royal addressees must arise from Cassiodorus' conscious selection, not from the impress of events. The years of Cassiodorus' first tenure as *quaestor* in the late 500s were a period of conflict and reconciliation with Byzantium, as Constantinople under Anastasius encouraged Frankish disruption of Theoderic's network of western alliances, and dispatched naval forces against Italy. Resolution cannot have been reached without the aid of many more letters sent from Theoderic's court than the two preserved by Cassiodorus.[14] Similarly, the breakdown of relations between Italy and Constantinople under Justinian and the consequential outbreak of war, straddled by Cassiodorus' times in office as *magister officiorum* and praetorian prefect of Italy in the mid-530s, was accompanied by negotiations with other western powers – including the Franks, the Burgundians, the Goths in Spain, and the Vandals – of which there is no trace in the *Variae*. The distribution of imperial and royal letters in the *Variae* is unlikely to reflect the proportions of letters originally written. Nor does the division of mostly royal diplomatic letters in the early books, and exclusively imperial letters in Book X, represent any simple thematic emphasis, such as a division between Theoderic's good rule, accompanied by peaceful negotiations, in the earlier books, and the domestic and international crises of the monarchs of Book X.[15] Theoderic's ultimately

[14] *Variae* I, 1 and II, 1.

[15] Suggested by O'Donnell, *Cassiodorus*, 80.

vain diplomacy in 506/7, to prevent conflict between the Goths of Toulouse and the Franks of Clovis, is recalled in Book III; so, in Book IX, is the outbreak of conflict in 526/7 between the Ostrogothic court and the Vandals under Justinian's ally Hilderic (signalled by the murder of Amalafrida, sister of Theoderic and wife of Hilderic's predecessor as king).[16] It is the dominance of letters to Justinian and Theodora in Book X which appears the most disproportionate feature of the distribution of diplomatic correspondence throughout the *Variae*. The series of diplomatic letters in Book X may be attributed to the topicality of negotiations with Constantinople at the time of publication of the *Variae*; they may represent the majority of the occasions when Cassiodorus was requested to act in the capacity of *quaestor* while holding the office of praetorian prefect of Italy, and therefore the bulk of his available material. But as the cause for the number of imperial letters in Book X is not made apparent by the editor of the work, one should be wary of conjecturing a purpose for this selection, whether mundane or persuasive.

Detailed analysis of the *Variae* as a whole indicates that Cassiodorus employs distinctive vocabulary to differentiate letters to emperors and kings, and also to the Senate, from the dispositive letters concerning Italian administration. Cassiodorus uses certain words exclusively to describe diplomatic correspondence.[17] These are not strictly technical terms, and though some, such as *apices*, have a sense of grandeur, all come directly from the vocabulary of private correspondence.[18] Somewhat surprisingly, the term used most exclusively for letters to sovereigns is simply *litterae*. Diplomatic correspondence differs stylistically from administrative letters in the *Variae* not by explicit aggrandisement of the former, but by the sense of command in the latter. In a formal sense, correspondence between rulers is more a part of the tradition of the cultured epistolography of friendship than of a specifically bureaucratic, chancellery style.[19]

Other features, either of Cassiodorus' original composition of the letters or of his subsequent collection, set the diplomatic letters apart. Several titles of courtesy used to address recipients are reserved exclusively for rulers, some exclusively for the eastern emperors and empresses, though

16 *Variae* III, 1–4; IX, 1.

17 Fridh, *Terminologie et formules*, 65–72 (*apices, chartae, epistulae*, and *litterae*).

18 The meaning of 'correspondence' for *apices* in fact derives from a mundane calligraphic sense; Lewis and Short, s.v. *apex* II, D–E.

19 See Pseudo-Demetrius, *Epistolary Types*, c. 1 in Malherbe, *Ancient Epistolary Theorists*, 33 on the occasions for 'those in prominent positions' to adopt the style of letter classified as 'friendly'; for a later period: M. E. Mullett, 'The Language of Diplomacy', in Shepard and Franklin (eds.), *Byzantine Diplomacy*, 203–16. Cf. the letters of the Burgundian king Sigismund to the emperor Anastasius or Justin; Avitus of Vienne, *Epp.*, 46, 78, 93, 94.

a number of titles are shared with addressees of *illustris* rank or bishops.[20] The diplomatic letters generally do not have learned digressions such as grace the letters in the *Variae* to Symmachus and Boethius; the importance of the letters to rulers precludes distractions from the matters at issue. In general, these letters are clear and readily comprehensible, which cannot be said for all other letters in the *Variae*.[21]

A final distinctive feature of the diplomatic letters concerns references to envoys. The *Variae* is one of the most important sources of prosopographical information for the early sixth century, naming many officials otherwise unknown or poorly attested. This does not hold true for the envoys of the Ostrogothic monarchs. Almost all the letters to rulers conclude with a statement that the *legati* bearing the letter will more fully convey the Ostrogothic monarch's views orally. Like most ancient correspondence, the letters could be expected to be read publicly and possibly to circulate, thus serving as an introduction to discussions. Private negotiations could then be held with the envoys, for whom the written document served as a letter of credence.

The envoys were named in most if not all the original letters to emperors and kings, but in every case, as the letter stands in the *Variae*, the envoys' names have been removed and the words *ille et ille* substituted.[22] Similar deletions of specific information occur elsewhere in the *Variae*, but for no category of information or group of court functionaries

[20] Fridh, *Terminologie et formules*, 176–8, 190–1 (terms exclusively for rulers: *excellentia, virtus*), 191–4 (solely for eastern emperors or empresses), 187–91 (terms used also for other recipients of high rank: *fraternitas, potestas, prudentia, sapientia*).

[21] Digressions: the sole exception is Cass., *Variae* v, 2.2–3, to the king of the Haesti (on the origin of amber).

The diplomatic letters are particularly susceptible to modern readings which construe conventional rhetoric as articulated ideology and foreign policy. Most recently: Amory, *People and Identity in Ostrogothic Italy*, 50, 59, 61–6, where the assertiveness evident in many of the letters of Theoderic to western kings is construed as 'a condescending, at times sneering, tone' towards barbarian rulers (61), set in apposition to a schematised interpretation of the theme of *civilitas* in the domestic letters of the *Variae*. This alleged 'condescension', hardly an advisable approach to diplomatic communication, represents no more than a negotiating position.

Other aspects of Amory's treatment of Theoderic's letters to kings require amendment: the claim that, in the earliest diplomatic correspondence in the *Variae*, Theoderic asserted that he had 'no special relationship' (62) with the kings of the Franks and Burgundians (yet Theoderic was tied by marriage to both); the assertion that, after the battle of Vouillé, the Thuringians were more important to Theoderic's strategic interests than the Heruls, and consequently Theoderic pursued appropriately differentiated forms of alliance, a marriage-tie with the Thuringian king and 'adoption-in-arms' of the Herul ruler (63–4; neither the greater strategic importance of the Thuringians, nor the innate superiority of marital over adoptive ties, is demonstrated; Theoderic adopts a superior, paternal role in both pseudo-familial alliances).

[22] This occurs with such regularity that it can at least be said that envoys usually travelled in pairs, apparently acting jointly as principals of the embassy, e.g.: Cass., *Variae* I, 1; II, 41; III, 1, 2, 3, 4; IV, 43; VIII, 1; IX, 1; X, 32, 33, 35. For other examples: see below, chapter 6 nn. 67–8.

so consistently as the envoys in the diplomatic letters.[23] The potential prosopographical list of envoys serving the Ostrogothic court of Italy is thus substantially reduced. This is a significant loss, and not just statistically but qualitatively. Several narrative sources record embassies dispatched by the Ostrogothic kings, and give the names of the envoys, but the narratives record only embassies led by *optimates* of Italian society, including members of the Senate of Rome (in particular the *caput senatus*) or by the bishops of Rome.[24] The activity of embassies led by less prestigious figures is thus almost hidden from view. It is not the diplomatic correspondence in Cassiodorus' *Variae* but the edicts and encomiastic letters of appointment that record the function of non-senatorial servants of the court of Ravenna as envoys.

The substitution of *ille* for the envoys' names in the diplomatic correspondence is not made to conceal the identity of the individuals at the time of the *Variae*'s publication, for envoys are named several times in the other categories of letters.[25] Nor were envoys of insufficient rank to warrant commemoration with other high officials named in the *Variae*. Many of Theoderic's envoys held high office and were of aristocratic background, and some of less impressive origin were advanced to high office in part because of their services on legations.[26] Rather, the deletions reflect the literary and bureaucratic milieu of the *Variae*. Cassiodorus intended his collection to provide stylistic models for his successors in office, not only in the two books of *formulae*, but in the individual letters also. In the preface, Cassiodorus indicates that he considers his letters to rulers as one

[23] Traube, 'Index rerum et verborum' to Cass., *Variae*, 546–7, s.v. *ille*, usefully distinguishes the use of *ille* as a substitution for individuals, times, places, and other subjects. Almost all occurences of *ille* other than for persons are in the *formulae* of Books VI and VII. Nine times *ille* stands for private citizens who receive royal assistance; in all other occasions, *ille* represents court functionaries. The majority of these last cases are the envoys of the diplomatic letters; for no other type of court office are the names of the office holders consistently replaced by *ille*. Cassiodorus also uses *tot* to replace specific information in the letters. Such deletions of details occur also in other letter collections, e.g. the *Registrum* of Pope Gregory I; Dag Norberg, *In registrum Gregorii Magni studia critica* (Uppsala, 1939), II, 6 n. 3.

[24] The main extant source for names of envoys of the Ostrogoths is *Anon. Val. pars II*, which provides six names of senators (see n. 26) and Pope John I, whose ill-fated mission in 525 is recorded in many chronicle sources (see chapter 2 above, n. 11).

[25] Envoys are named in edicts (Cass., *Variae* I, 15 Agnellus; II, 6 Fl. Agapitus; XII, 20 Pope Agapitus), and in eulogies (I, 4 Cassiodorus' father; IV, 3–4 Senarius; V, 40–1 Cyprianus). Envoys received at Ravenna from the Senate or the province of Dalmatia are also named (VIII, 12 Arator; 15 Publianus).

[26] Commemoration of officials: Cass., *Variae, Praef.*, 9. Envoys of high rank: e.g. Fl. Rufius Postumius Festus (*Anon. Val.* XI, 53; XII, 64; *PLRE* II, 467–9); Fl. Anicius Probus Faustus iunior Niger (*Anon. Val.* XII, 57; *PLRE* II, 454–5); the senators Theodorus, Inportunus, Agapitus, and Fl. Agapitus, most of whom were members of the Decii family (*Anon. Val.* XV, 90; *PLRE* II, 30, 32, 592, 1098; John Moorhead, 'The Decii under Theoderic', *Historia* 33 (1984), 107–15). Advancement for diplomatic duties: Senarius (below), Cyprianus: *Variae* V, 40.5; Agnellus: *Variae* I, 15 (*PLRE* II, 35–6).

category, alongside those to high officials and to *humillimi*, to be imitated by his bureaucratic heirs.[27] For letters of appointment and other recurring occasions, Cassiodorus provides both the *formulae* of Books VI and VII and the actual letters of many individuals' elevations. No *formula* could be provided for diplomatic correspondence, but by deleting the detail of the envoys' names, Cassiodorus took a step towards removing the letters from their historical context, making them timeless stylistic models.[28]

Notwithstanding their distinctive features, the diplomatic letters are integrated into the body of the *Variae*, in rough conformity with the broad chronological sequence of the collection, rather than gathered into a separate book. Many are closely related in topic or circumstance with their adjacent letters. The letters to the Burgundian and Frankish kings which conclude the first two books are preceded by the famous letters to Boethius, requesting his aid in preparing suitable gifts to be given to the respective kings, and digressing indulgently on the subjects of engineering and music.[29] Two letters to western kings at the beginning of Book IV, sealing alliances, are followed by a pair of letters elevating a court servant to high rank as a reward for his services as an envoy.[30] Athalaric's letter to Justin opening Book VIII is the first of a series announcing his accession in 526. The eight letters are arranged in descending order of rank, from the emperor and the Roman Senate to outlying provincials.[31] The final four letters of Book X are also a series, concerning Vitigis' appeal to Justinian for peace, introduced by a letter to the emperor; again, precedence of rank is observed.[32] Cassiodorus highlights his letters to rulers, but intersperses

27 Cass., *Variae, Praef.*, 17. Similar collections of real diplomatic correspondence have been produced in modern times to serve as stylistic models: Charles de Martens, *Manuel diplomatique* (Paris, 1822), chap. 10: 'Des compositions diplomatiques', 174–93, 'Actes et offices diplomatiques', 195–575; Ernest Setow, *A Guide to Diplomatic Practice*, 4th edn, ed. Nevile Bland (New York, 1957), chap. 7: 'The Language of Diplomatic Intercourse and Forms of Documents', 57–77. On these and other modern works: Gordon A. Craig, 'On the Nature of Diplomatic History: the Relevance of Some Old Books', in P. G. Lauren (ed.), *Diplomacy: New Approaches in History, Theory, and Policy* (New York and London, 1979), 21–42.

28 On *ille* as part of the formulaic nature of the *Variae*: Mommsen, *Prooemium* to Cass., *Variae*, xxiii–xxiv; followed by Fridh, *Terminologie et formules*, 2; O'Donnell, *Cassiodorus*, 93; Barnish, Introduction to *Cassiodorus: Variae*, xviii.

There is no evidence to support the suggestion of Peter, *Der Brief*, 205–6 (followed by Krautschick, *Cassiodor*, 43), that the use of *ille* indicates that Cassiodorus compiled his collection from personal draft copies, written before the envoys were appointed; the use of *ille* and *tot* in other types of letters, including rescripts, indicates that the words are deletions from the originals.

Formula of royal correspondence: though cf. Marculf, *Formulae* I, 10 (a general greeting of friendship).

29 Cass., *Variae* I, 45–6; II, 40–1.

30 Cass., *Variae* IV, 1–4 (Senarius); see below.

31 Cass., *Variae* VIII, 1–8. Cf. the letters announcing the accession of Amalasuntha and Theodahad: X, 1–4.

32 Cass., *Variae* X, 32–5. For a comparable series of diplomatic letters, dispatched simultaneously to a descending order of officials, cf. *Ep. Austr.*, 25–39 (580s).

them among letters relating to other duties. He thus displays the variety, asserted in his preface, both of his correspondence and of his functions in office.[33]

Cassiodorus chose to give the letters to rulers emphasis by the prominent position they have in each book. This placement also draws attention to Cassiodorus' role, in the capacity of *quaestor*, in diplomatic exchange. As with the other functions of the *quaestor*, this role centred on eloquence. The diplomatic letter, though only one part of communication between powers, served as a formal introduction to negotiations of great moment. It was essential, therefore, that letters to rulers displayed skilled command of the forms of communication, that is to say, of rhetoric. Rhetorical skill is the common factor between the function of the *quaestor* and the duties of envoys. The oratorical talents of envoys were crucial to the success of their missions; Sidonius establishes eloquence as the defining characteristic of Avitus in order to cast him as a legate.[34] Eloquence is also the foremost feature of diplomatic correspondence, conveying a mystique of authority.[35] It is this lesson which Cassiodorus offers to his successors in office, and for this reason he draws attention to his letters to emperors and kings in the monument to his public career.

Diplomatic affairs do not bulk large in the dispositive letters, the edicts and rescripts, of the *Variae*. Only one letter commissions an individual to undertake a mission on the court's behalf. At some date between late 509 and 511, the senator Fl. Agapitus was directed by Theoderic to travel to Constantinople. Agapitus, already a mature figure, had held high office in Ravenna since *c.* 502, had been prefect of Rome in 508/9, and had recently been raised to the rank of *patricius*. At least twice in the two years after completing his tenure as prefect of Rome, Agapitus had received instructions from Theoderic, in both cases to act as a civil magistrate. The direction to travel to Constantinople was a further instance of Theoderic exploiting the services of this senior member of the Senate of Rome to complete a specific commission, which was not part of the duties of any palatine office. It was customary for the court under Theoderic to deploy former holders of office and other senior figures in this way, and the tone of the letter is similar to others in the *Variae* which direct ex-officials (including Cassiodorus' father) to return to Ravenna in order to attend the king's *comitatus* or to perform certain unspecified duties without office.[36] Similar written summonses might have been issued when Theoderic sent

[33] Cass., *Variae, Praef.*, 15–17. [34] Above, chapter 3 at n. 62.

[35] Macpherson, *Rome in Involution*, 71–4.

[36] Cass., *Variae* II, 6; Mommsen, *Prooemium*, xxxii; Sundwall, *Abhandlungen*, 84–5; *PLRE* II, 'Fl. Agapitus 3', 30–2. Krautschick, *Cassiodor*, 60–1, dates Agapitus' tenure as prefect of Rome

other high-ranking individuals, not currently in court service, to the East, but this is the only extant example. Theoderic and his successors were keen to have their wishes presented in the eastern capital by senior representatives of the Roman Senate, especially those who held the position of *caput senatus*, president of the senate, as Agapitus would have during his tenure as urban prefect.[37] But other embassies, perhaps the majority, were led by legates drawn from the ranks of current palatine officers.[38] The letter to Agapitus contains no instructions, and makes no reference to any diplomatic correspondence to be conveyed to Constantinople. It is clearly not intended to act as a letter of credence for Agapitus, for the eastern court is described unflatteringly. Though the letter cannot be dated exactly, the termini for its original composition show that it is the product of the uneasy period of reconciliation between Ravenna and Constantinople, following Byzantine aggravation towards Italy in the middle of the decade.

As a source for the administrative arrangements for embassies, the value of the *Variae* is limited. Practical concerns for the dispatch of embassies are addressed in only two letters. In one, Theoderic provides for the protection, *tuitio*, of the private affairs of the *patricius* Agnellus, whom he sends as envoy to Africa probably *c.* 507/8, for the duration of Agnellus' absence. The interests of provincials absent from their home on embassies to the court had been protected by imperial law since at least the third century; this letter attests the extension of protection to a person sent on an embassy by the court. Theoderic himself, however, does not stand as

to 507/8, arguing that the embassy, undertaken after completion of his period in office, was associated with Cass., *Variae* I, 1 (to Anastasius) and the Byzantine naval attacks on the Italian coast in 508. There is no reason, however, that Agapitus' mission need be associated with the events of 508; Theoderic's court was in frequent contact with Constantinople. The dating of Agapitus' prefecture in *PLRE* is to be preferred. The embassy could have occurred at any date between September 509 (the date of appointment of the next attested prefect of Rome) and 511, the *terminus post quem non* of Cass., *Variae* I–IV.

Recall of former officers to perform specific duties for court: Cass., *Variae* III, 28 (to Cassiodorus senior, former praetorian prefect of Italy and *patricius*), III, 22 (to Artemidorus, former prefect of Rome); VII, 34 (*formula* for royal summons to the *comitatus*).

[37] E.g. Theoderic dispatched the *caput senatus* Fl. Rufus Postumius Festus to the emperor Zeno in 490, and again to Anastasius in 497; *Anon. Val.* XI, 53, XII, 64. He possibly sent Symmachus, also then *caput senatus*, to Constantinople as an envoy; *PLRE* II, 'Q. Aurelius Memmius Symmachus iunior 9', 1045. To protest Justin's treatment of Arians in the East, Theoderic sent four senators together with John, the bishop of Rome; *Anon. Val.* XV, 90. Theodahad also dispatched an embassy of senators to Constantinople; Procopius, *Wars* V, 4.15. At about this time, Cassiodorus drafted a letter in the Senate's name to Justinian, appealing for peace; Cass., *Variae* XI, 13. Wolfram, *History of the Goths*, 287. Prefect of Rome as *caput senatus*: Jones, *LRE*, 332, 531, 537.

[38] Below, on Cyprianus (n. 46) and Senarius; presumably Maximianus: *PLRE* II, 'Maximianus 7', 739–40.

Agnellus' protector, but appoints the ex-consul and *patricius* Fl. Rufius Postumius Festus, in his capacity as *caput senatus*. Presumably Agnellus, a *patricius* described elsewhere as *magnificus vir*, was a member of the senatorial order, and Theoderic made use of the obligations of Festus' position. The letter intimates that the absence of a person on an embassy opened the possibility of unscrupulous dealings or accusations against him; such exploitation is attested in earlier periods. The responsibility of the *caput senatus* in protecting the affairs of envoys sent by the court might well have applied to all instances of senators dispatched by the court, and very likely continued imperial precedent. The court thus co-opted the Senate into a supporting role for its administration. Who acted as protector of the affairs of the *caput senatus* when he served as an envoy – Festus himself had twice undertaken embassies to Constantinople on Theoderic's behalf while *caput senatus*, and other heads of the Senate are recorded as envoys – is unclear, and there is no reference in the *Variae* to similar protection of the affairs of non-senatorial court servants sent on legations.[39]

The second letter addressing practical arrangements concerns the financing of a mission. In 536, Theodahad sent Pope Agapitus to Constantinople, to answer charges that Theodahad had arranged the murder of Amalasuntha; Agapitus died while in the East. A letter sent by Cassiodorus in his own name as praetorian prefect to the treasury officials Thomas and Petrus reveals that the mission had been funded by moneys advanced to Agapitus from the royal treasury, at Theodahad's order. Agapitus, however, had been required to deposit vessels of the Church of Rome and a signed pledge with treasury officials to secure the advance of funds; the mission had thus been funded by pawning church plate to the royal treasury. Theodahad, through Cassiodorus, later annulled the pledge, returning the ecclesiastical vessels to the Church of Rome.[40] The letter is the only direct evidence extant for the financing of palatine embassies. Theodahad's release of the debt is represented as an act of generosity and piety; the implication is that it was not usual for the court to fund the expenses incurred on an embassy by a wealthy figure such as the bishop of Rome or, presumably, senators, even when an embassy was undertaken at the command of the king. As with the letter concerning the

[39] *Variae* I, 15. *PLRE* II, 'Agnellus', 35–6 (he had already been in Africa, perhaps on behalf of the court, two years previously; and was appointed to a high palatine office in 508–11), 'Fl. Rufius Postumius Festus 5', 467–9. Protection of provincial envoys: above, chapter 1, n. 71. Justinian, *Nov.*, 123.26, provides legal protection for bishops who travel as legates to Constantinople.

[40] Cass., *Variae* XII, 20; trans. Barnish 173–4 with note at 174 *fin*. For the context: *Liber pont.*, 59; Procopius, *Wars* V, 4, 6.

tuitio of a senatorial envoy, this document indicates the deployment of private resources, here financial, by the court in order to support diplomatic activities. Again there are parallels with provincial embassies to imperial centres in earlier periods, for most if not all of the costs of undertaking a provincial embassy were commonly borne by the envoy himself, even when civic or imperial funds were nominally available, as an assertion of wealth and status with the individual's community. Cassiodorus' letter, however, suggests a *quid pro quo* for this financial burden. Cassiodorus represents an embassy, at least to Constantinople, as an opportunity for cultivating ties and patronage through the generous distribution of gifts. Such an opportunity, Cassiodorus implies, had assisted Agapitus in his dealings with Justinian on doctrinal matters, conducted in parallel with the main, political purposes of the mission. By annulling Agapitus' debt to the court, Theodahad was enabling the Church of Rome to benefit from Agapitus' munificence in Constantinople, without having to bear the expense. This of course is only a generous interpretation put by Cassiodorus on an otherwise unattested situation; but it accords with evidence from earlier periods, and of Sidonius and Ennodius, of provincial embassies exploited by their leaders as opportunities for personal influence.

Both these letters, concerning *tuitio* and financing, are unique attestations of the particular arrangements concerned. Their example can be generalised only tentatively for regular practice in the Ostrogothic kingdom, or other areas or times. Both concern arrangements for embassies to be undertaken on behalf of the court by wealthy, socially prominent individuals, not currently holding secular office. There is no indication what arrangements for *tuitio* and financing of missions were made for embassies undertaken by non-senatorial court functionaries.

None of the *formulae* of Books VI and VII addresses arrangements for outgoing embassies. Several of the *formulae*, however, are more informative regarding incoming legations, and the responsibilities of a number of senior magistrates – the praetorian prefect of Italy, the *magister officiorum*, the *comes patrimonii*, and the *cura palatii* – for the provisioning and care of envoys. The legates whom these letters concern are primarily not emissaries of the cities or provinces under Theoderic's rule, but those of external *gentes*, who 'come from almost every part of the world'. In each case, the letters emphasise the need to impress the visitors with the abundance and hospitality of the court. Envoys of the *gentes* are expected to be *voraces*; the satisfaction of their appetites will redound to the praise of the state. Grandeur and munificence were tools commonly exploited in ancient diplomacy to command the respect of other parties.

The praetorian prefect and the *magister officiorum*, by their administration of *evectiones* (official travel warrants) and the *cursus publicus* (official means of transport and communication) were involved in the transportation, accommodation, and provisioning of envoys; the *comes patrimonii* and the *cura palatii*, through their provisioning of the royal court, were responsible for ensuring the palatial plenitude which would, amongst other things, impress visitors. The *magister officiorum* also controlled and stage-managed the official receptions of envoys, as his eastern counterpart did also in Constantinople.[41] Cassiodorus included a separate *formula* for the issue to foreign envoys of a *tractoria*, an official warrant which would ensure their provisioning and a speedy return home.[42] One edict, not a *formula*, demonstrates that responsibility for the provision of supplies to visiting envoys was not met solely from central government resources: the *comites*, *defensores*, and *curiales* of the city of Pavia were enjoined to provide transport by boat between their city and Ravenna and five days' provisions (*annonae*) to envoys from the Heruli travelling to Theoderic's court. Again, the need to impress the visitors with the copiousness of resources is enjoined.[43] This is the extent of administrative detail on embassies provided by the *Variae*.

Altogether, there is remarkably little evidence for organisation of embassies in the administrative documents of the *Variae*. This is partially because diplomatic activities were not confined within a single departmental structure; there was therefore no responsible magistracy which would generate or receive administrative correspondence specifically concerning the needs of embassies. Facilities for embassies, such as transport, were provided by the service departments of the praetorian prefect and *magister officiorum*, and so the needs of envoys were included under the general administration of, for example, the *cursus publicus* or the provisioning of the court. It is probably not by chance that the only two letters giving evidence of arrangements for specific embassies concern envoys who were not current servants of the court, for whom, therefore, specific provisions were needed. There is also a further systemic reason why administrative arrangements for embassies are little attested. The activities of envoys were part of the *arcana regia*, the privy affairs of the monarch,

41 Cass., *Variae* VI, 3.3, 6 (praetorian prefect), 6.4 (*magister officiorum*), 9.7–8 (*comes patrimonii* – quotation); VII, 5.1 (*cura palatii*); VII, 33 (*Formula tractoriae legatorum diversarum gentium*). *Legati gentium* are specified in all but VII, 5.1. The *legati* mentioned in IV, 47.1, concerning abuses of the *cursus publicus*, appear to be Theoderic's agents in Rome; cf. 47.2. Eastern court: Constantine VII Porphyrogenitus, *De cerimoniis aulae Byzantinae libri duo*, ed. J. J. Reiske (Corpus scriptorum historiae Byzantinae 7; Bonn, 1829–30), I, 87.

42 Cass., *Variae* VII, 33 (*Formula tractoriae legatorum diversarum gentium*).

43 Cass., *Variae* IV, 45. See below, chapter 6, at nn. 85–8.

and so were more likely to be organised directly by the imperial or royal consistory than through one of the palatine magisteries, leaving no documentation.[44]

SENARIUS, 'CEASELESS WAYFARER OF THE WORLD'

The third category of document in the *Variae*, the eulogistic letters of appointment for high officials, also contains only a small number of references to embassies. They provide, however, prosopographical details and indications of the potential advantages to individuals' careers which could come from participation in embassies. Several eulogies include the completion of embassies among tasks deserving acclaim. The praise for envoys' rhetorical skills in these passages is reminiscent of Cassiodorus' own pride in his diplomatic correspondence. Cassiodorus attributes the appointment of the former advocate Arator to a high position in the *officium* of the *patricius praesentalis* Tulvin in part to the eloquence Arator had shown when he had acted as an envoy to Theoderic's court, representing the province of Dalmatia.[45] In praising officers for their former embassies, Cassiodorus employs two literary topoi: the cunning of the Constantinopolitan court, and the fury of barbarian kings, both dangers to be overcome by the courage and eloquence of envoys. The *comes sacrarum largitionum* Cyprianus, best known as the accuser of Boethius, is praised for being impervious to the grandeur of the eastern court; his linguistic skills prevented his succumbing to Greek *argutia*. Cassiodorus' own grandfather is honoured for boldly withstanding the rage of Attila, and destroying the king's iniquitous pretexts for conflict with his arguments.[46]

[44] Cass., *Variae* IV, 3.3; for similar descriptions of proximity to the royal consistory: I, 4.10 (*imperiale secretum*); VIII, 12.8 (*arcana nostri imperii*); 18.3 (quote in text); XI, 6.3 (*consistorii nostri secreta*). Cf. Priscus' description of the organisation of Maximus' embassy to Attila in 449; Priscus, *Fr.*, 11.1–2 (*Fr. Class. Hist.*, 245–7); Sid. Ap., *Ep.* III, 7.3 (envoys trading in the *secreta dirigentium principum*); Ennodius, *Vita Epiphani*, 136 (Theoderic commissions Epiphanius to travel to Gundobad *secretius*). Recognition of the secrecy of the imperial and quasi-imperial consistorium extended well beyond diplomatic affairs; cf. Ambrose, *Ep.*, 75.20; Eunapius, *Fr.*, 50.

[45] Cass., *Variae* VIII, 12.2–4, 7; *PLRE* II, 'Arator', 126–7 with Barnish, *Cassiodorus: Variae*, 103 n. 3.

[46] Cyprianus: Cass., *Variae* V, 40.5; cf. II, 6.2 to Agapitus, who is warned that, when he travels to Constantinople, he must *contra subtilissimos disputare et in conventu doctorum sic agere, ne susceptam causam tot erudita possint ingenia superare*. The Byzantine courtiers are characterised as *artifices*.

(For Grecian deceits of another order met by an envoy of the Ostrogothic court: Maximianus, *Elegia* V (cited above, chapter 1 at n. 82): *Hic me suscipiens Etruscae gentis alumnum/Inuoluit patriis Graia puella dolis*. Such a liaison carried risks to the envoy: cf. below, chapter 6, at nn. 104–5.)

Cassiodorus senior: Cass., *Variae* I, 4.11–12, characterising the elder Cassiodorus' speeches as *veritas*. Cf. *Variae* IV, 3.2 on Senarius, discussed below.

Both Greek subtlety and barbarian irrationality are commonplaces, employed to provide a context for the praise of former envoys' eloquence.

The most informative of the letters of appointment are two written in the name of Theoderic concerning the elevation of a palatine officer named Senarius to the financial position of *comes patrimonii*.[47] Senarius had many times undertaken embassies for Theoderic. Several other sources relating to Senarius are extant which, together with Cassiodorus' letters, give a profile of a late Roman officer who specialised in the task of an envoy.

Senarius' appointment as *comes* was made for the indiction year commencing 1 September 509.[48] Following the usual practice of the *Variae*, two letters announce Senarius' appointment: one to the appointee and the other to the Senate of Rome. It is the only personal letter of appointment for a *comes patrimonii* in the *Variae*; the other *comites* mentioned in the collection might have received only a variant of Cassiodorus' standard *formula* for appointment to this office.[49] The *comitiva* of the *patrimonium*

[47] Cass., *Variae* IV, 3–4. For full text and translation, see appendix III.

On Senarius: Mommsen, 'Index personarum' to Cass., *Variae*, 499; Sundwall, *Abhandlungen*, 153–4; *PLRE* II, 'Senarius', 988–9; Roland Delmaire, *Les Responsables des finances impériales au Bas-Empire romain (IVe–VIe s.): études prosopographiques* (Collection Latomus 203; Brussels, 1989), 293–6, and Delmaire, *Largesses sacrées et* res privata*: l'*aerarium *impérial et son administration du IVe–VIe siècles* (Ecole française de Rome, Collection 121; Rome, 1989), 692; Christoph Schäfer, *Der weströmische Senat als Träger antiker Kontinuität unter den Ostgotenkönigen (490–540 n.Chr.)* (St Katharinen, 1991), no. 92, 103–4; Amory, *People and Identity in Ostrogothic Italy*, 413. On the *comitiva patrimonii*, below nn. 103–5.

Senarius is styled *comes privatarum* in the inscription of Cass., *Variae* IV, 3, 7, 11, and 13, and the respective entries in the *Capitula* of *Variae* IV in all manuscript families. He was, however, *comes patrimonii*, not *privatarum*; *Variae* IV, 3.2 and 4.2 and Senarius, *Epitaph*, line 15, *contra* Otto Seeck, 'Comes sacri patrimonii (c)', *RE* IV.1, 676; Barnwell, *Emperor, Prefects, and Kings*, 148, 150. The discrepancy does not occur with any of the other three *comites patrimonii* addressed in the *Variae*. Though Theoderic's officers sometimes performed the tasks of two posts simultaneously, only one was held formally, and the dual responsibility draws comment from Cassiodorus; Cass., *Variae* VIII, 13.2–3 (Ambrosius as CRP, also fulfilling the task of *quaestor*), *Praef.*, 7 and IX, 24.6, 25.8 (Cassiodorus acting as *quaestor* while *magister officiorum* and praetorian prefect). The appearance of *comes privatarum* in the inscriptions of the *Variae* appears to be a simple scribal error; Delmaire, *Les Responsables*, 295.

[48] Cass., *Variae* IV, 3.2: *per indictionem tertiam*. For the fifteen-year cycle of the indiction, beginning in 312: E. J. Bickerman, *Chronology of the Ancient World* (London, 1968), 78–9. The first year of the indiction cycle fell on 507/8; as all letters in *Variae* I–IV were written between 506/7 and 511, the third indiction to which Cassiodorus refers is that of 509/10. For the date: Krautschick, *Cassiodor*, 67–8 and Table 3, 76. Krautschick's assumption, however, that Senarius' tenure as *comes* lasted longer than one year, is unsupported. On the duration of tenure in financial *comitivae*: Delmaire, *Largesses sacrées*, 113.

[49] Other *comites patrimonii*: Julianus (Cass., *Variae* I, 16), Wilia (V, 18–20; IX, 13), Bergantinus (VIII, 23; IX, 3), unnamed (IV, 15, cf. *PLRE* II, 'Anonymus 35', 1225). *Formula* for appointment of *comes patrimonii*: VI, 9.

conveyed illustrious rank and full membership of the Senate on its incumbent, and consequently the king commends their new member to the *patres conscripti.* Though the two letters appear similar in tone and sequence of topic, close examination reveals a tactful tailoring of each to its recipient. The letter to Senarius emphasises the court's patronage of its servants and Senarius' personal qualities. The Senate's letter, however, dwells on Senarius' entry into the ranks of that body, and his obligations, in office, to the public good.

The promotion of virtuous servants, according to the letter to Senarius, redounds to the glory of their ruler.[50] For the officer, the acquisition of dignities is a reward for efficient and loyal service; even when commencing a new office, the promise of further advancement is held out as a spur to loyalty.[51] The 'good deeds' to which Senarius is exhorted are to serve the interests of the court, rather than those of the public in general, which receive scant attention.[52]

By contrast, the theme of reward for service is absent from the letter to the Senate. Instead, the second document states that the king's advancement of deserving servants benefits the public at large, rather than the ruler's glory or the individual, for 'whatever we give to such persons, we bestow rather for the general good'.[53] Theoderic vouches that Senarius will not abuse the authority of his office for personal profit, a concern not explicit in the letter to Senarius.[54] While the letter to Senarius does not even mention his entry to the Senate, his elevation in rank is clearly expected to be the main concern of the Senate. His career is briefly related in the second letter as evidence of his personal virtue, displaying his constancy, wisdom, administrative talents, and humility.[55] Cassiodorus mentions, with perhaps suspicious brevity, Senarius' equally meritorious family background (again unmentioned in the letter to the subject himself), and concludes with an exhortation to the Senate to welcome their new member, not to resent his advancement.[56]

The letter to Senarius reflects the background of court service and patronage within which officials pursued their careers, while that to the Senate echoes the traditional etiquette governing relations between the ancient body of the Roman aristocracy and the imperial court. Though the Senate was nurtured by Theoderic in the early part of his reign, the

[50] Cass., *Variae* IV, 3.1, lines 16–19.

[51] Efficiency: Cass., *Variae* IV, 3.2, line 23: *disposita laudabili assumptione complebes*; further advancement: 4, lines 4–5: *tanto studiosus gratiam quaere, quantum te locum beneficiis respicis invenisse.*

[52] *Bona*: Cass., *Variae* IV, 3.4, lines 5–7; public: 1, lines 19–20.

[53] Cass., *Variae* IV, 4.1, lines 10–11: *Quicquid enim talibus tribuimus, pro generali potius utilitate largimur.*

[54] Cass., *Variae* IV, 4.2. [55] Cass., *Variae* IV, 4.3–4. [56] Cass., *Variae* IV, 4.5.

adlection of a new member, whose career was based on palatine service rather than on a senatorial *cursus honorum*, still required tact.[57]

These concerns were inherent in all royal appointments to high office of illustrious rank. The letter to Senarius, however, also contains more individualised passages which indicate that Cassiodorus took pains to craft a letter agreeable to its recipient. The more personalised passages are those which laud Senarius' public career. Again it is useful to contrast the letter to the Senate with that to Senarius. The description of Senarius' career sent to the Senate is brief and factual. At some time after 493,[58] Senarius entered court service as a youth, performing such varied tasks (including 'discourse with the king', presumably membership of the royal *consistorium*; *exceptiones*, i.e. the duties of *exceptores*, stenographic officers in imperial *officia*; and the execution of embassies) that it was difficult to state in which office he had actually served.[59]

In the letter to the new *comes*, however, Cassiodorus dwells on Senarius' talents, rather than the progress of his career. He states that Senarius had served Theoderic in a twofold capacity, participating in Theoderic's *consilium* while acting as the king's agent.[60] It was as an official of the king that Senarius undertook embassies and performed the duties of *exceptor*. These tasks, briefly listed in the letter to the Senate, are elaborated by Cassiodorus in the address to Senarius. On Senarius' embassies, Cassiodorus says:

Often you have sustained the duty of an arduous embassy: you have withstood kings, an advocate not unequal to the task, constrained to reveal our justice even to those who, in their base obstinacy, were barely able to understand reason. The enraged authority of kings did not terrify you with its contentions; rather you subjected insolence to truth and, following our instructions, you forced the barbarians to their senses.[61]

57 Theoderic and Senate: below, at n. 95.

58 Cass., *Variae* IV, 4.3, lines 17–18: *In ipso quippe adulescentiae flore palatia nostra* [i.e. after the death of Odoacer in 493; cf. I, 4.6] . . . *intravit*. Ensslin, *Theoderich*, 295 makes Senarius' entry to court service in the early 500s, after the Laurentian schism, but without evidence. Sundwall, *Abhandlungen*, 154 wrongly sees *cana Libertas* in Cass., *Variae* IV, 4.5 as referring to Senarius, who was therefore 'wahrscheinlich schon im fortgeschrittenem Alter' in 509; *cana Libertas* in fact refers to the Senate, whereas Senarius is one of the *primaevi introeuntes*, i.e. a *homo novus* (cf. Traube, 'Index rerum et verborum' to Cass., *Variae*, 583, reading *cana Libertas* as the aged senators themselves). Senarius can have spent at most sixteen years between entering court service *in ipso . . . adulescentiae flore* after 493 and his advancement in 509. On the average age of the financial *comites*: Delmaire, *Largesses sacrées*, 94.

59 Cass., *Variae* IV, 4.3.

60 Cass., *Variae* IV, 3.2, lines 22–3: *diu namque nostris ordinationibus geminum mutuatus obsequium et consilii particeps eras et disposita laudibili assumptione complebas.*

61 Cass., *Variae* IV, 3.2, lines 24–8. The letter to the Senate refers to the 'honour of an embassy' (*in honorem legationis electus*, IV, 4.3), but without the emphasis of IV, 3.2.

Senarius is praised for the eloquence he displayed as *exceptor*; his compositions refreshed the minds of court officials as quickly as their duties tired them. His *humilitas*, praised in general terms in the letter to the Senate, is here more explicitly described as probity in dealing with the court secrets to which he had access.[62]

Allowing for brevity and the abstract style of the *Variae*, the letter to Senarius is unexpectedly precise in describing his experiences and talents. The features which Cassiodorus praises are not topoi but the characteristics of an individual court official. The letter proclaims Senarius' appointment and emphasises the bond of patronage between court and officer; but it also has every appearance of being a communication between two members of the same part of society, shaped to gratify its recipient by dwelling on just those features of Senarius' service in which he would have taken the most pride.

By a happy chance, this impression can be confirmed by a short, autobiographical text of Senarius' own. Senarius' epitaph has been preserved, one of a small number of epitaphs of secular office holders to survive from Ostrogothic Italy.[63] The epitaph is in poetic form, written in the first person. There is no reason to doubt that it is from Senarius' own pen; composing one's epitaph was a Roman tradition of long standing, and Senarius' eloquence is amply attested by Cassiodorus.

Following is the text of the epitaph with a translation:[64]

Cf. Cyprianus' letters of appointment as *comes sacrarum*: his embassy to Constantinople is mentioned in the letter to Cyprianus, but not in the letter to the Senate; *Variae* v, 40.5, 41. The imagery of withstanding enraged and unjust barbarian kings is similar to the description of the embassy of Cassiodorus' grandfather to Attila; *Variae* i, 4.11–12.

62 *Eloquentis ingenium*: Cass., *Variae* iv, 3.3, lines 28–32; *humilitas*: lines 32–4.

63 Other epitaphs: Praetextatus Salventius Verecundus Traianus, nominated prefect of Rome when he died in 533 (*CIL* vi, 32038; *PLRE* iii, 1333); Liberius, former praetorian prefect of Italy and the Ostrogothic province of Gaul, and *patricius* (*CIL* xi, 382; *PLRE* ii, 677–81; James J. O'Donnell, 'Liberius the Patrician', *Traditio* 37 (1981), 70–1); Seda, *cubicularius* of Theoderic (*CIL* xi, 310; *PLRE* ii, 987); Florentius, *pater pistorum* of Theoderic (and his wife Dominica and their son Apolenaris, *cancellarius* of the Byzantine praetorian prefect of Italy Longinus *c.* 568–74/5; *CIL* xi, 317; *PLRE* iii, 100, 410, 489); Iulius Felix Valentinianus, *comes domesticorum* (*CIL* vi, 32003; *PLRE* ii, 1137–8); possibly Decoratus, former *quaestor* (*PLRE* ii, 350–1). For Burgundian and Frankish Gaul, there are two epitaphs of former court officials, both poetic and both of men named Pantagathus, one a *rector* of Provence (*CIL* xii, 1499; *PLRE* iii, 963–4), the other a *quaestor* before becoming bishop of Vienne (MGH AA vi.2, p. 187; *PLRE* iii, 964–5).

64 Text from Pierre Pithou (ed.), *Epigrammata et poematia vetera* (Paris, 1590), 108; minor amendments have been included from Mommsen, 'Index personarum' to Cass., *Variae*, 499. For bibliography and transmission of the text, see appendix iv.

Ille ego sum mundi quondam sine fine viator
Senarius, membris tumulo, non nomine clausus,
principis invicti semper sublimis amore,
cuius in orbe fui vox regum, lingua salutis,
foederis orator, pacis via, terminus irae,
semen amicitiae, belli fuga, litibus hostis.
Novit et hoc Oriens, hoc ultimus axis Iberi,
hoc scit bruma rigens, scit et Africa solibus usta.
Bis denas et quinque simul legatio nostra
signat in orbe vias et numquam strata labore.
Cursus erat volucer, namque anno pervigil uno
bis maris Oceani, bis Pontica litora vidi
Europamque Asiamque sequens duo limina mundi.
His etiam meritis sociavimus agmen honorum:
aulica quippe comes rexi patrimonia clarus
et mea patricio fulserunt cingula cultu.
Me pietas, me sancta fides, me fovit honestas.
Saecla canant titulos: nam moribus astra tenemus.

I am that former, ceaseless wayfarer of the world,
Senarius, my limbs, but not my name, imprisoned by the tomb,
forever distinguished by the love of my unvanquished prince.
In the world I was his voice of kings, the language of security,
the orator of alliance, the path of peace, the boundary of wrath,
the seed of friendship, the banishment of war, the foe of strife.
This the East also knows, this the furthest clime of Spain,
this the numb North knows, this knows sun-scorched Africa.
Twice ten and five times our embassy
marked its paths upon the world and never failed in its task.
My passage was fleet, for, ever-watchful, in one year
twice I saw the shores of Ocean, twice those of Pontus,
traversing both Europe and Asia, the two limits of the world.
To these services we also joined the host of honours:
for, to my renown, as *comes* I guided the patrimonia of the palace
and my belt of office shone with patrician splendour.
I was fostered by piety, by sacred faith, by honesty.
Let the ages sing my titles: for by our virtues we grasp the heavens.

4 *regum*] *legum*: François Juret, letter to Pithou, Paris, Bibliothèque Nationale *Collection Dupuy* vol. 700, folio 128, cited *apud* Pithou, p. 463; wrongly seeing Senarius as a *quaestor*; cf. F. Juret, *Symmachus: Epistolarum* (Paris 1580) 11–12; Burman I 318.

8 *scit et Africa*] Mommsen omits *et*, following Hirschfeld, uncited (possibly private communication), but *et* is required by the metre.

10 *strata*] Pithou; *fracta* Hensius; Burman I 319.

13 *sequans*] Pithou, preferring however *secans* (*Epigrammata* 463); Mommsen's proposed *secantia* is unnecessary, cf. Burman II 723–24.

Like Cassiodorus' eulogy in the letters of appointment, Senarius' epitaph dwells on his services as an envoy. Eleven of the eighteen lines of the epitaph are dedicated to his journeys for the court. The first line of the poem is an epithet characterising Senarius as an envoy, and eight other such attributes follow. Senarius dwells on the geographical distance he had travelled and the range of courts he had visited, the number of embassies he had undertaken, and the constant success of his missions. His appointment as *comes patrimonii*, and his later rank as *patricius*, are attributed to these duties; his service in Theoderic's *consilium* and as *exceptor* pass unmentioned.

The epitaph complements Cassiodorus' letters on Senarius' appointment. The theme of royal patronage is present (line 3), as is a general appeal to the virtues (line 17). The poem itself is an expression of the author's pride in eloquence. But Senarius has greatly elaborated the theme of embassies. The epitaph is an indication of the status of the envoy's duties among servants of the court.

The literary merits of the poem deserve attention. Though brief, it is a skilful composition. The epitaph uses an abundance of metaphor, characteristic of late antique writing, but it is without the hyperbolic excess of Sidonius.[65] The hexameters are metrically correct, noteworthy though not unexpected from a contemporary of Boethius. Despite the solemnity of the imagery, Senarius has leavened the poem with several puns, including witty plays on conventions of epitaph. The word *viator* often appears as a vocative in the opening lines of Latin epitaphs, inviting the traveller passing by the graveyard to contemplate the former life of the tomb's occupant.[66] *Viator* also appears prominently in the first line of Senarius' epitaph, but as an epithet of the speaker himself, the 'former, ceaseless wayfarer of the world'. The phrase 'former, ceaseless' is paradoxical, also characteristic of late antique writing, in the collocation of *sine fine* with *quondam*, another word conventionally used in the opening lines of epitaphs.[67] The whole first line has Virgilian reminiscences: *sine fine* (which seems intended to modify *viator* but is close in proximity to *mundi*) suggests Virgil, *Aeneid* 1, 279: *imperium sine fine dedi*, Jupiter's gift of endless rule to Roman power; the opening words *Ille ego sum . . . quondam* recall those of the preliminary quatrain prefixed to the *Aeneid*: *Ille ego*

[65] Cf. Macpherson, *Rome in Involution*, 151–63. For the piling-up of the epithets of Senarius as an envoy in *Epitaph*, lines 4–6, cf. Ennodius, *Vita Epiphani*, 165, where Epiphanius is called *pacis suasor, concordia auctor, egregie moderator* (also *Christianae lucis iubar*).

[66] Richmond Lattimore, *Themes in Greek and Latin Epitaphs* (Urbana, 1942), 230–4. For examples: Maria Luisa Fele *et al.*, *Concordantiae in carmina latina epigraphica* (Hildersheim, 1988), II, 1257–8, s.v. *viator*.

[67] Roberts, *The Jeweled Style*, 20, 134–5, 140–1.

qui quondam gracili modulatus avena/carmen.[68] Another technical witticism is the choice of metre, hexameter. Senarius' name is an adjectival form of *sex*, six; Latin writers conventionally referred to verses with six feet as *versus senarii.*[69]

The final line invokes not only the Platonist belief in the astral origin of the soul, but more specifically the topos of eternal life in the heavenly sphere as the reward for those who serve the state well. The *locus classicus* in Latin literature for this belief is Cicero's myth of the dream of Scipio at the end of his *De re publica*, one of the favoured texts of fourth- and fifth-century Roman paganism.[70] The vitality of this theme in the late empire is demonstrated by the commentaries on Scipio's dream written by Favonius Eulogius and Macrobius in the late fourth and early fifth centuries.[71] Cicero's myth and its commentaries circulated in Italy in the time of Senarius, and formed an important part of the intellectual background of Boethius' *Consolation of Philosophy*. The imagery of elevation *ad astra* after death had long since been comfortably incorporated into both Neoplatonic philosophy and Christian discourse;

[68] The quatrain, possibly of first-century origin, is first attested in the late fourth and early fifth centuries; R. G. Austin, '*Ille ego qui quondam . . .*', *Classical Quarterly* n.s. 18 (1968), 107–15. Other allusions to the quatrain, contemporary to Senarius, include Dracontius, *De laudibus Dei*, ed. Frideric Vollmer, MGH AA 14.III, 654; and, less closely, the opening line of Boethius, *Philosophiae consolatio*, ed. Ludwig Bieler (CCSL 94; Turnhout, 1967), I *carm.* 1, line 1: *Carmina qui quondam . . .*, conflated with the closing lines of Virgil, *Georgics* IV, lines 564–5; cf. Bieler's note to Boethius, *ibid.*

[69] E.g. Quintilian, *Institutio oratoria*, ed. Jean Cousin, V (Paris, 1978), IX 4.73, 125, 140.

[70] Cicero, *De re publica*, ed. and trans. Esther Bréguet, 2 vols. (Paris, 1980), VI, esp. 13, 16, 23–4, 26. Late paganism: H. Bloch, 'The Pagan Revival in the West at the End of the Fourth Century', in Arnaldo Momigliano (ed.), *The Conflict Between Paganism and Christianity in the Fourth Century* (Oxford, 1963), 207–17; Philip Levine, 'The Continuity and Preservation of the Latin Tradition', in Lynn White Jr. (ed.), *The Transformation of the Roman World: Gibbon's Problem after Two Centuries* (Berkeley, 1966), 210–14.

[71] Macrobius: Macrobius, *Commentarii in somnium Scipionis*, ed. J. Willis (Leipzig, 1963). Date: Alan Cameron, 'The Date and Identity of Macrobius', *Journal of Roman Studies* 56 (1961), 1–11. Macrobius' concern with the *topos* of divine reward for service to the state is revealed particularly by his schema of the virtues. The Neoplatonists viewed virtues as the means to a philosophical release from worldly impurities and thence to a divine state. Macrobius summarises this view but discreetly subverts it to a more Ciceronian concept, seeing beatitude as the due reward for the 'civic virtues', primarily service to the state; Macrobius, *Comm.* I, 8, esp. 2–4, 12; P. M. Schedler, *Die Philosophie des Macrobius und ihr Einfluss auf die Wissenschaft des christlichen Mittelalters* (Münster, 1916), 89–90; Clemens Zintzen, 'Römisches und Neuplatonisches bei Macrobius', in P. Steinmetz (ed.), *Politeia und Res Publica: Beiträge zum Verständnis von Politik, Recht und Staat in der Antike* (Wiesbaden, 1969), 366–70; cf. Jacques Flamant, *Macrobe et le néo-platonisme latin à la fin du IVe siècle* (Leiden, 1977), 609–14.

Eulogius: Favonius Eulogius, *Disputatio de somnio Scipionis*, ed. and trans. Roger-E. van Weddington (Collectio Latomus 27; Brussels, 1957), especially 1, 2, p. 13, lines 14–16: *bene meritis de re publica patriaeque custodibus lactei circuli lucida ac candens habitatio deberetur*. Date: *PLRE* I, 'Favonius Eulogius 3', 294.

so too had the accompanying desire for worldly fame throughout the *secula*.[72]

The epitaph is a minor example of the *belles-lettres* which characterise holders of public office, and more generally the aristocracy, of the later empire. This literary context is an indication of Senarius' social position.

The rarity of Senarius' name has led to the supposition that it is a Latin rendering of a Gothic name, and that Senarius himself was therefore a Goth.[73] One other *comes patrimonii* under the Ostrogoths appears to have been Gothic.[74] But this reconstruction is false. Senarius' name, though rare, is not quite unique.[75] It is perhaps related to the once-common plebeian *nomina* Sextius and Sextilius, or the *praenomen* Sextus. The form and derivation of the name are typical of the single-name *signa* or *supernomina* which came to supersede both the ancient Roman system of *tria nomina*, and traditional individual names themselves, from the early fourth century onwards.[76] Senarius himself alludes to the Latin

[72] Circulation: *PLRE* II, 'Symmachus 9', 1046 (Symmachus and Macrobius Plotinus Eudoxius participate in improving the text of the elder Macrobius' Commentary on the *Somnium Scipionis*). Boethius, *Philosophiae consolatio*, esp. II, Pr. 7; Pierre Courcelle, *La* Consolation de Philosophie *dans la tradition littéraire* (Paris, 1967), 116–24. Neoplatonism: Franz Cumont, *Lux perpetua* (Paris, 1949; repr. New York, 1985), 142–88, 343–86. Christian imagery of elevation *ad astra*: e.g. Lattimore, *Themes*, 312; J. de Rossi, *Inscriptiones Christianae urbis Romae septimo saeculo antiquiores* II pars i (Rome, 1888), 20 no. 6 (in St Peter's, possibly fourth century); 113–14 no. 79 (probably fifth century); Prudentius, *Liber Cathemerinon*, in *Carmina*, ed. Ioannes Bergman (CSEL 61; Vienne, 1926), X, 89–92. Worldly fame: Iiro Kajanto, *Classical and Christian: Studies in the Latin Epitaphs of Medieval and Renaissance Rome* (Annales Academiae Scientiarum Fennicae ser. B no. 203 (Helsinki, 1980), 83–4.

[73] For 'Senarius' < Gothic *Sini-harjis ('ancient-army'): F. Wrede, *Über die Sprache der Ostgoten in Italien* (Strasburg, 1891), 117; Eduard Schroeder, *apud* Mommsen, 'Index personarum' to Cass., *Variae*, 499 (though Mommsen, 'Ostgothische Studien', 402 n. 2 denies that Senarius was a Goth); M. Schönfeld, *Wörterbuch der altergermanischen Personen- und Völkernamen* (Heidelberg, 1911), 202; Gerhard Köbler, *Gotisches Wörterbuch* (Leiden, 1989), 699; *PLRE* II, 'Senarius', 988; Henry Chadwick, *Boethius: The Consolations of Music, Logic, Theology, and Philosophy* (Oxford, 1981), 27; Hermann Reichert, *Lexicon der altgermanischen Namen* I: *Namen* (Vienna, 1987), 596 (Senarius a Goth, but with a Roman name); Moorhead, *Theoderic*, 72–3 n. 32 (Senarius a Roman, but with a Germanic name); Amory, *People and Identity in Ostrogothic Italy*, 273 n. 163 ('probably'), 413. ('Siniharjis' is also seen by Ernst Gamillscheg, *Romania Germanica: Sprach- und Siedlungsgeschichte der Germanen auf dem Bolden des alten Römerreichs*, 1st edn, I (Berlin, 1934), 323, as the Gothic root of several medieval French names, e.g. Signarius (more likely = 'signatory', cf. Du Cange, *Gloss.* VII, s.v. 'signarius', 480), Senarens.)

[74] *PLRE* II, 'Wilia 2', 1167; cf. below, n. 105.

[75] There are no Senarii in Aegidius Forcellini, *Lexicon totius latinitatis* VI: *Onomasticon*, ed. Joseph Perin (Padua, 1940); in *CIL*; in *PIR*; in A. Silvagni *et al.*, *Inscriptiones Christianae urbis Romae septimo saeculo antiquiores* (Rome, 1922–92); or elsewhere in *PLRE*. The feminine version of the name, however, appears in an inscription on a pin found in Sardinia, datable only to Christian times; *CIL* X, 2 8072.18. A Senario appears on an inscription in Saragossa; *CIL* II, Suppl. 5856.

[76] For Sextius, Sextilius, Sextus: Forcellini, *Onomasticon* VI, 621–2; *RE* II A.2, 2033–66; *PIR*[1] 3, 235–41; two Sextilii and one Sextius appear in *PLRE* I, but none in *PLRE* II or III. For names with 'ordinal' etymologies in the early Christian period: Iiro Kajanto, *Onomastic Studies in the Early Christian Inscriptions of Rome and Carthage* (Acta Instituti Romani Finlandiae 2.1; Helsinki,

etymology of his name in the choice of metre for his epitaph. Moreover, Senarius' title of *patricius*, which he attests in his epitaph, precludes Gothic ethnicity. Theoderic was scrupulous in ensuring that the patriciate, like the consulate and the highest civilian offices, was awarded only to Romans.[77]

Senarius can be placed in his proper context with the aid of the letters written by Ennodius as deacon of Milan in the 500s. Senarius appears in Ennodius' letters as part of the circle of high-born Italian aristocrats who dominated the most important offices of the court in Ravenna in the early part of Theoderic's reign, as their ancestors had done in the previous century. Some ten letters of Ennodius to Senarius are extant.[78] All appear to have been written while Senarius was at court in Ravenna.[79] Some are purely letters of friendship, maintaining the formal ties of *amicitia*, while others contain specific requests – for news, or for aid to a client.[80] Ennodius claimed Senarius as a relative, and letters of friendship outweigh those explicitly conveying requests, but it is clear that Senarius was a part

1963), 78–83, 125–37, 'Index of Personal Names' (including *Sextilius* and other names based on *primus* to *septem*).

Late antique names: *signa* and other *supernomina* were often formed with *-ius* endings (e.g. Senarius), like earlier family *nomina*; Ernst Fraenkel, 'Namenwesen', *RE* XVI.2, 1663; Iiro Kajanto, 'Les noms', in H. Zilliacus (ed.), *Sylloge inscriptionum Christianarum veterum Musei Vaticani* (Acta Instituti Romani Finlandiae I.1, I.2; Helsinki, 1963), 40–72, esp. 47, 65–6; Kajanto, *Onomastic Studies*, 31–49; Benet Salway, 'What's in a Name? A Survey of Roman Onamastic Practice from c. 700 BC to 700 AD', *JRS* 84 (1994), 136–7.

Senarius may have possessed more names than the one by which he is addressed in the extant sources. It was conventional for individuals with traditional names, whether in the *tria nomina* system or not, to be addressed by only one name; this is attested specifically for both imperial correspondence and personal letters, two categories by which Senarius' name is attested; Alan Cameron, 'Polynomy in the Late Roman Aristocracy: the Case of Petronius Probus', *Journal of Roman Studies* 75 (1985), 171–7; Amory, *People and Identity in Ostrogothic Italy*, 264. Verse epitaphs were unlikely to preserve more than the one, conventional name; cf. the epitaph of the praetorian prefect of Gaul and *patricius* Petrus Marcellinus Felix Liberius, *CIL* XI, 382 (called only 'Liberius').

77 Mommsen, 'Ostgothische Studien', 402 n. 2. The only Gothic *patricius* in Theoderic's Italy was the king himself, who had been granted the title by the emperor Zeno in the 470s, when the Ostrogoths were still in the Balkans; *ibid.*, 422 n. 2. Under Athalaric the general Tulvin was made *patricius praesentalis*, as was the praetorian prefect of Gaul Liberius; Cass., *Variae* VIII, 9–11; XI, 1.

78 Ennodius, *Epp.* I, 23; III, 11, 34; IV, 27, 33; V, 15; VI, 8, 27; VII, 5; VIII, 7; cf. V, 16 (Senarius mentioned). Dates: Sundwall, *Abhandlungen*, 1–83.

79 Sundwall, *Abhandlungen*, 11–12, 21, 25, 31–2, 32–3, 37–8, 44–5, 47, 51, 58. References to court service: *Epp.* III, 11, esp. lines 7–9; V, 15; VI, 27, lines 17–19; VII, 5; VIII, 7; cf. the titles of address employed by Ennodius to Senarius, e.g. *sublimitas tua*, *Epp.* I, 23, line 2; III, 11, line 34.

80 *Amicitia*: *Epp.* I, 23; III, 11, 34; IV, 33; VI, 8; VIII, 7 (conventional rebukes for not writing); V, 15–16 (invitation to Senarius to visit Ennodius); VII, 5: *religio amicitiae*. News: IV, 27; VII, 5. Aid: IV, 33 (concerning a disputed episcopal succession for the see of Aquileia; Sundwall, *Abhandlungen*, 32–4); VI, 27 (arranging a hearing of a dispute before Theoderic; Sundwall, *Abhandlungen*, 45–7, 49). On *amicitia* in late antique epistolography: Matthews, *Western Aristocracies*, 5–9; *ibid.*, 'The Letters of Symmachus', 58–68; more generally, Stanley K. Stowers, *Letter Writing in Greco-Roman Antiquity* (Philadelphia, 1986), 28–31, 58–70; Caroline White, *Christian Friendship in the Fourth Century* (Cambridge, 1992), 13–44; Conybeare, *Paulinus Noster*.

of the network of patronage, emanating from Ravenna, which features prominently in Ennodius' correspondence.[81]

Senarius' contacts, as revealed by the letters of Ennodius, range from up-and-coming court officers to members of the most important families of Rome.[82] Among the latter was Fl. Anicius Probus Faustus Niger, Ennodius' patron. Twice, Ennodius wrote to Senarius enquiring after Faustus' well-being.[83] Faustus was a member of a senatorial family with an impressive list of official honours. His father, Gennadius Avienus, consul in 450, was described by Sidonius Apollinaris as one of the two most influential men in Rome in the 460s.[84] Faustus himself was nominated consul by Odoacer in 490. Theoderic also honoured Faustus, appointing or retaining him as *magister officiorum* when he took power in 493 and later making him *quaestor c.* 505/6, about the time of Ennodius' letters to Senarius. In the late 500s, Faustus was made *patricius* and appointed praetorian prefect of Italy. His sons shared his prestige. Rufius Magnus Faustus Avienus held the consulate as a youth in 502, and his brother Fl. Ennodius Messala was also consul, in 506.[85]

A letter of Ennodius written in early 508 is addressed jointly to five correspondents in Ravenna: Liberius, Eugenes, Agapitus, Senarius, and Albinus.[86] It is the only one of Ennodius' letters written to a group, and suggests that the five individuals are closely associated. All were current or former holders of palatine offices. Liberius, the first named, was of an unknown family but had held important offices under Odoacer. He was courted by Theoderic when he and Odoacer shared rule of Italy.[87] Liberius served as Theoderic's praetorian prefect of Italy throughout most of the 490s and was made *patricius* in 500. He held no known offices in the 500s, but, upon the Ostrogothic acquisition of Provence from the Franks in 508/9, was appointed praetorian prefect of Gaul. He administered Provence throughout the remainder of Theoderic's reign and that

[81] Relations: Ennodius, *Ep.* I, 33, lines 9–10: *inter nos gemina vincula . . . caritatis et sanguinis*. Patronage network: Moorhead, *Theoderic*, 156–8.

[82] Junior officers: Pamphronius, who entered court service *c.* 506, with the aid of Ennodius: Ennodius, *Epp.* V, 16, cf. II, 16; IV, 14, 16; VII, 2; Sundwall, *Abhandlungen*, 16, 29; *PLRE* II, 285; Moorhead, *Theoderic*, 156.

[83] Ennodius, *Epp.* IV, 27, cf. 28; VII, 5, dated 506 and mid-508 by Sundwall, *Abhandlung*, 31–2, 51, cf. table 76, 79. Ennodius and Faustus: above, chapter 4 at n. 142.

[84] Faustus: *PLRE* II, 'Fl. Anicius Probus Faustus Niger 9', 454–6. Avienus: *PLRE* II, 'Gennadius Avienus 4', 193–4; Sidonius, *Ep.* I, 9.

[85] *PLRE* II, 'Rufius Magnus Faustus Avienus iunior 2', 192–3; 'Fl. Ennodius Messala 2', 759–60.

[86] Ennodius, *Ep.* VI, 12. Though there are are no other joint letters in his extant works, Ennodius several times wrote groups of letters simultaneously to members of this group at Ravenna, e.g. IV, 26–8 to Eugenes, Senarius, and Agapitus; VI, 7–9 to Faustus, his son Avienus, and Senarius; Sundwall, *Abhandlungen*, 31, 44.

[87] *PLRE* II, 'Petrus Marcellinus Felix Liberius 3', 677–81; O'Donnell, 'Liberius'.

of Athalaric. The tenure of Liberius' two prefectures was exceptionally long.

Albinus, another of the recipients of Ennodius' letter, was from a highly distinguished family, the Decii, which vied with the Anicii for eminence in fifth- and sixth-century Italy.[88] Albinus' grandfather had been consul under the emperor Majorian and was the second of the two men, along with Faustus' father, described by Sidonius as the most influential in Rome a generation earlier.[89] Albinus' father and two paternal uncles were consuls, *patricii*, and prefects of Italy or of Rome under Odoacer.[90] These honours were reproduced in the next generation. Albinus was Theoderic's first nominee as consul (in 493), and later *patricius* and praetorian prefect of Italy, probably succeeding his brother Theodorus. Theodorus was to be both consul and *patricius* before the end of the 500s, as were two other brothers of Albinus, Avienus and Inportunus.[91]

The ancestry of Eugenes and Agapitus, the remaining two addressees of Ennodius' letter, is unknown. They also held very high public office. Eugenes was *quaestor* in 506 and *magister officiorum* in 507; he was probably brother to the praetorian prefect of 503.[92] Agapitus held palatine offices in the 500s, became prefect of Rome late in the decade, and was made *patricius* by 511; he was consul in 517.[93] Like Senarius and several other recipients of Ennodius' letter, Agapitus was associated with Faustus Niger.[94]

Senarius' associates were powerful figures, both for their aristocratic status and for their control of the highest court offices. Faustus and Albinus represent two of the great Roman families which dominated public office and honours under the last western emperors. Under Odoacer, such families continued to receive positions of prestige. Theoderic followed this policy for the first two decades of his reign. During the 510s, for reasons which are not clear, Roman aristocrats are less visible in public

[88] *PLRE* II '(?Faustus) Albinus iunior 9', 51–2. Delmaire, *Les Responsables*, 294, wrongly identifies this Albinus as a lesser figure of the same name, identified in *PLRE* II as 'Albinus 6', 50. All the addressees of Ennodius, *Ep.* VI, 12 had received other communications from Ennodius (for Albinus 9: *Ep.* II, 21, mentioned in *Ep.* II, 22.1; *Carm.* II, 99), but not Albinus 6. In 507/11, Albinus 6 had only just reached the legal age of majority (Cass., *Variae* IV, 35.2); he is therefore an unlikely companion for four experienced officers of state. On the Decii: Moorhead, 'The Decii under Theoderic', 107–15; Moorhead, *Theoderic*, 147–51.

[89] *PLRE* II, 'Fl. Caecina Decius Basilius 11', 217–18.

[90] Father: *PLRE* II, 'Fl. Caecina Decius Maximus Basilius iunior 12', 217; uncles: 'Decius Marius Venantius Basilius 13', 218; 'Caecina Mavortius Basilius Decius 2', 349.

[91] *PLRE* II, 'Fl. Theodorus 62', 1097–8; 'Fl. Avienus iunior 3', 193; 'Fl Inportunus', 592.

[92] *PLRE* II, 'Eugenes', 414–16; 'Olybrius 5', 795–6.

[93] *PLRE* II 'Fl. Agapitus 3', 30–2.

[94] Agapitus and Faustus: Ennodius, *Ep.* IV, 28, cf. IV, 27 and Sundwall, *Abhandlungen*, 31–2. Liberius and Albinus were related to Faustus by marriage: Ennodius, *Epp.* II, 22; IX, 7.

office and honours; the leading families and the court of Ravenna might have become alienated.[95] Senarius' rise coincided with the period of close alliance between Ravenna and Rome. At some time after his tenure as *comes patrimonii* he was made *patricius*, but the epitaph is evidence that he held no further high office. The tone of the epitaph, however, makes it unlikely that Senarius harboured feelings of resentment towards the Ostrogothic regime. Perhaps the termination of his career represents no more than a lapse into *otium*; the office of *comes patrimonii* was one which the incumbent could exploit for self-enrichment, and was perhaps given as a reward before retirement from public life.[96]

It is unlikely that Senarius came from such a great family as that of Faustus or Albinus. His career of palatine service, unbroken by prolonged periods of *otium*, is uncharacteristic of members of the higher aristocracy.[97] His status in the late 500s stemmed from court service, rather than family prestige. He seems, however, to have been of senatorial class.[98]

Senarius' career was firmly based in Ravenna, not in the senatorial milieu of Rome.[99] Cassiodorus mentions Senarius' proximity to Theoderic: 'employed in the judgement of his ruler', he was 'worthy of discourse with the king', and privy to the secrets of the royal palace.[100] It is unclear in what capacity Senarius had such access to the king. His position appears to have been ambiguous. Cassiodorus never names Senarius' actual post prior to his appointment as *comes*, but refers to his 'double service', engaging in royal council while executing duties including the implementation of royal commands; dictation, stenography, and perhaps legal duties; and the completion of embassies. In stating that these duties fell beyond the scope of any one office, Cassiodorus acknowledges that Senarius' position had been outside traditional administrative arrangements, and his career unlike the conventional *cursus honorum*.[101] Similarities can been

[95] Honours of Roman senatorial class under Odoacer and Theoderic: Alan Cameron and Diane Schauer, 'The Last Consul: Basilius and His Diptych', *Journal of Roman Studies* 72 (1982), 138–9. Change in Theoderic's attitude in 510s: Sundwall, *Abhandlung*, 215–17; Bury I, 466; Moorhead, *Theoderic*, 147–53; Thomas S. Brown, 'Everyday Life in Ravenna under Theoderic: An Example of his "Tolerance" and "Prosperity"?', in *Teoderico il Grande e i Goti d'Italia*, 98. But cf. Ensslin, *Theoderich*, 295–6.

[96] Cass., *Variae* IV, 4.2; VI, 9.2.

[97] Jones, *LRE* I, 382–3, 558.

[98] Cass., *Variae* IV, 4.5: *originis quoque simili claritate resplendet.*

[99] On senatorial and palatine careers: Matthews, *Western Aristocracies*, 12–17; Matthews, 'Anicius Manlius Severinus Boethius', 26–8.

[100] Cass., *Variae* IV, 4.3: *ad imperantis conversus arbitrium . . . ad colloquia dignus*, cf. IV, 3.2: *consilii particeps. Arcana*: IV, 3.3, 4.4.

[101] Duties outside any one post: Cass., *Variae* IV, 3.2, 4.3. The phrase *sub exceptionis officio* (IV, 3.3; IV, 4.3) suggests that Senarius fulfilled the tasks of the *exceptores*, general clerks and shorthand writers in all palatine, praefectorial, and military *officia*; *Not. dig.*, 'Conspectus officiorum civilium'

seen between Senarius' career and those of other palatine officers under Theoderic.[102]

The illustrious position to which Senarius was advanced was of particular importance to Theoderic's administration. A recent addition to the two financial *comitivae* of the *largitiones* and *res privatae* established about the time of Constantine, the *comitiva patrimonii* administered all sources of income acquired by the Italian government since Odoacer's usurpation of 476. Primarily these sources consisted of revenues from lands in the conquered provinces of Sicily, Dalmatia, Pannonia, and Provence.[103] The revenue from the *patrimonium* in the West was distinct from that of the other financial *comitivae*, for it was treated as the private domain (*domus*)

and 'militium', 335–6; Jones, *LRE* I, 412, 427, 497; II, 565, 584, 587–8; idem, 'The Roman Civil Service (Clerical and Sub-Clerical Grades)', *Journal of Roman Studies* 39 (1949), 53–4 = his *Studies in Roman Government and Law* (Oxford, 1960), 213–14; H. C. Teitler, Notarii *and* Exceptores: *An Inquiry into the Role and Significance of Shorthand Writers in the Imperial and Ecclesiastical Bureaucracy of the Roman Empire (From the Early Principate to c. 450 AD)* (Amsterdam, 1985), 73–85. Mommsen, 'Ostgothische Studien', 420 n. 6, suggests that Cassiodorus refers to the post of *referendarius*, rather than the stenographic position, as neither Cassiodorus' praise of Senarius' oratorical skills in office, nor Senarius' advancement to an illustrious office, was characteristic of the lowly *exceptor*. Cassiodorus, however, does not usually employ euphemisms instead of titles of offices, and he uses the title *referendarius* elsewhere; Cass., *Variae* VI, 17 *Formula referendariorum* VIII, 21.4, 25 title. (There are no other *exceptores* named in the *Variae*; cf. XI, 25: a letter of appointment for a *primicerius* of the *exceptores* in the praetorian prefect's office.) It is possible that the status of the *exceptor*, unimpressive in the fourth and fifth centuries, had been inflated in the West by the early sixth century. The similar position of *tribunus et notarius* had been elevated from a stenographic post to an office with the rank of *clarissimus* from the fourth to the mid-fifth century; Jones, 'Roman Civil Service', 214; Teitler, Notarii *and* Exceptores 2, 68–72. Cf. the use of *exceptio* in Cass., *Variae* XI, 38.4 in the sense of 'literary composition'; and note that under the Ostrogoths the *scriniarius curae militaris*, charged with the financing of the army, was placed among the *exceptores* of the office of the praetorian prefect, a higher ranking than the post enjoyed in the East; Ernst Stein, *Untersuchungen über das* Officium *der Prätorianer Präfectur seit Diokletian* (Vienne, 1922; repr. Amsterdam, 1962), 70–1. The *formula* for appointment of *notarii* to the king's *consilium* begins: 'There is no doubt but that the king's confidences glorify his servants' (*Non est dubium ornare subiectos principis secretum*); Cass., *Variae* VI, 16.1. The theme of the probity required for such access to palatine secrets is reminiscent of Cassiodorus' praise of Senarius, *Variae* IV, 3.3, 4.4.

102 E.g. entry to court service as a youth: *Variae* VIII, 10.3–4 (the Amal Tulvin); proximity to the king, service as an envoy, and advancement to a financial *comitiva*: V, 40.2–4, 41.2–4 (Cyprianus); Wolfram, *History of the Goths*, 292.

103 On the *comitiva patrimonii*: *Codex Just.* I, 34 (Anastasius); Cass., *Variae* VI, 9; John Lydus, *De magistratibus* II, 27; Procopius, *Wars* V, 4.1; Theodore Mommsen, 'Ostgothische Studien', 401–3; Seeck, 'Comes', 676–7; Ernst Stein, 'Untersuchungen zur spätrömischen Verwaltungsgeschichte', *Rheinisches Museum für Philologie* n.s. 74 (1925), 384–7; Ensslin, *Theoderich*, 170–2; Jones, *LRE* I, 255, 292, 424–7; Wolfram, *History of the Goths*, 293; Delmaire, *Largesses sacrées*, 691–8; Delmaire, *Les Responsables*, 291–9; Barnwell, *Emperor, Prefects, and Kings*, 148–50. On the western *comitivae* under Theoderic: William G. Sinnigen, '*Comites consistoriani* in Ostrogothic Italy', *Classica et Mediaevalia* 24 (1963), 158–65; Sinnigen, 'Administrative Shifts of Competence under Theoderic', *Traditio* 21 (1965), 456–67. The office of *comitiva patrimonii* continued in the sixth century both in Byzantine Italy and in Visigothic Spain: Jean Durliat, *Les Finances publiques de Dioclétien aux Carolingiens (284–889)* (Beiheft zu Francia 21; Sigmaringen, 1990), 111 n. 111, 114, 160 n. 74.

of the king. Income from these lands was used directly for the expenses of the royal palace, and apparently for the payment of the Gothic offices, such as the *comes Gothorum*, created by Theoderic.[104] The claim that the office of *comes patrimonii* regularly formed an exception to Theoderic's practice of excluding Goths from high civil offices may be doubted, but it clearly was important for the operation of the royal palace.[105] It was natural that this post would be filled by a trusted palatine officer.

Theoderic's envoy was from a lesser family of the Roman senatorial class. Equipped with the traditional training in rhetoric which was the basis for public office, he entered palatine service at a young age at some time after 493, gaining a place at court sufficiently influential for his aid to be sought by Ennodius. He was in contact with some of the most important men in Italy. Amongst other duties, he repeatedly undertook embassies for the king, and came to be seen as a specialist in this task. For his services he was honoured in 509 with an important and lucrative post, *illustris* rank, entry to the Senate, and, later, with the patriciate. The ethos of such Roman aristocrats, upon whom the civil administration of the empire and the barbarian kingdoms depended, is shown by the laudatory tone of Cassiodorus' letters and Senarius' epitaph.

In the course of his career, Senarius undertook twenty-five embassies. This is an indication of the ubiquity of political communication in the western kingdoms; narrative sources do not record so many embassies dispatched by Theoderic for the whole of his reign, let alone only for the period to 509. Senarius' journeys clearly included missions of the highest political importance. He states that he communicated between rulers (he was the 'voice of kings'), and he stresses his role both in securing alliances and in restraining aggression. What were the circumstances of these journeys?

Some may have been within Italy. The communications of the court of Ravenna with both the Senate and the Church of Rome are termed *legationes* in the sources, indistinguishable from overseas embassies; missions

[104] Stein, 'Untersuchungen', 384; Ensslin, *Theoderich*, 172.

[105] Exception: Mommsen, 'Ostgothische Studien', 402; Stein II, 51; Ensslin, *Theoderich*, 171; Wolfram, *History of the Goths*, 293. The evidence is solely onomastic, resting on the unfamiliarity of the names of three of the four known *comites patrimonii*, Senarius, Wilia, and Bergantinus (even the fourth, Julianus, has been claimed as a Goth, on the basis of an erroneous manuscript reading; Thomas S. Burns, *A History of the Ostrogoths* (Bloomington, 1984), 171). Neither Senarius nor Bergantinus, however, was Gothic (for Bergantinus: Sundwall, *Abhandlungen*, 100–1; Ensslin, *Theoderich*, 171). Wilia, the sole probable Goth, held the office during the turbulent final years of Theoderic's rule, when the Ostrogoths faced hostility from the Vandals; Cass., *Variae* V, 18–19. At this time, relations between the government and sections of the Roman population of Italy had broken down (*Anon. Val.* XIV, 85), which may explain the appointment of a Goth to this office crucial for the operation of Theoderic's court.

to Rome may account for a number of Senarius' trips. The Laurentian schism, which divided the aristocracy and clergy of Italy over a disputed papal election in 498, necessitated many communications between Rome and Ravenna in the following years. It was perhaps in this context that Senarius made the acquaintance of John, a deacon of Rome, who played an active role in the affair.[106]

Senarius and Cassiodorus, however, emphasise travel to other courts, Senarius mentioning both Constantinople and the West, Cassiodorus stressing the courts of barbarian kings. Ennodius, too, gives contemporary evidence of journeys to *gentes*.[107] Even a score of long-distance voyages in the course of a career spanning perhaps a decade and a half is not incredible for pre-modern travelling conditions. Italy was connected with the eastern Mediterranean and North Africa by ancient sea-routes, and the inland waterways of Gaul, where many of Senarius' western missions may have taken him, were equally well exploited.[108] Senarius states that he travelled from Constantinople to the Atlantic coast twice in one year, showing that even 'shuttle diplomacy' of a sort was possible.[109]

The epitaph employs the four cardinal points to delineate the extent of Senarius' journeys.[110] *Oriens*, and later *Pontica litora*, evidently represent Constantinople, and 'sun-scorched Africa' stands for Vandal Carthage. The 'numb North' refers at least to Gaul, indicating the Frankish and Burgundian kingdoms, and perhaps beyond. The 'furthest clime of Spain' and 'the shores of Ocean' are problematic. If *ultimus axis* is meant to modify *Iberi* ('furthest', i.e. westernmost Spain), and is not merely a transferred epithet of Spain itself ('Spain, the furthest clime'), taken literally it can only refer to the kingdom of the Sueves in Gallaecia,

[106] Below, at nn. 144–5. Ennodius, in winter 507/8, asked Senarius to pray *per omnes sanctorum basilicas* for the illness he was experiencing in his eyes; *Ep.* VI, 8, cf. VI, 4. Vogel interprets this as a reference to the basilicas of Rome, implying that Senarius was in or travelling to the city at the time; 'Index nominum' to Ennodius, *Opera*, 359; followed by Delmaire, *Les Responsables*, 294. But cf. Sundwall, *Abhandlungen*, 44–5: Ennodius, *Ep.* VI, 8 was sent simultaneously with *Epp.* 6 and 9 to recipients in Ravenna, and was shortly followed by *Ep.* VI, 12, the letter to Senarius and four other addressees in Ravenna, discussed above at n. 86. There is no reason that Ennodius could not be referring to the basilicas of Ravenna.

[107] Ennodius, *Ep.* V, 15–16; below, at n. 130.

[108] Use of the inland waterways of Gaul for long-distance travel pre-dated Roman conquest; Strabo, *Geography*, trans. H. L. Jones (LCL; London, 1949), IV, 1.14, 3, 5.2; P.-M. Duval, 'Proues de navires de Paris', *Gallia* 5 (1947), 123–42. On riverine trade and travel in the Roman period: Louis Bonnard, *La Navigation intérieure de la Gaule à l'époque gallo-romaine* (Paris, 1913); A. R. Lewis, 'The Rhône Valley Route and Traffic between the Mediterranean and Northern Europe, AD 300–1200', *Res publica litterarum* 5 (1982), 139–50. Evidence of fifth- and sixth-century navigation: Constantius, *Vita Germani*, 23 (on the Saône); *Vita Genovefae*, 35–40, 51; Gregory of Tours, *Hist.* VI, 25; VII, 46; below, n. 122 (the Visigothic princess Galswintha, and Venantius Fortunatus). See McCormick, *Origins of the European Economy*, 77–82.

[109] Epitaph, lines 11–13. [110] *Ibid.*, lines 7–8.

with its capital at Braga. This is not impossible, although relations between Theoderic and the Sueves are not attested elsewhere. It is perhaps more likely, however, that by both *Iberus* and *maris Oceani . . . litora* Senarius means the kingdom of the Visigoths, which since 418 had embraced the Atlantic coastline of south-western Gaul and, from some time after the 470s, controlled the greater part of the Iberian peninsula.[111]

More precise information on Senarius' missions would be gained if he could be identified as one of the *legati* who were entrusted with the diplomatic letters preserved in the earlier books of Cassiodorus' *Variae*. But, as discussed above, it is just these diplomatic correspondences from which the names of court servants have been most consistently deleted. Nevertheless, some indication of Senarius' missions can be gained from the *Variae*. It may reasonably be assumed that Senarius' appointment as *comes patrimonii* in September 509 rewarded more than just his years of service to the court. The timing may have been determined by recent events in which Senarius played an important role, earning appointment to the *illustrissimate*. Certainly the years immediately preceding Senarius' advancement, from 504 to 509, gave ample opportunity for an envoy of Theoderic to engage in important negotiations.

The early years of Theoderic's rule in Italy were spent consolidating the Goths' military security by gaining recognition of Theoderic as ruler of Italy from the emperor Anastasius, and by establishing a network of marriage-alliances throughout the West, tying Theoderic to the royal houses of the Franks, the Vandals, the Goths of Toulouse, and the Burgundians.[112] These arrangements lasted until the mid-500s. In 504/5, Ravenna and Constantinople contested the control of Pannonia. The Ostrogoths succeeded in bringing the province under Italian control, but at the cost of good relations with the government of Anastasius. Soon afterwards, in 506/7, the stability of the West was threatened by tensions in Gaul between the Franks under their aggressive king Clovis and the Visigoths under Alaric II. Theoderic's interests had already been compromised recently by Clovis' eastern expansion, which had forced Alamannic refugees into Ostrogothic territory. Theoderic strove to prevent warfare between the Franks and the Visigoths through a combination of arbitration and deterrence, but to no avail. In 507, the forces of Alaric and

[111] Gothic occupation of Spain: Thompson, *Romans and Barbarians*, 190–4. For *maris Oceani . . . litora*, cf. Hydatius' description of the settlement of the Goths in Aquitania in 418: *Gothi . . . sedes in Aquitania a Tolosa usque ad Oceanum acceperunt*, Hyd., c. 69; modified by the author of the *Chr. Gall. 511*: *a Tolosa in Burdegalam* [Bordeaux] *ad Oceanum versus*, c. 565.

[112] Recognition: *Anon. Val.* XII, 57, 64. Marriage alliances: Ennodius, *Vita Epiphani*, 163; *Anon. Val.* XII, 63, 68, 70, 72; Jordanes, *Get.* LVII, 295–6; LVIII, 297; Procopius, *Wars* V, 12.22. Cf. Bury I, 461–2; Ensslin, *Theoderich*, 84–90; Ensslin, 'Romverbundenheit', 509–36; Wolfram, *History of the Goths*, 284–90, 306–15; Moorhead, *Theoderic*, 35–9, 51–4.

Clovis fought at Vouillé near Poitiers. Alaric was killed, and Clovis was able to penetrate Visigothic territory. While the Visigoths were able to retain Novempopulana in south-western Gaul, the Franks, allied with the Burgundians, took control of parts of Aquitania and Provence, gaining access to the Mediterranean. Despite diplomatic and military hindrance from Byzantium, Theoderic subsequently forced the Franks out of Provence in a series of engagements in 508/9. Provence was then ruled from Ravenna as the province of Gallia; Ostrogothic control was represented as the return of the region to the empire. This settlement was not challenged, and Italy was involved in no further known military conflicts with the Franks, the Burgundians, or Constantinople for the rest of Theoderic's lifetime.[113]

All the diplomatic letters included in the first four books of Cassiodorus' *Variae* concern these events. Those letters to Clovis and the Burgundian king Gundobad which stand at the end of the first two books respectively were written before the outbreak of hostilities in the West, as Theoderic still enjoys at least nominally good relations with his fellow kings.[114] The two letters to the kings of the Thuringians and the Heruli at the beginning of Book IV are usually dated after Vouillé, and seen as an attempt by Theoderic to forge new ties with powers surrounding the now hostile Franks and Burgundians.[115]

Theoderic's diplomacy is best displayed in the set of letters at the beginning of Book III, addressed to Alaric II, Gundobad, the kings of the Heruli, Warni, and Thuringians, and Clovis.[116] Written when the

[113] For these events and their consequences to 511: *Chron. Gall. 511*, cc. 688–91; Cassiodorus, *Chron.*, cc. 1348–9 (a. 508); Procopius, *Wars* V, 12–13; Jordanes, *Get.*, 296–305; *Chron. Caesar.*, s. aa. 507, 508, 510, 513; Marius of Avanche, *Chron.*, s.a. 509; Gregory of Tours, *Hist.* II, 35–8; III, 1, 2, 5, 21, 31; Isidore, *Hist. Goth.*, s. 36; Fredegar, *Chron.* II, 58; III, 24. Modern accounts: Bury I, 459–64; Stein II, 143–55; Ensslin, 'Romverbundenheit', 518–24; Eugene Ewig, 'Die fränkischen Teilungen und Teilreiche (511–613)', in his *Spätantikes und fränkisches Gallien: Gesammelte Schriften (1952–1973)*, ed. H. Atsma (Munich, 1976), I, 114–28; Erich Zöllner, *Geschichte der Franken bis zur Mitte des sechsten Jahrhunderts* (Munich, 1970), 65–6; Wolfram, *History of the Goths*, 243–6, 306–24, Moorhead, *Theoderic*, 173–88. No further known conflicts: though Theoderic ruled from Verona and Pavia from *c.* 519 *propter metum gentium* (*Anon. Val.* XIV, 81–3, 87), he returned to Ravenna *c.* 524 (after the death of Boethius; *ibid.* XV, 88). Theoderic's return followed the fall of the Burgundian king Sigismund to the Franks and the allegedly peaceful extension of Ostrogothic power into a large part of Burgundian territory (Moorhead, *Theoderic*, 213–26). These circumstances suggest that the *gentes* causing worry in *c.* 519 were the Burgundians.

[114] Cass., *Variae* I, 46; II, 41.

[115] E.g. Stein II, 50; Wolfram, *History of the Goths*, 318–20.

[116] Cass., *Variae* III, 1–4. There were six original letters; the kings of the Heruli, Warni, and Thuringians each received a copy of the same letter; *Variae* III, 3 title: *Epistula uniformis talis ad Herulem regem, ad Guarnorum regem, ad Thoringian regem* (not a single circular letter; cf. Bury I, 462 n. 1; Ensslin, 'Romverbundenheit', 519). Doubtless the original letters were differentiated by individual inscriptions, including the kings' names, and perhaps other elements omitted by Cassiodorus for publication. A later letter to the Thuringian king preserves his name, Herminafred (Cass., *Variae* IV, 1 title), but the later letters to the kings of the Heruli and Warni do

conflict between the Franks and the Visigoths was impending, the letters to Alaric II and Clovis attempt to dissuade the antagonists from conflict. Concerned that the neighbouring tribes might encourage the strife in the hope of profiteering, Theoderic wrote to them to enlist their aid in deterring Clovis from aggression.[117]

Two envoys, anonymous in the *Variae*, carried these letters to all six royal addressees, an arduous task which has received little attention. The *Variae* preserves the order in which the letters were to be delivered. The envoys were first to travel to Alaric II in southern Gaul, then to turn north-east to Gundobad, next to visit the courts of the Heruli, Warni, and Thuringians, and finally to approach Clovis. It was hoped that when the envoys reached the Frankish court, representatives of the Burgundians, Heruli, Warni, and Thuringians would accompany them to form a joint deputation. Wisely, Theoderic's letter to Clovis does not specify which rulers would support the Italian legates; at Vouillé, the Burgundians joined forces with the Franks, not the Visigoths.[118]

not (Cass., *Variae* IV, 2; V, 1). On the letters: Salvatore Pricoco, 'Cassiodore et le conflit franco-wisigothique: rhétorique et histoire', in Michel Rouche (ed.), *Clovis: Histoire et mémoire* (Paris, 1997), I, 739–52.

117 Date: there is no internal evidence for the date of these letters. The length of the envisaged journey of the envoys (see below) assumes that open conflict, though brewing, is not immanent; otherwise Theoderic could have dispatched envoys directly to Clovis. The letters were probably written in late 506 or early 507, before the onset of summer made large-scale campaigning likely; Mommsen, *Prooemium* to Cass., *Variae*, xxxiv; Krautschick, *Cassiodor*, 57, 75. Other evidence supports late 506; below, at n. 130. The battle itself is securely dated to 507, but there is no evidence of the time of year at which it occured (*Chron. Caesar.*, s.a. 507; *Chron. Gall.* 511, s.a. *XV Anastasii* and cf. s.a. *XIX Anastasii* = 511 by consular and indiction dating – on this basis, *XV Anastasii* is 507).

A date of late 506/early 507 for Cass., *Variae* III, 1–4, and so for *Variae* I, 45–6; II, 40–1, implies either that Cassiodorus' tenure as *quaestor* commenced in the indiction year beginning September 506, not September 507 as is usually accepted, or that he drafted important diplomatic correspondence before holding the quaestorship, while still *consiliaris* to his father, at the time praetorian prefect of Italy; Mommsen, *Prooemium* to Cass., *Variae*, xxvii–xxviii; A. van de Vyver, 'La victoire contre les Alamans et la conversion de Clovis', *Revue Belge de Philologie et d'Histoire* 16 (1937), 35, 50; *PLRE* II, 55–7. The latter explanation is unsatisfactorily urged by Krautschick, *Cassiodor*, 55–7.

118 Route of the envoys: Cass., *Variae* III, 1.4: Theoderic's envoys 'will both sufficiently intimate our instructions to you and hasten to our brother Gundobad and the other kings with your desires' (*uobis et mandata nostra sufficienter insinuent et usque ad fratrem nostrum Gundibadum uel alios reges cum uestra uoluntate deproperent*); cf. 2.3. The kings of the Heruli, Warni, and Thuringians are enjoined: 'send your envoys together with my own and those of our brother King Gundobad to Clovis the king of the Franks' (*legatos uestros una cum meis et fratris nostri Gundobadi regi ad Francorum regem Luduin destinate*), 3.2. It is clearly the same pair of envoys who are to visit all the kings: 1.4 (above); 4.4: 'we have seen fit to send to your excellency our envoys A and B, through whom we have also sent our writings to your brother, our son King Alaric' (*ad excellentiam uestram illum et illum legatos nostros magnopere credidimus dirigendos, per quos etiam ad fratrem uestram, filium nostrum regem Alaricum scripta nostra direximus*). Ludo Moritz Hartmann, *Geschichte Italiens im Mittelalter* I (Leipzig, 1897), 157–8.

The envoys' route cannot be charted, as there is no record of the residences of the kings of the Visigoths, Franks, and Burgundians at this time; the very localities of the lesser tribes are unsure. The scale of the journey, however, may be appreciated. Alaric II may have been in his capital Toulouse, or perhaps further north, near the border of Visigothic and Frankish territories on the Loire.[119] The capital of the Burgundian kingdom at this time appears to have been at Vienne, though Lyons, Geneva, and Valence were all used as royal residences in the early sixth century.[120] The Thuringians occupied lands to the north-east, perhaps modern lower Bavaria. The larger part of the Heruli lived at this time on the middle Danube, where they were in contact with the Lombards further to the east, but a smaller group had occupied part of the Belgian coastline from the mid-fifth century. The little-known Warni probably still dwelt on the North Sea littoral, beyond the Franks. Clovis may have been in residence at Tours, where he later celebrated his victory over the Goths.[121] The envoys' journey circumscribed some half-dozen modern European states.[122] Even allowing for the inland waterways and Roman roads which made such travel possible, Theoderic must have assumed that his agents would have a considerable period, perhaps months, before hostilities could begin, to enable them to circulate among the five kings prior to approaching Clovis.

A clear vision of dispute settlement procedure underlies the letters. Though Theoderic warned of punitive action if Frankish aggression continued, he appealed to Clovis to accept arbitration.[123] The planned joint

For a comparable journey, accumulating envoys of three kings across four kingdoms: Fredegar, *Chron.* IV, 31 (envoys of the Gothic king of Spain Witteric and of both the Frankish kings Chlothar II and Theudebert II to the Lombard king Agilulf in Italy, *c.* 607); other journeys in which embassies had to travel to successive courts, modifying their mission depending on their reception at each court: Priscus, *Fr.*, 39.1 (a Constantinopolitan envoy negotiating between the rebel *magister utriusque militiae* Marcellinus of Dalmatia, Geiseric, and the western imperial court; *Fr. Class. Hist.*, 343); Gregory of Tours, *Hist.* IX, 16 (to accommodate different reactions of two Frankish kings to a marriage proposal).

119 Cf. Gregory of Tours, *Hist.* II, 35.

120 Gregory of Tours, *Hist.* II, 32–4; H. H. Anton, 'Burgunden II: Historisches', in *Reallexikon der germanischen Altertumskunde*, 2nd edn ed. J. Hoops *et al.*, IV (Berlin, 1981), 243.

121 Locations of Thuringians, Heruli, and Warni: Schmidt, *Ostgermanen*, 2nd edn, 127–8, 549–53, 558–60; *Westgermanen* 28, 332–4; Wolfram, *History of the Goths*, 190, 258, 318–19. Clovis: Gregory of Tours, *Hist.* II, 38.

122 Cf. the itineraries of the Visigothic princess Galswintha, travelling from Narbonne to Rouen via Marseilles, Poitiers, and Tours; and of Venantius Fortunatus who, after passing through northern Italy, Noricum, and along the Danube, journeyed around Gaul along the Rhine, Moselle, Meuse, Aisne, Seine, Loire, and Garonne river valleys; Venantius Fortunatus, *Opera poetica*, ed. F. Leo (MGH AA 4.1), *Carm.* VI, 5 *De Gelesuintha*, 142, lines 214–15, 229–36; *Vita Sancti Martini* IV, lines 630–80; Venantius Fortunatus, *Opera pedestria*, ed. B. Krusch (MGH AA 4.2), *Praefatio* 2, lines 2–7. These journeys, however, were undertaken at a more leisurely pace than that of Theoderic's envoys.

123 Punitive action: Cass., *Variae* III, 3.2, 4.4.

embassy to Clovis would not include representatives of his antagonists, the Visigoths, but only envoys of five nations not directly involved in the conflict. The letter to Clovis urges him to choose arbitrators (*iudices, medii*) from among these friendly nations in order to mediate the dispute.[124] Cassiodorus refers to such arbitration as *leges gentium*, a phrase reminiscent of the *ius gentium* of classical jurisprudence, with strong contemporary moral force.[125] This image of an assembly of kings acting as moderators may have been a tactful way of presenting a hoped-for military alliance against Clovis; there are, however, comparable instances of similar interstate arbitration, involving the Ostrogothic monarchs.[126]

Whatever the underlying causes of the conflict, it was precipitated only by a diplomatic insult, not a physical act of aggression by either side.[127] Theoderic therefore reprimands Clovis for not attempting to resolve the dispute himself by diplomatic negotiations with Alaric: 'it lacks sense to set arms in motion immediately at the first embassy'.[128] The four letters are more explicit than many in the *Variae* in describing their circumstances and the aim of their dispatch. Nevertheless, the success of the mission rests on the envoys, for whose oral persuasions the letters act as validations.[129]

Two letters of Ennodius, one to Senarius, the other to his friend Pamphronius, suggest that Senarius was involved in this lengthy mission. The letters, sent to Ravenna soon after 1 September 506, express Ennodius' great relief at Senarius' recent return from 'the distant borders of the *gentes*' and 'the farthest parts of the world'.[130] Such allusions to the official duties of Ennodius' correspondents or to current political events are

[124] Cass., *Variae* III, 4.3.

[125] Cass., *Variae* III, 3.2: *leges gentius quaerat [Luduin]*. See below, chapter 6 at nn. 181–94.

[126] Procopius, *Wars* IV, 5.12–25 (Amalasuntha suggests arbitration by Justinian over occupation of Sicily). Cf. Procopius, *Wars* VII, 34.26–7, 34 (Gepid envoys to Justinian protest that they have sought and been refused arbitration by their enemies, the Lombards, as a ploy to claim moral ascendancy); cf. Fredegar, *Chron.* II, 58 (a burlesque).

[127] Cause: not a Catholic crusade, as represented by Gregory of Tours, *Hist.* II, 37; cf. Moorhead, *Theoderic*, 178–9. No physical aggression yet: Cass., *Variae* III, 1.3.

[128] Cass., *Variae* III, 4.3: *impatiens sensus est ad primum legationem arma protinus commouere.*

[129] Cass., *Variae* III, 1.4, 2.3, 3.4, 4.4.

[130] Ennodius, *Ep.* V, 15: *de prolixis gentium finibus*; 16: *ab ultimus terrarum partibus*. Date: Sundwall, *Abhandlungen*, Table 77, 37–8, followed by *PLRE* II, 'Pamphronius', 825, 'Senarius', 989. Reference to Pamphronius' recent appointment to a palatine office simultaneous with the return of Senarius fixes the date to about 1 September, the beginning of the indiction; Ennodius, *Ep.* V, 16.3. The year can be deduced from the manuscript order of Ennodius' works, which appears to retain the chronological order of their composition between 503 and 513; Vogel, Introduction to Ennodius, *Opera*, liii–liv; Vogel, 'Chronologische Untersuchungen zu Ennodius', *Neues Archiv* 23 (1898), 53–4. The firmest *termini* for the two letters are provided by contempory references to the western consuls of 506 and 510; Ennodius, *Carm.* II, 32, *Ep.* VIII, 1; Vogel, 'Untersuchungen', 53. *Epp.* V, 15 and 16 were written after the death of bishop Marcellianus of Aquileia, a supporter of the schismatic antipope Laurentius, *c.* late 505/early 506 (Sundwall, *Abhandlungen*, 32–4), and the commencement of the quaestorship of Eugenes, which apparently began at an irregular time early in 506 (Vogel, 'Untersuchungen', 63–74; Sundwall, *Abhandlungen*, 35–6, 115; followed by

rare in his correspondence. It is clear from Ennodius' words that Senarius' mission had been to barbarian peoples, not to Constantinople or elsewhere in Italy; that it had been potentially dangerous; and that it had travelled far. There is a break of some months between these letters and Ennodius' previous correspondence with Senarius; presumably, Senarius was absent during this period.[131] The dates of Ennodius' letters strongly suggest that the mission from which Senarius had recently returned was part of Theoderic's involvement in Gaul. In no other letter does Ennodius refer to Senarius' many journeys. His emphasis on the distance travelled, and his relief at his friend's return, would be understandable if the embassy concerned was the lengthy mission outlined in *Variae* III, 1–4.[132]

Senarius states that all his missions were effective. Cassiodorus' praise for his embassies implies general, or at least memorable, success, as does Senarius' promotion to *comes patrimonii*. Though war between the Franks and Visigoths did break out, there is evidence that Theoderic's appeals to the antagonists in Gaul gained a moratorium on the conflict. Ennodius' *Panegyric* on Theoderic, delivered after Ennodius' letters greeting Senarius' return but before the battle of Vouillé early in 507, describes the Burgundians as in perpetual alliance with Theoderic; Ennodius passes in silence over the Franks and Visigoths.[133] Yet by spring 507 the Burgundian prince Sigismund had set out with his army to support Clovis against the Visigoths.[134] The *Panegyric* was therefore composed when the Gothic–Burgundian alliance seemed firm, before it was later reneged. The sequence of events can be reconstructed as follows: the mission of *Variae* III, 1–4, undertaken late in 506, secured the agreement of the Burgundians, Heruli, Warni, and Thuringians to oppose Clovis; the *Panegyric* was composed during the winter of 506/7, when relations between the Franks and the Visigoths were still unsettled; by spring the Burgundians had decided to support the Franks instead of the Goths; later in the

Krautschick, *Cassiodor*, 56, n. 2; *PLRE* II, 415). The letters were written before the delivery of Ennodius' *Panegyric* on Theoderic, which pre-dates Vouillé, probably early in 507, also before *Carm.* I, 3, delivered on 18 April of that year; Sundwall, *Abhandlungen*, 42–3. Senarius' return was therefore *c.* early September 506.

[131] Ennodius, *Ep.* IV, 33, early 506; Sundwall, *Abhandlungen*, Table 77, 32–3.

[132] Sundwall, *Abhandlungen*, 37–8, sees the mission mentioned by Ennodius as part of Theoderic's diplomacy before Vouillé, without associating it with Cass., *Variae* III, 1–4; cf. Schäfer, *Der weströmische Senat*, 103 n. 727. Ensslin, *Theoderich*, 368 n. 14, suggests that Senarius might have undertaken the embassy which carried *Variae* II, 41 to Clovis; Shanzer, 'Two Clocks', 248–9, suggests that Senarius may have carried *Variae* I, 46 to Gundobad.

[133] Ennodius, *Panegyricus dictus Theoderico* X, 54. Date: Sundwall, *Abhandlungen*, 42–4.

[134] Karl Binding, *Das burgundisch-romanische Königreich (von 443–532 n. Chr.)* (Leipzig, 1868; repr. Aalen, 1969), 193–7, 292, based on Avitus of Vienne, *Epp.*, 45, 91, 92 (nos. 40, 81, 82 in Sirmond's edition, *PL* 59). Gregory of Tours, *Hist.* II, 28 refers to Clovis sending embassies to Burgundia *saepius*.

summer the Visigoths were defeated at Vouillé. If Senarius was one of the envoys who bore the original copies of *Variae* III, 1–4, his claim to success either overlooks the calamity of the Visigothic defeat of 507, or, more likely, includes a remission in hostilities gained in 506/7, before the Burgundian allegiance was switched to the Franks. Such a moratorium suggests that the progress to war in Gaul was considerably more protracted than the sparse narratives of the chronicles suggest.

In the aftermath of conflict with the Franks, Theoderic sought new support in western Europe through a marriage alliance with the king of the Thuringians and the adoption-in-arms of the king of the Heruli. Letters to the kings of these people immediately precede the letters of Senarius' appointment as *comes patrimonii* in Cassiodorus' *Variae*, perhaps suggesting his association with these negotiations.[135]

For two years following the battle of Vouillé, the security of Ostrogothic Italy was compromised. Provence was first occupied by the Franks and Burgundians, but then annexed to the Italian administration. Though the Ostrogoths pushed the Franks out of Provence by military strength, the antagonists may have reached some form of negotiated settlement, for there were no further border conflicts between the Ostrogoths and the expansionist Franks during the next two decades. The court of Anastasius attempted to distract Ostrogothic efforts in Provence by launching naval attacks on the east coast of Italy, a tactic criticised even at Constantinople, and Byzantine support of the Franks was displayed by the grant of an honorary consulate to Clovis. Yet by late 508/9, Ravenna and Constantinople were reconciled.[136]

Senarius' advancement came after, and very likely because of, the resolution of the conflicts which had jeopardised the Italian kingdom for the previous five years. The period 507/9 in particular must have seen much 'shuttle diplomacy' between Italy, Constantinople, and Gaul.[137] Senarius owed his advancement to *comes patrimonii* to the international hostilities of 504–9.

There is little evidence of Senarius' career after his appointment as *comes patrimonii*. The *Variae* preserves three letters giving him instructions while

[135] Cass., *Variae* IV, 1, 2. Date: Krautschick, *Cassiodor*, 54, 76.

[136] Annexation of Provence: Cass., *Variae* I, 24; III, 16–18, 32, 40; IV, 16.1; Procopius, *Wars* V, 12.45. Byzantine naval attacks: Marcellinus *comes*, *Chron.*, s.a. 508. Clovis' honorary title: Gregory of Tours, *Hist.* II, 38; Michael McCormick, 'Clovis at Tours: Byzantine Public Ritual and the Origin of Medieval Ruler Symbolism', in Evangelos K. Chrysos and Andreas Schwarcz (eds.), *Das Reich und die Barbaren* (Vienna and Cologne, 1989), 155–80; Ralph Mathisen, 'Clovis, Anastase et Grégoire de Tours: consul, patrice et roi', in Rouche (ed.), *Clovis: histoire et mémoire* I, 395–407. Reconciliation: Cass., *Variae* I, 1; Moorhead, *Theoderic*, 186–7.

[137] Cf. epitaph, lines 11–13.

in office, a minor indication of Senarius' relative importance still in Cassiodorus' mind at the time of editing his collection.[138] He was awarded the patriciate at some time after his tenure as *comes*, since he is not addressed as *patricius* by Cassiodorus.[139] Ennodius' last letter to Senarius was written early in 510, and it may be assumed that Senarius served only one year as *comes patrimonii* and was not in residence in Ravenna between the expiry of his office and the end of Ennodius' extant letters in early 513.[140] His epitaph indicates that he held no further high office after the *comitiva patrimonii*.

Senarius nevertheless remained in contact with Ennodius and the royal court. In 515/16, Bishop Avitus of Vienne wrote to Senarius to ask for news of an embassy led by Ennodius to Constantinople. The legation had been dispatched by Pope Hormisdas in an attempt to resolve the Acacian schism which had estranged the churches of Rome and Constantinople since the 480s. Senarius appears to have been in Ravenna at the time; Avitus also wrote to the bishop of the city on the same issue. Avitus might have written to Senarius as much for his contacts with the court as for his personal ties with Ennodius, for the embassy had been commissioned by Hormisdas after consultation with Theoderic. Avitus claimed to have often benefited from Senarius' assistance in the past.[141]

[138] Cass., *Variae* IV, 7, 11, 13. See also IV, 15 and *PLRE* II, 'Anonymus 35', 1225; the arrangement of letters in the *Variae* favours the identification of this unnamed *comes* with Senarius rather than his predecessor Julianus, as all the letters to Senarius are contained in Book IV; cf. Cass., *Variae* I, 16 to Julianus; Delmaire, *Les Responsables*, 295.

[139] Epitaph, line 16. The title, however, is not used in either the letter of Avitus of Vienne to Senarius, *c.* 515/16, or that of John the Deacon, *c.* 509/23, discussed below. On *patricii* under Theoderic: Mommsen, 'Ostgothische Studien', 422–3; Wilhelm Heil, *Der konstantinische Patriziat* (Basel and Stuttgart, 1968), 52–3, 128–32; Wilhelm Ensslin, 'Aus Theoderichs Kanzlei', *Würzburger Jahrbücher für die Altertumswissenschaft* 2 (1947), 75–85; Evangelos K. Chrysos, 'Die Amaler-Herrschaft in Italien und das Imperium Romanum: Der Vertragsentwurf des Jahres 535', *Byzantion* 51 (1981), 461–2. Theoderic's policy on the appointment of *patricii* did not follow the provisions of *Cod. Just.* XII, 3.3 (Zeno), limiting the grant of the patriciate to former praetorian prefects, prefects of Constantinople, *magistri utriusque militiae, magistri officiorum*, and consuls. Instead he anticipated Justinian's *Nov.* LXII, 2.5, extending candidacy to all holders of offices with *illustris* rank (i.e. *quaestors* and the financial *comites*). Possibly this reflects late fifth-century imperial practice in the West; Ensslin, 'Aus Theoderichs Kanzlei', 75. Nevertheless, award of the patriciate to financial *comites* was rare in Italy. Of twelve financial officers known from the Ostrogothic regime in Italy, only Senarius and Cyprianus, the accuser of Boethius, held the patriciate under Theoderic (the patriciate of Bergantinus is not attested before 538; *PLRE* II, 225). Several eastern *comites sacrarum largitionum* held the patriciate in the late sixth century; *PLRE* III, 'Elias 2', 437; 'Petrus 9', 1000; 'Fl. Se . . . ', 1118; 'Theodorus 34', 1256; 'Fl. Victor 3', 1372.

[140] Ennodius, *Ep.* VIII, 7; Sundwall, *Abhandlungen*, Table 81, 58.

[141] Avitus of Vienne, *Opera*, ed. Rudolf Peiper (MGH AA 6.2), *Epp.* XXXIX (Senarius), XL (bishop Peter of Ravenna); XLI–XLII. Cf. Ensslin, *Theoderich*, 298; Danuta Shanzer and Ian Wood (trans.), *Avitus of Vienne: Letters and Selected Prose* (TTH 38; Liverpool, 2002), 123–5. Delmaire, *Les Responsables*, 289, considers that Senarius had retired to Rome when he received the letter from Avitus. On the Acacian schism: Jedin and Dolan, 429–36, 616–24; Chadwick, *Boethius*, 29–46; Moorhead, *Theoderic*, 54–60, 194–200.

A final source, which contains a fragment of a letter by Senarius, reveals another aspect of this late Roman civil servant's relations with the court of the Ostrogothic king: the problem of divergent faiths. At some time between 509 and 523, Senarius wrote to John, one of the seven deacons of Rome, generally identified as the later Pope John I.[142] Senarius' letter is lost but John's reply is preserved.[143] John had played an active if ambivalent role in the Laurentian schism following the disputed papal election of 498. He was a close friend and spiritual adviser of Boethius.[144] From John's letter it is clear that he and Senarius were previously acquainted. The old favour done by Senarius, to which John refers, might have been performed in an official capacity, perhaps in the troubled times of the Laurentian schism.[145]

Like Boethius, Senarius sought religious instruction from John, but of a liturgical rather than theological nature. Senarius made two requests: he asked for copies of certain texts, and wanted John's reply to a series of questions. One of the texts he requested was *De haeresibus*, possibly Augustine's work of that title to which a continuation had been added in the mid-fifth century.[146] The original questions Senarius asked cannot

[142] Identity of John the Deacon and Pope John I: Altaner, *Patrologie*[7], 464; *Clavis patrum latinorum*[2], ed. Eligius Dekkers (Bruges, 1961), § 950; Chadwick, *Boethius*, 28; Moorhead, *Theoderic*, 204–11; reservations in *PCBE* II, 'Iohannes 18, 22, 26, 28', 1070–1, 1072, 1074–5, 1080. Date: John addresses Senarius as *Dominus meritus illustris*, *Ep.* 1, therefore after *illustris* rank was conveyed on Senarius in September 509; and before John's election as pope on 13 August 523. The reference to unorthodox liturgical practices in Africa in *Ep.* 8 does not necessarily refer to Arian oppression of the Catholic church, and so does not help date the letter, *contra* Delmaire, *Les Responsables*, 296.

[143] Editions: John the Deacon, *Epistola ad Senarium*, ed. Jean Mabillon, *PL* 59, 399–408; André Wilmart (ed.), *Analecta Reginensia: extraits des manuscripts latins de la reine Christine conservés au Vatican* (Studi e Testi 59; Vatican City, 1933), 170–9; Wilmart's edition is cited here. On the transmission of the text: *ibid.*, 153–7.

[144] Boethius describes John as his spiritual father and dedicates to him three of his theological tractates. At the time Boethius wrote the fifth tractate (an early theological work), John already possessed a collection of Boethius' writings, which might have been the earlier dialectical writings rather than the theological works; Boethius, *Tractates*, ed. E. K. Rand, trans. H. F. Stewart and S. J. Tester in *The Theological Tractates and Consolation of Philosophy* (LCL; London, 1973), II *dedicatio* and *praef.*, III *dedicatio*, V *dedicatio*; cf. Chadwick, *Boethius*, 180; Moorhead, *Theoderic*, 205–6. John shared an interest in Aristotelian philosophy with Boethius: John the Deacon, *Ep.* 14, cf. Boethius, *Philosophiae consolatio* I, 16.15; Joachim Gruber, *Kommentar zu Boethius*, De consolatione philosophiae (Berlin, 1978), 155–6; Chadwick, *Boethius*, 27; Moorhead, *Theoderic*, 210.

The bearer of Senarius' letter, Renatus, played an important role in the preservation of Boethius' dialectical works; Chadwick, *Boethius*, 255–7; *PLRE* II, 'Marcius Novatus Renatus 1', 939.

[145] John the Deacon, *Ep.* 1. The statement of Delmaire, *Les Responsables*, 294 that Senarius had represented Theoderic at the Synod of Rome in 502 is only conjectural; cf. Sundwall, *Abhandlungen*, 11 on Ennodius, *Ep.* 1, 23.

[146] Request: John the Deacon, *Ep.* 1, lines 8–9. *De haeresibus*: 9, lines 17–19: *De Pelagianis autem, Eutycianis sive Nestorianis aperta et vulgata sunt omnia, quae, in libro de haeresibus cum legeritis, plenius*

be exactly reconstructed. John states that he has reordered and rearranged the topics Senarius had raised into separate discussions as he saw fit. He preserves an abbreviated fragment of only one set of Senarius' enquiries; the pragmatic style of that fragment is different from that of John's letter (and gives little hint of Senarius' own eloquence).[147]

Nevertheless, John's reply concentrates on three main topics which seem to reflect the central concerns of Senarius' letter: baptism, liturgical practices peculiar to the Church of Rome, and ecclesiastical offices. John provides distinctions between the offices of bishop and priest, and acolyte and exorcist, and justifies liturgical practices unique to Rome mainly on the basis of tradition, defending a diversity of practices between churches. His explanation of the roles and forms of baptism and catechesis occupies the greatest length. The letter breaks off during a philosophical consideration of the effects of improper baptism.

Senarius also asked John's opinion on which former heretics joining the Catholic church required rebaptism. The general principle in John's reply is that if an individual has previously received baptism in the name of all three Persons of the Trinity, even if confessing erroneous differences between the Persons, he is not to be rebaptised. John specifies that this includes heretics 'like those who, at the time, followed Arius'.[148] Other contemporary heresies (Pelagianism, Eutychianism, and Nestorianism) do not require discussion, as their situation is well known; instead John refers Senarius to the copy of *De haeresibus* being forwarded. That work, if correctly identified as the expanded version of Augustine's treatise, does not provide instructions for the reconciliation of these or other heretical groups. The question of rebaptism, then, appears to have required clarification in regard only to Arian congregations, though

poteritis advertere. Augustine: *De haeresibus*, ed. R. Vander Plaetse, C. Beukers, and G. Morin (CCSL 46; Turnhout, 1969), 262–351; continuation: *ibid., Appendix*, 347–51. The fullest recension appears to date from the third quarter of the fifth century (from references to the heretic Timothy as still alive in exile, and the narrative of Eutyches up to his exile); *Appendix* 1, IIIA; cf. Gennadius, *Liber de viris illustribus*, ed. Ernst Cushing Richardson (TU 14.1; Leipzig, 1896), cc. 83, 94. The text sent by John cannot have been the *Indiculus de haeresibus*, wrongly attributed to Jerome and Gennadius, as the *Indiculus* does not discuss the Pelagians (significantly, it has a chapter on Predestinationism instead); *PL* 81, 636–46, Pseudo-Gennadian continuation, cc. 51–63; cf. Augustine, *De haeresibus*, c. 81 (Pelagians). On the relationship between the fifth-century continuations of *De haeresibus* and the *Indiculus de haeresibus*: Gustav Krüger, *Lucifer Bischof von Calaris und das Schisma der Luciferianer* (Leipzig, 1886; repr. Hildersheim, 1969), 64–6; G. Morin, 'Le *Liber dogmatum* de Gennade de Marseille et les problèmes qui s'y rattachent', *Revue Bénédictine* 24 (1907), 450–3.

[147] Reordering: John the Deacon, *Ep.* 1, lines 26–9. Fragment: *Ep.* 2. John discusses the following topics: baptism and catechesis (3–7); roles of bishops and priests (7–8); rebaptism of heretics (9); the roles of acolytes and exorcists (10); three separate points of the liturgy of Rome (11, 12, 13); death without proper baptism (14, incomplete).

[148] John the Deacon, *Ep.* 9: *uti qui illo in tempore Arrium sunt secuti.*

the other groups he named were still active in areas which influenced Italy.[149]

John's opposition to rebaptism was in accord with the usual policy of the Catholic church for the reception of proselytes since the early fourth century.[150] His reason, however, is somewhat unusual. Earlier arguments for the validity of baptism performed by heretics proceed from the proposition that the condition of the priest performing the ceremony does not affect the sacrament itself. John does not use this argument, but considers only the necessity for a Trinitarian baptismal formula. His thought was possibly influenced by Augustine, who was much studied in the circle of Boethius in Rome.[151] The focus of John's statement is on correct baptismal liturgy, rather than the theology of baptism.

A restatement of the prohibition of rebaptism in the early sixth century was obviously relevant to relations between the Catholic and Arian churches then coexisting in Italy. There is evidence of Arians converting to the Catholic church during the reign of Theoderic.[152] The creeds labelled 'Arian' from the time of the Council of Nicaea onwards varied greatly. Not all may have used Trinitarian baptismal formulae, though the little evidence available suggests that most did.[153] The liturgy of

[149] Pelagianism in Provence, the Christological heresies in the Monophysite controversies of the East.

[150] E.g. Pope Siricius, *Ep.* I, 2 (on Arians), in Victor Saxer, *Les Rites de l'initiation chrétienne du IIe au VIe siècle: esquisse historique et signification d'après leurs principaux témoins* (Spoleto, 1988), 574–5; Pope Gelasius, *Ep.* XII, 10 (on Macedonians and Nestorians) in Thiel, *Epistola*, 357–8; Pope Anastasius II, *Ep.* I, 7 (on Acacian schismatics), *ibid.*, 620–2 (preserved in the papal *decretalia* of Dionysius Exiguus); Pope Vigilius, *Ep.* I (II), 3 (*PL* 69, 18). Cf. Jedin and Dolan, 709–10.

[151] Condition of priest: references as previous note. John Chrysostom argued that while the condition of the priest did not affect the validity of baptism, an orthodox Trinitarian baptismal formula was necessary; Arian baptism was therefore invalid. This belief was not followed in the West; Thomas M. Finn, *Early Christian Baptism and the Catechumenate: West and East Syria* (Collegeville, MN, 1992), 13–14. Augustine: Chadwick, *Boethius*, 175. John mentions consulting *maiorum volumina* in preparing his reply to Senarius' questions; *Ep.* I. Augustine specified that a Trinitarian formula was needed, but implicitly accepted Arian baptism; Maria Andrelita Cenzon Santos, *Baptismal Ecclesiology of St. Augustine: A Theological Study of His Antidonatist Letters* (Rome, 1990), 278–314.

Later in the sixth century, Pope Vigilius also was concerned over improper Trinitarian formulae in baptism; Vigilius, *Ep.* I, 6 (*c.* 538) in Saxer, *Les Rites de l'initiation chrétienne*, 581–2.

[152] Moorhead, *Theoderic*, 95–6; Brown, 'Everyday Life', 86, 94; though evidence based solely on individuals with Germanic names who are attested as Catholic, but not expressly attested as formerly Arian, is invalid; cf. Amory, *People and Identity in Ostrogothic Italy*, 263–74.

The belief that Theoderic forbade Catholics from proselytising to Arianism (Brown, 'Everyday Life', 94 n. 74; Amory, *People and Identity in Ostrogothic Italy*, 258), based on Theodore Lectore, *Kirchengeschichte* II, 18, reads too much into this eastern source.

[153] Late fourth-century 'Arian' groups such as the Eunomians and Macedonians used Trinitarian baptismal formulae; R. P. C. Hanson, *The Search for the Christian Doctrine of God: The Arian Controversy, 318–381* (Edinburgh, 1988), 636 n. 170; 769.

the church of Theoderic's Goths is unknowable because of the extreme paucity of extant Gothic Arian writings.[154] Some evidence, however, is offered by iconography and theological tracts. The mosaic medallion on the dome of the Arian baptistry in Ravenna portrays the baptism of Christ by John the Baptist, beneath the Holy Spirit in the form of a dove. This iconography is shared with contemporary Catholic representations of the baptism of Christ, suggesting that a Trinitarian baptismal formula was employed in the Gothic church.[155] One anti-Arian tract, written in Naples perhaps during the Ostrogothic period, also seems to presume that baptism in the name of the Holy Spirit as well as the Father and Son is common to Catholics and Arians.[156] It would seem that John's statement countered unconventional suggestions that Gothic proselytes required rebaptism to join the Catholic congregation.

This attention to rebaptism suggests a context for Senarius' letter to John. There is no doubt that Senarius himself was an orthodox and active member of the Catholic church.[157] His interest seems to have been to justify the practices and organisation of the Catholic church in Rome to someone outside the church, presumably an Arian; for this reason he wrote to one of the deacons of Rome. As his enquiries are liturgical not theological, his interest might have been to proselytise rather than to engage in Christological apologetic. Reassuring prospective converts that rebaptism would not be required would be a major step towards easing a

[154] On the Gothic liturgy: Klaus Gamber, *Die Liturgie der Goten und der Armenier: Versuch einer Darstellung und Hinführung* (Studia Patristica et Liturgica 21; Regensburg, 1988), 9–44, 89–96. The limited evidence for the Gothic Arian liturgy suggests that it conserved the structure and details of the fourth-century eastern church, adopted at the time of conversion, and consequently differed little from the Catholic liturgy; *ibid.*, 32; Jacques Zeiller, 'Etude sur l'Arianisme en Italie à l'époque ostrogothique et à l'époque lombarde', *Ecole française de Rome: Mélanges d'archéologie et d'histoire* 25 (1905), 131–2.

[155] Friedrich Wilhelm Deichmann, *Ravenna: Geschichte und Monumente*, 3 vols. (Wiesbaden, 1969–76), I, 210 (Holy Spirit), 211–12 (date); II.1, 255–8; III, plate 252; Spiro K. Kostof, *The Orthodox Baptistery of Ravenna* (New Haven and London 1965), 87–9.

[156] *Contra Varimadum arianum diaconum* (*PL* 62, 351–434), II, 17 410D: 'For if the Holy Spirit is not equal in the substance of divinity with the Father and the Son, why is nothing accomplished without it in the sacrament of holy baptism?' (*Si enim Spiritus Sanctus in dietatis substantia Patri et Filio non coaequatur, cur in sacramento sacri baptismatis nihil absque illo completur?*). On the *Contra Varimadum*: G. Morin, 'Pour un prochain volume d'anecdota', *Revue Bénédictine* 24 (1907), 269–70; W. Ensslin, 'Varimadus', *RE* VIII A.1, 382; W. Teuffel, W. Kroll, and F. Skutsch (eds.), *Geschichte der römischer Literatur* III, 6th edn (Leipzig, 1916), § 418.15.

[157] John the Deacon, *Ep.* 1: *quantus pectori vestro* [ms. *nostro*] *divini cultus ardor insidat, catholica sollicitudine non celastis.* Avitus of Vienne, *Ep.* XXXIX, presumes Senarius' familiarity with the affairs and procedures of the church of Rome, and his interest in the resolution of the Acacian schism; cf. esp. lines 14–15: *vestram* [sc. *fidelium laicorum*] *in catholica religione rem gerimus* [*sacerdotes ecclesiae*]. Cf. Ennodius, *Epp.* VI, 8.2: *inploro ut per omnes sanctorum basilicas pro adflictione mea deum rogare non desinas*; VII, 5.1: *Christianae mentis [tuae] integritas.*

tentative change of confessions.[158] So too would justifying the liturgical practices of the Catholic church, as the barbarian Arian communities appear to have been more conservative in liturgy than in theology.[159] The letter of Avitus of Vienne indicates that Senarius was interested in the reconciliation of Rome and Constantinople over the Acacian schism, as indeed was Theoderic; Senarius' enquiries to John suggest that he was active in promoting his faith in a second way, in discussions with members of the Arian, largely Gothic congregation with whom his court service brought him into frequent contact.

Catholic subjects of the Vandals and Burgundians engaged in theological debates with their Arian rulers in defence of Nicene Christology. Evidence of similar debates in Ostrogothic Italy is minimal, though the Arian church flourished under Theoderic.[160] For most of his reign, Theoderic successfully managed a pluralistic religious policy; only in the final years did sectarian conflicts disturb public life. Hostile references to his religion come only after his death, as part of *damnatio memoriae*; the Arianism of Odoacer was similarly disparaged posthumously.[161] The church of Rome was more concerned with the Christological struggles of Chalcedonianism, Monophysitism, and Nestorianism current in Constantinople than with the Arian church of the barbarians. Given the legacy of religious conflict of the fourth and fifth centuries, however, it is unlikely that coexistence of Catholic and Arian congregations in Italy was ever anything but delicate.

Senarius' epitaph and his letters of appointment in Cassiodorus' *Variae* indicate the political and social values attached by high civil servants to their positions: consciousness of their dependence upon the favour of their ruler; exploitation of the social status which high rank conveyed; the deployment of their literary culture, the distinguishing mark of their class, in the court milieu; and pride in their achievements in office, in Senarius' case the exceptional vigour of arduous travel and the successful advocacy of his king's interests before foreign rulers. His interest in the settlement of the Acacian schism, and his apparent concern with the conversion of Gothic Arians, give a glimpse of his life outside official

158 Cf. the Arian synod in Toledo under the Visigothic king Leuvigild, *c.* 580, which renounced the old Arian requirement of rebaptism for proselytes from Catholicism, thus more readily attracting converts; John of Biclar, *Chron.*, s.a. 580.2; Jedin and Dolan, 712.

159 Jedin and Dolan, 713.

160 Jedin and Dolan, 707–22; Altaner, *Patrologie*⁷ §§ 111.2–4. On Catholic–Arian dialogue in Italy: Moorhead, *Theoderic*, 89–97; Amory, *People and Identity in Ostrogothic Italy*, 195–235.

161 Theoderic: Moorhead, *Theoderic*, 91–4. Odoacer: Gelasius, *Ep.*, 95 (*PL* 59, 63), but note that Gelasius had supported Odoacer's co-religionist Theoderic in the struggle between the two kings.

duties. These religious activities reveal the ambiguity in which a court servant, pursuing a successful career under a ruler of divergent faith, could operate. Senarius prepared his epitaph for posterity with a traditional concern for his worldly fame, a fame resting upon the favours he had received from Theoderic.

The eloquence of rhetoric, the art of communication and persuasion, was fundamental to contacts between rulers in late antiquity, as it was for all aspects of imperial government and public life. The writings of Cassiodorus and Senarius illustrate the role of traditional forms of epistolography and spoken eloquence in communications among imperial and barbarian rulers in the early sixth century. The style of the diplomatic letters represents a direct continuation of the rhetorical tradition of epistolography, and has stylistic forebears in fifth- and sixth-century communications between emperors, high officials, the Senate, provincial councils, and important members of the Christian church.[162]

Undertaking an embassy was traditionally a sign of distinction in classical Mediterranean culture. This honour only increased in the new context of the fragmented West. Within provincial communities, the prestige of completing a successful embassy prompted competition between local magnates seeking the role of civic patron, most obviously by bishops who sought to appropriate the role. At imperial and royal courts, the need for monarchs ceaselessly to send and receive emissaries was impressed on the workings of government not by generating bureaucratic changes to facilitate diplomatic communication, but by shifting those most important elements of late antique society, rank and honour, in favour of court servants who served as envoys. Senarius' career and epitaph show that legatine tasks now stood to be rewarded with high public office, and the financial rewards and social rank which followed. It is natural that the documents which preserve the details of his career, his letters of appointment and his epitaph, belong to genres largely concerned with encomium.

[162] Fridh, *Terminologie et formules*, 5–8, 27–28; Macpherson, *Rome in Involution*, 70.

Chapter 6

NEGOTIUM AGENDUM

> Vitigis, leader of the Goths, worsted in war [by Belisarius], sent two envoys to Chosroes, the king of the Persians, to persuade him to march against the Romans. In order that the real character of the embassy might not be at once obvious, the men whom he sent were not Goths but priests of Liguria who were attracted to this enterprise by rich gifts of money. One of these men, who seemed to be the more worthy, undertook the embassy assuming the pretended name of bishop, which did not belong to him at all, while the other followed as his attendant ... Vitigis also entrusted to them a letter written to Chosroes and sent them off.
>
> Procopius, *Wars* II, 2.1–2; VI, 22.20. Cf. II, 2.3–12, 14.11–12; VI, 22.17–25

The authors studied in previous chapters give some intimation of the constant activity and complexity of political communication throughout the late and post-imperial world. The interchange of communication between different levels of authority, using well-maintained traditions, continued to serve a central role in public administration as it had under the earlier empire. But, as Procopius' vignette demonstrates, political communication also shaped crucial political developments in the fifth and sixth centuries.

The role of two nameless members of the lower Italian clergy in triggering the conflict of 540–4 between the late antique 'super-powers' of the eastern Roman empire and Sassanian Persia dramatically illustrates the potential of late antique patterns of communication. Procopius' account of the prelude to renewed Roman–Persian conflict emphasises the flow of strategic information and diplomatic interchange throughout the Mediterranean, Iran, the Caucasus, and the Arabian peninsula.[1] Persians, Armenians, and Italians are all alert to the progress of Justinian's

[1] Procopius, *Wars* II, 1–4, decribes communications between Persia and the Lakhmid Arabs, the Goths of Italy, and the Armenians; and Constantinopolitan embassies to the Lakhmids, the Utigur Huns, and Chosroes. For the context: Bury II, 89–113; Stein II, 485–92; Lee, *Information and Frontiers*, 111, 113; Ifran Shahid, *Byzantium and the Arabs in the Sixth Century* I (Washington, DC, 1995), 209–18.

ventures in other parts of the Mediterannean world.[2] Vitigis' embassy constituted a meeting of two parallel diplomatic offensives against Justinian: in Italy, Vitigis attempted to gain allies against the east Roman forces from amongst the Franks in Gaul and the Lombards in central Europe (while simultaneously negotiating with Belisarius and Justinian); in Persia, Chosroes sought among the buffer states and client kings neighbouring Rome and Persia in the Caucasus and the Arabian peninsula for *causae belli* with Constantinople. In Procopius' narrative, Vitigis' embassy is followed by a legation from Armenia, also under attack by Justinian's forces, sent to Chosroes for the same ends. The Goths and Armenians gave Chosroes the pretexts he desired, while Vitigis succeeded in gaining an eastern distraction for imperial attention.

Procopius' narrative assumes a common protocol for the dispatch and reception of embassies in centres of authority within and adjacent to the Roman empire, employing letters of credence, formal audiences and orations, and in particular the high status of the envoys themselves. The Armenian delegation included a local lord; an earlier Roman embassy to Chosroes included a senior general and a civil magistrate who was also honorary consul and *patricius*, both with previous experience in negotiation with Rome's south-eastern neighbours.[3] The clerics sent by Vitigis were smaller beer, chosen for subterfuge and unlikely to have had prior acquaintance with international diplomacy. Yet the king judged them fit for this crucial task. Presumably, like Ennodius in Milan, their clerical positions had exposed them to ecclesiastical and perhaps municipal or provincial legations, forms of 'internal' communication applicable to external diplomacy. The arrogation by one cleric of the title of bishop, at which Procopius takes offence, was clearly an attempt to convey greater status on the embassy; there are comparable instances of secular officials being elevated to higher positions in preparation for an embassy.[4] Vitigis' legates adapted themselves to the expectations of their recipient.

These shared practices were conventional. Though there is no sense of constitutionalism associated with them – they were not agreed upon by any 'international' forum – they were to some extent prescribed by the routine procedures of Roman imperial reception of provincial and other embassies. Imperial legislation, for example, ordered embassies to present sealed letters from their principals outlining their purposes;[5] the automatic preparation of a letter to accompany the oral presentations of

[2] Persia: Procopius, *Wars* II, 1.1; Armenians: 3.52; Italians: VI, 22.15–17.

[3] Armenian envoy: Procopius, *Wars* II, 3.29–31 (Bassaces; *PLRE* III, 177); Roman envoys: 1.9–10 (Strategius and Summus; *PLRE* II, 1034–6 and 1038–9).

[4] See below, n. 51.

[5] *CTh* XII, 12.4, 10, 11; cf. below at nn. 117–20.

Vitigis' envoys, despite the potential danger posed by a written message should it fall into the wrong hands, may be a habitual continuation of this requirement by the king's chancellery. Some basic patterns of communication can be assumed to arise from any situation in which two communities or states are brought into contact. But the Roman admininstrative and cultural context is central to understanding the practices of the fifth and sixth centuries throughout the Roman and post-Roman world and beyond.

The following chapter essays a sketch of the conventions of practice and thought which formed the framework for legatine traffic. The evidence is discussed under two main headings: first, the few but instructive sources which are prescriptive accounts of procedures for the reception of embassies; second, the larger and more varied evidence which can be deduced, often with caveats, from narrative and other accounts of embassies.[6]

PRESCRIPTIVE ACCOUNTS OF RECEPTIONS

There are two short prescriptive accounts of the reception of envoys at the imperial court of Constantinople, both originating in the early sixth century. One is written from the perspective of the court, the other from that of the office of a frequent correspondent with the imperial court, the bishop of Rome. They therefore offer contrasting as well as complementary information.[7]

De ceremoniis aulae Byzantinae

A lengthy section of the work now known as *De ceremoniis aulae Byzantinae*, initially compiled at the order of the tenth-century Byzantine emperor Constantine VII Porphyrogenitus, records protocol used at the eastern imperial court in the fifth and sixth centuries for a number of ceremonial occasions. Part if not all of this record of earlier practice is

[6] For earlier outlines of diplomatic procedures in late antiquity, see above, chapter 1, n. 78.

[7] One other prescriptive account of the dispatch and reception of envoys is the short text *On Envoys* (Περὶ πρέσβεων) which forms chapter 43 of *The Anonymous Byzantine Treatise on Strategy* in *Three Byzantine Military Treatises*, ed. and trans. George T. Dennis (Corpus fontium historiae Byzantinae 25; Washington, DC, 1985), XLIII, but which also circulated independently; Douglas Lee and Jonathon Shepard, 'A Double Life: Placing the *Peri Presbeon*', *Byzantinoslavika* 52 (1991), 15–39 (I am grateful to A. D. Lee for drawing this article to my attention). Lee and Shepard have called the traditional mid-sixth-century date of the text into doubt; moreover, the identity and position of the author is quite unknown (Dennis, *Three Byzantine Military Treatises*, 3 for speculations). It is cited below, however, as comparative evidence for attitudes.

attributed in the text to the *patricius* Peter, who had twice served as envoy from Justinian to Theodahad on the eve of the war in Italy, and was subsequently appointed *magister officiorum* from 539 until his death in 565; twice while in this office, Peter undertook legations to the shah Chosroes. The data seem to have been excised from a history of the post of the *magister officiorum* which Peter wrote during his lengthy tenure.[8] This section of *De ceremoniis* includes two pairs of chapters detailing procedures for the reception, first, of envoys sent by a western imperial colleague who is to be recognised at Constantinople, and second, of envoys from the Persian shah.

Though the account of procedures for the reception of western imperial envoys is prescriptive, the text includes brief descriptions of two specific western embassies to Constantinople, from the emperor Anthemius in 467 and from the Gothic king of Italy Theodahad in 534.[9] The description of the embassy from Anthemius cites verbatim the proclamation of the eastern emperor Leo recognising Anthemius as his colleague. The embassy from Theodahad is one of the very few embassies attested by two different sources.[10] Throughout the prescriptive account, the *magister officiorum* is assigned responsibility for receiving the envoys and for arranging their audience; he ensures that the envoys are met (whether at their entry into Constantinople or earlier is not specified), and that lodgings and money for expenses are provided. The focus of the two chapters is

[8] Constantine VII Porphyrogenitus, *De cerimoniis* I, 84–95. I am most grateful to Ann Moffatt of the Australian National University for providing me with an extract of her forthcoming translation and commentary on *De cer.* for the series *Byzantina Australiensia.* On sources for Byzantine court ritual: M. McCormick, 'Analyzing Imperial Ceremonies', *Jahrbuch der Österreichischen Byzantinistik* 35 (1985), 1–20. On Constantine VII: I. Ševčenko, 'Re-reading Constantine Porphyrogenitus', in Shepard and Franklin, *Byzantine Diplomacy*, 167–95, with detailed review of earlier literature. On *De cer.*: J. B. Bury, 'The *Ceremonial Book* of Constantine Porphyrogenitus', *English Historical Review* 22 (1907), 209–27, 417–39; Albert Vogt (ed.), *Constantin Porphyrogénète: le livre des cérémonies, Commentaire*, vol. I only to date (Budé; Paris, 1935; repr. 1967), xv–xxxiii; Averil Cameron, 'The Construction of Court Ritual: The Byzantine *Book of Ceremonies*', in D. Cannadine and S. Price (eds.), *Rituals of Power: Power and Ceremonial in Traditional Societies* (Cambridge, 1987), 106–36; *Oxford Dictionary of Byzantium* I, 595–7; Franz Tinnefeld, 'Ceremonies for Foreign Ambassadors at the Court of Byzantium and their Political Background', *Byzantinische Forschungen* 19 (1993), 193–213. On *De cer.* I, 84–95: Bury, '*Ceremonial Book*', 212–13; Arthur E. R. Boak, 'The Master of the Offices in the Later Roman and Byzantine Empires', in Arthur E. R. Boak and James E. Dunlap, *Two Studies in Later Roman and Byzantine Administration* (London, 1924), 93–6; Vogt, *Commentaire* I, xxii–xxiii. Only *De cer.* I, 84–5 is explicitly attributed to Peter *patricius*.

On Peter *patricius* and his history of the *magister officiorum*: John Lydus, *De mag.* II, 25–6; Stein II, 723–9; *PLRE* III, 'Petrus 6', 994–9; P. Antonopoulos, 'The Less Obvious Ends of Byzantine Diplomacy', in Shepard and Franklin, *Byzantine Diplomacy*, 315–19. Ceremonial occasions described in *De cer.* I, 84–95 include: appointment of various palatine officers; recognition of a western colleague and reception of his envoys; reception of Persian envoys; and imperial proclamations.

[9] *De cer.* I, 87, naming Anthemius' envoy Heliocrates, and Theodahad's Liberius.

[10] Cf. Procopius, *Wars* V, 4.15–24.

the procedure for conducting the envoys into and from the imperial presence, and particularly the observation of precedence in rank. The rank of western palatine officials is to be equated with that of their eastern counterparts for the purpose of their disposition in audiences; no provision is made for envoys who are not court officials.

The western envoys meet first with the *magister officiorum*, who investigates the purpose of their mission; even at this initial meeting, the envoys are to be arranged by rank. When the envoys are later summoned to court, they are conducted by an official of equal rank (or a representative) to assemble in the *schola* of the *magister officiorum*, after which they greet other court officials and change into chlamyses.[11] When the silk curtain veiling the emperor is raised, the envoys enter the *consistorium*, perform obeisance, and state their purpose to the emperor.[12] Initially, the members of the legation form a discrete group, but after the emperor proclaims his acceptance of his western colleague, they disperse among other officials attending the consistory, according to their rank. This disposition, and the equation of rank, are visible affirmations of the unity of the empire: officials are servants of the one imperial authority, whether in Rome, Ravenna, or Constantinople.[13] On the occasion of Leo's recognition of Anthemius, both the current prefect of Constantinople and his predecessor declaimed panegyrics on both emperors, perhaps in their capacity as presidents of the Senate of Constantinople. The proceedings may be recorded – presumably this is the source of Leo's proclamation recognising Anthemius – and the emperor may choose to hold impromptu discussions with the envoys, though it is assumed that a formulaic exchange will be the norm. During a later audience, the western envoys again assemble with their eastern counterparts, and receive a donative determined by their rank. Upon their departure from the imperial *consistorium*, the *magister officiorum* receives letters from the emperor, and in turn formally presents them to the envoys for transmission to the western *augustus*.

That this procedural outline concentrates on observation of precedence in rank and on the role of each palatine official is a function of *De ceremoniis*

[11] For the palatine officials involved in different stages of the reception of envoys and their introduction into the imperial presence: Mary Whitby, 'On the Omission of a Ceremony in Mid-Sixth Century Constantinople: *candidati, curopalatus, silentarii, excubitores* and Others', *Historia* 36 (1987), 466, 468–83.

[12] For the curtain (*De cer.* I, 87, 89 (Reiske 394, 406)) cf. Fredegar, *Chron.* II, 62.

[13] In the early fifth century, too, palatine officials and military commanders passed conspicuously from the jurisdiction of one emperor to another at certain public occasions: Gillett, 'Olympiodorus of Thebes', 23 n. 100 (joint imperial appointment of senior officials at the time of the dynastic wedding of Valentinian III and Licinia Eudoxia in 437); *PLRE* II, 'Fl. Ardabur Aspar', 166 and Bagnall *et al.*, *Consuls LRE*, 403 (the eastern general Aspar as western consul for 434).

(and, possibly, of the original text of Peter *patricius*) as a practical handbook for court procedure. A more significant element of the description is the public and ceremonial nature of the reception of the embassy. One of the duties of the *magister officiorum* clearly is to carry out the substantive communications between the emperor and the envoys in private, to ensure that issues are decided before the actual audience. The procedure of the later formal audience, carried out before the full consistory, is ritual, not negotiation. The presentation of panegyrics, and the ritual for the presentation of letters, stresses the ceremonial nature of the formal audience.

The following two chapters of *De ceremoniis* detail the procedures for the reception of envoys from the Persian shah.[14] This section is considerably longer than the account of western imperial officials, for it details not only the stage-managing of the envoys' presence at court, but also the accommodation and care they are to receive from the time they cross into Roman territory, and provisions for an extended stay in Constantinople; the comparable details for the lodging of western envoys are perfunctory. Though the text is prescriptive, it is very likely that substantial parts describe the actual reception of specific Persian embassies at Constantinople. To illustrate the summons into the imperial presence given to the Persian envoy by the *magister officiorum*, the text reads: 'the *magistros* summons [the envoy] as follows, for example: "Let Iesdekos, the envoy of Chosroes the king of the Persians, and those who accompany him, be called." '[15] The Persian envoy is identified as Isdigousnas Zich, a senior palatine official at Ctesiphon who undertook three embassies to Constantinople between 547 and 557, dying *en route* to Constantinople a fourth time in 567. Peter *patricius* met Isdigousnas possibly as many as five times: in his capacity as *magister officiorum* from 539 to 565, he will have overseen the Persian noble's three visits to Constantinople; as an envoy himself twice to Chosroes in 550 and 561, Peter met Isdigousnas at Daras and probably at Ctesiphon. A number of senior palatine officials from Constantinople and Ctesiphon were extensively involved in embassies between the two powers in the time of Justinian; Peter and Isdigousnas are striking because their careers intertwined.[16] The account of *De ceremoniis* is perhaps a compilation of several visits to Constantinople by Isdigousnas and other Persian envoys.

[14] *De cer.* I, 89–90. [15] *De cer.* I, 89 (Reiske 405).

[16] On Isdigousnas (Yazd-Gushnasp): Stein II, 503–4 ('le représentant principal de son souverain dans toutes les négociations avec l'Empire'); N. Garsoïan, 'Byzantium and the Sasanians', in *The Cambridge History of Iran* III.1 (Cambridge, 1983), 574; *PLRE* III, 'Isdigousnas Zich', 722–3 (not citing *De cer.*); Tinnefeld, 'Ceremonies for Foreign Ambassadors', 194–5 (reading *De cers.* I, 89–90 as a description exclusively of Isdigousnas' visit of 547/8, but the provision in the text of alternative procedures, i.e. arrangements for when the emperor is in Chalcedon (*De cer.* I, 89 (Reiske 403)), indicates that the author is drawing on observations of several occasions).

There are several procedural differences between the receptions of the western imperial and Persian legations. Though similarities between the functions of palatine officials in Ctesiphon and Constantinople were observed by contemporaries, Persian envoys were not equated with Roman counterparts; consequently, expressions of honour through the selection of officials to greet the envoys were a matter for the judgement of the *magister officiorum*; and at court, the Persian envoys were conducted by *chartularii* of the *scrinium barbarorum*, part of the *officium* of the *magister*. When Persian and other 'barbarian' embassies were received, an armed guard was provided in the consistorium by the palatine forces known as the *candidati*; no guard was present for the reception of western imperial envoys.[17] It was expected that the envoy would present gifts to the emperor from both the shah and himself; procedures for a ritualised exchange of gifts, including an assessment of the worth of the Persian items, are given. Essential elements, however, were the same as for the reception of western imperial envoys: the *magister officiorum* acted as host, intermediatory, and perhaps substantive negotiator with the envoy, as well as stage-manager of the envoy's imperial audiences, which took place in the full *consistorium*.

The types of situations described in these two sections of *De ceremoniis* are very specific. There is no outline of procedures for the reception of western imperial legates who are not palatine officials, or whose mission concerns issues other than recogition of a new emperor. Nor is there provision for representatives of the Roman Senate, of the see of Rome, of rulers of the kingdoms in the former Roman West, of barbarian leaders beyond imperial boundaries, or of the constant flow of eastern provincial and municipal embassies to court. Peter *patricius*, during his tenure

Elements of *De cer.* I, 89 which may refer to Isdigousnas' embassies: provisions to prevent a Persian annexation of Daras under cover of a Persian embassy (*De cer.* I, 89 (Reiske 399); cf. Procopius, *Wars* II, 28.31–44, concerning the embassy of 547/8; Tinnefeld, 'Ceremonies for Foreign Ambassadors', 207–8); the provision of travelling expenses for 206 days (*De cer.* I, 89 (Reiske 400); cf. the length of Isdigousnas' stays in Constantinople in 547/8 and 550/1: Procopius, *Wars* II, 28.31–44 (ten months), VIII, 11.4–10, 17.9 (about a year)).

Other Constantinopolitan officials extensively involved in embassies and negotiations with Persia: *PLRE* II, 'Rufinus 13', 954–7; *PLRE* III, 'Alexander 1', 41–2; 'Hermogenes 1', 590–3. Persian officials: Mebodes, successor to Isdigousnas (Menander Protector, *Fr.*, 9.3; *PLRE* III 'Mebodes 2', 868–70); other Persian envoys are listed at *PLRE* III, 1538–9.

[17] Similarities of palatine offices: Menander Protector, *Fr.*, 6.1 *bis* (Blockley, 55, 65) with *PLRE* III, 722: Isdigousnas as *cubicularius* or *praepositus sacri cubiculi*; Menander Protector, *Fr.*, 23.9 (Blockley, 209–11): Persian equivalents to *a secretis* and *magister officiorum* (the *astabadh*; A. Christensen, *L'Iran sous les Sassanides*, 2nd edn (Copenhagen, 1944), 136, 352, 521); cf. Procopius, *Wars* I, 5.4: Persian *chanaranges* equivalent to Roman *strategos*; cf. 6.18, 11.25; I, 11.26: equivalent to *magister officiorum*. On Sassanian court officials: *ibid.*, 132–6; V. G. Lakonin, 'Political, Social and Administrative Institutions', in *Cambridge History of Iran* III.2, 681–746, esp. 709–13.

Persons assigned to honour and lead Persian envoys: *De cer.* I, 89. *Candidati*: *De cer.* I, 87, 89; Whitby, 'On the Omission', 466, 483.

as *magister officiorum*, would have overseen legations from each of these provenances. The two specific types of diplomatic receptions selected for inclusion in *De ceremoniis* by its compilers possibly were seen as having germane parallels to their own time, and potentially useful for adaption to current needs.[18] The passages, however, give brief indications of arrangements for other types of embassies. The account of the reception of western imperial envoys mentions in passing that they are exempt from being summoned into the imperial presence within the consistory, as other envoys are, and that armed guards flank the emperor when barbarian envoys are received; both details appear in the account of Persian envoys.[19] The reference to the embassy sent from Theodahad in 534, which was led by the *patricius* and praetorian prefect of Gaul Liberius and which concerned the imminent hostilities between Constantinople and Ravenna, may suggest that the legation was treated as if it had been dispatched by an imperial colleague; at any rate, Liberius' rank was recognised and equated with the eastern prefecture.[20]

Pope Hormisdas, Indiculi

The second prescriptive account of the reception of envoys at Constantinople consists of two sets of instructions, *indiculi*, written by Pope Hormisdas: the first to the legates (including his friend Ennodius of Pavia) he sent to the emperor Anastasius in August 515, the second to members of a later embassy, also to Anastasius, dispatched in January 519. Both embassies were sent in an endeavour to resolve the Acacian schism.[21] The legations were provided with a letter to present to the emperor on

[18] Cf. McCormick, 'Analyzing Imperial Ceremonies', 6.

[19] Exemptions of western imperial legates from summons and armed guards: *De cer.* I, 87 (Reiske 394), cf. I, 89 (Reiske 404–5). Armed guards: above, n. 17; in later Byzantine practice: cf. D. C. Smythe, 'Why Do Barbarians Stand Round the Emperor at Diplomatic Receptions?', in Shepard and Franklin, *Byzantine Diplomacy*, 305–12.

[20] *De cer.* I, 87 (Reiske 396). Unlike the reference to the embassies of Isdigousnas, this detail cannot reflect the personal observation of Peter *patricius* (not appointed *magister officiorum* until 539) who was not in Constantinople at the time of Liberius' arrival there, but *en route* to Theodahad in Ravenna; Procopius, *Wars* V, 4.17–25 (Peter and Liberius met during their journeys). During this embassy, Liberius appears to have deserted Theodahad; he remained in the East during the course of the war in Italy, and was appointed to offices by Justinian; *PLRE* II, 'Petrus Marcellinus Felix Liberius 3', 679–70. It is possible that the treatment of Liberius' embassy may reflect Justinian's overtures for support to a leading representative of the Italian administration, rather than conventional treatment of representatives of the Ostrogothic regime; the source, however, does not indicate that Liberius' treatment was unconventional.

[21] *Collectio Avellana*, 116 (with *Collectio Avellana*, 115, 116a, 116b); 158 (= Hormisdas, *Indiculi* of 515, 519). A good account of the place of these embassies in the complex negotiations between Anastasius and Hormisdas is J. P. Kirsch, 'Hormisdas', *Catholic Encyclopaedia*, 1st edn, VII (New York, 1910), 470–1. Useful summaries of the *indiculi* in *PCBE* II, 'Magnus Felix Ennodius', 626 (515), 'Iohannes 27', 1076 (519).

each occasion; Hormisdas' instructions outlined how the envoys were to conduct themselves in the East before their imperial audience and how they should argue their case during it.

The *Indiculus* of 515 is longer and more detailed than that of 519, for two reasons. First, in 515, Hormisdas expected his legates to insinuate a delicate political threat to the emperor. At the time of the embassy, Anastasius' hold on imperial power was threatened by his rebellious *magister utriusque militiae* Vitalian, who played on orthodox sentiment against Anastasius' sympathy for Monophysitism. Hormisdas hoped to exploit Anastasius' insecurity. In addition to the letter to Anastasius which he provided for his legation, he also wrote a second letter to Vitalian himself. Hormisdas' instructions in the *Indiculus* of 515, to keep this second letter secret until they had been ushered into the imperial presence and given permission to speak, occupy a good part of the document.[22] The second factor which extends the length of the *Indiculus* of 515 is the protracted and detailed outline of a hypothetical debate between the emperor and the envoys during their audience.[23] The later *Indiculus* also includes instructions as to how the legates should endeavour to conduct their interview, but it is far less circumstantial.[24]

The two sets of instructions outline a similar course of events. Hormisdas anticipates that his legations will be met by eastern bishops. The envoys are to join in communion with welcoming bishops, and accept their *libelli* of faith should they be offered; the Greek bishops may even wish to accompany the Roman envoys. The legates may also accept the customary elements of *hospitalitas*, accommodation and, if convenient, transport; to decline would appear hostile and militate against their claim to be pursuing church unity. The envoys are, however, very strictly instructed to decline with grace any offers of food or invitations to *convivia*.[25] Once in Constantinople, Hormisdas expects the legation to be assigned accommodation (*mansio*) by the emperor. The emperor will send unspecified persons to their lodgings, but Hormisdas warns the envoys not to receive any other guests before their audience. In both sets of instructions, much of Hormisdas' advice to his legates concerns informal means of negotiation, hospitality, and other contacts outside the court and *consistorium*, not the formal protocol of official receptions described by *De ceremoniis*; Hormisdas does not even specify which court official (the *magister officiorum*) will visit the envoys at their lodgings. The social restrictions

22 *Collectio Avellana*, 116.1–6.

23 *Collectio Avellana*, 116.7–27.

24 *Collectio Avellana*, 158.5–11.

25 *Collectio Avellana*, 116.1–3, 158.1–2. Invitations by eastern bishops are to be declined *blanda excusatione*; cf. Ennodius, *Vita Epiphani*, 92 (Epiphanius excuses himself from Euric's *convivium*).

he places on his envoys are safeguards against the substance of their purpose becoming known in advance of the formal imperial reception.[26] After their audience, the legates may receive at their lodgings any who are known to support the papal case; such visitors are to be exploited to advance the embassy's aims.[27]

The lengthy account of the envoys' audience and hypothetical dialogue with Anastasius in the *Indiculus* of 515 is difficult to square with the procedure of *De ceremoniis*. Hormisdas envisages the envoys delivering his letter to the emperor without its contents having been previously revealed. Should the emperor ask them what the letter concerns during their audience, they are to parry until he has read it. Only after he has done so are they to reveal that they possess a similar letter to be delivered to Vitalian, thus bluntly flagging Hormisdas' willingness to treat with the rebel; the envoys are to refuse the expected demand to see the second letter. In the following postulated debate, Anastasius seeks to defend the orthodoxy of himself and the eastern churches with arguments for which Hormisdas provides crushing responses.[28] Read as a set of practical instructions, the document seems disingenuous in its failure to anticipate any process of filtering the letters and arguments of embassies well before the legates are permitted into the presence of the emperor and his consistory, and in its depiction of an extended, contrary interview. Conventionally, letters were delivered sealed to the emperor or other recipient, as Hormisdas instructs his envoys to insist.[29] Yet even without the explicit evidence of *De ceremoniis* for the role of the *magister officiorum* in discussing the matters of embassies prior to the granting of an imperial audience, it is difficult to imagine any ruler, let alone one with the palace resources of the eastern emperor, engaging in open and unpremeditated debate with the representatives of a party known to be quarrelsome.[30] Hormisdas would be hopeful at best to think that dialogue between his legates and the emperor would follow the tortuous path he outlines, and that the emperor would accept the repeated rebuffs Hormisdas proposes. More realistic information on Constantinopolitan court procedures was readily available to the bishop of Rome, from the frequent contact between East and West over the Acacian schism. The scenario drawn by Hormisdas, of his bishops resolutely denying the emperor's demands and

[26] For receptions by local clergy as opportunity for the envoy's purpose to be revealed in advance: cf. Ennodius, *Vita Epiphani*, 151 (bishop Rusticius of Lyons welcomes, questions, and advises Epiphanius).

[27] *Collectio Avellana*, 116.4, 158.3.

[28] *Collectio Avellana*, 116.5–9 (handing over of letter; Vitalian), 10–27 (debate).

[29] Cf. *CTh* XII, 12.5, Procopius, *Wars* V, 7.21, *De cer.* I, 89 (Reiske 406).

[30] See Procopius, *Wars* V, 7.13–25 for an instance of an impromptu royal audience backfiring.

outwitting him with rhetorical skill and theological certitude, recalls the dramatic descriptions of envoys in the saints' *Vitae* and secular eulogies discussed in previous chapters, rather than the procedural formulae of *De ceremoniis*. Hormisdas' instructions may have been intended more as an exhortation to his envoys than a practical guide to what could be expected at the eastern imperial court.

DESCRIPTIVE ACCOUNTS: PERSONNEL AND PROTOCOL

There is no prescriptive account equivalent to *De ceremoniis* of the procedures for the reception of envoys at any western court, whether of the emperors, senior magistrates, kings, or bishops, or at provincial or town councils. A composite picture can be pieced together from descriptions in narrative sources, but only as a very rough approximation. Unlike the work of Constantine VII and perhaps Peter *patricius*, none of the sources which describe the dispatch or reception of embassies in the West professes to be prescriptive or even accurately descriptive. The protocol they intermittently report, assuming it to be chronologically accurate for the narrative setting and not anachronistic retrojection or dramatic artifice, need not apply to different courts or different times other than those of the scene at hand. Like other late antique secular protocols and ceremonial, the procedures described below represent attested practices from a range of options; conventions should not be taken as binding.[31] Several of the authors of the works most fruitful for descriptions of embassies had experience as legates themselves; in addition to Hydatius and Ennodius, this includes Gregory of Tours, who provides many useful comparanda for procedures in the fifth and early sixth centuries. Ennodius in particular, who gives the most circumstantial descriptions of the dispatch, reception, and return of embassies, has good claims to be a well-informed witness: he had personal experience of undertaking embassies to the court of Gundobad and perhaps Theoderic by the time he wrote the *Vita Epiphani*; he was acquainted with his subject during the time Epiphanius undertook his final three journeys; and he was close to many other individuals who undertook palatine, provincial, or ecclesiastical embassies. None the less, data drawn from *Vita Epiphani* must be used with caveats because of the literary nature of the work.[32]

[31] Cf. McCormick, 'Analyzing Imperial Ceremonies', esp. 2 (citing Peter *patricius*).

[32] There are rich descriptive sources for the conduct of embassies between the eastern imperial court and other powers, particularly Persia, thanks in part to the selections of the excerptors of Constantine VII (e.g. Priscus, *Fr.*, 11; Menander Protector, *Fr.*, 6.1), but also Procopius, *Wars*; Agathias, *Hist.*; Malalas, *Chron.* XVIII (Roger Scott, 'Diplomacy in the Sixth Century: The Evidence of John Malalas', in Shepard and Franklin, *Byzantine Diplomacy*, 159–65); these are drawn on below as comparanda.

Selection

The selection of envoys was a regular function of municipal and provincial bodies. Cities, assemblies, and other provincial bodies generally chose legates from among the ranks of their own nobles, though a professional orator, already familiar with the court to be approached, could be employed.[33] Under the empire, completion of a provincial embassy to court was often rewarded with specific immunities or privileges. The duty could also be exploited for patronage relations at the local level. The desirability of undertaking legations for social and possibly pecuniary rewards could therefore lead to fierce competition and even fraud.[34] Eulogistic sources which portray their subjects being petitioned by peers to undertake embassies, rather than actively seeking nomination, are somewhat sycophantic. Election to the episcopate was clearly no bar to undertaking legations on secular issues. Ennodius portrays Epiphanius comfortable among other Ligurian nobles; the Senate of Rome, which regularly chose from among its own senior members for legates to the western or eastern imperial courts or that of their successors in Ravenna, also on occasion selected bishops as envoys.[35] The increasing role of bishops from the late fifth century, as the church became the repository of rhetorical as well as other education, is to be expected.[36] None the less, the impression given by hagiographical sources, that bishops were preferred by provincial assemblies and by courts, is a function of the genre's exclusive focus on the honour of its subject. It is belied by references to provincial envoys by Hydatius and Sidonius which suggest that lay nobility outnumbered bishops until the 470s at least.[37] Similarly, nobles and professional rhetors, not clergy, appear as provincial envoys to the court of Theoderic in non-ecclesiastical sources.[38] As leading figures within the

[33] Selection from local nobles: e.g. Sid. Ap., *Ep.* v, 20. Use of professional orator: e.g. Arator, a Ligurian educated at Milan and Ravenna and former *advocatus*, served as envoy to Theoderic on behalf of the province of Dalmatia; Cass., *Variae* VIII, 12.3, 7.

[34] Privileges of undertaking embassies to imperial court: *CTh* VI, 22.1.2; VIII, 5.23; XII, 1.25, 36. Expectation of rewards: e.g. Sid. Ap., *Ep.* V, 20.2; Procopius, *Wars* II, 2.4; VII, 16.29 (debate on relative value of reward for envoy by honour from his host or from his homeland). Fraud: *CTh* XII, 12.15.

[35] Senate and bishops: Pope Innocent I, to Honorius (Zosimos V, 45.5); Cass., *Variae* X, 13.1 (*episcopi*); cf. Procopius, *Wars* VII, 16.4–32 (the deacon Pelagius, later pope).

[36] G. A. Kennedy, *Classical Rhetoric and Its Christian and Secular Tradition from Ancient to Modern Times* (Chapel Hill, 1980), 180–1; M. Heinzelmann, '*Studia sanctorum*: éducation, milieux d'instruction et valeurs éducatives dans l'hagiographie en Gaule jusqu'à la fin de l'époque Mérovingienne', *Haut Moyen-Age: culture, éducation et société* (Nanterre, 1990), 105–38.

[37] Hyd., cc. 219, 239 [215, 235] (the *vir nobilis* Palogorius, Opilio); cf. 251 [245] (the *praesens cives* Lusidius sent by Remismund to Anthemius). Sid. Ap.: *Carm.* VII, 207–14, 316–56 (Avitus); *Epp.* I, 5, 9 (Sidonius); V, 20 (Pastor); VII, 9.19 (Simplicius); VII, 12.3 (Tonantius Ferreolus).

[38] I.e. the lay advocate Arator (for Dalmatia) and Parthenius (presumably for Provence); *PLRE* II, 126–7, 833. Cf. Liebeschuetz, *Decline and Fall of the Roman City*, 154–7.

local political structures of both their provincial community and their own church, bishops could benefit from the prestige attached to completing an embassy, especially to the imperial court; but they might also well be wary of the potential for domestic intrigue developing during any prolonged absence.[39]

Palatine embassies comprised a wider range of representatives. Bishops were used as envoys by courts, as by provincial bodies. In selecting clergy for envoys, courts could choose to take into consideration the religious heterodoxy prevalent throughout the West, by choosing priests adhering to the confession, Nicene or Arian, of the recipient court.[40] In the envoy's delivery, a shared creed between the principal and recipient could be exploited in hope of winning favour.[41] Yet creed was not always a determining factor in the selection of envoys: the Arian Theoderic of Italy chose to send to his co-religionist Gundobad the Nicene Epiphanius of Pavia.[42] In addition to the bishops' own eloquence or the respect that their personal piety might command, rulers who dispatched clergy could hope to exploit the status of their office; on rare occasions, this included the bishops of Rome. Even such a senior dignitary was no guarantee of success: three times, the Ostrogothic kings of Italy sent senior clergy of Rome, two popes and one deacon who later also became pope, to Justinian, each time in vain.[43] Though Justinian warmly received Pope Agapitus, dispatched by Theodahad in 536 in the hope of forestalling the approaching naval forces, 'the emperor, not wishing to recall the army already dispatched to Italy because of the great expense to the imperial fisc, did not wish to hear the supplications of the Pope. But Agapitus

[39] Gorce, *Les Voyages, l'hospitalité, et le port des lettres dans le monde Chrétien des IVe et Ve siècles*, 35–40.

[40] Nicene to Arian: e.g. Theodosius II sends the Arian priest Bleda to Geiseric (Priscus, *Fr.*, 31.1). Arian to Nicene: Alaric I sends bishops from various Italian cities which he had captured to Honorius (Zosimos v, 50.2); Theoderic I of Toulouse sends Orientius to Aetius (*Vita Orientii*, 3); Theoderic of Italy and Theodahad send popes John I and Agapitus to Constantinople (*Liber pont.*, 55, 59); possibly Hyd., c. 101 [92]: the Suevic king Hermeric sends Bishop Symphosius *ad comitatum*. Jordanes, *Get.*, 234: Sueves send *locorum sacerdotes* to the Goths of Toulouse; it is not clear whether these are Arian or Nicene.

[41] E.g. Procopius, *Wars* v, 4.9 (Justinian to Frankish kings); vii, 34.24 (Lombards to Justinian); Gregory of Tours, *Hist.* ix, 16, 25: when the newly proselytised king of the Goths in Spain, Reccared, approaches the Frankish kings Guntram and Childebert II for peace and a marriage alliance *in fide se . . . adserebat unum* (Gothic Arianism had not precluded earlier Frankish–Gothic marriage alliances).

Avitus of Vienne, *Ep.*, 45 (MGH AA 6.2), encourages Clovis to use his legations to other peoples as opportunities for proselytism.

[42] Ennodius, *Vita Epiphani*, 136–77.

[43] John I, sent by Theoderic (Marcellinus, *Chron.*, s.a. 525; *Anon. Val. pars post.*, 15.88–93; *Liber pont.*, 55); Agapitus, sent by Theodahad (*Liber pont.*, 59; Liberatus of Carthage, *Breviarium causae Nestorianorum et Eutychianorum* (*PL* 68), 21); the deacon Pelagius, a former papal *apocrisiarius* to the imperial court, sent by Totila (Procopius, *Wars* vii, 21.18–25). Cf. Leo I, attached to the embassy of Valentinian III to Attila (Prosper, *Chron.*, 1367).

carried out the embassy of Christ, as he was His servant', by bringing about the excommunication of the Patriarch of Constantinople, Anthimus.[44] Perhaps the most important reason for the use of bishops as envoys was to serve as oath-takers. At the conclusion of successful negotiations, oaths were sworn between the recipient of the embassy and the envoys, to whom their principal had delegated this right; the office of bishop constituted a trustworthy proxy.[45] As with provincial embassies, ecclesiastical sources give the misleading impression that clergy dominated palatine legations; the random prosopographical evidence suggests that this is not true.[46]

Like provincial bodies too, rulers employed leading private citizens as their envoys. This was particularly the case with rulers of Italy, both emperors and kings, who employed members of the Roman Senate in their intercourse with the eastern imperial court; the imperial court of Constantinople also employed members of the eastern Senate.[47] There

[44] Liberatus of Carthage, *Breviarium*, 21: *Imperator autem pro multis fisci expensis ab Italia destinatum exercitum avertere nolens, supplicationes papae noluit audire. At ille, quod suum fuit, Christi legatione fungebatur.*

[45] Ennodius, *Vita Epiphani*, 72, 91; *Ep. Austr.*, 42 (the emperor Maurice to the Frankish king Childebert II): *in scriptis pollicita atque per sacerdotis firmata et terribilibus iuramentis roborata.*

[46] *Contra* Ennodius, *Vita Epiphani*, 136. Several times, Gregory of Tours mentions that an embassy consists of both bishops and leading officials or nobles, but names only the former (*Hist.* VI, 3; VI, 31; X, 19: Egidius of Rheims (but cf. VII, 14: Egidius' companions are named, probably to implicate him in the treason of which he is ultimately accused; one of his companions is the *dux* and trouble-maker Guntram Boso, see *PLRE* III, 571–4); IX, 18: Namatius of Orléans, Bertram of Le Mans, *cum comitibus et aliis viris magnificis*; IX, 38: [*legati*] *inter quos episcopi erant*). For other sixth- and seventh-century Gallic embassies combining bishops and palatine officials: *Ep. Austr.*, 25–39 (the bishop Ennodius, the *spatharius* Grippo, the *cubicularius* Radan, and the *notarius* Eusebius), 42 (the bishop Iocundus and the *cubicularius* Chotro); Fredegar, *Chron.* IV, 30 (bishop Aridius of Lyons, Rocco, and the *comestabuli* Eborinus; *c.* 607), 85 (Bishop Chanibert of Cologne and the *maior domus* Pippin; a. 641).

Named bishops who undertake embassies in Gregory of Tours include: *Hist.* V, 40: Elafius of Châlons-sur-Marne; V, 26, 29, 40: Eunius of Vannes; VI, 3: Leudovald of Bayeax; IX, 20: Gregory himself, and Felix, possibly bishop of Châlons-sur-Marne, cf. IX, 41 (signature list) and *PLRE* III, 'Felix 7', 482. Abbots: VII, 30: abbot of Cahors and another *clericus*; X, 31 § 17: Gunthar, abbot of St Venantius. Cf. M. Weidemann, *Kulturgeschichte der Merowingerzeit nach den Werken Gregors von Tours* (Mainz 1982), I, 133–4.

For secular envoys in Gregory of Tours, see below, n. 49.

[47] Western emperors: e.g. Rufius Antonius Agrypnius Volusianus, sent by Valentinian III to Theodosius II concerning arrangements for the dynastic wedding of 437 (*Vita Melania* II, 19–24); Anicius Olybrius was possibly sent by Valentinian III to Constantinople; he was certainly sent by the emperor Leo I to Geiseric (Malalas, *Chron.* XIV, 45; *Chron. Pasch.*, s.a. 464); Gennadius Avienus, sent by Valentinian III to Attila (Prosper, *Chron.*, 1368); the deposed emperor Romulus sends envoys from the Senate on behalf of Odoacer to Zeno (Malchus, *Fr.*, 14; this seems to be a separate embassy from the one sent by Odoacer himself, to which Zeno gives a separate reply, cf. Candidus, *Fr.*, 1: another embassy from Odoacer to Zeno). Italian kings: Theoderic: the *caput senatus* Fl. Rufius Postumius Festus, twice, in 490 and *c.* 497 (*PLRE* II, 467–9); the *viri inlustris* Fl. Anicius Probus Faustus Niger and Iranaeus (*PLRE* II, 454–5, 625), possibly the *caput senatus* Symmachus (*PLRE* II, 1045); the former prefect of Rome and *patricius* Fl. Agapitus (Cass.,

are, however, also examples of kings in the former provinces employing local nobles.[48]

Courts, however, could draw on resources not available to provincial authorities. Almost any palatine functionary could be dispatched.[49] At least five factors, none of which operated in isolation, determined the selection of palatine officials as legates.[50] The rank attached to the official's post, or to him personally, could signify the degree of respect being paid to the recipient; *patricii* and individuals of consular rank were used and indeed demanded in the most important missions, and many *viri inlustris* are attested as envoys; some were elevated to high ranks specifically in preparation for the undertaking of embassies.[51] The proximity to the emperor and his decision-making process conveyed by membership of the *consistorium* made *notarii* frequent envoys. Certain officials were involved in matters closely associated with communication with other parties, and so were logically chosen to undertake embassies as a consequence of their involvement; this included the *magister officiorum* and

Variae II, 6); possibly the *vir clarissimus* Renatus (*PLRE* II, 939); Theodorus, Inportunus, Agapitus, and Fl. Agapitus (*PLRE* II, 30, 32, 592, 1098). Theodahad: Liberius, Opilio, and other senators (Procopius, *Wars* V, 4.15). See above, chapter 5, nn. 26, 36–7. Eastern emperor: Procopius, *Wars* VI, 29.1–5; VIII, 24.11–30; cf. VIII, 25.7–10: an alliance with the Lombards is signed by Justinian and twelve members of the Senate of Constantinople.

48 Hyd., c. 251 [245]: the Suevic king Remismund sends the *praesens cives* Lusidius to Anthemius.

49 To the evidence in chapter 5 for the court of Theoderic in Italy, add officers of the courts of sixth- and seventh-century Merovingian Gaul and Visigothic Spain, indicated by actual post or the rank of *vir inlustris*. For Gaul: Gregory of Tours, *Hist.* III, 33 (Secundinus); X, 2 (Evantius, *rector Provinciae*; Grippo, *spatharius*, cf. *Ep. Austr.*, 25, 43); *Ep. Austr.* 25 (Radan, *cubicularius*; Eusebius, *notarius*, cf. *PLRE* III, 'Eusebius 8', 468); 42 (Chotro, *cubicularius*); 43 (Babo, *vir inlustris*); *Epistolae Arelatenses genuinae* (MGH Epp. 3), 38 (Modericus, *vir inlustris*, a. 538), 48, 54 (Rufinus, *vir inlustris*, aa. 556, 557); Fredegar, *Chron.* IV, 30 (*comestabuli* Eborinus); Marculf, *Formulae* (MGH Legum section 5: Formulae), I, 9, 11 (envoys in formulae are assumed to be *viri inlustris*); Ganshof, 'Merowingisches Gesandschaftswesen', 171. For Spain: Gregory of Tours, *Hist.* V, 43 (Agila, *vir inlustris*, cf. *PLRE* III, 'Agila 2', 27); *Epistolae Wisigoticae* (MGH Epp. 3), 13 (Guldrimirus and Tatila, *viri inlustris*, *c.* 610–12; Tatila is possibly the same as the envoy Totila, *ibid.*, 9 lemma).

Other envoys whose positions are not specified may also have been palatine staff. For Gaul: e.g. Gregory of Tours, *Hist.* IV, 40 (Warmarius *Francus*; Firminus *Arvernus*); V, 36 (Heraclius); VI, 18 (Ansovald, a *prior* of Chilperic; Domegisel, cf. VII, 7); VII, 14 (Sigivald); VIII, 13 (Felix); VIII, 44, IX, 13 (Baddo, *senior* of an embassy from Fredegund); IX, 28 (Ebregisel); *Ep. Austr.*, 18 (Iohannis; Missurius). For Spain: Gregory of Tours, *Hist.* VI, 40 (Oppila). Ganshof, *Middle Ages*, 38–9; Weidemann, *Kultergeschichte*, I, 103–6.

50 *On Envoys* in Lee and Shepard, '*Peri Presbeon*', 30 = *Anon. Byz. Treatise on Strategy* XLIII, lists the selection criteria of envoys as piety, a lack of criminal convictions, prudence, and a willingness to risk their safety for the public good. The illustration of these qualities with classical exempla underscores the literary nature of this list, though the point about convictions perhaps relates to the need for status.

51 Demand: e.g. Attila's demand in 448 for envoys of consular rank; Priscus, *Fr.*, 11.1, 11.2, 13.1 (*Fr. Class. Hist.*, 234, 247, 283); Croke, 'Anatolius and Nomus', 165–6. Elevation: Malchus, *Fr.*, 5, 20 (*Fr. Class. Hist.*, 411, 439); R. Mathisen, 'Patricians as Diplomats', 34–49; Elton, *Warfare in Roman Europe*, 182–3 n. 15.

members of his office, and the *quaestor*, whose duties involved the oversight of visiting envoys and drafting of diplomatic correspondence as well as counsel to the ruler.[52] The individual's talents in oratory might particularly recommend him.[53] Finally, there is a striking number of individuals who undertook multiple palatine embassies, recommended apparently by their previous experience in undertaking legations, whether to the same party or another.[54] As the writings of Cassiodorus and Senarius demonstrate, palatine officials drew status and personal gain from successful completion of embassies.[55] It was not uncommon for palatine legates to be charged with more than one task, negotiating ecclesiastical issues for an episcopal court while conducting political affairs with the emperor or king to whom they had been sent.[56]

Besides civilian magistrates, military commanders, too, could serve as envoys. Hydatius is the only fifth-century source to record as envoys

[52] Members of the office of the *magister officiorum*. e.g. Malalas, *Chron.* XVIII, 57 (Justinian dispatches a *magistrianus* to the Gothic king Athalaric).

[53] Lee, *Information and Frontiers*, 45 and n. 142. Oratorical skill was still an important criterion for selection of envoys in late sixth-century Merovingian Gaul: e.g. Gregory of Tours, *Hist.* III, 33 (Secundinus, *sapiens et retoricis inbutus litteris*), cf. V, 43 (Gregory derides an envoy from the Gothic king Leuvigild as *virum nulli ingenii aut dispositiones ratione conperitum*).

[54] E.g. Trygetius twice, from Valentinian III to Geiseric 435 and Attila 452 (Prosper, *Chron.*, 1321, 1367); Censorius three times, from Aetius to the Sueves in Gallaecia (above, chapter 1, Table 1, nos. 3, 5, 6); Consentius *quotiens*, from Valentinian III to Theodosius II (Sid. Ap., *Carm.* XXIII, 228–62); Faustus Niger twice, from Theoderic to Zeno and Anastasius (above, n. 47); Phylarchus twice, from Leo to the renegade *magister utriusque militiae* Marcellinus of Dalmatia and then to Geiseric in 462/3, and to Geiseric again in 467 (Priscus, *Fr.*, 39.1, 52; *Fr. Class. Hist.*, 343, 361); Senarius twenty-five times, including twice to 'the East' and twice to 'the West' in one year, from Theoderic (Senarius, *Epitaph*, lines 9–13); Alexander three times and Peter *patricius* four times, from Justinian to the Persians and the Ostrogoths (*PLRE* III, 41–2, 996–7), the deacon Pelagius, by Pope Vigilius to Justinian, by the city of Rome to Totila three times, and by Totila to Justinian (Procopius, *Wars* VII, 16.4–32; 20.23–5; 21.17, 18–25); Secundinus *plerimque legationem*, from the Frankish king Theudebert I to Justinian (Gregory of Tours, *Hist.* III, 33); Bishop Egidius of Rheims three times, from Childebert II (Gregory of Tours, *Hist.* VI, 3, 31; VII, 14); Ebregisel *saepe*, for Frankish rulers to Visigothic Spain (Gregory of Tours, *Hist.* IX, 28); the abbot Gunthar *saepe*, between Frankish kings (Gregory of Tours, *Hist.* X, 31 § 17); the *spatharius* Grippo, from Childebert II to the emperor Maurice (*Ep. Austr.*, 25–39, 43–7; Gregory of Tours, *Hist.* X, 2, 4; see Paul Goubert, *Byzance avant l'Islam* II.1: *Byzance et les Francs* (Paris, 1956), 165 73). For eastern examples, see Lee, *Information and Frontiers*, 45–7 (emphasising the increase throughout the fourth to sixth centuries in evidence for individuals repeating embassies). For a later period, cf. McCormick, *Origins of the European Economy*, 175–81, 229–32.

[55] So too in late sixth-century Gaul: e.g. Secundinus, who undertook many embassies for the Frankish king Theudebert, *ob hoc iactantia sumpserat et nonnulla contra rationem exercebat* (Gregory of Tours, *Hist.* III, 33).

[56] E.g. on the Acacian schism: the *vir inlustris* Latinus and *vir spectabilis* Medusius, 476 (*Collectio Avellana*, 57); the western *magister officiorum* Andromachus, *c.* 489 (*PLRE* II, 89); the *patricius* Fl. Rufius Postumius Festus, *c.* 497 (*Collectio Avellana*, 102); the eastern *magister scrinii memoriae* Gratus, in 518 (*PLRE* II, 519; Moorhead, *Theoderic*, 116 n. 62). On the Three Chapters controversy: an unnamed *legatus* from a royal court in Gaul (either Childebert I, Chlothar I, or Theudebald; *PLRE* III suggests the latter: 'Leudardus', 786) (*Epistolae aevi Merowingici collectae* (MGH Epp. 3) 4).

western generals, either imperial or Gothic; some are dispatched by the senior general in the field, notably Aetius, others by their imperial or royal court.[57] Eastern generals appear as envoys in the classicising historians, and the Merovingian kings of late sixth-century Gaul also dispatched *duces* and military *comites* on embassies.[58] The western kings could also employ a further class of representative: their own royal heirs. In 515/16, the Burgundian king Gundobad sent his son Sigismund, *patricius* and *rex*, to the emperor Anastasius in Constantinople *officio legationis*. The aim of the journey was perhaps to secure imperial support for Sigismund to succeed his father in ruling southern Gaul; the unspecified official title conferred on Sigismund in Constantinople may have been the token of recognition. Gundobad had earlier employed Sigismund on domestic legations.[59]

The commissioning of provincial and palatine embassies differed significantly. Provincial embassies were appointed publicly, at municipal or other councils, where the matter of the legation was discussed and its members elected.[60] Palatine embassies presumably could arise from discussions in the *consistorium*, and could be dispatched with attendant publicity if it suited the court's purposes. The only accounts of the commissioning of legations dispatched by rulers, however, stress the secrecy

[57] Chapter 2, Table 2, nos. 3, 5, 6 (the *comes* Censorius and Fretimund, dispatched by the *magister utriusque militiae* Aetius); 7 (the *comes Hispaniarum* Mansuetus and the *comes* Fronto; whether they were sent by the imperial court or by Aetius is unclear); 10 (the *comes* Fronto, sent by the emperor Avitus in Rome); 16 (envoys sent by the *magister utriusque militiae* Nepotian and the *comes* Suneric); 25 (the general Cyrila sent by Theoderic II). Avitus as *magister utriusque militiae* approached the Goths in 455, allegedly as *legatus*; Sid. Ap., *Carm.* VII, 402.

[58] For the East: Blockley, *East Roman Foreign Policy*, 134 and 239 n. 27. Gaul: Gregory of Tours, *Hist.* VII, 10 (Ragnovald); VII, 14; VII, 36 (Guntram Boso); VII, 14 (Sigisvald, cf. *PLRE* III, 'Sigisvaldus 3', 1150–1); possibly IX, 2 (Bodegisel, brother of the *dux* Bobo); possibly Fredegar, *Chron.* IV, 30 (Rocco; cf. *PLRE* III, 1088).

[59] Avitus of Vienne, *Ep.*, 9. Conferral of title: Avitus, *Ep.*, 78; *PLRE* II, 1109 (perhaps *magister utriusque militiae*; both Sigismund's father Gundobad and his grandfather Gundioc held this title while kings of the Burgundians). Imperial support for succession: cf. Priscus, *Fr.*, 20.1 (Frankish prince secures support for succession from Valentinian III and Aetius); Cass., *Variae* VIII, 1.3 with Moorhead, *Theoderic*, 213 (apparent acceptance of Eutharic as successor to Theoderic of Italy by the emperor Justin, indicated by sharing of consulate and adoption-in-arms, though unlike Sigismund and the Frankish prince, Eutharic clearly did not travel to the imperial court to secure recognition; Cass., *Variae* VIII, 1.3).

Internal embassy: Avitus, *Ep.*, 38 (to Vienne), though note that he met there the *maior domus* of the deacon and doctor Helpidius, who had ties to the court of Theoderic in Italy (*PLRE* II, 'Helpidius 6', 537).

[60] Sid. Ap., *Carm.* VII, 336–8 (Avitus selected by a Gallic provincial council); *Ep.* I, 9.5 (Sidonius acting for the Arverne); *Ep.* V, 20 (selection of an envoy by an unspecified council, presumably of the *civitas* of Clermont); *Epp.* VII, 6.10, 7.4 (a southern Gallic assembly, including bishops, with involvement in embassies from the western emperor); Hydatius, *Chron.*, 96, 239 [86, 235] and cf. chapter 2 at nn. 75–83; Constantius, *Vita Germani*, 19 (Germanus elected by *civitas*); Ennodius, *Vita Epiphani*, 53–8, 81–2 (Epiphanius selected by council of Liguria).

both of discussions and of the selection of the members; such business is part of the *secreta* of the court.[61]

Provincial envoys to court were constrained to adhere closely to their commission, outlined in the letters of credence with which they were supplied, though literary narratives often overlook this restriction on their subject's independence.[62] Palatine legates may sometimes have enjoyed, or been burdened with, a greater latitude in independently assessing a situation after arrival at their host's court and negotiating an outcome accordingly.[63] It was presumably in order to allow time for assessment and negotiation that some embassies remained for up to a year at their host court.[64] The imprecision of some diplomatic letters in Cassiodorus' *Variae* may also have been intended to allow scope for independence by the envoys. Nevertheless, there is explicit evidence for even very senior and experienced legates needing to seek new instructions when situations changed significantly.[65]

Though envoys are often named singly in eulogistic sources, it appears to have been common for the leadership of legations to have been entrusted to two envoys, sometimes more.[66] This is most evident from the sixth-century evidence of Cassiodorus' *Variae*, in which diplomatic letters refer with formulaic regularity to their bearers, who are to deliver the substantive message orally, as *ille et ille*. Pairs of envoys appear to have been customary in the fifth and seventh centuries also, for both palatine and provincial embassies.[67] Dispatching two colleagues afforded companionship in the labour of their travels and negotiations; a back-up in the

[61] Priscus, *Fr.*, 11.1–2 (*Fr. Class. Hist.*, 245–7); Sid. Ap., *Ep.* III, 7.3; Ennodius, *Vita Epiphani*, 136; above, chapter 5 at n. 44. The planned assassination of Attila in the excerpt from Priscus of course necessitated clandestine discussions, but it is striking that Theoderic's plans to redeem Italian captives, an act of largesse to his subjects, should have been discussed secretly.

[62] *CTh* XII, 12.4, 11. Cf. below, at n. 117.

[63] Cf. *On Envoys* in Lee and Shepard, '*Peri Presbeon*', 30–1 = *Anon. Byz. Treatise on Strategy* XLIII: 'The envoys must exercise judgement and be alert to opportunities, not necessarily carrying out all they have been instructed to do, unless they have been ordered to accomplish something at all costs'; like the criteria for selecting envoys (above, n. 50), this may reflect literary influences.

[64] Below, at n. 93. [65] Procopius, *Wars* V, 4.20–1.

[66] *CTh* XII, 12.7 (380?) limits provincial embassies to three envoys, XII, 12.9 (382) suggests one or two for diocesan embassies; both laws are attempts to rationalise and restrict the number of municipal envoys to court.

[67] Cassiodorus: see above, chapter 5 at n. 22, for Theoderic's outgoing embassies, with Cass., *Variae* I, 4.11 (Cassiodorus' grandfather and Carpilio, son of Aetius, to Attila). For embassies received from other western kings: Cass., *Variae* V, 1, 2, 44; VIII, 1 (though the *formula* for travelling provisions for foreign envoys provides for only one: VII, 33). Other examples: Prosper, *Chron.*, 1367 (Trygetius, Gennadius Avienus, and Pope Leo I to Attila, though Leo's role may have been to ransom captives rather than to act as a negotiator; see above, chapter 4 at n. 5); Priscus, *Fr.*, 11.1, 11.2 (three envoys), 14.2, 15.3–4 (*Fr. Class. Hist.* 243, 263, 297); Malchus, *Fr.*, 20 (*Fr. Class. Hist.*, 243, 263, 297, 437); Ennodius, *Vita Epiphani*, 123–4, 146; *Collectio Avellana*, 57, 102 (three envoys); Procopius, *Wars* II, 2.1; III, 24.7; VI, 22.20, 29.1–5; VII, 21.18; Gregory of Tours, *Hist.* IV, 40; VI, 18; VII, 30, 32; IX, 20; X, 2 (three envoys); Gregory the Great, *Registrum* XIII, 7, 9; *Ep. Austr.*, 18, 20, 42, 43–7

not-uncommon event that one should die *en route*; and a possible mutual check on dealings with the other party.[68] Even where several envoys undertook a mission, however, one individual may have been awarded or assumed a place of seniority.[69] No source mentions the size of the retinue which travelled with any embassy; Constantius' claim that the smallness of Germanus' entourage showed his humility is an indication that large retinues were common, as part of a display of status directed at both the envoy's home community, and the party he approached.[70]

Accommodation and transportation

The imperial court at Constantinople provided lodging for envoys from the western emperor, the bishop of Rome, and the Persian shah.[71] Provincial envoys to western courts, however, had to shift for themselves. This was the case even for those provincial envoys to the western imperial court or that of its Ostrogothic successors who were provided with transport via the *cursus publicus*: Sidonius Apollinaris, travelling to Rome in 467 to make representations on behalf of the Auvergne, was supplied

(cf. *ibid.*, 25–39: four envoys). Seventh century: Fredegar, *Chron.* IV, 40, 62, 73, 85; assumed in Marculf, *Formulae* I, 9. Ganshof, 'Merowingisches Gesandschaftswesen', 170–1.

Some instances of only one envoy being named may arise from the eulogistic nature of the source, which ignores its subject's partners, or from distance from events (e.g. Ennodius in *Vita Epiphani* does not mention partners in Epiphanius' journeys of the 470s, but does name partners for two of the three journeys of the 490s). Other embassies, however, clearly consisted of only one principal legate, sometimes drawing comment, e.g. Constantius, *Vita Germani*, 28 (*unus*), 30 (*iter illius comitatu proprio solitarium*); Procopius, *Anecdota* XVI, 2 (maliciously associating Peter *patricius*, as the sole envoy on his first legation for Justinian to Theodahad, with the murder of Amalasuntha; Peter was accompanied by a second envoy, Athanasius, on his return to Italy (Cass., *Variae* X, 19, 20, 22, 23, 24; Procopius, *Wars* V, 3.30, 4.17–31; cf. V, 6.25–7, 7.11–25; *PLRE* III, 142, 994–5)). Of his two embassies to Persia, Peter alone is recorded on the journey to Ctesiphon in 550 (Procopius, *Wars* VIII, 11.2–4), but he had at least one fellow envoy, Eusebius, when he negotiated with Chosroes' nominee Isdigousnas at Daras in 561 (Menander Protector, *Fr.*, 6.1 *bis* Blockley 65, 71). There is a noticeable change to one envoy in legations from Italy in the time of Theodahad (Cass., *Variae* X, 19, 20, 22, 23, 24; XI, 13 from the Senate of Rome).

68 Companionship: e.g. Priscus, *Fr.*, 11.2 (*Fr. Class. Hist.*, 247, 263). Death *en route*: e.g. Rufius Antonius Agrypnius Volusianus (*Vita Melania* II, 19–24; *PLRE* II, 1185); Isdigousnas (*PLRE* III, 723); Gregory of Tours, *Hist.* X, 2. Mutual check: e.g. Procopius, *Wars* I, 22.15; V, 4.23–5 (Theodahad's envoys to Justinian, Liberius, and Opilio).

69 Procopius, *Wars* II, 2.1–2 (quoted at head of chapter 6); VI, 22.19; Gregory of Tours, *Hist.* VIII, 44 (Baddo, *senior habebatur*). A clear description of two envoys participating jointly in an audience is *ibid.*, IX, 20 (Gregory and Felix).

70 Constantius, *Vita Germani*, 19, 20, 30. Gregory of Tours, *Hist.* VI, 2, describing a shipwreck of an embassy returning from Constantinople to Tours, refers to *multis puerorum* of the envoys drowning.

71 For envoys of western emperor and shah: *De cer.* I, 87, 89 (Reiske 393, 401–2). Of the pope: *Collectio Avellana*, 116.4, 158.3 (= Hormisdas, *Indiculi* of 515, 519): *mansio*.

with a travel warrant (*evectio*), but took accommodation in Rome first at an inn, then with a leading private citizen.[72] Germanus too, who also enjoyed *evectio*, lodged at a *diversorium* when in Ravenna, and Vivianus resided in a humble *hospitium* in Toulouse, chosen for its proximity to the tomb of St Saturninus. The mundanity of these accommodations could be exploited as signs of the humility of the bishops by their eulogists.[73] The same is true of their transport. Germanus' transportation by horse is *exigua*; Vivianus travelled by ox-drawn carriage, 'though high in his mind, yet lowly in his custom, so that the priest could trample underfoot with holy humility the pomp of the proud'.[74] In fact, bishops undertaking embassies could expect to receive hospitality from their peers, including transport, accommodation, and invitations to meals.[75]

Evectio, including transport by horse or boat and food, was provided for subjects of the Ostrogothic kings to travel to court, and for emissaries of other kings.[76] It is uncertain whether other western kings provided transport to their courts for their own subjects, and if so, for how long the resources of the *cursus publicus* operated outside Italy. The title in the *Theodosian Code* concerned with transport provisions for provincial and other embassies travelling on embassies to court is amongst those not included in the *Breviarium* of Alaric II.[77] The *Code* also omits the parallel provisions for the transport and accommodation of government officials in the course of their duties, and the role of the *cursus publicus* in the supply of the army (along with all other references to the Roman army).[78]

[72] *Evectio*: Sid. Ap., *Ep.* I, 5.2; cf. V, 20.2–3. Inn: *Ep.* I, 5.9: *deversorium*. Citizen: *Ep.* I, 9.1: the former prefect of Rome Paulus (cf. *PLRE* II, 'Fl. Synesius Gennadius Paulus 36', 855, though if this identification is correct, it is odd that Sidonius' friend Paulus directed him to the patronage of Caecina Basilius, not Gennadius Avienus, who would have been his relative; cf. *Ep.* I, 9.2). Cf. Duncan-Jones, *Structure and Scale in the Roman Economy*, 146–50. Imperial provisions for *evectio*: *CTh* VII, 1.9; VIII, 5.57; XII, 12.6.

[73] Constantius, *Vita Germani*, 19, 20, 44 (*evectio*); 35 (*diversorium*); *Vita Viviani*, 5.
Ennodius suggests less humble lodgings for Epiphanius at Lyons and Ravenna: *Vita Epiphani*, 167; 190: *domus*; by the sixth century, *domus* often referred to a substantial dwelling, including a royal or episcopal palace.

[74] Constantius, *Vita Germani*, 19. *Vita Viviani*, 4 (*quamvis altus mente, humilis habitu . . . ut superborum pompam sacratissimus pontifex sancta quadam abiectione calcaret*), 5 (*boves*). Vivianus' carriage, however, was presumably not provided at public expense.

[75] *Collectio Avellana*, 116.3, 158.2 (= Hormisdas, *Indiculi* of 515, 519). Gorce, *Les Voyages*, esp. 137–89. For the central Middle Ages, cf. Ciggar, *Western Travellers to Constantinople*, 39–42.

[76] Cass., *Variae* VI, 6.4; VII, 33 (the term *subvectio* is also used, e.g. IV, 45).

[77] *CTh* XII, 12: *De legatis et decretis legationum*; Mommsen, *Theodosiani libri XVI*, I, 2: *tituli*. The omission of this title may indicate the end of public financing of municipal embassies within Gothic territories, but hardly of embassies themselves; cf. John F. Matthews, 'Interpreting the *Interpretationes* of the *Breviarium*', in Mathisen (ed.), *Law, Society, and Authority in Late Antiquity*.

[78] Travel warrants for officials (*tractoria*): *CTh* VIII, 6.1–2. Omission of provisions for army: Matthews, 'Interpreting the *Interpretationes*', 19–20.

From the provisions in the *Code* for the maintenance and prevention of abuse of the *cursus publicus*, one law is preserved (concerning penalties for the misappropriation of official horses and wagons).[79] The editors of the *Breviarium* seem to have assumed the continued existence of the *cursus publicus*, and made provision for the prevention of abuse, but specified none of its purposes: provision of the army, transport for government officials, or transport of municipal embassies. This silence is equivocal, and reflects the different primary functions of the *Code* as a near-complete record of imperial legislation, and of the *Breviarium* as an efficient, shorter reference source for law in a provincial region (a function seen, for example, in the omission of the bulk of the title on the *cursus publicus* in order to reduce the lengthiest and most repetitive title in the *Code* to a single title concerned with criminal misuse). The *Breviarium* does not provide a template of administrative arrangements.

The title in the *Breviarium* on the *cursus publicus* includes, like most titles, a legal gloss (*interpretatio*); it differs little from the original law except that the word *evectio* is expanded to *publica evectio*. The qualification perhaps reflects a looser semantic range and more general application for *evectio* in the early sixth century.[80] The phrase *publica evectio* is used also by one hagiographic source in reference to transport provided by a Gothic king in Gaul in the late fifth century. The same work also mentions the provision at royal command of transport and accommodation, and suggests the maintenance of *mansiones*, staging posts of the *cursus publicus*, in the Burgundian kingdom of the early sixth century. The value of this evidence is ambiguous: the extant text is Carolingian but seems to be based on an earlier work composed close to the narrative time.[81] *Publica evectio* is used by Gregory of Tours for transport provided at royal command, and *evectio* is used by other pre-Carolingian sources also.[82] What if any public system existed to provide this transport in sixth- and seventh-century Gaul is unknown.

There is some evidence to suggest that governments in the western kingdoms did continue to ensure the availability of transport and provisions for embassies and those travelling on official business, but that the responsibility for actually providing these services and goods shifted

[79] *Cursus publicus*: *CTh* VIII, 5.1–66; *CTh* VIII, 5.59 = *Breviarium* VIII, 2.1 with *interpretatio*.

[80] *CTh* VIII, 5.59 = *Breviarium* VIII, 2.1, *interpretatio*.

[81] *Vita Marcelli* (for date and edition, see chapter 4 above, n. 136) V, 3 (*evectio publica* from the Pyrenees region to Toulouse); IX, 2 (Gundobad provides accommodation for Marcellus' return voyage from Lyons to Die *sub octavo lapide Viennensis urbis in fiscali praedio mansionem*). *Evectio* is attested only in pre-Carolingian sources (see following note); the terminology of the second passage is consistent with a Carolingian composition.

[82] Gregory of Tours, *Hist.* IX, 9 (587); cf. II, 24 (set in the 470s). Pre-Carolingian sources: Niermeyer, *Lexicon*, 383 s.v. *evectio*.

away from central government and onto the shoulders of land-holders. In Cassiodorus' *Variae*, cities and land-holders were, as under earlier imperial law, required to provide public services (*munera*) to support the *cursus publicus*, such as the provision of additional horses.[83] The government continued to maintain its own staff for land- and boat-post; public rowers (*dromonarii*) for the river-post, co-ordinating with land-post by horse and maintained at government expense, are explicitly attested for the river Po, which brought travellers to the royal court in Ravenna.[84] Yet in one injunction, Theoderic orders municipal officials of the city of Pavia to provide boat transport and provisions for foreign envoys travelling to court.[85] A more general provision appears in the Burgundian law code, the *Liber constitutionum*, under the title 'Against the refusal of hospitality for the envoys of foreign peoples and for travellers', which obliges all classes to provide accommodation for envoys of the royal court, legates from foreign peoples, and those travelling (presumably to the court) on private business; foreign envoys are entitled also to food.[86] Transport is not mentioned as part of this public levy; it may still be provided from government resources, or perhaps is now the private responsibility of travellers themselves. Subsequent early medieval law codes and *formulae* contain similar provisions.[87] Several sixth-century literary sources may describe private provisioning of embassies as a public levy.[88] The requirement for landowners to provide *hospitalitas* to travellers and envoys seems not to come directly from imperial law, but recalls similar *munera*. The shift in provisioning of travellers on official business in the early medieval kingdoms probably proceeds from

[83] Imperial practice: *CTh* VIII, 5.64, XV, 3, Jones, *LRE*, 462, 749, 832–3, 1349 n. 22. Cass., *Variae* XII, 15.6–7 of 533/7 (for the city of Squillace in Bruttium, Cassiodorus as praetorian prefect commutes the costs of provision of *annona* and *paraveredi* to the government through taxation concession).

[84] Cass., *Varaie* II, 31; IV, 15.

[85] Cass., *Variae* IV, 45, before September 527. For the municipal authorities involved: Liebeschuetz, *Decline and Fall of the Roman City*, 124–5.

[86] *Liber constitutionum*, ed. L. R. De Salis, MGH Legum sectio I, tom. 2.1 (Hanover, 1892), XXXVIII, 2 (*convivia regis*), 3 (*legatis . . . extranearum gentium*), 7 (*in causa privata iter agens*). On *Liber constit.* XXXVIII and *hospitalitas*: Ganshof, 'Merowingisches Gesandschaftswesen', 177; Goffart, *Barbarians and Romans*, 40–50, esp. 41–3, 48. The limits of *hospitalitas* are briefly outlined in *Collectio Avellana*, 116.3, 158.2 (= Hormisdas, *Indiculi* of 515, 519).

[87] Marculf, *Formulae* I, 11; for Frankish, Lombard, and Anglo-Saxon law codes: Barnwell, 'War and Peace', 136 n. 49.

[88] Ennodius, *Vita Epiphani*, 149–50: provisions given to Epiphanius and Victor of Turin by *incolae* as they travel to Lyons (Ennodius twice mentions that goods had to be bought by the hosts to provide for the travellers); this is described as personal hospitality rather than fulfilment of a levy. Gregory of Tours, *Hist.* VI, 45: the procession of the Frankish princess Rigunth to Spain where she is to be married to the Gothic prince Reccared, accompanied by a *magna legatio* from Spain, travelled *expense de diversis civitatibus in itinere*; this royal procession, however, may not reflect usual practice.

breakdown of the western *cursus publicus* after the end of imperial administration, though its appearance in Ostrogothic Italy, where the *cursus publicus* was apparently healthy enough to be abused by officials as it had been in imperial times, underscores its descent from imperial administrative practices.[89]

Embassies generally travelled along well-established routes, whether by road, river, or sea. The account by Sidonius Apollinaris of his journey in 467 from southern Gaul to Rome by road and river, in order to petition the emperor Anthemius, is one of the best extant descriptions of the conditions of travel in late antique Italy.[90] At times of crisis, when many legations passed back and forth between protagonists, the use of the main *viae* could lead to embassies from the different parties meeting *en route* and exchanging information which modified their purposes or necessitated new instructions.[91] The duration of embassies could vary enormously, depending not so much on travel time as how protracted the actual negotiations were.[92] *De ceremoniis* indicates that the eastern court expected to entertain some Persian envoys for the better part of a year, and Gregory of Tours mentions envoys of the Frankish kings returning to Gaul from Constantinople in 581 after a three-year absence.[93] By contrast, Senarius boasts of visiting *volucer* both Constantinople and 'the shores of Ocean', presumably Toulouse, twice within a year.[94] When, in late 537, Belisarius and Vitigis agreed to an armistice while Gothic envoys were sent under Roman safeguard to Justinian, three months was considered sufficient time for the journey to Constantinople and back;

[89] Abuses in Ostrogothic Italy: e.g. Cass., *Variae* IV, 47; V, 5; V, 39.14; in imperial times: *CTh* VIII, 5 (one of the longest titles in *CTh*).

[90] Sid. Ap., *Ep.* I, 5; cf. Rutilius Namatianus, *De reditu suo*.

[91] Hyd., 219 [215] = above chapter 2, Table 1, nos. 25–6; Procopius, *Wars* V, 4.20–1 (Peter *patricius*, *en route* to Italy, meets the embassies to Justinian first of Amalasuntha, then of Theodahad); Menander Protector, *Fr.*, 9.3 (the possiblility of embassies crossing paths is intentionally exploited).

[92] Cf. McCormick, *Origins of the European Economy*, 470–4. On travelling times, at least for government-sponsored voyages: A. M. Ramsay, 'The Speed of the Roman Imperial Post', *Journal of Roman Studies* 15 (1925), 60–74; Duncan-Jones, *Structure and Scale*, 7–29; cf. McCormick, *Origins of the European Economy*, 469–500.

[93] *De cer.* I, 89 (Reiske 400); Gregory of Tours, *Hist.* VI, 2. Two fourth-century sources for Roman journeys to barbarian neighbours appear to suggest similar time scales, but in fact may not. *CTh* XII, 12.2 (?357) permits Roman envoys to barbarian groups in Ethiopia and Arabia to reside at Alexandria for up to a year *en route*; this attests not the length of time taken by the actual journey to these buffer states, but presumably of preparations before departing Roman territory. The Egyptian *protector* Abinnaeus spent three years after 336 escorting Blemmye envoys from Constantinople to their *patria* before reporting back to the court in Asia Minor; *The Abinnaeus Archive: Papers of a Roman Officer in the Reign of Constantius II*, ed. H. I. Bell *et al.* (Oxford, 1962), p. 1, lines 5–10; *PLRE* I, 1; T. D. Barnes, 'The Career of Abinnaeus', *Phoenix* 39 (1985), 368–70. The Blemmyes, however, had arrived in Roman territory as *refugae*, and the task of returning them to their homeland may have involved more than mere travelling.

[94] Senarius, *Epitaph*, lines 11–13.

this period covered winter, when sailing conditions were difficult though not altogether suspended.[95]

Patrons, friends, and lovers

Sidonius' host in Rome provided not only accommodation but also aid in seeking a powerful patron from among the leading senators, who could aid Sidonius' mission on behalf of his province, as well as advance Sidonius' personal interests. Local patronage for envoys to Rome had an ancient tradition.[96] Ennodius' letters reveal him actively pursuing support at Ravenna for projected embassies to court.[97] Local patronage, particularly by senior members of a ruler's *consistorium*, could determine the fate of the issue at hand; Theoderic's support for Symmachus in the disputed papal election of the early 500s was attributed by the disgruntled losers to bribery of his court officials.[98] The episcopacy provided a valuable network: Epiphanius received assistance in the form of local advice, if not actual advocacy at court, in Lyons from the Catholic bishop Rusticius, and had contacts at Ravenna; Pope Hormisdas suggested to his envoys to Constantinople that supportive locals could help win their case.[99] As with patronage relations in other contexts, the cult of saints annexed this function, at least in literary representations.[100]

Residence in the city of an envoy's destination gave the opportunity to strike up new friendships, later maintained by exchanges of letters.[101] Ennodius met Laconius, a palatine official of Gundobad, in Lyons and

95 Procopius, *Wars* VI, 6.33, 7.13–15, 22.22; for date: *PLRE* III, 201. Cf. Procopius, *Wars* VII, 37.17, 39.25, 29: a similar agreement, but apparently over the summer; *Liber pont.*, 61: Pope Vigilius is arrested in Rome on 22 November, and arrives at Constantinople on 24 December, having stopped *en route* at Catina in Sicily long enough to perform December ordinations there. Winter sailing conditions: Vegetius, *Epitoma rei militaris*, ed. C. Lang (Stuttgart, 1872), IV, 39; Duncan-Jones, *Structure and Scale*, 20, 25 and references at nn. 33–4; McCormick, *Origins of the European Economy*, 458–64.

96 Sid. Ap., *Ep.* I, line 5. E. Badian, *Foreign Clientelae (264–70 BC)* (Oxford, 1958), esp. 154–67.

97 Moorhead, *Theoderic*, 156–8.

98 Symmachus: *Fragmentum Laurentianum* (*Liber pont.*), 52. Cf. Malchus, *Fr.*, 15 (Theoderic in Thrace believes he has the support of high officials within Constantinople); Fredegar, *Chron.* IV, 45 (Lombard envoys succeed in terminating tribute to the Frankish kings through bribes to three mayors of the palace).

99 Epiphanius: Ennodius, *Vita Epiphani*, 151 (Lyons); 190 (Ravenna). Hormisdas: *Collectio Avellana*, 116.4.

100 E.g. *Vita Viviani*, 5 (Vivianus seeks *patrocinium* of St Saturninus of Toulouse); Gregory of Tours, *Hist.* VIII, 6 (Gregory as envoy of St Martin to king Guntram: *a domino meo in legatione ad te directus sum*). Patronage and cult of saints: Brown, *Cult of the Saints*, 55–68.

101 For an insightful account of the interrelationships between duty and personal relations in a comparable function, the carrying of private letters: Conybeare, *Paulinus Noster*, 31–40: 'The carrier's message therefore ends up consisting partly in his entire comportment while he stays with the correspondent' (38).

kept up an intermittent correspondence for the next decade. Parthenius, a grandson of the emperor Avitus, met the poet Arator as a student in Ravenna when acting as a representative from Provence to Theoderic perhaps *c.* 508; they spent happy times together, reading Caesar's *Commentaries* and Christian (presumably Gallic) poets. The two were still in contact in 544 when Arator, by this time a cleric of the church of Rome, sent a copy of his verse composition of the Acts of the Apostles from Rome to Parthenius, now *magister officiorum* and *patricius* under the Merovingian kings in Gaul. Q. Aurelius Memmius Symmachus, father-in-law of Boethius, while in Constantinople probably as an envoy of either Theoderic or the Senate of Rome, met the grammarian and panegyricist Priscian in Constantinople, and was later dedicatee of three of Priscian's works.[102] Literary products could be offered to a host ruler also. Anthimus, a *comes* of the court of either the eastern emperor or Theoderic in Italy, apparently served as an envoy to his ruler's namesake, the Frankish king Theuderic I in Gaul, to whom he later wrote a treatise in epistolary format on the medical properties of food and diet.[103]

More licentious ties, too, could be cultivated, though with legal and emotional risks. In Procopius' *Wars*, Theodahad makes a veiled threat to Peter *patricius* that the common respect for the security of envoys could be justly ignored if the legate was accused either of insulting a ruler or of adultery; the latter charge was perhaps more easily concocted.[104] The poet Maximianus devotes an elegy to his regrets for an affair with a younger woman he encountered in Constantinople, where he had been sent, presumably by Theoderic, to seek peace.[105]

Stages of reception, audience, and departure

Ennodius, in *Vita Epiphani*, describes five receptions of Epiphanius as an envoy at imperial and royal courts. The few details given in these accounts, and passing references in other sources, recall the protocol of the

[102] Ennodius and Laconius: Ennodius, *Opera* 38, 86, 252 = *Epp.* II, 5; III, 16; V, 24. Parthenius and Arator: Arator, *Epistula ad Parthenium*, *PL* 68, 245–52; *PLRE* II, 'Arator', 127, 'Parthenius 3', 833–4. Symmachus and Priscian: Priscian, *De figuris numerorum; de metris Terentii; de praeexercitamentis rhetoris: libri tres*, in *Grammatici latini*, ed. H. Keil (Leipzig, 1859; repr. Hildersheim, 1981), *Praef.*, 405; *PLRE* II, 'Q. Aurelius Memmius Symmachus iunior 9', 1045.

[103] Anthimus, *De observatio ciborum*, ed. E. Liechtenham in *Corpus medicorum latinorum* (Leipzig, 1915–68), VIII; trans. S. H. Weber, *Anthemius: De observatione ciborum* (Leiden, 1924). *PLRE* II, 'Anthimus 2 and 3', 100.

[104] Procopius, *Wars* V, 7.15–16, 18; similarly Menander Protector, *Fr.*, 9.3 (Blockley, 109). Intercourse (presumably with slaves) was offered as part of hospitality amongst the Huns; Priscus, *Fr.*, 11.2 (*Fr. Class. Hist.*, 261).

[105] Maximianus, *Elegia* V.

fifth- and sixth-century passages of *De ceremoniis*.[106] Similarities in procedure are probably not examples of western kings imitating the trappings of the imperial court, but represent the continuity of procedures maintained in the *praetoria* of senior provincial magistrates, together with a degree of inevitability as to how arrangements for receiving representations are to be made.[107]

Ennodius' embassy narratives present a more or less consistent outline of procedures for the stages of the reception of an embassy and an audience, somewhat compressed for literary effect. In each narrative, after the emperor or king receives advice of the arrival of the legation, court servants are sent to greet the envoys, who are then summoned to court.[108] Ennodius mentions the formal grant of *licentia* within the *consistorium* for the envoy to speak to the ruler.[109] Following this permission are Epiphanius' speeches and the rulers' replies, Ennodius' oratorical set pieces.[110] Upon the satisfactory conclusion of discussions, action is taken immediately to put agreements into effect: Anthemius makes an oath; a pact is formed with Euric; Theoderic and Gundobad delegate the administration of their decisions to court officials.[111] After the journey home, it is conventional for a legate to report in person to court, even if he is not a palatine official.[112]

This sequence of events conveys an impression of immediacy, but there are indications of a more leisured pace, allowing time not only for rest from the exertions of travel, but also for informal contacts.[113] Though each scene usually progresses directly from the embassy's arrival to its reception by the ruler, Ennodius once indicates that some period of time passes between the arrival of the embassy in its city of destination and its audience, when Gundobad dispatches court officials to determine on

[106] Brief but consistent descriptions of procedure are given also in Gregory of Tours, *Hist.* VI, 31, 34; VIII, 13, 44; IX, 1; at greater length: IX, 20 (Gregory's own embassy to King Guntram).

[107] Continuity of provincial practice: McCormick, *Eternal Victory*, 231–59. Inevitable procedures: cf. the expectations of the Constantinopolitan envoys to Attila in 448 (Priscus, *Fr.*, 11.2 (*Fr. Class. Hist.*, 251)) and to the shah Hormisdas in 579 (Menander Protector, *Fr.*, 23.9 (Blockley, 209–11)) that failure to observe familiar protocol constituted a calculated insult.

[108] Ennodius, *Vita Epiphani*, 60–1 (received by *officia palatina tota*); 86; 123 (*suscepti reverenter*); 152 (*omnis Christianorum principi adsistentium turba*).

[109] Ennodius, *Vita Epiphani*, 62 (*licentia*); 124 (*agendi aditus*). Cf. Gregory of Tours, *Hist.* VI, 31 (*Quibus intromissis ad regem, data suggestione, dixerunt*).

[110] Ennodius, *Vita Epiphani*, 63–71, 86–91, 124–34, 154–67, 185–9.

[111] Ennodius, *Vita Epiphani*, 72 (*accepto etiam pro concordiae firmitate ab Anthemio sacramento*); 91 (*initio etiam pactionis vinculo*); 135 (Urbicus, presumably *quaestor* to Theoderic); 168–71 (Laconius, perhaps *consiliarius* to Gundobad). Only Epiphanius' final embassy, to Theoderic in Ravenna in 496, lacks narrative confirmation of the decision reached; most other elaborations of detail are also absent from this scene.

[112] Ennodius, *Vita Epiphani*, 75, 95, 179–80, above, chapter 4 at nn. 232–4.

[113] Exertions of travel: cf. Gregory of Tours, *Hist.* VII, 9.

which day Epiphanius wishes to come to court.[114] One embassy scene concludes with Epiphanius departing as soon as his audience is over, but twice Ennodius refers to actual or potential delays, to accommodate informal discourse: an invitation to the envoy to attend a royal *convivium* some days after his audience with Euric, and Epiphanius' many visits to and from local figures in Ravenna, after his final meeting with Theoderic.[115] (Envoys to the imperial court of Constantinople suffered much more restricted latitude; Procopius has one legate say that 'it is not easy for an envoy even to drink except by the will of those who watch over him'.[116]) These details are included solely for literary purposes: Euric's invitation is an opportunity for the display of Epiphanius' good judgement in politely declining the opportunity to share a table with Arian clergy; the bishop's busy visits to friends in Ravenna are prompted by prescience of his death. The reader is more likely to be impressed by the alacrity with which Epiphanius completes his purposes than by these auxiliary contacts. Ennodius generally compresses the successive stages of the reception and audience of the embassies for literary effect, similarly to the way Constantius telescopes Germanus' episcopal career.

There are no references in *Vita Epiphani* to the presentation of letters from the envoy's principals to the various rulers in their *consistoria*, prior to the delivery of Epiphanius' speeches. This omission is probably literary licence. Late fourth-century imperial legislation specified the presentation of letters from an embassy's principal, stating the mission entrusted to envoys (*mandata*), as a prerequisite for securing an audience at court.[117] Descriptions of receptions in other sources indicate that letters were routinely presented after the envoy entered his host's presence and greeted him, and before he received permission to speak.[118] Peoples outside the

[114] Ennodius, *Vita Epiphani*, 152–3 (*constitutus ergo videndi regem dies*).

[115] Hasty departure: Ennodius, *Vita Epiphani*, 72: (*discessit festinans ad Liguriam reverti*). Delays: 92 (Epiphanius declines an invitation from Euric to his *convivium*, because he is planning to depart for Italy the day after the next, i.e. two days after his interview with the king – the implication being that the *convivium* would not be organised until after that time, and that an embassy was expected to remain for longer than a few days after completion of the formal audience); 190 (Epiphanius pays visits to *omnibus*, including *Christianae multitudinis turbas*, before his final departure from Ravenna). Cf. *Collectio Avellana*, 116.4 (Hormisdas envisages his envoys in Constantinople receiving guests at their lodging after their imperial audience). But cf. Gregory of Tours, *Hist.* VIII, 44 (failure of envoys to depart immediately is suspicious); IX, 20 (the Frankish king Guntram and two envoys proceed directly from their audience to a church service for Easter Sunday, then to the king's *convivium*).

[116] Procopius, *Wars* V, 7.18; cf. Procopius' outrage at the freedom of movement allowed to Isdigousnas in Constantinople, *Wars* VIII, 15.20.

[117] *CTh* XII, 12.4, 10, 11.

[118] To the sources at n. 29 above, add: *Collectio Avellana* 116 (= Hormisdas, *Indiculus* of 515), 5–7 (*Praesenti itaque imperatori lietteras porrigite cum tali allocutione 'salutat pater vester, deum cotidie*

empire or its former territories adopted the custom of sending letters to validate their dispatched representatives when dealing with imperial representatives or their successors, using Latin as a common language of diplomacy.[119] Diplomatic letters, as well as introducing the matter of negotiation, acted as letters of credence for the envoys named in their text. The act of accepting a proffered letter from the envoy's principal perhaps constituted the *licentia* for the legate to address the ruler in full.[120] Sometimes, however, separate letters of credence were also written, to be presented alongside or in lieu of a letter addressing the matter of the embassy.[121] Ennodius' omission of letters is perhaps intended to focus attention on Epiphanius' oratory; his principals' letters could suggest an alternative source of persuasion.

Ennodius' formulaic presentation of the audience as consisting essentially of two speeches, the envoy's oration and the ruler's reply, appears to be an accurate rather than stylised description of common practice, at least for initial meetings. *De ceremoniis* too portrays the audience as consisting of a petition and reply; Procopius, who regularly presents embassy narratives as speech and reply, has a Roman envoy on behalf of Vitigis seek dispensation from Belisarius to discuss matters in the format of a dialogue rather than in the conventional oration and reply.[122] Doubtless, much depended on the groundwork laid during preliminary meetings between the envoys and court officials, and on subsequent discussions, whether further formal audiences in the ruler's *consistorium* or informal settings such as *convivia*. The fifth- and sixth-century sections of *De ceremoniis*, however, note the emperor's option to hold extempore discussions

rogans et confessionibus sanctorum apostolorum Petri et Pauli vestrum regnum commendans . . .'), 158 (= Hormisdas, *Indiculus* of 519), 4 (*cui [imperatori] praesentati salutantes litteras nostras offerte, suggerentes*); Gregory of Tours, *Hist.* VIII, 13 (*Felix legatus, salutatione praemissa, ostensis litteris, ait*).

119 *CTh* XII, 12.5. Second- and fourth-century examples in Elton, *Roman Warfare in Europe*, 186 and n. 28; Linda Ellis, 'Dacians, Sarmatians, and Goths on the Roman–Carpathian Frontier: Second–Fourth Centuries', in Ralph W. Mathisen and Hagith S. Sivan (eds.), *Shifting Frontiers in Late Antiquity* (Aldershot, 1996), 118. Both Attila and his leading chiefs had secretaries to prepare Latin and perhaps Greek letters to the emperors, prizing 'literary skills'; Priscus, *Fr.*, 11.2, 14 (*Fr. Class. Hist.*, 263, 289). Procopius, *Wars* VIII, 19.8, comments on the Utrigar Huns as being exceptional in not using letters. Cass., *Variae* IV, 1 and V, 1, responses to friendly embassies from the kings of the Thuringians and Warni, mention the receipt of gifts and envoys (IV, 1.3), but do not specify letters.

120 Letter of credence: e.g. Priscus, *Fr.*, 11.2 (letter of Theodosius II to Attila establishes the rank of the envoy Maximinus; *Fr. Class. Hist.*, 247). *Licentia*: note *Collectio Avellana*, 116.5–7 (insistance of Hormisdas that his envoys pass their letter to the emperor Anastasius before answering any questions).

121 E.g. *Ep. Wisigotica*, 4; Marculf, *Formulae* I, 9.

122 Procopius, *Wars* VI, 6.11–13. Cf. Blockley, *History of Menander* for the possible historicity of the speeches and replies in Menander's account.

with legates during the audience, and some narrative accounts describe such dialogues.[123]

The actual speeches of *Vita Epiphani* appear to be all from Ennodius' pen; the style however need not be excessively florid for a genuine oration. The only extant record of what purports to be the text of an actual speech delivered by an embassy in late antiquity is Peter *patricius*' oration opening negotiations with the Persian envoy Isdigousnas at Daras in 561; his address is no less ornate and structured than those Ennodius offers.[124] The stress on oratorical skills of envoys in panegyric, hagiography, and other eulogistic sources indicates that a Sophistic presentation remained the central element of audiences. One of Epiphanius' speeches is concluded with a genuflection, a flourish from the rhetor's repertoire.[125] A framework of mutually assumed consent to convention enabled such perorations to fulfil their role; if, however, one of the participants chose to breach practice, the conventional bombast of formal speeches could be curtly deflated. The emperor Maurice, in a letter reprimanding the Frankish king Childebert II for his failure to undertake promised attacks on the Lombards in Italy, wrote sharply: 'Why then do you weary your envoys, whom you think it so necessary to send across the vast distance of land and sea, to no purpose? Boasting with their rash speeches, they do nothing useful.'[126]

Most of the embassies in *Vita Epiphani* end with an indication that the newly wrought agreement would be immediately put into effect, Theoderic and Gundobad issuing instructions to court servants, Anthemius and Euric making formal commitments to *pactiones*. Ennodius refers to Anthemius' oath (*sacramentum*); oaths to conclude *pactiones* immediately following an audience are attested elsewhere.[127] Written treaty documents, conveyed between signatory parties by envoys, are attested

[123] *De cer.* I, 87 (Reiske 395). Dialogues: e.g. Procopius, *Wars* V, 7.13–25 (n. 30 above); Gregory of Tours, *Hist.* VII, 14; IX, 20.

[124] Peter *patricius, apud* Menander Protector, *Fr.*, 6.1, 3 (Blockley 55–9), with Isdigousnas' reply; though, since Peter himself apparently preserved the document, perhaps as part of a report to Justinian's court, the speech could well be a polished version. Another text apparently derived from a report by a Constantinopolitan envoy is Malalas, *Chron.* XVIII, 56; Scott, 'Diplomacy in the Sixth Century', 161.

[125] Ennodius, *Vita Epiphani*, 164, not an act of obeisance: cf. *De cer.* I, 87, 89 (Reiske 395, 406): envoys to the eastern emperor perform obeisance on entering his presence.

[126] *Ep. Austr.*, 42: *Et si hoc est, quid per tanta spatia terrae atquae maris inaniter sine responsu necessarios vestros ligatarios fatigatis, iuvenalis sermonis, qui nihil utilitatis induxerunt, iacantes?* Cf. Blockley, *History of Menander*, 11–12.

[127] Procopius, *Wars* VI, 29.5; Gregory of Tours, *Hist.* e.g. VI, 3 (*data susceptaque de pace sacramenta pactionibusque firmatis*), 31, 34; *Ep. Austr.*, 42 (*terribilibus iuramentis roborata*).

also.[128] Most known cases of written treaties involve the eastern imperial court from the mid-sixth century. Whether this reflects the development of diplomatic protocol between the eastern imperial court and Persia and subsequently applied to the West, or whether documentary treaties were used throughout the West as a natural extension of Latin written culture, is unclear.[129]

Court personnel

Ennodius' accounts are by no means full. Whereas the *formulae* of Cassiodorus' *Variae* agree with *De ceremoniis* that the *magister officiorum* has oversight of visiting envoys, Ennodius' narrative makes no mention of a *magister officiorum* in association with Epiphanius' embassy to Anthemius in Rome or his two legations to Theoderic in Ravenna. Neither does Pope Hormisdas in his *Indiculi*, though he understood the role of the *magister officiorum* in regard to overseeing envoys.[130] The absence from the accounts of Ennodius and Hormisdas of any reference to the palatine official who most closely supervises visiting envoys stems in part from their literary emphases; it may also indicate that palatine officials did not intrude on the actual conduct of court business as much as seems to be suggested by the writings of Cassiodorus and Peter *patricius* who were, after all, writing for fellow bureaucrats.

Ennodius does mention three palatine officials, one each at the courts of Euric, Theoderic, and Gundobad: Leo, Urbicus, and Laconius respectively. Their inclusion has been interpreted as an indication that they held pre-eminent places at the kings' courts as Roman administrators and ameliorators of their barbarian lords, a role comparable to that sometimes supposed for Cassiodorus.[131] The text of *Vita Epiphani* itself suggests different functions. The three officials serve to dramatise pertinent aspects

[128] Procopius, *Wars* VI, 29.5–6 (treaty between Justinian and Vitigis, partitioning Italy, to be signed by Belisarius); Gregory the Great, *Registrum* IX, 229 (treaty between Justinian and an unnamed Gothic king of Spain); Gregory of Tours, *Hist.* IX, 20 (treaty of Andelot between Guntram and Childebert II); cf. Menander Protector, *Fr.*, 6.1 (full text plus details of reproduction and verification of treaty of 561 between Justinian and Chosroes). M. Wielers, *Zwischenstaatliche Behiehungsformen im frühen Mittelalter (Pax, Foedus, Amicitia, Fraternitas)* (diss., Münster, 1959).

[129] Development of protocol between Constantinople and Ctesiphon: Blockley, *History of Menender*, 17–18.

[130] *PLRE* II, 'Symmachus 4', 1043. On the *magister officiorum*: Cass., *Variae* VI, 6.4; Blockley, *East Roman Foreign Policy*, 134–7.

[131] E.g. Reydellet, *La Royauté*, 151–2; E. Ewig, 'Residence et capitale pendant le haut moyen âge', in his *Spätantikes und Fränkisches Gallien: Gesammelte Schriften*, ed. H. Altsma (Munich, 1976), 367 n. 29.

of the narrative. Urbicus, presumably *quaestor* at Theoderic's court in 494, and Laconius, possibly *consiliarius* to Gundobad, are both mentioned only after Epiphanius' orations to their masters, when they are charged with the execution of the agreements Epiphanius has negotiated. Like the references to the oath sworn by Anthemius and the pact agreed to by Euric after their interviews with Epiphanius, the role of these officials is strictly limited to narrative confirmations of the success of Epiphanius' negotiations.[132] Leo, perhaps *consiliarius* of Euric in Toulouse, appears twice, framing Epiphanius' speech to Euric, which he attends. Though it is possible that Leo was in charge of overseeing the protocol of the audience, the text does not say this. His presence at the historical meeting could be attributed to his position, attested by both Ennodius and Sidonius Apollinaris, as a senior adviser of Euric.[133] His role in the text, however, is as an appreciative audience, able to give well-informed praise to Epiphanius' eloquence, for when he is first introduced, Leo is described not only as the 'moderator and judge' of Euric's counsels, but also as a figure 'to whom already more than one prize for declamation had come deservedly on account of his eloquence'; that Leo was 'gripped by such great awe at his oratory' underscores the force of Epiphanius' rhetoric.[134] The functions of these characters in praising Epiphanius indirectly attest the importance of two aspects of the procedure of embassies: oratorical delivery, and positive confirmation of an agreement in the envoy's presence.

Besides their functions at a narrative level, these three palatine officials may also serve literary ends at the level of the reception of the text. Laconius was a friend and correspondent of Ennodius; Urbicus, otherwise unattested, may have been one of Ennodius' associates at Theoderic's court. Leo enjoyed a reputation in Gaul as an arbiter of literary taste.[135] It was customary for the authors of late antique letter collections to include revised or new letters to specific friends for their delight; thus the published collections of letters, as well as the original epistles, contributed to the cultivation of *amicitia*.[136] Similar aims may have influenced the naming and praise of select palatine officials in *Vita Epiphani*.

132 Ennodius, *Vita Epiphani*, 135 (Urbicus), 168–71 (Laconius); cf. 72 (Anthemius' *sacramentum*), 91 (Euric's *pactio*).

133 Ennodius, *Vita Epiphani*, 85; Sid. Ap., *Epp.* IV, 22.3; VIII, 3.4.

134 Ennodius, *Vita Epiphani*, 85: *consiliorum principis et moderator et arbiter Leo nomine, quem per eloquentiae meritum non una iam declamationum palma susceperat*; 89: *tanto adlocutionis ipsius tenebatur miraculo*.

135 Laconius: Ennodius, *Opera* 38, 86, 252 = *Epp.* II, 5; III, 16; V, 24. Urbicus: the dramatic date of Ennodius, *Vita Epiphani*, 135, is 494; Ennodius' extant letters commence in 501 (Sundwall, *Abhandlungen*, 3–4, 72); earlier correspondence between Ennodius and Urbicus is possible. Leo: *PLRE* II, 662; Ennodius, *Vita Epiphani*, 85.

136 Sid. Ap., *Ep.* IX, 14.1; Cass., *Variae*, *Praef.*, 9; Gillett, 'Purposes', 49–50.

Ceremonial

Leo's first appearance in *Vita Epiphani*, more informative of actual protocol, is as the only palatine official named in association with the reception of an embassy: '[Leo] with great joy proclaimed to public notice the arrival of the bishop.'[137] The passage is an explicit reference to the public announcement of the reception of an envoy. There are other indications that the arrival and departure of embassies was a publicly observed event, attended by ceremonial akin to the *adventus* liturgies for the reception of the emperor and other public figures.[138] The hagiographical embassy-narratives repeatedly describe the *occursus* of populations of towns meeting bishops both during their journeys and at their destination, prompting Germanus of Auxerre to attempt to hide his identity when entering towns; in Arles, a watch is maintained for the expected arrival of his legation.[139] Constantius also mentions the 'regular practice' of the praetorian prefect of Gaul in meeting a provincial embassy at some distance outside the city; as was traditional with ceremonies of reception, the distance at which the recipient meets the embassy is an indicator of honour.[140] Malchus records the ceremonial reception, outside the city, of envoys from the emperor Zeno by the 'men of rank' and other inhabitants of the provincial city of Lychnidus in Macedonia.[141] The record of the arrival of Persian envoys into Constantinople in sources derived from the putative Constantinople city chronicles suggests that these were

137 Ennodius, *Vita Epiphani*, 85: *qui cum summo gaudio adventum pontificis indicavit notitiae publicae*. The phrase *summo gaudio* may reflect the phraseology of public proclamation.

Reception by officials: in Rome, Epiphanius is ushered in to his audience with Anthemius by *officia palatina tota*, *Vita Epiphani*, 61.

138 On imperial *adventus*: S. MacCormack, 'Change and Continuity in Late Antiquity: The Ceremony of the *adventus*', *Historia* 21 (1972), 721–2. Imperial ritual was an extension of ubiquitous aristocratic practices celebrating the arrival or departure (*discessus*) of magnates: McCormick, *Eternal Victory*, 252–8; Thomas F. Mathews, *The Clash of Gods: A Reinterpretation of Early Christian Art*, 2nd edn (Princeton, 1999), 24–5; David Noy, *Foreigners at Rome: Citizens and Strangers* (London, 2000), 142.

139 *Occursus*: e.g. Constantius, *Vita Germani*, 21, 23, 30, 35; cf. Ennodius, *Vita Epiphani*, 59, 85, 149 (*fama* of Epiphanius draws crowds from the cities he approaches on his journeys). Secrecy and watch: Constantius, *Vita Germani*, 32, 35. From at least the late fourth century, *adventus* rituals greeted bishops entering or re-entering their own sees (McCormick, 'Analyzing Imperial Ceremonies', 15 n. 47; J. George, *Venantius Fortunatus, a Latin Poet in Merovingian Gaul* (Oxford, 1992), 74–7); the receptions described by Constantius and Ennodius may have been extensions of these practices to visiting bishops.

140 Praetorian prefect meets embassies: Constantius, *Vita Germani*, 24: *Ingrediente longissimo praeter consuetudinem famulatur occursu* (cf. the late evidence of Stephanus Africanus, *Vita Amator*, 5: Amator is received by the praetorian prefect of Gaul Julius; *PLRE* II, 642). Tradition: McCormick, *Eternal Victory*, 211 and n. 102 (citing Augustus, *Res gestae* XII, 1). Distance: in addition to the last citation from *Vita Germani*: Ennodius, *Vita Epiphani*, 151 stresses that Bishop Rusticius of Lyons crosses the Rhône to greet the Italian legation.

141 Malchus, *Fr.*, 20 (*Fr. Class. Hist.*, 443).

urban ceremonial occasions; it is argued above that the prominence of references to embassies in the *Chronicle* of Hydatius also reflects public formalities.[142] The regularity of such ritual is probably an important factor militating against its record: frequently repeated ceremonies, even of important events such as imperial accessions, tend not to be recorded by contemporary sources because of their very banality.[143]

The departure of a legation too could be an occasion for public observation. A passage of *Vita Epiphani* may represent public ritual for the departure of a legation.[144] The brusque dismissal of unwelcome envoys recorded in several sources may have been known to the authors because of intentional publicity on the part of the court, and recorded as eloquent breaches of convention.[145]

Other elements of the hosting of embassies were also for public consumption. The formal audience of the legation in the imperial or royal *consistorium*, though limited to the small circle of the ruler's leading officials and advisers, was not a privvy occasion. Procopius casually describes such interviews as 'in public' (δημοσίᾳ).[146] In times of conflict, the regular presence of senior officials and other important subjects at the reception of an embassy could be anticipated and exploited as an opportunity to spread disinformation and distrust between a ruler and his leading magnates.[147] References to secret dealing on secondary matters between envoys and rulers – 'to put a word in your ear', as one envoy put it – underscore the public nature of the ostensible communications.[148] Ceremonial of the audience could be elaborate, including, like many other late antique public ceremonies, the delivery of panegyrics.[149] *Convivia* and other informal meetings between ruler and envoy also exposed

[142] Persian envoys: *Consularia Constantinopolitana* (MGH AA 9; Burgess, *Chronicle*), s.aa. 358, 384; *Chron. Pasch.*, s.a. 384; Marcellinus *comes*, *Chron.*, 384.1. Hydatius: above, chapter 2 at nn. 51–2.

[143] McCormick, 'Analyzing Imperial Ceremonies', 7 ('The banality of ceremonies, in particular, profoundly affected the surviving evidence'), 8–9.

[144] Ennodius, *Vita Epiphani*, 92 (read as the abandonment of Roman provincials by the ceding of the Auvergne to Euric by e.g. Courcelle, *Histoire littéraire*, 180, but cf. above, chapter 4, at n. 224).

[145] Hyd., 238 [234]; Gregory of Tours, *Hist.* VII, 14.

[146] Procopius, *Wars* V, 7.13 (quotation; Theodahad in Ravenna with envoys from Justinian); V, 20.8 (envoys of Vitigis before Belisarius, his commanders, and the Senate of Rome); VIII, 4.12–13 ('for there were many who heard their speeches'); Agathias, *Hist.* I, 5.3 (Gothic envoys before Frankish kings and 'all the high officials').

[147] Procopius, *Wars* V, 4.22, cf. 7.21–5; III, 16.12 (Justinian writes to the 'archons' of the Vandals).

[148] Secret dealing alongside public negotiations: Procopius, *Wars* V, 2.4, 9; 4.17–19; VI, 2–5, 7–25 (Theodahad and Justinian); V 3.13–16, 8–29 (Amalasuntha and envoys of Justinian); VI, 29.26–30 (Goths and Belisarius); VII, 2.17 (Eraric and Justinian); VIII, 4.12–13 (Tetraxite Goths and Justinian); Gregory of Tours, *Hist.* VII, 30; VIII, 13, 28; VI, 3; VII, 32; IX, 16 (quotation: *Iussit . . . dominus noster ponere verbum in auribus vestris*); X, 19 (Bishop Egidius).

[149] John Lydus, *De mag.* III, 28; *De cer.* I, 87 (Reiske 395); Ennodius, *Pan. Theod.*, 77.

legates to leading members and satellites of the court, as well as providing informal opportunities for negotiation.[150]

Ritual for the reception of embassies served several functions for the host ruler. For domestic purposes, the tableau of a ruler receiving embassies from foreign powers or from subjects impressed the importance of his rule upon his court and subjects. The number of legations a ruler received, and the distance they had travelled, was an indicator of his importance in affairs beyond the boundaries of his own realm. Multitudes of envoys are a feature common to Roman imperial panegyric, the propaganda of the Persian shahs, and the public projection of the western kings.[151] The equation of a ruler's importance with the range and foreignness of legations he receives is nowhere more explicit than in the short panegyrical poem Sidonius Apollinaris wrote for the Gothic king Euric.[152] The same message was aimed at foreign envoys, who could be shown their host's influence in other parts of the world. The historian Priscus, who seems to have participated in an embassy from Constantinople to Valentinian III in Rome *c.* 450, witnessed a diplomatic ceremony involving another legation: the 'adoption-in-arms' by the *magister utriusque militiae* Aetius of a Frankish prince, who had himself come to Rome from the Rhineland on an embassy.[153]

[150] *Vita Orientii* 5; *Vita Viviani* 6; Ennodius, *Vita Epiphani*, 92; Cass., *Variae* VI, 3.6, 6.4, 9.7–8; VII, 5.1, 33. Informal settings for negotiation. e.g. Sid. Ap., *Epp.* I, 2.8 (description of losing to the Gothic king Theoderic II at a board-game *ut causa salvetur*); VII, 12.3; Priscus, *Fr.*, 11.1 (*Fr. Class. Hist.*, 245); Procopius, *Wars* III, 24.9–15; Gregory of Tours, *Hist.* IX, 20.

[151] E.g. Roman imperial: *Pan. lat.* X (II) 3.4; Claudian, *Cos. Stilich.* II, 184–207. Persian shahs: the ninth century *ekphrasis* by Al Buhturi of mosaics in the palace of Ctesiphon, perhaps depicting Chosroes I Anoushirvan, trans. in A. J. Arberry, *Arabic Poetry* (Cambridge, 1965), 72–80, *versus* 46. Royal: Ennodius, *Pan. Theod.* XII, 60; XXI, 92; cf. Cass., *Variae* XI, 1.7, 11 (on Amalasuntha, regent to Athalaric in Italy). Also a stock image in non-panegyrical works, e.g. Sid. Ap., *Ep.* I, 2.4 (*gentium* to be understood as parts of Gaul, not foreign peoples); Pope Symmachus, *Ep.*, 10 to the emperor Anastasius; *PL* 62, 67, cited by Amory, *People and Identity*, 205 n. 50. Cf. Barnwell, 'War and Peace', 138.

[152] Sid. Ap., *Ep.* VIII, 9.5 *versus*, lines 21–54.

[153] Priscus, *Fr.*, 20.1. Date: Thompson, *Attila*, 221; *PLRE* II, 906. This ceremony in Rome recalls the Roman republican practice of foreign leaders swearing oaths of friendship in the temple of Jupiter Capitolinis; the pagan temple of Isis at Philae was still used for this purpose in the mid-fifth century; Priscus, *Fr.*, 27.1 (*Fr. Class. Hist.*, 323). The visit of the Frankish prince to Rome, however, was probably necessitated by the presence there of Aetius, perhaps in connection with the recent, permanent relocation to Rome by Valentinian III; Gillett, 'Rome, Ravenna', 144, 147–8.

The diplomatic tie of adoption *per arma* is identified as 'barbarian' by Procopius, *Wars* I, 11.22 and Cass., *Variae* IV, 2.1, 2, though not necessarily exclusive to the northern barbarians; Procopius' example involves the Persian royal family (the proposed adoption of Chosroes, son of the shah Cavades, by the emperor Justin I). In Procopius, *Wars* I, 11.22, it is proffered by Justin's *quaestor* Proclus as a form of adoption inferior to Roman adoption by written document, but it is unclear whether Proclus means that adoption ὅπλων σκευῇ is inferior because it precludes inheritance, i.e. of the empire (cf. Procopius, *Wars* I, 11.17–18), or whether the term is a figure

With regard to visiting envoys, the ceremonial involved in the reception of an embassy established a backdrop with its own messages of reassurance or intimidation. On the one hand, ceremonial could signify the degree of respect the host wished to pay to the embassy and its principal (just as the rank of a dispatched envoy conveyed the degree of honour the sender wished to pay to the recipient). Justinian received the Persian legate Isdigousnas in late 550 '[not] simply as an envoy, but counted him worthy of much more friendly attention and magnificence'; the citizens of Constantinople were disgruntled at the scale of this public μεγαλοπρέπεια.[154] Procopius presents a dialogue between the Gothic king Totila and the deacon of Rome (later Pope) Pelagius, debating in what manner it is most appropriate for a host to honour an envoy.[155]

On the other hand, disrespect and displeasure could be demonstrated by manipulation of protocol, and could be aimed at undermining the envoy himself or at sending an aggressive message to his principal. When Totila received Pelagius, the king spoke first; according to Procopius, Pelagius took this reversal of the usual order of speech and reply as a deliberate insult, calculated to pre-empt his mission and make him appear ineffectual before the citizens of Rome who had sent him.[156] Delayed and cold receptions, restrictions on the envoy, and brusque dismissal without the informal meetings and negotiations which conventionally followed an audience all conveyed the host's displeasure.[157] Most blunt was refusal to receive an embassy at all, which could express annoyance with the

of speech for conquest (so H. B. Dewing, n. to Procopius, *Wars* I, 11.22). Analogues are available to both options from the few examples available. For preclusion from inheritance: Cass., *Variae* VIII, 9.8 (the Goth Gensimund, adopted presumably by Theoderic, is not a member of the Amal family for purposes of succession to the throne); for an attribute of military defeat and submission: Jordanes, *Get.*, 273–7 (the Suevic king Hunimund is defeated by the Gothic king Theodemer and adopted under duress, but later rebels and kills Theodemer). The custom marks submission of one ruler to a superior; cf. Jordanes, *Get.*, 289 (the emperor Zeno adopts Theoderic the Amal, probably when he was *magister utriusque militiae praesentalis* and *patricius*; *PLRE* II, 1079). Notwithstanding the comparison made by the *quaestor* Proclus between Roman adoption by written document and barbarian adoption, adoption-in-arms could be carried out by letter: Cass., *Variae* IV, 2 (Theoderic adopts the king of the Heruli); presumably VIII, 1.3 (the emperor Justin had adopted Eutharic, nominated successor of Theoderic). See Amory, *People and Identity*, 64 n. 97.

154 Procopius, *Wars* VIII, 11.7 (trans. Dewing).

155 Procopius, *Wars* VII, 16.9–32. Cf. Malchus, *Fr.*, 17: the emperor Zeno 'received the envoys [of the Vandal king Huneric] in a friendly manner, bestowed upon them the honour due to ambassadors, [and] sent them away laden with the appropriate gifts'.

156 Procopius, *Wars* VII, 16.27–32.

157 Brusque dismissal: never more so than Gregory of Tours, *Hist.* VII, 14 (horse dung and other filth thrown on envoys – note that Gregory specifies that this happens to the envoys *euntes*, i.e. as they formally depart); cf. Hyd., 238 [234]; Procopius, *Wars* VII, 21.25; VIII, 24.5; Malalas, *Chron.* XVIII, 57 (Justinian abuses Vandal envoys from the Vandal usurper Gelimer). Other obnoxious changes to convention: Priscus, *Fr.*, 11.2 (Hunnic envoy Orestes insulted at not being invited to a *convivium* as his partner Edeco was; Roman envoys offended at being asked to state the purpose

envoys themselves, or an equivalent of the modern refusal of diplomatic recognition; this was a reaction recorded particularly for representatives of usurpers.[158] The ramifications of insulting an envoy were pertly exploited by Gregory of Tours when King Guntram was proving particularly intractable on a domestic issue. Gregory reports: ' "Listen, O King! I have been sent by my lord on an embassy to you. And what will I answer him who sent me, when you refuse to give me a response?" Stupefied, [the king] said, "And who is your lord who sent you?" Smiling, I said to him, "The holy Martin sent me." ' Guntram acceded to Gregory's petition.[159]

On the other hand, ritual also displayed to visiting envoys the scale of resources and strength of the host's forces. Cassiodorus' *formulae* stress that the ostentation of meals and *convivia*, and of palace architecture, were vehicles for important political messages.[160] Similarly, hosts ensured that envoys witnessed public ceremonies other than those put on specifically for their benefit. The *patricius* Symmachus, sent by the eastern imperial court to Italy during the consulate of Theoderic's nominated successor Eutharic in 519, was 'amazed at the riches given to the Goths and the Romans' during the consular celebrations.[161] Military parades were

of their mission before reaching Attila's court; *Fr. Class. Hist.*, 249, 251); Gregory of Tours, *Hist.* IX, 20 (Guntram's warmer reception of envoys from Fredegund than of Childebert II is noted by the latter's legate); Menander Protector, *Fr.*, 9.3 (the emperor Justin II throws the Persian envoy Mebodes into confusion by his cold reception, in direct contrast to that given to his predecessor, Isdigousnas).

158 Priscus, *Fr.*, 23.3, 41.2 (*Fr. Class. Hist.*, 317, 347); Procopius, *Wars* VII, 37.6–7; Gregory of Tours, *Hist.* IX, 1, 16 (the Frankish king Guntram refuses to receive envoys from the Gothic king Reccared, but sends messengers to them to learn their mission). Withdrawal of recognition: Malalas, *Chron.* XVIII, 57 (Gothic king Athalaric refuses to receive Gelimer's embassies, on Justinian's instructions); usurpers: below, n. 182.

159 Gregory of Tours, VIII, 6: *'Audiat, o rex, potestas tua. Ecce! a domino meo in legatione ad te directus sum. Vel quid renuntiabo ei qui me misit, cum nihil mihi responsi reddere vellis?' At ille obstupefactus ait: 'Et quis est dominus tuus qui te misit?' Cui ego subridens: 'Beatus Martinus', inquio, 'misit me.'*

160 *Convivia*: Cass., *Variae* VI, 3.6, 6.4, 9.7–8; VII, 5.1, 33; architecture: VII, 5.1; cf. Priscus, *Fr.*, 11.1 (*Fr. Class. Hist.*, 245). Gregory of Tours, *Hist.* IX, 20 gives a characteristic perspective on the effect of a royal *convivium* on himself as an envoy: 'he invited us to his dinner, which was not more weighed down with dishes than lavish with gaiety' (*convivio nos adscivit, quod fuit non minus oneratum in fercolis quam laetitia opulentum*); cf. Sid. Ap., *Ep.* I, 2.6.

Priscus, *Fr.*, 13.1 [8] shows an alternative exploitation of conventions of display: at a lavish dinner for leading nobles as well as envoys from Constantinople, Attila ostentatiously eats simple food with wooden plates and cups, and eschews the ornamentation of clothes and weapons which mark other Hunnic leaders' claims to status; the Roman envoys are suitably impressed. Similar acts of signal restraint appear as exempla of humility in hagiography, e.g. Sulpicius, *Dialogi* II, 6; Constantius, *Vita Germani*, 35.

161 Cass., *Chron.*, 1364: *stupente etiam Symmacho Orientis legato divitias Gothis Romanisque donatas.* Cf. Zacharias Rhetor, *Historia ecclesiastica* IX, 17, cited by Lee and Shepard, '*Peri Presbeon*', 35 (Persian envoys witness Belisarius' triumph parade in Constantinople after the defeat of the Vandals). For a later period: McCormick, 'Analyzing Imperial Ceremonies', 9 n. 25. At Procopius, *Wars* VI, 29.7–15, 22, 30, Belisarius addresses his army in the presence of two senatorial envoys from Justinian, in order to preclude any suspicion of secret dealing with the Goths on his part.

a blunter demonstration of strength. One group of Suevic envoys to Toulouse in 467–8 was present at a muster of the Gothic army, while a second Suevic legation witnessed the arrival at Rome of the massive fleet assembled against Vandal Carthage.[162] Senatorial envoys to Roman emperors had been similarly treated to demonstrations of military strength and the spectacle of foreign suppliants.[163] Such displays required strict stage management, for whatever their benefits, they had the potential to be disastrous if proceedings went out of control. In 555, a Persian envoy accompanied Justinian to races held in commemoration of the anniversary of the foundation of Constantinople. But the emperor was embarrassed in front of the envoy when the crowd in the hippodrome chanted in protest at a current bread shortage; Justinian inflicted harsh punishments.[164] By the same token, manipulation of what the envoy saw included restrictions on what he should not see or learn; it was desirable, from the host's point of view, for the envoy to witness parades of military might, but not to learn exact details of the actual strength of army resources.[165]

Just as diplomatic correspondence observed the forms of letters of friendship, so many aspects of the reception of embassies followed the outward conventions of hospitality. This included not only invitations to *convivia* and the provision, in certain cases, of accommodation, but also the exchange of gifts, ritualised as part of the ceremonial of the reception of embassies. Gift-exchange between rulers via embassies had an ancient tradition throughout the Mediterranean region and Iran; sources tend particularly to record exotica. The eastern emperors continued this traffic with the Persian shahs and lesser rulers.[166] The exchange of presents was such a regular element of the reception of Persian embassies that officials of the imperial vestry had the duty of assessing the gifts brought by Persian envoys to ensure that presents of similar worth were offered in return, and additional doors into the *consistorium* were available to accommodate the delivery of horses.[167] Western rulers, too, exchanged gifts through embassies. Cassiodorus' letters show a regular commerce of gifts among

[162] Hydatius, *Chron.*, 243, 247 [238, 241]; Gillett, 'Accession of Euric', 20–2; Gillett, 'Rome, Ravenna', 132, 152. See also Procopius, *Wars* II, 21.1–14; III, 7.9. *On Envoys* in Lee and Shepard, '*Peri Presbeon*', 30 = *Anon. Byz. Treatise on Strategy* XLIII.

[163] Matthews, *Western Aristocracies*, 32–3.

[164] Malalas, *Chron.* XVIII, 121.

[165] E.g. '*Peri Presbeon*', 30 = *Anon. Byz. Treatise on Strategy* XLIII; Nikephorus, *Short History*, ed. and trans. Mango, 11. Lee, *Information and Frontiers*, 166–70.

[166] E.g. Marcellinus *comes*, *Chron.*, s.aa. 448.1, 496.2 (gifts of a tiger, an elephant, and two giraffes to the eastern emperor from *provincia India* (Axum? cf. Croke, *Chronicle of Marcellinus*, 109)); Malalas, *Chron.* XVIII, 36 (embassy to the shah Cavades announcing Justinian's accession bears gifts, 529).

[167] *De cer.* I, 89 (Reiske 405 (doors), 407 (assessment)).

western kings; Theoderic enlisted the aid of Boethius in preparing items for the Burgundian king Gundobad and the Frankish Clovis.[168] Royal and imperial gift-exchange is attested earlier in the *Chronicle* of Hydatius, and later, regularly, in the many royal embassies in the *Histories* of Gregory of Tours.[169]

One gift had the striking fate to be owned by at least two kings and by the two leading generals of the eastern and western halves of the fifth-century empire: Zercon, a Moor whose severe hunched back, stammer, and quick wit condemned him to a life as an object of humour. Given as a gift to the eastern *magister utriusque militiae* Aspar in Proconsular Africa either by a leading citizen of Carthage or, perhaps, by the Vandal king Geiseric, Zercon subsequently passed as war booty into the possession of Bleda, co-ruler of the Huns with his brother Attila. Regarding Zercon as an unwanted gift, Attila, after his murder of Bleda, gave him to the western *magister utriusque militiae* Aetius, who in turn presented Zercon back to Aspar.[170]

Not only the principals but the envoys themselves could give and receive gifts. The historian Priscus cynically observed that Attila exploited this practice as a way of enriching favourite subjects.[171] As with other aspects of ceremonial, alterations to the customary protocol of gift-giving could be powerful means of negotiation. The Constantinopolitan senator and *patricius* Severus, sent by the emperor Zeno to Geiseric to negotiate

[168] Cass., *Variae* I, 45–6 (to Gundobad, a sundial and water-clock); II, 40–1 (to Clovis, a harpist); IV, 1 (the Thuringian king Herminifrid, when marrying Amalaberga, niece of Theoderic, sends in addition to the bridal *pretia* of a herd of horses, gifts including domesticated beasts (*beluasque morigeras*)); V, 1, 2 (gifts of swords and amber from the kings of the Warni and Haesti respectively); Theoderic sends unspecified return gifts to the Thuringian, Warni, and Haesti kings.

[169] Hydatius, *Chron.*, 226 [222] (Theoderic II of Toulouse and the Suevic ruler Remismund). Gregory of Tours, e.g. *Hist.* IV, 40; VI, 2 (one-pound gold medallions from the emperor Tiberius II to the Frankish king Chilperic, and other gifts), 3, 34, 40; VIII, 35; IX, 1, 16 (*acceptisque ac datis muneribus*), 25, 28 (a large golden salver decorated with jewels, and wooden dishes with gold and jewel decorations, from Brunhild, mother of king Childebert II, to the Gothic king Reccared), 29. Also *Ep. Austr.*, 18 (gifts from Justinian to the Frankish king Theudebald).

[170] Priscus, *Fr.*, 13.1–3 (*Fr. Class. Hist.*, 287–9). A possible chronology for the travels of Zercon is as follows. Given to Aspar 'in Libya': between Aspar's arrival in 431 as part of the eastern fleet against the Vandals, and his departure, sometime between 434 and 441 (*PLRE* II, 166; for departure *c.* 441: Thompson, *Attila*, 81; for late 434: Clover, *Geiseric the Statesman*, 43–53, who postulates some form of treaty between Aspar and Geiseric). Capture: during a Hunnic raid on Thrace, probably the push which reached Constantinople in 443, at which Aspar and his fellow generals were defeated (Thompson, *Attila*, 84). Death of Bleda: 445 (*PLRE* II, 230). Presentation to Aetius: between 445 and 449, the date of Priscus' embassy to Attila, possibly as part of the negotiations transferring to the Huns part of Pannonia near the Save (Priscus, *Fr.*, 11.1 (*Fr. Class. Hist.*, 243); *PLRE* II, 27).

[171] Envoys receiving gifts: *De cer.* I, 90 (Reiske 408); Malchus, *Fr.*, 17 (the emperor Zeno and envoys of the Vandal king Huneric); *Vita Epiphani*, 188 (though here the gifts given to envoys 'pro ipsorum quiete' could mean subsidies to be passed on to the envoys' principals). Attila: Priscus, *Fr.*, 10, 14.1 (*Fr. Class. Hist.*, 243, 293).

a truce, declined the king's offer of gifts. Not money and valuables, said Severus, but the handing-over of Roman captives, was an appropriate gift for an envoy; Geiseric, impressed by his personal integrity, concurred.[172] The cultivation of ties through gift-exchange, however, was not restricted to the long-distance exchange of monarchs and generals and their representatives. Private petitioners to provincial authorities took gifts to lubricate their demands.[173] Somewhat more surprisingly, emperors, kings, and senior magistrates are attested giving gifts to provincial envoys.[174]

The ceremonial of an imperial or royal audience demanded ritual clothing. At the imperial court of Constantinople, envoys from the West changed into dark-coloured chlamyses before entering the imperial presence.[175] Clothing projected multiple symbolic messages in different contexts. In the tableau of authority which a formal reception entailed, the ritual symbolism of power overrode even religious ideology. Lupicinus, abbot of a monastery in Burgundian Gaul, imitated St Martin in his extreme poverty of clothing, an inversion of social conventions intended to make a bold statement of humility. Yet, when undertaking intercessions at the court of the Burgundian kings, even Lupicinus put shoes on.[176]

No late antique source attests any distinctive emblem marking envoys, with one exception. In a scene set in 585, Gregory of Tours describes two *legati* dispatched from the Merovingian royal usurper Gundovald to king Guntram, 'with staffs [*virgae*] consecrated according to the manner of the Franks, so that they should not be interfered with by anyone, but should return after their embassy with the king's response'. This is one of the very few apparently Frankish customs Gregory describes, but its mention is not incidental. Gregory's unique reference to this token of inviolability bodes ill for the envoys, for only a few lines later they are put in chains, set on the rack, beaten, interrogated under torture, and thrown into prison, a characteristically Gregorian punch-line.[177]

172 Malchus, *Fr.*, 5 (*Fr. Class. Hist.*, 411); see above, chapter 4, n. 191.

173 E.g. Sid. Ap., *Ep.* IV, 8.5.

174 Sulpicius, *Dial.* II, 5 (the emperor Valentinian I to Martin); Constantius, *Vita Germani*, 24 (praetorian prefect of Gaul Auxiliaris to Germanus); *Vita Viviani*, 6 (Theoderic I of Toulouse to Vivianus); Ennodius, *Vita Epiphani*, 188 (general reference to the many gifts Theoderic bestows on envoys).

175 *De cer.* I, 87.

176 *Vies des Pères du Jura* [*Vita Lupicini*], ed. Martine, 63. On clothing symbolism in saints' *Vitae*: Lynda L. Coon, *Sacred Fictions: Holy Women and Hagiography in Late Antiquity* (Philadelphia, 1997), 52–70.

177 Gregory of Tours, *Hist.* VII, 32–3: *cum virgis consecratis iuxta ritum Francorum ut scilicet non contingerentur ab ullo, sed exposita legatione cum responsu reverterentur* (the names of the envoys, Zotanus and Zahulfus, are interpolated in only one late manuscript; Krusch-Levison, n. *ad loc.*). W. Goffart, 'Foreigners in the *Histories* of Gregory of Tours', in his *Rome's Fall and After* (London, 1989), 275–7; E. James, 'Gregory of Tours and the Franks', in Murray (ed.), *After Rome's Fall*, 60.

In the classical Greek and early republican period also, heralds and other messengers bore staffs as tokens of their peaceable office. The custom appears in Virgil, and several late antique Latin commentators gloss the *virga* of envoys as a *pacis signum*.[178] It seems unlikely that the practice Gregory reports had any direct continuity from the classical convention; an iconographical attribute such as a staff would probably have been worked into literary descriptions of envoys by authors such as Sidonius Apollinaris or Ennodius. It is striking that a golden staff (*aurea virga*, χρυσέην ῥάβδον) was an emblem of office of several early sixth-century officials of the imperial court of Constantinople and the Ostrogothic royal court of Ravenna: the *cura palatii* (*curopalatus* in Constantinople), the decurions of the *silentarii*, and the ostiary.[179] The duties of the *cura palatii* and decurions included the reception and conduct of foreign and western imperial envoys, but there is no indication that they bore their staffs when conducting legations. Rather, the ceremonial function of the golden staffs was associated with the person of the ruler: the *cura palatii* and decurions bore them before the emperor or king when he travelled; the ostiary carried his staff when introducing high officials into the imperial presence.[180] It is possible but by no means certain that the staffs mentioned by Gregory of Tours (which he does not describe as golden) represent a transfer of these imperial emblems to envoys, as a token of the royal authority they represent.

Ius gentium

Eulogies of individuals who had undertaken embassies to rulers often stress the dangers they faced from hostile recipients; several sources refer to envoys who were imprisoned or killed by their host. Such acts could be deliberate provocations or, in the case of captivity, insurance against attacks.[181] The position of legates was precarious in times of war, and

178 '*Virga*', in *Dictionnaire des antiquités grecques et romaines* (Paris, 1919; repr. Graz, 1969), v, 924–5. Virgil, *Aeneid* IV, 242. Servius, *In Vergilii carmina commentarii*, ed. A. F. Stocker *et al.*, III (Oxford, 1965), 333–5, on Vergil, *Aeneid* IV, 242 (late fourth century); Varro *apud* Nonius Marcellus, *De compendiosa doctrina*, ed. W. Lindsay (Oxford, 1903), 528 (Nonius: early fourth century); Placidus, *Liber glossarum* in *Corpus glossariorum latinorum* V, ed. G. Geotz (Leipzig, 1894), 550, line 8 (mid-fifth century).

179 Whitby, 'On the Omission', 468–83; ostiary at 469–70 n. 55.

180 *Cura palatii*: Whitby, 'On the Omission', 466; decurion: 478–9.

181 Provocation: Hyd., cc. 121, 139 [113, 131]: the *comes* Censorius, captured by the Sueves in 440, executed during a period of Suevic–imperial hostility in 448; *The Chronicle of Pseudo-Joshua the Stylite*, trans. Trombley and Watt, 50, 54: the shah Cavades I holds Anastasius' envoy Rufinus during the seige of Amida, releasing him in order to spread news of the city's destruction; Gregory of Tours, *Hist.* IV, 40: Persarmenians kill Persian envoys, then seek miliary aid from the emperor Tiberius; Nikephorus, *Short History*, VII: the shah Chosroes II imprisons envoys of the

envoys from or associated with usurpers in particular could not expect to travel with impunity.[182] Yet by and large, embassies seem to have travelled without molestation in late antiquity. The great majority of legations throughout the West, supplications for tax relief or other petitions, faced no greater threats than the vicissitudes of travel. In times of tension, practical considerations were paramount in safeguarding legations: the necessity to maintain channels of communication outweighed the urge to give way to pique. Escorts could be provided to ensure the safe conduct of envoys sent by an antagonist, either by force of arms or by the moral force of priests.[183] But the office of envoy carried its own degree of protection. A scene from the *Histories* of Gregory of Tours dramatically shows the potential ramifications of assaulting members of an embassy. Grippo, an experienced Frankish envoy stopping over in Byzantine North Africa *en route* to Constantinople, faces down an angry mob which has already killed his two fellow legates over a misunderstanding, saying:

> We don't know what's supposed to have happened, but look! my companions on this journey, who had been sent to the emperor, cut down by the sword! God will judge our injuries and their death by your destruction, since you have butchered us, innocent as we are and coming in peace. Nor will there any longer be peace between our kings and your emperor, for we came in peace and to give aid to your empire. Today I call God as witness that your crime is to blame that the promised peace between our leaders will not be kept.[184]

emperor Heraclius. Insurance: Procopius, *Wars* v, 7.22; vi, 22.23–4: Theodahad imprisons Peter *patricius* and Athanasius for the first three years of hostilities with Constantinople, cf. vi, 22.23; possibly *Ep. Wisigoticae*, 13: the Frankish king Theuderic II captures envoys of the Gothic king Gundemar during a period of border conflict between Gaul and Spain, *c.* 610–12.

182 War: e.g. Hyd, c. 224 [220]: envoys from Aegidius to the Vandals travel via the Atlantic, presumably to avoid hostilities from the Goths of Toulouse or their allies the Sueves (cf. Gregory of Tours, *Hist.* viii, 35: ships from Gaul to Gallaecia attacked by orders of the Gothic king Leuvigild); Gregory of Tours, *Hist.* v, 26, 29, 40: envoys of Bretons held by Frankish king Chilperic; *ibid.*, vi, 2: envoys of the Frankish king Chilperic, shipwrecked when returning from Constantinople, find it safer to enter Gothic territory in Spain than lands controlled by Chilperic's cousin Guntram.

Usurpers: fourth-century examples in Elton, *Warfare in Roman Europe*, 193–4 and nn. 50–1. Olympiodorus, *Fr.*, 39.2 = Philostorgius xii, 13: Theodosius II and envoys of the usurper John; Eunapius, *Fr.*, 37: Valens and Gothic envoys, sent in association with pact between Goths and the usurper Procopius; Malalas, *Chron.* xviii, 57: Justinian abuses and dismisses envoys of Vandal usurper Gelimer; Gregory of Tours, *Hist.* vii, 30, 32, 33: Frankish king Guntram imprisons and tortures envoys of the usurper Gundovald. Note especially *ibid.* ix, 28: Guntram imprisons envoys on suspicion of travelling to the usurper Gundovald, but on learning that they in fact are travelling to the Gothic king Reccared on behalf of Brunhild, mother of king Childebert II, Guntram releases the envoys; yet at the time, Guntram was in a state of *inimicitia* with Reccared and refused to receive Gothic embassies; cf. *ibid.* ix, 1, 16, 20.

183 Soldiers: Zosimos, v, 45.5; Procopius, *Wars* vi, 7.15. Priest: Priscus, *Fr.*, 20 (*Fr. Class. Hist.*, 443).

184 Gregory of Tours, *Hist.* x, 2: *Quae gesta fuissent, nos ignoramus, et ecce! socii iteneris mei, qui ad imperatorem directi fuerant, gladio sunt prostrati. Iudicavit Deus iniuriam nostram et mortem illorum de interitu vestro, quia nos innocentes et in pace venientes taliter trucidatis. Nec ultra erit pax inter regis nostros*

The praetorian prefect of Africa, and later the emperor Maurice, go to great lengths to molify Grippo and his king, Childebert II.

Greco-Roman authors explained the free movement of legations, and other elements of interstate relations, by invoking the classical Roman legal concept of *ius gentium*. The term originally referred to a body of law which originated perhaps in praetorian ordinances of the early Roman republic, intended to control relations between Roman citizens and foreign traders by specific applications of Roman legal provisions to peregrines. The need for these laws was superseded by the expansion of Roman power throughout the Mediterranean. By the time of the early imperial juriconsultants, the term *ius gentium* had become understood in a much broader sense, in relation to *ius naturale* and *ius civilis*, as a body of legal concepts common to all peoples, distinct from the universal imperatives of living creatures or the legislative provisions of individual states. *Ius gentium* applied to that part of private law which involved human concepts deemed to be ubiquitous, such as most contracts, and also customs controlling relations of states to each other in war or peace. It is in this broad sense, in contrast to natural and civil law, that the term is defined in Justinian's *Institutes* (derived from the second-century jurist Gaius). The concept was largely one of moral value rather than practical application.[185]

According to the jurisconsultants, *ius gentium* precluded the physical punishment of envoys or their restraint in the outbreak of war, but the concept affected the conduct of embassies in a broader way than specific legal definitions.[186] The term, loosened from a specifically legal context, became part of the public discourse of state affairs. Roman literary authors of the republic and early empire, particularly the historians Livy, Tacitus, Sallust, and Quintus Curtius Rufus, freely employ the term as a set of sacred standards which declared *nefas* certain activities in wartime, including the violation of foreign envoys or the commencement of war without just cause.[187] A century after Justinian's commissioners restated

imperatoremque vestrum. Nos enim pro pace venimus et pro adiutorio rei publicae inpertiendo. Testem hodie invoco Deum, quia vestra excitavit noxa ut non custodiatur inter principes pax promissa. Cf. *ibid.* X, 4: Maurice sends to Childebert twelve suspects, with the right to execute them if he wished.

185 Justinian, *Institutes* I, 1.2.2. Kunkel, *An Introduction to Roman Legal and Constitutional History*, 75–83, 100; A. A. Schiller, *Roman Law: Mechanisms of Development* (The Hague, 1978), 525–30; Max Kaser, *Ius gentium* (Forschungen zum Römischen Recht 40; Cologne, 1993); P. Stein, *Roman Law in European History* (Cambridge, 1999), 12–13.

186 Pomponius *apud Digest* L, 7.17 (cf. Procopius, *Wars* VI, 7.14; VI, 22.23). Cf. Ulpian *apud Digest* XLVIII, 6.7: provision for punishment under *lex Julia* for anyone harming *legatos oratores comitesve*. Kaser, *Ius gentium*, 33–5. For examples of historical instances of *ius gentium* cited for the protection (or prosecution) of envoys: Jerzy Linderski, 'Ambassadors Go to Rome', in E. Frézouls and A. Jacquemin (eds.), *Les Relations internationales* (Paris, 1995), 452–4 n. 4 with references.

187 *ThLL* VI, s.v. *gens* II F2a for references. Cf. Herodian VI, 4.6.

Gaius' definition in the *Institutes* and *Digest*, Isidore in his *Etymologies* defined *ius gentium* exclusively in terms of actions concerning peaceful or warlike relations, revealing the influence of literary over jurisprudential sources:

The law of peoples [concerns] the occupation of dwelling-places, construction, fortification, wars, captivities, slavery, the recovery of rights, treaties of peace, armistices, the sanctity of not violating envoys, and the prohibition of marriage between those who are born in foreign lands. It is called the law of peoples, because almost all peoples use this law.[188]

A similar concept of the *religio* of envoys' inviolability informs several fifth- and sixth-century narratives, which display an expectation that the 'name of envoy' at least ought to offer protection.[189] In Eunapius, war erupts between Valens and the Gothic king Athanaric when the emperor imprisons Gothic envoys without regard for their ἀξιώματα.[190] Priscus makes Attila threaten that he would impale an interpreter attached to a Roman embassy but that it would outrage the θεσμός of envoys.[191] Procopius has two Gothic kings, Theodahad and Totila, preface speeches with professions that 'the position of envoys is revered and in general has become respected among all people'; the phrase ἐς πάντας ἀνθρώπους in particular recalls *ius gentium*.[192] Both Menander Protector and Theophylact Simocatta indicate the barbarity of the khagans of the Avars by referring to their disregard of the 'universal laws of envoys'.[193] Amongst Latin authors before Isidore, the concept appears in Cassiodorus' *Variae*: writing in the name of Theoderic, the phrase *leges gentium* refers not to inviolability of envoys but to the process of mediation which the king encourages in order to prevent conflict between Clovis and Alaric II.[194] These references to *ius gentium* are small signs of the continuity from imperial to post-imperial times of the mental frameworks within which political communication occurred.

188 Isidore, *Etymologiarum sive originum libri XX*, ed. W. M. Lindsay, 2 vols. (Oxford, 1911), V, 6: *Quid est ius gentium: Ius gentium est sedium occupatio, aedificatio, munitio, bella, captivitates, servitutes, postliminia, foedera pacis, indutiae, legatorum non violandorum religio, conubia inter alienigenas prohibita. Et inde ius gentium, quia eo iure omnes fere gentes utuntur.*

189 E.g. Priscus, *Fr.*, 9.2; Procopius, *Wars* V, 7.17.

190 Eunapius, *Fr.*, 37.

191 Priscus, *Fr.*, 11.2 (*Fr. Class. Hist.*, 254).

192 Procopius, *Wars* V, 7.14; VII, 16.9; cf. VIII, 20.20. Cf. *On Envoys* (Lee and Shepard, '*Peri Presbeon*', 30 = *Anon. Byz. Treatise on Strategy* XLIII): 'When envoys are sent to us, they should be received with honour and liberality, for everyone treats envoys with respect.'

193 Menander Protector, *Fr.*, 12.4; Theophylact Simocatta, *Hist.* VI, 2.13.

194 Cass., *Variae* III, 3.2; cf. I.3; 2.3; 4.3, 4. Further allusions to mediation: above, chapter 5, n. 126.

Negotium agendum

Justinian's wars and after

The wars undertaken in North Africa, Italy, and Spain at Justinian's command began with a diplomatic démarche of the highest order. The use of lengthy speeches as part of Procopius' classicising historiographical style highlights the role of open communication in military tactics and strategy.[195] Tactfully critical of Justinian's decision to commence hostilities against the Vandals in the face of good counsel, Procopius portrays Justinian actively seeking *causae belli* against first the Vandals, then the Ostrogoths. Justinian uses his envoys to Carthage and Ravenna in order to negotiate in secret while spreading disinformation in public.[196] Both the imperial and the Ostrogothic courts sought strategic advantage through opening negotiations for military support with neighbouring powers, particularly the Franks in Gaul but also the Lombards in central Europe and Persia.[197] Several times, the Ostrogothic and imperial courts negotiated directly to end the conflict. Agreement was reached in 540 to end hostilities by partitioning Italy along the Po, but Belisarius overthrew this deal (to preclude charges of disloyalty on Belisarius' part, Procopius is careful to note that Belisarius' actions in this affair are at all times conducted in full view of the imperial envoys sent to ratify the peace treaty).[198] On the battlefield itself, generals dispatched frequent embassies to their counterparts and to the cities in dispute, to make economical use of their force; the brutal taking of Naples at the beginning of the war informed subsequent negotiations between generals and urban populations.[199] Through all these exchanges, the Gothic leadership, as much as the Roman generals and court, made use of the skills of trained orators and observed the protocols of embassies.[200]

195 Averil Cameron, *Procopius and the Sixth Century* (London, 1985), 148–50, 212.

196 Critical: Procopius, *Wars* III, 10.1–21; Roger Scott, 'The Classical Tradition in Byzantine Historiography', in Margaret Mullett and Roger Scott (eds.), *Byzantium and the Classical Tradition* (Birmingham, 1981), 73–4. *Causae belli*: III, 9.10–26; V, 2.23–4.31. Secret negotiations and disinformation: above, nn. 147–8.

197 Imperial approaches to Franks: Procopius, *Wars* IV, 4.8–10; VI, 28.7–23; VIII, 20.10, 24.11–30. Gothic approaches to Franks: V, 13.26–9; VI, 28.7–23; VII, 37.1; VIII, 34.17; Agathias, *Hist.* I, 1.7, 3.1, 5.1–6.1; to Lombards: Procopius, *Wars* VI, 22.11; to Persians: II, 2.1–2; VI, 22.17–20.

198 Justinian and Gothic kings negotiate for peace settlement: Procopius, *Wars* VI, 6.33, 7.13–15, 22.22; VI, 28.7–29.30 (Belisarius' intervention); VII, 21.18–25; VII, 37.6–7; VIII, 24.4–5.

199 Armistices and other communications between generals: e.g. Procopius, *Wars* V, 20.8–21.1; VI, 7.21–4; VII, 22.8–17, 37.11. Cities: see below, nn. 223–35.

200 Oratory: most obviously at Procopius, *Wars* VII, 21.18 (Totila sends to Justinian the *rhetor* Theodorus with the deacon Pelagius, who was a former papal *apocrisiarius* to Justinian and three times an envoy of the city of Rome to Totila himself; VII, 16.4–32; 20.23–5). Protocol: e.g. VI, 29.1–5 (Justinian observes rank in sending senators to negotiate peace with Vitigis); VII, 16.4–32 (Totila and the deacon Pelagius discuss correct ways of honouring envoys).

Procopius exploits the dramatic potential of embassy narratives with portraits of bold and eloquent envoys before hostile monarchs, images drawn from the same secular ethos as Cassiodorus' eulogies of court servants.[201]

Formal embassies constituted the infrastructure for this communication and negotiation. Letters too played an important role in communication, not only the short notes of credence conventionally sent with envoys but also substantive letters intended to be independently persuasive. Procopius, however, carefully distinguishes between communications which depend on the orations and negotiations of envoys, and those for which substantive letters (including field dispatches), borne by mere letter-bearers, are the effective means of communication.[202] The traditions and conventions of formal embassies which had constituted a significant part of the internal administration of the Roman empire, and which provided the medium of political exchange throughout the prolonged break-up of the Roman West, continued to serve as the framework of communication during the essentially internal conflict of the war between Constantinople and Italy.

Justinian's wars redirected the channels of political communication throughout the West. The long fifth century is characterised by the graduated fragmentation of the western imperial provinces among, for the most part, small groups of more-or-less allied barbarian groups, living within the territories they controlled and assuming control of Roman political institutions with varying degrees of consensus and legitimacy. The wars of the 530s and 540s, by contrast, were large-scale annexations of territories by an external force. The Constantinopolitan intrusion had clear precedents: the eastern campaigns of Theodosius I and Theodosius II to suppress western usurpers in 388, 394, and 424; naval campaigns against the Vandals in the 430s and 460s; interference with the Ostrogothic kingdom in the mid-500s. Justinian's wars, however, never really ended. The Byzantine toehold in Spain prompted conflict there until the 620s; the imperial presence in Italy, sharply reduced after the Lombard invasion of 568, was contested until the advent of the Normans in Italy in the early eleventh century. The historical memory of Justinian's wars, as much as the actual imperial presence in Italy and Spain, sustained the constant possibility of further attempts on the West, beckoned not least by the

[201] E.g. Procopius, *Wars* v, 7.13–25 (Peter *patricius* and Theodahad); vii, 16.4–32, 20.23–5 (the deacon Pelagius and Totila). For dramatic embassy narratives in earlier Greek historians: Priscus, *Fr.*, 23.3, 31.1; Malchus, *Fr.*, 5 (*Fr. Class. Hist.*, 317, 335, 411).

[202] Letter-bearers: e.g. Procopius, *Wars* vi, 24.1–11; 26.1–15, 25–26; vii, 9.6–20, 10.15–16.

bishops of Rome. This potential was briefly realised with the prolonged expedition to Italy and Sicily by the emperor Constans II from 662 to his death in 668.[203] Throughout the fifth century, the politics of the western kingdoms were essentially provincial: contact with imperial authorities was largely with senior civil and military magistrates at Arles, rarely with the imperial court in Rome or Ravenna.[204] After Justinian, every western ruler had to be mindful of distant Constantinople.

New terminology

Just as the dominance of France in early modern times bequeathed to modern diplomacy a heavily Francophone vocabulary, so Constantinople's position affected language of political communication in the early Middle Ages. From the early sixth century, the standard Latin term for an envoy, *legatus*, came to be displaced by a new term, *legatarius*. The first attested users of the term were Greek-speakers or translators from Greek, including the *legatarius* Anthimus, sent by either the imperial or the Ostrogothic court to the Frankish king Theuderic I.[205] Italian and Gallic authors of the sixth century continued to use *legatus*, but *legatarius* appears in the extant correspondence between the Frankish royal court and the imperial court of Constantinople, written in the 540s and 580s; it appears to have been adopted by the Frankish chancelleries in imitation

[203] Popes: e.g. Gregory the Great, *Registrum* XIII, 41. Constans II: *Liber pont.*, 79; Paul the Deacon, *Historia Langobardorum* V, 6–12; Judith Herrin, *The Formation of Christendom* (Princeton, 1987), 263–5. Frankish concern at the presence of Constans: Bede, *HE* IV, 1: the Neustrian *maior domus* Ebroin detained Hadrian, the abbot sent in 664 by Pope Vitalian to accompany Theodore of Tarsus to Canterbury, on suspicion of undertaking a mission from Constans to the Anglo-Saxon kings, detrimental to the Frankish kingdoms. (Ebroin detained the north African Hadrian, not the Greek Theodore, possibly because Hadrian's monastery was at Naples, which Constans had visited (W. Levison, *England and the Continent in the Eighth Century* (Oxford, 1946), 13–14; J. M. Wallace-Hadrill, *Early Medieval Europe* (Oxford, 1975), 63–4; Wood, *Merovingian Kingdoms*, 176); perhaps also because Hadrian had previously travelled through Gaul twice *diversis ex causis*.)

[204] Gillett, 'Accession of Euric', 31–2.

[205] Greek speaker: Anthimus, *De observatio ciborum, inscriptio*; *c.* 511–533 (nb. c. 64: *nos Graece dicimus*). Translators: Epiphanius, *Historia tripartita* VII, 24.9; X, 33.1; XI, 15.18; after 553 (Epiphanius' origins are not known, but he was employed by Cassiodorus to translate large amounts of Greek material; *legatarius* is not used in Cassiodorus' own writings); Rusticus *deaconis, Synodicon* in *Acta conciliorum oecumenicorum*, ed. E. Schwartz (Berlin, 1922–3), I, 4.2, p. 63 line 2; after 565 (on Rusticus: *Encyclopedia of the Early Church*, ed. A. Di Berardino, trans. A. Walford (Cambridge, 1992), II, 747). The only attested user who may antedate the early sixth century is the glossator Placidus, *Liber glossarum*, 550, line 8; ?mid-fifth century.

Legatarius continued to be used also in its traditional sense as an heir; *ThLL* VII, s.v. 1101; Niermeyer, *Mediae latinitatis lexicon minus* (Leiden, 1984), s.v. 593–4.

of imperial usage.[206] From the seventh century *legatarius* appears interchangeably with *legatus* in Frankish sources.[207]

From the mid-sixth century also, the term *apocrisiarius* is first attested for representatives sent by the bishops of Rome, often for prolonged periods, to the imperial court in Constantinople. The title of this office comes from Constantinopolitan chancellery usage. *Apocrisiarius* (or *responsalis*) was a generic term for messengers, including agents dispatched by senior magistrates to the imperial court, and by the patriarchs to each other as well as to the court, to convey and bring back communiqués. Justinian legislated to restrict the number of episcopal *apocrisiarii* at court; this perhaps had the effect of more distinctively restricting the term to 'registered' agents, especially in the West.[208] By the second half of the sixth century, it was conventional for papal *apocrisiarii* to reside in Constantinople for substantial periods, to maintain on-going communications with both the emperors and the patriarchs of the city, instructed by regular correspondence from Rome. Papal *apocrisiarii* resided also at the imperial exarchate in Ravenna.[209] Several attested *apocrisiarii* of the bishops of Rome subsequently became pope, including Vigilius, Pelagius I, Gregory I, and Martin; some were installed by direct imperial

[206] *Ep. Austr.*, 18 (the Frankish king Theudebald to Justinian, 547) uses *legatus*, but *legatarius* is used exclusively in 19 (the Frankish king Theudebert I to Justinian, *c.* 534–47), 25–39, 43–4, 46, 48 (Childebert II and Brunhilda to Maurice), 42 (Maurice to Childebert), all 584 or later. Ganshof, 'Merowingisches Gesandschaftswesen', 167–8. At *Ep. Austr.*, 20, the term *Visigothorum*, a Byzantine not a western usage, may be another Constantinopolitan influence on Frankish diplomatic correspondence: Andrew Gillett, 'Jordanes and Ablabius', in Carl Deroux (ed.), *Studies in Latin Literature and Roman History* X (Collection Latomus 254; Brussels, 2000), 482 n. 52.

Italian and Gallic writers: *legatarius* is not used by e.g. either Gregory the Great or Gregory of Tours. The latter uses *legatus* interchangeably as both a second declension singular and a fourth declension plural; examples of the latter include *Hist.* IV, 40; VIII, 44 (both uses); IX, 1; cf. M. Bonnet, *Le Latin de Grégoire de Tours* (Paris, 1890; repr. Hildesheim, 1968), 355–9. Gregory also uses both *missus* and *nuntius*, sometimes synonymously with *legatus* (e.g. V, 4; VI, 19; VIII, 18; IX, 13), sometimes apparently with a distinction between a *legatus* undertaking negotiation, a *nuntius* merely conveying a message (e.g. VI, 31, p. 300 line 5; VII, 24; IX, 18). Venantius Fortunatus, *Carm.* XI, 1.28 (MGH AA 4.1), once uses *legatarius* (often spelt *ligaturius*) for a pun, describing Christ delivered bound by Pilate to the Jewish judges: *ligatus dominus, magis legatarius, pax inter partes extitit.*

[207] Marculf, *Formulae* I, 11; Fredegar, *Chron.* II, 58; IV, 31, 45, 51, 71, 73 (Fredegar uses *legatarius* and *legatus* interchangeably; his plural for the former is *legataries*); *Lex Ripuaria*, 68.

[208] Justinian, *Nov.* 6.2, 3; 123.25. J. Pargoire, 'Apocrisaire', *Dictionnaire d'archéologie chrétienne et de liturgie* I.2 (Paris, 1924), 2537–55, esp. 2537–47; O. Treitinger, 'Apocrisiarius', in *Reallexikon für Antike und Christentum* I (Stuttgart, 1950), 501–4.

[209] Date: Pargoire, as for preceding note. The term does not appear in *Liber pont.* until the entry for Silverius (536–7). The envoys of Pope Leo I, sometimes suggested as the first *apocrisiarii* to the imperial court in Constantinople, are referred to only as *legatii* by Vigilius in his letter to Justinian on the Three Chapters, *Collectio Avellana*, 83.285. Instructions: Gregory the Great, *Registrum epistolarum* IX, 187, 189, 237; IX, 29 (Gregory refers to his *responsales* in numerous letters to other recipients, e.g. III, 7, 64; V, 39, 44; VII, 27; VIII, 11).

intervention.[210] The maintenance of representatives in Constantinople was a crucial element in relations between the bishops of Rome and the empire. Pope Gregory I initially withdrew his *apocrisiarius* when Phocas usurped power and killed Maurice.[211] The Frankish kings in the late sixth century also sometimes maintained representatives at the imperial court for periods of several years, and sought to gain the support of papal *apocrisiarii* for the appeals of their own envoys to the emperors.[212]

Embassy narratives from Merovingian Gaul

The *Histories* of Gregory of Tours give the clearest narrative indication of the regularity of communications between Constantinople and a western realm. Merovingian Gaul is the early medieval kingdom for which the most plentiful evidence is available.[213] Nevertheless, the chance survival of a score of diplomatic letters between Merovingian rulers and the imperial court in the letter collection known as *Epistolae Austrasicae* intimates a far busier interchange than Gregory attests.[214] Embassies occupy a prominent place in Gregory's narrative. Among external communications, embassies to and from Visigothic Spain are the most frequently recorded, though Gregory also mentions legations from Lombard Italy, Breton Armorica, Suevic Gallaecia, and a number of other regions and peoples.[215] Even more frequent are the many legations between the multiple Merovingian rulers.[216] Gregory makes no distinction in terminology or description between these latter, 'internal' embassies and those to other courts. His narrative is to a degree shaped by references to embassies: many chapters of the *Histories* open with the dispatch or arrival of an embassy, which

[210] Vigilius and Martin: *Liber pont.*, 60; 76. Pelagius I: Procopius, *Wars* VII, 16.5; Liberatus of Carthage, *Breviarium*, 22, 23. Gregory I: John the Deacon, *Vita Gregorii magni* (*PL* 75), 26; Paul the Deacon, *Vita Gregorii magni*, 7 (*apocrisiarii* also appear at *Liber pont.*, 75, 78).

[211] Gregory the Great, *Registrum* XIII, 38.

[212] Prolonged Frankish embassies at Constantinople: Gregory of Tours, *Hist.* VI, 2 (Chilperic's envoys to Tiberius II return after three years). Support of *apocrisiarius* for Frankish embassy: *Ep. Austr.*, 32 (Childebert II to the *apocrisiarius* Honoratus). Cf. Gregory the Great, *Registrum* XIII, 7, 9 (referring to appeal by Frankish rulers to assist in maintaining relations with the emperor).

[213] Gregory of Tours, *Hist.* e.g. IV, 40; VI, 2; VIII, 18; X, 2, 3, 4. On relations between the empire and the Merovingians: Goubert, *Byzance avant l'Islam*, II.1: *Byzance et les Francs* ; Ganshof, *Middle Ages*, 1–55; E. Ewig, *Die Merowinger und das Imperium* (Opladen, 1983); Barnwell, 'War and Peace'.

[214] *Ep. Austr.*, 18–20, 25–48.

[215] Visigothic Spain: Gregory of Tours, *Hist.* IV, 27, 28; V, 40, 43; VI, 18, 29, 33, 34, 40, 45; VII, 10; VIII, 28, 35, 37, 45 (*crebro*); IX, 1, 16, 28. Lombard Italy: IX, 25, 29. Bretons: V, 26; IX, 18. Suevic Gallaecia: V, 41. Avars: IV, 23. Saxons: IV, 14. Also Burgundy and Visigothic Aquitania, before Clovis' conquests: II, 28 (*saepius*), 32, 35; and Ostrogothic Italy: III, 31.

[216] Gregory of Tours, *Hist.* III, 24; IV, 49, 50; V, 17; VI, 3, 11, 19, 31, 36; VII, 5–7, 14; VIII, 13, 36, 44, IX, 20, 38, X, 15, 28. Also with Merovingian usurpers: IV, 16; VII, 30, 32–3. Ganshof, 'Merowingisches Gesandschaftswesen', 166, 168–9.

precipitates the following action. Gregory, predictably, gives precedence to bishops as envoys, but he also presents sufficient data to indicate the continued use of secular legates trained in traditional rhetorical skills.[217]

Gregory's writings are an early example of a medieval literary tradition employing embassies as a narrative device. Whereas Procopius is conscious of the time-delay involved in the sending and return of embassies, and the distinction between an embassy's principal and its members, Gregory sometimes (though not always) elides these distinctions. The embassy thus becomes the voice of its principal, and receives a reply directly from the recipient. Scenes of the reception of embassies therefore become dialogues between the two rulers.[218]

Gregory's seventh-century redactor and continuator Fredegar also features prominent embassy narratives. As well as including embassies in that part of his *Chronicle* composed by himself, covering the first half of the seventh century, Fredegar improves upon several narratives in his summary of Gregory (though not in his summary of Hydatius, another of Fredegar's major sources, perhaps because none of Hydatius' embassies concern the Frankish kingdom).[219] More than Gregory, Fredegar's embassy narratives are literary constructs, not mere data. Fredegar is aware of the confrontational drama inherent in scenes of audiences, which had been exploited not only in classicising historiography such as Procopius' works, but also in late antique hagiography and eulogy.[220] More distinctly the work of Fredegar is his exploitation of the potential in embassy narratives for dramas of concealment and deceit. Embassies invest in a single individual the transfer of confidential information over sometimes very long distances; the legate is, by definition, an outsider at a foreign court, privileged by virtue of the potential his presence bears for his principal's displeasure and hostility. The envoy, therefore, can be a catalyst for dramatic stories: by acting as a trickster, concealing or distorting his information; by intervening with impunity in local power struggles; and by conveying news of exotica from afar. Fredegar's embassy narratives are linked by recurring motifs, arising either from the legations themselves or from stories brought back by envoys from foreign climes: wronged queens

[217] See above, nn. 46 and 49, and below, nn. 232–3.

[218] Pizarro, *Rhetoric of the Scene*, 94–5; Pizarro, *Writing Ravenna*, 88 n. 35, 118 n. 39.

[219] Fredegar, *Chron.* II, 53, though placed after lengthy extracts from Hydatius, in fact expands upon a passage of Gregory of Tours, *Hist.* II, 7. Other expansions of passages from Gregory: II, 57; III, 11, 18–19, 58. Embassies in Fredegar's own composition: IV, 9, 30, 31, 35, 37, 38 *fin*, 40, 45, 49, 51, 62, 68, 69, 71, 73, 85. On Fredegar: W. Goffart, 'The Fredegar Problem Reconsidered', in his *Rome's Fall and After* (London, 1989), 319–54; Roger Collins, *Fredegar* (Authors of the Middle Ages: Historical and Religious Writers of the Latin West 4, Aldershot, 1996).

[220] E.g. Fredegar, *Chron.* II, 58: Clovis' envoy to Alaric II, Paternus (not in *PLRE* II, probably rightly; the name is used also for a seventh-century Frankish envoy at IV, 62).

restored to their rightful places through the intervention of envoys; new 'instructions' improvised by envoys to trick their hosts or intervene in conflicts; duels; fantastic elements including a magic potion and astrology; the frequent occurrence of the figure twelve; and in almost all of Fredegar's embassy narratives, deceit of one form or another, usually perpetuated by envoys on their hosts.[221] Procopius too presents a number of embassy narratives with strong elements of *fabulae*; these are set safely in the past.[222] By contrast, Fredegar's motifs occur somewhat more often in the part of the *Chronicle* which he composed himself, covering more recent history, than in his interpolations into earlier works. They suggest the influence of romance fiction on Fredegar's approach to historiography.

Municipal embassies in the sixth century

There is sufficient evidence for formal embassies among western rulers during the later sixth and seventh centuries, given the decline of extant evidence from the latter part of this period, to indicate that patterns of communication between heads of state were maintained.[223] Municipal and provincial legations are also attested, though far less clearly. In part this reflects changing sources. Secular eulogies for provincial magnates or court servants, such as appear in the letters of Sidonius and Cassiodorus, are lacking for this latter period (though, even in the writings of Gregory of Tours, there are indications of the status which accrued to palatine envoys, described in Gregory's characteristically deprecating manner[224]). The encomiastic image of bishop as envoy, developed in the *Vitae* of Germanus of Auxerre and Epiphanius of Pavia, seems no longer to have attracted hagiographers by the late sixth century.[225] When fifth-century texts were reworked in later centuries, references to embassies were often omitted. In the active cycle of hagiographical texts produced at Auxerre,

[221] Queens: Fredegar, *Chron.* IV, 51, 71 (cf. Cass., *Variae* IX, 1; Gregory of Tours, *Hist.* III, 31 for the precarious position of princesses married to foreign courts), cf. IV, 9 (the Christian queen of Persia in hiding at Constantinople). Improvised instructions: IV, 51, 68, 71. Duels: IV, 51, 64. Magic potion and astrology: IV, 49, 65. Figure twelve: II, 62 (Gelimer flees Belisarius with twelve followers, and kills twelve youths in combats), IV, 45 (twelve Lombard dukes each send envoys to the emperor Maurice, and to the Frankish kings). Deceit: II, 53 (Aetius, Theoderic II, Attila; expanding an already folkloristic story found in Gregory of Tours, *Hist.* II, 7), 57; III, 11; IV, 45, 49, 68, 69.

[222] Procopius, *Wars* I, 2.12–15, 3.8–14 (envoy as privileged outsider; cf. 3.15–4.35 for further oriental *fabulae*); III, 7.6–10, 22.3–12; cf. Scott, 'Classical Tradition in Byzantine Historiography', 73.

[223] Cf. Barnwell, 'War and Peace'.

[224] Gregory of Tours, *Hist.* III, 33 (Secundinus).

[225] E.g. no embassy narratives in Gregory of Tours' *Miracula* or the hagiographic chapters of the *Historiae*, though he often mentions bishops as envoys in the *Historia*. In his brief account of Germanus of Auxerre, Gregory (or his source) transforms the bishop's journey to Italy into a pilgrimage; above, chapter 4, n. 89.

Germanus' missions were relegated to a minor place.[226] Chroniclers redacting Hydatius' work, with the partial exception of Fredegar, deleted his accounts of embassies, and did not write their own.[227] By default, narrative *historia*, a genre almost absent for the fifth-century West, is the source most likely to register the occurrence of embassies.

Procopius' *Wars* and Gregory of Tours' *Histories*, the two lengthiest extant works of the sixth century, give considerable attention to palatine embassies. Municipal embassies do, however, appear in their narratives at crucial times: when a city faces a siege or is otherwise threatened with changing masters. Procopius records embassies to both the east Roman and the Gothic armies from Italian cities facing siege, most importantly Naples (before its occupation and slaughter of its population by the Byzantine army) and Rome.[228]

The most substantial account by Gregory of exchanges of embassies involving cities concerns a dispute in 584 between the Frankish kings Guntram and Childebert II involving the towns of Tours and Poitiers, which both kings seek to subjugate. The towns send and receive envoys from the two kings and their generals; moreover, Tours and Poitiers repeatedly exchange *legati* with each other.[229] What authority represented the towns is unclear; one can hope for, but not expect, such information from Gregory. Though Gregory mentions 'the bishop and citizens' of Poitiers as the recipients of an embassy, he refers only to *nos* when describing the dispatch of legations from Tours.[230] This exchange of embassies amongst cities, generals, and the king is recorded only because it involved Gregory's own see, which suffered considerable harm in the process. There are few other indications in Gregory's works of similar activity, though the cause for this traffic in embassies, attempts by Frankish monarchs to annex cities controlled by their fellow kings, occured repeatedly.[231] Elsewhere, Gregory describes bishops, including himself, sending envoys to Frankish kings and generals, and even treating with raiding Bretons.[232] His privileging of bishops as principals of non-palatine legations is to be expected, and should not be taken as a necessarily accurate picture of

[226] Texts associated with existing cults: above, chapter 4, n. 89–90.

[227] Above, chapter 2, nn. 18–19.

[228] Procopius, *Wars* V, 8.6–25 (Naples); VII, 16.4–32 (Rome); VI, 19.4–5 (Urbinus), 21.27 (Milan).

[229] Gregory of Tours, *Hist.* VII, 12 (*Tornici* to Guntram), 13 (Childebert's *dux* Gararic to Tours; *Toronici* to *Pectavis*: *rursum . . . remissis*; Poitiers to Tours), 24 (Guntram to Poitiers; Poitiers to Guntram).

[230] Gregory of Tours, *Hist.* VII, 13: *episcipo et civibus.*

[231] Cf. Gregory of Tours, *Hist.* III, 21 (Cabrières receives envoys from Theudebert).

[232] Gregory of Tours, *Hist.* III, 34; V, 4, 31; VIII, 18. Bishops also send *legationes* to citizens of their sees: V, 11; VII, 47. Cf. n. 46 above: Gregory privileges bishops over palatine officials both as principals and as named envoys.

exclusive authority over secular affairs by bishops; Gregory's views on the role of bishops distorts his representation of social structures.[233] One isolated reference in Gregory describes *Franci* sending envoys to a king to express allegiance; it is unclear what body this word represents.[234]

The references to municipal legations in Procopius and Gregory of Tours, though sparse, indicate that by the late sixth century, as for the medieval period as a whole, the right to send and receive formal legations remained general, not an exclusive attribute of sovereigns and their immediate agents. Municipal embassies are likely to have continued for as long as towns were politically and economically important, whether under the control of late incarnations of *curiae*, of comital appointees of kings, or of their bishops.[235] Embassies sent by towns and bishops, like the frequent legations among Frankish monarchs, represent the afterlife of Roman administrative practices of 'internal diplomacy'.

Two general points emerge from this survey of legatine practices. First, much of the evidence for the conduct of embassies, and indeed attestation of individual legations, comes not from documentary material, but from writers as different as Ennodius, Procopius, Gregory of Tours, and Fredegar, who exploit narrative accounts of embassies for a variety of literary strategies. Their exploitation depends upon considerable familiarity among contemporaries with the practice and conventions of communication by formal embassies. Knowledge was not merely general but detailed; Fredegar, in a *fabula* concerning Justinian, casually mentions a suppliant bribing the palatine servant who draws the silk curtains to usher petitioners into the imperial *consistorium*.[236] Secondly, ceremonial was an important element in the practice of communication. Negotiations could occur within the formal situation of audiences, or in informal settings such as *convivia*, other public displays, or even talks at the envoy's accommodation; the actual protocol used in any one situation could be variable.

[233] Martin Heinzelmann, *Gregory of Tours: History and Society in the Sixth Century*, trans. Christopher Carrol (Cambridge, 2001).

[234] Gregory of Tours, *Hist.* IV, 51.

[235] On authority in early medieval cities, see C. Wickham, *Early Medieval Italy: Central Power and Local Society, 400–1000* (London, 1981), 80–92; E. James, *The Origins of France: From Clovis to the Capetians, 500–1000* (Houndmills, 1982), 43–63, esp. 56–7; Roger Collins, *Early Medieval Spain: Unity in Diversity, 400–1000* (Houndmills, 1983), 88–108; W. Liebeschuetz, 'The End of the Ancient City', in J. Rich (ed.), *The City in Late Antiquity* (London, 1992), 1–49, esp. 15–25, 35–6; Liebeschuetz, *Decline and Fall of the Roman City*, esp. 124–36; D. Nicholas, *The Growth of the Medieval City from Late Antiquity to the Early Fourteenth Century* (London, 1997), 1–53, esp. 31; S. T. Loseby, 'Gregory's Cities: Urban Functions in Sixth-Century Gaul', in Ian Wood (ed.), *Franks and Alamanni in the Merovingian Period: An Ethnographic Perspective* (Woodbridge, 1998), 239–84, esp. 245–9. *Vitae sanctae Balthildis*, 6 (ed. Bruno Krusch in MGH SRM 2) seems to refer to hereditary curial obligations, *c.* 657/65.

[236] Fredegar, *Chron.* II, 62.

But ritual conventions framed all contact. Though differing degrees of respect may be paid to different parties through varied ceremonial practices, the right to engage in formal communication was open to all elements of society. Exchanges of embassies between monarchs are the best-attested examples of political communication, and those which draw the most attention from moderns. But these exchanges, 'diplomatic' in the modern sense, are only one manifestation of wider practices. Exchanges of embassies in late antiquity represent participation in formal patterns of communication, not in constitutional structures of sovereignty.

CONCLUSION

Formal embassies were an aspect of public life which continued from the later Roman empire through the fifth and sixth centuries into the time of the early medieval kingdoms. Originating in the exchanges of *civitates* before the rise of Roman hegemony, the 'internal diplomacy' of embassies played a fundamental part in the administration of the Roman empire. Cities, provincial councils, and other bodies communicated directly with the emperor and his senior magistrates, raising and resolving issues outside those addressed by bureaucratic administration, and maintaining the political cohesion of the vast empire through regular affirmations of loyalty. The conventions of the Second Sophistic, which flourished in the first and second centuries AD with a resurgence in the newly Christian empire of the fourth century, formalised the rhetorical practices of embassies, while imperial legislation regulated their conduct in regard to access to imperial officials, obligations and recompense for envoys, and the provision of state facilities to assist the undertaking of the journeys involved. Municipal and provincial embassies were thus officially coopted into the machinery of government. This system of internal communication was important to the functioning not only of the empire as a whole, but also of local society, where the successful completion of the burden of undertaking legations brought social advantage through prestige and perhaps rewards from the emperor. The traffic in embassies was essentially one-way: embassies from cities and provinces approached the imperial centre and returned with the authority's reply. The central government did not regularly need to delegate emissaries to represent itself to its constituents in the same manner.

Communications between the imperial government and external forces occurred largely through military channels. Only rarely were the conventions of internal communications transplanted to outside environments. The use of Sophists as envoys to foreign powers, however, begins to be attested in fourth-century relations with Sassanian Persia. The acceptance of permanent confrontation with an equally powerful neighbour, and a shared Hellenistic heritage, made possible two partial shifts: in the locus of communication, from military borders to the palaces of administrative centres; and in the medium, from displays of arms to rhetorical argument. Such civilian modes of negotiation, however, were not customary in treating with tribal groups on any of the empire's borders.

Officially regulated traffic in provincial and civic embassies continued throughout the fifth century within the areas under imperial rule, best demonstrated by Sidonius Apollinaris' provincial embassy to the emperor Anthemius in Rome in 467. The governments of Odoacer and the Ostrogothic monarchs maintained this machinery; Theoderic received legations not only from cities within Italy, but also from the provinces of Dalmatia and Provence. It is unclear whether the resources of the kingdoms in Gaul or Spain were sufficient to permit government assistance to civic legations, but there is evidence that in Gaul assistance was provided for emissaries to and from the royal court at least by public levy.

Whether or not governmental infrastructure was available, the habit of civic legations continued within the former western provinces after rule had devolved onto barbarian kings. The borders of each kingdom were not restrictions to diplomatic traffic. Hydatius shows Gallaecian provincials approaching imperial officials and the Gothic royal court in Gaul; Sidonius' letters reveal several appeals to the kings at Toulouse from Roman citizens of the Auvergne while still under imperial rule. Though the sources tend to advance bishops as representatives of regional communities, lay envoys elected by municipal councils or provincial assemblies continued to form the bulk of traffic. Close attention to provincial embassies shows regional communities as far more active in the political processes of the fifth century than may otherwise be supposed. Cities could organise their own defence; more characteristically, cities sought through embassies to avoid becoming theatres of war between competing forces, whether imperial or barbarian. There are indications that in the early fifth century, provincial and municipal bodies negotiated with barbarian monarchs as separate entities, not as impotent subjects.

The fragmentation of political power in the West throughout the fifth century, and the complex layering of authority and interstate relationships, gave rise to the need for royal courts themselves regularly to adopt the use of embassies to communicate with other rulers and even distant regional communities. Even rulers outside the former Roman territories adopted Mediterranean conventions of public communication, as Attila's use of Latin secretaries demonstrates. Within the former empire, rulers made use of the channels and conventions of imperial 'internal diplomacy' to communicate with other kings and with the imperial courts at Rome, Ravenna, and Constantinople. The use of Roman bishops and magnates by the Suevic kings in western Spain in the early 430s are the earliest datable examples; the earliest extant diplomatic letters written by western monarchs are those composed for Theoderic of Italy by Cassiodorus, and for the Burgundian king Sigismund by Avitus of Vienne, in the 500s and 510s. There is no reason to think that these attested communications were innovations, or that administrative patterns of oral and epistolary communication had suffered any substantial interruption in the course of the fifth century.[1]

Exchanges of communication throughout the West are rarely evidenced for the fifth century, not because of infrequency but because of the nature of the sources which are, on the one hand, generally exiguous for political events, and on the other, not concerned to record regular phenomena. The only extensive narrative record of the exchange of embassies is Hydatius' *Chronicle*, which shows a constant exchange of embassies between many participants, particularly in the later part of the work; even so, Hydatius gives most attention to the high politics of embassies between courts. It is Hydatius' choice to record embassies, not the frequency of traffic in Gallaecia, which is unusual. Sidonius Apollinaris refers with complete familiarity to embassies between regional communities, Gothic and Burgundian rulers, and imperial authorities, mainly in the context of praising individuals who had undertaken embassies. Modern studies often misinterpret the significance of individual embassies attested by the sources by failing to realise the context of ubiquitous exchange.

The necessity for courts to employ emissaries only enhanced the traditional status accruing to those who undertook civic legations. Courts employed leading citizens, including clergy, as envoys, to exploit their social status; courts also utilised the military experience of generals. When communicating with Constantinople in particular, the royal court of Italy sought to be represented by members of the highest Roman elites: the presidents of the Senate, and the bishops of Rome. But rulers also dispatched their own officials, perhaps in the great majority of cases. Educated in rhetoric as part of their early training in order to secure government posts, palatine officials were naturally able to undertake the same function that their counterparts in municipal posts performed. The images of professional orators, Sophists and philosophers, as upright and bold defenders of communities were absorbed as one aspect of the professional ethos of palatine officials, and are reflected in the letters of Cassiodorus and the *Epitaph* of Senarius.

As an important part of the politics of the post-imperial world, embassies participated in the public discourse of power. Ceremonial ritual

[1] Note the casual reference to correspondence between the royal court of Toulouse and Pope Hilary concerning the filling of a vacant see in 462; *Epistolae Arelatenses genuinae*, 15.

attended the dispatch and reception of embassies, and envoys became themselves the recipients of honour at courts, in addition to their role as registers of the degree of cordiality exchanged by their principals and hosts. The formal audience, with its protocols of restricted entry and its conventions of speech and reply, was itself a ritual around which other elements of ceremonial could be constructed.

The conditions of the fifth and early sixth centuries conspired to elevate the prestige of the duty of legation. The survival of provincial communities, or at least their prosperity under new rulers, could depend upon the representatives of their emissaries; court officials were ceremonially honoured by hosts when undertaking embassies, and rewarded by their ruler when successful. The envoy became a potent image to be appropriated and exploited, as works in a variety of genres attest. Sidonius' *Panegyric* on Avitus is a unique attempt to transfer the respect owed to envoys to imperial eulogy, prompted by the awkward circumstance of Avitus' position as a usurper. It is a work of propaganda, delivered at the specific occasion of Avitus' consular celebrations, to a precise audience, the Senate of Rome. These circumstances underscore his presumption of a ready acquaintance with the phenomenon of provincial and imperial envoys to western kings. Constantius, Ennodius, and the anonymous biographers of Orientius of Auch and Vivianus of Saintes also appropriated the secular image of the envoy for the subjects of their hagiography, a genre whose specific circumstances are less readily identifiable than those of panegyric. The new provincial elite of aristocratically born bishops sought to graft the trappings of prestige associated with their social origin onto episcopal office. Ennodius reveals explicitly the model of palatine legations which underlay his portrait of Epiphanius. The briefer secular eulogies of Cassiodorus and Senarius exemplify the same professional ethos which Ennodius seeks to appropriate.

By happy chance, these sources speak to each other in enlightening ways. Sidonius employs specific literary strategies in order to manipulate details of Avitus' career into an endless series of arduous legations on behalf of his local or wider community. Constantius and Ennodius employ strikingly similar techniques to achieve very similar images, suggesting at least indirect influence rather than parallel development. The account by Ennodius of Epiphanius' supplication to the Burgundian king Gundobad almost exactly mirrors that of the classicising historian Malchus concerning the senator and *patricius* Severus before Geiseric. Ennodius describes Epiphanius as eschewing the rewards for service sought by palatine envoys; Cassiodorus presents the career promotions of Senarius and other Italian palatine officials as just such rewards; while Senarius in turn chooses this same theme to commemorate himself.

Conclusion

The developments of the fifth century wrought significant changes on the former Roman West, as former provinces and prefectures separated or fragmented into autonomous kingdoms. Royal courts inserted a new layer of authority into the complex of governmental, civic, and ecclesiastic administration. These changes, however, occurred within the context of an active tradition of internal political communication within the Roman empire, flourishing in the late fourth century. The flexible conventions of formal embassies readily adapted to new circumstances. Provincial embassies, which before primarily conveyed expressions of loyalty to the imperial government or petitioned for minor adjustments to taxation regimes, now sought to ameliorate kings and emperors seeking to annex, plunder, or punish their cities. Central courts, formerly the recipients and dispensers of decisions to embassies, now regularly dispatched palatine functionaries or grandees to represent their own interests. The traffic in embassies within and among the western kingdoms and the empire evident in the late sixth century is a visible element of continuity from the imperial past; and indeed, this traffic and its conventions maintained a kind of unity within the 'diplomatic bloc' of the Mediterranean world. The framework for the political changes of the late antique West was formed by the largely unrecorded travails and persuasions of countless envoys.

Appendix 1

CHRONOLOGY OF CONSTANTIUS, *VITA GERMANI*

I GERMANUS' EPISCOPATE AND DEATH[1]

The traditional chronology, set out in Levison, depends on the reconciliation of seven sources, the reliability of none of which is demonstrable. The only absolute year dates are:

i. Prosper, *Chron* s.a. 429 (Germanus to Britain), a *terminus ante quam* for Germanus' election;

ii. Constantius, *Vita Germani*, 25, 42 (the *augusta* Galla Placidia alive when Germanus visited Ravenna; she died 27 November 450[2]), a *terminus ante quam* for Germanus' death.

A possible further year date is provided by:

iii. [Honoratus Massiliensis], *Vita Hilarii episcopi Arelatensis*, 21 (Germanus involved in attempts in 444/5 to depose Celidonius of Arles), a possible *terminus post quam* for his death.[3] This source, however, is not contemporary; it may have been written after 477 or later.[4] The testimony of the *Vita* has been questioned. The author seeks to exonerate his controversial subject, who was reprimanded by both papal and imperial authority; the revered figure of Germanus appears in *Vita Hilarii* not casually but specifically to support Hilarius over one of the main issues of contention.[5]

Other evidence comes from reconciling day-dates in liturgical and other documents of the church of Auxerre:

iv. the date for the death of Amator, Germanus' predecessor as bishop of Auxerre, is given as 1 May in the late sixth-century *Kalendarium Autissiodorensis*, a

[1] On the dates of Germanus' episcopate: Levison, 'Bischof Germanus von Auxerre und die Quellen zu seiner Geschichte', 98–101, 117–43; Levison, Introduction to 'Vita Germani', 225–7; P. Grosjean, 'Notes d'hagiographie celtique 29: le dernier voyage de S. Germain d'Auxerre', *AB* 75 (1957), 180–2; E. A. Thompson, 'A Chronological Note on St Germanus of Auxerre', *AB* 75 (1957), 135–8; Mathisen, 'The Last Year of Saint Germanus of Auxerre', 153–4; Thompson, *Saint Germanus*, 55–70; Ian Wood, 'End of Roman Britain', 14–16; R. Scharf, 'Germanus von Auxerre – Chronologie seiner *Vita*', *Francia* 18 (1991), 1–19.

[2] *PLRE* II, 889.

[3] Honoratus Massiliensis, *Vita Hilarii episcopi Arelatensis*, ed. Cavallin, 79–109.

[4] Cavallin, *Praefatio* to *Vita Hilarii*, 39.

[5] On Hilarius and Celidonius: R. W. Mathisen, 'Hilarius, Germanus, and Lupus'. The acquaintance (not expressly a close friendship) of Hilary and Germanus is attested in Constantius' *Vita Germani*, 23. Doubts on *Vita Hilarii*: Thompson, *Saint Germanus*, 57–60; Wood, 'End of Roman Britain', 15.

reconstructed local church calendar preserved in Gallic recensions of the *Martyrologium Hieronymianum*;[6]

v. *Vita Amatoris*, written by the priest Stephanus Africanus also in the late sixth century as part of a literary promotion of the cult of St Germanus, likewise gives Amator's date of death as 1 May, and specifies that this was the *quarta feria*.[7] In the decades before 429, 1 May fell on a Wednesday only in 407, 412, and 418;

vi. the first service in the late seventh/early eighth century *Missale Gallicanum vetus*, a mass in honour of St Germanus, states that he was bishop for thirty years;[8]

vii. the *Gesta episcoporum Autissiodorensis*, written in the 870s by Hericus, a monk of the monastery of St Germanus in Auxerre, and the canons Alagus and Rainogalus, includes an abridged, interpolated version of Constantius' *Vita Germani* which states that Germanus was bishop for thirty years and twenty-five days.[9]

Germanus' thirty-year episcopate, if it were to include the year 444/5 (iii above), must have begun on 418, not 407 or 412 (see v above). The year of his death must therefore have been 448.

The fragility of this construction is obvious. It depends on a saint's *vita* with a clear agenda, and on ecclesiastical records, dating from between one to four centuries after Germanus' life, set down to support a flourishing local cult. Levison described the dates 418 to 448 as only approximate, but these dates have calcified on the basis of his

[6] *Martyrologium Hieronymianum*, ed. J. B. de Rossi and L. Duchesne, AASS Nov II pars I (Brussels, 1894), 53 (death of Amator), 98, 124, 128 (on the *Kal. Autiss.*: xl–xliii). The *Kal. Autiss.* also gives anniversary dates for the death of Germanus (31 July), the reception of his body into Auxerre (22 September), and his burial (1 October). For the liturgical cycle of early medieval Auxerre and its attendant writings: Yitzak Hen, *Culture and Religion in Merovingian Gaul,* AD *481–751* (Leiden, 1995), 97–100.

[7] Stephanus Africanus, *Vita sancti Amatoris episcopi Autissiodorensis*, AASS Mai I, 51–61, c. 31. Literary promotion of cult: Introduction to *Vita Amatoris*, 51–2: letters of bishop Aunarius of Auxerre and Stephanus Africanus. Aunarius commissioned Stephanus to set the *vita* of Germanus (presumably Constantius') to verse, and to write a prose life of Amator. The verse *vita* of Germanus, if completed, is not extant.

[8] *Missale gallicanum vetus (Cod. Vat. Palat. lat. 493)*, ed. L. C. Mohlberg (Rome, 1958), I, *Contestacio*, 3–6 at 5; also ed. J. Mabillon, *PL* 72, 339–82, at 342 (on the *missale*: 219).

[9] Hericus, Alagus, and Rainogalus, *Gesta pontificum Autissiodorensium*, ed. L.-M. Duru, *Bibliothèque historique de l'Yonne* I (Auxerre, 1850), c. VII, p. 315: *annos XXX, dies XXV*; Levison, Introduction to *Vita Germani*, 226 n. 9 (the edition of the *Gesta* by P. Labbé, as reprinted in *PL* 138, c. 7, p. 226, gives Germanus' episcopate as *annos 25, dies 30*). On the *Gesta*: Duchesne, *Fastes épiscopaux* II, 432–3, 438–44.

The authors of the *Gesta* give data in a formula derived from *Liber pont.* (Duchesne, *Fastes épiscopaux* II, 433), including consular, regnal, and papal dates. The account of Germanus also includes a citation from *Liber pont.*, c. 44 (an anachronistic reference to Valentinian III as emperor residing in Ravenna, where Germanus would die). The dates, clearly the authors' reconstruction, are not sound; e.g. it is unlikely that Germanus pursued a secular career as early as the reigns of Valentinian (presumably I) and Gratian (i.e. in or before 375); the *Gesta* gives Celestine (d. 432) as the last pope during Germanus' lifetime, but states that his successor, Alodius, came into office four years after the death of Germanus, during the pontificate of Leo I (440–61); *Gesta*, cc. VII, VIII, p. 321, 322; Duchesne, *Fastes épiscopaux* II, 439.

authority.[10] There is some external corroboration for the anniversary dates given by the *Kal. Autiss.*, but none for the length of Germanus' episcopate.[11] Testimony for the latter is late; the *Vetus missale Gallicanus* provides only the most formalised presentation of Germanus' episcopate, and in the *Gesta episc. Autiss.*, a striking number of early bishops of Auxerre are recorded as having thirty-year episcopates.[12] Moreover, the *Gesta episc. Autiss.* is not internally consistent, and fails to coordinate the episcopates of Germanus and his predecessor Amator.[13]

The only dates which can be adduced for Germanus' journeys are Prosper's reference to the trip to Britain in 429, and inscription evidence for Auxiliaris in office as praetorian prefect of Gaul 435/7.[14] Auxiliaris' known predecessor and successor in office are attested for July 425 and 439, but it is likely that Auxiliaris was praetorian prefect until 439, and therefore most improbable that he was in office in the 420s or early 430s.[15] Constantius falsely makes Germanus' trip to Arles occur immediately after the first trip to Britain.[16] He appears misleadingly to collapse in time all the public events of Germanus' career.

The reference to the patriciate of Sigisvult, for which there is no firm dating, does not help date Germanus' final mission.[17] In any case, the reference need not be chronologically accurate for the narrative setting; Constantius may well have used a title of honour which the general acquired at a subsequent date, just as manuscript headings often describe authors with all their known titles, not just those held at the time of composition of the particular work which follows. Bagaudae unrest is attested for the years 435, 437, and 448; the Armorican revolt in *Vita Germani* cannot be firmly identified with any one of these, though Tibatto, named by Constantius as leader of the Armorican revolt, is attested in the 435/7 disturbances.[18] A final external attestation of the chronology of Germanus' career appears in the *Chron. Gall. 452* under the year 433: 'Germanus, bishop of Auxerre, was renowned for his miracles

[10] Levison: Introduction to 'Vita Germani', 225, 226. The years 418–48 as episcopate: e.g. Borius, Introduction to *Vie de Germain*, 44–5, 106; Heinzelmann, 'Studia sanctorum', 112 § 1; *PLRE* II, 'Tibatto', 1119. Critique: Mathisen, 'Last Year', 152–3 and n. 8.

[11] Anniversary dates: Grosjean, 'Le dernier voyage de S. Germain d'Auxerre', 180–2.

[12] I.e. the fourth, sixth, seventh, and eighth bishops, including Germanus, his predecessor Amator, and his successor Alodius. This round figure may be a hagiographic convention, or may reflect actual commemorations of the thirtieth anniversaries of the bishops' elevations, akin to imperial *tricennalia* (cf. Ennodius, *Dictio in natale Epiphani in annum tricensimum sacerdotii*, title and line 154); records of such celebrations perhaps served as a source of information for later archivists.

[13] The *Gesta episc. Autiss.*, 7, gives 1 May as the date of Amator's death (cf. *Kal. Autiss.*, 53 and *Vita Amatoris*, c. 31) and states that Germanus was ordained thirty days afterwards, i.e. 31 May. But *Gesta episc. Autiss.* also gives 31 July as the date of Germanus' death (cf. *Kal. Autiss.*, 98; Grosjean, 'Le dernier voyage de S. Germain', 180–1), and states that he was in office for thirty years and twenty-five days, i.e. his episcopate must have begun on 7 July. Levison, Introduction to *Vita Germani*, 226.

[14] *PLRE* II, 'Auxiliaris 1', 206.

[15] *PLRE* II, 1246; Mathisen, 'Last Year', 151–2 n. 4.

[16] Constantius, *Vita Germani*, 19 (*reditu* [sc. *a Britannia*] *venerabilium sacerdotum . . . expectatio propriae civitatis beatum Germanum . . . ambiebat*). Levison, 'Bischof Germanus von Auxerre', 127.

[17] Sigisvult: the only other attestation of this title is the forged *Processus habitus circa Sixtum papam III* (*Gesta de purgatione Xysti*) in Mansi, *Sacrorum conciliorum* V, 1061–70; on which: *Liber pont.* I, cxxvi–cxxvii, 196. Barnes, '*Patricii* under Valentinian III', 158–9, adduces evidence for Sigisvult's patriciate in 443.

[18] *Chron. Gall. 452*, s.aa. 435, 437, 448.

and the strictness of his life.'[19] The *Chron. Gall. 452* includes several similar floruits; almost all occur before 400, and are entered at what the chronicler takes to be the beginning of the subject's public life.[20] The few entries after 400, however, are placed in the middle of subjects' careers. This appears to be the case for Germanus.[21] The *Chron. Gall. 452*, unfortunately, sheds little light on the chronology of Germanus' episcopate.

In the last four decades, several attempts have been made to establish a firm new date for Germanus' death; all have been unsuccessful. Thompson proposed but retracted 445;[22] Mathisen argued for 446, but was refuted by Thompson and Wood;[23] both Thompson and Wood independently suggested 437, but have been disproved by Mathisen.[24] The most recent contribution to the debate, by Scharf, again proposes 445. His argument, however, does violence to the text of *Vita Germani* in order to support a thorough reconstruction of the events of Germanus' career, producing two separate Armorican rebellions and two unrelated journeys to Ravenna.[25] Scharf's detailed argument depends on questionable assumptions of prosopography and authorial intent, e.g. identifying the *cancellarius* Volusianus as the son of the former prefect of Rome and praetorian prefect of Italy Rufius Antonius Agrypnius Volusianus, said to be named by Constantius because of the fame of the embassy undertaken by the ex-prefect to Constantinople in 437. There is no evidence that the two Volusiani were related – the name was not uncommon – and the ex-prefect's embassy, known by a chance reference in the *Vita* of Melania the Younger, need not

[19] *Chron. Gall. 452*, 114, s.a. 433 (*Germanus episcopus Altisiodori virtutibus et vitae districtione clarescit*).

[20] *Chron. Gall. 452*, cc. 4 (Martin of Tours, s.a. 379); 35 (Claudian, s.a. 396); 37 (Prudentius, also s.a. 396); 41 (Paulinus of Nola, s.a. 399); 42 (John Chrysostom, s.a. 400); 44 (Pelagius, s.a. 401). Though the chronicler's dates are not necessarily correct for the beginning of the episcopate or public literary career of each subject, they are consistently early, and clearly meant to indicate the beginning, not end or highpoint, of each subject's careers (cf. the more detailed accounts of the careers of Ambrose, cc. 8, 13–15; and Augustine, cc. 17, 47, 81).

[21] E.g. *Chron. Gall. 452*, c. 104 (Cassian, s.a. 429), like the entry for Germanus, has no evident significance in relation to the beginning or end of the subject's career.

[22] Thompson, 'Chronological Note', 135–8, Grosjean, 'Le dernier voyage de S. Germain d'Auxerre' (in the same volume of *AB*). Retraction: E. A. Thompson, 'Britain, AD 406–410', *Britannia* 8 (1977), 311–12 and n. 35; Thompson, *Saint Germanus*, 55.

[23] Mathisen, 'Last Year', 153–4. Refutation: Thompson, *Saint Germanus*, 56 n. 9; Wood, 'End of Roman Britain', 15 n. 109.

[24] Thompson, *Saint Germanus*, 55–70; Wood, 'End of Roman Britain', 14–16. Refutation: R. W. Mathisen, 'The Last Year of Germanus of Auxerre'. Further objections to both Thompson's and Wood's arguments can be adduced. Thompson suggests that Valentinian III left Ravenna after Germanus' arrival, but before his death, to attend his wedding in Thessalonika; but the *Vita* implies Valentinian's presence at the time of Germanus' death: the emperor funded Germanus' funeral cortège, and the *Vita* mentions the presence in Ravenna of the *augusta* Galla Placidia and the *praepositus sacri cubiculi* Acolus, members of the imperial household who must have attended Valentinian on his journey to the East; Constantius, *Vita Germani*, 43–4. The description of Valentinian as *iuvenis* is not, as Thompson suggests, inconsistent with a narrative date in 448, when Valentinian was aged twenty-nine, for it accords with a classical schema of descriptions of ages in which one was *iuvenis* between the ages of thirty and forty-five: Varro *apud* Censorinus, *De die natali*, ed. K. Sallmann (Leipzig, 1983), XIV, 2; this schema was current in the fifth century, e.g. Sid. Ap., *Carm.* XIV, *Praef.*, 3; Gillett, 'The Birth of Ricimer', 383–4 n. 23. *Vita Severi*, central to Wood's chronology, is at earliest an early seventh-century work, as *Vita Severi*, 10, mentions the Merovingian queen Brunhild (567–613).

[25] Scharf, 'Germanus', 16.

have been renowned.[26] Other unsupported assumptions marr Scharf's argument: the Armorican rebellion is linked with Aetius' settlement of the Alans in northern Gaul and therefore dated to 437, though Goar's army appears in *Vita Germani* only as a punitive force employed by the western army with no clear association with the settlement;[27] the reference to the patriciate of the *magister utriusque militiae* Sigisvult, anachronistic for 436/7, is dismissed because the only other text to mention it is the forged account of the trial of Pope Sixtus III – but the status of that work does not implicate the validity of the unrelated *Vita Germani*;[28] Germanus' alleged 'second' and fatal trip to Ravenna is made part of his support for Hilarius of Arles in the Celidonius affair, with no evidence from either *Vita Germani* or *Vita Hilarii*.[29] The liberties taken by this thesis, in order to reconcile Constantius' account with fragile prosopographical constructions and texts with which *Vita Germani* frankly cannot be harmonised, are unwarranted.

Despite attempts at greater precision, the only firm dates for Germanus' episcopate continue to be the two long known: Prosper's assignment of Germanus' voyage to Britain in 429 (presumably, though not necessarily, the first of the two trips to Britain that Constantius attributes to Germanus[30]); and the death of the *augusta* Galla Placidia in November 450. These are *termini ante quam* for Germanus' ordination and death respectively.

II CONSTANTIUS' COMPOSITION OF *VITA GERMANI*

The only internal evidence for the publication of *Vita Germani* is the two letters to the bishops Patiens of Lyons, who commissioned Constantius to write the work, and Censurius of Auxerre, who put it into circulation. Both Patiens and Censurius were recipients of letters from Sidonius Apollinaris, written after his own accession to the episcopate, perhaps *c.* 469. Patiens held the episcopate from 449 to before *c.* 494; Censurius died before 511.[31] It is unclear from *Vita Germani* whether Lupus of Troyes and Severus of Trier, Germanus' companions on his two trips to Britain, were still alive at the time of composition (Lupus held the episcopate from *c.* 426/7 to between 476 and 511; Severus died some time before 477[32]). These episcopal dates provide only the *termini c.* 469–94.

The construction of a church dedicated to St Germanus, by Victorius, *comes* of the Auvergne under Euric during the 470s, attests a growth of Germanus' cult,

26 Volusiani: *PLRE* II, 1182–5. Embassy: *The Life of Melania the Younger*, trans. Elizabeth A. Clark (New York, 1984), c. 58. The ex-prefect's embassy was part of many unattested contacts between the western and eastern courts prior to the imperial wedding of 437; Gillett, 'Date and Circumstances of Olympiodorus of Thebes', 22 n. 96.

27 Scharf, 'Germanus', 8–9.

28 Scharf, 'Germanus', 10. Barnes, '*Patricii* under Valentinian III', 164.

29 For the dubious evidence of *Vita Hilarii*: above, at n. 5. Scharf, 'Germanus', 18.

30 Chadwick, *Poetry and Letters*, 255–6, suggests that the second trip to Britain is a doublet of the first. Chadwick is refuted by Wood, 'End of Roman Britain', 14, who cites the references to two voyages in *Vita Genovefa*, 2–4, 9. But this is inconclusive: the references demonstrate only that the author of Genovefa's *Vita* had read *Vita Germani*, rather than *Vita Lupi*, which records only the first journey to Britain.

31 Duchesne, *Fastes épiscopaux* II, 163, 445.

32 Duchesne, *Fastes épiscopaux* II, 453–4; III, 36, with *PLRE* II, 'Arbogastes', 128–9 for date.

of which Patiens' commission to Constantius to compose the *Vita* may have been another contemporary expression.[33]

Sid. Ap., *Ep.* VIII, 15.1 provides a possible *terminus ante quam* for the publication of *Vita Germani*. Prosperus, bishop of Orléans, asked Sidonius to write an account of Attila's raid on Gaul, in order to praise the role played by Annianus, Prosperus' predecessor, in defending Orléans. In politely declining the commission, Sidonius specifically compares Annianus with Germanus of Auxerre and Lupus of Troyes: 'you wish that the holy Annianus, a great and consumate priest, the equal of Lupus and not unequal to Germanus, be celebrated with the greatest praises'.[34] This is the sole reference to Germanus in Sidonius' letters, though the cult of St Germanus was active in the Auvergne; Lupus, however, was a frequent correspondent of Sidonius.[35] It has been thought that this reference, in conjunction with the evidence of *Vita Germani* that Lupus accompanied Germanus to Britain, attests a close association between Germanus and Lupus during their life.[36] The context of Sidonius' reference, however, could suggest another explanation: Sidonius might have mentioned Lupus and Germanus because they were two bishops whose lives had already been 'celebrated', in *vitae* circulating within Sidonius' circle. As such, the *vitae* would be available literary models, showing bishops of a previous generation as community leaders in quasi-historical narratives. Sidonius' reference is too elusive to permit a definitive interpretation; but, if his allusion is not to written texts, it is difficult to explain why he should choose these two bishops specifically as yardsticks for comparison. If Sidonius had read the *Vitae* of Germanus and of Lupus, then Constantius must have written *Vita Germani* before the publication of Sidonius' penultimate book of letters, in the late 470s.[37]

[33] Victorius: Gregory of Tours. *Hist.* II, 20; *PLRE* II, 'Victorius 4', 1162–4. Levison, Introduction to *Vita Germani*, 230; Harries, *Sidonius Apollinaris*, 122.

[34] Sid. Ap., *Ep.* VIII, 15.1: *laudibus summis sanctum Annianum, maximum consummatissimumque pontificem, Lupo parem Germanoque non imparem, vis celebrari.*

[35] Sid. Ap., *Epp.* VI, 1, 4, 9; IX, 11; mentioned IV, 17.3; VII, 13.1; VIII, 14.2, 15.1; *Carm.* XVI, 111.

[36] Chadwick, *Poetry and Letters*, 258–9; cf. Mathisen, 'Hilarius, Germanus, and Lupus', 163–4.

[37] Date of publication of Sidonius' letters: Harries, *Sidonius*, 7–9.

Appendix II

CHRONOLOGY OF THE LIFE OF EPIPHANIUS OF PAVIA

The chronology for the life of Epiphanius offered in chapter 4 differs by one year from that of e.g. Cook and Cesa.[1] *PCBE* offers a chronology similar to chapter 4, but without a full justification.[2] The central datum in any reconstruction of the chronology of Epiphanius' life is the date of his embassy to Euric, during the reign of Nepos, in the eighth year of Epiphanius' episcopate.[3] Cook places the embassy in spring 475 on the following basis: Nepos ruled in Italy from 19 or 24 June 474 (summer) to 28 August 475 (summer); Ennodius indirectly refers to the season during which Epiphanius undertook the embassy as spring by a passing mention of spring rains; therefore only spring 475 is possible. But the evidence in the *Vita* of the season in which Epiphanius undertook his embassy is very slight. In fact, as far as it goes, the text suggests summer, not spring: during stops at *mansiones* on the journey to Toulouse, Epiphanius regularly draws apart from his retinue to pray by himself, under the shade of trees for protection from the sun, where, prostrate on the verdant grass, his tears water the soil which is parched for want of rain.[4] This is hardly an explicit time indicator, but it has the virtue at least of autopsy, for Ennodius accompanied Epiphanius on the journey to Toulouse. The references to the heat of the sun, the verdant grass, and the dry soil suggests the heat of summer, not the rains of spring. If the journey was undertaken in summer, then the summer of either 474 or 475 is possible.

Nepos was made *caesar* in Ravenna at an unknown date in early 474, prior to his elevation as emperor in Rome in June; presumably from this point he controlled northern Italy.[5] His summons of the Ligurian council is more probably to be dated to his period as *caesar* than after his imperial elevation: he was, as *caesar*, in northern Italy, whereas he is attested in Rome between his imperial elevation and his expulsion by Orestes.[6] Before marching on Glycerius in Rome, he will have wished to protect his rear from Gothic intrusions, which Epiphanius' mission aimed to prevent. *Vita*

[1] Cook, *Life of St Epiphanius*, 9 n. 6; Cesa, Introduction and Commentary to *Vita del Epifanio* 14 n. 19, 165–8.

[2] *PCBE* II, 'Epiphanius 1', 637–41. [3] Ennodius, *Vita Epiphani*, 81.

[4] Ennodius, *Vita Epiphani*, 84: *eligebat secessum nerorea fronde conclusum. ubi conexis arborum brachiis nox domestica texeretur, quod solum refugus per umbracula opaca sol nesciret, et totum vivrdanti cespite gratia naturalis sterneret, ibi profusus in oratione continuis fletibus exortem pluviarum terram oculorum imbribus inrigabat.*

[5] See above, chapter 4, nn. 226–7.

[6] *Auctarii Havn. ad Prosper. ordo priores*, s.a. 475.1; *Anon. Val.* II, 7.36; Gillett, 'Rome, Ravenna', 154–5.

Epiphani does not explicitly attest Nepos' personal presence in Pavia, either when Epiphanius is appointed or when he returns, though Ennodius' wording is perhaps intended to imply this.[7] But Nepos' consultation with the *lumina* of Liguria on an issue of regional defence is likely to be understood as a function of the proximity of the new ruler. The embassy to Euric will then have been made in summer 474.

Epiphanius undertook the embassy in the eighth year of his episcopate; therefore his episcopate commenced 466. He was bishop for thirty years, i.e. to winter 496. His mission to Theoderic in Ravenna to plead for the restoration of civic rights took place not two years before his final journey to Theoderic and death, i.e. in 494.[8] This places the mission to plead for legal rights not long after Theoderic's defeat of Odoacer in 493.[9]

Ennodius gives Epiphanius' age at death (traditionally 21 January) as fifty-eight, which gives 438 as the year of his birth.[10] The *Vita* specifies Epiphanius' age at the time of his appointment to the offices of lector, subdeacon, deacon, and bishop.[11]

The chronology offered by Vogel in his MGH edition of *Vita Epiphani* uses a letter of Gelasius, *Ep.* 15 *bis*, to bishop Rusticius (or Rusticus) of Lyons, dated 25 January 494, which purports to have been borne by Epiphanius *en route* to Gundobad.[12] The letter forms part of a dossier of fifth-century documents which Jérome Vignier claimed to have found in the seventeenth century, and which was declared a forgery by J. Havet, coincidently in the same year in which Vogel's edition was published.[13] The forger interestingly makes Epiphanius a messenger from Gelasius to the bishops of Gaul, commissioning him to gather support for Gelasius in the Acacian schism while undertaking his secular embassy.

7 Ennodius, *Vita Epiphani*, 94 (Epiphanius' return): *Nepoti . . . insinuat*. It is noteworthy, however, that when the Ligurian council nominates Epiphanius as envoy in 471, the bishop is first called to meet Ricimer before setting out to Rome (58); there is no equivalent meeting between Epiphanius and Nepos after his nomination in 474. Nepos' need to protect rear from Goths before advancing on Rome, cf. Burgundian transalpine raids on Liguria in similar circumstances *c*. 491, during Theoderic's assaults on Odoacer; Moorhead, *Theoderic*, 24.

8 Ennodius, *Vita Epiphani*, 81, 182, 195.

9 Cook, *Life of St Epiphanius*, 9 n. 6, places the embassy for legal rights in 495.

10 Age: Ennodius, *Vita Epiphani*, 195. Day date: Cook, *Life of St Epiphanius*, 242–3 n. 6.

11 Ennodius, *Vita Epiphani*, 8 (lector), 18 (subdeacon), 20, 26, 34 (deacon), 34 (bishop).

12 Vogel, *Preface* to Ennodius, *Opera* (MGH AA 7), xviii–xix. Letter: *PL* 59, 138–40.

13 J. Havet, 'Questions Mérovingiennes II: les découvertes de Jérome Vignier', *Bibliothèque de l'Ecole des Chartes* 46 (1885), 205–74, at 254–8; cf. Cook, *Life of St Epiphanius*, 4 n. 19, 222–3; W. Ullmann, *Gelasius I: Das Papsttum an der Wende der Spätantike zum Mittelalter* (Päpste und Papsttum 18; Stuttgart, 1981), 227 n. 36.

Appendix III

SENARIUS' LETTERS OF APPOINTMENT: CASSIODORUS, *VARIAE* IV, 3 AND 4

TEXT (ED. MOMMSEN)

IV, 3: Senario v.i. comiti privatarum Theodericus rex

Ad ornatum palatii credimus pertinere aptas dignitatibus personas eligere, quia de claritate servientium crescit fama dominorum. Tales enim provehere principem decet, ut quotiens procerem suum fuerit dignitus aspicere, totiens se recta iudicia cognoscat habuisse. Moribus enim debet esse conspicuus, qui datur imitandus. Facile est quemque sibi degere: multis autem electum vivere decet. Cape igitur per indictionem tertiam illustris comitivae nostri patrimonii dignitatem, quam tibi non inmerito tribuit regalis auctoritas. Diu namque nostris ordinationibus geminum mutuatus obsequium et concilii particeps eras et disposita laudabili assumptione complebas. Subisti saepe arduae legationis officium: restitisti regibus non impar assertor, coactus iustitiam nostram et illis ostendere, qui rationem vix poterant cruda obstinatione sentire. Non te terruit contentionibus inflammata regalis auctoritas, subiugasti quin immo audaciam veritati et obsecitus ordinationibus nostris in conscientiam suam barbaros perculisti. Quid studium tuum longa lucubratione sollicitum et laboris continui inculpabile referamus obsequium? Usus es sub exceptionis officio eloquentis ingenio: favebat ipse sui delectatus auditor, dum meliora faceres, cum recitare coepisses. Pronuntiatio tua nostrum delectabat arbitrum, quia tantum dictantium reficiebas animum, quantum se lassare poterat cura cognitantum. Fuit quoque in te pars altera vitae laudabilis, quod arcana nostra morum probitate claudebas, multorum conscius, nec tamen, cum plura nosses, elatus. Collegis gratia, superioribus humilitate placuisti. Sic omnium pro te factus est unus animus ex magna diversitate sociatus. Carpes certe probatae institutionis gratissimum fructum, quando provectus tuus ita potuit omnes laetos efficere, ut universi in te iudicent sua desideria profecisse. Tuere igitur hanc virtutum amabilem praeclaramque constantiam nostraeque domus auctoritate subnixus tanto studiosius gratiam quaere, quantum to locum beneficiis respicis invenisse. Tende itaque adhuc bonis actibus tuos ad potiora successus, sciens gratiam nostram in illo semper augeri, qui se dignum adepto culmini desiderat inveniri.

IV, 4: Senatui urbis Romae Theodericus rex

Gloriosum quidem nobis est, patres conscripti, honores passim impendere, sed laudabilius bene meritis digna praestare. Quicquid enim talibus tribuimus, pro generali potius utilitate largimur. Cunctis siquidem proficit recti tenax provectus nec locus relinquitur iniuriae, cum ad bonos pervenit regula disciplinae. Hoc itaque praeclaro desiderio illustrem virum Senarium comitivae patrimonii dignitate subveximus, qui venalitatis obscura animi claritate refugiat, qui calumnia non laetetur, nec patrimonii auctoritate suffultus de nostro sibi faciat terrore compendium, sed ius aequabile possittenere cum ceteris, unde nobis placere respicit servientes. Haec de illo futura promittere praeteritorum facit temporum fides. In ipso quippe adulescentiae flore palatia nostra meritis maturus intravit et, quod robustas quoque fatigat aetates, nullo deceptus novitatis errore ad imperantis conversus arbitrium effectum bonarum praestitit iussionum, nunc ad colloquiia degnus, nunc ad exceptiones aptissimus, frequenter etiam in honorem legationis electus, cuius multiplex meritum incertum apud nos reddebat officium. Non enim unius loci vir debet dici, a quo multa videntur impleri. Sed haec amplius commendabat humilitas, quae tam clara quam rara est. Novum est enim sub amore principis custodire modestiam, quia gaudia semper animos inquietant: modus enim raro laetis rebus imponitur, qui magis in tristibus invenitur. Verum inter haec stupenda meritorum originis quoque simili claritate resplendet, ut haereas, qua parte sit ditior, cum copiosius utraque possideat. Habent ergo singulatim distributa praeconium, iuncta miraculum. Quapropter, patres conscripti, assurgat primaevis introeuntibus cana Libertas. Nihil de genio vestro subtrahitur, quando venientium novitas honorabiliter invitatur. Parentes publici de clementia nominati, duplex vos ratio benignitatis invitet: incipiens mereatur gratiam, provectus favorem.

TRANSLATION (INCORPORATING SOME READINGS FROM FRIDH'S EDITION)

IV, 3: King Theoderic to Senarius, vir inlustris, comes privatarum

1 We believe that part of the ornamentation of the palace is the selection of fit persons for official dignities, since the fame of rulers grows from the renown of their servants. For it is proper that a prince should advance such men that, whenever he deigns to look upon one of his foremost officers, he knows that his judgement is sound. One granted the opportunity to be emulated should be of outstanding character. It is easy for such a person[1] to live for himself, but, once appointed to office, it is proper that he live for the many.

2 Take, therefore, for the course of the third indiction, the dignity of the illustrious *comitiva* of our patrimony, which royal authority gives to you, not undeservedly. For, long having derived a double service from our instructions, you have both participated in our council and fulfilled tasks set before you with praiseworthy diligence. Often you have sustained the duty of an arduous embassy: you have withstood kings, an advocate not unequal to the task, constrained to reveal our justice even to those who, in their base obstinacy, were barely able to understand reason. The enraged authority of kings did not terrify you with its contentions; rather you subjected insolence to truth and, following our instructions, you forced the barbarians to their senses.

[1] *quemque* Mommsen; *qualemque et sim.* mss., CCSL 96; Åke Fridh, *Contributions à la critique et à l'interprétation des* Variae *de Cassiodore* (Göteborg, 1968), 56–7.

3 Why should we rehearse your efforts, care-worn by the exertions of long nights, and the blameless service of your uninterrupted labour? In the office of the *exceptio* you employed your talent for eloquence; even a listener pleased with his own compositions favoured yours, when, once you began to speak, you produced better. Your oration gave delight to our halls of judgement, since you refreshed the minds of those employed in composition as quickly as the care of their concentrations exhausted them. Yet another part of your life was praiseworthy: you kept our secrets concealed by the probity of your character, aware of many things, yet, though you knew much, not proud of it.

You pleased your colleagues with your grace, your superiors with your humility.
4 Thus all share a single opinion about you, united in this despite their great diversity. You surely pluck the most favoured fruit of proven principles when your advancement can make everyone rejoice, so that all consider that in you their own desires have been promoted.

So protect this beloved and splendid constancy of virtue and, supported by the authority of our domain, seek our grace all the more zealously as you reflect that you have found opportunity for benefit. Direct the happy issue of your good acts to date towards yet better ones, knowing that our favour always grows greater towards him who desires to be found worthy of the eminence he has reached.

IV, 4: King Theoderic to the Senate of Rome

1 It is indeed glorious for us, conscript Fathers, to weigh out honours far and wide, but it is more praiseworthy to furnish fitting rewards to those who well deserve them. For whatever we give to such persons, we rather bestow for the general benefit. A man tenacious in truth, once advanced, profits all, nor does there remain opportunity for harm when the rule of discipline takes hold of good men.

2 And so, from this splendid desire, we have borne aloft the *vir illustris* Senarius. May he shun the darkness of corruption with the clarity of his mind, may he not rejoice in injustice, nor, supported by the authority of our patrimony, profit from fear of us, but may he avail to hold equitable justice with others, reflecting that thus do our servants please us. His faithful service in times past promises this future for him.

3 In the very flower of his youth he entered our palace, already mature in his merits, and performed what exhausts even those in their prime: not led astray by unfamiliarity when employed in his ruler's judgement, he put good commands into effect, now worthy for discourse, now well suited for *exceptiones*, often also chosen for the honour of an embassy. His manifold merits performed no fixed office for us, for one by whom many tasks are completed ought not be called by the title of only one post.

4 But his humility, as renowned as it is rare, more fully recommends his merits. For it is a novelty that he preserved his modest bearing under the love of his prince, since joy always unsettles minds; tact, usually found in sad affairs, is rarely employed in happy ones.

5 Moreover, amidst these admirable merits, he shines alike with the splendour of his ancestry; so you may be at a loss in which respect he is the richer, when he has both so lavishly. His virtues distributed one by one cause praise, but joined together they raise wonder.

Therefore, conscript Fathers, let hoary Liberty arise for youthful entrants. Your genius is nothing lessened when the novelty of newcomers is honourably invited. Named as you are 'Fathers of the People' from your clemency, a two-fold cause for benevolence summons you: taking up his place in the Senate, he deserves your grace; advanced in office, your favour.

Appendix IV

THE TEXT OF SENARIUS' EPITAPH

The text was first published by Pierre Pithou in 1590 among anonymous epitaphs, despite Senarius' name in line 2.[1] Pithou edited Latin poems from manuscripts, inscriptions, and earlier printed editions, but gave no indication of provenances for individual poems. After his edition was typeset, but before publication, Pithou sought advice on this and other poems from the philologist François Juret, editor *inter alia* of Symmachus' *Epistolae*; unfortunately, Juret's extant reply sheds no light on the source of the epitaph.[2] It is thus unclear whether, in the sixteenth century, the epitaph was preserved in the original inscription or in a syllogue. The latter, however, appears more likely; certainly, the epitaph does not appear in early collections of Latin inscriptions.[3] It is therefore not possible to determine the locality of Senarius' tomb.[4]

All later editions and citations appear to be derived from Pithou's.[5]

[1] Pithou (ed.), *Epigrammata et poematia vetera*, 108, 463.

[2] *Collection Dupuy*, vol. 700, folio 128, Paris, Bibliothèque Nationale; cf. Pithou, 463 n. to p. 108. Burman (below, n. 5) wrongly cites Juret's edition of Symmachus, *Epistolarum ad diversos libri decem* (Paris, 1580), I, 17, 20 (*recte* 11–12) as an earlier edition and commentary on the epitaph. On Pithou: Donald R. Kelley, *Foundations of Modern Historical Scholarship: Language, Law, and History in the French Renaissance* (New York, 1970), 241–70.

[3] E.g. Janus Gruterus, *Inscriptiones antiquae totius orbis Romani* (Heidelberg, 1602), rev. Joannes Georgius Graevius (Amsterdam, 1707); Paulus Aringhus, *Roma subterranea novissima* (Rome, 1651). Mommsen did not include the epitaph in *CIL*, presumably because it cannot be localised.

Pithou's suggested emendations (*Epigrammata*, 463; 'Epitaph', lines 4, 13) suggest palaeographic rather than epigraphic corrections.

[4] The epitaph of Liberius, the praetorian prefect of Italy and Gaul and *patricius* with whom Senarius was associated, was preserved at Ravenna (*CIL* XI, 382); epithets of other palatine officials under Theoderic are preserved at Ravenna (*CIL* XI, 268, 310, 317) or Rome (*CIL* VI, 1794 and 31933, 32003) (Otto Fiebiger and Ludwig Schmidt (eds.), *Inschriftensammlung zur Geschichte der Ostgermannen* [vol. I] (Akademie der Wissenschaften in Wien, Philosophisch-historische Klasse, Denkschriften 60.3; Vienna, 1917), nos. 182–4, 187–8). *Contra* Schäfer, *Der weströmische Senat*, 190, Ennodius' claim of a family tie with Senarius need not make the latter of north Italian origin.

[5] I.e. Friedrich Lindenbrog, *Codex legum antiquarum* (Frankfurt, 1613), 1379 (citing lines 15–16); Avitus of Vienne, *Opera*, ed. J. Sirmond (Paris, 1643), repr. in Sirmond's *Opera varia* II (Paris, 1696), 76–8 (omitting lines 5–6) = *PL* 59; Thomas Reinesius, *Syntagma inscriptionum antiquarum comprimis Romae veteris* (Leipzig and Frankfurt, 1682), XX, 182 940 (lines 1–5 only, incorporating Juretus' unnecessary reading *legum* for *regum*); Pieter Burman the Younger, *Anthologia veterum latinorum epigrammatum et poematum* I (Amsterdam, 1759), II, 133 318–19, 734; II (Amsterdam, 1773), 723–34; rev. Henric Meyer, I (Leipzig, 1835), 256, notes 210; Pasquale Amati, *Collectio Pisaurensis omnium poematum carminum fragmentorum latinorum*, IV (Pisauri, 1746), 449; Cass., *Variae*, 'Index personarum', 499; Otto Fiebiger (ed.), *Inschriftensammlung zur Geschichte der Ostgermannen* [vol. III] (Akademie der Wissenschaften in Wien, Philosophisch-historische Klasse, Denkschriften 72.2; Vienna, 1944), 10 no. 8.

NOTE ON EDITIONS, COMMENTARIES, AND TRANSLATIONS OF MAJOR SOURCES

HYDATIUS

Hydatius Lemicus, *Continuatio chronicorum Hieronymianorum*, ed. T. Mommsen (MGH AA 11), 1–36.
The Chronicle *of Hydatius and the* Consularia Constantinopolitana*: Two Contemporary Accounts of the Final Years of the Roman Empire*, ed. and trans. R. W. Burgess (Oxford 1993), 70–123.
Hydace, *Chronique*, ed. and French trans. Alain Tranoy, I [trans.], II [notes] (Sources chrétiennes 218, 219; Paris, 1974).

References give Mommsen's section numbering, followed by Burgess' in square brackets, except where these coincide.

Tranoy's edition employs the flawed revision of Hydatius' chronology proposed by Christian Courtois, 'Auteurs et scribes: remarques sur la Chronique d'Hydace', *Byzantion* 21 (1951), 23–54; cf. Muhlberger, *Fifth-Century Chroniclers*, 200–4, 279–312; Burgess, *Chronicle*, 27–31. On Hydatius' preface: Pierre Nautin, 'L'Introduction d'Hydace à sa continuation de la *Chronique* d'Eusèbe et Jérôme', *Revue d'Histoire des Textes* 14–15 (1984–5), 143–5.

English translation: Burgess, *Chronicle*. Translations here are my own.

For commentary: Tranoy's edition (above); Thompson, *Romans and Barbarians*, 137–229; Muhlberger, *Fifth-Century Chroniclers*, 193–266; Burgess, 'Hydatius', I; Cardelle de Hartmann, *Philologische Studien*. For recent work on late antique Gallaecia: Alberto Ferreiro, 'Sueves and Martin of Braga: Historiography and Future Research Projects', in Erwin Koller and Hugo Laitenberger (eds.), *Suevos-Schwaben: Das Königreich der Sueben auf der Iberischen Halbinsel (411–585)* (Tübingen, 1998), 37–62.

SIDONIUS APOLLINARIS

C. Solius Apollinaris Sidonius, *Opera*, ed. Jacques Sirmond (Paris, 1602) = *PL* 58, 435–752.

Gaius Solius Apollinaris Sidonius, *Epistulae et Carmina*, ed. Christian Luetjohann *et al.* (MGH AA 8).
C. Sollius Apollinaris Sidonius, ed. P. Mohr (Teubner; Leipzig, 1895).
Sidoine Apollinaire, *Poèmes et Lettres*, ed. and French trans. André Loyen, 3 vols. (Budé; Paris, 1970).

Loyen's edition is cited here.

English translations: *The Letters of Sidonius*, trans. O. M. Dalton, 2 vols. (Oxford, 1915) [*Epp.* I–II]; Sidonius, *Poems and Letters*, I, trans. W. B. Anderson; II, trans. W. B. Anderson [and E. H. Warmington] (LCL; London, 1936, 1965), based on Luetjohann, Mohr, and some independent manuscripts. Except where otherwise noted, translations are from Anderson, with some silent emendations.

Commentary on *Carm.* VII: A. Loyen, *Recherches historiques sur les panégyriques de Sidoine Apollinaire* (Paris, 1942; repr. Rome, 1967), 35–58; Loyen, *Sidoine* I, 181–6; Harrison, 'Verse Panegyrics of Sidonius Apollinaris', esp. 126–45; Portmann, *Geschichte in der spätantiken Panegyrik*, 99–105, 114–15.

CONSTANTIUS, *VITA GERMANI*

Constantius, 'Vita Germani episcopi Autissiodorensis', ed. W. Levison (MGH SRM 7), 225–83.
Constance de Lyons, *Vie de Saint Germain d'Auxerre*, ed. and French trans. R. Borius (Sources chrétiennes 112; Paris, 1965).
BHL 3453.

Levison's edition is cited here, except where otherwise noted.

English translation: F. R. Hoare, *The Western Fathers* (London, 1954), 281–320; repr. in T. F. X. Noble and T. Head (eds.), *Soldiers of Christ: Saints and Saints' Lives from Late Antiquity and the Early Middle Ages* (University Park, PA, 1995), 75–106. Translations here are my own, with useful reference to those of Hoare and Borius.

VITA ORIENTII

Vita (I) sancti Orientii episcopo Ausciorum in Novempopulania, ed. Godefroid Henskens, AASS Mai I.
BHL 6344.

Translations here are my own.

VITA VIVIANI

Vita Bibiani vel Viviani episcopi Santonensis, ed. B. Krusch (MGH SRM 3), 92–100.

BHL 1324.

Translations here are my own.

ENNODIUS, *VITA EPIPHANI*

Ennodius, *Vita Epiphani*, ed. J. Sirmond (1611) = *PL* 63, 207–40.
Ennodius, *Opera omnia*, ed. G. Hartel, CSEL 6 (Vienne, 1882), 331–83.
Ennodius, *Opera*, ed. F. Vogel (MGH AA 7), 84–109.
Ennodio, *Vita del beatissimo Epifanio vescovo della chiesa pavese*, ed. and Italian trans. Maria Cesa (Biblioteca di Athenaeum 6; Como, 1988).
BHL 2570.

The section numbering used in Vogel's and Cesa's editions is cited here.

English translation: *The Life of St Epiphanius by Ennodius*, trans. Genevieve Marie Cook (Washington, 1942), repr. with alterations in *Early Christian Biographies*, ed. R. J. Deferrari (Washington, 1952), 301–51. Translations here are my own, with valuable reference to Cook's.

Commentary: Cesa, *Vita del Epifanio*, 119–212.

CASSIODORUS, *VARIAE*

Cassiodorus Senator, *Variae*, ed. Theodore Mommsen (MGH AA 12).
Cassiodorus, *Variarum libri XII*, ed. Å. J. Fridh (CCSL 96; Turnhout, 1973), including *De anima*, ed. James W. Halporn, 501–75.

Mommsen's edition of the letters, and Halporn's edition of *De anima*, are cited here.

English translations: *The Letters of Cassiodorus*, trans. Thomas Hodgkin (London, 1886), an abridged translation; *Cassiodorus: Variae*, trans. S. J. B. Barnish (TTH 12; Liverpool, 1992), a selection. Translations here are my own, with valuable reference to Hodgkin and Barnish. For Cass., *Variae* IV, 3–4, see appendix III.

SENARIUS, *EPITAPH*

Pierre Pithou, *Epigrammata et poematia vetera* (Paris, 1590), 108.
Mommsen, 'Index personarum' to Cass., *Variae*, 499, reproduces Pithou's text with minor amendments.

On the transmission of the text, see appendix IV.

The translation here is my own.

BIBLIOGRAPHY

SOURCES

Agathias, *Historiarum libri quinque*, ed. Rudolf Keydell (Corpus fontium historiae Byzantinae 2; Berlin, 1967); trans. J. D. Frendo (Corpus fontium historiae Byzantinae 2a; Berlin, 1975)

Al-Buhturi, trans. in A. J. Arberry, *Arabic Poetry* (Cambridge, 1965), 72–80

Ammianus Marcellinus, *Rerum gestarum libri qui supersunt*, ed. Wolfgang Seyferth, 2 vols. (Teubner; Leipzig, 1978); trans. J. C. Rolfe, 3 vols. (LCL; London, 1935–9)

Anthologia graeca, trans. W. R. Paton, 5 vols. (LCL; London, 1916–18)

Anthologia latina, ed. F. Bücheler and A. Reise, 2 vols. (Teubner; Leipzig, 1894); ed. D. R. Shackelton Bailey, 1 vol. to date (Teubner; Stuttgart, 1982)

Anthologia veterum latinorum epigrammatum et poematum, ed. Pieter Burman the Younger, 2 vols. (Amsterdam, 1759, 1773); rev. Henric Meyer, 2 vols. (Leipzig, 1835)

Athanasius, *Vie d'Antoine*, ed. and trans. G. J. M. Bartelink (Sources chrétiennes 400; Paris, 1994)

Augustine, *De haeresibus*, ed. R. Vander Plaetse, C. Beukers [and G. Morin] (CCSL 46; Turnhout, 1969)

Aurelius Victor, Sextus, *Liber de Caesaribus*, ed. Fr. Pichlmayr (Teubner; Leipzig, 1961)

Ausonius, *The Works of Ausonius*, ed. R. P. H. Green (Oxford, 1991); trans. H. G. E. White, 2 vols. (LCL; London, 1961)

Avitus of Vienne, *Opera*, ed. Rudolf Peiper (MGH AA 6.2; Berlin, 1883); trans. Danuta Shanzer and Ian Wood (TTH 38; Liverpool, 2002)

Bede, *Historia ecclesiastica*, ed. and trans. B. Colgrave and R. A. B. Mynors (Oxford, 1969)

Biblia sacra iuxta vulgatam versionem, ed. R. Weber and R. Gryson, 4th edn (Stuttgart, 1994)

Bibliorum sacrorum latinae versiones antiquae, ed. P. Sabatier (Rheims 1743–9; repr. Turnhout, 1983)

Bischoff, Bernhard, and Wilhelm Koehler, 'Eine illustrierte Ausgabe der spätantiken Ravennater Annalen', in W. R. W. Koehler (ed.), *Medieval Studies in Memory of A. Kingsley Porter* 1 (Cambridge, MA, 1939), 125–39

Boethius, Anicius Manlius Severinus, *Philosophiae consolatio*, ed. Ludwig Bieler (CCSL 94; Turnhout, 1967)

Boethius, Anicius Manlius Severinus, *The Theological Tractates and Consolation of Philosophy*, ed. E. K. Rand, trans. H. F. Stewart and S. J. Tester (LCL; London, 1973)

Byzantinische Diplomaten und östliche Barbaren, trans. Ernst Doblhofer (Byzantinische Geschichtsschreiber 4; Graz, 1955)

Cassiodorus, *Variae epistolae*, ed. T. Mommsen (MGH AA 12; Berlin, 1894); *Variarum libri XII*, ed. Åke J. Fridh (CCSL 96; Turnhout, 1973); (selected trans.) *The Letters of Cassiodorus*, trans. Thomas Hodgkin (London, 1886); (selected trans.) Cassiodorus, *Variae*, trans. S. J. B. Barnish (TTH 12; Liverpool, 1992)

Censorinus, *De die natali*, ed. Klaus Sallmann (Teubner; Leipzig, 1983)

Choricius of Gaza, *Opera*, ed. Richard Förster and Eberhard Richtsteig (Stuttgart, 1922; repr. 1972)

Chronica minora, ed. T. Mommsen, 3 vols. (MGH AA 9, 11, 13; Berlin, 1892–8)

The Chronicle of Pseudo-Joshua the Stylite, trans. Frank R. Trombley and John W. Watt (TTH 32; Liverpool, 2000)

Chronicon Paschale, 284–628 AD, trans. Michael Whitby and Mary Whitby (TTH 7; Liverpool, 1989)

Cicero, *De re publica*, ed. and trans. Esther Bréguet, 2 vols. (Budé; Paris, 1980)

Claudian, *Carmina*, ed. J. B. Hall (Teubner; Leipzig, 1985); trans. M. Platnauer, 2 vols. (LCL; London, 1922)

Codex legum antiquarum, ed. Friedrich Lindenbrog (Frankfurt, 1613)

El código de Eurico, ed. Alvaro d'Ors (Rome, 1960)

Constantine VII Porphyrogenitus, *De administrando imperio*, I, 2nd edn, ed. Gy. Moravcsik, trans. R. J. H. Jenkins (Corpus fontium historiae Byzantinae 1; Washington, DC, 1967); II, *Commentary*, ed. R. J. H. Jenkins (London, 1962)

Constantine VII Porphyrogenitus, *De cerimoniis aulae Byzantinae libri duo*, ed. J. J. Reiske, 2 vols. (Corpus scriptorum historiae Byzantinae 7; Bonn, 1829–30); ed. Albert Vogt, vol. 1 only to date (Budé; Paris, 1935; repr. 1967)

Constantine VII Porphyrogenitus, *Excerpta de legationibus*, ed. C. de Boor, in *Excerpta historica iussu imperatoris Constantini Porphyrogeniti confecta*, ed. U. P. Boissevain, C. de Boor and T. Büttner-Wobst, 1 (Berlin, 1903)

Constantius, *Vita Germani episcopi Autissiodorensis*, ed. W. Levison (MGH SRM 7; Hanover, 1920); *Vie de Saint Germain d'Auxerre*, ed. and trans. René Borius (Sources chrétiennes 112; Paris, 1965)

Contra Varimadum Arianum diaconum, *PL* 62, 351–434

Corpus haereseologicum, ed. Franciscus Oehler, 3 vols. (Berlin, 1856–61)

Corpus inscriptionum latinarum, ed. T. Mommsen *et al.*, 17 vols. (Berlin, 1863–1986)

Corpus legum ab imperatoribus Romanis ante Iustinianum latorum, ed. Gustav Haenel (Leipzig, 1857)

Corripus, Flavius Cresconius, *In laudem Iustini Augusti minoris libri IV*, ed. and trans. Averil Cameron (London, 1976)

Corripus, Flavius Cresconius, *Iohannidos seu de bellis Libycis libri VIII*, ed. J. Diggle and F. R. D. Goodyear (Cambridge, 1970)

Demosthenes, *Oration 19: De falsa legatione*, in *Demosthenes*, II, trans. C. A. Vince and J. H. Vince (LCL; London, 1926)

Dolbeau, François, 'La *Vie* en prose de saint Marcel, évêque de Die', *Francia* 11 (1983), 97–130

XII panegyrici latini, ed. R. A. B. Mynors (Oxford, 1964); trans. as *In Praise of Later Roman Emperors; The* Panegyrici latini; *Introduction, Translation, and Historical Commentary, with the Latin Text of R. A. B. Mynors*, trans. C. E. V. Nixon and Barbara Saylor Rodgers (Berkeley, 1994)

Early Christian Biographies, ed. R. J. Deferrari (Washington, DC, 1952)

Edictum Theodorici Regis, in *Fontes iuris Romanii antejustiniani*, ed. S. Riccobobo *et al.*, II (Florence, 1940)

Ennodius, *Opera*, ed. William Hartel (CSEL 6; Vienna, 1882); *Opera omnia*, ed. Frideric Vogel (MGH AA 7; Berlin, 1885)

Ennodius, *The Life of St Epiphanius by Ennodius*, trans. G. M. Cook (Washington, DC, 1942)

Ennodius, *Vita del beatissimo Epifanio vescovo della chiesa pavese*, ed. and trans. Maria Cesa (Biblioteca di Athenaeum 6; Como, 1988)

Epistolae Romanorum pontificum genuinae, ed. Andreas Thiel (Braunsberg, 1867; repr. Hildersheim, 1974)

Epistulae Austrasicae, ed. W. Gundlach (MGH Epp. 3; Berlin, 1892)

Epistulae imperatorum pontificum aliorum (Collectio Avellana), ed. Otto Guenther (CSEL 35; Vienna, 1895)

Eugippius, *Vita S. Severini*, in *Opera*, ed. P. Knoell (CSEL 9; Vienna, 1885); trans. P. Regerat (Sources chrétiennes 374; Paris, 1991); trans. L. Bieler and L. Krestan (Fathers of the Church; Washington, DC, 1965)

Eunapius of Sardis, *Vitae sophistarum*, ed. G. Giangrande (Rome, 1956); trans. in Philostratus and Eunapius, *Lives of the Sophists*, trans. Wilmer Cave Wright (LCL; London, 1921)

Eutropius, *Breviarium ab urbe condita*, ed. C. Santini (Teubner; Leipzig, 1979)

Excerpta Valesiana, ed. J. Moreau, rev. V. Velkov (Teubner; Leipzig, 1968); trans. J. C. Rolfe, in *Ammianus Marcellinus*, III (LCL; London, 1939)

Festus, Rufius, *The* Breviarium *of Festus: A Critical Edition with Historical Commentary*, ed. J. W. Eadie (London, 1967)

Fiebiger, Otto, and Ludwig Schmidt (eds.), *Inschriftensammlung zur Geschichte der Ostgermannen*, 3 vols. (Kaiserliche Akademie der Wissenschaften in Wien, Philosophisch-historische Klasse, Denkschriften 60.3; Vienna, 1917, 1939, 1944)

Fragmenta historicorum Graecorum, ed. Carl Müller, IV (Paris, 1851)

The Fragmentary Classicising Historians of the Later Roman Empire: Eunapius, Olympiodorus, Priscus, and Malchus, ed. and trans. R. C. Blockley, 2 vols. (ARCA Classical and Medieval Texts, Papers and Monographs 6 and 10; Liverpool, 1981, 1983)

Fredegarius Scholasticus, *Chronicarum libri IV*, ed. B. Krusch (MGH SRM 2; Berlin, 1888)

Fulgentius: Selected Works, trans. R. B. Eno (Washington, DC, 1997)

Gennadius, *Liber de viris illustribus*, ed. Ernst Cushing Richardson (TU 14.1; Leipzig, 1896)

Gildas, *De excidio Britonum*, ed. T. Mommsen (MGH AA 13; Berlin, 1898); trans. M. Winterbottom (Arthurian Period Sources 7; London, 1978)

Die Gotische Bibel, ed. Wilhelm Streitberg, I 2nd edn, II 3rd edn (Heidelberg, 1919; repr. Heidelberg, 1960)

Gregory the Great, *Registrum epistolarum*, ed. P. Ewald and L. M. Hartmann (MGH Epp. 1 and 2; Berlin, 1891, 1899); *Registrum epistolarum*, ed. Dag Norberg (CCSL 140, 140A; Turnhout, 1982)

Gregory of Tours, *Historiarum libri X*, ed. B. Krusch and W. Levison (MGH SRM 1.1; 2nd edn, Hanover, 1951); trans. O. M. Dalton, 2 vols. (Oxford, 1927)

Gregory of Tours, *Libri octo miraculorum*, ed. B. Krusch (MGH SRM 1.2; Hanover, 1885)

Grierson, Philip, and Melinda May (eds.), *Catalogue of Late Roman Coins in the Dumbarton Oaks Collection and in the Whittemore Collection: From Arcadius and Honorius to the Accession of Anastasius* (Washington, DC, 1992)

Honoratus Massiliensis, *Vita Hilarii episcopi Arelatensis*, ed. S. Cavallin, *Vitae sanctorum Honorati et Hilarii episcoporum Arelatensium* (Publications of the New Society of Letters at Lund 40; Lund, 1952)

Hydatius Lemicus, *Continuatio chronicorum Hieronymianorum*, ed. T. Mommsen, in *Chronica minora* 2, 1–36; *Chronique*, ed. and trans. Alain Tranoy, 2 vols. (Sources chrétiennes 218, 219; Paris, 1974); *Cronicón*, ed. and trans. Julio Campos (Salamanca, 1984); *The* Chronicle *of Hydatius and the* Consularia Constantinopolitana: *Two Contemporary Accounts of the Final Years of the Roman Empire*, ed. and trans. R. W. Burgess (Oxford, 1993)

Inscriptiones latinae Christianae veteres, ed. Ernest Diehl, 3 vols. (Berlin, 1961)

Inscriptiones latinae selectae, ed. Hermann Dessau, 3 vols. (Berlin, 1892–1916)

Isidore, *Etymologiae*, ed. W. M. Lindsay (Oxford, 1911)

Jerome, *Die Chronik des Hieronymus*, ed. Rudolf Helm (Die griechischen christlichen Schriftsteller der ersten drei Jahrhunderte 47 = Eusebius' Werke 7; Berlin, 1956)

John the Deacon, *Epistola ad Senarium*, ed. Jean Mabillon, *PL* 59, 399–408; *Epistola ad Senarium*, in André Wilmart (ed.), *Analecta Reginensia: extraits des manuscripts latins de la reine Christine conservés au Vatican* (Studi e Testi 59; Vatican City, 1933)

John Lydus, *On Powers, or The Magistracies of the Roman State*, ed. and trans. A. C. Bandy (Philadelphia, 1983)

Jordanes, *Romana et Getica*, ed. T. Mommsen (MGH AA 6.1; Berlin, 1882); *Getica*, trans. C. C. Mierow (Cambridge, 1915)

Julian, *Œuvres complètes*, ed. and trans. J. Bidez, 1 (Budé; Paris, 1932); trans. Wilmer Cave Wright, 3 vols. (LCL; London, 1913)

Justinian, *Corpus iuris civilis*, ed. T. Mommsen, P. Krüger, R. Schöll, and W. Kroll (Berlin, 1872–95; repr. Dublin and Zurich, 1968–70)

Lamirande, Emilien, *Paulin de Milan et la* Vita Ambrosii*: aspects de la religion sous le Bas-Empire* (Montreal, 1983)

Leges Burgundionum, ed. L. R. De Salis (MGH Leges 2.1; Hanover, 1892)

Libanius, *Selected Works*, trans. A. F. Norman, 2 vols. (LCL; London, 1969–77); *Autobiography and Selected Letters*, trans. A. F. Norman, 2 vols. (LCL; Cambridge, MA, 1992)

Liberatus of Carthage, *Breviarium causae Nestorianorum et Eutychianorum*, *PL* 68

Luxorius, *Luxorius: A Latin Poet among the Vandals*, trans. M. Rosenblum (New York, 1961)

Malalas, John, *The Chronicle of John Malalas*, trans. E. Jeffreys *et al.* (Byzantina Australiensia 4; Melbourne, 1986)

Marcellinus *comes*, *Chronicon* in *Chronica minora*; trans. in *The Chronicle of Marcellinus: Translation and Commentary*, trans. Brian Croke (Byzantina Australiensia 7; Sydney, 1995)

Martyrologium Hieronymianum, ed. J. B. de Rossi and L. Duchesne (AASS Nov II pars I; Brussels, 1894)

Maximianus, *Elegiae*, in *Poetae latini minores* V, ed. E. Baehrens (Teubner; Leipzig, 1879)

Menander Protector, *The* History *of Menander the Guardsman*, ed. and trans. R. C. Blockley (ARCA Classical and Medieval Texts, Papers and Monographs 17; Liverpool, 1985)

Menander Rhetor, ed. and trans. D. A. Russell and N. G. Wilson (Oxford, 1981)

Merobaudes, Flavius, *Reliquiae*, ed. F. Vollmer (MGH AA 14; Berlin, 1905); Frank M. Clover, *Flavius Merobaudes: A Translation and Historical Commentary* (American Philosophical Society, Transactions, n.s. 61.1; Philadelphia, 1971)

Namatianus, Rutilius Claudius, *De reditu suo sive iter gallicum*, ed. Ernst Doblhofer, 2 vols. (Heidelberg, 1972); trans. in *Minor Latin Poets*, trans. J. W. Duff and A. Duff (LCL; London, 1934)

Nikephorus, *Short History*, ed. and trans. Cyril Mango (Corpus fontium historiae Byzantinae 13; Washington, DC, 1990)

Nonnos, *Dionysiaca*, trans. W. H. D. Rouse (LCL; Cambridge, MA, 1940); ed. and trans. N. Hopkinson and F. Vian, VIII (Paris, 1994)

Nonnosus, in Photius, *Bibliothèque, codex* 3

Notitia dignitatum, ed. Otto Seeck (Berlin, 1876)

Orientius, *Commonitorium*, ed. R. Ellis (CSEL 16; Vienna, 1888); trans. M. D. Tobin (Washington, DC, 1945)

Orosius, Paulus, *Historiarum adversum paganos libri VII*, ed. C. Zangemeister (CSEL 5; Vienna, 1882)

Passio S. Sabae Gothi, ed. H. Delehaye, in 'Saints de Thrace et de Mésie', *Analecta Bollandiana* 31 (1912), 216–21

Patrick, St, *St. Patrick: His Writings and Muirchu's Life*, ed. and trans. A. B. E. Hood (Arthurian Period Sources 9; London, 1978)

Paul the Deacon, *Historia Langobardorum*, ed. L. Bethmann and G. Waitz (MGH Scriptores rerum Langobardicarum; Hanover, 1878), 12–87

Paul the Deacon, *Historia Romana*, ed. H. Droysen (MGH AA 2; Berlin, 1878 = MGH Scriptores in usum scholarum; Berlin, 1879)

Paul the Deacon, *Vita Gregorii magni*, *PL* 75, 41–60

Paulinus of Pella, *Eucharisticos*, ed. W. Brandes, in *Poetae Christiani minores* I (CSEL 16; Vienna, 1888)

Photius, *Bibliothèque*, ed. René Henry, 8 vols. (Paris, 1959–77); partial trans. in *The Library of Photius*, trans. J. H. Freese (New York, 1920); Photius, *The Bibliotheca*, trans. N. G. Wilson (London, 1994)

Pithou the Younger, Pierre (ed.), *Epigrammata et poematia vetera*, ed. (Paris, 1590)

Placidus, *Liber glossarum*, in *Corpus glossoriarum latinorum* IV, ed. G. Goetz (Leipzig, 1894)

Plutarch, *Precepts of Statecraft*, in *Moralia* X, trans. Harold North Fowler (LCL; London, 1936)

Plutarch, *Pyrrhos*, in *Vies*, ed. and trans. Robert Flacelière and Emile Chambry, VI (Budé; Paris, 1971)

Possidius, *Vita Augustini*, *PL* 32, 33–66

Priscian of Caesarea, *De laude Anastasii imperatoris*, trans. Patricia Coyne (Lewiston, NY, 1991)

Procopius, *Opera omnia*, ed. J. Haury, rev. G. Wirth, 4 vols. (Teubner; Leipzig, 1962–4); trans. H. B. Dewing (LCL; London, 1914–40)

Robertson, Anne S. *Roman Imperial Coinage in the Hunter Coin Cabinet* V: *Diocletian (Reform) to Zeno*, ed. (Oxford, 1982)

Roma subterranea novissima, ed. Paulus Aringhus (Rome, 1651)

Roman Imperial Coinage VI–X, ed. C. H. V. Sutherland, R. A. G. Carson, and J. P. C. Kent (London, 1966–94)

Salvian, *De gubernatione Dei*, ed. C. Halm (MGH AA 1; Berlin, 1877); *De gubernatione Dei*, ed. F. Pauly (CSEL 8; Vienna, 1883); trans. E. M. Sanford (Columbia University Records of Civilization; New York, 1930)

Sidonius Apollinaris, *Opera*, ed. Jacob Sirmond (Paris, 1602) = *PL* 58, 435–752; *Epistulae et Carmina*, ed. Christian Luetjohann *et al.* (MGH AA 8; Berlin, 1887); *Poèmes et Lettres*, ed. and trans. André Loyen, 3 vols. (Budé; Paris, 1970); *The Letters of Sidonius*, trans. O. M. Dalton, 2 vols. (Oxford, 1915); *Poems and Letters*, trans. W. B. Anderson [and E. H. Warmington], 2 vols. (LCL; London, 1936, 1965); *Brief, Buch I*, ed. and trans. Helga Köhler (Bibliothek der klassischen Altertumswissenschaften n.s. 2, 96; Heidelberg, 1995)

Socrates, *Ecclesiastica historia*, ed. Robert Hussey, 3 vols. (Oxford, 1853); trans. anon., rev. A. C. Zenos (NPNF ser. 2, 2; Oxford, 1891)

Sozomen, *Ecclesiastica historia*, ed. J. Bidez and G. C. Hansen (GCS 50; Berlin, 1960); trans. E. Walford, rev. C. D. Hartranft (NPNF ser. 2, 2; Oxford, 1891)

Stephanus Africanus, *Vita sancti Amatori episcopi Autissiodorensis* (AASS Mai 1), 51–61

Sulpicius Severus, *Vie de S. Martin*, ed. J. Fontaine, 3 vols. (Sources chrétiennes 133–5; Paris, 1967–9)

Symmachus, Q. Aurelius, *Quae supersunt*, ed. Otto Seeck (MGH AA 6.1; Berlin, 1883)

Syntagma inscriptionum antiquarum comprimis Romae veteris, ed. Thomas Reinesius (Leipzig and Frankfurt, 1682)

Themistius, *Orationes*, ed. H. Schenkl, G. Downey, and A. F. Norman, 2 vols. (Leipzig, 1951, 1971)

Theodoret, *Kirchengeschichte*, ed. L. Parmentier and F. Scheidweiler, 2nd edn (GCS 44; Berlin, 1954); trans. B. Jackson (NPNF ser. 2, 3; Oxford, 1892)

Theodoros Anagnostes, *Kirchengeschichte*, ed. G. C. Hanson, 2nd edn (GCS n.s. 3; Berlin, 1995)

Theodosiani libri XVI, ed. T. Mommsen and P. Kruger, 3rd edn (Berlin, 1962); trans. C. Pharr (Princeton, 1952)

Theophanes Confessor, *The* Chronicle *of Theophanes Confessor*, trans. Cyril Mango and Roger Scott (Oxford, 1997)

Theophylact Simocatta, *Historiae*, ed. C. de Boor and P. Wirth (Leipzig, 1887; repr. 1972); trans. M. Whitby and M. Whitby (Oxford, 1986)

Three Byzantine Military Treatises, ed. and trans. George T. Dennis (Corpus fontium historiae Byzantinae 25; Washington, DC, 1985)

Three Byzantine Saints, trans. E. Dawes and N. H. Baynes (London, 1948)
Vegetius Renatus, Flavius, *Epitoma rei militaris*, ed. C. Lang (Teubner; Leipzig, 1885)
Venantius Honorius Clementianus Fortunatus, *Opera pedestria*, ed. B. Krusch (MGH AA 4.2; Berlin, 1885)
Venantius Honorius Clementianus Fortunatus, *Opera poetica*, ed. F. Leo (MGH AA 4.1; Berlin, 1881)
Victor of Tunnuna, *Chronicle*, ed. T. Mommsen (MGH AA 11), 178–206; ed. Carmen Cardelle de Hartmann (CCSL 173a; Turnhout, 2001), 1–55
Victor of Vita, *Historia persecutionis Africanae provinciae*, ed. K. Halm (MGH AA 3.1; Berlin, 1879)
Vie de sainte Mélanie, ed. and trans. D. Gorce (Sources chrétiennes 90; Paris, 1962); trans. Elizabeth A. Clark (New York, 1984)
Vies des Pères du Jura, ed. F. Martine (Sources chrétiennes 142; Paris, 1988)
Vita Bibiani vel Viviani episcopi Santonensis, ed. B. Krusch (MGH SRM 3; 92–100)
Vita Fulgentii, *PL* 65, 117–50
Vita Lupi episcopi Trecensis, ed. B. Krusch (MGH SRM 3; Hanover, 1896; and 7; 1920)
Vita sanctae Genovefae virginis Parisiensis, ed. B. Krusch (MGH SRM 3; Hanover, 1896)
Vita (I) sancti Orientii episcopo Ausciorum in Novempopulania, ed. Godefroid Henskens (AASS Mai 1)
The Western Fathers; Being the Lives of Martin of Tours, Ambrose, Augustine of Hippo, Honoratus of Arles, and Germanus of Auxerre, trans. F. R. Hoare (New York, 1954)
Zosimus, *Historia nova*, ed. and trans. F. Paschoud, 3 vols. (Budé; Paris, 1979); English trans. Ronald T. Ridley (Byzantina Australiensia 2; Sydney, 1982)

MODERN STUDIES

Adams, Jeremy Du Quesney, *The* Populus *of Augustine and Jerome; A Study in the Patristic Sense of Community* (New Haven, 1971)
Adcock, Frank, and D. J. Mosley, *Diplomacy in Ancient Greece* (London, 1975)
Albertini, E., *Les Divisions administratives de l'Espagne romaine* (Paris, 1923)
Amory, Patrick, *People and Identity in Ostrogothic Italy, 489–554* (Cambridge, 1997)
Ando, Clifford, *Imperial Ideology and Provincial Loyalty in the Roman Empire* (Berkeley, 2000)
André, Jean-Marie, and Marie-Françoise Baslez, *Voyager dans l'antiquité* (Paris, 1993)
Arce, Javier, 'El catastrofismo de Hydacio y los camellos de la *Gallaecia*', in *Los ultimos Romanos en Lusitania*, ed. A. Velazquez *et al.* (Merida, 1995), 219–29
'La *Notitia dignitatum* et l'armée romaine dans la *diocesis Hispaniarum*', *Chiron* 10 (1980), 593–608
Bachrach, Bernard S., *The Anatomy of a Little War: A Diplomatic and Military History of the Gundovald Affair (568–586)* (Boulder, CO, 1994)
Early Carolingian Warfare; Prelude to Empire (Philadelphia, 2001)
A History of the Alans in the West from Their First Appearance in the Sources of Classical Antiquity through the Early Middle Ages (Minneapolis, 1973)
Badian, E., *Foreign Clientelae (264–70 BC)* (Oxford, 1958)

Bibliography

Bagnall, R. S., Alan Cameron, S. R. Schwartz, and K. Worp, *Consuls of the Later Roman Empire* (American Philological Association, Philological Monographs 36; Atlanta, 1987)

Bakhrouchine, S., and E. Kosminski, 'La diplomatie du moyen âge', in V. P. Potiemkine (ed.), *Histoire de la diplomatie*, 79–153

Barker, J. Craig, 'The Theory and Practice of Diplomatic Law in the Renaissance and Classical Periods', *Diplomacy and Statecraft* 6 (1995), 593–615

Barnes, T. D., *Ammianus Marcellinus and the Representation of Historical Reality* (Ithaca, NY, 1998)

Constantine and Eusebius (Cambridge, MA, 1981)

The New Empire of Diocletian and Constantine (Cambridge, MA, 1982)

'*Patricii* under Valentinian III', *Phoenix* 29 (1975), 155–70

'Who Were the Nobility of the Roman Empire?', *Phoenix* 28 (1974), 444–9

Barnish, S. J. B., 'Ennodius' *Lives* of Epiphanius and Antony; Two Models for the Christian Gentleman', *Studia Patristica* 24 (1993), 13–19

'Transformation and Survival in the Western Senatorial Aristocracy, c. AD 400–700', *Papers of the British School in Rome* 56 (1988), 138–40

Barnwell, P. S., *Emperor, Prefects, and Kings; The Roman West, 395–565* (London, 1992)

Kings, Courtiers and Imperium; The Barbarian West, 565–725 (London, 1997)

'War and Peace; Historiography and Seventh-Century Embassies', *Early Medieval Europe* 6 (1997), 127–39

Bash, A., *Ambassadors for Christ; An Exploration of Ambassadorial Language in the New Testament* (Tübingen, 1997)

Bauslaugh, Robert A., *The Concept of Neutrality in Classical Greece* (Berkeley, 1991)

Bayless, W. N., 'The Peace of 439 AD: Avitus and the Visigoths', *The Ancient World* 1 (1978), 141–3

'The Political Unity of the Roman Empire during the Disintegration of the West, AD 395–457' (diss., Brown University, 1972)

Baynes, Norman H., 'A Note on Professor Bury's *History of the Later Roman Empire*', *Journal of Roman Studies* 12 (1922), 207–29

Berger, Adolf, *Encyclopedic Dictionary of Roman Law* (Philadelphia, 1953)

Berschin, W., *Biographie und Epochenstil im lateinischen Mittelalter*, 3 vols. (Stuttgart 1986–91)

Bibliotheca hagiographica latina (Brussels, 1898–9); *Novum supplementum*, ed. H. Fros (Brussels, 1986)

Binding, Karl, *Das burgundisch-romanische Königreich (von 443–532 n. Chr.)* (Leipzig, 1868; repr. Aalen, 1969)

Blockley, R. C., 'Doctors as Diplomats in the Sixth Century AD', *Florilegium* 2 (1980), 89–100

East Roman Foreign Policy: Formation and Conduct from Diocletian to Anastasius (ARCA Classical and Medieval Texts, Papers and Monographs 30; Leeds, 1992)

'Roman–Barbarian Marriages in the Late Empire', *Florilegium* 4 (1982), 63–77

Rome and Persia: International Relations in Late Antiquity (Ottawa, 1985)

'Subsidies and Diplomacy; Rome and Persia in Late Antiquity', *Phoenix* 39 (1985), 62–74

Boak, Arthur E. R., and James E. Dunlap, *Two Studies in Late Roman and Byzantine Administration* (Ann Arbor, 1924)

Bonnard, Louis, *La Navigation intérieure de la Gaule à l'époque gallo-romaine* (Paris, 1913)
Bowersock, G. W., *Augustus and the Greek World* (Oxford, 1965)
Fiction as History: Nero to Julian (Berkeley, 1994)
Greek Sophists in the Roman Empire (Oxford, 1969)
Bowersock, G. W., Peter Borwn, and Oleg Grabar, *Late Antiquity: A Guide to the Postclassical World* (Cambridge, MA, 1999)
Braund, David, 'Priscus on the Suani', *Phoenix* 46 (1992), 62–5
Rome and the Friendly King: The Character of the Client Kingship (London, 1984)
Braund, David (ed.), *The Administration of the Roman Empire, 241 BC–AD 193* (Exeter, 1988)
Briant, Pierre, 'La Boulè et l'élection des ambassadeurs à Athènes au IVe siècle', *Revue des Etudes Anciennes* 70 (1968), 7–31
Brown, Peter, *Augustine of Hippo: A Biography* (London, 1967)
The Cult of the Saints: Its Rise and Function in Latin Christianity (Chicago, 1981)
Power and Persuasion in Late Antiquity: Towards a Christian Empire (Madison, 1992)
The World of Late Antiquity: From Marcus Aurelius to Muhammed (London, 1971)
Brown, T. S., *Gentlemen and Officers: Imperial Administration and Aristocratic Power in Byzantine Ravenna* (Oxford, 1984)
Burgess, R. W., 'Consuls and Consular Dating in the Later Roman Empire', *Phoenix* 43 (1989), 143–57
'Hydatius; A Late Roman Chronicler in Post-Roman Spain: A Historical Study and New Critical Edition of the Chronicle' (diss., University of Oxford, 1988)
'The Third Regnal Year of Eparchius Avitus: A Reply', *Classical Philology* 82 (1987), 335–45
Burns, Thomas S., *A History of the Ostrogoths* (Bloomington, 1984)
Bury, J. B., 'The *Ceremonial Book* of Constantine Porphyrogennetos', *English Historical Review* 22 (1907), 209–27, 417–39
History of the Later Roman Empire: From the Death of Theodosius I to the Death of Justinian, 2 vols. (London, 1923; repr. New York, 1958)
'A Note on the Emperor Olybrius', *English Historical Review* 1 (1886), 507–9
'The *Notitia dignitatum*', *Journal of Roman Studies* 10 (1920), 131–54
'The Treatise *De administrando imperio*', *Byzantinische Zeitschrift* 15 (1906), 517–77
The Cambridge Ancient History XIII: *The Late Empire, 337–425*, ed. Averil Cameron and Peter Garnsey (Cambridge, 1998); XIV: *Late Antiquity: Empire and Successors*, ed. Averil Cameron, Bryan Ward-Perkins, and Michael Whitby (Cambridge, 2000)
Cameron, Alan, *Claudian: Poetry and Propaganda at the Court of Honorius* (Oxford, 1970)
'The Empress and the Poet; Paganism and Politics at the Court of Theodosius II', *Yale Classical Studies* 27 (1982), 217–89
'The Fate of Pliny's *Letters* in the Late Empire', *Classical Quarterly* n.s. 15 (1965), 289–98
'Wandering Poets; A Literary Movement in Byzantine Egypt', *Historia* 14 (1965), 470–509
Cameron, A. M., and A. D. E Cameron, 'Christianity and Tradition in the Historiography of the Later Empire', *Classical Quarterly* 58 (1964), 316–28

Cameron, Alan, and Diane Schauer, 'The Last Consul; Basilius and His Diptych', *Journal of Roman Studies* 72 (1982), 126–45
Cameron, Averil, 'Agathias on the Early Merovingians', *Annali della Scuola Normale Superiore di Pisa* 3rd ser. 37 (1968), 95–140
'Agathias on the Sassanians', *Dumbarton Oaks Papers* 23 and 24 (1969–70), 67–183
'Cassiodorus Deflated', *Journal of Roman Studies* 71 (1981), 183–6
Campbell, J. B., *The Emperor and the Roman Army, 31 BC–AD 235* (Oxford, 1984)
Cardelle de Hartmann, Carmen, *Philologische Studien zur* Chronik *des Hydatius von Chaves* (Palingenesia 47; Stuttgart, 1994)
Carney, T. F., *Bureaucracy in Traditional Society; Romano-Byzantine Bureaucracy Viewed from Within* (Lawrence, KS, 1971)
Carson, R. A. G., *Coins of the Roman Empire* (London and New York, 1990)
Castritius, H., 'Zur Sozialgeschichte der Heermeister des Westreiches nach der Mitte des 5. Jh.; Flavius Valila *qui et* Theodovius', *Ancient Society* 3 (1973), 239–41
Cenzon Santos, Maria Andrelita, *Baptismal Ecclesiology of St. Augustine: A Theological Study of His Antidonatist Letters* (Rome, 1990)
Chadwick, Henry, *Boethius: The Consolations of Music, Logic, Theology, and Philosophy* (Oxford, 1981)
Chadwick, Nora K., *Poetry and Letters in Early Christian Gaul* (London, 1955)
Chastagnol, André, *Le sénat romain sous le règne d'Odoacre* (Bonn, 1966)
Christensen, Arne Søby, 'The *Vita* of Saint Germanus of Auxerre and Fifth-Century History', *Studies in Ancient History and Numismatics Presented to Rudi Thomsen* (Aarhus, 1988), 224–31
Chrysos, Evangelos K., 'Die Amaler-Herrschaft in Italien und das Imperium Romanum; Der Vertragsentwurf des Jahres 535', *Byzantion* 51 (1981), 430–74
'Gothia Romania; zur Rechtsgrundlage des Föderatenstandes der Westgoten im vierten Jahrhundert', *Dacoromania* 1 (1973), 52–64
'Legal Concepts and Patterns for the Barbarians' Settlement on Roman Soil', in Chrysos and Schwarcz (eds.), *Das Reich und die Barbaren*, 13–23
'Some Aspects of Roman–Persian Legal Relations', *Kleronomia* 8 (1977), 1–60
'The Title Βασιλεύς in Early Byzantine International Relations', *Dumbarton Oaks Papers* 32 (1978), 31–75
Chrysos, Evangelos K., and Andreas Schwarcz (eds.), *Das Reich und die Barbaren* (Vienna and Cologne, 1989)
Chrysos, Evangelos K., and Ian Wood (eds.), *East and West; Modes of Communication* (The Transformation of the Roman World 5; Leiden, 1999)
Ciggar, Krijnie N., *Western Travellers to Constantinople: The West and Byzantium, 926–1204: Cultural and Political Relations* (Leiden, 1996)
Clarke, G., *et al.* (eds.), *Reading the Past in Late Antiquity* (Rushcutters Bay, NSW, 1990)
Clauss, Manfred, *Der Magister officiorum in der Spätantike (4.–6. Jahrhundert); das Amt und sein Einfluss auf die kaiserliche Politik* (Vestigia 32; Munich, 1980)
Clover, F. H., 'The Family and Early Career of Anicius Olybrius', *Historia* 27 (1978), 169–96
'Geiseric and Attila', *Historia* 22 (1973), 104–17
'Geiseric the Statesman: A Study of Vandal Foreign Policy' (diss., University of Chicago, 1966)

Collins, Roger, *Early Medieval Spain: Unity in Diversity, 400–1000* (Houndmills, 1983)
Collins, Wilkie, *Antonina, or The Fall of Rome*, 2nd edn (London, 1872)
Conybeare, Catherine, *Paulinus Noster: Self and Symbols in the Letters of Paulinus of Nola* (Oxford, 2000)
Coon, Lynda L., *Sacred Fictions: Holy Women and Hagiography in Late Antiquity* (Philadelphia, 1997)
Courcelle, Pierre, *La* Consolation de Philosophie *dans la tradition littéraire* (Paris, 1967)
Histoire littéraire des grandes invasions germaniques, 3rd edn (Paris, 1964)
Late Latin Writers and Their Greek Sources, trans. H. E. Wedeck (Cambridge, MA, 1969)
Courtois, Christian, 'Auteurs et scribes: remarques sur la chronique d'Hydace', *Byzantion* 21 (1951), 23–54
Les Vandales et l'Afrique (Paris, 1955)
Cracco Ruggini, L., 'The Ecclesiastical Histories and the Pagan Historiography: Providence and Miracles', *Athenaeum* 55 (1977), 107–26
Craig, Gordon A., 'On the Nature of Diplomatic History: The Relevance of Some Old Books', in Paul Gordon Lauren (ed.), *Diplomacy: New Approaches in History, Theory, and Policy* (New York and London, 1979), 21–42
Cramer, Peter, *Baptism and Change in the Early Middle Ages, c. 200–c. 1150* (Cambridge, 1993)
Croke, Brian, 'AD 476: The Manufacture of a Turning Point', *Chiron* 3 (1983), 81–119
'Anatolius and Nomus: Envoys to Attila', *Byzantinoslavica* 42 (1981), 159–70
'City Chronicles of Late Antiquity', in G. Clarke *et al.* (eds.), *Reading the Past in Late Antiquity* (Rushcutters Bay, NSW, 1990), 165–203
Count Marcellinus and His Chronicle (Oxford, 2001)
'Evidence for the Hun Invasion of Thrace in AD 422', *Greek, Roman, and Byzantine Studies* 18 (1977), 347–67
'Mundo the Gepid: From Freebooter to Roman General', *Chiron* 12 (1982), 125–35
'The Origins of the Christian World Chronicle', in Croke and Emmett (eds.), *History and Historians in Late Antiqity*, 116–31
Croke, Brian, and A. M. Emmett (eds.), *History and Historians in Late Antiquity* (Sydney, 1983)
Curtius, Ernst Robert, *European Literature and the Latin Middle Ages*, trans. Willard R. Trask (Bollingen Series 36; New York, 1953)
Daly, Lawrence J., 'The Mandarin and the Barbarian: The Response of Themistius to the Gothic Challenge', *Historia* 21 (1972), 351–79
Daly, William D., '*Christianitas* Eclipses *Romanitas* in the Life of Sidonius Apollinaris', in T. F. X. Noble and J. J. Contreni (eds.), *Religion, Culture and Society in the Early Middle Ages: Essays in Honor of R. E. Sullivan* (Kalamazoo, 1987), 7–26
Deichmann, Friedrich Wilhelm, *Ravenna: Geschichte und Monumente*, 3 vols. (Wiesbaden, 1969–76)
Delbrueck, R., *Die consular Diptychen und verwandte Dankmäler* (Berlin, 1929)
Delehaye, H., *Legends of the Saints*, trans. V. M. Crawford (1907; repr. Norwood, PA, 1974)

Delmaire, Roland, *L'Empire romain et les barbares d'occident (IVe–VIIe siècle); scripta varia* (Paris, 1988)
La Formation de l'Europe et les invasions barbares, 2 vols. (Paris, 1979)
Largesses sacrées et res privata*: l'aerarium impérial et son administration du IVe–VIe siècles* (Ecole française de Rome, Collection 121; Rome, 1989)
'The Osmosis of Late Roman and Germanic Aristocracies', in Chrysos and Schwarcz (eds.), *Das Reich und die Barbaren*, 75–86
Les responsables des finances impériales au Bas-Empire romain (IVe–VIes.); études prosopographiques (Collection Latomus 203; Brussels, 1989)
Dill, Samuel, *Roman Society in Gaul in the Merovingian Age* (London, 1926)
Roman Society in the Last Century of the Western Roman Empire, 2nd edn (London, 1910)
Dizionario patristico e di antichità Christiana, 2 vols. (Rome, 1984)
Dorey, T. A. (ed.), *Empire and Aftermath: Silver Latin II* (London and Boston, 1975)
Drinkwater, John, and Hugh Elton, (eds.), *Fifth-Century Gaul: A Crisis of Identity?* (Cambridge, 1992)
Du Cange, Charles du Fresne, *Glossarium mediae et infirmae latinitatis*, ed. C. P. Carpenter and G. A. L. Henschel, 10 vols. (Niort, 1883–7; repr. Graz, 1954)
Duchesne, L., *Fastes épiscopaux de l'ancienne Gaule*, 3 vols. (Paris, 1910–15)
Duncan-Jones, Richard, *Structure and Scale in the Roman Economy* (Cambridge, 1990)
Durliat, Jean, *Les Finances publiques de Dioclétien aux Carolingiens (284–889)* (Beihefte zu Francia 21; Sigmaringen, 1990)
Dvornik, Francis, *The Origins of Intelligence Services: The Ancient Near East, Persia, Greece, Rome, Byzantium, The Arab Muslim Empire, The Mongol Empire, China, Moscovy* (New Brunswick, NJ, 1974)
Eckstein, Arthur M., *Senate and General: Individual Decision-Making and Roman Foreign Relations, 264–194 BC* (Berkeley, 1987)
Elliott, Alison Goddard, *Roads to Paradise: Reading the Lives of the Early Saints* (Hanover and London, 1987)
Elton, Hugh, *Warfare in Roman Europe AD 350–425* (Oxford, 1996)
Ensslin, Wilhelm, 'Aus Theoderichs Kanzlei', *Würzburger Jahrbücher für die Altertumswissenschaft* 2 (1947), 75–85
'Beweise der Romverbundheit in Theoderichs des Grossen Aussen- und Innenpolitik', *Centro italiano di studi sull'alto medioevo, Settimane di studio* 3 (Spoleto, 1956), 509–36
Theoderich der Grosse, 2nd edn (Munich, 1956)
'Zum Heermeisteramt des spätrömischen Reiches', *Klio* 23 (1930), 306–25; 24 (1931), 102–47, 467–502
Erskine, Andrew, *Troy between Greece and Rome: Local Tradition and Imperial Power* (New York, 2001)
Ewig, E., *Die Merowinger und das Imperium* (Opladen, 1983)
Spätantikes und fränkisches Gallien: Gesammelte Schriften (1952–1973), ed. H. Atsama, 2 vols. (Munich, 1976)
Fele, Maria Luisa *et al.* (eds.), *Concordantiae in carmina latina epigraphica*, 2 vols. (Hildersheim, 1988)
Ferrary, Jean-Louis, '*Ius fetiale* et diplomatie', in Frézouls and Jacquemin (eds.), *Les Relations internationales*, 411–32

Finn, Thomas M., *Early Christian Baptism and the Catechumenate: West and East Syria* (Collegeville, MN, 1992)

Flamant, Jacques, *Macrobe et le néo-platonisme latin à la fin du IVe siècle* (Leiden, 1977)

Fontaine, Jacques, 'Une clé littéraire de la *Vita Martini* de Sulpice Sévère: la typologie prophétique', in *Mélanges offerts à Mademoiselle Christine Mohrmann* (Utrecht, 1963) 84–95

'Hagiographie et politique, de Sulpice Sévère à Venance Fortunat', *Revue d'Histoire de l'Eglise de France* 62 (1976), 113–40

Forcellini, Aegidius (ed.), *Lexicon totius latinitatis* v and vi: *Onomasticon*, ed. Joseph Perin (Padua, 1940)

Fornara, Charles William, *The Nature of History in Ancient Greece and Rome* (Berkeley, 1983)

Fouracre, P., 'Merovingian History and Merovingian Hagiography', *Past and Present* 127 (1990), 3–38

Fowden, Garth, *Empire to Commonwealth: Consequences of Monotheism in Late Antiquity* (Princeton, 1993)

Fraenkel, Ernst, 'Namenwesen', *RE* xvi.2, 1611–70

Frézouls, E., and A. Jacquemin (eds.), *Les Relations internationales* (Paris, 1995)

Fridh, Åke, *Contributions à la critique et à l'interprétation des* Variae *de Cassiodore* (Göteborg, 1968)

Terminologie et formules dans les Variae *de Cassiodore; études sur le développement du style administratif aux derniers siècles de l'antiquité* (Studia graeca et latina Gothoburgensia 2; Stockholm, 1956)

Gagé, L., 'L'empereur romain et les rois', *Revue Historique* 221 (1959), 221–60

Gamber, Klaus, *Die Liturgie der Goten und der Armenier: Versuch einer Darstellung und Hinführung* (Studia Palistica et Liturgica 21; Regensburg, 1988)

Ganshof, F. L., 'Merowingisches Gesandschaftswesen', in *Aus Geschichte und Landeskunde: Forschungen und Darstellungen* [*Festschrift* for Franz Steinbach] (Bonn, 1960), 166–83

Le Moyen Age, vol. I of *Histoire des relations internationales*, ed. P. Renouvin (Paris, 1953); trans. Rémy Inglis Hall as *The Middle Ages: A History of International Relations* (New York, 1970)

Garnsey, Peter, and Richard Saller, *The Roman Empire: Economy, Society and Culture* (Berkeley, 1987)

Geary, Patrick J., *Living with the Dead in the Middle Ages* (Ithaca, NY, 1994)

George, Judith, *Venantius Fortunatus: A Latin Poet in Merovingian Gaul* (Oxford, 1992)

Gessel, Wilhelm, 'Germanus von Auxerre (um 378 bis 448); die *Vita* des Konstantius von Lyon als homiletische Paränese in hagiographischer Form', *Römische Quartelschrift für Christliche Altertumskunde und Kirchengeschichte* 65 (1970), 1–13

Gibbon, Edward, *The History of the Decline and Fall of the Roman Empire*, ed. J. B. Bury, 7 vols. (London, 1926); ed. David Womersley, 3 vols. (London, 1994)

Gillett, Andrew, 'The Accession of Euric', *Francia* 26.1 (1999), 1–40

'The Birth of Ricimer', *Historia* 44 (1995), 380–4

'The Date and Circumstances of Olympiodorus of Thebes', *Traditio* 48 (1993), 1–29

'Jordanes and Ablabius', in Carl Deroux (ed.), *Studies in Latin Literature and Roman History* x (Collection Latomus 254; Brussels, 2000), 479–500

'The Purposes of Cassiodorus's *Variae*', in Murray (ed.), *After Rome's Fall*, 37–50

Review of R. W. Burgess (ed. and trans.), *The* Chronicle *of Hydatius and the* Consularia Constantinopolitana (Oxford, 1993), *Journal of Roman Studies* 87 (1997), 312–13

'Rome, Ravenna, and the Last Western Emperors', *Papers of the British School in Rome* 69 (2001), 131–67

'Was Ethnicity Politicized in the Earliest Medieval Kingdoms?', in Gillett (ed.), *On Barbarian Identity*, 85–121

Gillett, Andrew (ed.), *On Barbarian Identity: Critical Approaches to Ethnicity in the Early Middle Ages* (Studies in the Early Middle Ages 4; Turnhout, 2002)

Goffart, Walter, *Barbarians and Romans, AD 418–584: The Techniques of Accommodation* (Princeton, 1980)

The Narrators of Barbarian History (AD 550–800): Jordanes, Gregory of Tours, Bede, and Paul the Deacon (Princeton, 1988)

Rome's Fall and After (London, 1989)

Gorce, Denys, *Les Voyages, l'hospitalité, et le port des lettres dans le monde chrétien des IVe et Ve siècles* (Paris, 1925)

Gordon, C. D., 'Subsidies in Roman Imperial Defence', *Phoenix* 3 (1949), 60–9

Goubert, P., *Byzance avant l'Islam* II.1: *Byzance et les Francs* (Paris, 1956)

Greatrex, Geoffrey, 'Lawyers and Historians in Late Antiquity', in Mathisen, *Law, Society, and Authority in Late Antiquity*, 148–60

Grierson, P., and M. Blackburn, *Medieval European Coinage* I: *The Early Middle Ages (5th to 10th Centuries)* (Cambridge, 1986)

Griffe, E., *La Gaule chrétienne a l'époque romaine*, 3 vols., 2nd edn (Paris, 1964–6)

'L'hagiographie gauloise au Ve siècle: la *Vie de saint Germain d'Auxerre*', *Bulletin de Littérature Ecclésiastique* 66 (1965), 289–94

Grosjean, Paul, 'Notes d'hagiographie céltique 27–29', *AB* 75 (1957), 158–85

Gruen, Erich S., *The Hellenistic World and the Coming of Rome*, 2 vols. (Berkeley, 1984)

Guilland, Rodolphe, *Recherches sur les institutions byzantines*, 2 vols. (Berlin, 1967)

Titres et fonctions de l'Empire byzantin (London, 1976)

Günther, Rigobert, 'Apollinaris Sidonius – Eine Untersuchung seiner drei Kaiserpanegyriken', in G. Wirth *et al.*, *Romanitas–Christianitas: Untersuchungen zur Geschichte und Literature der römischen Kaiserzeit* (Berlin, 1982), 654–60

Hägg, Tomas, and Warren Treadgold, 'The Preface of the *Bibliotheca* of Photius Once More', *Symbolae Osloenses* 61 (1986), 133–8

Hague, Barry John, 'Cultures in Collision: The Barbarization of the Western Roman Empire in Ideology and Reality (c. 370–530 AD)' (diss., Cambridge University, 1987)

Haldon, John, *Warfare, State and Society in the Byzantine World, 565–1204* (London, 1999)

Handbuch der lateinischen Literatur der Antike V: *Restauration und Erneuerung: die lateinische Literature von 284 bis 374 n. Chr.*, ed. R. Herzog (Handbuch der klassischen Altertumswissenschaft 8.5; Munich, 1989)

Hanning, Robert W., *The Vision of History in Early Britain: From Gildas to Geoffrey of Monmouth* (New York, 1966)

Hansen, Mogens Herman, *The Athenian Assembly in the Age of Demosthenes* (Oxford, 1987)
The Athenian Democracy in the Age of Demosthenes (Oxford, 1991)
The Athenian Ecclesia II (Copenhagen, 1989)
Hanson, R. P. C., *The Search for the Christian Doctrine of God: The Arian Controversy, 318–381* (Edinburgh, 1988)
Harnack, A., Militia Christi: *The Christian Religion and the Military in the First Three Centuries*, trans. I. M. Gracie (Philadelphia, 1981)
Harries, Jill, 'The Roman Imperial Quaestor from Constantine to Theodosius II', *Journal of Roman Studies* 78 (1988), 148–72
Sidonius Apollinaris and the Fall of Rome, AD 407–485 (Oxford, 1994)
Harries, Jill, and Ian Wood (eds.), *The Theodosian Code* (Ithaca, NY, 1993)
Harrison, Geoffrey, 'The Verse Panegyrics of Sidonius Apollinaris: Poetry and Society in Late Antique Gaul' (diss., Stanford University, 1983)
Hartmann, Ludo Moritz, *Geschichte Italiens im Mittelalter* I (Leipzig, 1897)
Hasenstab, B., *Studien zur Ennodius: ein Beitrag zur Geschichte der Völkerwanderung* (Munich, 1890)
Studien zur Variensammlung des Cassiodor Senator: ein Beitrag zur Geschichte der Ostgothenherrschaft in Italien (Munich, 1883)
Hauken, Tor, *Petition and Response: An Epigraphic Study of Petitions to Roman Emperors 181–249* (Monographs from the Norwegian Institute at Athens 2; Bergen, 1998)
Havet, J., 'Questions mérovingiennes II: les découvertes de Jérome Vignier', *Bibliothèque de l'Ecole des Chartes* 46 (1885), 205–74
Heather, Peter, 'The Anti-Scythian Tirade of Synesius' *De regno*', *Phoenix* 42 (1988), 152–72
'The Crossing of the Danube and the Gothic Conversion', *Greek, Roman, and Byzantine Studies* 27 (1986), 289–318
Goths and Romans, 332–489 (Oxford, 1991)
Heather, Peter, and John Matthews, *The Goths in the Fourth Century* (TTH 11; Liverpool, 1991)
Heil, Wilhelm, *Der konstantinische Patriziat* (Basel and Stuttgart, 1968)
Heinzelmann, Martin, *Bischofsherrschaft in Gallien: zur Kontinuität römischer Führungsschichten vom 4. bis zum 7. Jahrhundert* (Beiheft der Francia 5; Munich, 1976)
'Gallische Prosopographie, 260–527', *Francia* 10 (1982), 615–16
Gregory of Tours: History and Society in the Sixth Century, trans. Christopher Carrol (Cambridge, 2001)
'Neue Aspekte der hagiographischen Literatur', *Francia* 1 (1973), 27–44
'*Studia sanctorum*: éducation, milieux d'instruction et valeurs éducatives dans l'hagiographie en Gaule jusqu'à la fin de l'époque mérovingienne', in *Haut Moyen-Age: culture, éducation et société* (Nanterre, 1990), 105–38
Heinzelmann, M., and J.-C. Poulin, *Les Vies anciennes de sainte Geneviève de Paris: études critiques* (Paris, 1986)
Helm, Rudolf, 'Untersuchungen über den auswärtigen diplomatischen Verkehr des römischen Reiches im Zeitalter der Spätantike', *Archiv für Urkundenforschung* 12 (1932), 375–436; repr. in Olshausen and Biller (eds.), *Antike Diplomatie*, 321–408
Hen, Yitzak, *Culture and Religion in Merovingian Gaul, AD 481–751* (Leiden, 1995)

Henken, Elissa R., *The Welsh Saints: A Study in Patterned Lives* (Cambridge, 1991)

Herrin, Judith, *The Formation of Christendom* (Princeton, 1987)

Hill, David Jayne, *A History of Diplomacy in the International Development of Europe* I (New York, 1905)

Hillgarth, J. N., 'Coins and Chronicles: Propaganda in Sixth-Century Spain and the Byzantine Background', *Historia* 15 (1966), 483–508

'Historiography in Visigothic Spain', *Centro italiano di studi sull'alto medioevo, Settimane di studio* 17 (Spoleto, 1970), 261–311

Hodgkin, Thomas, *Italy and Her Invaders*, 8 vols. (Oxford, 1880–99)

Holder-Egger, Oswald, 'Untersuchungen über einige annalistische Quellen zur Geschichte des fünften und sechsten Jahrhunderts', *Neues Archiv der Gesellschaft für Ältere Deutsche Geschichtskunde* 1 (1876), 13–120, 213–368; 2 (1877), 47–111

Holum, Kenneth G., *Theodosian Empresses: Women and Imperial Dominion in Late Antiquity* (Berkeley, 1982)

Hoops, J. *et al.* (eds.), *Reallexikon der germanischen Altertumskunde*, 4 vols. (Strasburg, 1911–19); 2nd edn, 7 vols. to date (Berlin, 1967–)

Isaac, Benjamin, *The Limits of Empire: The Roman Army in the East* (Oxford, 1992)

James, Edward, *The Origins of France: From Clovis to the Capetians, 500–1000* (Houndmills, 1982)

Jedin, Hubert, and John Dolan (eds.), *History of the Church*, trans. Anselm Biggs, 3 vols. (Freiburg and Montreal, 1965–9)

Jeffreys, Elizabeth, Brian Croke, and Roger Scott (eds.), *Studies in John Malalas* (Byzantina Australiensia; Sydney, 1990)

Jones, A. H. M., 'The Constitutional Position of Odoacer and Theodoric', *Journal of Roman Studies* 52 (1962), 126–30

The Later Roman Empire, 284–602: A Social, Economic and Administrative Survey, 3 vols. (Oxford, 1964)

'The Roman Civil Service (Clerical and Sub-Clerical Grades)', *Journal of Roman Studies* 39 (1949), 38–55

'Were Ancient Heresies National and Social Movements in Disguise?', *Journal of Theological Studies* 10 (1959), 280–98

Jones, A. H. M., J. R. Martindale *et al.* (eds.), *The Prosopography of the Later Roman Empire*, 3 vols. (Cambridge, 1971–92)

Jones, C. P., *Kinship Diplomacy in the Ancient World* (Cambridge, MA, 1999)

Kaegi, W. E., *Byzantium and the Decline of Rome* (Princeton, 1968)

Kaser, Max, *Ius gentium* (Forschungen zum Römischen Recht 40; Cologne, 1993)

Kaster, Robert A., *Guardians of Language: The Grammarian and Society in Late Antiquity* (Berkeley, 1997)

Khadduri, Majid, 'Diplomacy, Islamic', in *Dictionary of the Middle Ages* IV (New York, 1984), 197–201

Kienast, Dietmar, 'Presbeia', *RE* Suppl. XIII, 499–628

Klauser, Theodor, Ernst Dassmann *et al.* (eds.), *Reallexikon für Antike und Christentum* (Stuttgart, 1950–)

Klebs, E. *et al.* (eds.), *Prosopographia imperii Romani saec. I. II. III.*, 3 vols. (Berlin, 1897–8); 2nd edn ed. E. Groag *et al.*, 5 vols. to date (Berlin and Leipzig, 1933–87)

Klingshirn, William, *Caesarius of Arles: The Making of a Christian Community in Late Antique Gaul* (Cambridge, 1993)

'Charity and Power: Caesarius of Arles and the Ransoming of Captives in Sub-Roman Gaul', *Journal of Roman Studies* 75 (1985), 183–203

Köbler, Gerhard, *Gotisches Wörterbuch* (Leiden, 1989)

Koller, Erwin, and Hugo Laitenberger (eds.), *Suevos-Schwaben: das Königreich der Sueben auf der Iberischen Halbinsel (411–585)* (Tübingen, 1998)

Kostof, Spiro K., *The Orthodox Baptistery of Ravenna* (New Haven and London, 1965)

Krautschick, Stefan, *Cassiodor und die Politik seiner Zeit* (Bonn, 1983)

Kulikowski, Michael, 'Barbarians in Gaul, Usurpers in Britain', *Britannia*, 31 (2000), 325–45

'Nation versus Army: A Necessary Contrast?', in Gillett (ed.), *On Barbarian Identity*, 69–84

'The *Notitia Dignitatum* as an Historical Source', *Historia* 49 (2000), 358–77

'The Visigothic Settlement in Aquitania: The Imperial Perspective', in Ralph W. Mathisen and Danuta Shanzer (eds.), *Society and Culture in Late Antique Gaul: Revisiting the Sources* (Aldershot, 2002), 26–38

Kunkel, Wolfgang, *An Introduction to Roman Legal and Constitutional History*, 2nd edn, trans. J. M. Kelly (Oxford, 1973)

Lécrivain, C., 'Un épisode inconnu de l'histoire des Wisigoths', *Annales du Midi* 1 (1889), 47–51

'Note sur la Vie de Saint Orientius, évêque d'Auch', *Annales du Midi* 3 (1891), 257–8

Lee, A. D., *Information and Frontiers: Roman Foreign Relations in Late Antiquity* (Cambridge, 1993)

'The Role of Hostages in Roman Diplomacy with Sasanian Persia', *Historia* 40 (1991), 366–74

Lee, Douglas, and Jonathon Shepard, 'A Double Life: Placing the *Peri Presbeon*', *Byzantinoslavika* 52 (1991), 15–39

Levison, Wilhelm, 'Bischof Germanus von Auxerre und die Quellen zu seiner Geschichte', *Neues Archiv* 29 (1903), 97–175

Levy, Ernst, 'Reflections on the First "Reception" of Roman Law in Germanic States', *American Historical Review* 48 (1942), 20–9

West Roman Vulgar Law: The Law of Property (Memoirs of the American Philosophical Society 29; Philadelphia, 1951)

Lewis, A. R., 'The Rhône Valley Route and Traffic between the Mediterranean and Northern Europe, AD 300–1200', *Res Publica Litterarum* 5 (1982), 139–50

Liebeschuetz, J. H. W. G., *Barbarians and Bishops: Army, Church and State in the Age of Arcadius and Chrysostom* (Oxford, 1990)

The Decline and Fall of the Roman City (Oxford, 2001)

'The End of the Ancient City', in John Rich (ed.), *The City in Late Antiquity* (London, 1992), 1–49

'The End of the Roman Army in the Western Empire', in John Rich and Graham Shipley (eds.), *War and Society in the Roman World* (Leicester-Nottingham Studies in Ancient Society 5; London, 1993), 265–76

Linderski, Jerzy, 'Ambassadors Go to Rome', in Frézoul and Jacquemin (eds.), *Les Relations internationales*, 452–78

Lot, Ferdinand, 'Du régime de l'hospitalité', *Revue Belge de Philologie et d'Histoire* 7 (1928), 975–1011

The End of the Ancient World and the Beginning of the Middle Ages, trans. P. and M. Leon (London, 1931)
'La *Vita Viviani* et la domination wisigothique en Aquitaine', in *Mélanges Paul Fournier* (Paris, 1929), 467–77
Lot, Ferdinand, Christian Pfister, and François L. Ganshof, *Les Destinées de l'Empire en Occident de 395 à 888* (Paris, 1928)
Lotter, F., *Severinus von Noricum: Legende und historische Wirklichkeit* (Stuttgart, 1976)
Lounghis, T. C., *Les Ambassades byzantines en Occident depuis la fondation des états barbares jusqu'aux croisades (467–1096)* (Athens, 1980)
'Ambassadors, Embassies, and Administrative Changes in the Eastern Roman Empire Prior to the Reconquista', in Chrysos and Schwarcz (eds.), *Das Reich und die Barbaren*, 143–53
Loyen, André, *Recherches historiques sur les panégyriques de Sidoine Apollinaire* (Paris, 1942; repr. Rome, 1967)
Sidoine Apollinaire et l'esprit précieux en Gaule aux derniers jours de l'Empire (Paris, 1943)
Luttwak, E. N., *The Grand Strategy of the Roman Empire from the First Century AD to the Third* (Baltimore and London, 1976)
Maas, Michael, *John Lydus and the Roman Past: Antiquarianism and Politics in the Age of Justinian* (London and New York, 1992)
MacCormack, Sabine, *Art and Ceremony in Late Antiquity* (Berkeley, 1981)
'Change and Continuity in Late Antiquity: The Ceremony of the *adventus*', *Historia* 21 (1972), 721–52
'Latin Prose Panegyrics', in Dorey (ed.), *Empire and Aftermath*, 142–205
McCormick, Michael, 'Analyzing Imperial Ceremonies', *Jahrbuch der Osterreichischen Byzantinistik* 35 (1985), 1–20
'Clovis at Tours: Byzantine Public Ritual and the Origin of Medieval Ruler Symbolism', in Chrysos and Schwarcz (eds.), *Das Reich und die Barbaren*, 155–80
Eternal Victory: Triumphal Rulership in Late Antiquity, Byzantium, and the Early Medieval West (Cambridge and Paris, 1986)
'Odoacer, the Emperor Zeno, and the Rugian Victory Legation', *Byzantion* 47 (1977), 212–22
Origins of the European Economy: Communications and Commerce, AD 300–900 (Cambridge, 2001)
Mackie, Nicola, *Local Administration in Roman Spain AD 14–212* (British Archaeological Reports, International Series 173; Oxford, 1983)
McKitterick, Rosamond (ed.), *The Uses of Literacy in Early Medieval Europe* (Cambridge, 1990)
McLynn, Neil, *Ambrose of Milan: Church and Court in a Christian Capital* (The Transformation of the Classical Heritage 22; Berkeley, 1994)
MacMullen, Ramsay, 'The Epigraphic Habit in the Roman Empire', *American Journal of Philology* 103 (1982), 233–46
Romanization in the Time of Augustus (New Haven, 2000)
Macpherson, Robin, *Rome in Involution: Cassiodorus'* Variae *in Their Literary and Historical Setting* (Poznan, 1989)
Maenchen-Helfen, Otto J., *The World of the Huns: Studies in Their History and Culture*, ed. Max Knight (Berkeley, 1973)

Maguinness, W. S., 'Locutions and Formulae of the Latin Panegyrists', *Hermathena* 48 (1933), 117–38

'Some Methods of the Latin Panegyrists', *Hermathena* 47 (1932), 42–61

Malherbe, Abraham J., *Ancient Epistolary Theorists* (Sources for Biblical Study 19; Atlanta, 1988)

Mandouze, André, *Prosopographie chrétienne du bas-empire* 1: *Prosopographie de l'Afrique chrétienne (303–533)* (Paris, 1982)

Mandouze, André, Charles Pietri, Luce Pietri *et al.* (eds.), *Prosopographie chrétienne du Bas-Empire*, 2 vols. to date (Paris, 1982, 1999)

Markus, R. A., 'Chronicle and Theology: Prosper of Aquitaine', in C. Holdsworth and T. P. Wiseman (eds.), *The Inheritance of Historiography, 350–900* (Exeter, 1986), 31–43

'The End of the Roman Empire: A Note on Eugippius, *Vita Sancti Severini*, 20', *Nottingham Medieval Studies* 26 (1982), 1–7

Martens, Charles de, *Manuel diplomatique* (Paris, 1822)

Mathews, Thomas F., *The Clash of Gods: A Reinterpretation of Early Christian Art*, 2nd edn (Princeton, 1999)

Mathisen, R. W., 'Avitus, Italy, and the East in AD 455–456', *Byzantion* 15 (1981), 232–47

'Emigrants, Exiles, and Survivors: Aristocratic Options in Visigothic Aquitania', *Phoenix* 38 (1984), 159–70

'Epistolography, Literary Circles, and Family Ties in Late Roman Gaul', *American Philological Association, Transactions* 111 (1981), 95–109

'Hilarius, Germanus, and Lupus: The Aristocratic Background of the Cheldonius Affair', *Phoenix* 33 (1979), 160–9

'The Last Year of Saint Germanus of Auxerre', *AB* 99 (1981), 151–9

'Patricians as Diplomats in Late Antiquity', *Byzantinische Zeitschrift* 79 (1986), 35–49

'Resistance and Reconciliation: Majorian and the Gallic Aristocracy after the Fall of Avitus', *Francia* 7 (1979), 597–627

Roman Aristocrats in Barbarian Gaul: Strategies for Survival in an Age of Transition (Austin, 1993)

'Sidonius on the Reign of Avitus: A Study in Political Prudence', *American Philological Association, Transactions* 109 (1979), 165–71

'The Third Regnal Year of Eparchius Avitus', *Classical Philology* 80 (1985), 192–6

Mathisen, Ralph W. (ed.), *Law, Society, and Authority in Late Antiquity* (Oxford, 2001)

Mathisen, Ralph W., and Hagith S. Sivan (eds.), *Shifting Frontiers in Late Antiquity* (Aldershot, 1996)

Matthews, John, 'Anicius Manlius Severinus Boethius', in Margaret Gibson (ed.), *Boethius: His Life, Thought, and Influence* (Oxford, 1981), 25–31

'Gallic Supporters of Theodosius', *Latomus* 30 (1971), 1073–99

'Gesandtschaft', trans. R. Werner-Reis, *Reallexicon für Antike und Christentum* x (Stuttgart, 1977), 653–85

'Hostages, Philosophers, Pilgrims, and the Diffusion of Ideas in the Late Roman Mediterranean and Near East', in F. M. Clover and R. S. Humphreys (eds.), *Tradition and Innovation in Late Antiquity* (Madison, WI, 1989), 29–49

'Interpreting the *Interpretationes* of the *Breviarium*', in Mathisen (ed.), *Law, Society, and Authority in Late Antiquity*, 11–32

'The *Letters* of Symmachus', in J. W. Binns (ed.), *Latin Literature of the Fourth Century* (London, 1976), 58–99

'Olympiodorus of Thebes and the History of the West (AD 407–425)', *Journal of Roman Studies* 60 (1970), 79–97

'A Pious Supporter of Theodosius I: Maternus Cynegius and His Family', *Journal of Theological Studies* n.s. 18 (1967), 438–46

The Roman Empire of Ammianus (London, 1989)

Western Aristocracies and Imperial Court, AD 364–425 (Oxford, 1975)

Mattingly, Garrett, *Renaissance Diplomacy* (Boston, 1955: repr. New York, 1988)

Mause, Michael, *Die Darstellung des Kaisers in der lateinischen Panegyrik* (Palingenesia 50; Stuttgart, 1994)

Max, Gerald Edward, 'Majorian Augustus' (diss., University of Wisconsin, 1975)

Meslin, M., *Les Ariens d'Occident* (Paris, 1967)

Millar, D. A., 'The Logothete of the Drome', *Byzantion* 36 (1966), 438–70

Millar, Fergus, *The Emperor in the Roman World (31 BC to AD 337)* (London, 1977)

'Emperors, Frontiers and Foreign Relations, 31 BC to AD 378', *Britannia* 13 (1982), 1–24

'Government and Diplomacy in the Roman Empire during the First Three Centuries', *International History Review* 10 (1988), 345–77

The Roman Empire and Its Neighbours (New York, 1967)

Momigliano, Arnaldo, 'Cassiodorus and the Italian Culture of His Time', in his *Studies in Historiography* (London 1966), 181–210

Mommsen, Theodor, 'Ostgothische Studien', *Neues Archiv der Gesellschaft für Ältere Deutsche Geschichtskunde* 14 (1889), 225–49, 453–544; 15 (1890), 181–6; repr. in his *Gesammelte Schriften* VI (Berlin, 1910), 362–484

'Rede zum Geburtstag des Kaisers (1855): Apollinaris Sidonius und seiner Zeit', in his *Reden und Aufsatze* (Berlin, 1905), 132–43

Römisches Staatsrecht, 3rd edn, 3 vols. (Leipzig, 1887; repr. Graz, 1952)

Moorhead, John, 'Boethius and Romans in Ostrogothic Service', *Historia* 27 (1978), 604–12

'Clovis' Motives for Becoming a Catholic Christian', *Journal of Religious History* 13 (1985), 329–39

'The Decii under Theodoric', *Historia* 33 (1984), 107–15

'Italian Loyalties during Justinian's Gothic War', *Byzantion* 53 (1983), 575–96

'The Last Years of Theodoric', *Historia* 32 (1983), 106–20

'*Libertas* and *Nomen Romanorum* in Ostrogothic Italy', *Latomus* 46 (1987), 161–8

Theoderic in Italy (Oxford, 1992)

Moravcsik, Gyula (ed.), *Byzantinoturcica*, 2nd edn, 2 vols. (Berlin, 1958)

Mosley, D. J., 'Diplomacy by Conference: Almost a Spartan Contribution to Diplomacy?', *Emerita* 39 (1971), 187–93

'Diplomacy and Disunion in Ancient Greece', *Phoenix* 25 (1971), 319–30

Envoys and Diplomacy in Ancient Greece (Historia Einzelschriften 22; Wiesbaden, 1973)

'Greeks, Barbarians, Language, and Contact', *Ancient Society* 2 (1971), 1–6

'The Size of Embassies in Ancient Greek Diplomacy', *American Philological Association, Transactions* 96 (1965), 255–66

Moss, J. R., 'The Effects of the Policy of Avitus,' *Historia* 22 (1973), 711–31

Mosshammer, A., *The Chronicle of Eusebius and the Greek Chronographic Tradition* (Lewisburg, PA, 1979)

Mostert, Marco (ed.), *New Approaches to Medieval Communication* (Utrecht Studies in Medieval Literacy 1; Turnhout, 1999)

Muhlberger, Steven, 'Eugippius and the *Life of St. Severus*', *Medieval Prosopography* 17 (1996), 107–24

The Fifth-Century Chroniclers: Prosper, Hydatius, and the Gallic Chronicler of 452 (ARCA Classical and Medieval Texts, Papers and Monographs 27; Leeds, 1990)

'Heroic Kings and Unruly Generals: The "Copenhagen" Continuator of Prosper Reconsidered', *Florilegium* 6 (1984), 50–70

Murray, Alexander Callander, *From Roman to Merovingian Gaul: A Reader* (Readings in Medieval Civilizations and Cultures 5; Peterborough, 2000)

'The Position of the *Grafio* in the Constitutional History of Merovingian Gaul', *Speculum* 61 (1986), 787–805

'*Post vocantur Merohingii*: Fredegar, Merovech, and "Sacral Kingship"', in Murray (ed.), *After Rome's Fall*, 121–52

Murray, Alexander Callander (ed.), *After Rome's Fall: Narrators and Sources of Early Medieval History: Essays Presented to Walter Goffart* (Toronto, 1998)

Musset, Lucien, *The Germanic Invasions: The Making of Europe, AD 400–600*, trans. E. and C. James (University Park, PA, 1975)

Näf, B., 'Die Zeitbewusstsein des Ennodius und der Untergang Roms', *Historia* 39 (1990), 120

Nautin, Pierre, 'L'introduction d'Hydace à sa continuation de la *Chronique* d'Eusèbe et Jérôme', *Revue d'Histoire des Textes* 14–15 (1984–5), 143–53

Norberg, Dag, *In registrum Gregorii Magni studia critica*, 2 vols. (Uppsala, 1939)

Noy, David, *Foreigners at Rome: Citizens and Strangers* (London, 2000)

Obolensky, D., 'The Principles and Methods of Byzantine Diplomacy', in *Actes de XIIème Congrès des études byzantines* 1 (Belgrade, 1963), 45–61

O'Donnell, James J., *Cassiodorus* (Berkeley, 1979)

'Liberius the Patrician', *Traditio* 37 (1981), 31–72

O'Flynn, J. M., *Generalissimos of the Western Roman Empire* (Edmonton, 1983)

Olshausen, Eckart, and Hildegard Biller (eds.), *Antike Diplomatie* (Wege der Forschung 462; Darmstadt, 1979)

Oost, Stewart Irvin, 'Aetius and Majorian', *Classical Philology* 59 (1964), 23–9

Galla Placidia Augusta: A Biographical Essay (Chicago, 1968)

Ostrogorsky, George, *History of the Byzantine State*, trans. Joan Hussey (Oxford, 1980)

Pauly, A. F. von, G. Wissona *et al.* (eds.), *Realencylopädie der classischen Altertumswissenshaften*, 2nd edn (Stuttgart and Munich, 1893–1978)

Penella, Robert J., *Greek Philosophers and Sophists in the Fourth Century AD: Studies in Eunapius of Sardis* (ARCA Classical and Medieval Texts, Papers and Monographs 28; Leeds, 1990)

Perrin, Odet, *Les Burgondes: leur histoire des origines à la fin de leur royaume (534). Contribution à l'histoire des invasions* (Neuchatel, 1968)

Peter, Hermann, *Der Brief in der römischen Literatur* (Leipzig, 1901; repr. Hildersheim, 1965)

Phillipson, Coleman, *The International Law and Custom of Ancient Greece and Rome*, 2nd edn, 2 vols. (London, 1911)

Pitts, Lynn F., 'Relations between Rome and the German "Kings" on the Middle Danube in the First to Fourth Centuries AD', *Journal of Roman Studies* 79 (1989), 45–58

Pizarro, Joaquín Martínez, *A Rhetoric of the Scene: Dramatic Narrative in the Early Middle Ages* (Toronto, 1989)

Writing Ravenna: The Liber pontificalis *of Andreas Agnellus* (Ann Arbor, 1998)

Pohl, Walter (ed.), *Kingdoms of the Empire: The Integration of Barbarians in Late Antiquity* (The Transformation of the Roman World 1; Leiden, 1997)

Pohl, Walter, and Helmut Reimitz (eds.), *Strategies of Distinction: The Construction of Ethnic Communities, 300–800* (The Transformation of the Roman World 2; Leiden, 1998)

Portmann, Werner, *Geschichte in der spätantiken Panegyrik* (Europäische Hochschulschriften, series 3: Geschichte und ihre Hilfswissenschaften 363; Frankfurt am Main, 1988)

Potiemkine, Vladimir P. (ed.), *Histoire de la diplomatie*, trans. X. Pamphilova and M. Eristov, I (Paris, 1946)

Potter, David S., *Literary Texts and the Roman Historian* (London, 1999)

Premerstein, A. M. von, 'Legatus', *RE* XII.1, 1133–41

Prostko-Prostynski, Jan, Utraeque res publicae*: The Emperor Anastasius I's Gothic Policy (491–518)* (Poznan, 1994)

Quasten, Johannes, and A. di Berardino, *Patrology* III and IV, trans. P. Solari (Utrecht, 1960, 1986)

Queller, Donald E., 'Diplomacy, Western European', in *Dictionary of the Middle Ages* IV (New York, 1984), 201–14

The Office of Ambassador in the Middle Ages (Princeton, 1967)

Reichert, Hermann, *Lexicon der altgermanischen Namen*, 2 vols. (Vienna, 1987)

Reydellet, Marc, *La Royauté dans la littérature latine de Sidoine Apollinaire à Isidore de Séville* (Paris, 1981)

Rhodes, P. J., *The Athenian Boule* (Oxford, 1972)

Riché, P., *Education and Culture in the Barbarian West, Sixth through Eighth Centuries*, trans. J. J. Contreni (Columbia, 1976)

Rouche, Michel, *L'Aquitaine des Wisigoths aux Arabes, 418–781: naissance d'une région* (Paris, 1979)

Rouche, Michel (ed.), *Clovis; Histoire et mémoire*, 2 vols. (Paris, 1997)

Rousseau, Philip, 'In Search of Sidonius the Bishop', *Historia* 25 (1976), 356–77

Saint Germain d'Auxerre et son temps (Auxerre, 1950)

Salzman, Michele Renee, *On Roman Time: The Codex-Calendar of 354 and the Rhythms of Urban Life in Late Antiquity* (Berkeley, 1990)

Sawyer, P. H., and I. N. Wood (eds.), *Early Medieval Kingship* (Leeds, 1977)

Saxer, Victor, *Les Rites de l'initiation chrétienne du IIe au VIe siècle: esquisse historique et signification d'après leurs principaux témoins* (Spoleto, 1988)

Schäfer, Christoph, *Der weströmische Senat als Träger antiker Kontinuität unter den Ostgotenkönigen (490–540 n.Chr.)* (St Katharinen, 1991)

Schäferdiek, Knut, 'Der germanische Arianismus', *Miscellanea Historiae Ecclesiasticae* 3 (1968), 70–83

Die Kirche in den Reichen der Westgoten und Suewen bis zur Errichtung der westgotischen katholischen Staatskirche (Berlin, 1967)

Schanz, Martin, Carl Hosius, and Gustav Krüger (eds.), *Geschichte der römischer Literatur bis zum Gesetzgebungswerk des Kaiser Justinians*, 4 vols. (Handbuch der klassischen Altertumswissenschaft 8; Munich, 1914–35)

Scharf, R., 'Germanus von Auxerre – Chronologie seiner *Vita*', *Francia* 18 (1991), 1–19

Schmidt, Ludwig, *Geschichte der deutschen Stämme bis zum Ausgang der Völkerwanderung* I: *Die Ostgermanen*; II: *Die Westgermanen* (Munich, 1934–41)

Geschichte der Wandalen, 2nd edn (Munich, 1942); *Histoire des Vandales*, trans. H. E. del Medico (Paris, 1953)

Schönfeld, M., *Wörterbuch der altergermanischen Personen- und Völkernamen* (Heidelberg, 1911)

Schwarcz, Andreas, 'Die Liguria zwischen Goten, Byzantinern, Langobarden und Franken im 6. Jahrhundert', in Laura Balletto (ed.), *Oriente e occidente tra medioevo ed età moderna* (Genoa, 1997), 1109–31

Scott, Roger, 'The Classical Tradition in Byzantine Historiography', in Margaret Mullett and Roger Scott (eds.), *Byzantium and the Classical Tradition* (Birmingham, 1981)

'Diplomacy in the Sixth Century: The Evidence of John Malalas', in Shepard and Franklin, *Byzantine Diplomacy*, 159–65

Seeck, Otto, *Geschichte des Untergangs der antiken Welt*, 6 vols. (Berlin and Stuttgart, 1910–21)

Regesten der Kaiser und Päpste für die Jahre 311 bis 476 n. Chr.: Vorarbeit zu einer Prosopographie der christlichen Kaiserzeit (Stuttgart, 1919)

Seibert, Jakob, *Historische Beiträge zu den dynastischen Verbindungen in hellenistischer Zeit* (Wiesbaden, 1967)

Serguiev, V., 'La diplomatie de l'antiquité', in Potiemkine (ed.), *Histoire de la Diplomatie*, 7–76

Setow, Ernest, *A Guide to Diplomatic Practice*, ed. Nevile Bland, 4th edn (New York, 1957)

Shahîd, Ifran, *Byzantium and the Arabs in the Fourth Century* (Washington, DC, 1984)

Byzantium and the Arabs in the Fifth Century (Washington, DC, 1989)

Byzantium and the Arabs in the Sixth Century I (Washington, DC, 1995)

Rome and the Arabs: A Prolegomenon to the Study of Byzantium and the Arabs (Washington, DC, 1984)

Shanzer, Danuta, 'Two Clocks and a Wedding: Theoderic's Diplomatic Relations with the Burgundians', *Romanobarbasica* 14 (1998), 225–58

Shepard, Jonathan, and Simon Franklin (eds.), *Byzantine Diplomacy* (Aldershot, 1992)

The Roman Citizenship, 2nd edn (Oxford, 1973)

Sinnigen, W. G., 'Administrative Shifts of Competence under Theodoric', *Traditio* 21 (1965), 456–67

'*Comites consistoriani* in Ostrogothic Italy', *Classica et Mediaevalia* 24 (1963), 158–65

Sivan, H. S., 'Sidonius Apollinaris, Theoderic II, and Gothic–Roman Politics from Avitus to Anthemius', *Hermes* 117 (1989), 85–94

'An Unedited Letter of the Emperor Honorius to the Spanish Soldiers', *Zeitschrift für Papyrologie und Epigraphik* 61 (1985), 273–87
Smith, Julia M. H., '*Fines imperii*: The Marches', in Rosamond McKitterick (ed.), *The New Cambridge Medieval History* II: *c.700–c.900* (Cambridge, 1995), 169–89
de Souza, Philip, *Piracy in the Graeco-Roman World* (Cambridge, 1999)
Stallknecht, Bernt, *Untersuchungen zur römischen Aussenpolitik in der Spatantike (306–395 n. Chr.)* (Bonn, 1969)
Stancliffe, C., *St Martin and His Hagiographer: History and Miracle in Sulpicius Severus* (Oxford, 1983)
Stein, Ernst, *Histoire du Bas-Empire*, trans. J.-R. Palanque, 2 vols. (Paris, 1959)
Untersuchungen über das Officium *der Prätorianer Präfectur seit Diokletian* (Vienne, 1922; repr. Amsterdam, 1962)
'Untersuchungen zur spätrömischen Verwaltungsgeschichte', *Rheinisches Museum für Philologie* n.s. 74 (1925), 347–94
Stevens, C. E., 'Marcus, Gratian, Constantine', *Athenaeum* 35 (1957), 316–47
Sidonius Apollinaris and His Age (Oxford, 1933)
Stockton, David, *The Classical Athenian Democracy* (Oxford, 1990)
Stowers, Stanley K., *Letter Writing in Greco-Roman Antiquity* (Philadelphia, 1986)
Stroheker, K. F., *Eurich, König der Westgoten* (Stuttgart, 1937)
Germanentum und Spätantike (Zurich, 1965)
'Politische Kräfte in der Auslösung des Weströmischen Reiches', *Orpheus* 1 (1954), 68–75
Der senatorische Adel im spätantiken Gallien (Tübingen, 1948)
Sundwall, J., *Abhandlungen zur Geschichte des ausgehenden Römertums* (Helsinki, 1919)
Weströmische Studien (Berlin, 1915)
Syme, Ronald, *Tacitus*, 2 vols. (Oxford, 1958)
Täckholm, U., 'Aetius and the Battle on the Catalaunian Fields', *Opuscula Romana* 7 (1969), 259–75
Talbert, Richard J. A., *The Senate of Imperial Rome* (Princeton, 1984)
Teillet, Suzanne, *Des Goths à la nation gothique: les origines de l'idée de nation en occident du Ve au VIIe siècle* (Paris, 1984)
Teitler, H. C., Notarii *and* Exceptores*: An Inquiry into the Role and Significance of Shorthand Writers in the Imperial and Ecclesiastical Bureaucracy of the Roman Empire (from the Early Principate to c. 450 AD)* (Amsterdam, 1985)
Teodorico il Grande, Atti de XIII Congresso internationale di studi sull'alto medioevo, 2 vols. (Spoleto, 1993)
Teuffel, W. S., *History of Roman Literature*, rev. L. Schwabe, trans. George C. W. Wurr, 2 vols. (New York, 1967)
Teuffel, W., W. Kroll, and F. Skutsch (eds.), *Geschichte der römischer Literatur*, 3 vols. in various editions (Leipzig, 1900–20)
Thompson, E. A., 'A Chronological Note on St Germanus of Auxerre', *AB* 75 (1957), 135–8
'The Foreign Policy of Theodosius II and Marcian', *Hermathena* 76 (1950), 58–78
The Goths in Spain (Oxford, 1969)
A History of Attila and the Huns (Oxford, 1948)

'Olympiodorus of Thebes', *Classical Quarterly* 38 (1944), 43–52
Romans and Barbarians: The Decline of the Western Empire (Madison, WI, 1982)
Saint Germanus of Auxerre and the End of Roman Britain (Studies in Celtic History 6; Woodbridge, Suffolk, 1984)
The Visigoths in the Time of Ulfila (Oxford, 1966)
Torres Rodríguez, Casimiro, *El Reino de los Suevos* (La Coruña, 1977)
Townsend, W. T., and W. F. Wyatt, 'Ennodius and Pope Symmachus', *Studies in Honor of E. K. Rand* (New York 1938), 277–91
Treadgold, Warren T., *The Nature of the* Bibliotheca *of Photius* (Washington, DC)
Twyman, B. L., 'Aetius and the Aristocracy', *Historia* 19 (1970), 480–503
Vallejo Girves, Margarita, 'Relaciones del reino visigodo de Tolosa con el imperio. Elpapel de las embajadas', in Antonio Mendez *et al.* (eds.), *Los Visigodos y su mundo* (Madrid, 1997), 73–9
Van Dam, Raymond, *Leadership and Community in Late Antique Gaul* (Berkeley, 1985)
Van de Vyver, A., 'Cassiodor et son œuvre', *Speculum* 6 (1931), 244–92
'La victoire contre les Alamans et la conversion de Clovis', *Revue Belge de Philosophie et d'Histoire* 15 (1936), 859–914; 16 (1937), 35–94; 17 (1938), 793–813
van Uytfanghe, Marc, 'Heiligenverehrung II', *Reallexikon für Antike and Christentum* 14 (1988), 150–83
Vogel, Frideric, 'Chronologische Untersuchungen zu Ennodius', *Neues Archiv der Gesellschaft für ältere deutsche Geschichtskunde* 23 (1898), 53–4
Walbank, F. W., *The Hellenistic World* (Cambridge, MA, 1981)
Wallace-Hadrill, J. M., *The Barbarian West: The Early Middle Ages, AD 400–1000*, 3rd edn (London, 1967)
Early Germanic Kingship in England and on the Continent (Oxford, 1971)
The Long-Haired Kings and Other Studies in Frankish History (London, 1962; repr. Toronto, 1982)
Watson, Lynette, 'Representing the Past, Redefining the Future: Sidonius Apollinaris' *Panegyrics* of Avitus and Anthemius', in Mary Whitby (ed.), *The Propaganda of Power: The Role of Panegyric in Late Antiquity* (Leiden, 1998), 177–98
Wattenbach, W., and W. Levison, *Deutchlands Geschichtsquellen im Mittelalter: Vorzeit und Karoliner* (Weimar, 1952)
Weidemann, Margarete, *Kulturgeschichte der Merowingerzeit nach den Werken Gregors von Tours*, 2 vols. (Mainz, 1982)
Wells, Peter S., *The Barbarians Speale: How the Conquered Peoples Shaped Roman Europe* (Princeton, 1999)
Whitby, Mary, 'On the Omission of a Ceremony in Mid-Sixth Century Constantinople: *candidati, curopalatus, silentarii, excubitores* and Others', *Historia* 36 (1987), 462–88
White, Caroline, *Christian Friendship in the Fourth Century* (Cambridge, 1992)
Whittaker, C. R., *Frontiers of the Roman Empire: A Social and Economic Study* (Baltimore, 1994)
'Landlords and Warlords in the Later Roman Empire', in John Rich and Graham Shipley (eds.), *War and Society in the Roman World* (Leicester-Nottingham Studies in Ancient Society 5; London, 1993), 277–302
Wickham, Chris, *Early Medieval Italy: Central Power and Local Society, 400–1000* (London, 1981)

Wielers, Margaret, 'Zwischenstaatliche Beziehungsformen im frühen Mittelalter (*Pax, Foedus, Amicitia, Fraternitas*)' (diss., Münster, 1959)

Wietersheim, Eduard von, *Geschichte der Völkerwanderung*, ed. Felix Dahn, 2nd edn, 2 vols. (Leipzig, 1880, 1881)

Wolfram, Herwig, *History of the Goths*, trans. T. J. Dunlap (Berkeley, 1989)

Wolfram, H., and A. Schwarcz (eds.), *Anerkennung und Integration: Zu den wirtschaftlichen Grundlagen der Völkerwanderungszeit, 400–600* (Vienna, 1988)

Wood, Ian N., 'The End of Roman Britain: Continental Evidence and Parallels', in M. Lapidge and D. Dumville (eds.), *Gildas: New Approaches* (Studies in Celtic History 5; Woodbridge, Suffolk, 1984), 8–17

The Merovingian Kingdoms, 450–751 (London, 1994)

The Merovingian North Sea (Alingsås, 1983)

'The Use and Abuse of Latin Hagiography in the Early Medieval West', in E. Chrysos and I. Wood (eds.), *East and West: Modes of Communication* (The Transformation of the Roman World 5; Leiden, 1999), 93–109

Woolf, Greg, *Becoming Roman: The Origins of Provincial Civilization in Gaul* (Cambridge, 1998)

Wozniak, F. E., 'Byzantine Diplomacy and the Lombard–Gepidic Wars', *Balkan Studies* 20 (1979), 138–58

'Diplomacy, Byzantine', in *Dictionary of the Middle Ages* IV (New York, 1984), 193–7

Wrede, F., *Über die Sprache der Ostgoten in Italien* (Strasburg, 1891)

Yver, G., 'Euric, roi des Wisigoths', in *Etudes d'histoire du moyen âge dédiées à Gabriel Monod* (Paris, 1896), 11–46

Zeiller, Jacques, 'Etude sur l'Arianisme en Italie à l'époque ostrogothique et à l'époque lombarde', *Ecole Française de Rome, Mélanges d'Archéologie et d'Histoire* 25 (1905), 127–46

Zimmermann, Odo John, *The Late Latin Vocabulary of the* Variae *of Cassiodorus, with Special Advertence to the Technical Terminology of Administration* (Washington, DC, 1944; repr. Hildersheim, 1967)

Zöllner, Erich, *Geschichte der Franken bis zur Mitte des sechsten Jahrhunderts* (Munich, 1970)

INDEX

In the Index, as throughout the book, familiar forms of names have been given where they exist; otherwise, the forms as given in *PLRE* have been used. Greek and Persian names have been Anglicised. The terms 'Ostrogoth' and 'Visigoth' have been retained for convenience, though it should be recalled that these are Byzantine labels, and were not used within the respective kingdoms for self-identification.

Index

Index

Index

Index

Index

Cambridge Studies in Medieval Life and Thought
Fourth series

Titles in series

1 The Beaumont Twins: The Roots and Branches of Power in the Twelfth Century
D. B. CROUCH

2 The Thought of Gregory the Great*
G. R. EVANS

3 The Government of England Under Henry I*
JUDITH A. GREEN

4 Charity and Community in Medieval Cambridge*
MIRI RUBIN

5 Autonomy and Community: The Royal Manor of Havering, 1200–1500*
MARJORIE KENISTON MCINTOSH

6 The Political Thought of Baldus de Ubaldis*
JOSEPH CANNING

7 Land and Power in Late Medieval Ferrara: The Rule of the Este, 1350–1450*
TREVOR DEAN

8 William of Tyre: Historian of the Latin East*
PETER W. EDBURY AND JOHN GORDON ROWE

9 The Royal Saints of Anglo-Saxon England: A Study of West Saxon and East Anglian Cults
SUSAN J. RIDYARD

10 John of Wales: A Study of the Works and Ideas of a Thirteenth-Century Friar*
JENNY SWANSON

11 Richard III: A Study of Service*
ROSEMARY HORROX

12 A Marginal Economy? East Anglian Breckland in the Later Middle Ages
MARK BAILEY

13 Clement VI: The Pontificate and Ideas of an Avignon Pope*
DIANA WOOD

14 Hagiography and the Cult of Saints: The Diocese of Orléans, 800–1200
THOMAS HEAD

15 Kings and Lords in Conquest England*
ROBIN FLEMING

16 Council and Hierarchy: The Political Thought of William Durant the Younger*
CONSTANTIN FASOLT

17 Warfare in the Latin East, 1192–1291*
CHRISTOPHER MARSHALL

18 Province and Empire: Brittany and the Carolingians
JULIA M. H. SMITH

19 A Gentry Community: Leicestershire in the Fifteenth Century, *c.* 1422–*c.* 1485*
ERIC ACHESON

20 Baptism and Change in the Early Middle Ages, *c.* 200–1150*
PETER CRAMER

21 Itinerant Kingship and Royal Monasteries in Early Medieval Germany, *c.* 936–1075*
JOHN W. BERNHARDT

22 Caesarius of Arles: The Making of a Christian Community in Late Antique Gaul*
WILLIAM E. KLINGSHIRN

23 Bishop and Chapter in Twelfth-Century England: A Study of the *Mensa Episcopalis**
EVERETT U. CROSBY

24 Trade and Traders in Muslim Spain: The Commercial Realignment of the Iberian Peninsula, 900–1500*
OLIVIA REMIE CONSTABLE

25 Lithuania Ascending: A Pagan Empire Within East-Central Europe, 1295–1345
S. C. ROWELL

26 Barcelona and Its Rulers, 1100–1291*
STEPHEN P. BENSCH

27 Conquest, Anarchy and Lordship: Yorkshire, 1066–1154*
PAUL DALTON

28 Preaching the Crusades: Mendicant Friars and the Cross in the Thirteenth Century*
CHRISTOPH T. MAIER

29 Family Power in Southern Italy: The Duchy of Gaeta and Its Neighbours, 850–1139*
PATRICIA SKINNER

30 The Papacy, Scotland and Northern England, 1342–1378*
A. D. M. BARRELL

31 Peter des Roches: An Alien in English Politics, 1205–1238*
NICHOLAS VINCENT

32 Runaway Religious in Medieval England, *c.* 1240–1540*
F. DONALD LOGAN

33 People and Identity in Ostrogothic Italy, 489–554*
PATRICK AMORY

34 The Aristocracy in Twelfth-Century León and Castile*
SIMON BARTON

35 Economy and Nature in the Fourteenth Century: Money, Market Exchange and the Emergence of Scientific Thought*
JOEL KAYE

36 Clement V*
SOPHIA MENACHE

37 England's Jewish Solution, 1262–1290: Experiment and Expulsion*
ROBIN R. MUNDILL

38 Medieval Merchants: York, Beverley and Hull in the Later Middle Ages*
JENNY KERMODE

39 Family, Commerce and Religion in London and Cologne: A Comparative Social History of Anglo-German Emigrants, *c.* 1000–*c.* 1300*
JOSEPH P. HUFFMAN

40 The Monastic Order in Yorkshire, 1069–1215
JANET BURTON

41 Parisian Scholars in the Early Fourteenth Century: A Social Portrait
WILLIAM J. COURTENAY

42 Colonisation and Conquest in Medieval Ireland: The English in Louth, 1170–1330
BRENDAN SMITH

43 The Early Humiliati
FRANCES ANDREWS

44 The Household Knights of King John
S. D. CHURCH

45 The English in Rome, 1362–1420: Portrait of an Expatriate Community
MARGARET HARVEY

46 Restoration and Reform: Recovery from Civil War in England, 1153–1165
GRAEME J. WHITE

47 State and Society in the Early Middle Ages: The Middle Rhine Valley, 400–1000
MATTHEW INNES

48 Brittany and the Angevins: Province and Empire, 1157–1203
JUDITH EVERARD

49 The Making of Gratian's *Decretum*
ANDERS WINROTH

50 At the Gate of Christendom: Jews, Muslims and 'Pagans' in Medieval Hungary, *c.* 1000–*c.* 1300
NORA BEREND

51 Making Agreements in Medieval Catalonia: Power, Order, and the Written Word, 1000–1200
ADAM J. KOSTO

52 The Making of the Slavs: History and Archaeology of the Lower Danube Region, *c.* 500–700
FLORIN CURTA

53 Literacy in Lombard Italy, *c.* 568–774
NICHOLAS EVERETT

54 Philosophy and Politics in the Thought of John Wyclif
STEPHEN E. LAHEY

55 Envoys and Political Communication in the Late Antique West, 411–533
ANDREW GILLETT

56 Kings, Barons and Justices: The Making and Enforcement of Legislation in Thirteenth-Century England
PAUL BRAND

**Also published as a paperback*

Lightning Source UK Ltd.
Milton Keynes UK
UKOW03f0305210117
292498UK00001B/244/P

9 780521 096386